'Truly encyclopaedic ... showing that success is up to us
– an exciting prospect in an enthralling read.'
— Donald Kaberuka, President: African Development Bank

'Observer, writer and participant: Greg Mills's sparkling
combination of talents has produced an invaluable understanding
of *Why States Recover*.'
— Luisa Dias Diogo, former Prime Minister, Mozambique

'Greg Mills pinpoints how states recover – at its heart it's down to
the will of the locals.'
— Tendai Biti, opposition spokesperson on finance, Zimbabwe

'Greg Mills challenges us all in capturing the essence of state failure
and its counterpoint, recovery: Security is imperative but must be
in harness with governance, the economy and, above, all,
democratic politics with leadership to match.'
— Raila Odinga, former Prime Minister, Kenya

'A first-rate analysis, which synchs with Somaliland's own
experience: state recovery is all about the power of local ownership.'
— President Ahmed Silanyo, Somaliland

'Mills's message is clear and convincing: Recovery in failed states
is possible, and up to the locals.'
— Tim Butcher, author of *Blood River*

'An entertaining adventure of how states fail; an enterprising
manual for their success.'
— David Kilcullen, author of *The Accidental Guerrilla* and *Out of the Mountains*

'From Afghanistan to Zimbabwe, Mugabe to Mandela, Greg Mills
finds failures, assesses interventions and analyses recovery, arriving
at a refreshing premise: Success, like failure, is down to politics.'
— Lindiwe Mazibuko, Democratic Alliance, South Africa

'The style is as the underpinning research: personal and eye level; the conclusions spot on.'

— Tony Leon, former leader of the official South African opposition; author of *The Accidental Ambassador* and *Opposite Mandela*

'There is simply no one else in the world who has the first-hand knowledge to write this, never mind the analytical and writing skill to pull it off.'

— Ray Hartley, Editor-at-large, Times Media; author of *Ragged Glory*

'Greg Mills is a remarkable person – courageous, indefatigable, thoughtful and deeply experienced. He has studied state formation on the ground in some of the most difficult environments on earth. His insights are wise, pragmatic and illuminating.'

— Rory Stewart MP, author of *The Places in Between* and *The Prince of the Marshes*

'More important than understanding why states fail is grasping why they recover – and this excellent book offers practical insights gleaned from personal experience in challenging places.'

— Lieutenant General Sir Nicholas Carter, Commander: UK Land Forces, recently Deputy Commander: ISAF

'Seldom does a writer analyse the problem and also identify the solution. Greg Mills manages both in *Why States Recover*, an entertainingly personal and compelling read.'

— F.W. de Klerk, former President of South Africa

'Interviewing rebel generals in Angola and the Congo, tracking petrol tankers in Afghanistan and on the road in Latin America and Asia's tiger economies, Greg Mills melds compelling reportage and analysis in search of the answer to *Why States Recover*.'

— Patrick Smith, Editor of *Africa Confidential*

'Greg Mills meets Andy McNab and Paul Collier ... though Mills speaks with his own voice and from his own experiences, offering reason to be more optimistic about the future. Read this book.'

— Professor Christopher Coker, London School of Economics

WHY STATES RECOVER

When the contest is only with native rulers, and with such native strength as those rulers can enlist in their defence, the answer I should give to the question of the legitimacy of intervention is, as a general rule, No. The reason is, that there can seldom be anything approaching to assurance that intervention, even if successful, would be for the good of the people themselves ... The liberty which is bestowed on them by hands other than their own, will have nothing real, nothing permanent.

— John Stuart Mill

WHY STATES RECOVER

Changing Walking Societies into Winning Nations –
From Afghanistan to Zimbabwe

*

GREG MILLS

HURST & COMPANY, LONDON

First published in the United Kingdom in 2014 by
C. Hurst & Co. (Publishers) Ltd.,
41 Great Russell Street, London, WC1B 3PL
© Greg Mills, 2014
All rights reserved.

Printed in India

Distributed in the United States, Canada and Latin America by
Oxford University Press, 198 Madison Avenue, New York, NY
10016, United States of America

The right of Greg Mills to be identified as the author
of this publication is asserted by him in accordance with
the Copyright, Designs and Patents Act, 1988.

A Cataloguing-in-Publication data record for this book
is available from the British Library.

ISBN: 978-1-84904-461-5

This book is printed using paper from registered sustainable
and managed sources.

www.hurstpublishers.com

CONTENTS

✳

ABOUT THE AUTHOR

*

Educated at Diocesan College, and the universities of Cape Town and Lancaster, from where he received a MA and PhD, since 2005 Greg Mills has directed the Johannesburg-based Brenthurst Foundation. Previously, from 1996 to 2005, he was national director of the South African Institute of International Affairs. He has run government advisory teams on Kenya, Lesotho, Liberia, Mozambique, Malawi, Rwanda, Zambia and Zimbabwe, and was assigned as a Danish Africa Commissioner in 2008–10. He undertook four deployments in Afghanistan with the International Security Assistance Force (ISAF) between 2006 and 2012, including a stint as the commander's adviser and head of the Prism strategic analysis group during the ninth iteration of ISAF in 2006. In 2013 he was appointed a member of the African Development Bank's High-Level Panel on Fragile States, and in 2014 a Visiting Senior Fellow at Singapore's S. Rajaratnam School of International Studies. He is on the visiting faculty of the NATO Defence College, the Royal College of Defence Studies, and the South African National Defence College.

ACKNOWLEDGEMENTS

*

My varied professional experiences as a government adviser and the exposure they have offered provide the basis for this book's case studies, observations and conclusions. They need also, in this regard, be considered in the light of four other, related publications: *Why Africa is Poor: And What Africans Can Do About It* (Greg Mills, 2010), *Victory Among People: Lessons from Countering Insurgency and Stabilising Fragile States* (David Richards and Greg Mills eds, 2011), *Africa's Third Liberation: The New Search for Prosperity and Jobs* (Greg Mills and Jeffrey Herbst, 2012) and *Somalia: Fixing Africa's Most Failed State* (Greg Mills, J. Peter Pham and David Kilcullen, 2013). The role of General Lord David Richards, who retired as the United Kingdom's Chief of Defence Staff in July 2013, and who was my boss in Afghanistan in 2006, in these projects and the professional assignments that underpinned them, is gratefully acknowledged.

I confess now that, at the onset of my advisory roles in Afghanistan and elsewhere, I instinctively believed outsiders could change conditions of failure by presenting an alternative logic to insiders and simultaneously by getting the formula for external engagement 'right'. Thus this book is not a justification of some prior personal muse that we should not intervene in the affairs of other states; to the contrary, I had exactly the opposite prejudice. This volume details what was a process of personal discovery. Inevitably, it presents the perspective of an outsider, since that is what I am, but with an emphasis on the limitations on that perspective, and the absolutely essential requirement to recognise that rescuing failed states depends on insiders, to whom people coming from outside like me can at best offer only partial support. This is a book fundamentally about what insiders should do, the need for domestic learning processes, and the necessity for space to be left for these processes to take effect; and about what outsiders should not do, and when and how not to get engaged.

The research behind this volume is thus based not on hours spent in libraries, but mostly on time in the field, endeavouring to turn theory into effect, political intent into practical realities, and moral principles into life-changing actions, all the time dealing with volatile, destructive and sometimes violent political circumstances, the very underlying conditions that usually got these countries in trouble in the first instance. Such a task is never easy, almost always messy, sometimes downright dangerous and inevitably controversial.

Writing about the reasons for failure always risks becoming a target of politicians or even nationalistic ire. People do not want to and rarely like hearing about the domestic or personal roots of their difficulties, preferring to externalise them and make them someone else's fault. It is as much human nature as it is politically expedient to point fingers elsewhere. But there would be little value to this book if it avoided asking and answering the hard questions about why failure exists. Few have apparently read Franz Kafka's comment that 'I think we ought to read only the kind of books that wound or stab us. If the book we're reading doesn't wake us up with a blow to the head, what are we reading for? So that it will make us happy, as you write? ... we need books that affect us like a disaster, that grieve us deeply, like the death of someone we loved more than ourselves, like being banished into forests far from everyone, like a suicide. A book must be the axe for the frozen sea within us.'

It is also easier not to get involved and to stay at home, but there is the moral dilemma of inaction. As Theodore Roosevelt observed, 'The only man who never makes mistakes is the man who never does anything.' While it is usually better for outsiders to do as little as possible, doing nothing – often while saying everything – undermines support for values, concerns for human rights and a shared, global responsibility towards others. It makes light of commitments to democracy, notions of a global commons and the responsibility of leadership. It should make it difficult for us to complain when terrorism, engendered by a sense of unfairness and alienation omnipresent in the losers, comes home to roost violently in our societies. It also recognises the disjuncture between today's world of endlessly making empty pronouncements and, as Roosevelt intimates, actually doing things; between policy and principles on the one hand, and the media on the other, the latter sometimes less a policy tool for politicians than a vacuous popularity contest in itself.

None of the experiences and learnings detailed here would have been possible without the support of the Oppenheimer family, and Jonathan and Jennifer Oppenheimer in particular, who initiated the Tswalu Dialogue in 2002 and established the Brenthurst Foundation in 2005. It remains a re-markable privilege to be able to traipse around the bush looking for answers to problems that have plagued generations. A generous writer-in-residence fellowship at Bellagio from the Rockefeller Foundation in May 2013 permit-ted this book's more rapid completion. The generosity of the Foundation and assistance of its staff, especially Pilar Palacia and Elena Ongania, is gratefully appreciated, as is the wisdom and companionship of the other resident fellows. Jeffrey Herbst, Christopher Clapham, Dianna Games, Stuart Doran and Donald Kaberuka provided important feedback on the overall manuscript, while Anthony Arnott was a great help in digging out statistical data, often after hours, helped also by Adrian Kitimbo and Zika Amalu. Leila Jack and Ghairoon Hajad provided important back-up on the Brenthurst side, where Terry McNamee helped to hold the fort during my frequent absences. Nelius Uys and his team were always on hand to sort out usually self-inflicted computer maladies. Stephan Malherbe, Dave Kilcullen, Ron Suskind, Ray Hartley, Stephen Ellis, Do Duc Dinh, Bill Rollo, Jacob Kolster, Mohamed Yonis, Eddie Keizan, Michael Spicer, Mark Shaw, Michael Holman, Mohamed Harun, Afeikhena Jerome, Andrew Stewart, Michael Faborode, Hugh Blackman, Jeff Sims, Nel Marais, Andy Sparkes, Nora Ahmetaj, Steve Caley, Alan Doss, Karin Landgren, Torben Brylle, Palo Conteh, Yero Baldeh, Peter Pham, Edward Clay, Johnny Clegg, Rod Hagger, Patrick Esnouf, Brad Anderson, John Robertson, Susan Thomson, Mauro de Lorenzo, Tim Butcher and Francis Omaswa were thoughtful commenta-tors and contributors to various aspects of the book, while Anthony Arnott, Daniel Pinhassi, Rakiya Omaar, Dolly Afun-Ogidan, Nel Marais, Patrick Mazimhaka, Dianna Games, Lyal White, Juan Carlos Pinzon, Schoeman du Plessis, Malcolm Ferguson, Johann Smith, Jeffrey Herbst, Sharon Polanksy, Thomas Vester, Olusegun Obasanjo, Robert Lloyd George, Janet Wilson, Nic and Angela Jooste, Rod Hagger and Doug Meisel, and Tim Carson provided collegial company and hospitality during sundry study trips. Lieutenant General Sir Nick Carter, Major General Dickie Davis and Brigadier Ewen McLay were hospitable and thoughtful colleagues during stints in Afghanistan based in Kandahar in 2010 and Kabul in 2012.

The research on Singapore and the Southeast Asia region was conducted, in part, during a Distinguished Visitor's Programme offered by its Ministry of Foreign Affairs in November–December 2013. Thanks go in particular to High Commissioner Bernard Baker and Ambassadors Barry Desker and Verghese Mathews in this regard, and to Joyce Davamoni who herded this wayward guest with aplomb and patience.

Any mistakes and contrarian opinions are, of course, mine alone. I am reminded in this respect of George Orwell's observation of the criticism he received about *Burmese Days*, his tough portrayal of the underbelly and wickedness of colonial society. 'I dare say it's unfair in some ways,' he wrote simply, 'and inaccurate in some details, but much of it is simply reporting what I have seen.'

The Pan Macmillan team of Andrea Nattrass, Terry Morris, Sally Hines and Laura Hammond, among others, expertly brought the draft to publication.

On the home front Amelia, Beatrix and William have not only steadfastly borne the brunt of the regular absences behind these observations and re-flections, but have always offered much encouragement to this occasionally febrile author. The challenges they face, including some of those my genera-tion has not managed well, recall George Bernard Shaw's remark: 'We are made wise not by the recollection of our past, but by the responsibility for our future.' In the hope it can assist them in avoiding the mistakes of the past and repeating its successes, it is to this next generation that this book is dedicated.

Greg Mills
JOHANNESBURG
MAY 2014

INTRODUCTION

❋

Countries can change for the better. But outsiders cannot fix state failure. Insiders are largely as responsible for their recovery as for their decline, since it is local politics, customs and rules that overwhelmingly shape their choices and thus their destiny.

The costs of failure and the potential rewards of recovery are enormous. Today the bulk of the world's poor – totalling 1.1 billion of the planet's seven billion people – live in failed or failing states.[1] Not only is their lack of development and progress a missed opportunity for all, but their problems are unlikely to remain at home in a world increasingly connected by the flows of people, capital, goods, technology, information and news.

Such statistics have a tragic, human dimension.

During 2013, Italian authorities were kept very busy intercepting boats filled to the gunwales with refugees fleeing failure in search of a better life and security. In a few days that September, for example, four vessels loaded with more than 700 people from Syria, Egypt, Eritrea, Nigeria and Ghana got into difficulty off Sicily. In two separate incidents the following month, 383 migrants drowned when their vessels capsized. According to the European border agency Frontex, more than 12 000 illegal migrants were detected off Sicily and 8 000 off the island of Lampedusa in the third quarter of 2013 alone,[2] the hazardous Mediterranean passage only one stage in a longer, gruelling ordeal for most. In October, the decomposing bodies of 87 migrants, among them 52 children, were discovered in the Sahara Desert. The two trucks carrying the migrants had broken down while trying to reach Algeria. Their passengers' corpses were found in groups in a wide radius around a well they were trying to reach. Some had been eaten by jackals. They were fleeing one of the world's poorest countries, Niger, second from last on the United Nations Human Development Index.[3]

The quicker the situations that give rise to such desperate migration can be turned around, the better. History teaches that the period of recovery for failed states is at least as long as the period of decline.

Failure is not a problem solely for Westerners trying to fix countries in places such as Afghanistan or trying to stop people from reaching their shores. While often politically more palatable, imposed regional solutions are no more useful and likely to succeed if they do not follow the local lead. As recovery success stories from Singapore to Colombia illustrate, the road from state weakness to strength is most likely under decisive domestic leadership that is committed to popular welfare and concerned less with inspiration of grand vision and governance frameworks, and more with the detail of policy content and perspiration of execution.

Recovery contains huge benefits. As one measure, the number of people living in conditions of extreme poverty has fallen fast since the end of the Cold War a quarter of a century ago.[4] Between 1990 and 2010, for example, nearly a billion people were lifted out of extreme poverty, their number falling by more than a half as a share of the total global population to 21 per cent. This was principally a result of economic growth, and growth in turn a product of better security, governance and policy.[5]

Though most welcome, however, such improvements are not uniform. To the contrary, despite improving global income averages, inequality has opened chasms between state success and failure. For every country 'with a catch-up story' of development, notes the Princeton economist Angus Deaton, 'there has been one with a left-behind story'.[6]

The helplessness of outside actors is most notable in failed, failing or weak states – generically referred to as 'fragile' – where a combination of governance, societal and economic factors leave citizens vulnerable to instability and shocks, and prey to bad leadership.[7] This does not, however, suggest external actors should do nothing. On the contrary, the stakes are high. It has been estimated that annual economic losses from armed conflict in Africa alone totals $18 billion, and that between 1990 and 2007 the cost of armed violence and conflict to the continent was $300 billion, about the same as the volume of aid flows over this time. Oxfam has calculated that conflict shrinks the economies of affected African countries by at least 15 per cent per year, and that compared to peaceful countries, these countries have, on average, 50 per cent more infant deaths and the same share of additional undernourished people, 20 per cent more adult illiteracy, more than 12 per cent less food per person, 2.5 times fewer doctors per patient, and life expectancy is reduced by five years.[8]

There is good reason why these fragile states have been a central concern over decades for international and national as well as public and private organisations. Could better ways have been found to assist?

Dilemmas for the outsider

Einstein famously was taken to remark that the definition of insanity was 'doing the same thing over and over again and expecting different results'. That saying is repeated often enough to ensure insanity in itself, not least because its central message is frequently ignored.

When it comes to engaging with fragile states, external actors apparently do the same thing over and over again in expectation that things will get better – or at least that they will not get worse. The template for engagement in these environments has a bureaucratic architecture – it is delivered by a (usually) foreign bureaucracy and presumes that there is a semblance of the same to receive and digest the aid, advice, equipment and support that comes in this package. The local receiving bureaucracy is convinced or, through the promise of money, conditioned to put in place the procedures and policies to digest this money.

This method is based on the (false, as it often turns out) presumption of the existence of a functional rump of a state on which to latch, engage and build. Such a task is also complicated by the increasing diffusion and degradation of power, and especially asymmetry of military power, as a result of which outsiders speak with many voices and local spoilers can easily upend fragile international political will. As a measure, while the number of democracies worldwide has doubled since the end of the Cold War, the margins of victory are often almost negligible, forcing governments into complex coalitions, without a strong mandate for action. By 2013, for example, 30 of 34 Organisation for Economic Cooperation and Development (OECD) nations, a group of the world's most advanced economies, had parliamentary coalitions. The rise of non-governmental organisations (NGOs) and other arms of civil society also further constrain the exercising of power. Political power is, in simple terms, easier now for people to obtain, through the blogosphere for example, but is also harder to retain and to use.

The spread of asymmetrical warfare is another indicator of the extent of state power 'diffusion'. The 9/11 attacks are, for example, estimated to have cost Al-Qaeda around $500 000. The cost of that action and, in particular, the response totals an estimated $3.3 trillion. Put differently, for every $1 spent by Al-Qaeda, the United States (US) alone has spent $7 million.[9] Piracy offers further evidence of this asymmetry, where a huge naval presence is required in the Gulf of Aden to stop small groups in speedboats, and imperfectly so. There are other examples: improvised explosive devices, the modern equivalent of a mine, have accounted for three-quarters of the military wounded in Afghanistan and Iraq; during the Second World War, mines were responsible for less than 5 per cent of casualties.[10]

Such diffusion is exacerbated by the absence of an over-riding plan by outsiders, where improved tactics are often the substitute for a lack of prevailing strategies and goals. During the Cold War, there was a predominant strategic objective. From the West's vantage, this was to defeat or at least deter the Soviet Union and the Eastern bloc. Everything was geared to this end, including support for dictatorial regimes from Mobutu Sese Seko's Zaire to Anastasio Somoza's Nicaragua, which may have been odious, but were seen as 'on-side'. Hence, President Harry Truman's alleged saying about the Nicaraguan strongman, 'He may be a bastard, but he's our bastard.'

Now countries engage and deal with problems, less according to national security and economic interests, but on more amorphous moral, humanitarian grounds, mostly on the basis that the less engagement, the better. While the military has become a preferred tool of diplomacy, given the difficulties of the situations into which foreign assistance is inserted, it is a blunt instrument, not always well adjusted for such a task, or for the change that such a role entails. And the art of strategy is increasingly lost in these circumstances, not least when it comes to finding solutions to complex regional political problems, such as those between Afghanistan and Pakistan. This strategic element includes not only an ability to determine where problems lie and how to solve them, but their prioritisation in 'separating the essential from the merely important'.[11]

Regardless, many books and studies on the subject of fragile states have promoted improved external methodologies and even a 'New Deal'[12] for engagement by donors. If careful and clever, outsiders can make positive interventions at critical junctures and stabilise situations by helping to stop the fighting where there is violence, providing aid to get, and keep, things moving in the right direction, offering strategic direction and advice, supplying technical skills and capital, and furnishing a temporary security umbrella through the presence of peacekeepers and military trainers. Aid can make a difference as a humanitarian salve or if aligned to the development priorities set by locals, but it can also easily offer the wrong incentives, providing authoritarian rulers 'with cash and services to prop themselves up – while punishing their enemies'.[13] With the humanitarian aid industry worth an estimated $18 billion annually,[14] there is a continuous need to guard against tautological institutional self-interests inherent in promoting intervention.

Even though their first premise has to be 'do no harm', outsiders can quite easily and quickly make things worse by lessening the effect of bad domestic policy choices in the troubled country, distracting and undermining leadership's responsiveness to the local electorate, or fuelling a 'war' economy of advice and aid.[15] Donors are usually also badly aligned to helping the private sector. Most outside helpers, like many domestic politicians, have little practical experience of competitive commerce and often are ideologically antagonistic towards private enterprise.

Instead, without local leadership and ownership of the problem and solution, outsiders risk setting the stage for the next cycle of violence and instability. This is particularly so as these troubled states move from the 'stabilisation' phase of post-conflict recovery (characterised by peacekeeping, a surge of aid, a political settlement and demobilisation of armed groups) to that of 'development' (better policy, rehabilitated infrastructure, improved governance and private sector growth). The reinvention of external phraseology, for example replacing 'stability' with the need for 'resilience', the use of pillars and processes,[16] and the reliance on an aid technocracy, together highlight an implicit danger inherent in external responses to state fragility, not least in overlooking the indigenous political character of the cause.

Attempting state recovery, or peace-building, in a series of sequenced, neat actions is made more difficult by a tendency by outside donors to revert to 'pet projects' in devising solutions. Gender empowerment, youth unemployment and climate change are, for example, three contemporary fads to which homage apparently has seemingly always had to be paid. Of course these are important drivers of change, and women and youth, especially, are affected disproportionately by conflict, whether in the cityscape or as smallholder farmers in the rural areas. Nonetheless, establishing a sense of priorities and strategies to deal with fragility implies a choice, and the approach cannot always be the same for every situation no matter the bureaucratic institutional inertia.

Such scepticism is founded on the history of development aid, thick with the wreckage of failure, especially in rural Africa. Not that such mistakes are ever admitted; their proponents have a personal and professional vested interest in keeping the dream and system alive. Bureaucracies seldom, if ever, do themselves out of a job. 'Western powers have adopted new, often contradictory, aid policies every decade or so, never publicly acknowledging their mistakes or owning up to the collateral damage they have inflicted on African lives,' reflects Howard French in his assessment of economist Jeffrey Sachs' Millennium Village scheme.[17] Regardless, some NGOs, multilateral institutions and consultants perversely justify their own existence by the presence of failure and the pursuit of the aid remedy. Aid proponents and agents too often eerily, and without apparent self-awareness, fit author V.S. Naipaul's description of American travellers in his book *An Area of Darkness*, 'whose privilege it was to go slumming about the world and sometimes scrounging, exacting a personal repayment for a national generosity'. It seems that many grand initiatives to help are based less on sound historical and empirical argument than ego. 'It's not about Africa, it's about Tony,' as Cambridge University's Christopher Clapham put it regarding Tony Blair's Africa Commission and his subsequent governance initiatives.[18]

The notion that more aid with improved, clearer instructions could do the job better than it has in the past ignores the social, environmental and, above all else, domestic political roots of the development challenge. There are good reasons why systems are the way they are, and dollops of money, together with ideology, have a poor track record in attempting changes, especially those of a linear, utopian, wholesale nature: notably, Mao's Great Leap Forward, *Ujamaa* village collectivisation schemes in Tanzania or, more recently, Sachs' Millennium Villages. Of course, aid can be better spent – and this book will suggest some fresh areas and new methods, particularly for improving prospects for private sector growth in conditions of state fragility. But money is not usually the only reason for failure or success.

This book focuses on three issues: why and how some states are fragile; where and why reforms succeed and some states recover; and the role of insiders and outsiders in this process. It is not a high-altitude academic survey; rather it offers an eye-level approach in describing how these processes occur and what these circumstances 'look like'.

In so doing, it attempts to provide an understanding of the role of personalities, the influence of interests and politics and the path of power. It offers little theory, however, in endeavouring to keep to the observation made by Benjamin Caffey about George C. Marshall, the great American public servant, that his 'greatest attribute was his ability to reduce complex problems to their fundamentals'.[19]

To reiterate, the contrasting stories here of failure and success show that it is principally up to the locals to get and keep things right and to set and own the political, policy and investment framework to create a path to recovery and, ultimately, prosperity. This is not least because failure, fragility and state *dysfunctionality* is mostly the result of their own choices rather than an immutable cultural, geographic or climatic destiny.

This begets a prior question, however: what lies beneath these choices?

The answer in academic jargon is in the term 'political economy': the study of who gets what, when and how (the core questions of the discipline of politics) in the context of scarcity (the issues or patterns of production and distribution – key issues of the discipline of economics). Political economy describes a country's operating system, the intersection between politics and economics. In so doing, the book is especially focused on the relationship in particular between security and economics, how one might provide an essential framework for the other, and how the recovery and development phase might best proceed from that of initial security stabilisation.

The notion of a 'political economy' suggests, as will be illustrated in the following case studies, that reforming one aspect, one comparatively easy target, of a state is a necessary but insufficient component to reform. If the cycles of fragility, collapse and violence that affect more than a billion people require, at their core, national not foreign ownership of the problem, they also require bringing security, governance and development together. As World Bank President Robert Zoellick wrote in the World Development Report of 2011, which focused on fragile states (as have numerous other reports),[20] underlying this condition are 'recurrent cycles of weak governance, poverty, and violence ... [which] drag down neighbours with violence that overflows borders, because conflicts feed on narcotics, piracy, and gender violence, and leave refugees and broken infrastructure in their wake'. Zoellick concluded that 'separate disciplines are not well integrated to address the inter-related problems'.[21]

State failure, therefore, not only encompasses security issues but also bad politics, poor governance, divided societies and weak economics. Each circumstance is unique and demands a specifically tailored recovery process, though some general guidelines are possible. The answer to their recovery lies at the intersection of these aspects of politics, security, society and economics. Fixing just one dimension – improving governance or economic policy, for example – is rarely going to produce the wholesale systemic change nearly always required for state recovery, reform and development progress. Sometimes outsiders cannot even instigate the reform processes necessary for the recovery of such states, despite the presence of a plethora of well-wishers, consultants and fellow travellers endeavouring to do so.

Overall, where there is violence, there is need to get the security (likely led by the military) 'bit' of stabilisation right, where foreigners might play an important role. If you do not get that aspect right, then it does not matter how good the other bits are, which include the rule of law, governance and economics. The governance and economic dimensions of recovery are not possible without security and peace.

The security aspect cannot, however, succeed alone. The commitment of substantial military and financial resources to circumstances as diverse as Iraq and Afghanistan illustrates that there is no such thing as a 'security solution' to a country's problems. Security 'crackdowns' might provide space, but a political and economic solution is fundamentally required for even medium-term stability. Neither is the solution just the need for better policy, or more resources, whether this is in the form of technical skills, infrastructure or finances. It is all of these aspects, and more.

Given that they involve, largely, choices by domestic actors, reform and recovery processes are inevitably deeply fraught and highly politicised. This is especially the case in fragile states where the politics are already turbulent and costly, relegating the country to a condition of underdevelopment, insecurity and poverty. This situation is amplified by the need for the continuous generation and influx of people, skills, technology and capital to enable recovery and reform.

Walking societies

Take Malawi, which since independence in July 1964 has been regarded as one of the world's poorest countries. (According to the World Bank,[22] in 2012 it ranked 211th out of 213 countries and territories,[23] its nominal annual per capita income of $320 placing it above only Burundi and the Democratic Republic of Congo.)[24] Its level of poverty was all the more remarkable in that it had not been the result of war, and that it had gone in 30 years from 50 per cent richer than its neighbour to the east and south, Mozambique, to twice as poor.[25]

Through the haze on the road travelling from the capital Lilongwe to Lake Malawi, I saw long lines of Malawians traipsing along the road. Some were pushing laden bikes, others carrying wood, water or food. Water shortages in the north demand that women leave their homes in the early hours of the morning and walk up to 40 minutes to fetch water from the closest source.[26] Others were simply walking.

'We are a walking society,' said the Malawian seated next to me in the four-wheel-drive vehicle as it hurried down through a bucolic rural setting of villages, roadside maize and lazy green fields to the lakeside town of Salima. 'We walk into town in search of work, we walk home, we walk here, there and everywhere. But,' he warned, 'this is not a good thing. It wastes time, it is unproductive. Those lucky to have work can only work six hours a day. The rest of the time they are walking. It is a metaphor for our lack of productivity.'

Formal sector jobs are scarce in Malawi. The population was just four million at independence in 1964; half a century later it hovered around 15 million. Of this, 170 000 are employed in the civil service, and just 5 per cent have wage-earning jobs in the private sector. About 80 per cent of Malawians depend on agriculture for survival, with the sector providing just under one-third of gross domestic product (GDP). The bulk of income comes from tobacco farming, providing a livelihood for 200 000 commercial and smallholder farmers, and three-quarters of the country's export income, bringing in an annual average of $300 million during the 2000s.

It is a nation that has been living on borrowed time and donated money. Its balance of payments deficit – the difference between imports and exports – has remained consistently at about 50 per cent, again the shortfall being funded by foreign taxpayers. Stir in some bad policy and this explains why the country was, at the start of 2012, bankrupt and broken.

When the late President Bingu wa Mutharika, first elected in 2004, went, in the words of more than one of his ministers, 'bonkers', refusing to liberalise the exchange rate and angering the donors with his excesses (including the purchase of a $20-million private jet), things started to fall apart. Yet he kept subsidising fuel and farm inputs, stoking domestic growth and demand for consumer imports. With an artificial exchange rate in place, this only worsened the country's balance sheet, ensuring an exchange rate adjustment was always going to be significant and most likely painful.

The former president might not feel quite the same way, of course, but it was a bonus for Malawi that Bingu possessed a sense of timing. His fatal heart attack in early April 2012 opened the way for his successor, Joyce Banda, who immediately had to set about tackling the twin tasks of spending less and prioritising economic growth. There was no time to waste. Not only did she have to pull her cabinet straight, not an easy task in a fractious and temporarily leaderless political environment, but she also had to deal with the immediate challenge of freeing the Malawian currency from its artificial peg, putting the conditions for stability and growth in place. Even though the currency was immediately liberalised, her government strained to shake off ingrained bad habits. Although some donors were quick, for example, to condemn her regime and suspend aid over a September 2013 corruption scandal known as 'cash-gate', graft was not invented under her watch. Rather it had become a way of life over the previous two decades. Malawi's contemporary political economy has been founded on patronage, with corruption and 'middleman' practices of rent-seeking, enrichment and redistribution as the tools.

Short donor memories were not helped by clumsy government actions. Still, donor outrages over her regime's (lack of) governance smacked of certain hypocrisy, not least since the largest recent corruption scandals had been perpetrated and institutionalised through Bingu's seed and fertiliser schemes, a favourite programme at the time of some donors and United Nations (UN) agencies. As one vice president of the UN's International Fund for Agricultural Development naively commented about Bingu's food self-sufficiency drive: 'It was a very bold decision to provide subsidies for seeds and fertilizers.'[27] Yet as *The Guardian* noted about the late president's term in office: '[He] made himself the country's biggest landowner, built a vast mansion with suitcases of cash stashed under the bed, went on two-week-long holidays to Macau and appointed his brother as foreign minister.'[28]

The walking society that is Malawi shows more than technocratic reforms are necessary. Mrs Banda or any other political leader would not be able to do this alone. It would require leading Malawians in a different direction and altering their way of doing things. 'Malawians have a mindset,' noted my passenger about his compatriots, 'which comes from working three months a year on their crops and spending the other nine watching the moon and the sun.'

A sense of a lack of ownership of the future would seem, at a glance, to be related to the nature of both colonial and post-independence government, and the absence of a culture of responsibility on the part of leadership and others in government. In Malawi, as in other societies, patronage 'big-man' politics has been pervasive. Leaders have mostly not been held accountable to institutions, to parliament and to the written law. They have routinely only consulted informally with elites, formed around family, tribal or sectarian groups, in the absence of countervailing, institutionalised incentives.[29] These elites are the main beneficiaries of the distribution of political favours and preferential economic benefits. Limits on the excesses of self-interest have been attenuated by the need for legitimacy, functionality and historical legacy, including colonialism.

Recovery as an iceberg

Complex problems, in other words, which have taken many years to form, layer and harden, require assiduously applied strategies to analyse and solve them. They involve domestic political cycles, policy choices and long-term processes of state- and institution-building, consolidation and maturation. And they involve selfless leadership. Mancur Olson, for example, argues in *Power and Prosperity* of the difference between 'roving bandits' (an anarchical environment) where the incentive is only to steal and destroy, and 'stationary bandits' (authoritarianism) where there is an incentive to encourage security and a degree of economic success, since the leader will expect to be in power long enough to take a share of that success, the seeds of civilisation and eventual democracy.[30]

These aspects demand understanding the nature of society, its formation and its operation, and the journey from traditional to modern examples. Here the role of identity in economic distribution runs through many of the country cases. For example, in Rwanda, a prominent and emotionally powerful example of a country rising from the ashes,[31] the question is whether the country's post-genocide economic gains are building national over ethnic identities; or whether they are a strategy for the political elite to rule in ways that are removed from peoples' daily experiences and that allow this elite to create a state that suits its own needs.

If policy is the tip of the reform iceberg,[32] other issues below the surface need to be addressed, including culture, mindset, customs and tradition. In 1999, the eminent Harvard political scientist Samuel Huntington provided his answer as to why some countries take off economically and others do not: 'For decades, economists have grappled with the question, "Why have some countries developed economically and become prosperous, while others remained mired in backwardness and poverty?" They have not been able to find a convincing economic answer. This question struck me with particular force some years ago when I happened to run across economic data on Ghana and South Korea from 1960. At that time, these two countries had almost identical economic profiles in terms of per capita GNP, relative importance of their primary, manufacturing, and service sectors, nature of their exports, and amounts of foreign aid. Thirty years later South Korea had become an industrial giant, with high per capita income, multinational corporations, a major exporter of cars and electronic equipment, while Ghana still remained Ghana. How could one account for this difference in performance? Undoubtedly many factors were responsible, but I became convinced that culture was a large part of the explanation. South Koreans valued thrift, savings, and investment, hard work, discipline, and education. Ghanaians had different values.'[33]

According to this perspective, three phrases are said to define Malawi's circumstances: *Choncho nanga titani?* (literally, Oh, well, what else can we do), *katangale* (corruption) and *nsanje* (jealousy). Transformation requires altering this pernicious combination of jealousy, corruption, handouts and fatalistic resignation that has characterised Malawi's political economy. Yet this does not have to be Malawi's destiny if East Asia, a region (as we will see) viewed in the 1950s by some as a development basket case because of cultural factors, is a guide.

Changing the attitude of helplessness and alienation that lies behind such a 'walking society' is important in delinking it from its traumatic past and a fantasy of helplessness. This is true in other countries well beyond Malawi's and Africa's borders.

Grappling with terms

The term 'failed' states, first apparently used by Madeleine Albright to describe Somalia in August 1993,[34] was followed by the development of the expressions 'failing' and then 'fragile' states. Such terminology is, *The Guardian* has concluded, rather 'like Jabba the Hutt after a night at an all-you-can-eat pizzeria: broad and ill-defined'.[35] This is little helped by further attempts, such as that by the World Bank, to redefine them as 'low-income countries under stress or "LICUS"'. The very notion of a 'failed' state itself has been rejected by some since it 'implies no degree of success or failure, no sense of decline or progress ... a binary division between those countries that are salvageable and those beyond redemption. It is a word,' says *The Guardian*, 'reserved for marriages and exams.'[36]

Rankings and labelling of fragility (and failure) are increasingly resisted by the very states they seek to describe on the grounds that they know more about their domestic circumstances than outsiders, and that such 'external assessments can ignore important early signs of progress, destroying citizen confidence and killing off progress.'[37] As President Ellen Johnson Sirleaf, who has led Liberia magnificently from the ashes of decades of war from 2005 to the point where the West African nation might contemplate a development take-off, puts it: 'Fragile states do not lack the political will to achieve sustained growth.'[38]

In sum, it is both a confusing and controversial debate.

Economic growth and per capita income figures are often an expedient shorthand to identify poor and weak countries based on their trajectory and absolute levels. This is the Bloomberg thesis, the three-time New York City mayor motto being: 'In God we trust; everyone else, bring data.' Such empiricism helps to steer qualitative insights, with all their risks of personal prejudices and other frailties.

GDP is, however, an imperfect measure of failure: the OECD maintains, for example, that whereas most fragile states were low-income a decade ago, nearly half (21) of the 47[39] that the OECD classifies as 'fragile', were middle-income countries by 2013.[40] Moreover, five of the ten fastest-growing countries between 2001 and 2010 were also fragile – Angola, Chad, Ethiopia, Nigeria and Rwanda. Despite this broad definition, none of the OECD's 47 is from the Arab world, notable when one considers the state of Iraq or Syria.[41]

A further general problem with statistics, whatever their reliability (and in situations of failure, statistics are often a first casualty of weak governance),[42] is that they ameliorate the extremes. What does an 'average' life expectancy in Angola, for example, convey about the prospects of longevity for a young child born into Luanda's masseques or slums? What can GDP per capita inform us about the reality of wealth divides in terms of access to education, health care and finance, the sum of future prospects, where 'slumdog millionaires' are enough of an exception for movies to be made about them? What might statistics tell us about the relationship between these sprawling city slum belts and politics?

This book seeks rather to describe, pinpoint and understand less the statistical character than the qualitative micro-terrain of these states, along with the defining declivities and idiosyncrasies of the personalities, the policy substance and shifts, the hard and human infrastructure and, above all, the type of politics, all of which combine to create a pathology of failure. This exists across a wide and varied spectrum, from Somalia at one extreme to, for example, Kenya or even Argentina at another. Countries can contain both elements of perfect functionality and failure for different communities; indeed, some constituencies prosper under conditions of failure. And failure can occur in terms of extreme violence and the collapse of the state through the failure to deliver basic common goods to democratic failure through authoritarianism.

The abiding commonality for states on this spectrum of failure is that they fail their citizens while usually enriching their elites. And while the notion of being such a failure implies a certain apathy and helplessness, to the contrary it is precisely local ownership of this 'state of being' and consequent action that will ultimately ensure state recovery and success.

Qualitative aspects – the attitudes, policies and situations that tell the history, explain the present and point to the likely future of fragile states – help to provide insights beyond the statistical exoskeleton in trying to explain these situations. These traits are seldom observable from the sanitary bubble of business class and international hotel chains, chauffeured transport and meeting halls. This is not the high-altitude Africa, to take the continental example where the bulk of fragile states are located, of safaris by celebrities or former prime ministers and presidents, whose arrogance is only matched by their ignorance and surreal, antiseptic experiences, somewhere between Animal Planet and Live Aid.

Just as there is a continuum of failure, there is a spectrum of intervention.

At the more benign end of the interventionist scale are actions, such as support for NGOs and other aspects of civil society, budget support, military training, democratic institutions and practices, and technical inputs and expertise, ranging through humanitarian assistance, governance conditionalities, structural adjustment support and post-conflict reconstruction to the protection of civilian populations, peace-support operations, including peacekeeping and peace enforcement, and at the extreme, regime change. The manner of delivery of such support depends, too, on a range of factors: whether the country is considered a wider threat, the scale and extent of the humanitarian issue, whether this is a bilateral or multilateral or even continental involvement, and, again at the furthest extreme, whether global conventions, including that on genocide, are invoked. In assessing the utility of this method, this book considers examples from the full spectrum of operations.

The trends that are driving these wars appear to be unstoppable.

Where things are already difficult, in many cases they are facing escalating strain. The shorthand for this world is in managing the expected increase in population numbers. The world took 64 000 years to reach one billion, in 1820, reflecting a history of wars, famines, pandemics and the slow pace of improvement of technology and governance. Then numbers started to accelerate as, in particular, communications and transport improved and industrial manufacturing took hold. The second billion took just over 100 years, in 1926, the third following by 1960 despite a fall in fertility numbers in the richer countries as affluence spread. As hundreds of millions escaped destitution, rates of mortality fell and population numbers exploded. Four billion were added in little more than a half-century. The fourth billion came in 1975, the fifth in 1988, and the six-billion mark during the year 2000. Accumulation kept accelerating. Seven billion was reached in December 2011.[43] The challenge is not in absolute numbers alone. It is about what people want and where people will be living. The growth in urban and littoral areas will be greater over the next 30 years than the number of people that lived on the planet in 1950. While the world population (at current fertility levels) is anticipated to increase from seven billion to around the nine-billion mark in 2040, Asia and Africa will make up three-quarters of this number, the latter at almost two billion – twice as many people as today.[44] The problem is not the numbers per se, given that at least in Africa the continent's population density (27 square kilometres) is little more than half the global average (45 square kilometres), but rather the inability or unwillingness to prepare adequately for this future. If the regions and countries that will experience this bulge can prepare properly in terms of infrastructure, services and health and education systems, it is possible to envisage a demographic dividend as the dependency ratios (the number of people working compared to the young and old dependent on them) fall and a surge of high-energy, young people arrive in the job market. In Africa, for example, the dependency ratio (measured as a percentage of the population under the age of fifteen or over 65) is anticipated to drop from over 80 per cent in 2010 to under 60 per cent in 2050 as, with ageing populations, this rises from 50 per cent in Europe and North America to over 60 per cent during the same period.

The impact, however, goes beyond managing their physical accommodation to a more complex intersection of improved connectivity, the globally fed and media-linked aspirations of a swell of energetic but restless young people, and stresses over the provision of basic services, not least housing, health care, education, water, electricity and food. One lesson from the Arab Spring is that the movement of people to the city from rural areas creates political as well as economic linkages, feeding not only people into the cities, but political and social stress as well as economic tensions. As David Kilcullen writes in *Out of the Mountains*, the Tunisian unrest started outside of Tunis in the town of Sidi Bouzid, but quickly reached into the capital, spreading rapidly through digital means along more ancient paths of kinship. Quickly, 'the synergy between virtual and real-world activism escalated into revolution'.[45]

The future, without proper preparation and selfless politics, looks bleak.

Being younger has consequences because young people have different outlooks, demands, tastes, mentality, aspirations, expectations, values and, critically, patience. The density of cities amplifies by the speed and volume at which everything from people to money, illness to goods, now moves. These changes are far more global and more inclusive than at any stage in history, with lower barriers of entry for its participants than ever before. Whereas when there is a gap between supply and demand, in economic terms, you have inflation; when you have a gap between people, aspirations, patience and the ability to manage these aspects, you have uncertainty and probably violence.[46]

It is not as if these challenges have remained unrecognised, especially in weak, uncertain environments. The so-called 'Principles for Good International Engagement in Fragile States and Situations' (or Fragile States Principles), which were endorsed at the 2007 OECD's Development Assistance Committee, recognise that such states face extreme development challenges such as weak governance and administrative capacity, chronic humanitarian crises and persistent social tensions and violence or the legacy of civil war. They also recognise that any sustainable and durable exit from such poverty and insecurity will need to be driven by their own leadership and people. The Principles, therefore, emphasise the need to: take 'context' as the starting point; ensure activities do no harm; focus on state-building as the central objective; prioritise prevention; recognise the links between political, security and development objectives; promote non-discrimination as a basis for inclusive and stable societies; align with local priorities; agree on practical coordination mechanisms between international actors; act fast, staying engaged long enough to give success a chance; and avoid pockets of exclusion, or so-called 'aid orphans'.[47]

A failure to adhere to such principles can lead to great frustration.[48] It is important that we not only learn but also learn to *apply* the lessons of the recent past when it comes to intervention. Even though there are, as this book posits, severe constraints on the utility of external actions and actors, the difference between success and failure will reside in the difference between those that learn the lessons of the past and those that do not. As Vietnam shows of an earlier generation of conflict and liberation, and Iraq and Afghanistan in particular remind us, mistakes and lessons are quickly forgotten, perhaps even deliberately erased to ease the institutional conscience, only to be re-learnt.

This book examines three dozen country case studies from Afghanistan to Zimbabwe to identify the role for external actors, and to detail strategies for recovery and help to devise a political economy for success. As they will show, the key determinant of success or failure is less the assistance the international community can provide than the willingness and ability of the locals to seize the opportunity – the moment of stability – sometimes created by their presence.

What lies behind the selection of its case studies?

The eminent Oxford economist Paul Collier helps in where to start looking by identifying 58 countries – amounting to a billion people – which are slipping behind the rest of the world for reasons of conflict, possession of few economic advantages save natural resources, being landlocked (often with bad neighbours) and poor governance. While, of course, not all fragile states are African, 70 per cent of Collier's 'Bottom Billion'[49] are in Africa.[50]

This group is overlaid with the states identified in the *Foreign Policy* and Fund for Peace's Failed State Index.[51] This is based on twelve primary social, economic and political indicators: demographic pressure; refugees and internally displaced people; group grievance; human rights and brain drain; uneven economic development; poverty and economic decline; state legitimacy; public services; human rights and rule of law; security apparatus; factionalised elites; and external intervention. The vast majority (23) of the bottom 'high-alert'[52] 35 countries ranked in 2013, for example, in the Failed States Index are in Africa. Somalia topped the Index for the sixth straight year, while the rest of the top-ten list comprised, in order: Somalia, Democratic Republic of Congo, Sudan, South Sudan, Chad, Yemen, Afghanistan, Haiti, Central African Republic and Zimbabwe.

Most of the case studies examined in this volume are taken from this Bottom Billion/Failed States group of 65 countries.

Nearly all of these states (with the notable exception of Venezuela and Argentina) have received considerable amounts of aid. As one illustration, donor flows to the Bottom Billion/Failed State Index group amount to $70 per capita, more than three times the global average, and approximately 45 per cent of all official development assistance. In the case of Afghanistan and Kosovo, there has been an extraordinary international peace-building and aid effort over a sustained period of time, emblematic for critics and supporters of what is wrong and right with international relations in terms of motive and commitment.

Some of the countries examined here have fought bitter civil conflicts in the twenty-first century (Angola, Iraq, Syria, Congo, Colombia, Afghanistan, Uganda, for example); others have been largely stable. Some have collapsed, with a consequent exodus of people, skills and financial capital. Most are democratic, even though they might be overwhelmingly considered as weak and, in some cases, 'authoritarian democracies'.

These are not from just one continent – even though Africa is the home of the bulk of fragile states – but include examples from Latin America, South, Central and East Asia, Europe and the Middle East, islands, littoral and land-locked states, and examples from different sub-regions within continents. There are very big states (Congo or Nigeria) and very small (Rwanda or Kosovo). They have different colonial histories, with a variety of colonisers, over vastly different historical timescales. The case studies contain examples of countries with Islamic governments, and those with secular regimes. Some have experienced bloody wars of liberation, others not. Some have enjoyed political transitions through negotiation; in the case of others this has only occurred after bitter, bloody and otherwise destructive struggles. Most have been deeply integrated with the global economy, even though at times on unfavourable terms of trade, and are active in the global political system, but some (Myanmar is one extreme example) have been isolated, not only economically, but politically as well.

They share many other features. Most fall into the low-income bracket. They are nearly all dependent on commodity exports, especially oil and gas. They are all, as will be seen, countries that export what they produce, and import what they consume. Many are riven by fault lines, whether these be around ethnicity, religion or race. They have weak governance regimes, with a poor record on tackling corruption. Their leadership invariably centres on individuals rather than institutions, yet these leaders have proven over time to be part of the problem.

Different types of failure

The case studies here exhibit different types of failure.

The presence of international peacekeepers is usually an indicator that things have come badly unstuck. The costs of and commitment to such international missions, bilateral and multilateral, civilian and military, peacekeeping and building, peacemaking and enforcement, UN-mandated or otherwise, have steadily increased over the past 70 years, and during the 2000s in particular. In sum, the direct costs of twenty-first-century global peacekeeping and peace-building ventures are estimated by mid-2013 to be over $2 trillion.[53] And the demands continue. In October 2013, for example, the African Union endorsed a 35 per cent increase in its force fighting Al-Shabab in Somalia, taking the total to 23 966. At the same time, the UN appealed for an increase in troops and more helicopters for its 12 000-strong peacekeeping mission in Mali in order to stabilise the north and protect civilians from attacks by Islamist groups. And while France was planning to reduce its contingent of 3 200 troops in Mali to 1 000, at the same time it was aiming to lift its presence in the Central African Republic to try to stop the violence there from spiralling further out of control.[54]

Let us call this type of fragility 'collapse', even though sub-state elements can actually prosper in such a setting, and money can be made especially by short-term speculators and traders. Of the three basic political institutions that Francis Fukuyama identifies – the state, rule of law and accountable government[55] – as components of good, competent, inclusive societies, this 'fragility category' is one where all three have disintegrated.

Such collapse can be the result of a military defeat – such as Germany or Japan after the Second World War. These circumstances were easier to recover from, given that the inner stuffings of talent and knowledge still existed within these states. The type of state failure resulting in collapse that is described here occurs where there has been a less dramatic and more insidious version of hollowing out of capacity as a result likely of a political system geared towards extraction and rent-seeking rather than a more inclusive vision of popular welfare, ultimately ending in a version of collapse from which it is more difficult to recover.

Collapse does not occur, however, where there was no state to begin with. One symptom of state fragility is taken as the inability of the state to extend power to its extremes – to its 'ungoverned spaces' to use the contemporary parlance. Yet this weakness has never, however, in Africa at least, been a definition of state failure. African regimes inherited countries from their colonial masters, who were unable to extend power throughout their capitals let alone to the extremities of their state boundaries, which helps to explain why at its outset in 1963, the Organisation of African Unity declared a moratorium on the continent's borders. The costs of not having such power extension as a precondition for the recognition of African post-colonial statehood can be seen in contemporary terms in the situation in Mali, as but one example, where long-time smuggling routes along such spaces have intersected with perhaps no less criminal but decidedly more ideological groupings. Both these groups, criminal and political, share the intent to take advantage of the absence of state authority, not least by cutting a profit in the process – so-called 'conflict entrepreneurs'.

Let us call this a failure to build the state, where basic services and 'common' goods, including health and education, along with infrastructure, are seldom anticipated or delivered. This failure not only undermines the relationship between the state and its citizens, increasing the likelihood of violent rupture, but the absence of lack of hard (roads, ports, railroads, electricity) and soft (systems, skills) infrastructure makes improvements difficult.

These are very difficult places to survive in, let alone prosper.

This, to take a continental example, is not the high-growth Africa of a swelling middle class, burgeoning consumerism, improving education, unstoppable investment flows and improving agriculture output, where the efficiencies of cellular technology have transformed lives, freeing up previously paralysed commerce and communications. That Africa exists, in pockets within some countries, and certainly in spirit and intent, but not across the continent.

This is then an Africa not benefiting from rapid urbanisation, the demographic dividend and the density of nascent mega-cities, but a continent where, already, 200 million live in slums, the highest number of any continent. These urban areas are in this scenario not promising nodes of development, but suffocating situations of disorder and decay, futureless and hopeless, of endemic unemployment and fragmentary education, where services, where they exist, were designed for a fraction of the current population.

They are the pressure cooker where politics attempts to manage high expectations. These are post-modern places of hardship and hard edges of violence and its corollary of insecurity, where its people are 'not indestructible ... but badly in need of rescue'.[56] They include the touts risking life and limb to sell bootleg books while dodging manic traffic on the highways through Lagos, the glowering youths loitering on Monrovia's street corners with little to do, the prostitutes loitering under Abidjan's street lights beneath my hotel window, some painfully young, haggling and hassling their way through the night, or the great human waves making their way into Kinshasa's mega-city in the morning to look for work, and drifting back, bobbling spots in the moving dust, mostly empty-handed come sundown.

This is the African antidote to the euphoric, celebrationist consultancy trying to sell an upbeat vision of the continent along with its services or a fund talking up prospective returns on investment. This is not the romantic Africa, but one of rutted and potholed roads, ubiquitous evidence of a lack of investment and maintenance regimes and of a failure of governance. It is the Africa of the streets far beyond the hotel lobby, of sitting in a locomotive *clank-clanking* its way across the East African escarpment while shooting the breeze with the guard and driver about family and goals, not being served by white-coated waiters in five-star luxury during bouts of policy-sightseeing or, the military equivalent, 'counter-tourism'. It is the Africa where people have made a plan in the absence of their governments having one; where digital technology remains, cellphones aside, tantalisingly out of reach, but where the old analogue ways no longer work for spares, skills or systems.

Democratic failure

In great part, the answer to achieving development lies in better checks and balances, on better and more accountable government – in a word, democracy. It depends less on wresting political control from other nations, no matter how dramatic and important that was a half-century ago, than it does on deliberate and steady processes of nation-building, on parliamentary processes, for example, rather than individual personalities, and on assiduously building internal capacity and a domestic revenue base through taxation, investment, good governance and the rule of law as opposed to seeking rapid development solutions through populist redistribution or external aid.

There are clear empirical links between the strength and health of democracy and governance. Excluding East Asia, autocracies have median growth rates 50 per cent lower than even weak democracies. There are good reasons for this beyond that democracy is 'nice to have' for human rights sensitivities. For one, as the former UN Secretary General Kofi Annan noted at the turn of the century: 'Democracies have far lower levels of internal violence than non-democracies … In an era when more than 90 percent of wars take place within, not between, states, the import of this finding for conflict prevention should be obvious.'[57] When it comes to explaining East Asia's development success, those supportive of a more authoritarian development-type state are prone to leave out the other critical bits from their supporting analysis exhibited by high-growth Asian countries. The focus on production not subsidisation, efficient and small civil service, and an overwhelming drive to diversify through competitiveness are but a few policy characteristics and concerns. Indeed, East Asia has used its inclusive growth (that not just benefiting co-opted elites) to enhance regime legitimacy in spite of a lack of liberal democracy.

As the work by the African Center for Strategic Studies' researcher Joseph Siegle illustrates,[58] democracies do a much better job of creating 'accountability institutions': that is, those institutions focusing on rule of law, providing checks against executive power, controlling corruption, ensuring bureaucratic efficiency and separating political allegiance from public opportunity. Greater openness tends to lead to better decision-making with improved information flows, while also ensuring fairer allocation of opportunity through increased accountability and more efficiency in markets. And democracies are better at keeping wealth, too. When things are going badly, there are more public alarm bells and more responsiveness. Not only are democracies more likely to avoid conflict (80 per cent of inter-state conflicts are initiated by autocracies; and 80 per cent are won by democracies), but democracies tend to have more systematic succession mechanisms – if you have a poor leader, you can replace the person without too much upheaval, at the same time offering norms for legitimacy and government. As Siegle's published work in 2010 showed, since the end of the Cold War, only nine of 85 autocracies worldwide have realised sustained economic growth. Moreover, 48 of these autocracies had at least one episode of disastrous economic experience (defined as an annual contraction in per capita GDP of 10 per cent or more) during this period.

More recent econometric analysis by Cornell academics Nic van der Walle and Takaaki Masaki substantiates further the link between democracy and growth.[59] In their analysis of 43 (of 49) countries in sub-Saharan Africa for the period of 1982–2012, the authors find 'strong evidence that democracy is positively associated with economic growth', and that this 'democratic advantage' is more pronounced for those African countries that have been democratic for longer periods of time.

In terms of governance and democracy, there has been much progress made in Africa, the site in 2013, according to the African Development Bank, of 20 of the 36 states classified worldwide as fragile, home to some 200 million people.[60] In the 1970s, there were just 41 democracies worldwide, which increased to 76 in 1991. By 2013, 90 regimes were considered to be 'free', while there were 118 electoral democracies.[61] Africa has experienced a parallel democratic revolution between 1980 (when they numbered three) and today, when more than 40 countries regularly hold multi-party elections. Even though some of these processes are undoubtedly flawed, the progress towards representative democracies is unmistakeable, in part because the alternatives have delivered such miserable results in Africa as elsewhere. Democracy assists in ensuring that the 'political' aspect lurking under the iceberg, shaping economic choices, is at least more responsive to public demands. Or, as the Ethiopian prime minister, Hailemariam Desalegn, explains: 'If we don't deal with rent-seeking behaviour, elections will only end up being zero-sum, rent-seeking exercises.'[62]

Still, there is a discussion about the value of democracy and, it is hinted, the preference of a benign 'developmental dictatorship' in late-developing economies. A combination of low literacy levels, the distraction and financial cost of regular domestic election cycles, and a preference for a strong figure 'who can just get things done' are all whispered as reasons for a 'strongman', an 'authoritarian advantage' – what might be, in an African context at least, modelled a 'Kigali consensus' after the policies pursued in Rwanda post-genocide: no electoral or redistributive distractions from the task of economic growth, yet with little chance of losing power.

But the problem of such a model is that many fragile states have already experienced such one-party or one-man leadership, and it has worked less like Lee Kuan Yew's Singapore than a caricature of a tinpot and often extremely brutal dictatorship. Also, imagine if the literacy level argument had been applied to South Africa in 1994; the legacy of apartheid would have disproportionately favoured whites over disenfranchised blacks. It is an unconscionable argument. Democracy is an imperfect but infinitely preferable system, and not just from a human rights perspective or as a tool for ongoing peaceful domestic conflict resolution. Authoritarian regimes tend to run things badly in the absence of the checks and balances present in democratic states. As Masaki and Van de Walle observe, 'In Africa, the disastrous economic management of the 1970s and 1980s had no doubt many causes, but it did suggest that the region's authoritarian governments, unlike perhaps those of East Asia, were not adept at promoting economic growth.'

Related to this third sort of 'democratic' failure, there is another type of contemporary state fragility that has a profound impact on the quality of governance. This type may, indeed, be the outcome of a restorative process of order under the international community, which results in a peace settlement, the establishment of democratic institutions and elections.

This type of fragility is, however, created when people vote for democracy but get a dictator, strongman or authoritarian government instead, even if they are more sophisticated, savvy and have better (and more highly paid) public relations than their Cold War prototype. These are not the lumbering, crude caricatures of authoritarianism à la North Korea or the old Soviet Union, the totalitarian misnamed 'People's Democracies' or 'Democratic Republics', but a much more sophisticated variant, where democracy and its necessary institutions – including parliament and NGOs – are permitted only up to a point. Hence, the existence of legislation in such states around foreign funding of NGOs (but never on state funding), for example, overstuffed presidencies, control of television especially, looking after 'friends' and regulatory interference in independent businesses or NGOs, all the time 'blending repression with regulation'.[63] Authoritarianism is also used as a justification to deal with poverty, despite the clear correlation, especially outside Asia, between economic performance and democratic governance. This is where the media is emasculated or wholesale owned and controlled by government or its lackeys, contrary to Thomas Jefferson's counselling that eternal vigilance is an essential element of a democratic system.

These states are also those where government apparatus may be employed as a lever to crush the opposition, tamper or sometimes wholesale rig the election results, and where the law is employed to reinforce party interests. The late Venezuelan strongman, Hugo Chávez, is said to have ruled along the lines of the mantra, 'To my friends, everything, for my enemies, the law'.[64]

Such 'authoritarian democracy' – authoritarianism with democratic language, institutional facade, procedures and trappings – otherwise known as 'virtual democracy', is usually bad news for the economy since the state has proven pathologically maladroit at picking winners, often because such arrangements are primarily geared to elite interests and/or their cranky economic schemes. All of this is likely to extract a further huge cost in terms of accountability, corruption, transparency, the rule of law and public and private sector efficiency. Democracies generally, as the foregoing quantitative analysis illustrates, perform better given that governance institutions and the rule of law are stronger, that they protect people and business alike.

Businesses that reinvest over decades, which are the sort most worth attracting, desire policy predictability and the rule of law, where the judiciary is independent and fair in protecting private investors against malignant government and other actions.

*

These three types of state failure are overlapping, inter-related and can affect each other. A failure to deliver basic goods and services and a failure of democracy can lead to violent collapse. And despite the differences between these three types – outright collapse, a failure to build the state and authoritarian democracy – in all there is one constant: the deliberate failure and neglect of the state to provide for all of its citizens.

Sometimes this choice is by design and even necessity. Robert Mugabe deliberately targeted opposition supporters by removing them from the farms and the towns to which they had migrated. All the while he distributed the proceeds to a small clique of his ruling party, at the same time running the country into the ground. It was also deemed necessary to destroy those who were seen as trying to sabotage the rule of Mugabe's Zimbabwe African National Union-PF party (such as the white farmers who were backing the opposition), and the economy was collateral damage.

Mobutu followed a similar path in Congo, the country temporarily from 1971–77 also known as Zaire. There he ran the country down to ensure that it could not unite against him. We can call this failure by dividing and ruling; his cabinet game of musical chairs being one feature of this system. The man born in 1930 as Joseph-Désiré Mobutu, who renamed himself Mobutu Sese Seko Kuku Ngbendu wa Za Banga (the all-powerful warrior who, because of his endurance and inflexible will to win, goes from conquest to conquest, leaving fire in his wake), described by former Kinshasa Central Intelligence Agency (CIA) station chief, Larry Devlin, as a 'political genius' if an 'economic spastic',[65] survived three decades through a combination of brutal repression (including public hangings of opponents), regular rotations of ministers (over 50 full cabinet changes in three decades), huge inflows of foreign aid (estimated at $9 billion during Mobutu's years, with the US the third-largest donor after Belgium and France), nationalisation of foreign interests (including the rich copper and cobalt mines), the development of a personality cult and the perfection of patronage politics (including the management of state interests by political cronies). His image of Mao-style abacost suit, thick-framed Buddy Holly glasses, walking stick and leopard-skin toque was the more benign aspect of his idiosyncratic bent that went with his Zairianisation or *authenticité* campaign. Underlying it all was a far less attractive mix of repression, spite, nepotism and corruption.

Like Mobutu, Mugabe's Zimbabwe and Chávez's (and, following his death, Nicolás Maduro's) Venezuela fall into this 'political genius, economic spastic' category. In both, the apparent folly of property seizures, along with the wide difference between the official and black-market foreign exchange rate, have been used for party and personal financial advantage, where access to largesse is offered as a political preference. And there are other, similar environments where failure or dysfunctionality of key institutions is acutely deliberate, and in the interests, too, of key supporters. This applies, for instance, to customs and border facilities, where slowing down traffic provides opportunity for arbitrage.

This type of democratic failure does not have to be as obvious as the demagogue caricature of Mugabe or even Chávez. It can happen even in societies recognised as shining examples of post-conflict transition, such as South Africa. The ruling party's regard for the institutional components that keep government accountable and honest – parliament, the judiciary, civil society – have led respected commentators such as Alex Boraine, hardly known for polemical outburst, to question whether South Africa is on the brink of becoming a failed state, a status driven both by a historical disregard for democratic niceties, where a combination of identity politics along with personal and ruling party self-interest trumps governance and policy niceties. Boraine cites Burma's Nobel Peace laureate Aung Sang Suu Kyi's observation in this regard: 'It is not power that corrupts, but fear; fear of losing power corrupts those who wield it.'[66]

Leadership gets away with such subversion partly because their electorate is too busy surviving to care; or supports them actively or through their apathy; or democracy is weak; or where foreign aid organisations have helped to reduce the social pressures, which otherwise an inept government would have felt at the polls. Governments use all means, fair and foul, to deflect these pressures and stay in power, from traditional gerrymandering of constituencies and campaigning to appeal to ethnic racial fears and expectations à la Kenya, to outright vote tampering, addition and rigging à la Zimbabwe. Racial, ethnic and religious identity also plays its part. The suppressed rage over the colonial era pervades, and is employed by political leadership to explain exclusion and deprivation as the fault of others, though this argument is now overlaid with narrow domestic interests and 'insider' identities.

This is not to suggest that everyone does badly in these environments. Far from it. These transactions can enrich and entrench elites, especially largesse delivered less systemically than driven through personalities, often at the expense of the broader public and of economic growth and development.

A spectrum of failure

There appears to be no single reason or a tipping point at which a state becomes officially 'failed', an imaginary dividing line between success or normality and failure. This explains the difficulty in defining such states, and especially in categorising them. Failed, fragile, weak, collapsed, vulnerable, moribund, straggling, struggling, crisis, quasi-failed, 'non-state', broken, invisible, insufficient, stillborn, phantom, Michael Jackson, or even, as will be explained, Potemkin states, should be viewed on a spectrum or continuum rather than a balance sheet of failure.

Countries that work for some, at least for the relatively well-heeled visitor, can work against the locals. Think Kenya. There are those that significantly and continuously under-perform, lurching from crisis to crisis, a roller coaster of political and economic collapse, but do not explode into violence and become the focus of international aid groups, one external metric of failure. Think Argentina.

The strains of fragility – of governance, economics, politics and society – intersect and play out differently in different circumstances. While many states are fragile, there is a group at one extreme that threatens to explode or implode, and is as a result prioritised by external actors. At the other extreme, there are authoritarian democrats; states that might work for now, but whose lack of democratic governance threatens to undermine both their standards of governance and prospects of growth.

Yet, there are common features on this spectrum, the product of circumstance, policy and personality. Seldom is collapse or failure not in the interests of one group or another within the countries examined here – and it can even be a choice, a course of action deliberately and frequently assiduously pursued regardless of the consequences for many citizens. This is a short-term game; while this environment may benefit different groups, the transaction costs are ultimately as ruinous for the privileged elites, if only they knew it, as they are for the nation.

The essays in this volume are thus not intended to compare countries with each other item by item. Instead, they aim to highlight the abovementioned themes and those political, economic and societal commonalities that contribute to failure and to recovery. Rather than labelling states, by its use of case studies, this book seeks to identify and describe their operations, drivers and symptoms.

This analysis is guided by the questions: how should the international community best intervene, if at all, in fragile situations so as to offer the optimum chance of stability and recovery? Why has economic recovery in post-conflict countries proven so problematic? Why and how do countries develop effective state institutions? What is the relationship between legitimacy, leadership, policy choices, economic growth and political and social stability? Do states evolve naturally, at their own pace and in their own way, or are they shaped by leaders and ideas, or even by external intervention? Can the enemies of political order – partisanship and cronyism – in the form of family, kinship or tribal ties operating at the expense of the wider society, be managed not just through the establishment of rules, but the institutions required to make necessary reforms take effect and the legitimacy to ensure that they are followed? Put differently, what are the critical aspects of state success and how might outsiders and locals work to transform those 'walking' into 'winning' societies and 'losers' into better-functioning states?

The book deliberately dwells less on the details of the 'what' and 'how' in analysing the role of local and foreign institutions in bringing about success, but attempts to shed light on 'why' some foreign interventions are more successful than others, and 'why', also, states recover, evolve and develop. The conclusion summarises the difference between vicious and virtuous cycles and the role to be played by insiders and outsiders in a range of actions from humanitarian intervention, peacemaking and conflict resolution, to peacekeeping, development assistance and peace-building.

In this regard Simon Sinek, the strategic communications guru, offers a relevant assessment of *why* some enterprises are more successful than others. All, he says, of course know what they produce and how they produce them, but the factor that distinguishes the best from the rest is answering the 'why' question beyond just the need to make money, appreciating the true purpose of their organisation.[67] For Bata, for example, it has been the aim to put shoes on people's feet that has kept it in business for 120 years; or in the case of Steve Jobs and Apple, a desire to challenge the status quo, not just to build computers, but to put them in the home. As Jobs put it, 'What it represents is as important as what it is' – the aim being not just to sell computers, but to change what people do with a computer.[68]

Thus, this is not a book simply about 'what' is required to ensure success and the mechanics of the process, but about the political and power relationships that underpin them, domestically, between the public and private sectors, for example, and internationally, between donors and recipients. It is a book fundamentally about people and social currency, not just about the technology of change, the identification and replication of best practice, and manufacturing the right set of policy choices. It is a book about finding ways of doing things differently, not just better.

*

Of course, fragile state situations are not uniformly negative. At the most human level, there is constant testament to – and sometimes amazement at – how people find the means to carry on in the most difficult of circumstances. There have clearly been significant improvements in many of the countries detailed here. No one should, for a moment, think that Sierra Leone, for example, for all of its significant challenges, is not considerably better off now than it was during the succession of military regimes, downright bestiality and outright civil war of the 1990s. Ditto Liberia, or Guinea, Nigeria, Somalia and Afghanistan, among many others.

While ending conflict is the critical first step to recovery, change requires more than that. Removing the conditions that led to conflict in the first place demands a different and long-term operating system – one that aims to invest in people, governance and infrastructure. The path to this future and the metrics of advancement are more difficult and complex to discern.

This book does not then ask the question: is peace better than war? While there are groups who profit from war, the answer to that is as obvious as the question ridiculous. It asks instead: is there a common path to be found in changing societies from losers into winners?

Understanding why states recover and reform, and the role possible by insiders and outsiders in this process, the importance of strategy, and especially the role for institutions, policy and for leadership, is where this study now turns.

PART 1

∗

PATHOLOGIES AND
THREADS OF FAILURE

You have to wash with the crocodile in the river,
you have to swim with the sharks in the sea,
you have to live with the crooked politician,
trust those things that you can never see.

— Johnny Clegg, 'Cruel, Crazy, Beautiful World'

According to legend, Grigory Potemkin, the governor of Russia's southern provinces, erected fake mobile villages along the banks of the Dnieper River in order to fool his lover, Empress Catherine II, during her six-month visit to Crimea in 1787, an area devastated during the wars of conquest by the Russian army. To impress the empress and display progress of rebuilding and evidence of Russian settlement, Potemkin ensured that the queen was to see new villages from her barge. As soon as she had passed, the villages were disassembled and rebuilt downstream overnight to further amaze her on her journey through the newly conquered territories.

The term 'Potemkin village' is now used to describe any construction built to deceive others into thinking that a situation is better than reality. It is an appropriate term for the worst end of a fragile state spectrum. It also fittingly describes the fruitlessness of external actions, where the method pursued by outsiders from military trainers to donor agencies is that more aid delivered in smarter ways will deliver stability and development because this is what the locals want. This logic assumes that there is a rump of local state capacity to graft onto, to work with, and that the interests of the elites with whom the outsiders deal accord in large measure with the interests of their broader societies.

South Sudan is, at first glance, such a Potemkin state, with a pre-market economy, feudal in character, devoid of all bar the most basic of infrastructure, dependent on raw materials for export income, without necessary skills and with a volatile and fragile national identity, with a narrow sense of community among its peoples and the absence of a modern outlook.[1]

Certainly, its airport at the capital, Juba, presented the worst possible face to the visitor arriving at Africa's 55th and the world's newest country.[2]

To say there were chaotic conditions and surly staff would be an understatement, an experience not out of place on a *Dogs of War* set. A few glass cubicles smeared with many layers of fingerprints welcomed me into the arrivals room, behind which sit apparently Soviet-trained cadres, unsmiling to a fault. Those wanting a visa on arrival are in for a gruelling, begrudging rip-off process lasting, for my colleague, an hour, and costing a mere $100 for a single-entry stamp.[3]

Then there was the peculiar luggage-inspection process. Bags were passed from a trolley outside through a hole in the wall, and a rugby scrum ensued whereby these were identified, gripped and lugged to a nearby table. There men looked through our clothes and other belongings after which a pink chalk cross was made on the bag.

This enabled us to get through the guard at the exit of the classroom-sized space, hosting more than 100 heaving besandled *aidistas*, peacekeepers in camouflaged fatigues, diplomats and officials sweating into their suits, as well as mere mortals. After the guard, sitting on his plastic perch, had thumbed through our passports, asked to see the all-important yellow fever certificate and checked on the presence of those mysterious pink crosses, it was a few steps to the next guard at the exit who did much the same thing, again intent on identifying those elusive pink 'X's.

Outside, the usual throng of touts positioned themselves between travellers and a hangar-sized tin-roof, open-sided structure reportedly donated by North Sudan on the South's independence and divorce from them in July 2011. The northerners were clearly not especially gracious or generous. After all, the two Sudans had fought a 22-year civil war that left more than a million people dead.

Leaving the country was even more of an ordeal. The check-in counter amounted to a table, around which crowded dripping passengers and the 'agents' of those too important (or rich) to enjoy the check-in experience in person. Our bags were weighed separately, and taken somewhere else where we had to seek them out using a bag tag once the check-in process was completed. The check-in involved one person looking through your passport and procuring the boarding card and another filling your name in on a form, after which the first person printed the bag tag – all of this while physically winning the airport pushing-and-shoving equivalent of the Superbowl. Then the passport is stamped in yet another ramshackle cubicle but not before going through more manual searches (the X-ray machine was down and serving as a stool-cum-table) and yet another patting down by yet another official. Then, only, are passengers allowed to enter the single departure lounge, Juba's answer to the Black Hole of Calcutta.

The process was more form than substance, highlighting who was in charge. One foreign aviation assessment says Juba's airport security is 'non-existent', with 'no proper training, no money and limited capacity'. It was a metaphor for the new country.

Oh, and it was all absolutely filthy.

Yet, by April 2013, an estimated 1.5 million passengers were using this facility annually, with no fewer than 25 flight movements daily.

This is the same South Sudan, which, in the opinion of its own supporters, had neglected health and education expenditure and where 80 per cent of the budget went on the salaries of officials. The army and police forces alone comprised not fewer than 210 000 people. Investment in basic services had lagged as a result; as the cities have swelled and housing sprung up, water sanitation has become of great concern.

This was the government, too, that had failed to get power projects up and running. The largest investor, SABMiller, with an $81-million stake in a brewery in Juba, generates more power (6 MW) than the government in the capital city. All of South Sudan's power was, by the start of 2013, provided by diesel generators. And the cost of transporting fuel to run them meant that in Juba power worked out to be $3 per kW/h (or 30 times the cost in South Africa), and as much as $30 kW/h in Malakal, 1 500 kilometres to Juba's north.

This has made South Sudan 'an extremely expensive place' to do business, said foreign investors and operators. The situation was compounded by poor roads, low skills and high salaries. While a security guard in Nairobi cost a company $300 per month to hire, in Juba this was $650. South Sudan exemplifies the truism that countries are poor because they are expensive, and expensive because they are poor.[4] The absence of land title and thus collateral for loans is also a significant and continuously cited constraint to growing entrepreneurship.

This is the same country that had become increasingly intolerant of foreign workers, especially towards the large number of fellow East Africans from Uganda and Kenya. Outside investors were uneasy about pending stipulations on at least partial local ownership of foreign-owned companies.

This was the South Sudan ruled by the Sudanese People's Liberation Movement (SPLM), a political party fraught with the management of ethnic divisions, grappling with national and party democratisation, and where entitlement apparently held sway over free market competition. This was the SPLM where commanders and their martial methods trumped civil niceties, where the highest level of experience of politicians and civil servants at the time of independence was commanding a battalion in the field, and where old boy networks and the barrel of the gun from which political power and independence had sprung, remain more powerful than civilian institutions in upholding the rule of law. It is a place where an estimated $6 billion had gone missing from national accounts since the original Comprehensive Peace Agreement was signed with the North in 2005.

This was the movement where officials called each other 'Comrade' or 'General', where there was a Politburo, where the government saw, in the words of one diplomat, 'the China model as appropriate for their political system', with one-party instincts and identity rather than issue-based politics. It was a country still defined by war, and by its relationship with Khartoum, where 'government', says one diplomat, 'makes every decision on the basis of going back to war with the North'.

This was the same country that, with abundant land and water, could feed East Africa, but remained dependent on donors for more than a billion dollars in humanitarian food and other forms of aid. It was the country with one of the largest herds of cattle in Africa, over 10 million head, but where meat was imported, cows being a source of wealth and status, not of protein. It was an economy where virtually everything else, too, had to be imported, from corrugated iron to plastic bottles, sugar to septic tanks, cement to bottle tops, even meat and maize. The South Sudanese had either lost or never achieved an ability to sustain a complex urban market economy, a factor embedded in the anatomy of the new state.

Rich in oil but poor in development, on its independence in July 2011, South Sudan was one of the world's least developed places. Just over 15 per cent of its 11 million citizens own a mobile phone, for example, and there are few tarmac roads in a territory about the size of Texas, or bigger than Spain and Portugal combined, with most of the rest in disrepair.[5] Social pressures have increased as the towns have swelled with refugees and through population growth, the latter number up from 6.5 million at the turn of the century, two-thirds of them under 24 years old. Over half of the population lives below the poverty line, and just a quarter are considered literate. This is likely to get worse, too, before it improves. The population growth rate of 4.23 per cent (the third-highest in the world behind Libya and Zimbabwe)[6] will see South Sudan double its population in less than twenty years.[7]

This was a pre-market society, as mentioned above, divided along ethnic lines. And this was the South Sudan that exploded into inter-communal violence in

December 2013 as tensions between President Salva Kiir Mayardit and his one-time deputy, Riek Machar, descended into allegations of ethnic marginalisation, persecution, what the president claimed was an attempted *coup d'état* (and the critics claimed was a coup by Kiir against himself) and civil conflict.

Then there was another South Sudan, one slowly emerging out of 50 years of brutal civil war at the end of which, according to Kiir, 'everything was at zero' in terms of capacity, infrastructure, governance regimes, and financial and human capital. It has been the variant preferred by generally bullish businesses and investors, where it has been comparatively easy to make positive and tangible changes, thus garnering political support of the population.

This was the country with a government eager to make up for lost time; or the one where the president, in his inaugural address in Juba in May 2010, admitted the problems they faced. 'The civil service we inherited has been packed with ghost employees,' he said. 'That alone makes it neither civil, nor a service. Service demands competence while civility entails awareness of the public good. Drastic measures are, therefore, needed to exorcise the ghosts and build capacity of our public service at all levels.'

This was the country headed by a government that not only coped with the austerity budget forced on it by the breakdown in relations with the North and the cut-off in its oil revenue, but managed in March 2013 to negotiate a much better deal, dropping oil pipeline fees substantially. This was the country where the population was not only prepared to suffer war but continued economic hardship for its economic independence. The January 2011 referendum turnout and 98.83 per cent 'yes' vote for independence was indicative of this support and mood.

This was the country where SABMiller arrived in 2008 to set up a brewery and, three years later, was producing 6 million litres of beer, soft drinks and bottled water monthly. Not only did it have to bring its own power and water plants, but it had to cut its own royalty agreement with the local community, earning no less than $35 000 each month from its share of sales. This was the government where the Ministry of Commerce's one-stop-shop proved to be an ally of investors, and an expeditor of investment, something that cannot be said for similar bodies across Africa.

This was a country where construction had boomed, the horizon dotted with new housing, hotels, shiny banks and skeletal skyrises. It was the economy where 'huge potential', according to one investor, existed in the long term in agriculture, but immediately also in light industry around fast moving consumer goods, such as reconstituted milk powder and the bottling of cooking oil. Only 10 per cent of its 640 000-square kilometre land mass is cultivated although as much as 80 per cent is deemed arable. Similarly, logging has significant growth potential, with forests covering a third of the country.

The challenge is getting from the one South Sudan to the other, weaning it off donor support ($4 billion in aid had been expended in eight years since 2005) and managing a highly militarised society riven by ethnic fault lines forged in internecine violence.[8]

Which of these two 'South Sudans' might come out on top would seem to rest on how politics shapes economic choices – in essence, the nature of the political economy. Post-conflict recovery is after all not a technocratic process, but rather one that is deeply politicised and demands the continuous generation and influx of people, skills, technology and capital.

At one level, South Sudan's political economy has been framed by the relationship with its northern neighbour, Khartoum, and by other colonial experiences, by its regional relations, by oil, by liberation ideology and mythology, by its severe infrastructure and human constraints, and by a deep, abiding sense of ownership and nationalism. In this political economy, progress is entwined with personal and party interests and by a sense of expectation and entitlement, especially among former guerrilla commanders and fighters. That so many soldiers, estimated at 170 000, were placed and kept on the government payroll, was a tangible illustration of a 'rent-seeking peace'. Whereas before they struggled with the North for control of their political destiny, this has quickly translated into a struggle for control within South Sudan over the spoils of power.

The outbreak of violence between Machar and Kiir's factions in 2013 left, in a matter of weeks, at least 30 000 reportedly dead, and perhaps as many as three times this number. It revealed deep-seated differences that went beyond ethnic issues to personalities, an almost complete lack of governance, widespread corruption, and the overall absence of a workable, inclusive government. The challenges to patch up a peace appeared on paper insurmountable, not least since Kiir's military strength was a fraction of that of his rival, with perhaps just 50 000 loyal to the president. Without – and perhaps even with – a settlement, Kiir would be dependent on Ugandan troops for his hold on office. And the terms of such a settlement would have to amount to nation-building '101': to draft a constitution acceptable to both sides; demobilise armed forces, integrate them and build a new, professional army; and to hold elections – all things that would, in turn, require peace and stability to achieve. Unsurprisingly, African leaders have taken privately to talking of an 'African Union trusteeship' to create the space to enable South Sudan (among other countries) to build an inclusive and effective state.

At the same time, more space for the private sector would have to be created and the economy geared to encourage investment rather than the expectation that investor money is simply another faucet for redistribution and a free ride for party hacks. Then recovery might be possible. If not, and instability and corruption was to take a firm hold, South Sudan would not even rank as a failed state, but a stillborn one.

*

Not all African states, obviously, are like South Sudan, despite the desire to paint the continent as either 'hopeless' or 'rising'. Nor do all fragile states suffer the same combination of a highly militarised ethnicity, a virtual total lack of governance, weak or no infrastructure, and a national economy dependent on just one export. Indeed, few states neatly fit into one typology. State fragility, as was suggested in the Introduction, takes many forms. It should be viewed along a 'spectrum of fragility', where there are different underlying reasons of weakness even if the symptoms appear similar. External responses have to take this into careful consideration.

At the 'most frail' end of this list appear Potemkin states, those that have a facade – a semblance – of state attributes, on which there is very little for outsiders to latch on to, little that resembles the institutions and policies of a modern, responsive state, where the operating systems are feudal or 'pre-market'. Afghanistan, much of the Sahel, the Congo, South Sudan and parts of West Africa fall into this category. These states (or parts of them) are often mired in violence, where society's fault lines are not managed to a consensual national blur, but are prominent, jagged edges, sources of friction, contestation and violence. In Somalia, to take another example of this category, central authority has collapsed as the outcome of a prolonged civil war, with power devolving to often violent competing factions – warlords – fighting over the spoils of local commerce, power and international aid.

It is these states where large spaces remained ungoverned, at least by national authority, a feature not only of rural areas far from the capital, but of burgeoning urban concentrations, too. For example, Africa will, at current rates of population increase, see the continent quadruple its people to over four billion during this century. Two scenarios flow from this surge: on the one hand, that this leads to a demographic dividend and greater economic growth and prosperity as birth rates fall about the time skilled, healthy adults come into the job market; and on the other hand, where it becomes, as a result of this increase in numbers, more impoverished and its people more desperate, a place of stupefying, grinding poverty, where energies are exhausted in getting from one day, and meal, to the next, and where birth rates remain high in insecure conditions. It is asked of Africa, 'can it be the next China' as the destination for a wave of manufacturing investment? It should also be asked in the same breath, however, 'What will happen if it is not?', and the jobs required for its burgeoning numbers of youth do not materialise.

The trajectory is not hopeful. In 1992 there were an estimated 170 million malnourished people in sub-Saharan Africa. By 2012, despite a good economic growth decade for the continent, the best on record since independence, this figure was 234 million, the only region where this number of hungry had increased.[9] According to the World Bank, the number living in extreme poverty in Africa rose over 30 years from 1980 from 205 million to 414 million,[10] even though African GDP growth had increased from a paltry 1.7 per cent during the 1980s and 2.5 per cent annual growth in the 1990s, to over 5 per cent in the 2000s and an estimated 5.6 per cent in 2013.[11]

NUMBER OF POOR BY REGION (MILLIONS)

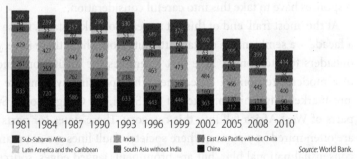

1981	1984	1987	1990	1993	1996	1999	2002	2005	2008	2010

■ Sub-Saharan Africa ▨ India ▨ East Asia Pacific without China
▨ Latin America and the Caribbean ▨ South Asia without India ■ China   *Source:* World Bank.

Where there is order within such environments, it is largely shaped to the advantage of elites, whose principal preoccupation in these circumstances is rent-seeking. While there is little capacity to govern to the extent of national borders, such boundaries can be regulated in topical parts, again to narrow financial advantage. Often, at these points of exit and entry, things do not work particularly efficiently, but for a reason, where traffic is slowed to create alternative means of leverage and economies. It is this category of fragile states that, in particular, prove impossibly difficult for outsiders to assist in their own image.

Along the fragility spectrum are those countries that look like they should work, with eloquent leadership that makes the right policy noises, especially in their consultations with donors and other outsiders, and seem to possess the right institutions for the task. But they miss the mark in terms of delivery, usually because the elites are uncommitted to these institutions beyond the conditions imposed by outsiders and because their own constituents are unwilling or unable to hold them to their electoral promises for reasons of apathy, ignorance, survival or identity. It is these states that display constant evidence less of collapse in the form of violence, but frailty in terms of poor social indicators, low growth and inter-communal tensions. These might also be countries 'in transition', either out of or into conditions of fragility.

At the farthest end of the range are those states that possess appropriate and often over-active democratic institutions, but instead of using these to their national advantage, they use them to contrarian aims, to subvert checks and balances on executive power and ensure, as best as possible, that government will not be turfed out by the electorate. Hugo Chávez's Venezuela has, as was indicated in the previous section, been a prototype.

There are all manner of contradictory examples along this spectrum. The definition is often political, as will be evinced, rather than empirical. Afghanistan under the Taliban actually worked quite efficiently, despite the remnants of an insurgency in the form of the Northern Alliance. The Hutu-led genocidal Rwandan state worked efficiently, albeit along ethnic lines, until 1994 when it organised the murder of one-tenth, or 800 000, of its people. Much the same could be said in reverse about the Tutsi regime in neighbouring Burundi. Similarly Khartoum worked well for most Northerners but not those in the South. President Suharto's 31-year (1967–98) Indonesian regime was hardly weak or fragile, even though it did not operate in the interests of the East Timorese.

Different extremes of failure have inevitably led to a taxonomy of states along the lines of strong, weak, failing and collapsed.[12] It is, of course, much easier to spot failure when it involves widespread violence and refugee flows, à la Sierra Leone, Afghanistan, Somalia or Liberia. It is much more difficult to judge when a state has pursued policies leading to a collapse in state functions and economic attributes just short of a loss of social control. When does the hollowing out of the middle class and the erosion of basic services become state failure? As will be seen, again, there are fragile states and failed ones, collapsed countries like Somalia, or an invisible one, such as the Congo, and South Sudan's apparently stillborn variant.

*

It is to a more eye-level examination of the point of intersection of the 'fragilities' of governance, political legitimacy, economics and society that this book now turns.

1

ARGENTINA

Living Beyond Means

✳

There is no place arguably more emblematic in Argentina than the Plaza de Mayo, Buenos Aires' independence square. At one end is the seat of government, Casa Rosada, the 'Pink House', from which balcony Eva Perón famously did her thing. On one side of the white obelisk independence memorial fly various banners railing against government and proclaiming solidarity with the 'disappeared' – the 10 000 or so who were killed by security forces during the bitter civil war in the mid- to late 1970s – and other victims of conflict.

It has been a site of high and continuous drama and demonstrations. In October 1945, mass crowds organised by the General Confederation of Labour trade union movement forced the release from prison of Juan Perón, later to become president. And it was here that 34 planes of the Argentine air force dropped 10 tonnes of ordnance on assembled crowds that were demonstrating in favour of embattled President Perón on 16 June 1955, killing 364. Having played a significant part in the 1943 military coup, Perón won power in the 1946 election, before escaping on a gunboat provided by Paraguayan leader, Alfredo Stroessner, in 1955 in the face of mounting debt and rampant inflation.

Of course, all this is scarcely remembered in contemporary Argentina. Claiming to be a Peronist is the most likely route to the Casa Rosada and, after the failure of the last non-Peronist government of Fernando de la Rua in December 2001, perhaps the only probable one. Since 1945 Peronism has won eight out of the ten presidential elections it has contested. As Perón said when he returned to Argentina in 1973, after eighteen years of exile in Franco's Spain, 'Argentines belong to different parties, but all of us are Peronists.'

Perón is, however, not remembered for the role of the military in politics and his policy and personal failures and excesses, including a penchant for underage girls. He is remembered rather for the manner in which he defined a new era of Argentine politics, defended neglected worker rights, added grand buildings to the already impressive Buenos Aires skyline, and in so doing reinstated national pride – even though the economy collapsed in the process.

*

Argentina's President Cristina Fernández de Kirchner was famously disparaged by her Uruguayan counterpart, José Mujica, the former guerrilla fighter and political prisoner, a man who drives a tatty VW Beetle and gives away around 90 per cent of his $12 000 monthly salary to charities to benefit poor people and small entrepreneurs. President Mujica was overheard saying, 'This old hag is even worse than the cross-eyed man', in reference to her late husband and predecessor Nestor, who had a lazy eye.[1]

No doubt her country's inclusion in a volume dealing with failed states will raise an anguished howl of disbelief across the South Atlantic. How could Argentina, in the 1930s rated the world's sixth most powerful economy, its capital termed the 'Paris of the South', be considered a failure? The answer is simple: despite all that wealth, the country's 41 million people still find the means to live above it. Dysfunctional politics and egomaniacal politicians have contrived to turn prosperity into economic and policy dysfunctionality and periodic failure. Even though per capita income was, in 2012, $11 600, making it an upper middle-income country, Argentina is locked into systemic crises, from which there seems to be no willing way out. This has an impact on poverty and inequality: Argentinians being termed (by the World Bank) as 'poor people in a rich country'.[2] 'Official poverty' in Argentina amounted, in 2013, to 2.5 million people but private, independent estimates put this figure at 11 million.[3] This is a government that has, since the mid-1990s, reneged on international borrowings, and seized private assets and pensions, and got away with it. Well, no one declared war on it, but they have not got away with it in economic terms.

The greatest crisis that Argentina is mired in, which is common to many other weak states, is the belief that its problems are caused by others, not themselves. To remedy this, a mindset change would seem to be necessary.

But to enable this, a majority of voters would have to own up to that reality, something they have spent much of the past century avoiding.

Cry for me

On taking office on 4 June 1946, Perón's stated goals were social justice and economic independence. He raised workers' wages, nationalised key institutions (including the Central Bank), imposed protectionism to stimulate domestic industry, ensured universal franchise, and spent vast sums on new infrastructure and military modernisation. This quickly gobbled up the $1.7 billion of reserves accumulated during the war-time years, an appetite for public spending worsened by increased consumer demand for imports. Amidst growing union problems and worsening terms of trade, the exchange rate deteriorated from 4 to 30 pesos per dollar and consumer prices rose nearly fivefold.

The story of Argentina since that time has been of a cyclical nature: crisis followed by austerity and then boom, and once more bust and recovery. For example, following the last military junta, which collapsed in the aftermath of the Falklands-Malvinas war in 1982, the government of Raúl Alfonsin (1983–89) encountered hyper-inflation as it attempted to tackle a debt problem. Despite the so-called austral plan introducing a new currency, by 1989 inflation had reached 5 000 per cent annually. The economy shrank by 7 per cent that year, with per capita GDP falling to its lowest level since 1964.

Alfonsin was followed by Carlos Menem, another to claim a Peronist label. The first of his two terms as president is generally regarded as the most successful, the second being characterised more by corruption allegations and less by reform.

In the first term, Menem's finance minister, Domingo Cavallo, introduced a series of reforms in 1991, pegging the value of the peso to the US dollar one-to-one, ending runaway inflation. This 'convertibility plan' was accompanied by the privatisation of utilities, including the state oil entity Yacimientos Petroliferos Fiscales (YPF), the post office, gas, electricity, state pensions, railways and water. The resultant inflow of investment not only brought down inflation but ensured the modernisation of key sectors, though the cost was an increase in unemployment.

Pegging should, however, have been a short-term measure, establishing a new framework for investment and growth. Indeed, its originator, Cavallo, saw the end of the tequila crisis[4] in 1997 as a most opportune moment, when the peso would likely have increased in value if convertibility had been abandoned.[5]

Instead, because the peg was politically popular, it went on for a decade, swelling debt as a way of increasing consumption. This is not unlike what occurred in southern Europe in the wake of the 2008 financial crisis.

Menem was re-elected in 1995. After his attempt to run for a third term in 1999 was ruled unconstitutional, opposition candidate De la Rúa defeated Menem's nominee Eduardo Duhalde for the presidency. De la Rúa inherited an economic crisis. Despite a $38-billion line of International Monetary Fund (IMF) credit in December 2000, things continued to deteriorate, and De la Rúa appointed Cavallo again as finance minister in March 2001. A massive shorting of Argentine bonds was followed by at least $40 billion in domestic capital flight, leading Cavallo to impose an account freeze (known as 'el corralito' – the small fence) on 1 December 2001. With the IMF, World Bank and Inter-American Development Bank cancelling loans of $5 billion, amidst widespread rioting, De la Rúa tendered his resignation on 21 December. After a tumultuous time that saw several leadership changes, Duhalde took over, de-pegging the faltering peso, and overseeing the biggest sovereign default ever of more than $60 billion.

The political stage was thus set for rule by the Kirchners, husband first and then wife, Nestor and Cristina, from 2003.

Burdened with debt of $178 billion, the first priority of President Nestor Kirchner (2003–07) was to reschedule $84 billion in debts with international organisations. Over three-quarters were restructured for approximately one-third of its nominal value. In December 2005, Kirchner announced the cancellation of Argentina's debt to the IMF in full in a single cash payment. In October 2008, the cash-short government secured the transfer of $30 billion in private pension holdings to its own control, effectively reversing the privatisation under Cavallo fifteen years earlier. This helped to feed consumption under the Kirchners.

By the time his wife Cristina won the election in November 2007, the country seemed to be well on the path to recovery. However, its stability had less to do with the government than met the eye. During the 1990s, the private sector made considerable investment in new farming techniques, notably 'no-till' injected seeding, along with the extensive use of herbicides and genetically modified seeds. As a result, crop production overall increased from 20 million tonnes to 93 million tonnes[6] between 1995 and

2010, although the area under cultivation (some 40 million hectares) increased only by 25 per cent. With increasing substitution of maize for soya (with comparative yields of 5 tonnes per hectare and 15 tonnes per hectare respectively), coupled with another 15 million hectares of land being made available, this figure could surge past 150 million tonnes by 2015.

Coupled with an increase in Chinese demand, even by the mid-2000s the country was in the midst of an agriculture export boom on the back of soya. In 1995, Argentina exported 2 million tonnes in soya; by 2010 this figure had increased to 56 million tonnes. 'Soya,' says one Argentine agricultural expert, 'is meat.' As the graphs illustrate, this has been on the back of Chinese (and other) increases in meat consumption.

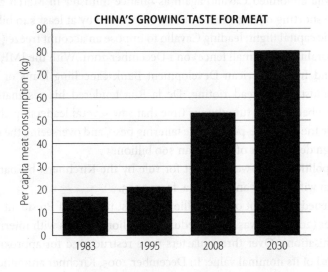

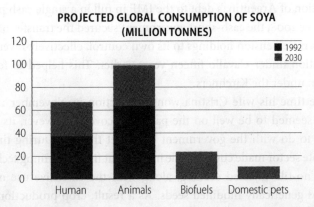

Source: ISK Argentina.

The government was quick to recognise this windfall, imposing a 35 per cent export tax (officially known as a 'retention'), bringing in an estimated extra $8 billion from soya alone in 2011. Argentina is the third-largest soybean-producing country behind the US and Brazil, and the biggest exporter of processed soybean products, including soybean meal, oil and biodiesel. In 2008, the government vainly attempted to raise this tax to 44 per cent, leading to demonstrations by farmers.

At the same time, the Argentina economy showed every sign of over-heating, reflecting rampant consumerism and low public and private investment. A 2011 *Economist* ranking of six indicators – inflation, the constancy of growth, labour markets, credit expansion, real interest rates and external balance of trade – put Argentina at the top of the overheating tables.[7] Wage increases in the second half of the 2000s averaged 25 per cent annually, a process that has been led by government and the unions. The government also kept interest rates to under 10 per cent although inflation was running at least fifteen points higher, encouraging rampant spending, with collapse only prevented by the extraordinarily positive (soya) terms of trade. No surprise that during Cristina's government, the Instituto Nacional de Estadisticas y Censos (Institute for Statistics and Census) was encouraged to 'produce' data favourable to government's view on the economy, including unemployment and inflation levels, together with the aforementioned low calculation of national poverty. Indeed, since 2012 *The Economist* newspaper no longer includes Argentina data (and inflation rates) on their official list of figures. They have made it clear that these cannot be trusted.[8]

Peronist, pliant and pernicious

To be a contemporary Cristianista is to follow the traditionalist route of Peronism: a strong centralised government, with authoritarian traits, acting in a corporatist fashion with pliable business interests, strong sentiments against foreign interference and distribution of wealth to favoured groups through subsidies and welfare payments. It has strong populist urges, ex-plaining, for example, the president's Fútbal para Todos (Football for All), a $170-million project for the free broadcasting of games, and the public works' Plan Trabajar, or gas and fuel subsidies. The intention behind all of this has been to stay in power, not to diversify or grow the economy. Just as Perón ran down the country's record foreign reserves in 1945 by funding pet projects, Cristina's government has spent an estimated $30 billion annually on social projects and subsidies. 'Today,' said Eduardo Menem in 2011, the brother of the former president, and himself a 22-year veteran senator and Peronista, 'we have a subsidy for gas, electricity, public transport, even some types of food, all paid for by the *retentions*. But what happens if the demand for soya changes?' he asked.

In April 2012, the government expropriated 51 per cent of shares in the YPF oil firm from the Spanish oil giant Repsol, which then controlled 57.4 per cent, offering little compensation.[9] In November 2011, YPF, which was privatised in 1993, had announced a major find of one billion barrels of shale oil, the third-largest recoverable store worldwide after China and the US. (In February 2014, Repsol settled on $5 billion in government compensation, less than half that sought.)[10] Earlier, Nestor Kirchner had also returned to the original corporatist Peronist vision and brought companies such as the national airline, Aerolineas Argentinas, back under state control.[11]

Needless to say, the early signs of the impact of the YPF nationalisation looked worrying for government. Neither Argentina's nor YPF's production increased as a consequence of the asset grab. Argentina was also not able to close its trade deficit in energy, which the government had promised. This should not have been surprising, since Argentina's oil production is primarily based on old discoveries with shrinking reserves. Indeed, it has led to the conclusion that a 'rational populist would have postponed the expropriation until the point when foreign investors had put their money into Argentina.'[12] But rational, Cristina was not.

Little wonder the Argentine literary great, Jorge Luis Borges, who hated Perón, said, 'Peronists are neither good nor bad, but incorrigible.' But Argentines themselves have caused this malaise, being unwilling to bite the long-term development bullet, by saving today for tomorrow. As former president De La Rúa notes, 'I think that Argentines learnt nothing from the crisis [in 2001]. I think people see me and Dr Cavallo as being responsible. They did not take the experience and produce better policies, but rather returned to the policies of the past.'[13]

Argentina has a redistributive, rent-seeking economy, a type familiar to other fragile states. Where the former has soya, many of the latter have minerals or oil. As Cavallo reflects: 'The government is somewhat leftist, somewhat statist, somewhat populist and definitely opportunist.' Or as Menem puts it, 'Our economic problems have deep political roots. Each government that takes office tries to change everything. This makes it impossible to feel safe as an investor as we lack the legal conditions to encourage this. Only in the 1990s did investors return because of the right legal conditions.'

Yet, so long as China (and a few others) continue to buy from Argentina, the party is likely to continue. As Alfonso Prat-Gay, the former Central Bank governor under Nestor, has observed: 'Cristina has benefited from an effective 11 per cent increase in tax-to-GDP revenues, an extra $50 billion. Yet,' he notes, 'Argentina remains a natural resource producer – worse than that, a single crop exporter, and with none of the attempts of previous eras to build a manufacturing sector.' The failure of industrialists to invest and the high pace of consumption together explain why the manufacturing balance of payments' deficit leapt to $24 billion, or 6 per cent of GDP, by 2012.

If and when foreigners stop buying, or other cheaper producers or natural resource substitutes are discovered, it will be over and the crisis will ensue. And so the cycle repeats itself in Argentina. Many Argentines apparently believe this cycle is inevitable, hence the estimated $1 billion in monthly capital flight since the mid-2000s. Or in Prat-Gay's view: 'The environment in Argentina does not favour the long-term investor. The incentive structure is to take the most out of today and let someone else pay for the future. But even though the government makes incredibly stupid mistakes in the interests of power, Argentina will always come back as it is such an incredibly wealthy country.' The costs of this boom-bust cycle and wasted potential have been considerable. As one banker put it in 2011: 'In 1940, we were once the tenth largest economy worldwide. In 1960, Brazil had just one-quarter of our GDP. Now they have six times our figure and we are outside the top 25 largest global economies. And it will only worsen,' he says, 'given Argentina's inability to gain foreign investment.'

Examples of the costs of the stop-go, boom-bust political short-termism abound. Today the name of Di Tella is best known in Buenos Aires as the private university in the leafy suburbs. Once, however, Siam Di Tella was an icon of Argentine industry, and one of the country's examples of industrial rise and fall. Founded in 1911 by an Italian immigrant, from a start in making baking machines, a contract with YPF saw it build fuel dispensers and grow into a leading manufacturer. From there it diversified into fridges and even motorcycles and cars, building Lambretta scooters and Riley motor cars under licence. Losses from the vehicle sector, however, led to a partnership with government. But a combination of a free trade regime in the 1970s plus poor management saw Di Tella's factories closed and sold off. One son, Guido, became foreign minister under Menem; another, the sociologist and former secretary of culture in Nestor Kirchner's presidency, Torcuato, a staunch Cristianista, became the country's ambassador to Rome.

The hope for politicians taking a longer-term view resides in the emergence of a new generation – one less vested in the traditional divides between protectionism and free trade, less interested in the use of power for power's sake but instead, as Alan Clutterbuck of the RAP Foundation, trying to bridge these traditional divides, says, 'in delivering a long-term vision'. Eduardo Menem argues that this generational change will be an inevitable consequence of having '30 years of democracy, the longest era in our history, which is generating a new kind of leadership'.

Until then, there are positive lessons others can learn from Argentina.

On the upside is the democratic-mindedness of Argentines, willing to take their rights to the streets; on the downside, the cost of politics to economic reform initiatives and the weakness of institutions. For some African countries, in particular, the growth of farming and the management of Argentina's natural resources offer some guide to future opportunities. But this has had little to do with the government; rather it was the result of the private sector making progress in spite of government, a common feature among fragile states.

*

The waiters at Papa Frita in Buenos Aires are a metaphor for the country, po-faced in their shabby white coats and bow ties, shuffling between tables in studied, ossifying disinterest. The restaurant was great, like the country, some time ago. While the early wealth of Argentina is visible in the grand boulevards of Buenos Aires and its grandstanding baroque facades, translating the country's natural wealth into long-term prosperity has proven more difficult. It has been the archetypal boom-and-bust economy. Despite its wealth on paper, its people have borne the brunt of this dysfunction, and yet are principally at fault. It is they who have sought radical solutions to their country's failings, so permitting extreme leadership, on the populist left and the right, and entrenching the dysfunctionality and accelerating decay.

2

GUINEA

A Great Balancing Act

*

Come five 'o clock and the streets of Conakry come alive with football. They are mostly not watching it or even listening to it, but playing it. Men aged between five and 25 throng the streets, one game after another along the tarmac, colourfully bedecked in Real Madrid, Manchester United, Barcelona and Arsenal strips, their own bright national colours of yellow, green and red, or their own home-grown and sewn kit.[1]

It is one of the few available palliatives from a tough existence, even though poverty, grinding and endemic, is hardly the sole measure of deprivation. It also comes in the form of the vaguer distinction between public and private space – people living, eating, cooking, washing, dancing and, yes, playing sport on the streets – and the absence of opportunity for the most basic services, education and jobs.

Football offers a straw to grasp at, a moment not only for escapism or an outlet for frustration, but, for the lucky talented few, a route off the streets via hopes of multimillion-pound and -euro contracts from famous clubs, a dream something even serious and educated Guineans admit to. Such fantasy highlights the plight and desperation of a burgeoning youth population, more than 60 per cent of Guinea's nearly 11 million people, virtually all of whom are self-employed or unemployed, but many of whom are, as one foreign investor warns, 'highly politicised'.

'The President [Alpha Condé] told me,' said Fodé Idrissa Touré, popularly known as Briqui Momo, then the presidential counsellor, 'that the biggest danger for us is the youth, the unemployed, for which there is no easy solution.' Touré had made his fortune in the Ivory Coast. He then came back to

Conakry and built a multi-storey building in the city. Each time he would finish a stage, he would stand on the roof and throw money to the people in the street. It was then that he had received his nickname: Momo is a term for old people and briqui for the packs of money.

As population numbers have expanded more than threefold since independence in 1958, Guinea's government and economy have fallen behind. 'The youth,' says one vice governor of the Reserve Bank, Nianga Komata Goumou, 'is the fundamental question for our country.' His concerns were heightened by an advert the Bank placed in 2013 for six posts, including three economists. 'We received 8 000 applications.' This is repeated in the shortage of opportunity for businesses. 'Recently, the Ministry of the Interior,' he adds, 'published a tender for the construction of university accommodation. No fewer than 250 companies presented offers.'

This illustrates the West African nation's great balancing act – between local realities and global expectations; the need for macroeconomic prudency alongside rapid economic growth and job creation; ethnic politics; matching the impulses of nationalism with the needs of foreign investors; and ensuring political stability, sound policy and democracy.

As its youth kick their heels along with their footballs, can Guinea develop before it explodes?

Realising enormous wealth

The country appears to have the natural resources to do so. On paper at least, it is enormously wealthy, though there is no country that has such a large gap between potential and reality.

Not only is it blessed with one-third (or 16 billion tonnes) of the world's known bauxite reserves, but it has abundant stores of uranium, diamonds, gold and other metals, including an estimated 6 billion tonnes in iron ore reserves, one-quarter of the world's store. The Simandou mountain range in Faranah province, near the border with Sierra Leone and Liberia where Rio Tinto and Vale have concessions, is said to be a giant iron lump. The same applies to Nimba Mountain in the neighbouring Forestiere province to the south.

Guinea similarly enjoys enormous hydropower potential, given its status as one of the wettest countries in West Africa. Coastal rainfall averages 4 300 millimetres a year, half of which falls in July and August. And its mountain ranges mean that it is known as the 'water tower' of West Africa.

Yet Guinea, for all of its water resources and perfect hydro topography, produced just 220 MW of electricity in 2013, the capital Conakry subject to frequent stoppages and the rural areas, where two-thirds of the population lives, permanent outages. When Rusal closed its mine and smelter in April 2012 following a labour dispute, not only did 2 800 jobs go, but so did all electricity supplies to the 100 000 people in the inland city of Fria.

From the air, Conakry sits in the middle of a maze of rivers, inlets and islands, rice paddies forming perfect postage stamps of orderliness and, from an altitude, apparent prosperity. It is Africa's Mekong Delta, a potential bread basket for the region. 'Spit on a seed here and it grows,' reflected one donor. But on the ground, instead of exporting its produce, in 2013 Guinea concluded a five-year, 300 000-tonne rice import deal with Vietnam to meet its annual domestic rice consumption estimated at 1.2 million tonnes.

There might be water, water everywhere, but there is also so little to drink. According to the UN, 50 per cent of the Guinean population does not have reasonable access to an improved water source (20 litres per person per day from a source within 1 kilometre is the UN definition). Moreover, water quality in the urban areas has 'strongly deteriorated' over the past decade, the result of a lack of investment and maintenance, and the growth of urban areas. Conakry, which housed a million people in the 1990s, has swelled to more than double that number. Unsurprisingly, cholera and other waterborne diseases, including diarrhoea, have been considered to be endemic.

More than half a century since independence, agriculture employs 80 per cent of the workforce. There is very limited light industry – just soft drinks, beer, palm oil and other minor agro-processing. Bauxite and alumina make up more than one half of all export earnings, even though this has fallen dramatically since Rusal's closure. This situation is a far cry from the co-lonial days when the country was a major exporter of bananas, mangoes, pineapples, coffee, peanuts and palm oil.

Guinea ranks in the bottom twenty poorest places on earth. With average annual per capita income of just over $500, half of Guineans were living be-low the poverty line by 2013. The reasons for such destitution are many and complex, but essentially boil down to one factor: politics.

The cost of bad politics

Under Ahmed Sékou Touré, Guinea took the hard road in breaking with France, which had colonised the territory in the 1890s. Sékou Touré, the son of a poor Muslim farmer with limited education (his schooling consisted only of attendance at a Koranic school and one year of studies at a French technical school in the colonial capital of Conakry before his expulsion), had found a job with the postal service. He worked his way up the political ranks via the unions, and 'seized the presidency via speeches'.[2] He was alone among his West African Francophone colleagues in spurning, via a referendum, President Charles de Gaulle's 1958 offer to France's colonies to take independence or integrate into a Franco-African community. Sékou Touré declared, in response to De Gaulle's threat that those who refused the French offer should be prepared to 'assume the consequences', that he preferred 'poverty in freedom than riches in slavery'. He soon got his wish as the angry De Gaulle immediately gave Guinea its independence on 2 October 1958 – but only after removing the entire French colonial infrastructure, including all 4 000 administrators, physicians and teachers. The recalled teachers constituted three-quarters of all educators in the newly independent country. Some of the departing officials allegedly even took away imported office equipment, including telephones and light fixtures. Not only did aid cease but all financial ties were cut by the government in Paris, including a planned $80-million investment programme.

Although this guaranteed Sékou Touré legendary African liberation status, it got him off to an exceptionally poor development start, from which Guinea has never recovered.

There was worse to come. A convinced Marxist even before the break with France, Sékou Touré turned to the Soviet bloc for assistance. Two days after the Guinean National Assembly declared independence, the new country was recognised by the Soviet Union. By December 1958, the new regime had been offered an arms deal by Czechoslovakia. By February 1959, the Kremlin concluded a trade agreement with the government in Conakry. In August 1959, the Communist Party of the Soviet Union sent delegates to attend the fifth congress of the Parti Démocratique de Guinée (PDG). Sékou Touré paid an official visit to Moscow in November 1959, reciprocated by Soviet Premier Nikita Khrushchev the following January.

Sékou Touré's limited years of education had apparently left him with a permanent inferiority complex and he proceeded to prove just why. Awarded the Lenin Peace Prize in 1961, the first president renamed the country the People's Revolutionary Republic of Guinea. The state seized farms, imposed price controls and generally enforced a social, political and economic monopoly.

Moreover, the isolation from the West bit hard and deep, and was compounded by poor policy choices and increasingly intolerant politics. Abetted by his new communist bloc patrons, Sékou Touré led his country into a period of totalitarian rule and economic ruin. In 1961, the Guinean government announced that it had discovered a 'conspiracy of teachers'. A large number of teachers and their students – some as young as the primary grades – were arrested, together with trade unionists and PDG cadres whose loyalties were questioned by the regime. Governments of Soviet bloc countries where Guinean students were pursuing their studies, including the Soviet Union, Czechoslovakia and the German Democratic Republic, were asked to arrest the students and summarily repatriate them, so that they might be interrogated. In 1967, Sékou Touré announced a 'cultural revolution' along the lines of the Chinese model. He had visited Mao Zedong in Beijing in September 1960 and pronounced his 'high regard' for the political and economic system installed by the 'Great Helmsman'. A little volume, modelled on the Chinese leader's *Little Red Book* and entitled *Thoughts of Sékou Touré*, was published, with the Guinean people being commanded to purchase and 'meditate' on its contents. Another aspect of this 'cultural revolution' was a hasty decision to abolish the French language and give equal status as official languages to no less than eight local languages. As a result of this last measure, less than 40 per cent of the Guinean populace now has a rudimentary knowledge of the official language, once again French.

The one-party state, declared in 1961, favoured Sékou Touré's own Mandinka ethnic group (around one-third of the population) over the majority Fula (40 and more per cent). It is said that the first question in Guinea is your name, the second your tribe. Ethnic politics plays a – perhaps *the* – major role in elections, with complex alliance-building.

In all, it was a textbook case of how to mess up an economy, permitted by the absence of opposition, the Cold War political climate of the time, and outright, cold-blooded ruthlessness. More than a million people fled, and as many as 50 000 were imprisoned, tortured, kept in dire conditions, and executed or died at the Camp Boiro, a Soviet-style concentration camp, and others like it countrywide.

Deeply paranoid, Sékou Touré's leadership style hardened, following an unsuccessful Portuguese-led invasion in 1970. Six years later he accused the Fula population of colluding to overthrow his government. More reprisals followed.

After almost three decades in power, Sékou Touré died suddenly on 26 March 1984, ironically in a hospital in the arch ideological enemy's heartland in Cleveland, Ohio, having been rushed there after taking ill in Saudi Arabia. By then Guinea's economy was in such a parlous state that even he had recognised the imperative for reform before his death.

This was too little, too late. Within days of his passing, a group of army colonels staged a military coup, and Lansana Conté, a soldier and farmer, became the country's new president. The advent of the 'Second Republic' was effectively a counter-Sékou Touré revolution. Even though Conté had been a loyal follower of Sékou Touré, he was from the army rather than the ruling party and was a Soussou, unlike the former president.

Perhaps that is why his regime showed some promise, at least initially, with a new currency, a new constitution and instatement of a multi-party system by 1991. Although he won three elections, corruption thrived while the economy stagnated under Conté. The levels of corruption were not helped by conflicts in neighbouring Liberia and Sierra Leone, which encouraged widespread smuggling, a role that Conté navigated well. Increasingly isolated and unwilling to enter into dialogue with opposition leaders, Conté was not helped by failing health, which left him unable to walk or speak in the final years of his rule. Little wonder that, by 2007, Guinea's youth violently took to the streets, calling for a new government. Despite a new prime minister in Lansana Kouyaté, the situation continued to worsen with an army mutiny over unpaid wages the following year, rising food prices, street violence and worsening banditry and criminality.

The streets of Conakry, dusty and functional, dirty and crowded, confused and dotted with container-shops but absolutely not pretty, became pretty dangerous. They remain that way for the most part.

Arriveés de junta

On 24 December 2008, less than 24 hours after Conté did the only honourable thing left to him by dying, an unknown army captain, Moussa Dadis Camara, staged a bloodless coup as head of the National Council for Democracy and Development, declaring that he had no interest in power other than for the purposes of 'cleaning the nation' and holding elections.

The reality was quite different, of course. The coup was said to be 'largely about drugs – in Lansana Conté's last years, the chief protector of the drugs trade was his son Ousmane. The latter wanted to take over from his dad as president. Dadis was a key distributor of drugs in the army. He and his friends took power and exposed Ousmane as the centre of the drug trade, thereby getting some international support that they otherwise hardly merited.'[3]

Regardless, change was as good as a rest from politics as usual. Dadis' initial popularity was fuelled, Hugo Chávez-style, by his domination of the news, quickly nicknamed 'The Daddis Show'. This did not last long. His behaviour and policies became increasingly wayward. 'I would go to the presidential palace four times a week,' recounts one former adviser. 'I would get to the palace at around midnight and be ushered into a room with Dadis and his team. They would quickly fall asleep and I would wait there until they had woken, all still in the same small room, to resume the meeting around six in the morning.' The president worked only at night because he was afraid of assassination, even though the most dangerous people were the ones surrounding him. This was no way to run his personal life, let alone a country.

Less than a year in office, on 28 September 2009, the junta ordered its soldiers to attack people protesting Dadis' presidential ambitions. Then, on 3 December 2009, the head of the presidential guard shot the man he was supposed to protect in the head at a military base during a dispute about the rampage and mass rapes on 28 September. Vice President Sékouba Konaté took over with Dadis flown out of the country to receive medical care.

Then, following an agreement between Dadis and Konaté brokered by Burkina's president, Blaise Compaoré, Guinea returned to civilian rule via elections in July 2010. Promising reform of the security sector and the review of mining contracts, Alpha Condé, a 72-year-old self-declared Trotskyite Sorbonne graduate, 'professional militant', and leader of the opposition Rally of the Guinean People, won the presidential run-off that November. With just 20 per cent of the vote in the first round, he had to play pretty serious and shrewd tribal politics to get there though. The outcome was assessed to be, in the words of one observer, more 'a vote against the Fula than for Alpha'.

Although Guinea prides itself on never having had a civil war in a region where this is exceptional, the junta 'almost broke the country', according to Condé's economic adviser Idrissa Thiam. As one indicator, he says, 'The total government debt relative to the banking system was ten times greater at the time of the 2010 election than it was when Dadis took over in 2008.' It was 'very simple', he says. 'What they did was to increase spending tenfold. And the only way to finance this was to print money. Today we are paying for the costs of them printing money.'

Indeed, by 2013 Guinea was 'top of the bill', as one European diplomat described it, in every of one the 'bad' metrics: incompetence, government capacity, skills, education, corruption, organisation and destruction of infrastructure. In each of these measures it was a failed state. Even though it has not been at war with itself, it was nonetheless one of the six countries that by then were the focus of the UN's peace-building commission.[4]

The donors regardless returned with democracy. They had reason to be pleased, as Condé immediately did much right, at least in stabilising the macroeconomic environment.

Despite his historical ideological orientation, Condé steadfastly followed an IMF-supervised austerity budget, curbing spending and thereby bringing down the fiscal deficit from 13 per cent to 2 per cent of GDP between 2011 and 2012, and reducing inflation from 22 per cent to 13 per cent over the same period. Perhaps this was of little surprise given the president's famously parsimonious living habits. These improvements were 'triggers' for the implementation of a Highly Indebted Poor Country (HIPC) debt cancellation moment in September 2012, which cut $2 billion, or two-thirds, of the country's outstanding debt. The Paris Club scrapped a further $600 million a few months later. The World Bank also returned after the election with nearly $300 million committed across fifteen projects, of which one-third was earmarked for education.

At the same time, the government launched a series of reforms aimed at improving efficiency and capacity, especially through creating a common information and communications technology platform. The government also recognised the need to 'rejuvenate' large chunks of the 120 000-strong civil service by employing the youth and women. Many of the old guard, educated and installed under the Sékou Touré regime of the 1960s and 1970s, remain, with all of their bad habits.

Moreover, aid, while helping to create the right conditions and slowly improving institutional capacity, cannot alone solve the other side of the stability coin – increasing economic output.

The growth plan

Condé's government has possessed a development vision – for Guinea to be an 'emerging country' by 2030 – although this has proven difficult to implement. Three pillars of sectoral growth have been identified to drive this: mining, agriculture and infrastructure.

With regard to the latter, there have been ambitious plans to increase electricity output thirtyfold to 6 000 MW, starting with the Chinese-constructed 240-MW Kaleta Dam, due to be completed by 2016. The government has hoped that agriculture will take off with 'improved extension services' and linking smallholders to larger commercial ventures. The reality is, however, that clarity on land tenure is a prerequisite for large-scale foreign investment. A more likely route to expansion is through improved smallholder yields and regional trade, using the mines as growth poles.

Mining is, unsurprisingly, the key sector. The government aimed for $20 billion worth of investment by 2015, the year the giant Rio Tinto project was supposed to start exporting iron ore via a $12-billion, 650-kilometre new railway and port facility. This single project was expected to create 10 000 direct jobs in the construction phase alone, and to increase GDP threefold to $15 billion.

The government's grand $20 billion target could be realised, at least on paper, with eight bauxite, four iron and 'many more' gold projects planned, and ongoing alluvial diamond diggings. According to one experienced diamantair, the country formally exports 'at least' $400 million in stones annually, although this figure could be 'closer to $1 billion' if smuggling was taken into account, even though corruption in customs has reputedly significantly reduced this tax take.

Initially the government made some progress, with Rio Tinto agreeing to a $700-million payment in April 2011 to secure their concession. The government, however, insisted that its vision of finally completing the long-mooted Transguinean Railways, tying the country north to south, be realised. It initially demanded majority ownership of the line and the inclusion of passengers along with non-iron freight. The reality is that the shortest way to the export markets for the miners is via Liberia. Guinea's government lacked its $6-billion share to put into the project, and adding passenger and other cargo into the mix has only over-complicated matters, adding to already significant project costs.

The result is that the projects soon sunk into limbo. This stalemate occurred against the backdrop of declining world ore prices and an original (though subsequently reworked) mining code that posited a tax and royalty regime pegged to the more lucrative era. By 2013 Rio Tinto had downsized its local operation, only one bauxite mine (the state-owned Societé des Bauxites de Kindia) operated, there was a deadlock in the dispute with government around ownership of the Vale/BSGR iron ore concession, and BHP Billiton was apparently intent on selling its Mount Nimba holding.

Rather than accept the need to not let the perfect be the enemy of the good and find a way to get the projects moving, the government claimed that the resources companies did not want to invest in the mines. 'They want to protect their mines elsewhere, and keep ours for later,' said the director general in the Ministry of Mines. 'We want the railway,' he pouted, 'since that decision was taken 30 years ago, as it will have more benefits than just mining.'

The government steadfastly stuck to its guns on the railway. Progress was, however, made on other aspects, including on transparency around mining transactions. In February 2013, the government published online all mining deals, including those with majors Rio Tinto, Vale and BHP Billiton.

Instead of a united negotiating front and process, the government 'deliberately fragmented the negotiations with Rio Tinto', as one Conakry-based diplomat observed. 'There is little interest in doing this and being transparent, since this reduces the scope for corruption.' And, 'while the president is receiving lots of advice from people, he is taking much less'. In part, this is down to the knowledge and motives of the advisers themselves. 'It is prestigious for [Condé] to have Tony Blair and his African Governance Initiative here. But his presence is easily manipulated,' said the diplomat, 'and Blair does not know the country well, if at all, no matter how well meaning he might be.' The extent to which the government – and the president – would prioritise longer-term national (and regional) interests over their shorter-term domestic financial and political ones was also, the diplomat noted, evident in the lip service paid to the Mano River Union and the rhetoric around regional integration. 'If they really wanted regional integration, then the railway would go through Liberia,' he noted, 'but doing so does not allow the opportunity for the government to fill its pockets.'

As hinted at above, the controversy over the mines was not all the government's doing; far from it. The rights to the Simandou deposit were given to Rio Tinto in 1997. After the Guinean government declared that the Anglo-Australian company was developing the mine too slowly, in

July 2008, Rio Tinto was stripped of its licence. In terms of the exploration permits, half of the deposit was then granted to Beny Steinmetz Group Resources (BSGR), a company that had, until then, been focused on diamonds. Despite Rio's protests, the government deal with BSGR was ratified in April 2009. Amidst rumours that the concession had been acquired through bribes with the famously corrupt (Lansana) Conté (who once reportedly remarked, 'If we had to shoot every Guinean who had stolen from Guinea there would be no one left to kill'), Steinmetz then sold on a 51 per cent stake in his Simandou operation to the Brazilian mining giant Vale for $2.5 billion, for what was reportedly at that stage a $160-million investment by BSGR. At the time the government budget in Guinea was less than half of this figure.[5] Paul Collier, an adviser to the Condé government, had a less-than-sanguine view of such operators: 'Their technical competence is a social-network map ... They know how to get a contract – *that* is their skill,' said the Oxford-based economist.[6]

Thus, it should be of little surprise that, according to Briqui Momo, who passed away in September 2013, the president 'believes the mining industry is against him'. While he realised, the counsellor said, 'that the sector is key to the country's future, we also realise that we don't have a lot of time'. He noted that 'our assumption is that the mining companies might have put money here, but that they are gaining much more in their operations outside, which are more important to them. How else do you explain that Rio Tinto has been here for fifteen years and not exported even a tonne of ore?' he asked.

While it could catalyse the economy, mining will not answer all, or even most, of Guinea's development woes. That will depend on having effective systems of governance to gather and then redistribute the tax income efficiently through improvements in services and infrastructure. There is a grave danger for the mines in operating in isolation from other general improvements, leading to 'rising expectations and driving predatory behaviour', warns one mining executive.

Here Guinea is not alone in finding a balance between fiscal austerity and creating the conditions for political stability. After all, its population, like others, cannot eat macroeconomic numbers. But Guinea is, based on its past profligate record, carefully constrained by its HIPC agreements. It cannot take any loan above the World Bank's 'cost of administration' interest rate, an effective 2 per cent. And any loan has to have a 35 per cent grant component.

These tensions have reflected the wider consolidation of the democratic process, such as the delay in staging the legislative elections, supposed to be held six months after Condé's win in 2010, and the contentious results when they were finally held in September 2013: Condé's party took 53 of the 114 parliamentary seats, with the main opposition, which said it would not recognise the result, securing 37.[7] With the process marred by 'irregularities', according to international observers, donors became very uncomfortable and some were hesitant to further commit funds to Guinea.

No mission impossible?

The country's plight has been exemplified by its ranking on global corruption tables, 154th out of 174, for example, on the 2012 Transparency International Corruption Perception Index, one place below the paragon of Paraguay and one above Kyrgyzstan. This reflects a deeper malaise within Guinean society, where the nuclear family unit is exceptionally fragmented, with fatherless children and single mothers fast becoming the norm. The extent of social dislocation and apparent lack of commitment to a common good seems to indicate that things are rotten to the core. 'Go to a minister's house,' says one observer. 'He has his own generator, his own water tank, and can use his authority to fix his road. He does not need a commitment to people, to the community, to the law, and to social rules.'

Thus, change will have to involve more than just words, visions or promises on institutional reforms and go to the heart of changing mindsets and operating systems embedded in the country's human software. African governments, and Guinea is no exception, prefer to argue that corruption demands both those seeking and those willing to pay a bribe. But this sidesteps the fact that most (at least Western-oriented) companies would prefer not to have to do so, not least since this makes them vulnerable to the vagaries of personalities rather than institutional processes and they usually have well-scrutinised systems and strictures back home. Those that do are usually presented with no option or would like to take a short cut. Changing this climate is always going to be difficult. The head of customs, for example, earned just $200 a month in Conakry in 2013 and the average government employee just $70. It will be difficult to attract skilled diaspora back home on this basis. While Liberia's transitional system of a better-paid core of civil servants – through its Senior Executive Service attracting skilled nationals on long-term contracts at higher salaries – has merit, Guinea could not afford this system without a strong relationship with donors.

Drafting an achievable plan for Guinea's recovery is, however, not 'mission impossible'. Drawing on the insights of country watchers, the suggestions are that it would need to build on the macroeconomic stability created by the IMF intervention and international supervision by, first, putting a government in place where delivery and technocratic capacity – not jobs for pals – were the key criteria. As one donor reflected, 'It would need to reduce the number of ministers from its current top-heavy 44 and replicate the success of the better ministries such as foreign affairs, environment, higher education and especially finance.'

Second, it would have to start planning things in a coordinated way, stopping 'the deal making, working with the international community, namely the donors and the investors'.

Third, it would need to succeed with one mega-project by actually making it happen. Such a deal 'would change the face of the country' in terms not only of image, but jobs, stability and indirect job opportunities. This should involve 'an infrastructure BOT [Build, Operate, Transfer] deal, and the government should use the savings from this to instead rebuild the three critical links: coastal, Conakry-Bamako and the Conakry-Forestiere roads'. Such a move would also, given that any mining railway should go through Liberia to the port of Buchanan, 'see the country living up to its Pan-Africanist rhetoric'.

Fourth, there would need to be reform in customs, establishing a 'machine' for funding the state. As a critical step, this would need to include external, professional auditors for mining exports. Also, fifth, the 'highly corrupt and politically tainted' system of rice import subsidies would need to be removed to boost domestic production.

A sixth step would be to clean up the public administration, with the strict enforcement of performance contracts and mandatory retirement ages. More controversially, this would also have to tackle the tricky issue of professionalising the 22 000-strong armed forces, especially the estimated 7 000 militia members who came in during the junta, who are 'badly trained, ill-educated and have nowhere to go'.

In Guinea, overall, there is a need to turn the government into one from where decisions are made impulsively by a chaotic presidency to one that has an evidence-based approach. Without this, Guinea is likely to stumble along, a perpetually disappointing outcome of nepotism, populism, tribalism, indigenisation and administrative dysfunction. As noted above, dealing with the corruption that oils the system but corrodes much else will have to involve more than transparency of mining contracts. An important aspect of such a change is undoing a national personality forged around the practice and expectation of payback and the scarcity of licit opportunity outside government.

A long and winding road

It is going to be a long and dangerous haul. In July 2011, Condé survived at least one attempted coup, which implicated associates of Konaté. In late February 2013, political violence erupted in Guinea after protesters took to the streets to voice their concerns over the transparency of the planned May 2013 elections, but they also revolved around inter-ethnic clashes between the Fula and Condé's Mandinka tribe.

This has led to frustration and, invariably, indifference. 'If we had to prioritise the top ten things that have made the greatest impact on Guinea,' observes one foreign investor who, unusually, has lived there for more than twenty years, 'cellphones would be first, the arrival of the Chinese second, and democracy down in tenth place'. While the government recognises, correctly, the importance of education, especially of a technical sort, this is at best a medium-term solution. In short, it is stuck in a bind, between generations, between old and new ways, and between stability and growth. If it does not find a way forward – and no one else is going to (or can) do this for it – a cycle of instability, populism and more 'lost decades' looms.

Idrissa Thiam says Sékou Touré is remembered for bringing 'enthusiasm for freedom' even though 'he destroyed his own people, leading to much resentment'. Conté, by comparison, 'brought hope and liberalised the economy before he was overcome by corruption'. Condé's government, he says, 'wants to be remembered as an exporter of food and power, and establishing ourselves as a significant mining country'. But this will require, first, thinking imaginatively about how to spend without breaking its pact with international donors; and, second, altering the country's political economy from one where tribalism, patriotism, nepotism, rural-urban divides, patronage and poverty are closely entwined to operate in a pernicious manner, to a more prosperous future based on transparency and competitiveness. No easy or simple task.

*

Conakry's Musée National is a sad, crumbling place. This tells its own story of years of government neglect. But when you are geared towards survival and tourists are few and far between, what is the point of investing in it? A collapsing apartment block frames the Musée's compound. A dog enveloped by flies, its ears wounded and bleeding, lay panting at the feet of the statue of the first governor, Eugene Noel Ballay, who set out Conakry. Under the bearded Frenchman's arms is a naked local youth, being protected and nurtured, we were told, by the colonialist. Amidst the various busts and statues in the littered courtyard were Sékou Touré and his father.

As history has softened his worst excesses, and subsequent leaders have failed to come up with fresh ideas and answers, Sékou Touré has started to look a little better in recent years. 'Guinea is at a crossroads,' admitted Thiam, 'but I believe we know what we have to do.'

Setbacks should not be necessary or, indeed, destiny, no matter the political explanation or justification. One Guinean business person described his country's travails since independence as the 'inevitable path of progress, no different to the trials and tribulations of Europe and the United States centuries before'. That may be correct, but the difference is that Guinea's journey is happening within a high-pressure digital world where expectations are high and where choices could be informed by the successes and failings of others. There are few more destabilising combinations than young people without jobs and with globally fed aspirations.

Guinea has so far battled to find a balance between local political demands and the policy realities for economic growth. Doing so is imperative if it is going to sweep the youth along in a new wave of nationalism, not the one of the 1960's variety, but rather one fuelled by improving prosperity. After all, not everyone can expect to play for the real Real Madrid.

3

HAITI

128 Shades of Grey

*

Behind the fluttering blue-and-red Haitian flags and the green mesh fence on the Champs de Mars in Port-au-Prince is the site of the National Palace, destroyed in the January 2010 earthquake that claimed 220 000 lives, including one-fifth of the public service. More than 300 000 were injured and 1.5 million people were left homeless. In the aftermath of this devastating event, the Caribbean country became a focus of international relief efforts, with celebrities to the fore, the National Palace being pulled down by Hollywood actor Sean Penn's J/P Haitian Relief Organization NGO.[1]

In the wake of the earthquake, the American televangelist Pat Robertson said that Haiti's collapse was down to a 'pact with the devil' it made 200 years ago.[2] This explained, he said, why Haiti suffers and is currently the poorest country in the Western hemisphere, while the Dominican Republic – which shares the 30 000 square metres of the Caribbean island of 'Hispaniola' – is relatively well off. 'That island of Hispaniola is one island,' Robertson observed. 'The Dominican Republic is prosperous, healthy, full of resorts, et cetera. Haiti is in desperate poverty.'

The devastating earthquake and other regular natural disasters only compounded Haiti's poor growth and stability record, tipping it over an already precarious edge and widening the gap with the Dominican Republic, which it once ruled. Even before the disaster, Haiti was a major recipient of Western aid. Haiti has teetered on the edge of being a failed state while other Caribbean islands have moved ahead, primarily through tourism and other services, a bellwether of progress.

Nearby Aruba, with just 100 000 inhabitants, for example, receives

1.6 million tourists a year despite limited offerings aside from good weather, ship cruises and charter flights, in the process lifting per capita GDP to over $23 000 annually.[3] The Dominican Republic's 10 million people cater for four million tourists each year, helping to lift per capita income levels to over $5 000. Haiti only accommodated 30 000 tourists in 2012, and many of these were day-trippers from the Dominican Republic or NGO types.

It is little wonder that its per capita income has remained stuck at $700. Not only has it missed out on globalisation's benefits, but the industries that were once there, including factories producing, famously, 90 per cent of US baseballs along with shoes, electrical items and other sporting goods, shut down in the face of the American embargo in the 1990s. As a result, unemployment is over 75 per cent of its 10-million population. Four million Haitians live and work abroad, including 1.5 million in the Dominican Republic and at least one million in the US, contributing as much as $4 billion annually in remittances, in so doing taking some of the heat and hardship out of the economy. The majority that remain, one-third of whom are squeezed into the capital Port-au-Prince, scrape by as *marchand* street vendors, *bouretye* cart pullers, and in other menial jobs, while those out 'beyond the mountain' scratch a living as peasants on small plots, disconnected from global and even domestic markets and apparently far from the concerns of the city-based elite.

The earthquake then only exposed the historical fault lines of Haitian society and politics – race, inequality, personalised law and order, weak governance and fractious politics. Despite its proud history as the second country in the hemisphere after the US to achieve its independence and its status as the first independent black republic, which continues to inspire people inside and outside its borders, Haiti's reconstruction path is a fraught and difficult one.

Why has this been the case, and what does this say about Haiti's prospects for recovery and the role to be played by the international aid community, there and elsewhere?

Green and brown

Satellite imagery of Haiti and the Dominican Republic bears out this distinction.[4] One is relatively denuded of trees, mostly brown compared to the Dominican Republic's forested green. It was not always like this.

Eighty years ago, more than 60 per cent of Haiti's land was forested; by 2006, this figure had shrunk to less than 2 per cent. In the absence of alternatives, two-thirds of Haitians, their population numbers having climbed from four to over 10 million in 50 years, depend on charcoal for cooking and livelihoods. Little wonder the patches of brown have spread across the border in a desperate attempt to find wood, where Dominican forest cover is over 20 per cent. The UN reports that in the process, 25 to 30 Haitian watersheds have been largely degraded or altered with all their wildlife habitats 'destroyed or seriously damaged'.[5]

Other statistics back up such visuals. At the time of the earthquake in 2010, the UN, for example, ranked the Dominican Republic 90th out of 182 countries on its Human Development Index; Haiti was at 149th. In the Dominican Republic, average life expectancy is nearly 74 years; in Haiti, 61. As the poorest country in the Western hemisphere, it is little surprise that Haiti has been beset with problems of political stability. To address this, the UN has repeatedly sent peacekeeping missions to maintain order there since the mid-1990s.

The most recent iteration, the United Nations Stabilization Mission in Haiti (MINUSTAH) was established on 1 June 2004 by Security Council Resolution 1542,[6] succeeding a Multinational Interim Force authorised by the Security Council in February 2004. This followed the departure of then President Jean-Bertrand Aristide for exile following widespread violence. Following the completion of presidential elections in 2011, MINUSTAH focused on restoring a 'secure and stable environment, to promote the political process, to strengthen Haiti's government institutions and rule-of-law-structures, as well as to promote and to protect human rights'. This has been at a considerable cost. As of November 2012, its strength totalled 9 988 uniformed personnel (made up of 7 297 troops and 2 691 police) plus 451 international civilian personnel and 1 317 local civilian staff.

While providing a platform for recovery, this by itself is not going to lever the country out of its plight, and nor should it be expected or attempt to do so.

There has also been a lot of money spent in the process. MINUSTAH's 2012 budget was $650 million. And even before the earthquake, Haiti was a recipient of a steady flow of international largesse, yet with little long-term effect, as the funds focused on the symptoms of the systemic problems underlying the perpetual crises, and by directly addressing them, bypassed the very government it needed to strengthen. As one Haitian noted in testimony to a June 2011 US Senate hearing on rebuilding Haiti, 'Haiti's status quo has been ineffectual for 200 years.'[7]

Regardless, faced with a humanitarian catastrophe, aid to Haiti tripled between 2009 and 2010, increasing from $1.12 billion ($142.1 million in relief and $977.6 million in development funding) to an estimated $3.27 billion ($1.55 billion in relief and $1.73 billion in recovery and development funding). Aid from bilateral and multilateral donors has become a much larger resource than the Haitian government's own revenue, providing 130 per cent of government's internally generated revenue in 2009 and an estimated 400 per cent of revenue in 2010.[8] In January 2012, figures released by the UN show that US$4.5 billion was pledged for reconstruction projects in 2010 and 2011, although only 43 per cent had been delivered.[9]

Haiti has involved a big international commitment. Yet recovery has been slow, partly because the international community has battled to deliver aid in an environment where governance is poor and the underlying conditions that led to the crisis in the first instance have still, in large measure, persisted.

Indeed, Robertson's devil aside, understanding the difference with the Dominican Republic helps to pinpoint these reasons, and chart a better way forward for Haiti and international partners.

Up and down, black and white

To some extent the difference is geographic and topographic.

Haiti's semi-arid climate has made cultivation challenging. Deforestation has only exacerbated the problem, causing massive soil erosion to the extent that in the case of regular flooding, as a UN expert puts it, 'houses simply get washed down Haiti's hills and valleys'. But, it should be said, Israel performs better with much less water and arable area.

To an extent it is historical – and racial.

Carlos Despradel is a former Reserve Bank governor of the Dominican Republic, a country whose turbulent relationship with Haiti lends it to having little sympathy towards its western neighbour. He puts the difference in stark terms. 'If you hate white people – and there is little doubt Haitians had good reason for it 200 years ago – then you have Haiti. You don't get foreign investment, and instead you get emigration. This started when the remaining French colonists fled the country for New Orleans and Cuba, leaving people in power, essentially slaves and their descendants, who did not know how to rule.'

Yet the history is not simply black and white. The colony of Saint-Domingue (the site of present-day Haiti) was once the richest French colony in the 'New World', a result of the profits from the sugar, coffee and indigo industries, based on slave labour. By the end of the eighteenth century, there were 40 000 French colonists on the island (Canada had only 65 000 around this time), but more than ten times the number of slaves, who were brutally exploited. Around half of the world's sugar and coffee came from the colony, where 8 000 plantations provided around 40 per cent of France's foreign trade.

The Haitian Revolution, which ended with the founding of the Haitian republic on 1 January 1804, began as a slave revolt on Saint-Domingue that started thirteen years earlier in the wake of the French Revolution. After the evacuation of a French expeditionary force, almost wiped out by dengue fever, from the once prosperous colony, the slave leader Jean-Jacques Dessalines came to power. Following the proclamation of independence, he gave the order that all white men should be put to death, an order that practically eradicated all white Haitians and resulted in the deaths of as many as 5 000 people. In terms of the 1805 constitution, all citizens were defined as 'black', and white men were banned from owning land.

Still, the subsequent tensions and divisions around race in Haiti were more complex. While the French left the Caribbean, race still played its part in the system. The colonial jurist and historian Moreau de Saint-Méry, for example, had counted and categorised eleven racial combinations in the colony of Saint-Domingue. He also argued that ancestry should be traced back seven generations, bringing it to 128 combinations.[10]

The expulsion of the French after such a vicious struggle 'atomised' politics and people in Haiti. Initially, following Dessalines' assassination in 1806, this saw the country split into two – a royalist north and a mixed-race-dominated south around Port-au-Prince. The destruction of the plantation and education system followed, entrenching marginalisation and poverty. Not only did the country's early independence ensure, ironically, that Haiti received none of the 'late colonial benefits' of local involvement in the administration, but it left behind a divided society. The mixed-race elite used their French connections to dominate the economy in the cities, and they apparently did not give much, if anything, to the masses and the peasant society outside. Crisis followed crisis, government and leaders turned over with rapidity and mostly with violence, and foreign intervention came hard on the heels of local upheaval and geo-political changes.

The US exerted its influence in the face of increased German presence in the early twentieth century by sending in the Marines, resulting in a nearly twenty-year occupation from 1915. This negative influence continued during the Cold War, with US support for the Duvalier regime (Papa and Baby Doc Duvalier, father and son, ruled for three decades from 1957–86) on account of their stated anti-communist credentials, even though they worsened an already fragile governance regime. This cannot have improved the scepticism felt about outsiders, starting with the massive reparations that had to be paid to France as compensation for French slaveholders and landowners in order to receive diplomatic recognition, a payment that was only completed in 1947.

For all of the external dimensions, the problems (and the solutions) had their origins then, as now, at home. Not for nothing emerged the saying in Paris, '*riche com un Creole*'. As a result, leadership, even when 'black' and autocratic as with the Duvaliers or democratic as in Jean-Bertrand Aristide and not of mixed-race descent, are seen to 'dance to the tune of a rich elite', who pursue their political interests through money, influence, business and violence. Gangs, known as Les Bases, have equally been a political feature. Another is the operation of a black market economy, visible in the houses of Pétionville and the gated community of Vivy Mitchell, paid for with money that apparently easily circumvents state books.

As one foreign official notes, 'Ten to twelve wealthy families continue to run the place, using a combination of violence, intimidation, criminality and monopolies to cement their power. Haiti was, for example, once nearly self-sufficient in rice production. Now it produces only about 10 per cent of its needs. The Duvalier regimes suppressed local rice production in favour of imports, of course benefiting an importing coterie.'[11]

Such relationships and rivalries have also been overlaid with cult practices – Vodou (voodoo) by another name.[12] During the years of Papadocracy, for example, the rural *houngan* priests were mainstays in the Tontons Macoutes paramilitary.[13] Catholic rituals are frequently complemented by Vodou. Add to this a dose of '*se pa fot mwen*' (it is not my fault, in Creole) and responsibility is routinely abrogated to someone else, another country or higher authority.

For example, the Chile earthquake that took place almost the same day as Haiti's in 2010 was several times stronger, yet killed less than 1 per cent as many people, and Chile was back on its feet in a week even though there were instances of looting in poorer areas. Haiti's recovery was still a work in progress three years later. This comparison speaks to improved building standards, readiness and response mechanisms. Better evidence of the importance of human development and an attitude of self-help and local ownership would be difficult to concoct.

It also reflects attitude. As the Costa Rican economist Alberto Trejos has noted, 'Haiti is very African in this regard. While the reason is obviously not race directly, it may be indirectly, as race conditions the way the rest of the world relates to Haitians – that it expects the world to come to its assistance, and the world expects and wants to do so.'[14] For example, take the comment of Jonathan Katz in *The Big Truck That Went By* when describing the 'failure' of the international community to deliver aid to Haitians on the scale promised (and expected): '[T]he legacy of the response has been a sense of betrayal.'[15] Importantly, this reflects the absence of social contract in Haiti. 'The social fabric is missing,' says a UN official who has spent much time in Africa. 'It's a dog-eat-dog environment, one where there is a marked absence of solidarity and trust at all levels, there is no land title, and where rule is only established by the gun and violence. In this environment, politics is about intimidation not delivery.' It is a history blighted by political instability. In its 210-year history there have been 56 presidents, of which 26 were overthrown or assassinated.[16] Since 1986, there have been more than a dozen heads of state, a handful of coups and military regimes, and a US-led military intervention.

This has created a fragile state, where structural problems of poor governance, institutional weakness, selfish leadership, and fractious politics persist, one result of which is that the country 'inevitably gets whacked', says a senior UN official, 'hardly able to pull itself together before the next crisis hits'. Thus, he adds, one 'cannot separate humanitarian crises from development needs'.[17] In great part, then, Haiti's plight has been a result of policy and choice, a point emphasised by its neighbour's performance.

Rolling success next door

Growth performance between Haiti and the Dominican Republic has diverged remarkably over the past half-century.[18]

In 1960, the Dominican Republic and Haiti had the same per capita real GDP at just below $800. By 2005, the Dominican Republic's per capita real GDP had tripled to about $2 500, whereas that of Haiti had halved to $430. As a result, the Dominican Republic and Haiti have been at opposite ends of the growth and development spectrum within Latin America and the Caribbean, with the Dominican Republic achieving one of the highest average real GDP growth rates at above 5 per cent, and Haiti the lowest at about 1 per cent. The reason according to the IMF: '[P]olicy decisions since 1960 have played a central role. In particular, the Dominican Republic has consistently outperformed Haiti and the rest of Latin America in terms of structural measures and stabilization policies, while Haiti has been subject to numerous political shocks that have severely affected its growth performance.'[19]

These differences are evident not only in the history of political stability of the two neighbours, but in the contemporary conditions for doing business. According to the 2014 World Bank Doing Business Indicators, Dominican Republic ranked 117th (out of 189 countries), while Haiti was at 177th.[20] Haiti ranked 163rd out of 175 placings on Transparency International's 2013 Corruption Perception Index; the Dominican Republic 123rd.[21]

Even though it is not a stellar global performer then, and has been beset by its own problems of military juntas and racial intolerance, the Dominican Republic was able to treble its economic output during the 1990s. Moreover, it is not as if the country does not share all the challenges of a difficult neighbourhood (the nearest major chunk of land is the US base at Guantanamo Bay in Cuba), or has not had its share of US military interventions (in 1905, 1916–24 and again in 1965 with 42 000 US Marines) and violent political leadership.

Rafael Trujillo, known as 'El Jefe' or 'The Boss', ruled Dominicans brutally from 1930 until his assassination in 1961 by disenchanted military officers, an event made famous in literary circles by Mario Vargas Llosa's harrowing and loosely biographical *Feast of the Goat*. Although his rule was exceptionally bloody, being responsible for 50 000 deaths, Leonel Fernandez, a three-term Dominican president who stepped down in August 2012, admits that Trujillo's rule brought the country stability and prosperity. 'Our dictatorship could be criticised on human rights and political grounds where they were reactionary, but on economic matters it was progressive.'[22]

Or as Carlos Despradel observes, 'Trujillo unified the country, which until then was under the control of various caudillos, or warlords. He ruthlessly integrated. Those against him he killed, and he became the richest man in the country in the process. But he also stabilised the economy, improved education and health care, and paid our foreign debt.' This could be contrasted with the rule of the Duvalier family. Following the downfall of the Trujillo dictatorship, the Dominican Republic's economic transition followed, says President Fernandez, various clear stages.

First, state-owned enterprises were transferred from Trujillo's personal coffers to state control. This stage was followed by a second, in 1969, involving the creation of Zona Francas, or duty-free export promotion zones.

The first Zona Franca was established by a private company at La Romana about two hours' drive east of the capital Santo Domingo. The success was quickly emulated by government. Within twenty years there were 35 such zones or parks hosting 350 factories.

These zones now include pharmaceutical, apparel, electrical and medical equipment companies, employing 160 000 workers and exporting $4 billion worth of goods.

At the same time, the government embarked on a tourism drive, intent on gaining a share of the US market. As Carlos Morales, the current foreign minister, remembers: 'When we started, tourism only provided 0.3 per cent of GDP. Today it is very different. The Dominican Republic has jumped from 1 200 to over 70 000 hotel rooms in four decades.'

Tourism has rapidly grown into a four-million-visitors-a-year industry worth $4 billion. This is, says President Fernandez, 'the wave of the future', the country diversifying away from simply 'beaches and sun' to more sophisticated golf and other estates.

Again La Romana was in the forefront with the Casa de Campo development, now housing 72 holes of golf and a world-class marina among its many facilities, a regular port of call for cruise liners.

A second stage involved the creation of the Caribbean Basin Initiative in 1983, allowing unilateral tariff-free access to the US market. In the 2000s this was transformed into the reciprocal Central American Free Trade Area.

The third stage followed in the 1990s when half of the government's stake in the twenty state-owned enterprises in sectors from sugar to electricity was sold off, and the entities commercialised. As a result, foreign direct investment has risen rapidly during the 2000s, along with a threefold increase in GDP to $60 billion between 2004 and 2012.

And in all this, the economy remains buoyed by remittance flows (another $4 billion), mainly from 1.5 million Dominicans working in the US, and by the more traditional sectors of agriculture and mining, the latter mainly gold and ferry nickel.

Agriculture has also diversified away from sugar and corn to higher-value fruits. Sugar exports were over one million tonnes in the 1960s, halving as special preferences fell away. But tobacco remains a bulwark. While Cuba gets the kudos, the Dominican Republic is the world's largest manufacturer of cigars. Its 300 million 'premium' hand-rolled cigars (plus three billion machine-made units) are more than the combined production of Cuba (150 million), Nicaragua (100 million) and Honduras (80 million). This industry is worth a further $3.5 billion in exports. Unlike Cuba, where cigar rollers have to find ways to supplement the standard state wage of $19, topped up by some incentives, the 35 000 Dominican cigar workers earn around $400 a month. There are apparently some advantages to not living in a workers' paradise, even though wealth inequality in the Dominican Republic remains, as with much of the region, stubbornly high and, with shades of Haiti, a racial tone prevails. Ten per cent of the population is estimated to control half the economy and 40 per cent of Dominicans continue to live below the poverty line.

Regardless, the Dominican Republic's development story is one of low wages (the average wage in the free zones is $160), and continuous private sector-led innovation and diversification, especially in tourism and industry. It is difficult to get away from these development tenets where there is excess unskilled labour.

And Haiti shows how one can get it very badly wrong, in which case aid makes little difference. It also illustrates that proximity to rich countries matters little, too, if the 'operating system' is pear-shaped.

Haiti's aid business

Haiti's international aid apparatus has been portrayed as a mess, 'driven by inefficiency, ignorance and greed, a failure of good (and not-so-good) intentions'.[23]

With media estimates putting the number of NGOs at 12 000, it is little wonder that the country has been termed an 'NGO Republic', with foreign-led organisations rushing to Haiti, especially after the earthquake, and building a powerful 'parallel state accountable to no one but their boards and donors'. The bashing does not stop with the NGOs. The UN is, among others, portrayed as being out of touch and uncaring, such as in the view, below, describing the stabilisation mission: 'Several miles northwest of downtown sits the Logistical Base, or Log Base, the headquarters for the United Nations and its recovery efforts. Here, it's a different world. Within the massive blue-and-white compound are revamped trailers, golf carts and more glistening public toilets than any other place in Haiti. (Log Base is germ – and cholera! – free.) Flowers line the walkways, and machines blow a cool mist into an outdoor restaurant whose menu, on one random day, included sushi, jasmine rice, German potatoes, Brazilian cheese bread, halaal shawarma and Häagen-Dazs ice cream. The American dollar, not the Haitian gourde, is the currency of choice.'[24]

Such views, however, fail to distinguish between various UN agencies. The UN is viewed as one lump, just as are all donors, perceptions about whom have suffered in Haiti from the relative gulf between commitments and delivery on aid. At the International Donors' conference 'Towards a New Future for Haiti' held on 31 March 2010, just eleven weeks after the quake, donors pledged $5.3 billion for Haiti's recovery, to be disbursed over two years. The Interim Haitian Reconstruction Commission, also known as the Clinton Commission after the former American president who headed it, was set up to spend the money quickly and wisely.

By the end of 2012, a little over half of this money had been delivered. Of course, this was a reflection of the state of governance in the Haitian government. Donors were reluctant to allow funds to flow through the government for reasons of both efficiency and corruption.

Similarly, there has been a tension about the UN's role, how effective it is, and whether it should stay or it should go. Fingers have been pointed at its slowness in training the police, a key mission, with just 900 officers being turned out in 2012, for example, in the planned expansion from 6 500 to 14 000.[25]

The critique has further included commentary not only about the number of NGOs, the relative wealth of foreign versus local NGOs, the extent of their overheads and the comfort of expatriate living standards, but about the technical efficiency of their solutions. The reluctance of foreign donors to spend money through Haitian governmental institutions is also seen to undermine the government's authority, and to prevent properly tailored and more effective programmes from being carried out. Yet the framing of Haiti as a failure has become a cottage industry 'written by journalists in search of failure and disaster, especially', says a UN official, 'given the closeness of Haiti to the US and Canada, where they regard it as their mission'. The international community is accused both of spending too much and too little. And these tensions are rising as the international commitment suddenly ramps down.

Here the debate on the NGO numbers has been misleading, at best. According to the UN, although 'the problem is getting the figures right, given that NGOs do not always report what is spent', $1.2 billion was raised for humanitarian relief immediately following the earthquake, reducing to $200 million in 2011 and $50 million in 2012 (with a supplement of $25 million on account of Hurricane Sandy). Another $50 million was to be spent in 2013. To these numbers had to be added 'several billion more' spent through the Red Cross and other agencies and not generated through the UN appeal. All of this is spent through 80 humanitarian partners. Indeed, far from the 12 000 claimed NGOs, the government recognises just over 500 in the country.

And, of course, money has been wasted. But if money was going to be well spent in Haiti, then the NGOs would not be there in the first place. And while it is easy to criticise the presence of the UN, the mission should not close, says Mariano Fernández, a Chilean diplomat who headed MINUSTAH until February 2013, until it is clear that it would never have to return. And that condition would require a much more competent state.[26]

Moreover, the criticism understates the achievements, both of the donors and of government. Yet, there is a need to differentiate between the NGOs themselves. They range from 'zillions of evangelical-based T-shirt brigade types' along with the 'traditional' deliverers of humanitarian relief such as Save the Children and Plan International, and new players from Brazil such as Viva Rio, with relevant experience in pacification programmes from Brazilian *favelas*. Then there are the 'celebrity humanitarians' including Mr Penn, although he receives pretty high marks from locals given the duration he has spent living among Haitians.

Still, the aid focus would have inevitably to shift in two respects. First, from how the international community and the government of Haiti could together migrate from humanitarian to development assistance; and second, how the Haitians could help themselves.

Bridging the humanitarian-development divide

The co-founder of a worldwide provider of telecommunications solutions in emerging markets and developing countries, Laurent Lamothe was appointed Haiti's prime minister in May 2012, following a spell as foreign minister. An articulate and visibly energetic man, as befits a former Davis Cup tennis player, he is a passionate defender of his country's progress.

While he acknowledges that the country still faces 'many problems and challenges', including 52 per cent living 'in extreme poverty, 350 000 homeless, and 75 per cent unemployed', he prefers to highlight the delivery record. 'Nearly 80 per cent of the people living in camps after the earthquake are now returning to their communities, while 95 per cent of the debris has been collected, enough to fill 4 000 Olympic-size swimming pools', he stated in January 2013. 'We have moved 77 per cent of people back into their homes and have created subsidies for micro-enterprises, as well as subsidies for the most vulnerable, including young mothers and the disabled, reaching more than four million people in 2012.' This links with the introduction of free education at the primary level, with nearly 1.3 million children attending school free of charge in 2012, up from just 50 per cent enrolment in 2006. 'For many of them,' he says, 'this is the first time. We will also teach reading and writing to more than 300 000 adults in 2013.'

On law and order, 'We have dismantled five of the largest criminal organisations in the country, and this is reflected in our crime statistics. Haiti,' he says, 'has the same homicide rate as Long Beach, California.' The government has also rebuilt 735 kilometres of roads and opened up a new, $300-million industrial park in the north. 'There is the feeling that this year, 2013, is the year of the private sector in Haiti.'

But at the same time he has acknowledged that politics is the reason for the disaster in the first instance. A key reason for the continuing misery, the wrenching tales of suffering and of good intentions gone awry with the human and financial assistance pouring into Haiti, is the underlying problems that got them there. As the prime minister observes, 'Bad performance was due to the fact that Haiti's previous governments were more interested in political control at all cost than in economic and GDP growth. Bad governance, managerial incompetence and lack of decision-making contributed to putting the country down the wrong path and kept it poor.'[27]

This analysis squares with that of the international community. 'Development will never work if you have a bunch of Neros fiddling in the political system,' says one foreign diplomat. 'There need to be clear political rules of the game, in other words, without which the only vision for the country is one of a 'winner takes all'.

And if the diagnosis of the problem is similar, so, too, is the proposed solution. Lamothe says: 'We will move the country from being a charity to investment by: first, identifying the main sources of diversified economic growth; second, by highlighting those to the world; third, by conducting

Doing Business reforms: reforms in business and electricity will contribute to better economic performance; fourth by identifying new sources to increase the GDP, such as in mining; and fifth, by having NGOs follow a road map of priorities established by the government of Haiti.' His government hopes to achieve this by involving a combination of outside actors (such as those working under Clinton's co-chairmanship in the 35-strong Presidential Advisory Council) and internal reforms.

In this regard, there is little here that the international community would disagree with, at least in a technical sense. In transiting from a humanitarian to a development agenda, says Nigel Fisher, then the UN mission's deputy for development and humanitarian issues, 'we have to move away from the whole traditional, north-south, charity-based humanitarian experience, involving too many people that do not know the environment and end up simply displacing and not supporting government'. To do so, there is a need for international agencies to get to know the country before crises happen, but also to focus on strengthening national capabilities, through mentoring key government departments, building up local communities and not simply central government capacity, and through local procurement with transparent contracting and focusing expenditure on the types of areas that improve the link between foreign money and the local economy. This includes rural roads, the building of dams, cleaning of canals and reforestation to give both immediate relief and to link the peasantry to the mainstream economy.

In part, this requires a clear, preferably single priority – 'not ten'. Surveys consistently illustrate that what people want is 'jobs, jobs and jobs with education in fourth place'. Such a single, over-riding goal would help to clarify and coalesce the response: dealing with land tenure, overbearing customs procedures and port costs and the efficiency of government all have a logic and relevance.

All this, Fisher says, can be reflected in the international community changing its mindset from a 'cargo cult' – 'where we give Haiti what we have' – to one that gives them 'what they want'. But that is only half of the deal.

This necessary degree of focus requires, at its heart, immense political will intent on changing the very system that got Haiti into the mess it is.

The underlying reasons of failure

Haiti is not the Dominican Republic. One indicator is in the number of Haitians, not fewer than 1.5 million, who take jobs in their eastern island neighbour.

But then it is also not Somalia, Congo or pre-Ellen Johnson Sirleaf Liberia either. Infrastructure is degraded and weak by the standards of the Dominican Republic, and many people live in terrible conditions, vulnerable to disease, as the cholera outbreak in 2011 showed, where there were no fewer than 20 000 cases each week. And there are less visible but no less insidious threats, including the omnipresent risk of violence and kidnappings from prowling Haitian gangs.

Haitians still take their *tap tap* taxis on the plunging streets of Port-au-Prince, and those roads are mostly still intact, if increasingly clogged with traffic. Children walk in smiling and laughing groups to school, their regimented uniforms and the girls' neatly ribboned hair standing out in the crowded streets. Refugees live in ordered tents, some such as those in the Jean-Marie Vincent camp near the Belair *favela* in the capital, with paved roads. Sure it cannot be easy sharing and in some of these 500 camps countrywide there are 80 to a latrine. Regardless, this is certainly not Kitchanga in the eastern Congo, where refugees live under leaves, sticks and plastic, easy prey for marauding government soldiers and militias.

Haiti is more fragile than failed, then; a country in the grip of a perverse racial system and trapped in a mindset of violence, entitlement, bad government and poor leadership. Getting out of it is going to require undoing 200 years of history, unpicking vested interests and installing a sense of local responsibility along with governance. In all, this is no easy task. Getting there requires acknowledging why things went wrong. It also requires building a competitive economic base. Above all, as intimated above, it demands changing the Haitian mindset, from victim to being in charge.

In abolishing the plantations that were associated with slavery and by giving each family its own plot of land in the process, Haiti was turned from a producing and export economy to a subsistence, remittance and aid-dependent one. To reiterate, now it produces little more than 40 per cent of its own food 'in a good year', and despite a big effort made in the 1980s to turn the country into a 'little Taiwan' (which was latter destroyed by the 1990s' embargo), it has no manufacturing save for a small textile and handicrafts sector, their brightly painted pressed-tin animals lining the tourist routes. It is difficult to imagine how industry can progress with electricity at $40c kW/h, where the state provider ran a $230-million loss in 2012, and just 28 per cent of subscribers paid their bills. Even the baseball plant has been struck out. Fuel is also dependent on a low interest arrangement with Venezuela via its PetroCaribe preferential fuel-financing scheme for

Caribbean countries,[28] and highly susceptible to political shocks, notably a change of heart of regime (or both) in Caracas.

The most valuable export, as noted, is Haiti's people who bring in the aforementioned $4 billion in remittances annually, even though the country has a number of strategic advantages, not least its location just 90 minutes from Miami and its tourism potential. Perhaps the most damning condemnation of Haiti's system is that its people prosper when they leave it behind and are widely admired for their productivity and work ethic.

If Haiti is to make progress, it will not depend on what the international community does, but rather in how it deals itself with underlying problems of race, violence and inequality. While Haiti will inevitably be a focus of sporadic international charity efforts, at best the humanitarian aid community can only deal with the symptoms.

4

KENYA

Off the Rails or Back on Track?

✳

No doubt there are also many Kenyans who will take umbrage with their country being included in a volume on failed states. But there are two Kenyas, with a huge divide between them in wealth, privilege and opportunity. And the vast difference between these two worlds, as much the conditions among the 'have-nots', ensure Kenya fails a large chunk of its citizenry.

It is the difference between the four-wheel drives, overseas educations, big homes and expensive suits of the elite hanging out smoking cigars and sipping house ales on black-and-white chequer chairs at Nairobi's swish Capital Club, annual membership not less than $10 000, compared to the plight of those living in and working the Kibarani rubbish mound on the outskirts of Mombasa, where several thousand people live in abject poverty, picking their livelihood through the mountains of putrefying waste, searching for recyclable material to sell to make a living. There is no clean water, sanitation, schools or permanent housing.

Their situation is sadly not unique. For Kibarani read the relatively well-known Kibera township in Nairobi, 25 minutes away from the Capital Club as the Matatu flies, one of the ubiquitous barely roadworthy minibus taxis, so named after their original rate per passenger of just 3 (tatu) shillings.[1]

Often the centrepiece of visits by furrow-browed foreign dignitaries, some 800 000, said our guide Mildred, live in Kibera's 16 square kilometres of dust, sewerage splash and stench. The rail track, festooned with plastic rubbish, cuts through the area of Gatuwekera. Metalworkers, cycle-repair shops, electricians distinguishable by their throbbing music, shoemakers, drinking dens and smoky open-air grills, barbers named 'Scizor Cutz' and

'Lamborghini', and charcoal sellers, the bundles in small buckets of 60 and 50 shillings each, ply their trade on the dirt roadside. The site of much election violence in 2007–08, Kibera's walls and doors are daubed with signs the likes of 'Peace maker is you' and 'Peace wanted alive'. Security is much improved, say the locals, with assault rifle-toting soldiers in camouflage on regular view, but it is still a tough, vulnerable existence. 'The rate of HIV is 50 per cent', says Everlyne Shiangala, the chairperson for the Power Women Group Kibera, a small cooperative selling handmade gifts to inquisitive tourists. Outside her corrugated-iron market two giggling tots practised their skipping using a piece of packaging as a Matatu lurched past with 'Spread God not Virus' on its rear window.

Still, Kibera is relatively upmarket, chaos to the uneducated eye, but with relative organisation and social structure. It is far worse in the lesser-known Mukuru Kwa Njega slum in the capital's industrial area, a vicinity earmarked by spewing avalanches of litter, including 'flying toilets', plastic bags filled with excrement. The sight and smell cannot be avoided, although the inhabitants appear invisible to government concern.

Just under half of Kenya's 44 million people live below the poverty line, an estimated 3.9 million of them in slums.[2] The slums remain deprived of central and local government services in part because the government refuses to reform their town planning laws. Official Kenyan projections suggest the numbers of Kenyans living in urban settlements will increase from 32 per cent to 54 per cent by 2030.[3]

North of Mombasa, a city itself of apparently limitless litter and limited interest to collect it, is Mtwapa, said to be a party town 'which never sleeps' and where 'even the dogs have girlfriends'.[4] The reality is less appealing – the open drain alongside the road a floating porridge of waste and water, a town where the goats nibble and tiptoe on top rather than in between the piles of litter. 'Goats in the street', is the rule of one colleague, 'and I eat only Pizza Margherita'. His Mtwapa diet would be a bit starchy.

The Kenyans living in the failed version of their state are the clientele, if they are lucky, who frequent the *mitumba* shops selling second-hand clothing passed down from richer Western donors. They are the ones who mount a daily struggle to put food on the table.

And it is not that it is much better outside the cities. Most of Kibarani's waste-pickers are jobless migrants from the surrounding rural areas. These are the families lining the railway track to Mombasa, the snotty-nosed children running among the goats and chickens, waving to the train in which their more fortunate brethren travel. But in the third-class passenger section there is little laughter, just the jar of screaming children and tired, scolding parents, and the stare of faces etched deeply by poverty and, more than that, weariness.

When the train manager was asked how this sight, inside and out, made him feel, he tapped his heart. 'Sore in here,' he choked.

Whether they are mounting the stalls flanking the road from Diani to Mombasa, dragging carts laden with cement, water, tomatoes, steel re-bar or every other imaginable item over the Mombasa ferry and beyond, these are the Kenyans left out and behind. They live amidst high levels of insecurity and accept personal risk most Westerners baulk at. Their transport is at best a *boda-boda* motorcycle (so named because they made their name in taking people across the no-man's-land between borders), probably without a helmet, or a sweaty, uncomfortable place in an overloaded and badly driven purple-and-yellow striped Matatu taxi, where even the badges are pop-riveted on to prevent them from being prised off and extra locks are added to the rear door. Their experience of justice is a *sorgah* stick-wielding (swagger stick) predatory police-man or, if they are lucky, a roadside court, where the police serve as arresting officer, judge, jury and executioner – unless you can pay for your 'pardon' upfront.

For one group the state has worked, and perhaps too well. In the short term at least they are not overwhelmingly adversely affected by the corruption, nepotism, tribalism and the high costs and poor delivery of services – in essence, the failure of the state to deliver. This environment, which has cost the majority so much, either benefits them or can be circumvented. Ultimately, the transaction costs of staying afloat in business and ahead in politics and life are as ruinous for the privileged group, as they are for the nation. They have to lend a crutch for indigent relatives and friends. And if they do not feel an unease about their growing alienation from the mass of their fellow citizens, they may one day discover what deep trouble they are in.[5]

The other group survives in spite of the corruption, predation, missed opportunities, waste, squander and squalor. This includes the estimated 80 per cent of Kenyans who work in the informal sector.

The gap in income and living standards between these two Kenyas does not, economists say,[6] hurt those living in poverty, which includes half of those in the capital city, but is the kindling that can quickly turn violent. The political violence around the 2007 presidential election, for example, claimed more than 1 100 lives, thousands more injured, over 600 000 displaced, and more than 40 000 houses, farms and many businesses looted or destroyed.[7]

The distance between these worlds is not narrowing, and is unlikely to do so without something radical happening. For example, even though poverty came down from 56 per cent of the population in 2002 to oscillate between 44 and 46 per cent between 2008–14,[8] there was a 30.5 per cent increase in poverty levels through 1996 to 1999.[9]

According to traditional economic theory, à la Rostow,[10] traditional society (like the one most Kenyans operate in) develops through increased investment in transport and infrastructure and an agricultural revolution. This allows the division of labour in areas other than subsistence agriculture. In these theoretical surrounds, through diversification the industrial sector comes to dominate the economy with primary goods playing a lesser role, with widespread consumption of consumer goods (such as cars) being driven by the much greater disposable income of domestic consumers – the stage of 'high mass consumption'.

Yet, the demands of such a growth cycle – including improving skills and the need for extensive capital formation – are considerable hurdles, especially in small markets. One effect is 'dualism' – essentially where one sector of the economy makes progress – our Kenyan elite – and where another – the rest of society – gets increasingly left behind.

Moreover, Kenya's anticipated population increase militates against things being very different. By 2045, in 30 years, Kenya's population is projected to nearly double to 80 million. Many Kenyans will be living in its cities, both due to migration, and as towns expand to become cities. This offers tremendous opportunities for development and economies of scale, especially in the delivery of essential infrastructure and services. Already 800 000 young Kenyans join the labour market annually. Yet most of this cohort can only acquire menial work if they are lucky enough to find any at all.

The Kenyan workforce was, *circa* 2013, over 20 million people, with just five million in wage-earning jobs, the remainder in farming or self-employed. Only 1.3 million work in the private sector. Twenty-five years before, the share of the informal sector in the job market was just at 20 per cent.

This especially affects Kenya's young people under 35, two-thirds of the population. Most are unemployed and poorly educated. More than 40 per cent have never attended or completed primary school, and under one-fifth have completed secondary school, partly because they are sent out to work and fend for themselves at a very early age.[11] It is a shocking statistic that more than 50 per cent of workers under the age of fifteen, some 1.9 million Kenyans, work 66 hours a week or longer.

*

Something will have to shift or things will change for the worse in Kenya, where the underclass grows faster than the middle class. In understanding why things are this way and what might be done to remedy matters, one does not have to look much further than the railway.

Another walking society

The short cut I took to Nairobi's main station got me out of the car at the old railway works, the one with the banners advertising male circumcision as a means to reduce the spread of HIV transmission, and over the wood-and-steel bridge spanning the tracks. Underneath were long lines of disused waggons and tankers, on top thousands of hurrying commuters. But they were not taking the train. 'They are walking home from school and from work. It's quicker,' said the railway official in reference to Nairobi's infamous traffic, 'and cheaper.' At the foot of the bridge in the descending dusty evening gloom were several stalls selling fried, steaming food – some chicken and a few ball-like 'things' – to the hungry masses. Where they carried on straight towards the city, it was a sharp turn right to the railway station and the Nairobi-Mombasa 'Lunatic Express'. Nairobi's origins are as a railway depot at the turn of the nineteenth century and into the twentieth century, the last piece of flat ground before the Uganda Railway huffed and puffed its way up and through the highlands towards Lake Victoria.

The area, halfway between Mombasa and Kampala, was named after the Masai 'Enkare Nyorobi', meaning cool waters. A 1 600-metre elevation made it comfortable for living and relatively malaria-free. Now the 'ugly mess' of a city of 3.5 million is anything but comfortable and has little to commend it;[12] a giant 'jam', as the locals term it, of traffic and smog, testament to both a failure to keep pace with population and urban growth, and to devote resources to long-term infrastructure investments.

One hundred years ago, Kenya and East Africa were full of colonial promise and ambition. The railway was the region's imperial centrepiece. Now it is an illustration of all that is wrong with Kenya's governance and how it might be put right.

This controversial and costly exercise is not for nothing known as the Lunatic Express. The motive was less trade, but British regional intentions as 'a giant metal spike nailing together British territory and providing a direct link between the Indian Ocean and the lake which was the source of the Nile' intended to check German colonial intentions in what are now mainland Tanzania, Burundi and Rwanda.[13] Regardless, working in relentless heat, and confronting disease and other hardships to lay over a million sleepers, the Kenyan stretch of the railway was built in just five years, finishing at Kisumu on the top tip of Lake Victoria. This brought other unintentional and longer lasting consequences. Built mainly by 32 000 Indian labourers brought over specifically, nearly 7 000 of this cohort remained behind, forming the basis of the Asian community so prominent in regional commerce.

The transition from ox-wagon to steam engine cost over £5 million, or £200 million in contemporary cash values, and poignantly the lives of 2 500 labourers in its construction, including some 28 of them to two maneless lions dubbed the 'man-eaters of Tsavo'. And it was controversial, even for the time. Tension existed between those who felt Britain had no right to exert its authority over local 'tribesmen' and those who believed it afforded strategic control over the entire area.

The railway metaphor

It was, ultimately, as much a technological masterpiece as imperial political statement. Requiring no fewer than 177 curves to manage the steep climb over the 520 kilometres from Mombasa to Nairobi, including the famous 'spiral' near the port, it became, in the words of Winston Churchill, one of the 'finest expositions' of the 'British art of muddling through ... Through everything – through the forests, through the ravines, through troops of marauding lions, through famine, through war, through five years of excoriating Parliamentary debate, muddled and marched the railway.'[14]

Railways are a simile for what is wrong (or right) with any country, and how fixing them shows a way of putting governance right. The sheer complexity and the enormity of the challenge of running and making a railway work on time and efficiently also illustrates the leadership and governance challenge. An almost fascist-like zeal is required to make a modern railway work. Iran's Shah Mohammad Reza Pahlavi, for example, sought to emulate Turkey's Mustafa Kemal Atatürk and bring modernity and order to his country. He was photographed standing at the railway station with his large pocket watch, confirming the on-time arrival of a passenger express. No doubt this was staged. Most of the well-known examples are best remembered, apart from Atatürk, for their dictatorial tendencies rather than their successful or enduring models of modern governance. Mussolini is the standing riposte to the 'make the trains run on time' argument, usually used as a joke. Regardless, a nation that can successfully run a railway, on time, efficiently and profitably is in general well run itself. The examples are many – and just so the opposite. If the answers to the question 'do the railways work?' are 'terrible' or 'what railway?', governance is usually poor.

Transport is everywhere the province of powerful special interests, the politically well connected. In Kenya, the railway was neglected partly for the same reason railways languished in the United Kingdom (UK) in the post-Second World War era: road transport was more effective, flexible and, above all in Kenya, made those who controlled trucks immensely prosperous and powerful. Likewise, those who owned road construction companies, secured or patrolled the highways, operated weighbridges, and so on. It also enabled those out of favour with government to develop their businesses nonetheless and spread the love, the gravy, round to more individuals. In the UK, there were at least two political parties, each with a different approach to transport policy. In Kenya, there has historically been no policy difference; just issues of personal and political funding. 'No donors,' reflects one former ambassador to the region, 'following the anti-public transport mood of their own countries, were interested in trying to fund the Kenyans to send good money after bad.'

As a result, with little investment since independence, and with not even one new kilometre of track added, by 2005 the Kenyan network was in, as one local employee put it, 'a terrible condition, with accidents very day'. With 3 600 employees and then carrying around half its peak annual traffic of 4 million tonnes, it was 'losing government a small fortune'.

The same year the railway was put up for a 25-year concession, the tender being won by a South African-led Rift Valley Railway (RVR) consortium. With the assets valued at over $800 million, the consortium was supposed to invest $40 million over five years and it committed to pay government a surprisingly high 11.1 per cent of top-line earnings.

But the money was not there and bickering between the six shareholders turned quickly to outright hostility. By 2010 the government had declared the venture to be in default, with an Egyptian private equity firm coming in as the new, majority owner of the concession with Kenyan and Ugandan partners.

By 2013 there was commitment to invest nearly $300 million in the rail network over five years, funded by an international consortium of donors, banks and businesses, starting with the rehabilitation of the curvy route and the fleet of 100 locomotives and 3 500 waggons, of which just 30 and 1 500 respectively were usable in 2013. 'The engines are so old,' said the former RVR chairman, Brown Ondego, 'that GE quoted 72 weeks to supply spares, which, eventually, we found in Mexico.' He was not wrong about their age or, as the bill for refurbishment and recapitalisation suggested, their condition.

On track for Mombasa

The passenger express shuddered into the night, lurching, rocking and bouncing through the lit suburbs of Nairobi. As the giant diesel-electric Montreal Engine Works' engine *doef-doefed* its way, the following carriages snaked past occasional bonfires on the side of the tracks, shadows around them moving furtively and probably innocently.

'It's very important to close the window,' the guard explained, 'or at least to leave the mesh up. We have bad people coming from outside.'

It is a taste of an older world, a sixties' variant at least. The cabin was testament to that era's baby-boomer consumer tastelessness and then exotic new materials: aluminium piping, fawn plastic and linoleum, an electric fan that did not work when I travelled in it and fluorescent lights flickering in the ceiling. A flopped-over ashtray was a reminder of past habits in a time before political correctness. A man tap-taps on the door, locked from the inside by a distinctly twenty-first-century steel bolt, and delivers an olive-green bag; it did not contain mail but bedding. The 'postman' folded down my bunk and made up the bed in a wink.

But forty winks were few and far between. The bucking and swaying of the carriage opened all the doors imaginable, the train clattering into the night with a cacophonic metallic slap of doors and walkway plates up and down the carriage. The toilets were rudimentary. The best had a bowl (but no seat), and few had hit the mark. Still, the smell did point to the location. The dining car was replete with no fewer than twelve overhead fans angling from the ceiling, none of them now chat-chattering their welcome draughts onto the red leather seats below. The fare of rice and chicken or stew was like the decor: functional, adequate, but forgettable.

Regardless, the members of the staff were trying very hard. Like the railway per se, they are endeavouring to make up for the lost years. Successive governments did not so much as display 'wilful neglect' towards the railway, says Michael Chege, an adviser to the minister of planning. On the contrary, 'they actively asset stripped'.[15]

The journey was slow. The first stop was a long one – 50 minutes – made just 45 minutes outside Nairobi. *Kerklats, kerklats* died out with *eeeeeeiiih-haaaadunk*. And then silence, save the North American accent speaking to her friend a continent away, by phone apparently, several doors down.

This stop, explained the train manager, was to let an oncoming goods train pass coming from Konza, the wannabe Kenyan high-tech hub. This had to be done in a station where there was a dual passing lane.

This single-track, single-user system was put in place during the colonial era. The system of 'hand-to-hand' control, ensuring only one train was on the line at the time, functioned very effectively when the signal system worked and when there was a regular frequency of stations along the lines to allow trains to pass. Now the stretches for single-train usage have spread, and consequently the journey time was longer and the waits more frequent.

Just fifteen of 50 stations that once existed on this section of the line remained open, the demise of the majority signalled by mostly roofless abandoned white buildings along the track: Mwanatibu, Buchuma, Wangala, Maungu and Ndara, among others, the detritus of a bygone era. Where water towers once stood to quench the steam trains, just the concrete legs remain, like upturned animals in the red-brown earth.

Signal systems had also been abandoned. For example, at Changamwe just outside Mombasa, alongside the bonded warehousing, the signal wires still neatly ran alongside the track to disappear into a disused station master's windowless control room.

Without a computerised onboard control system, a circular wicker carrier was frantically passed out at each station with an 'authority to proceed' slip tacked to it. The radio in the engine driver's cab was for communication on the train. On the day I travelled with him, he did, however, have his mobile phone as an emergency back-up, though there was no signal along the whole route.

According to the driver, Jared Boaz Akumu, a man with twenty years of experience and ready humour, six trains a day used the track. The maximum achievable speed was 72 kilometres per hour for the six weekly passenger services, and 65 kilometres per hour for the more frequent goods trains. At times the speed dropped to 15 kilometres per hour 'for safety', the driver explained.

The passenger train service could be up to three hours faster than the fifteen hours it took us if the rail-line was improved. As a result of the poor track condition, there were numerous 'capsizings', which, together with problems of engine reliability, caused frequent delays. In 2011 there were more than 300 derailments or other major incidents on the line. Little wonder the share of Kenya Railways freight nationally had fallen from 15 to 3 per cent, though usage rose in nominal terms from 1 060 million tonnes in 2009 to 1 135 million tonnes in 2012.[16] Even though the cost of a third-class passenger ticket was just $8 one way, the volume of passenger usage fell from 389 million (revenue passenger kilometres) in 2009 to 365 million three years later, with more people preferring to travel by road and by air. The car and truck journey over the 520 kilometres took less than half the time of a train. 'When you reach Nairobi on the train,' said my companion in Mombasa, 'you will leave young and arrive old.' Or, he added looking me up and down, 'you will leave fat and arrive thin.' 'Punctuality and reliability' were the two key reasons why passengers prefer other means of transport, said the train manager Frederick Omondi.[17] Up in the 1970s' vintage engine, many of the instruments and some of the controls were out of order when I rode the train in September 2013, including the electric brake and the vigilance pedal (for stopping the train if the driver fell asleep). The track, where one could see with the naked eye continuous bows and distortions, was littered with evidence of the 'capsizings' in the form of discarded old rail and broken bogeys. Of course, given that it is a single track, a major repair is difficult without closing the railway.

It is not as if there is no place for the train in Kenya. One only has to see the vast number of trucks – 2 200 each day in either direction – on the road that parallels the railway to realise the volumes. Given the demand for transport from Mombasa, there is plenty of upside potential. Though 60 per cent of Mombasa traffic is destined for Nairobi, the rehabilitation also of the whole 2 352-kilometre line to Kampala is seen as good business sense, especially with regional oil discoveries and the long time it is expected to develop an alternative port to the north in Lamu. The costs and benefits are widespread. The high cost of imports, especially of fuel, has driven Kenya's serial budget deficits, inflation and downward pressure on the shilling.

But getting the railway to work properly will additionally require 'fixing' Mombasa, an exercise in more than logistics and bureaucratic management.

In the opinion of the railway specialists, *sans* privatisation at the port, there is little way the handling times through the port can be lowered significantly from the 'six to seven days' it takes to get goods from ships to the waggons. It takes ten hours to manually load a grain train, for example, with each bag having to be 'manhandled' onto the waggons. Customs alone can take up to four days 'because of the bureaucratic mentality'. This mentality pervades all the way to Kenya's neighbours. It takes two to three days to move a train over the Uganda border, given that the goods have to be cleared *in situ* rather than at the point of origin by using electronic documentation up the line.[18]

And this mentality does not just pervade at the port.

Leave the energy and dirt of Mombasa heading south and there is another hurdle – a tailback of cars waiting for the Likoni ferry across the Kilindini harbour.

Many questions come to mind just looking around the town. Why has virtually not an inch of railway been added in Kenya in 100 years, or why has no bypass been built in the last 50 years to circumvent Mombasa's estuary? Why does Mombasa, which has a relatively wealthy city council, not arrange for its buildings to be painted or its rubbish collected? Why has development of Mombasa's Likoni ferry terminals stalled despite the presence of signs declaring its imminent (even ongoing) refurbishment?

The answer is that things happen only when the government is interested in getting them moving, whatever the logic (or its absence). When they could not care less, the lack of results speak for themselves.

It is not about money. As an official said of Mombasa, 'The money for the new bypass has been there for years. Truth is, no one is that interested to make it happen.'

This explains why the government would neglect the national railway for many years and then chastise the concessionaire for a failure to reinvest. Or why the government would then see fit to purchase (that is the right term) from the Chinese a standard gauge railway intended to go from Mombasa all the way to Uganda, of which the Mombasa-to-Nairobi segment alone would cost an estimated $3.5 billion. Paying for this would by the government's own admission require not only doubling Mombasa's annual throughput from the 2012 figure to 32 million tonnes, but increasing the percentage of rail freight to 50 per cent of the total. With the capital cost of the new standard gauge line and only an estimated 11 per cent speed advantage foreseen, this was going to be difficult, not least since the diversion measures to force businesses to use rail rather than road are likely to incur political resistance from interested parties.

Moreover, big efficiency improvements are possible less through more money but better management and less costly politics.

The cost of politics in Kisumu

By February 2013, the railway station in Kisumu had not seen a passenger in more than a year.

Opened in 1961, its well-swept platform and ticketing offices have a certain concrete charm, with signs outside pointing the way for 'upper class' and 'third class' passengers. But the grass is growing long between the tracks, a metaphor for Kisumu and Kenya itself.

Just up the road, from a giant billboard of presidential candidate Raila Odinga exhorting 'New Industries for More Jobs', sat the abandoned Kicomi textile factory behind wonky steel gates, founded in 1993, though one of the '9's had long since gone. Around the corner in Nyerere Road is the former factory of East African Breweries, now 'just a depot', muses the security guard. 'We make nothing here any more.' Such are the effects of the weakness of state institutions and the failure to keep pace with modern economic demands, overlaid with the politics of identity.

The first construction stage of the colonial railway stopped at Kisumu. There 'knocked-down' steel ferries constructed in Britain were lugged, assembled and used to connect Kenya via the lake with Uganda and Tanganyika. Not fewer than ten vessels were built this way in Kisumu by 1930, the largest over 1 100 tonnes.

And the once bountiful lake, with its shabby 'Hard Core' and 'Delta Force' hotels and myriad hostelries, was clogged solid with water hyacinth. Fishing was an excavation exercise, and many of the ships at the port had not moved in decades. The SS *Nyanza*, reputedly the oldest steamship in Africa, marooned, listing to the quay, was more *Das Boot* than Bogart. A green hyacinth carpet stretched out several kilometres beyond the dry dock where the SS *Uhuru* ('independence') was receiving a fresh coat of paint.

Quick to pick up on the *Uhuru* connection just weeks before the March 2013 election, Paul Wawasa, the self-appointed harbour tour guide, lamented how little had gone right since independence. The hyacinth, which thrives on sewerage, and the empty sheds as well as the absence of ferries since 1995, were evidence of how little Kenyans had contributed to building on what the 'British colonials had given us', he said.

The city, Kenya's third-largest behind Nairobi and Mombasa, was increasingly clogged, too, with the population, growing at over 4 per cent annually, straining essential services. It is best, like this author, described as clean but scruffy.

While the mayor and councillors spoke optimistically of the benefits of attracting tourism, fixing the railway and improving water and other basic services, Kisumu was stuck on the periphery. Chinese contractors were working to fix the 5 kilometres between the airport and the city, but the 130 kilometres in the other direction to Uganda via Busia remained potholed and tediously slow.

Those lucky enough to have a job would, like Mary serving tables at the smart 'international airport', be earning $50 per month, and grateful for that. But that amount was, she explained, not enough to live off let alone prosper and plan with. It made hollow the official ambition to use the city's ten universities and tertiary colleges to transform Kisumu into a centre of higher learning. Few had the luxury of money to attend classes. Traders were everywhere on the city's streets, but producers scarce, the largest employer the city council with 1 000 employees. The former mayor, Sam Okello, lamented, 'We were once a major producer of cotton. Now the ginneries have all gone.'

Kisumu's task had not been helped by the election violence that beset the region in 2007/08, pitting Odinga supporters against those of Mwai Kibaki, local Luo against outsiders. Such ethnic duelling reflects, in part, the colonial legacy. The settlement of white farmers followed the railway, in the process not only shaping the development of Kenya, but the movement of other ethnic groups as the white settlers first prospered and, later, many departed.

While whites have long since, following independence in 1963, ceased to be a political force, the fault lines of race have endured.

Political not rocket science

Despite 50 years of independence – indeed perhaps because of it – tribalism is deeply ingrained and institutionalised in Kenya. The elites are routinely blamed for their use of the tribal tool to garner support. But they do not operate alone. Frustration feeds off the absence of work opportunities and presence of everyday hardship. In 2007–08 the spark for serious election-related violence was provided by the belief that the Kikuyu were, again, pulling a fast one over the Luo and other, smaller ethnic groups. Or as Paul, the Kisumu guide, put it, 'In Africa, we choose people from our area because we think they are going to give us something.' He still (vainly, as it turned out) hoped, in the next breath, that Odinga the Luo would, for these reasons, become president in the 4 March 2013 election, illustrating the Kenyan saying about the link between political power, ethnicity and privilege: 'It's our turn to eat.'[19]

Famously President Barack Obama's father was Luo, originating from Kogelo, just 40 minutes from Kisumu. After the then junior senator visited the area in 2006, he had a primary school and a high school named after him, built on land donated by his father. The locals even renamed the local senator brew 'Obama'. This gave rise to the joke that there would be a Luo president in the US before Kenya, true as it turned out. For in Kenya politics is an ethnic game, and in the absence of the right ethnic alliances, the minority Luo (13 per cent) or, for that matter, Kalenjin (12 per cent) and Luhya (14 per cent) are always going to be sucking air against the Kikuyu (22 per cent).[20] The country remains very polarised, between ethnic groups and in terms of inequality.

In his 2006 lecture to Nairobi University, then Senator Obama said: 'It is painfully obvious that corruption stifles development – it siphons off scarce resources that could improve infrastructure, bolster education systems, and strengthen public health. It stacks the deck so high against entrepreneurs that they cannot get their job-creating ideas off the ground.'[21] This echoed President Kibaki's 2002 inaugural speech: 'Corruption will now cease to be a way of life in Kenya and I call upon all those members of my government and public officers accustomed to corrupt practice to know and clearly understand that there will be no sacred cows under my government.'[22] The anti-corruption line has become a political mantra, all eight presidential candidates in the March 2013 election having 'plans' to combat the scourge. Little wonder since, to quote Odinga, 'corruption has permeated every facet of our national life'.[23]

Deeds, however, need to equal words, starting with addressing the culture of impunity among senior bureaucrats and political leaders. Otherwise it would be a Lewis Carroll world: jam tomorrow, but never today.

Without such change, to invoke an Obama-ism, progress towards greater formal employment that Mary and her Kisumu friends hope for and all Kenya politicians at least publicly subscribe to, is likely to be faltering at best, especially given the numbers of young people coming onto the job market. Already youth under 35 comprise two-thirds of Kenya's 44-million population.

Yet, as the decline of its once proud railways, the chronic state of Nairobi's infrastructure, painfully slow operations at Mombasa, and many other examples illustrate, corruption and its political corollary, tribalism, remain integral to the Kenya scene. The necessary reforms require less rocket than political science. While the 2010 constitution is a step in this direction, especially in terms of the devolution of powers to the 47 counties, this makes funding still larger government systems even more stretched. In 2014, the wages of the 700 000 civil servants consumed more than half of the government budget, or 13.2 per cent of GDP, way more than the global benchmarks of 7 and 35 per cent respectively. The number of officials is boosted by so-called ghost workers, who do not exist but for whom someone draws a salary, while a 'good number' of those remaining 'do not engage in any productive labour'.[24]

It was Churchill who, on visiting Kenya as undersecretary of state for the colonies in 1907, remarked that 'every man in Nairobi was a politician and most of them were leaders of parties'.[25] Little seems to have changed in the last 100 years.

Every person a politician

The island of Lamu, tucked up against Kenya's border with Somalia, similarly reminds one of the old cliché, 'the more things change, the more they remain the same'. In the run-up to Kenya's bitterly contested 2013 general election, the island was bedecked with posters of candidates for president, MPs and, now, with the creation countrywide of 47 'counties', governors, too. The focus was especially on the presidency, on who would replace the somnolent Mwai Kibaki – his fellow Kikuyu tribesman Uhuru Kenyatta, or the candidate many say won the contested 2007 election, his prime minister, Raila Odinga? There seemed to be almost as many candidates as donkeys, and there are not fewer than 3 000 *Equus asinus* on the island, or one for every seven people.

Lamu is a tourist paradise, an enthralling mix of medieval buildings, narrow streets, warm people, spicy Swahili cuisine rich in coconut milk, and magnificent beaches.

It has, however, a bloody and sad history. Prosperity as an Arab slaving post was ended by the advent of British rule in 1873, the territory formally and violently incorporated into the Kenya protectorate within twenty years.

Fast forward nearly a century and Lamu and the surrounding islands of Manda and Kiwayu emerged as hot property on the global tourism scene. The waterfront is a string of restaurants, lodges and small hotels, all very much in the local tradition.

But this masks a security threat that put the industry flat on its back during 2012.

In September 2011, an English couple staying on Kiswayu were attacked by Somalis. One died and one was kidnapped. A fortnight later, a French woman was snatched from Manda and taken to Somalia where she later died. With most Western governments advising against travel to the area and travel insurance becoming costly if not impossible to get, tourism died with the victim. It has battled to recover.

The Somali terrorism link was rammed home by the complex attack on the Westgate shopping centre in Nairobi by Al-Shabab militants in September 2013. The attackers selected a venue frequented by foreigners, with nationals from Britain, Canada, France, the Netherlands, Australia, Peru, India, Ghana, South Africa and China among the dead. They deliberately targeted defenceless civilians, with shoppers and staff the victims of indiscriminate gunfire and grenades. The technology was as basic as the methods barbaric.

The attack goes with the neighbourhood – the challenge of Kenya having to live next door to the failed state of Somalia. Not only do these wars and their clan and religious fault lines travel over international boundaries, but they pick up recruits along the way. Of course, terrorism on this horrific scale and targeting the weak and defenceless is nothing new in East Africa. Kenya was the site of what was the largest atrocity perpetrated by Al-Qaeda pre-9/11. Two hundred and twelve were killed and 4 000 wounded in Nairobi, and eleven more were murdered in a simultaneous bombing in Dar es Salaam. In stressing the enduring international dimension, these attacks, on 7 August 1998, marked the date of the eighth anniversary of the arrival of US forces in Saudi Arabia.

As the Al-Qaeda affiliate Al-Shabab was pushed out of controlling urban centres in Somalia, it shifted its modus operandi in three ways: mounting a running insurgency across southern Somalia against the African Union Mission in Somalia (AMISOM); launching terrorist attacks in Somalia, especially in the cities of Kismayo and Mogadishu; and extending attacks across the region, especially to AMISOM troop contributors Uganda and Kenya, in so doing copycatting its bombing of the crowds watching the July 2010 World Cup screening in Kampala, which left 74 dead and a near equal number injured.

This is not the only challenge faced by Kenya, and especially those in Lamu.

Mention of Churchill reminds of the bitter counter-insurgency campaign fought in the First World War by colonial forces, including a good number of South Africans, against German-led troops commanded by the legendary Colonel Paul von Lettow-Vorbeck.

The German commander was good, so good that he was never defeated in battle and only surrendered after his countrymen had given up in Europe. The colonel's legend did not end there. He did not like Adolf Hitler apparently, though the Nazi leader was nonetheless keen to get the war hero on-side. When Vorbeck's nephew was later asked if it was true that his uncle had told Hitler to go fuck himself, the reply was, 'That's right, except that I don't think he put it that politely.'[26] The imperial German general was not the only and not even the most formidable enemy encountered.

Facing dysentery, typhoid, malaria and blackwater fever among other joys, twelve times as many British soldiers died of disease during the campaign than in combat. Many of them had brought a malaria cure before embarking from Southampton. Wrapped with a note that read 'Do not open until Mombasa', inside were two blocks of wood containing the instructions: 'Place the mosquito on one block and hit it hard with the other.'

Kenya's contemporary challenges centre on inclusive development. Realising its promise and simultaneously dealing with instability will require a modernising vision to manage a country with widening inequality. Indeed, Kenya's struggle against the scourge of terrorism of the type of the Westgate rampage is likely to be no different to others prosecuted elsewhere – increasingly complex, cutting across regional borders and addressing dimensions other than solely militant extremism, including problems of urban decay and overstretch, disenchantment and alienation. The 'feral cities' such as Nairobi are a breeding ground for such resentment. Kenya's National Crime Research Centre,[27] for example, has reported that 46 indigenous criminal gangs operate in Kenya, many exercising brutal control over Nairobi's slums such as Kariobangi, Dandora, Mathare and Kibera, the latter housing perhaps as many as one-quarter of the capital's population on 1 per cent of its land.[28] These figures could worsen before they improve as the urban areas swell with increased and uncontrolled migration and population growth. Wealth provides a partial shield to this menace, with more than 200 private security companies in Nairobi alone, often better paid and equipped than the police.

There is a further internal dimension to this terror. The domestic violence following the disputed 27 December 2007 election has had a greater impact on the overall Kenya population – rather than Nairobi's foreign and local elite – than the Westgate attack. As Sir Edward Clay,[29] the former British High Commissioner to Kenya, has pointed out, it is as much in the interest of the health of Kenya's internal governance that the domestic issues that gave rise to the election violence are resolved properly one way or another as it is that external terrorism does not strike again. Or as Giles Foden has put it in the Westgate aftermath, 'You can gesture at the transnational problem of Islamist terrorism all you like, but it's just hot air unless you invest in proper security on the ground in your own country, with the right safeguards to civil liberties.' He added: '[U]nless the corruption stops, and real investment is made in the social fabric, Kenya will once again be faced with systemic shocks it is hardly able to deal with.'[30] The 100 hours it took for Kenyan security forces to deal with the attack and the chaos that ensued raised additional questions about the standard of training and capacity – in other words again, governance.

Thus, only part of the answer to these security challenges is in expedited development, especially in updating infrastructure. Near Lamu on the mainland is the site of the mooted $25-billion Lamu Port Southern Sudan-Ethiopia Transport (LAPSSET)[31] rail, road, refinery, oil pipeline, resort and harbour project. Designed to service the needs not only of Kenya, but also South Sudan, Uganda and Ethiopia, despite originally being conceived in 1975, at the start of 2013, it was, however, little more than a bare patch in a mangrove forest.

Ambitious infrastructure projects are important for the long term, for Kenya's next 50 years. But progress will depend on politicians stopping their old corrupt ways.

'*Kitu kidogo*', a 'little something', is the Swahili code for requesting a bribe in Kenya. It is an endemic problem, from the policeman shaking down the truck driver to officials wanting their palms greased to issue a permit or contract, give customs release or even secure treatment from public hospitals. One 2002 study found urban Kenyans paid an average of sixteen bribes a month, with 60 per cent of respondents reporting that they routinely bribed the police.[32]

But the problem is that it is not always that 'little' or involving 'little', petty officials. The 1990s' Goldenberg[33] and 2005 Anglo Leasing[34] mega-scandals implicated senior members of government. Little wonder that Kenya was in 136th (of 177 countries) on Transparency International's 2013 corruption index, ranking countries by perceived levels of corruption, as determined by expert assessments and opinion surveys.[35]

It is not as if government is unaware of the problem, one reason why there has been some improvement in its ranking, from 159/178 in 2010, for example.[36] 'The heart of the problem,' says one official in the (Uhuru) Kenyatta administration, 'is in the government procurement system. The presidency has no fewer than 120 procurement officers, 10 per cent of the workforce. Multiple signatures are required on even the smallest procurement, each officer wanting something for their efforts. This is why the president has sent all of them back, and replaced them with ten officials from the Treasury.'[37]

Changing this institutional culture and national practice demands, he emphasised, action by leadership. Regardless, the public remains immensely suspicious, the more so when, at the outset, the standard gauge railway was clouded by controversy and financial scandal.[38]

At the junction between politics and infrastructure, changing the system will also require difficult development choices by government. Was it better, for example, to spend the best of $3.5 billion on a standard gauge rail system between Mombasa and Nairobi, or to plough that money into more electricity production?

It is a choice, as the fresh loans for the railway would take Kenya close to its debt ceiling, a figure that increased from $2.82 billion in 2008/09 to $6.12 billion five years later, fuelled by a combination of low growth and the suffocating public sector wage bill.[39] It was difficult to envisage the government's ambitious plans of spending $20 billion on new energy infrastructure coming to fruition in this environment.

Kenya's national grid produced just 1 600 MW for its 44 million people in 2013 (compared, say, to the South African ratio of just under 1 000 MW per million of its population, or the Singaporean one of over 2 000 MW per million people). As fast as new Kenyan power stations have come on line, shortages of power have led to regular brown-outs. Essentially, power has been privatised since individual people and firms had more installed capacity than the government – no business could afford to not have a back-up system in place. If $3.5 billion was spent on power – creating 3 500 MW – rather than a railway with a dubious revenue model, that would be an investment in the future, enabling citizens to read at night, children to do their homework after dark, householders to refrigerate their food, and, as has been the evidence from other areas, in lowering the birth rate with television-linked social transformation.[40] That the railway took precedence led to questioning about whether energy offered quite the scale of local procurement and tendering opportunities, a cynicism born out of experience.

Like the Lunatic Express, the standard gauge railway had become more than a business proposition, but rather a prestige project, a statement of political intent about what sort of country Kenya wanted to become, whatever the cost.

*

It is not all bleak. There are positives inherent in Kenya's macroeconomic management (especially when compared to the Arap Moi era) and in the new constitution – ones that should at least pose the question of whether these significant changes will be enough to assist the start of a new trajectory or whether the organic and historical ballast of rent-seeking – of political patronage and corruption – will still prove too much.

In the same vein, Kenya remains a relative diplomatic oasis for settling regional difficulties in South Sudan, Somalia and in the Great Lakes centring on the Congo. Its regional status as a 'little Switzerland', as one Nairobi business person put it, a safe haven for funds, helps to explain why the economy continues not only to survive but to prosper when the statistics suggest it should be flat on its back. Much of trade and other flows are conducted 'off the books', one reason why the middle class, to be found less at the Capital Club, perhaps, than with their families eating out at the Spur or Naked Pizza, continues to grow.

There is also a new generation of leadership less focused on power and feathering its own nest than ensuring a longer-term legacy. President Uhuru Kenyatta, a rich man before he came into office, says in this regard that 'there is a need to cater for future generations and not leave them with craters in the ground'.[41] His administration, in particular, is seized by the need to break the old ways of doing business and making money for politicians.

Whether the Kenyan glass is half full or empty might be indicated by liberalisation of key sectors in the economy. Kenya's extraordinary information technology revolution, epitomised by the M-Pesa digital banking technology, shows the way to how the country might develop. This system of cash transfers works brilliantly, mainly because the private sector runs it and the state is nowhere near it. The same applies to Kenya Airways, one of the best carriers in Africa. If such ingenuity and excellence, not Mombasa's stultifying statism or a tribally driven political economy, resembles the model for a new Kenya, then the glass is half full; put differently, its development strategy will finally be on track with a hope of ending the system of failure that affects so many Kenyans.

5

NIGERIA

A Cauldron of Superlatives

*

The sight of a South African Breweries Falcon 2000 corporate jet – registration, ZS-SAB – parked in front of a Mi-24 Hind helicopter gunship at Port Harcourt International Airport on 12 April 2013 sums up the challenges and opportunities of doing business in Nigeria and especially its restive Niger Delta region.[1] The levels of violence in Nigeria beggar belief, and would in many other national circumstances define state failure: military measures imposed by President Goodluck Jonathan, including the imposition of a state of emergency in May 2013 in the north-eastern states of Borno, Adamawa and Yobe, had the effect of increasing, not decreasing, violence. Some 2 226 people were killed in politically motivated attacks in Nigeria in the first five months since the imposition of the state of emergency. Of that total, 1 006, or 45 per cent, involved Boko Haram, the locally based Islamist movement.[2]

It did not mean that money could not be made despite this environment, to the contrary. SABMiller bought into its first brewery in Nigeria in 2009, when it acquired 75 per cent of Pabod Brewery in Port Harcourt. In 2011 it effectively swapped International Breweries in another Nigerian city, Ibadan, with its Castel operation in Angola. And in September 2012, SABMiller invested in a greenfield site in Onitsha in Anambra State. The investments quickly proved to be a big success, with the new brewery 'hitting capacity in its second month', and the other two almost immediately going through expansion plans.

And there was plenty of future upside anticipated. Nigeria's beer consumption has historically been about one-tenth of South Africa's, for example.

But doing business in Nigeria has required working around the environment. The infrastructure is inadequate, the roads, in Lagos as in Port Harcourt, a constant challenge in passenger patience and nerves and the driver's steel and skill. Choked and rutted to the point that the tarmac disappears on occasion altogether into dust or muddy dams of water, the drivers create additional lanes either side of the stream, cutting in on the lanes from left and right amidst much tooting and hooting. The Trans-Amadi Road through Port Harcourt's industrial area is an exercise in bone-jarring endurance, hardly the stuff of modern commerce, though testament to the remarkable energy, humour and resolve of Nigerians, who comprise about one in every five black people on the planet.[3] Their daily struggle for survival defies description.

Oil junkies

Vendors steadfastly ply their wares in the snarling traffic, holding up and waving everything from biscuits, airtime, socks, mops, apples, nuts, tissues, hankies and, naturally, newspapers. The lack of traffic pace lends plenty of time to study the aspirational slogans given to the number plate origins: 'Kano – City of Commerce', 'Bayelsa – The Glory of All Lands', 'Lagos – Centre of Excellence', 'Abuja – Centre of Unity' and 'Rivers – Treasure Base of the Nation'.

A treasure trove Rivers State certainly is, producing 300 000 barrels of oil per day from more than 100 wells. Overall, the Delta region's six states (Akwa Ibom, Bayelsa, Cross River, Delta, Edo and Rivers) are home to half of Nigeria's 159 oil fields and produce nearly two-thirds of all production.

Nigeria's oil and gas condensate output was, at the start of 2013, a little over two million barrels per day, under its agreed OPEC quota of 2.5 million, the shortfall a result mainly of insecurity in the Niger Delta, dropping nearly $3 billion in exports – a fall from 2.26 million to two million barrels per day – between the third and fourth quarters of 2012 for example. Regardless, oil and gas provided Nigeria with income of about $65 billion annually, accounting for over 90 per cent of exports and more than 80 per cent of government revenue. On the flip-side, the US has been the largest importer of Nigeria's crude oil; the West African nation providing about 10 per cent of US oil imports, ranking as the fifth-largest source for oil imports in the US. This volume accounts for 40 per cent of Nigerian oil exports.

Under the revenue-sharing formula for oil wealth, the nine oil-producing states receive 13 per cent of oil income, the remainder being shared between the other 27 and the federal government as well as 774 local government areas. But for many this has been insufficient. And they have a point when it comes to complaining about the level of poverty.

Out in the Delta, in the Imo River area, Shell continues to develop new wells. Near Imo River 1 wellhead, there is a complex series of well-protected flow stations, their pipes, valves and turbines shiny green behind tangles of razor wire. Yet, on the same road along which Nigeria's wealth is extracted, pumped and exported, the Etche people live in squalor and poverty. It might be worse elsewhere, perhaps, but it is bad and hopeless enough there, defined by the number of snotty-nosed, semi-clothed children running around, the pathetic small stores and half-completed buildings with hopeful signs like 'Laundry' and 'Tailor'. To supplement their income, men still hunt for 'bush-meat', including antelope and 'grass-cutters' (cane rats), and appear in small groups alongside the road, menacingly toting well-worn shotguns hoisted over their shoulders.

Little wonder that evangelistic churches are everywhere, possessing the loudest and brightest banners and slogans. The 'Reaper Life Bible Church', 'Breakthrough Church', 'Deeper Life Bible Club', 'City of God', 'Scatter the Gathered – Gather the Scattered', 'God Government Ministries International', 'Winners Chapel', 'Devil Stop There', and many others welcome converts, offering a spiritual road out of this hard life.

Endemic poverty

They have nothing to lose. According to a 2007 Amnesty International report, 70 per cent of the six million people in the Niger Delta live on less than $1 per day.[4] Poverty plus a sense of entitlement has led to widespread insecurity in the region, a source of terrorism, kidnappings and a low-tempo insurgency of a sort. Indeed, the guide book counsels, 'The threat of kidnap [in Port Harcourt and the Niger Delta region] remains extremely high, and we currently advise against travel here.'

For example, on 1 April 2013, twelve policemen were murdered along the Azusuama waterway in the Southern Ijaw area in Bayelsa State. A detachment of fifteen policemen were ambushed by militants while travelling down a creek in a wooden boat, the gun duel lasting 40 minutes. The bodies were stripped of their uniforms and rifles, then mutilated and burnt. Despite attempts to placate the Movement for the Emancipation of the Niger Delta and, in the north of Nigeria, Boko Haram through a combination of the military stick and the carrot of amnesty, Nigeria remains a violent place. In May 2014 President Jonathan said Boko Haram's campaign had claimed 12 000 lives, with a further 8 000 injured since 2009. The abduction of 276 schoolgirls by the Islamist movement from a boarding school in Chibok in north-eastern Nigeria in April 2014 underlined the powerlessness of the state to cope with this security and governance threat, notwithstanding the presence of 20 000 federal troops in those areas where Boko Haram was active.[5]

This explained the presence of the Hind at the airport.

Much of the anger has been directed against foreign oil workers and their companies. They certainly have their share of responsibility. From the time of the Biafran War between July 1967 and January 1970, international companies have colluded and supported the federal government in order to do business in Nigeria – and to extract the maximum possible profits. That is what they are expected to do best after all.

Over time, the international companies have become more sensitive to local needs, hence greater transparency over their oil payments to the federal government and more extensive and active corporate social responsibility programmes. This is why the government has been intent on trying to show it cares. In late April 2013, President Jonathan endorsed the creation of a special trust fund for the Delta region.[6]

Letting the people down

The US-based Nigerian writer Okey Ndibe has observed: 'In fact, one of the greatest crimes of which the Nigerian state is guilty is a failure to take Nigerians seriously. A government that takes its citizens seriously would recognize that its first and primary job is to secure the lives and property of its citizenry. On that score, the Jonathan administration – like its predecessors – has been woeful.'[7] But it has got away with it. The method for doing so, and for maintaining a degree of elite cohesion necessary for the preservation of Nigeria's 'federal character' by, inter alia, financing the indifference of regionalised opposition, is institutionalised patronage. And the mechanism is decentralisation through myriad states. Before and after independence in 1960, Nigeria was a federation of three regions, the Northern, Western and

Eastern. The Mid-Western Region was added in 1963. In 1967, the regions were replaced by twelve states by military decree. In 1976, seven new states were created, increasing the total to nineteen. A further two new states were created in 1987, followed by another nine and the Federal Capital Territory (now Abuja) in 1991, bringing the total to 30. In 1996, more were added, raising the number of states to 36.

In part, the fascination with the management of ethnic ties reflects the British colonial heritage. The British got on with the Hausa rulers in the North, believing that their sense of discipline and order offered the best means for 'indirect' rule. Hence, one logic behind the creation of additional representative states was to break up the larger ethnic units.[8]

In part, this concern is also down to the legacy of the Biafran War,[9] which cost an estimated 1.2 million lives, 80 per cent of them in the south-east among the Igbo, over 30 months. This war was fought over a combination of the right to self-determination and self-rule, and the security of the Igbo people against the North, in particular. It is viewed as the apogee of a period of violent state upheaval and overthrow, ending only with the return to democracy in 1999. But it represents a deeper malaise. As Johns Hopkins University's Peter Lewis argues, 'The First Republic ... suffered from an institutional design that encouraged ethnic segmentation and invidious regional competition for power. The regime quickly succumbed to communal polarization, political conflict, and social strife. The military stepped into the maelstrom with a coup in 1966. But the officers were themselves vulnerable to ethnic antagonism, leading to a countercoup and the ensuing civil war.'[10]

The history of the military in Nigerian politics is déjà vu. The first coup in January 1966, led primarily by Ibos (who dominated the officer corps), failed, though the death of the prime minister and finance minister, Festus Okote-Eboh (found in a Lagos lagoon, castrated, with his eyes gouged out), left the army chief of staff, Major General Aguiyi-Ironisi, overthrown and murdered in a coup the same year by Major General Yakubu Gowon. Gowon held power until 1975 when he in turn was tossed out in a bloodless coup. Murtala Mohammed, who succeeded Gowon, was assassinated in February 1976 in an abortive coup attempt, when a junior officer walked up to his car in the traffic and emptied two magazines of sub-machine gun ammunition into it. The army chief of staff, then Brigadier Olusegun Obasanjo, who had a distinguished war record leading the Third Division in Biafra, took over the reins temporarily before handing over to Shehu Shagari in 1979, in so doing signalling the end of the junta.

But Shagari only lasted until 1983 when overthrown in another coup by Muhammadu Buhari, who lasted two years until he was kicked out by General Ibrahim Babandiga, who ruled Nigeria until 1993, when he temporarily handed power to Ernest Shonekan. This civilian regime only lasted two months before being overthrown in turn by General Sani Abacha. Following Abacha's death in 1998, General Abdulsalami Abubakar assumed power and ruled until handing over to a civilian government in 1999, when Obasanjo won the election and again became head of state.

The costs of such systemic instability cannot be overstated in terms of setting back Nigeria's progress. Singapore's Prime Minister Lee Kuan Yew tells a tale about meeting a Nigerian minister at a Commonwealth conference in Lagos in 1966. He was seated opposite 'a hefty Nigerian, Chief Festus [Okotie-Eboh], their finance minister. The conversation', he recalled in 2000, 'is still fresh in my mind. He was going to retire soon, he said. He had done enough for his country and now had to look after his business, a shoe factory. As finance minister, he had imposed a tax on imported shoes so that Nigeria could make shoes.' Lee was 'incredulous'. 'I went to bed that night convinced that they were a different people playing to a different set of rules.' Three days later, Lee recalls, after he had arrived in Accra, there was a bloody coup in Lagos in which the prime minister (Abubakar Tafawa Balewa) and Chief Okotie-Eboh were killed.[11]

One impact of this can be seen in the perpetuation of Nigeria as 'one of the most hierarchical and unequal societies in the world'.[12] It is a country where tribalism matters, simply because there is not enough wealth to go around. This fuels a zero-sum mentality, where one group is seen as rich because another is viewed as poor, as expressed in the 'turn' of ethnic groups to rule as president, both to maintain political balance and a turn at the trough. In a vicious cycle, as Lewis has argued, 'Nigeria's deep communal divisions significantly impede state formation and economic growth and are themselves aggravated by political uncertainty and privation.'[13]

While the multinationals are an easy and visible target, the principal source of the tension is around government's own (in)efficiencies. Much of the oil wealth has been wasted. Despite an estimated trillion-dollar oil windfall since the mid-1960s, astonishingly the number of Nigerians living in absolute poverty rose from 19 million in 1970 (out of a total population then of 70 million) to 90 million 40 years later. It has the third highest number of poor people in the world, only behind China and India, both of which have nearly ten times Nigeria's population.[14] The rebasing of the

Nigerian economy in April 2014 changed this picture a bit, but not entirely. The size of the Nigerian economy almost doubled, from around $260 billion to $510 billion. The increase does not square with poverty figures as per the 2010 poverty survey, which according to Nigeria's National Bureau of Statistics had 60.9 per cent living in 'absolute poverty, and … this figure had risen from 54.7 per cent in 2004'.[15] Either the economy is not growing as fast as the rebasing suggests or inequality is growing very fast.

Rebasing or not, unless something changes, the poverty situation is likely to worsen. Nigeria's population increased fourfold since independence on 1 October 1960 to over 160 million half a century on, creating enormous and ongoing stress. At current rates, the number of Nigerians is expected to increase to over 500 million by 2050 and, barring changes in birth rates, is estimated to increase to over 900 million by the turn of the next century.[16]

Richer without oil?

The reasons behind this widespread poverty are thus a steep increase in the number of people, a lack of investment in education and infrastructure, violence and insecurity and, as is intimated above, a government and policy that, if it did not care less, has been unable to help much. In that environment, populism and radicalism, as represented by movements such as Boko Haram (literally, 'Western education is sinful') is not only likely, but unavoidable.

The oil economy has created its own negative incentives. As Chief Dixon Orike, a native of Port Harcourt, put it, 'Before oil, during the colonial times, our economy was dependent on agriculture, especially palm oil, but also a variety of other crops for export. Now we do nothing else other than oil and gas.'[17] (A London barrister in the early 1960s, Orike was a great survivor despite the tempestuous local political climate, and a warm and amusing host – interspersing his take of history with frequent bellows for 'HARRISON', his butler, to keep serving the champagne to wash down the surprisingly good Harcourt Chinese take-away.)

Indeed, Nigeria would probably have done better – by some estimations the economy would have been 25 per cent bigger – if the Delta had no oil. One effect of the hydro-carbon boom was to squeeze out the non-oil private sector, both because there was less incentive and the economic conditions were not right to export. In the 35 years until 2000, for example, the Nigeria government increased its role in the economy from 20 per cent to 40 per cent of non-oil GDP. Agriculture plummeted and manufacturing and utilities stagnated. Capacity utilisation in manufacturing went from 75 per cent (in 1975) to a plateau of around 40 per cent, and total factor productivity fell.[18] Nigeria became a nation, the Royal Africa Society's Richard Dowden observes, of 'junkies' on oil, which 'suffocated the economy, generated greed, fed regional jealousy, funded terrible regimes, started a war. Oil dreams wrecked Nigeria ...'[19]

It is not down to the resources, but the way in which they are managed. Although Indonesia, another oil producer with a complex religious and ethnic make-up, vast geographic expanse to govern and which suffered a dictatorship under Hajii Muhammad Suharto from 1967, the difference with Nigeria is stark. When the Indonesian strongman left power after 31 years in charge, his country had enjoyed an average annual economic growth rate of 7 per cent, adult literacy was 90 per cent (Nigeria's is 40 per cent) and manufacturing represented 40 per cent of exports.[20] In 1965, for example, Nigeria had a higher per capita GDP than Indonesia: by 1997, just before the financial crash, Indonesia's per capita GDP had risen to more than three times the level of Nigeria's. Both were corrupt dictatorships, but Indonesia's rulers had an over-riding commitment to popular welfare as was evident in the investment in education, health care and the economy. Nigeria's elite, by contrast, described by playwright Wole Soyinka as 'The Chosen', was apparently only interested in extracting and shipping offshore the country's wealth.

It is no wonder then that manufacturing industries, including the giant Michelin tyre factory, have largely given up the ghost in Port Harcourt, abandoning their operations for easier environments. To the negative impact of oil, add a further range of constraints to business. In addition to the clogged and chaotic roads, these include the cost and the logistical challenge of moving goods through the ports, the related (high) level of corruption and the lack of adequate and reliable power. Virtually every ingredient of manufacturers, such as in brewing, is imported, this in a country that, pre-oil, was a major agricultural producer. These problems are, of course, hardly unique to brewing or even business per se. Nigeria's growth is severely constrained by a shortage in electricity.

Never expect power always

The output of Nigeria's national electricity grid is just under 4 000 MW, or a tenth of South Africa's (which has less than a third of the people). According to its own road map on power sector reform, Nigeria has the biggest gap between supply and demand for electricity in the world.[21] Little wonder that NEPA, the former national provider, was known as 'Never Expect Power Always'. Unsurprisingly, it has been renamed as the Power Holding Company of Nigeria.

Plans to increase national supply tenfold by 2020 would cut business costs by an estimated 40 per cent, add 3 per cent to GDP, and reduce the impact of fuel theft, known as 'bunkering', estimated to cost $14 billion annually.[22] Nigerians also spent, in 2012, some $13 billion on diesel, most of which is imported (into a country with the world's ninth-largest gas reserves) to power generators, the electricity produced costing more than twice as much as from the grid.[23]

From the clogged road network in Lagos to electricity, the infrastructure backlog from years of bad decisions and stolen money is immense. One survey puts the level of investment required in Nigeria in order to make it a competitive global economy at $650 billion.[24] Such investment is not going to be made in a decade let alone a generation, however, and will, if it happens at all, be dependent on the end of monopolies and increased private sector financing. It means stuffing the shell of the Nigerian state, including ensuring it has responsibilities other than wealth redistribution.

There are some positive signs.

The return of democracy in 1999 initially under the hardy perennial Obasanjo, who had survived a stint in prison under Abacha, got rid of the worst excesses of corruption, allowing for the emergence of a new, entrepreneurial, younger business elite. Rather than spending it on philanthropy, Nigeria's – and Africa's – reportedly richest man, Aliko Dangote, for example, plans to invest half of his $16-billion fortune constructing a new oil refinery in Nigeria, which, despite being the continent's biggest oil producer, imports 80 per cent of its petrol. The new refinery, scheduled for completion in 2016, will produce about 400 000 barrels a day, nearly doubling the current capacity.

The financial services sector, to take another example, has boomed since the economy opened up, showing what Nigerians are capable of with even the tiniest reforms, where their energies are not simply geared towards surviving against the odds. Economic growth during the 2000s improved to average over 6 per cent, peaking at 8.4 per cent in 2010.[25] Technology has helped to get around the inefficiencies of government. In 1990 the country had just one telecoms operator with maybe 300 000 phone lines. Nearly a quarter of a century later its mobile phone sector had 110 million subscribers and not fewer than seven operators.[26] A South African business person working in information technology summed up Nigeria. 'There is so much need here, so much opportunity. The Nigerians I work with have an extraordinary appetite for business. The question is how we can get past the challenges and make it happen.'

Leadership's second chance: Olusegun Obasanjo

Nigeria epitomises Africa's second post-independence chance. Beset by poor leadership and its choices, corruption, ethnic division, military coups and dismal economic performance, the reinstatement of democratic rule in 1999 signalled a change in the country's fortunes. Just as sub-Saharan Africa enjoyed its best post-independence economic growth decade on record in the 2000s, Nigeria's economy had surged on the back of high oil prices and improvements in governance in general and the banking sector in particular.

Olusegun Obasanjo, 77 in 2014, was at the helm during this recent boom time. It was also his second turn at government leadership, having earlier assumed power in February 1976 after the assassination of Mohammed, who himself had seized power in a coup the previous year. By Obasanjo's own admission,[27] 'People invariably perform better in anything second time around. In my first term, I came in believing that what the Nigerians needed was the ownership of the economy for them to make the best of things. So we encouraged indigenisation,' says the former president. 'But it was a failure in many respects, given that, first, the Nigerians who were interested in economic matters usually had no entrepreneurial experience or capacity. Second, Nigerians were often fronting for other owners, for appearances' sake. Third, it did nothing to help foreign direct investment. And fourth, it placed obstacles in front of those wanting to make investments, where there should not have been any.

'So,' smiles Obasanjo, 'people tend to see me as a socialist and not especially private sector friendly, which is a misreading of the situation. When I had then a second chance, from 1999, I became the greatest proponent of the private sector. In one day during my second stewardship we had $100 million in foreign direct investment into the country. The economy boomed. The exchange rate appreciated over 1 000 per cent and we grew the economy at an average of 6.5 per cent annually for five years. This was more than just oil. Agriculture, for example, grew at over 7 per cent.'

There are few better placed to look at the overall lessons for leadership and at the impact of the military's role in African politics.

'My background,' he reminds, 'is military.' Obasanjo enlisted in the Nigerian Army in 1958, receiving his training in the UK at Aldershot and at the Defence Services Staff College, Wellington, and the Indian Army School of Engineering. Having served time with the UN peacekeeping mission in the Congo in the early 1960s, he moved rapidly up the ranks. Promoted to chief army engineer, he was made commander of 2 Area Command from July 1967. During the Nigerian Civil War, he commanded 3 Marine Commando Division, which, by taking Owerri, effectively ended that conflict. 'What I came to realise,' says Obasanjo, 'is that leadership qualities necessary for success in the military are not much different to those needed for success in the civilian sector. I came to realise also that most of the successful management techniques in fact came originally from the military, such as management by objectives, or critical paths. If you can manage men and material in the military in peace and in war, the only difference in politics is,' he stresses, 'money.'

But he argues that the Nigerian military 'went wrong by going into government back in 1965. People will tell you that the politicians should be blamed for their behaviour, for allowing it to happen. By the military coming in they destroyed politics beyond recognition and destroyed at the same time the military institution.' It also played, he says, to the tribal factor in Nigerian politics.

'I came back from Staff College in India on 13 January 1966. The man who led the coup – Patrick Chukwuma – was my best friend. [Major Chukwuma was later killed in the Biafran War.] He said later it was the greatest decision of his life. I came back and less than 48 hours later, the coup was launched. I was a major then. If he had told me and I said "yes", there was no role for me to play. If he told and me and I said "no", it was too late. He did not tell me. He concealed it completely. If he had told me, I would have been arrested. Six months later, there was another coup, decidedly factional, led by northern officers. I have learnt from this and subsequent events that it is an advantage not to have your tribe as your base, since this tends to encourage cronyism and family politics. The most important thing in a politician is trust. If when in government I surround myself with my tribal group, what reason is there for others belonging to other ethnic groups to trust me, to use me, and be able to say yes to me?'

By contrast, says Obasanjo, democracy 'may not necessarily produce better leadership [than the military], but it produces orderly changes of leadership. It enables people to be patient for their turn, rather than revert to a coup. A viable democratic dispensation,' he stresses, 'offers the possibility of alternative government, and avoids government complacency.' Little wonder that the former president's list of lessons from his three terms then are: 'identifying what to ignore as priorities; learning to ignore gossip; educating ignorant critics; ignoring red herrings; never acknowledging praise-singers; ensuring that people are properly credited or commended for their service. This is never to be done grudgingly, but instead publically, so that people know; and, sanctioning errors or mistakes made, and relating these sanctions to their magnitude and duration.'

Failure, but ...

Even though its citizens might baulk at the moniker, Nigeria is a failure for many – perhaps *most* – who live within its borders. Writing in 2006, Lewis succinctly summarised the country's plight: 'Central authorities cannot provide stable governance, in the sense of effective legitimate rule and essential public goods. The country's boundaries may provisionally be settled, but the basis of political community – the idea of Nigeria – is fiercely contested. Economically, Nigeria has experienced a steady decline since the oil windfall peaked more than twenty years ago. Slow growth and a rapidly rising population have yielded dramatic increases in poverty.'[28]

Getting Nigeria to work better in supplying more opportunities for all, and not just an elite, demands at its heart addressing what Nigerians refer to as the 'leadership conundrum'. The 'litany of political succession', involving 'six successful coups, numerous failed revolts, two abortive democratic regimes and three inconclusive democratisation programmes illustrates essential problems of leadership and institutional development in Nigeria'. Instead of 'setting out conditions for investment and capital formation', Nigeria's rulers have commonly emphasised 'short-term inducements for political accommodation', encouraging rent-seeking and 'fiscal perquisites' in order to ensure stability and control.[29]

The answer to Nigeria's development failure then lies in institutionalising the opposite set of conditions and policies, aimed at improved governance and policy predictability and transparency; but achieving those conditions risks undermining fragile ethnic and religious coalitions. Compromise, balance and muddling through are the messy result.

6

TUNISIA

And Other Springs

*

Three thousand seven hundred and twenty-four names are etched into the Wall of the Missing at the American cemetery in Carthage in Tunisia. A further 2 841 white headstones criss-cross the site. Among them is that of Foy Draper who won gold as part of the 4 x 100-metre relay at the 1936 Berlin Olympics, the team anchored to Hitler's racial annoyance by Jesse Owens, the African American winner of four gold medals at those Games. Captain Draper lost his life on 4 January 1943 when the Douglas A-20 Havoc twin-engine light-bomber he was co-piloting crashed on take-off near the Algerian border.

Tunis and its surrounds are dotted with Allied cemeteries. South-east of the capital, Massicault Cemetery houses the graves of 1 448 Commonwealth troops who were killed in the final advance on Tunis. One of twelve such sites in Tunisia where nearly 10 000 are commemorated, Massicault's simple symmetry and emotionally moving minimalism contrasts with the grubby, rubbish-strewn villages en route. Close to the city, perched on a hillside at Gammarth, not far from the picturesque seaside tourist town of Sidi Bou Said and its white-blue buildings, narrow streets and cosy squares, is the French war cemetery. Its terraces contain the remains of 4 190 French soldiers, their resting places each outlined by a white stone border, a distinctive Adrian steel helmet placed neatly under their cross. These were part of the 456 000-strong North African French army, including 150 000 Algerians, 85 000 Moroccans and 45 000 Tunisians.

Most of these soldiers, sailors and airmen lost their lives in Operation Torch, the Allied campaign to defeat German and Italian forces in North

Africa. On 8 November 1942, US and British forces landed at Casablanca, Algiers and Oran, the first major American action in the European-Mediterranean theatre in the Second World War.

The turning point, however, in the fight for the control of North Africa was 2 000 kilometres east and just over two months earlier at El Alamein in Egypt. An obscure railway halt 100 kilometres west of Alexandria, Tel el Alamein is now synonymous with the desert war. But it is only part of a series of battles that took place between December 1940 and May 1943 across the desert and up and down the Mediterranean coastline. It is possibly the best-remembered Second World War Commonwealth battle, as Prime Minister Winston Churchill noted: 'Before Alamein we never had a victory. After Alamein we never had a defeat.' El Alamein led to the subsequent rapid Allied advance into Libya and onwards. The remnants of General Erwin Rommel's once seemingly invincible Afrika Korps surrendered in Tunisia on 13 May 1943.

*

Differences between Carthage and around Massicault illustrate one driver of contemporary political change and economic challenges in Tunisia. While Carthage, once the centre of ancient civilisations and conquest, is now an upper-class suburb with its large homes, tennis clubs and classy, glassy restaurants, just 30 kilometres outside the city Massicault is in a relatively deprived, largely agricultural area, a bleak mix of scrappy livings and unkempt housing. 'A lack of regional development', observes Jaloul Ayed, a former minister of finance and 2014 prime ministerial candidate, is one of the reasons why the Arab Spring occurred, as 'there was no strategy to develop the regions of the country, and very little infrastructure across the country to ensure it was evenly spread. This is why,' he says, 'all revolutions in Tunisia have been triggered from the interior of the country.'

On 17 December 2010, a poor flower-seller, Mohamed Bouazizi, from Sidi Bouzid, a city in the centre of the country, set himself alight[1] after a run-in with police over his alleged refusal to pay a bribe. His death two weeks later triggered anger and protests, leading to the toppling of long-time president Zine el-Abidine Ben Ali Here, the first leader to go in what seemed then a heady Spring.[2]

Reminiscent less of the 1968 Prague Spring than the suddenness of collapse of the Soviet bloc of state in Eastern Europe's 1989 'Autumn of Nations', Ben Ali fled to Saudi Arabia on 14 January 2011 in the face of mounting protests. Within the month Egyptian President Hosni Mubarak had resigned as the '25 January' movement occupied Cairo's Tahrir Square and protestors fought battles with the army and police. Muammar Gaddafi was overthrown in Libya on 23 August 2011, and killed near Sirte on 20 October. In Sanaa in Yemen President Ali Abdullah Saleh signed a power transfer deal in exchange for immunity from prosecution. The Arab Spring was approaching its democratic climax. The bloody mess of Syria still lay ahead, a conflict that had claimed more than 100 000 dead in just three years from its onset in the form of protests sparked in the southern city of Deraa in March 2011 after the arrest and torture of teenagers who had painted anti-government slogans on a school wall.

Still, the underlying tensions that ejected Ben Ali so quickly, and which had been building for some time in Tunisia just as elsewhere across the region, have proven much more difficult and complex to resolve, reflecting years of governance and policy inadequacy.

At the heart, political and economic freedoms

Tunisia's Jasmine Revolution that brought down Ben Ali illustrates that sound macroeconomic policy, relative affluence and political stability is not always enough. Indeed, Tunisia's annual per capita income of $9 500 outstrips most African countries, ranking behind only oil-rich Equatorial Guinea, Seychelles, Gabon, Mauritius, Libya, Botswana and South Africa. The social and political problems are deeper than statistics, however, especially those so notoriously unreliable across this region.

Educated in the US and a musical composer in his spare time, Jaloul Ayed spent eighteen years working for Citibank, based in Morocco. He identifies three other reasons, in addition to that of the absence of regional development, for Tunisia's Arab Spring: the lack of political and economic space, related to the 'nepotism of Ben Ali and his family'; the type of economic growth; and high levels of unemployment, especially among the youth, linked to exponential population growth across the region.

Ben Ali and his family, he says, 'acted quite literally like the head of a mafia, controlling and spending the resources of the country'. He had ruled virtually unchallenged since taking over in a bloodless palace coup in November 1987 from the 'secular-socialist' independence leader Habib Bourguiba, a man seen as having brought modernity with a light touch over three decades from the time of independence from France in 1956. Bourguiba took an anti-Islamic line, while promoting women's rights, the abolition of polygamy and compulsory free education.

Inheriting an economically stable country, despite nominal multi-partyism, Ben Ali was re-elected president in 1989, 1994, 1999, 2004 and 2009, his popularity peaking with an (in fact) unbelievable 99.44 per cent majority. Changes to the constitution allowed him to run for re-election on the last two occasions.

A lack of opposition, however, permitted corruption to become entrenched. Ben Ali, his wife Leila and their extended family were at the centre of a web of nefarious dealings, living shamelessly lavish lifestyles. 'Because Ben Ali and his family had the largest slice of the economic pie,' says Ayed, 'if the private sector raised its head above the parapet, it would get chopped off.'

As a result, just below the surface of the impressive coastal infrastructure developments and high rates of economic growth, frustration was bubbling.

While unemployment was officially 14 per cent, in reality it was twice as much, with a widening chasm of income between the affluent coast and deprived interior, places such as Sidi Bouzid. Like elsewhere in North Africa, the economy remained dominated by the state, a 'shut up and get paid', cradle-to-grave system, dependent on redistribution through patronage, not growth through entrepreneurship.

These tensions were exacerbated by population growth. As regional population numbers have surged (in Egypt it leapt from 28 million in 1960 to 82 million 50 years later; in Tunisia from four million to just under 11 million), youth unemployment has steadily risen.

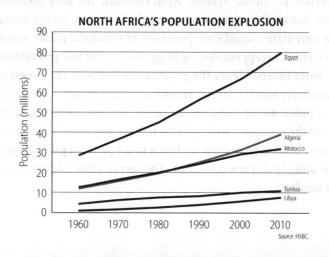

NORTH AFRICA'S POPULATION EXPLOSION

Source: HSBC.

As a result, the IMF has, for example, estimated that Arab economies must grow at least 6.5 per cent annually to keep up with population numbers, two percentage points higher than the average growth during the decade of the 2000s.[3] Equally dire, World Bank estimates have suggested that the region will need to create twice as many jobs – at least 50 million – during the 2010s to ensure social and political stability.

How the North African region might achieve this is unclear. The state there has a particularly poor record of entrepreneurship, governance and economic management. Moreover, it has lacked the necessary skills to match income with aspiration. For example, while Tunisia has enjoyed a burgeoning university system, the value of their skills is doubtful. 'The education system throughout North Africa is structurally flawed,' observed one locally based foreign banker in March 2013, 'especially at a tertiary level. You have to be a genius to be worth employing out of that system.'

'Bourguiba encouraged education on a large scale after independence,' recalls Ayed. 'He realised that Tunisia did not have natural resources and had to convert its people instead into these resources. I am one of those products. But it resulted in a large number of graduates who could not find a job.'

Around one million young Tunisians, including 70 000 university graduates, entered the labour market each year during the 2000s, a challenge to which the old Soviet-trained bureaucracy was unable to respond effectively. Instead, their tired and top-down, central-planning mindsets and discredited ideas were incapable of dealing with what one regional analyst refers to as the 'triple whammy of social unrest, economic upset and political uncertainty'.[4] 'In our system,' Ayed reminds, 'the state dominated the economy. Banks, the tobacco company, the insurance sector, energy – all of these were state-owned enterprises out of which the public was not getting very much except employing large numbers of low productivity, lazy people. Since independence the government had been the largest investor in the economy and the largest employee, which meant we ended up with a bloated public sector and a private sector that was not taking up the largest part of the economy, without which there was insufficient growth and investment. And even though we had 4 to 4.5 per cent growth over a long time,' he adds, 'it did not come from the sort of value-adding investments that we needed.'

The limits of offshoring

Economic growth under Ben Ali averaged 4.7 per cent during the 1990s. But when the 2008 slowdown happened in Europe, it hit Tunisia hard, which had positioned itself as a low-wage 'workshop for the European Union (EU)', the destination of 80 per cent of its exports. It had entered an 'Association Agreement' with the European Union in 1996, removing tariff and other trade barriers, and allowing Tunisians to work in the EU's agriculture sector.

Driven by incentives to attract low-wage export industries, the Tunisian model was vulnerable to both low-cost competition and a change in demand. 'This system was not as strong as people once believed it was,' says Ayed. 'Essentially Ben Ali pursued a policy of economic transformation through foreign companies establishing a manufacturing presence using cheap Tunisian labour. This resulted in thousands of companies weakly capitalised, very volatile and very vulnerable to a change in market conditions. Instead of a strategy to assist small and medium-sized companies, we had a weak financial system, with undeveloped instruments outside of the banking sector, such as the stock and bond markets, and the private equity sector. Even today,' he said in March 2014, 'there is too little money in the budget for investment, just €2.5 billion, much of which is for social investments, such as schools and hospitals, which is unlikely to create the sort of short-term impetus we require. And the type of investments we had were demand not supply driven; rather than being driven by Tunisian innovation it was led by European consumer demand.'

Such problems were worsened by strong barriers to entry into the Tunisian market, whether for importers or those trying to start a business. The market was protected – where political connections provided preferences – through licensing: famously, 'one person in Tunisia imported bananas', as an example of how difficult it was for local businesses to establish themselves. Little wonder that with the arrival of a moderate, interim government in December 2013, and the country's new constitution being agreed the following month, the focus shifted to pro-business reforms.[5]

Spring in their step?

The Arab Spring initially did little to help these challenges in the short term. If anything, it made things more difficult, with political instability

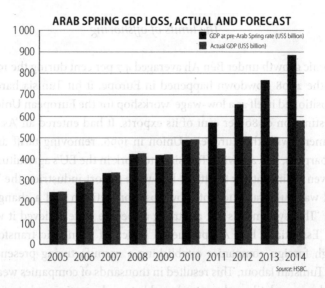

ARAB SPRING GDP LOSS, ACTUAL AND FORECAST

- GDP at pre-Arab Spring rate (US$ billion)
- Actual GDP (US$ billion)

2005 2006 2007 2008 2009 2010 2011 2012 2013 2014

Source: HSBC

worsening external investor and general perception, weakening investment and tourism revenues. It is estimated that the seven affected 'Spring' countries – Egypt, Libya, Tunisia, Jordan, Lebanon, Syria and Bahrain – lost as a result not less than $800 billion in actual and forecast cumulative GDP between 2010–14.[6]

Where exactly the political crisis characterised by the Jasmine Revolution might lead in Tunisia and elsewhere in the region is still, at the time of writing, unclear. At least it suggests that all bets should be off. My regional guide book, printed in June 2010, noted that 'there is no suggestion that the Tunisian government is anything other than in complete control. Politics still begins and ends with Ben Ali.' Its sudden change highlights the political and economic frailty of this region and those facing similar challenges of burgeoning youth and high unemployment.

Indeed, the Arab Spring reminds us that surface political calm should not be mistaken for social cohesion; that economic growth is not enough by itself, but can worsen inequality; and that previously seemingly invulnerable regimes can quickly fall. These are sometimes violent reminders of the potential consequences of an African demographic explosion unprecedented in world history, and of the grave dangers in placing faith in the maintenance of good relations with a generation whose values and aspirations leaders might not share or appreciate. They highlight the potentially intoxicating appeal of radicalism and populism in such circumstances, especially to unscrupulous leadership, promising the masses a short cut to prosperity, while destroying the basis of private, broad-based wealth creation. And these events illustrate the challenge of sustaining democracy in such an environment.

Avoiding an African Spring

The presence of French Transall C160 transports and Armee de L'Air refuelling tankers at Bamako-Sénou International Airport in Mali, along with a cluster of camouflage netting and a park of containers, indicates how the Arab Spring spread beyond the Sahara into the Sahel.

Mali had long been seen as a poster child for democratisation, development and recovery. In March 1991 Colonel Amadou Toumani Touré, then the head of the presidential guard, overthrew the regime of his boss, Moussa Traoré. Touré then presided over a year-long transition, producing a new constitution and staging multi-party elections, before handing over power to Mali's first democratically elected president, Alpha Oumar Konaré, on 6 June 1992. In 2002, Touré, widely known as 'ATT', won a presidential election of his own and was re-elected overwhelmingly in 2007, a position he retained until he was toppled in a military coup to the month 21 years after his own. His demise, however, 'came as little surprise to anyone who had been watching the steady erosion of state institutions, largely as a result of widespread corruption'.[7]

In January 2012, Tuareg rebels launched an offensive to take over northern Mali. By that March, army elements had staged a successful coup in Bamako as they were displeased over the civilian handling of the crisis. By April 2012, the Tuaregs declared the secession of a new state, Azawad, though by then they were embroiled with Islamists. Then, in January 2013, in response to threatening Islamist gains, France launched Operation Serval, quickly clawing back control of much of the north.

By April 2013, there were 2 500 French troops in the country, their role against separatists and jihadists bolstered by the presence of a 7 000-strong African Union force. While politically controversial, regional analysts were in no two minds as to what it has achieved. 'Without the French,' says one World Bank official based in West Africa, 'the Islamists would, by now, be in Dakar [in Senegal].'[8]

There were several reasons why the government in Mali proved to be, unexpectedly, so weak in the 2011 fight against the rebels, led in the north initially by a combination of Al-Qaeda in the Islamic Maghreb (AQIM), the National Movement for the Liberation of Azawad, an organisation fighting to make Azawad an independent homeland for the Tuareg people, the Islamist Ansar Dine, and the AQIM splinter Movement for Oneness and Jihad in West Africa.

Instability in the north was nothing new. It has, for years, been a largely 'ungoverned space', at least by the state, where cigarette and other forms of smuggling is a way of life; camels moving on camels. Bamako politicians and their families are believed to have benefited directly from the illicit economy, where the government and military elements 'tolerated or actively participated' in various smuggling schemes.[9]

Mali's north has been described as a 'war economy', 'where the military effort structures and justifies everything else'. Networked through tribe and marriage, employing Bedouin trading routes, whole communities are dependent on these activities. In this, 'AQIM's main financial resources are derived, directly or indirectly, from traditional banditry (smuggling, racketeering, extortion of public funds, levies on the trafficking of drugs, cigarettes or human beings, etc.), and justified by the issuing of various fatwa. Additionally, various right-of-way levies bring in an estimated €100 million annually. This is supplemented by hostage taking and ransoms, estimated to yield as much as '€50 million some years', an area of 'business' facilitated through both informal networks and global telecommunications.[10] The infamous 'Air Cocaine' incident in 2009 is a case in point, when a burnt-out carcass of a Boeing 727, believed to have been transporting 10 tonnes of the drugs, was found in the desert near the northern Malian town of Gao. While such activities have contributed to the breakdown of state structures and law and order, they are nothing new. The Sahara 'has always served as a transit point for a variety of goods as well as a market for goods from both sides of the desert', a vital part of local economies, especially from the end of colonial times, involving everything from 'subsidised powdered milk and other foodstuffs from Algeria' to 'counterfeit and black-market cigarettes, subsidised fuel, weapons and narcotics, including cannabis resin and hashish'. This was largely ignored by donors before 2012 in their desire to view Mali as a success story.

Pierre Buyoya, the former Burundi president, was, by 2014, the African Union's representative for Mali and the Sahel. He says the region has been a haven for 'all types of smuggling' and the corruption that accompanies this malaise: 'Drugs, human and cigarette trafficking along with kidnapping.'

These activities 'can corrupt anybody', he says, but has been absent. So when the rebels come from Libya, there was no state to resist them.' Thus, he adds, though 'solutions inevitably have a political and technical aspect, first and foremost the collapse of governance is a political problem.'[11]

Where the state breaks down completely or even in part, protection for criminal activities becomes a commodity in itself – and is priced as such. Mali illustrates that the term 'ungoverned spaces' is a misnomer. They are governed, but just not by the state. By accumulating illicit profits through the provision of protection, some groups strengthen themselves over others.[12]

Gaddafi's removal coupled with the influx of Al-Qaeda elements from Algeria tilted the balance between law and disorder. The Libyan strongman had long financially supported Bamako, notably in the construction of a new government centre, but also through investments in hotels and fuel. Malian migrants working in Libya channelled earnings back home.

Mali's democratic setback shows how fragile many African governments are to external shocks, and how quickly consistent growth and progress, even though it was consolidated over twenty years, can be overturned. Stir in corruption and other forms of criminality, take away Gaddafi's largesse and throw in the spread of weapons from lawless Libya and, voilà, Mali's government wobbled and was toppled. It shows, too, the limits of aid, not least that directed towards the Malian military, long supported by the West.

If Mali provides the questions, in spite of the undoubted progress made overall in governance and democratisation over the past twenty years, the challenges facing fragile states are formidable. A failure to meet the basics of political, economic and social security will, if the Arab Spring is anything to heed, result in social and political tensions and potentially a fruitful recruiting ground for extremist groups. Yet, meeting these challenges is no small order, not least given the rise in population numbers, especially in cities, and the absent corollary of employment and education opportunities, especially for Africa's burgeoning youth. These fundamentals should not be obscured by statistics of growth, 'freedom', democracy and peace, no matter the welcome improvements in this regard. Add to this the potential for outsiders to 'go after' natural resources with little regard for governance niceties, indeed sometimes deliberately to undermine such regimes, and African governments, their armed forces as well as external partners have a daunting task ahead. Finally, while the priority focus has understandably been on getting the military out of politics, given its history, and on changing the incentives in this regard, there is a no less formidable challenge: ensuring that the political economy operates in a way that favours competitiveness and efficiency, not political connections. While not ignoring the short-term benefits for stability of economic 'co-option', unless a globally competitive political economy is encouraged, a vicious longer-term cycle of economic under-performance and political meddling is likely.

One big lesson from the Arab Spring is in the need for Africa to increase economic growth rates to create jobs and give citizens a stake in stability. This requires, more than anything, an economic debate at home, not just visions directed at donors. Development policies have to take care to avoid developing a constituency of consistent losers: racial, tribal, sectarian, urban-rural, military-civilian, or between the public and private sector. This is especially important, given the immense demographic changes under way in many fragile states, especially in Africa. Without fresh political and economic direction, the potential for unstoppable, desperate migration is great, by which these states will impose themselves on the world, for good or ill.

*

As the Spring turned into less of a summer, perhaps, than an autumn, Mali, and to its north Libya, illustrated just how messy these transitions can be. In Tunisia, too, a relatively sophisticated and socially cohesive country with a manageably small population (at least by Egyptian comparisons), there was cyclical political turmoil after Ben Ali's departure, with no fewer than five governments appointed in just three years from 2011.

These events also illustrate that, despite the level of French and, later, African Union support in stabilising the violent situation in Mali, these countries will, to a great extent, have to work out their own future on their own.

Churchill, cited above, also said that the victory at Alamein in 1942 was 'not the end. It is not even the beginning of the end. But it is, perhaps, the end of the beginning.' Strategically, it was the last major victory achieved by the Allied side without US involvement. Cooperation was thereafter necessary to endure global peace and order. On the wall of the American cemetery in Carthage is a letter from President Dwight D. Eisenhower dated 21 July 1960. He wrote: 'The landings of the American forces on the shores of North Africa nearly eighteen years ago were the symbol and the noble expression of unity and determination in a great crusade.'

Unlike the Eisenhower era of unconditional support in a binary world, today external engagement in meeting these challenges is limited, before, during and after political changes.[13]

The World Bank, which announced in February 2014 $1.2 billion in funding for Tunisia's governance and legal reforms,[14] has, for one, been hamstrung in its efforts to assist by the fluid nature of the political environment and the backlog in legislative reforms. This reflects wider challenges, common to most recovery situations: changing the model from one of preferential elite access to contractual and licence opportunities granting economic privilege, to a more transparent system, while maintaining stability. In essence, setting the country onto a different path requires not only technocratic reforms, but a vision behind which people can unite, enabled by a great deal of political will and dollops of leadership. Similarly, despite the central role of North Atlantic Treaty Organization (NATO) members in removing Gaddafi from power by force in 2011, as will be seen later in this volume, the post-conflict relationship there, too, by the West has been minimalist.

Two additional factors militate against positive change from such uprisings: the traditional nature of these societies and the overtly political nature of those that have sought to take over. These situations are fraught with contradiction. The revolutionaries behind the Arab Spring, from Tunisia to Yemen, were motivated by a sense of political and social injustice, to be remedied by wider prosperity and great political plurality. But not all were driven by high liberal ideals rooted in the fight against socio-economic inequality and autocracy. Islamists did not, put differently, seek to take over only in poor countries. As the eminent Arabist Asher Susser has noted, 'the political forces [in these states] … are all deeply rooted in traditional politics, such as political Islam, sectarianism, and tribalism … . This does not necessarily mean that democracy will not develop in these societies sooner or later. However this is not the most likely eventuality, and certainly not an inevitable one.'[15]

Those seeking to influence these countries in a positive direction will have to show an alternative future; that democracy, the rule of law and liberal economics makes sense, not crony capitalism and authoritarianism or radicalism. To illustrate this future, a strategy to support such social transformation will have to rely on internal change agents. How to support them without undermining their political credibility is a challenge across the range of weak states, including in North Africa. Too often Western governments, the principal proponents and adherents of liberal values, have dabbled, providing ammunition to the detractors, never going far enough in their influence to make the antagonists irrelevant. If nothing else, Wikileaks shows that such external influence is a concern of autocrats. This is not to advocate George Bush-style social engineering à la Iraq, but could start with upholding values: holding those leaders dependent on external support to account for their actions and spending is a good place to start, since leadership is critical to realising these goals. As the former South African president Thabo Mbeki noted at the 2014 African Development Bank summit in Kigali about the roots of state failure, 'Conflict happens because of a failure of leadership.' Or as his Botswana counterpart, Festus Mogae, put it at the same event, 'The role of leaders is to take initiatives to deal with problems as they arise.' But when people come to power, he said, problems arise instead from their 'self-interest and greed' since 'they are too obsessed with self-importance.'

The Arab Spring and its aftermath challenge thus the thesis of driving all aid towards development, humanitarian causes and civil society. This has become a never-ending treadmill, an industry for civil society that can alleviate the worst problems but never resolve the undergirding issues. It does not make sense to push billions of dollars into patching up the socio-economic environment or humanitarian situation while tossing only a few crumbs the way of political actors.

7

UGANDA

Kettles, Pots and Land

*

‘They're black', responded the Ugandan driver to the question whether he could tell the Acholi apart.[1] His response came on the way to the northern Ugandan city of Gulu, the capital of a region ravaged by twenty years of barbaric bush war between government forces and the Lord's Resistance Army (LRA), led by Joseph Kony.

In January 1986, the National Resistance Army (NRA) led by a southerner Yoweri Museveni, still president 28 years later, overthrew the regime of President Tito Okello. In a tumultuous and violent history, Okello, an ethnic Acholi, had earlier, in July 1985, been part of a successful coup against President Milton Obote, who himself had come to power in 1966 via a coup, only to be similarly removed by his army commander, Idi Amin, when away at a Commonwealth summit in Singapore in January 1971. Kony's movement grew in 1988 out of the remnants of the Uganda People's Democratic Army (UPDA), itself formed by disaffected former officers in Obote's Uganda National Liberation Army (UNLA). Many UNLA troops and some officers were Acholi, which resulted in the group being blamed for the 300 000 deaths during the bush war with Museveni's NRA (about the same number who died at Amin's hands), especially in the West Nile region and in the Luwero Triangle. The war started in 1981 when Museveni accused Obote of having rigged the December 1980 elections in which the current president was a minority candidate.[2]

Alice in Wonderland

Following the fall of Kampala on 25 January 1986, a young woman from Gulu, Alice Lakwena, took control of much of the UPDA, transforming it into the Holy Spirit Movement. Presenting herself as a spirit medium, Lakwena held that the Acholi had turned away from God and thus required purification to defeat Museveni, setting the stage for a quasi-religious, cult-like dimension to the war in the north. Lakwena imposed a set of bizarre practices and beliefs on her followers, including a prohibition on taking cover during combat, treating stones with oils supposedly to turn them into grenades in combat, and the ruling that 'thou shalt have two testicles, neither less nor more'. Despite horrendous casualties among her youthful followers, many of whom were armed with little more than stones, she led a major campaign through eastern Uganda. After being bloodily stopped by the NRA at Jinja, Alice fled to Kenya where she died, a refugee, in January 2007.

After her forces fled, Alice's home district of Kitgum became the focus of thousands of armed Karimojong tribesmen from the east looking for plunder. As they swept through Acholi villages, the NRA mostly did not intervene, alternating between watching in pleasure as those 'stubborn northerners' lost their economy and livelihood in their cattle herds, and at times foraging themselves from the local population, which was already leaned on by the rebels.

Following the signing of the Pece Peace Accord in 1988, what was left of Lakwena's forces regrouped around two leaders. One was Alice's father, who called himself 'Rubanga Won' (God the Father), the other a young man from Odek village in Gulu district, Joseph Kony, who had joined the UPDA the previous year. Like Lakwena, to whom he was said to be related, Kony styled himself as a spokesperson of God, desiring a theocratic state based on the Ten Commandments. In his mind he was on a divine mission; in reality, with support from the Islamic government in Sudan as a proxy in its own war against the Ugandan-supported southern Sudanese People's Liberation Army, he was a player in a wider regional conflagration.

A brutal bush war ensued, precipitating a humanitarian crisis. Two million people were herded into so-called IDP (internally displaced people) camps under government guard. An estimated 100 000 civilians died from the poor conditions in these camps and from the fighting outside, and many more were badly brutalised, with over 30 000 children alone estimated to have been forcibly recruited as supporters, soldiers and concubines by Kony's rebels who specialised in extreme cruelty.

The war became infamous for its 'night commuters' or 'invisible children', the patter of small feet at dusk when children fled into Gulu for safekeeping from the marauding LRA. In March 2012, the Invisible Children organisation posted the 'Kony 2012' video on YouTube, which highlighted the LRA's forced abduction of children and brutal methods, in order to have Kony arrested by the end of 2012. The video went viral with over 100 million hits, creating controversy about both the methods of such pressure groups and their principal aim – for them, in simple terms, or for the Acholi.

A post-liberation insurgency

The LRA is a modern, 'post-liberation' insurgency. Whereas liberation movements usually aim to take control of the capital and ultimately secure the state by political agreement, such modern insurgencies, like Kony's, are characterised by highly decentralised groups that live off the land, often crossing over borders between states to do so, and terrorising people with seemingly no rationale except to profit and to fight. This makes mediation very difficult (since there is no discernible aim or rational ideology) and inevitably thus stresses military rather than political solutions. It also explains why it is so easy for these situations to return to conflict since greed, rather than grievance, lies at the root of the fighting.

This also helps to understand why it has taken so long to end the insurgency, but only in part. Some Acholi are more cynical. They believe Kampala's intention was to break the dominance of the military by the traditional Acholi (who were viewed as tall and athletic warriors by the colonialists). Olom Zachary, a former deputy minister in Museveni's government, and a US-educated agronomist, says the Acholi believe that far from not possessing the means to stomp out the LRA, the national Ugandan People's Defence Force was, as intimated above, rather interested in retributions against the Acholi, given their support for former presidents Amin, Obote and Okello, all northerners, and in the process earning itself extra privileges and resources from the conflict.

With fewer than 2 000 armed supporters remaining and under intense international pressure (including being the target of US special forces and the focus of a variety of mostly US-based advocacy movements), since 2010 Kony has been on the run, likely hunkered down in the Central African Republic, a job made easier by the fall of the regime of President Francois

Bozizé in March 2013 to the Seleka rebels, with whom Kony appeared to be allied.

The Ugandan government has taken to view Kony as no more than an 'altar boy' running, quizzically, a 'Christian fundamentalist organisation sponsored by Islamic fundamentalists'. In line with this posture, the Ugandan government has strategically used its position in the 'war against terror' through its central support (5 700 of a total of 17 700 troops in 2012) for the African Union Mission in Somalia (AMISOM), an attempt to bolster Western, especially US, support for the military and the Kampala regime. It also provides the military with a source of external succour: Ugandan troops with AMISOM earn an allowance of $600 per month, about ten times what they receive at home. The embers of the LRA have proven difficult to put out altogether. As one US special forces officer engaged in the campaign has noted: 'There remain some significant sanctuaries that no amount of support and enablement can stem.' Although the LRA is a cult with overtly religious rather than political aims, wider political reassurances for the Acholi would also have to play a part in solving this problem in the region and internally by diluting the divisions between the northern Acholi and those in Kampala. Although regional dynamics changed considerably with the emergence of the state of South Sudan in 2011, and the pressure on the LRA's top commanders has intensified both militarily and through high-profile amnesties, there have been many cases of over-optimism about the end of the conflict. In 2007, for example, then US Assistant Secretary of State Jendayi Frazer visited Uganda and stated that her country would capture Kony if the LRA did not swiftly sign a peace agreement. A year earlier she had said that the US would eliminate all remaining rebels by the end of that year. The Ugandan People's Defence Force has, too, been prone to regular and rash promises in this regard.

Although peace has returned to the area and Gulu itself, even if all rebels have not, prosperity remains elusive.

Given the absence of a clear ideology, ensuring that conflict does not return requires restoring law and order, including police and judicial structures, providing people and especially the ex-combatants with a sense of place and role, managing the trauma of violence, rebuilding destroyed infrastructure, and making sure that resources are distributed evenly to ensure that no one group is a permanent loser from conflict and perceives itself as such.

Moses Ali, like Idi Amin from the northern West Nile region and once a general and finance minister under the self-styled field marshal-come-president-for-life, had become the third deputy prime minister in Museveni's government. He emphasised the need for recovery and redistribution. 'We in the north,' he observed as he sat alongside me on a panel in Gulu to discuss global lessons from building peace in May 2012, 'are a very big casualty room. We are all victims of war. We need to be treated as victims. We need attention more than other people in Uganda.'

The role of agriculture

One way to post-conflict economic recovery in many countries is through agriculture. 'We have to transform agriculture from being a way of life into a business,' stated the minister of internal affairs, Hilary Onek, the only Acholi and, in May 2012, one of just two ministers from the north (the other being Moses Ali) in Museveni's 29-strong cabinet.

But this transformation has proven to be very difficult, not least since recovery not only requires getting people back on the land, itself a big enough challenge where trauma and mistrust is rife, but because competitiveness depends on the introduction of commercialisation. Add into this an innate suspicion of outsiders, less of white people in the case of the Acholi than people from the south, and things have proven tough.

'I am the custodian of our land for three generations,' says Chief Jeremiah, a man who gave up a job with Xerox to take up his hereditary post, 'my ancestors, the living and the unborn.' Jeremiah, who heads 45 000 people around Gulu, is a man caught between his modernising education and conservative inheritance.

It is not that there are no good examples. Bruce Robertson, a South African, had leased the West Acholi Co-operative Union cotton ginnery in 2009. An injection of finance and management proved to be just the tonic for its recovery. From producing 2 000 185-kilogram cotton bales in 2009, in 2014 the Gulu Agricultural Development Company aimed to produce 15 000 bales, or seven months of continuous 24-hour a day operations at its 50-year-old factory. The use of natural herbicides (a chili-based mixture) and fertilisers means that the cotton can be certified organic for key markets in the US and Japan. With 25 extension officers and 200 'lead' model farmers to assist, over 6 500 farmers are benefiting from seed and technical inputs, along with an 'organic premium' bonus payable at the end of each season.

Peace and investment has brought real dividends. In the 1990s, cotton production collapsed due to the war. By 2012, each farmer was earning $250 from their 0.9-acre average plots.

The company, whose motto is 'Cotton for Cash', is also evidence of what the private sector, local communities and donors can do in partnership. The Danish government had injected cash as an 'accelerator', enabling the 'hanging' of other services, including health and education, onto the extension schemes, and this partnership led to the planting of sesame and looking at the potential for organic chili.

A visit along a bumpy mud road – once off-limits to all bar the military – to the Amuru district 40 kilometres outside Gulu proved how, in their words, life had changed 'very, very much' for the farmers since the end of the war. Most had spent many years in the camps and were pleased to be back, even though they were 'not sure whether it would last'. The 'biggest change in their lives was that they have been able to come back to their land, plough it and produce their own food'.

But this is a tough life. Even though there is plenty of land, it is impossibly difficult to clear, with little mechanisation and no electrification. The Amuru farmers yearn for 'animal tractors', realising that the mechanical versions are out of their financial reach at a ploughing cost of $30–40 per acre. Although many owned bicycles and nearly one-quarter of the 40 or so gathered on mats outside the cooperative centre had mobile phones, they were reliant on solar power at $0.25c per phone charge. The vagaries of the market and the prices paid for cotton meant many found it difficult to meet primary school fees of $7–10 per child per term, let alone those of senior secondary at $150 per term. This was a large chunk of income for a community where each woman present had no fewer than six children, about the national average for Uganda and one of the highest in the world.

Little wonder there was stunned silence when they were asked if they felt that the government was doing enough for them. In private they said they needed more, especially roads and training in 'proper agronomy'. It costs $5 500 to move a container from Gulu to Mombasa, slashing the returns to the farmer, and less than one-third of this amount again from Mombasa to any major port worldwide. Such is the cost of inefficiencies, including transport monopolies.

Infrastructure, infrastructure, infrastructure

None of this is exclusively Acholi, however. Uganda remains beset by problems of road coverage and their standard and power generation and transmission countrywide, and by financing (one-quarter of government budget is from donors; its tax/GDP ratio is just 13 per cent) and corruption in moving from planning to delivery. With a total national grid in 2012 of just 305 MW in electricity production for its 33 million people, Uganda's electricity coverage is among the worst in the world, alongside Somalia, Sierra Leone and the Central African Republic. Little more than 10 per cent of its people have access, and very few in the rural areas. As with many other countries, Uganda has failed to foster a development and growth ideology, a practical model beyond vision documents that predictably have a year date in the title; one that focuses on hard economic choices and priorities instead of playing identity politics.

The dirt road to Amuru, for example, is criss-crossed by abandoned railway tracks, with only bits of the tracks visible on the road before disappearing into human-high grasses on the verges. These were built soon after independence to link up with those laid down by the British during colonial times, using Asian labour as far as Soroti in the south, the aim being to move tobacco out from Amin's West Nile region. The Asians stayed behind, becoming the key trading class and, in the process, a focus of Amin's opprobrium, resulting in their expulsion en masse in 1972. At the same time, the field marshal's insertion of various incapable lackeys and relatives to run the railways led to their collapse. Forty years on that tobacco had to be extracted by truck, pummelling the roads further.

There is little doubt that the government has had a difficult inheritance. 'If you think of where we were 30 years ago,' says the minister of trade, Peter Mudenge, 'when we were a net importer of everything and when one-quarter of the country was at war until 2006, a lot has been achieved. You must remember,' he stresses, 'that when the Jinja hydro-scheme was completed in 1952 it produced 180 MW. In 1986, when we took over, it produced just 60 MW.' Dr Mudenge, like his boss Minister Amelia Kyambadde, points to the completion of the 250-MW Bujagali hydro-dam as one positive development, along with the reversal of the government's once high dependency on foreign aid for 75 per cent of its budget. Even so, Uganda remains hopelessly behind the curve of electricity demand.

Donor handouts have done little to help communities, apart from inculcating a sense of entitlement, and little to change government's ways with their conditions. 'The president dismisses the donors on issues such as governance or corruption,' reflects one European ambassador, 'which is why we cannot justify budget support any longer and go for targeted programmes with particular ministries. All this, while other foreign actors have served to distort local pricing, notably the World Food Programme, which uses Uganda as a regional buying hub and, in the words of one aid specialist, 'is a law unto itself. They seem to take pride,' he says, 'in saying that we have never been bigger.'

This is why the Danes, for one, have shifted to stress the importance and terms of private sector interactions, in this case through the joint Agri-Business Initiative. But getting local people to understand – or accept – how the market works remains a challenge. Many farmers cannot – or do not want to – accept that some people can make money from adding value rather than physically tilling the soil. And suspicion abounds still of outsiders coming to grab land. 'I am from Kampala and here to help you,' is something few Acholi believe. 'People here would much prefer *wazungu* as an investor than another foreigner from the south,' commented one Acholi business person.

The usual formula adopted by people like me in advising how to translate land into commercial value is to stress the importance of land title in collateralising land, being able to borrow against it. 'But does that mean,' one woman asked at a seminar in Gulu, 'that we will lose our land if we cannot pay the loan?' Where land is only held by the living in trust for other generations, this is a difficult concept.

Thus the answer to agriculture as a means of recovery from war in environments like Gulu and its surrounds lies not in advocating one but rather a variety of approaches. There is also a need for a few large-scale commercial farms, both operating as examples for others and hubs for smallholders. There is a need for direct contracting between cooperative-type schemes that can supply inputs to smallholders in return for guaranteed sales from farmers' production. Government's role should be to strengthen both the systems and arteries of infrastructure, and to remove local fears of central government domination and vested interests by acting in the interests of communities.

And more than anything, there is a role for men like Chief Jeremiah in building trust between the old ways and the market, of facilitating introductions between private operators and local communities. With their leadership, suspicions might be managed and the market strengthened.

8

VENEZUELA

An Authoritarian Democratic Playbook

*

The digital board at Simón Bolívar International Airport carried an image of Hugo Chávez next to the flight arrival updates. It showed the former president, who died on 5 March 2013, hands clasped together in the rain, his green fatigues wet through. It slowly zoomed onto his face, which looks out as if into the far distant future. As it did the text appeared: *'Canta canta compañero. Que no cayo su corazon'* (Sing, sing colleague. So that your spirits don't fall).

In the year following Chávez's death, the future looked bleak for Venezuelans, the system created by the comandante threatening to be less the foundations of the new society he had promised than a house of cards.[1] The black market exchange rate between the new bolivar and the US dollar had leapt dramatically, the local currency losing two-thirds of its value on the black market during 2013. This has led to a surge in inflation and a shortage of basic goods as the government responded by imposing price controls to suppress the inflation, attempting to externalise the problem as being one of market speculators, profiteers and, in its own words, 'parasites'.

But it was the system itself that had given space to speculators to leverage the widening exchange rate differential and their access to so-called CADIVI[2] dollars at the official rate. Alice in Economic Wonderland ruled the day. Thousands of travellers thronged through the airport as flights in and out of Venezuela were booked up months ahead as citizens purchased their $3 000 foreign exchange allowance at the official rate and quickly 'round-tripped' to exchange their stipend at the unofficial rate, pocketing the difference.

In late 2013, the Venezuelan government seized the Manpa toilet paper factory in the northern state of Aragua to avoid shortages. National Guard officers who took control of the plant were ordered to monitor production and roll out distribution. Earlier the government was forced to import millions of stock items to counter a chronic shortage, which the regime of President Nicolás Maduro blamed on unscrupulous traders. His vice president, Jorge Arreaza, said authorities would 'not permit hoarding of essential commodities, or any faults in the production and distribution process.'[3]

The government, never short of conspiracy theories, believed it was, in toilet paper parlance, being ripped off. In response to the crisis, Maduro requested emergency powers over the economy, enabling him to rule by decree, a step further down the path of authoritarianism and populism initiated by Chávez's Bolivarian Revolution.

Ply as they might, the government had only itself to blame. Toilet paper was not the only product in short supply; the country was beset by regular shortages of food essentials including milk, sugar, cooking oil and the corn flour used to make *arepas*, Venezuela's national dish. According to Venezuela's Central Bank's scarcity index, one-fifth of goods were not available in the government-subsidised supermarkets such as Bicentanario (celebrating the bicentenary of the Bolivarian Revolution, which saw Venezuela get independence from Spain) established by Chávez.[4] By the start of 2014, inflation was running at more than 50 per cent per annum according to official statistics, but as much as 40 per cent per month unofficially;[5] the black market rate of the new bolivar and US dollar ten times the official one. At the latter rate it was the most expensive place in the world to live and survive, with a Burger King Whopper meal, for example, costing $22. But everyone only pretended to be paying such amounts, while quietly changing their money on the black market.

Regardless, the government sought targets to explain its troubles in order to avoid its own policies being fingered for blame. Long queues surrounded the Daka electronic stores after Maduro ordered their seizure in November 2013, accusing them of overcharging. He also announced the confiscation of the JVG store in the eastern part of the capital, Caracas, saying it was used by the wealthy elites of the city whom he described as 'thieves'. He said he would turn his attention next to those stores selling toys, cars, food items, textiles and shoes. He blamed Venezuela's economic woes on 'sabotage' by opposition forces. The opposition leader, Henrique Capriles Radonski, responded by saying that the situation proved the failure of the government's policies as a 'failed puppet of the Cuban government'.[6]

The seizures were politics by other means. For example, the government, then facing December 2013 municipal elections, was desperate to highlight that it was a profiteering conspiracy behind the shortages and burgeoning inflation, not the government itself.

In Catia, in the run-up to the election, activists in black uniforms with orange stripes, identified as members of the revolutionary People's Liberation Movement – or 'collectives' – forced shops in the west of the city to open at 10 a.m. and sell at 'fair prices', noting that after they had finished with the electrical appliances, they would do the same with hardware, clothing and footwear. The merchants, meanwhile, pointed out that in many cases, after selling the inventory in question, they would close their doors forever because of fees charged by these so-called collectives.[7] Behind the windbag revolutionary speeches and omnipresent banners and slogans exhorting the people to higher ideals and further action, was old-fashioned threat and menace that was keeping the opposition at bay, maintaining the privilege of the revolutionary elite, including its Cuban allies, and attempting to contain the failure of the regime's policies.

Maduro survived the elections, but by February 2014 politics had caught up with widening economic and social problems. Two months of public marches and protests followed, initially over rising crime but snowballing into anti-government rallies, in which 40 people were killed in two months, paralysing the country. By April, although the president remarked the protests were part of a 'fascist' US-backed plot against him,[8] he met with opposition leaders in crisis talks aimed at quelling the unrest.

*

Venezuela is a place of extremes. It has a fantastic endowment of natural resources, including the largest reserves of oil worldwide and significant stores of gold, coltan, copper, bauxite and nickel. Its problems have been externalised and epitomised by the great 'imperial power', the US, yet the US is Venezuela's number one import and export partner. It possesses rich farming areas and enjoys abundant rainfall. Yet, local industry has been destroyed by the past fifteen years of economic folly, and most food, like everything else, is imported. Caracas' wealthy reside in the valley of Manhattan-like areas of Chacao, which are overlooked by barrios, or slums, such as Petare, which climb up the mountainside. It is in these barrios that the bulk of the Latin American nation's 30 million people live, even after fifteen years of rampant redistribution led by Chávez. By the end of 2013, there were long waiting lists to purchase cars, which cost as much as ten times the price elsewhere, although petrol was ridiculously cheap, at 6 bolivars for a tank of 65 litres. At the official exchange rate of 6.3 bolivars to the dollar, that would be $0.95 per tank. Per litre, it would be $0.014. At the prevailing 'parallel rate' of 65, it was just $0.0014. So it was basically free: in other words, it is my right. With vast oil reserves, it has not been generating wealth that has been Venezuela's principal problem; it is the management of it.

Comandante Chávez was a charismatic, if pugnacious, political genius.[9] Like Margaret Thatcher, he was a game-changer, breaking the mould of Venezuelan elite-centred politics, putting the marginalised at the heart of national political concerns for the first time. He defied stereotyping, rising quickly to become a global icon, the only Venezuelan politician before or since Simón Bolivar who was widely known outside Latin America – a Millennium-Man politician.

Combining superb oratory, a sharp sense of humour and excellent communication skills with an alluring personality, Chávez sought common cause with the downtrodden through the liberation mythology of the Bolivarian Revolution, building an ideological and, later, business partnership with Fidel Castro's Cuba, while externalising his problems by blaming problems on, internally, the local elites and, outside, the 'imperialist' US. He was at once comical and dictatorial, a showman and an intellectual, an autocrat and democrat, launching a 1992 coup and respecting a 2007 referendum result on term limits against his intent.

In adding to the playbook of authoritarian democracies, Chávez not only fed off and widened existing wealth divisions, but created new ones. His populist alternative, focusing on its revolutionary symbols and slogans, the plight of the poor and the dispossessed and the use of redistribution as a means of instant social justice, has become a model for those elsewhere who seek a rapid way out from poverty and inequality. But not even a year after his death the country was a long way from a world that Maduro said would become a 'sea of happiness'.[10] The Bolivarian Revolution, launched fifteen years earlier, was eating itself, apparently proving Thatcher's aphorism: 'The problem with socialism is that eventually you run out of other people's money.' The problem in Venezuela is not only about money, however, but also about the erosion of basic political freedoms, contrary to the apparent spirit of the Bolivaristas but completely in line with their intent to maintain power.

Chávez died probably at the peak of his popularity, since the economic policies that underpinned his Bolivarian Revolution were largely illiterate and unsustainable, predicated on short-term redistribution and spending rather than long-term growth and investment. His attempted revolution was riddled with contradiction and fundamentally dependent on conflict as a strategy. Where there was once envy between Venezuela's classes, following Chávez, there has been hatred.

Regardless, his popularity spoke volumes about the historical polarisation of Venezuelan society.

A brief history of elitism

It is of little surprise that Chávez, born in 1954 as the second of seven children of school teachers, felt so impassioned about these two worlds. Sent to live with his grandmother, Rosa, Chávez was to describe his childhood as 'poor ... very happy', but where he experienced 'humility, poverty, pain, sometimes not having anything to eat', and 'the injustices of this world'.[11] Chávez carefully airbrushed his childhood to fit in with his political self-image. After all, his 'father had been a proud member of the Comité de Organización Política Electoral Independiente (COPEI), one of the "putrid" ruling parties, and despite his modest teacher's salary all six of his children went on to college education and decent careers. The state provided subsidised housing (Chávez lived in one with his grandmother) and free, rickety education and health care ... All this,' Rory Carroll reminds us in his biography of Chávez, 'became heresy. The comandante, the nation was told a thousand times, was born in extreme poverty, a mud hut, and grew up in a venal, vicious system.' By so doing, his 1992 coup was not a military uprising, but the 'cry of an oppressed people'.[12]

Enrolling in the Venezuelan Academy of Military Sciences at the age of seventeen, Chávez later pursued Political Science at Simón Bolivar University in Caracas where he developed a doctrine of Bolivarianism, inspired by the Pan-Americanist philosophies of the nineteenth-century, Spanish-Venezuelan revolutionary. In a military career lasting seventeen years, eventually rising to the rank of lieutenant colonel, during a staff appointment at the Military Academy of Venezuela, Chávez established the Revolutionary Bolivarian Movement-200 according to an oath – *Juramento en el Samán de Güere* – he made with his colleagues[13] on 17 December 1982.

Bolivar was the great Latin American liberator, bringing independence to the north-west of South America – contemporary Venezuela, Colombia,

Panama, Ecuador, Peru and Bolivia. Yet he died (some say of yellow fever, some poison, others syphilis, depending on where they stood politically) penniless, rejected and dejected in Santa Marta on the Colombian coast while waiting to escape to Europe in December 1830 at the age of 47. He summed up his life: 'There have been three great fools in history: Jesus, Don Quixote and I.' Bolivar's dream of a Gran Colombia, a unified republic comprising Colombia, Venezuela and Ecuador, did manifest, but quickly disintegrated despite (and perhaps because of) his dictatorial powers. The grand republic started amidst violence and some of its elements have since continued in that vein.

The post-independence period in Venezuela was characterised by instability, autocracy and even anarchy, the country being ruled by a series of military dictators, the caudillos. The first of these, General José Antonio Páez, controlled the country for eighteen years (1830–48). The period that followed involved an almost uninterrupted chain of civil wars, abbreviated by the rule of General Antonio Guzmán Blanco from 1870–88. A theatrical pattern of despotism and reformism was developing – and continues.

After Cipriano Castro's private army swept into power in Caracas from Colombia in 1899, the new government defaulted on its foreign debt. This led to a naval blockade by Britain, Germany and Italy in 1902. Six years later, Cipriano was overthrown by his junta colleague, General Juan Vicente Gómez. Under his rule, oil was discovered at Lake Maracaibo, which transformed the economy. Until that point it had been used by local Indians to plug the seams of their boats. By 1929, Venezuela was the second-largest oil-producing country (behind the US) and the largest oil exporter in the world. By 1935, the time of Gómez's death, the country's per capita income was the highest in Latin America. But with this sudden gush of foreign money came other problems that have since blighted the economy, including Dutch disease – the strengthening of the currency due to foreign inflows to the cost of diversification. For example, while agriculture accounted for about one-third of economic production in the 1920s, by the 1950s this had reduced to just one-tenth. As Dr Teodoro Petkoff, once the minister of economic planning, observes: 'In forty years we have been trying to solve the problem of the weight of oil in our economy. Nothing has changed, but nothing serious has been done to end this dependency. As a country we have failed in this.' Or as a Caracas-based business person has reflected: 'We don't have bad governments in Venezuela, only bad oil prices'.

The *gomecista* dictatorship system – so-named after Gómez's 27 years in power, sometimes as president but always the strongman – continued after his demise but with some relaxation, including the legalisation of political parties. This reform process was hastened by a 1945 coup that ushered in a democratic regime and was then set back by a further coup in 1948. The military junta led by Marcos Pérez Jiménez ignored the results of the election it staged in 1952, until it was forced out in January 1958. Yet, much of the infrastructure of modern Venezuela was laid down during his junta, including contemporary power supply and transmission and Venezuela's road network.

Two parties – Democratic Action and COPEI (the Social Democrats) – thereafter dominated politics until Chávez's ascendancy four decades later, known as the Puntofijismo period on account of the political pact that gave rise to it. In spite of challenges from left-wing guerrilla movements and economic instability caused by an explosion of debt during the 1970s and the collapse of oil prices in the 1980s, the system held. But the fall in oil prices and unbridled public spending sowed the seeds for Chávez's populist movement. With the devaluation of the (old) bolivar in 1983, standards of living fell sharply and political instability rose. Hundreds were killed in the Caracas and Guarenas riots of 1989 and two attempted coups followed in 1992, one staged on 4 February by Chávez when troops under his command stormed the presidential palace in the capital.

Pardoned in March 1994, Chávez was elected president in a landslide victory in 1998. Briefly ousted in a 2002 coup following popular demonstrations, he was quickly returned to power. He learnt one lesson from this attempted *golpe* (coup). The army had developed a Plan Avila following the 1989 Caracas riots, designed to stop protests. The military opposed Chávez's attempted activation of this plan, teaching him both to consolidate power and rely on his own resources in so doing.

The comandante also survived an August 2004 'recall' referendum to quickly consolidate his power in subsequent elections. The recall mechanism was introduced into Venezuelan law in 1999 under the new constitution drafted at Chávez's behest by the National Constituent Assembly that he had set up. Under its provisions, an elected official could be recalled via a referendum if a petition gathered signatures from at least 20 per cent of the relevant electorate. Thus, to order a presidential recall vote in 2004, 2.4 million signatures were needed.[14]

This proved to be a messy business. In August 2003, about 3.2 million signatures were presented by Súmate, a Venezuelan civil association, but were rejected by the National Electoral Council (CNE) on the grounds that they had been collected prematurely. Three months later, in November 2003, the opposition collected a new set of signatures, with 3.6 million names delivered in four days. The CNE again rejected the petition, saying that only 1.9 million were valid. The Supreme Court reinstated over 800 000 of the disputed signatures. The list of signatories was subsequently collected by the government and posted online in what became known as the Tascón List. Signatories working in government and the state oil company Petróleos de Venezuela SA (PDVSA; expressed as 'PADAVESA'), among other parastatals, were allegedly targeted as a result of their preferences. Unsurprisingly, a record number of voters defeated the recall attempt with a 59 per cent 'No' vote in favour of Chávez.

The comandante was re-elected in December 2006 and again, for a third term, in October 2012, although he was never sworn in due to his declining health. During his fifteen years in government, he perfected his brand of populist politics, using state resources to buy support and international relations to cement it.

The Cuban playbook

'Chávez,' according to Argelio Pérez, editor of the pro-government *Diario VEA* newspaper, 'inherited a place that was totally broken. The state of the economy was very poor. The economic crisis had led to a major intervention by the IMF, which resulted in a period of tremendous social consequences, pushing the price of gasoline beyond the cost of most ordinary people. Levels of poverty were very high, and there was no focus by government [until then] to change this.' Chávez was the result of a bad preceding twenty years. The early 1980s had seen over 100 per cent inflation, and between 1979 and 1999 the value of the bolivar to the dollar declined a hundredfold.

The situation was, says Modesto Ruiz, a member of parliament for the ruling Partido Socialista Unido de Venezuela (PSUV or United Socialist Party of Venezuela), founded in March 2007, 'ripe for change'. This explains why none of the traditional political parties fielded a candidate in the 1998 elections as they were badly discredited. It also explains why an environment for more radical strategies towards health and education appealed, 'and why the message of the need for democracy and legality rung hollow', says one Venezuelan business person, 'for the Chávistas'.

Milos Alcalay was a professional diplomat for 34 years, serving in Israel,

Brazil and as deputy minister of foreign affairs and Chávez's permanent representative to the UN, among other appointments. Alcalay resigned over the 2004 referendum controversy. Now an opposition member, he says that after 2004 there was a change in Chávez's political style from 'change through democracy to a revolution in autocracy and ultimately totalitarianism'. The publication of the Tascón List was a 'moment of apartheid' in Venezuela, polarising politics. Instead of working for solutions, he used confrontation as a strategy, seeing the opposition as an enemy that you have to 'crush' rather than convince or seek consensus with. Alcalay is among those who point to two distinct periods of Chávism – before 2004, when he was more pragmatic and less dictatorial, and after this period when he became increasingly arrogant and extreme in his methods. These methods also provided opportunity for corruption through contracts and skimming, and through foreign currency arbitrage for those with (government) access to preferential exchange rates.

This change also reflected, Alcalay says, growing ties with and influence of Cuba.

'Chávez came to Brazil in 1998 between his election and inauguration as president. He was desperate to see Castro at the Rio Summit, he was in awe of him and wanted to wait and meet with him in the lobby. When he appeared, Castro said "Stop. It is me that will come to you, not you to me." He managed [Chávez] brilliantly. He said, "Don't make yourself General; the people of Latin America will nominate you *Marshall* of the people." Venezuela under Chávez offered Cuba the possibility of a post-Soviet-era ally in exchange for ideological legitimacy. It was,' he reflects, 'a way out for Castro, the leader he says was 'a *widow* of the collapse of communism', the last East bloc-aligned Cold War-era leader standing.

The Cuban influence, he says, can be seen throughout the economy. Castro 'appointed Chávez the standard-bearer of the revolution'. The payback was initially in exchange for cheap (free) oil not only for Cuba, but others including El Salvador, Nicaragua and Bolivia, and cheap shots at US imperialism, capitalism and colonialism 'without actually confronting anyone militarily or physically'. The Cubans quickly gained a stronghold in key sectors of Venezuela's economy, including the ports, customs, control of the identification card system and some government industries such as electricity production. They also inserted themselves into the military hierarchy, especially in intelligence. As the exchange rate has bitten and redistribution taken hold, the economy has become totally dependent on imports for everything from consumer goods to maize and milk. In a vicious cycle, this favours those controlling the customs.

But the Venezuelan leader was far from being a simple stooge. 'He was charismatic and quite brilliant, a giant,' says Alcalay, 'and a sponge for information. When I met him in Brazil in 1998, he was given ten points for an agenda – regional integration, oil, blah blah. He soaked it all in, and when it came to the discussions, he elaborated on each of these aspects. I have never seen this ability in all my years as a diplomat.'

The necessity of conflict as a political tool

Chávez was a brilliant communicator, a figure who shrewdly appropriated the symbols and tools of the Bolivarian Revolution.

'He was both a Jekyll and Hyde character,' Alcalay adds. 'Chávez was honest in trying to solve problems. But like Mr Hyde he also needed to smash something, to have an enemy. But he could not achieve full destruction of the system because he was not competent enough to build something new.'

Politics had become war by other means. Newspapers speak of an 'economic counter-offensive' and of 'parasites engaged in economic warfare'. In the run-up to the December 2013 municipal elections, for example, near the Plaza Bolivar in Caracas, in front of the National Assembly was a tent handing out leaflets, promoting the PSUV. Inside was a poster with the photographs of several prominent business figures proclaiming '*RECONÓCELOS PUEBLO! RECOGNISE THESE PEOPLE – Enemigos de la Patria! Enemies of the Nation – Hambreadores del Pueblo! – Those who make the People Hungry – Sembradores de Odio! Sowers of Hate – PROHIBIDO OLVIDAR! PROHIBITED TO FORGET!*'. The tent stood opposite the art deco building that had once housed the La Francia gold and jewellery business, among those appropriated by Chávez's government.

While apparently a democrat working in the interests of the majority, Chávez and his followers learnt to use more authoritarian measures to intimidate and tie down their opposition, 'right out of the Cuban manual', reflected one opposition leader. As their position became more tenuous, menace quickly supplanted any pretence of democracy.

A PSUV poster plastered up around Caracas in October 2013 demonised, quite literally, the leaders of the opposition – presidential candidate Henrique Capriles, who received 49.12 per cent of the vote in the April 2013 election; Leopoldo López, a prominent opposition party organiser; and María Corina Machado, an outspoken anti-government parliamentarian who once called Chávez a 'thief' to his face – as the *trilogia de mal* (trilogy of evil). The poster blamed them for Venezuela's crisis: 'They're stealing your electricity. They're stealing your food. They're stealing your peace. No more violence.' The communications and information minister did not deny that the government was behind the posters, and described the opposition leaders as 'violent beings, militants of hatred and bitterness ... They are the fascists. Not those posters.' Maduro referred to the three politicians as 'mercenaries' and 'fascist parasites'.

Such blatant criminalisation of the opposition was a step up in a dangerous game that Chávez had started fifteen years earlier.[15]

Miguel Enrique Ontero's grandfather and father before him ran Venezuela's *El Nacional* newspaper group. He says the government has a 'target' of 'communications hegemony' for which the means are, first, 'physical aggression' towards journalists. 'In the last ten years, there have been 1 200 cases of violence against journalists, and no prosecutions. Seven years ago,' he said in November 2013, 'they bombed our newspaper offices. The suspect stayed in custody for just two hours, imagine two hours.' Second, says the Cambridge graduate, 'the powers of participation are controlled by the government. The justice system is not independent, the attorney general and auditor general are both militants in the ruling party, and the opposition is marginalised from all key commissions in parliament. The government also changes laws in favour of their point of view, including Le Resorte, the Law of Social Responsibility in Radio and Television, which although promoted as a means of increasing the production of Venezuelan-produced programmes and keeping off sex and violence when children might be listening or watching, it effectively silences opposition media by limiting their content. The government has also created, bought up and shut down radio and television stations, with direct access now to four television stations.' With approximately 850 radio stations countrywide, an estimated 500 were controlled by government.

The 'eyes of Chávez', posters and T-shirts with only his eyes visible, have become a metaphor for the Big Brother state. But they are among the more obvious manifestation of government attempts to intimidate and control the population. While some media outlets have been shut down completely, such as Radio Caracas Television, Alcalay notes that 'the methods are more sophisticated', involving the sponsorship of alternative media, the use of heavy fines to create 'auto-censorship', the transfer of power from the legis-lature to the executive, and control of civil society through a law preventing foreign funding. This is all, he notes, part of a 'strategy seeking enemies out-side and in who are intent on sabotage, in the government's terms'.

The government has used these stations to broadcast repetitively propa-ganda including the *cadenas*, apparently endless presidential broadcasts, which offer a caricature of a totalitarian state and 'insult and threaten the opposition and individuals, including me', highlights Ontero. In 2010, in order to be able to resume broadcasting, the cable television station RCTV-Internacional had to agree to register as a 'producer of national broadcast content', meaning it would have to comply with the requirement to carry the president's long speeches when they were transmitted by national network.[16] In his fourteen years in power, Chávez talked on his *cadenas* for a total of seven months and one day; while since his accession to the presidency Maduro has spoken on his *El Noticiero de la Verdad* (News of the Truth) twice every day. Then the government has used the justice system against dissidents, says Ontero, and business people who oppose them. 'There are 3 000 such people on trial here who have to go to the Department of Justice every two weeks,' he noted in November 2013. 'They are free but not free.'

The Chávez and Maduro regimes have also used government-organised protests as a means of destabilising more legitimate public events. By 2013 over 400 such contrived public displays were being organised daily by gov-ernment, 'serving as spoilers', says Benigno Alarcon of the Andrés Bello Catholic University, 'to prevent true public protests'.

Nelson Bocaranda Sardi, who runs a popular daily opposition radio pro-gramme from his Caracas studio, says that self-censorship is a very effective tool against opposition organs. 'People are afraid – afraid that they will not have their licence renewed, or they will not receive control dollars [at the of-ficial rate] to buy equipment or newsprint. Since we have to import everything now,' he says, 'and since they control the dollars, they control everything.'

This has been part of a wider strategy aimed less at national unity than fomenting division to ensure their continued hold on power. Professor Alarcon says, 'Chávez worked very hard to create divisions, not only between rich and poor people, but ethnic divisions, which never before existed, around race, between indigenous people versus immigrants. You can see this,' he reflects, 'in the new conception of the image of Chávez's face, no longer as a white man, but one with Indian features, even though he has Spanish parents.' But compensation based on redistribution and societal divisions is not a long-term recipe for success. From philosophy to private property, the goal has been the same. Just as Chávez was willing to target and appropriate the assets of those business people who opposed him politically, government supporters were keen to berate the private sector for not doing enough. 'Government,' says Argelio Perez, 'is in a huge battle for social and political change with those who want to prevent it and who are trying to resist their loss of privilege.' This 'investing class' is roundly criticised by the government for '*exfiltrating* money' from the country and for other 'economic crimes', including over-invoicing and profiteering.

Such a demonisation strategy has had its limits, since the government has realised that it cannot run things without the private sector. A writer with the opposition newspaper *Tal Cual* (That's the way it is), Teodoro Petkoff, once the planning minister under Chávez's immediate predecessor Rafael Caldera Rodríguez (1994–99), says that the 'government has learnt that it needs the private sector. Indeed, under Chávez the weight of oil has become heavier since for him, power was the issue. And power comes from money, and money comes from oil.'

The problem is that the more desperate the conditions, the more radical the government has become – though some have preferred to take this as a mark of success. Perez, for example, the pro-government *Diario VEA* editor, says, 'The social changes have created a new set of expectations and requirements for the national economy. Social changes have outpaced the ability of the economy to provide, though.' He adds, 'This is a consequence of the well-being of people and their circumstances.'

The economic insanity has caused the pages in the state cheque book to run short. While oil has been the historical means to ensure support and power in Venezuela, under the Chávez regime this source of income became even more important as the engine of redistribution and as other sectors atrophied, some by design, others neglect. Not for nothing has the state oil company PDVSA operated under the banner '*Revolución Gasifera Socialista*'. But it has its limits, as Chávez and, especially, Maduro have found out.

The socialist petroleum revolution

Venezuela has the world's largest known oil reserves, some 297 billion barrels, or 24.8 per cent of world share, more than Saudi Arabia (264 billion barrels, or 22.2 per cent).

Venezuela's considerable oil wealth – averaging 2.7 million barrels per day,[17] the world's fifth largest exporter – provided $1 000 per family per month, or $200 million per day in government income during the Chávez era. While the redistributive subsidy scheme has reduced malnutrition from 15 to just 5 per cent of the country's 30 million people, poverty has remained high. Despite this income and the country's socialist orientation, still an estimated 28 per cent of the population lives in poverty.[18]

On comparable data, Venezuela's poverty is twice Costa Rica's and four times Chile's, two nearby countries that do not enjoy such bounty.[19] Moreover, given that the price of a barrel of oil was, by the time of his death, about ten times what it was when Chávez was first elected in 1998, the record of his Bolivarian Revolution appears far worse. Indeed, two of the (many) ironies of the Chávez era are that the socialist revolution has depended on the global free market for a high oil price, and its main purchaser is the country most often denigrated by Caracas – the US.[20]

There have been several reasons for this poor performance, and for the shortages. First, oil production declined after Chávez took office in 1999 by roughly a quarter, and oil exports have dropped by nearly a half. In part, this is down to a doubling of domestic consumption because of subsidies, reduced demand from its major customer, the US (down from 1.7 million barrels per day to about one million by 2013), and a failure to invest in production facilities.

Output has been reduced by a blend of hostility to foreign investment and mismanagement of the state oil company, PDVSA, including the firing of 40 per cent of the workforce, along with management and 20 000 others, after a 2002 strike. By comparison, Colombia has increased its oil production from 200 000 barrels per day to one million, on account, it is said (somewhat chauvinistically) by Venezuelans, of their countrymen having departed for their neighbour after the PDVSA meltdown.

Such problems were compounded by a further 2006 nationalisation (oil companies were originally nationalised in 1976) of both upstream and downstream projects, forcing a renegotiation of contracts with foreign entities. Under these new conditions, PDVSA was to receive a minimum 60 per cent project share. While sixteen companies, including Royal Dutch Shell and Chevron, went along with the new rules, Exxon Mobil, Conoco Philips and others resisted.

The result?

First, the nationalisation exercise was a short-term gain for the 'supreme

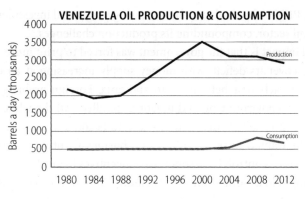

Source: US Energy Information Administration.

commander's' populism, but had a longer-term cost to the economy. Venezuela's huge reserves, including its Orinoco field, estimated perhaps to have as much as 513 billion barrels of recoverable oil, could potentially make the country one of the top three world producers. But these have effectively been off limits to foreign companies in the circumstances. Capital flight led to the imposition of currency controls (abolished in 1989) and several currency devaluations as the country increasingly exported what it produced and imported what it consumed. Such developments have posed a major self-inflicted economic threat to Venezuela, since the country depends on oil for 95 per cent of its exports and 45 per cent of its budget.[21]

Second, money has been wasted on Chávez's grand projects, both domestically and regionally. Billions of dollars have been channelled into secretive development funds, with little or no accountability. Regional fellow ideological travellers – including the Castro brothers' Cuba, Evo Morales' leftist regime in Bolivia, the Farabundo Marti National Liberation Front led by Mauricio Funes in El Salvador and the Sandinistas in Nicaragua under Daniel Ortega – have all received cheap oil and money. Domestic programmes were aligned to political needs. In the run-up to the 2012 presidential election, for example, Chávez made low-income and social housing a priority, launching a plan to build three million homes by 2018. As a result, during the first quarter of 2012, the construction sector expanded by 30 per cent, compared with the same period a year before. There was nothing wrong in improving housing, especially among the poor, but again the sustainability was questionable.[22] And rather than providing Venezuelans with jobs, many of the construction companies (and workers) were from abroad, notably Turkey, China and Iran.

In this, PDVSA has had to focus increasingly on social investments rather than the oil sector, compounding its production challenges.

A third impact is that the government was forced to print more and more money to cover its deficit, with money supply increasing at an estimated 60 per cent each year between 2010 and 2013. Foreign exchange became scarcer in this environment, and inflation spiralled. All the while, the state has attempted to ignore the market – and to become the market. Maduro said that he wanted to set legal limits on businesses' profit margins on all goods. Yet price controls have suppressed incentives to produce – with some goods being sold as something else (including milk) on which no price controls existed, or across the border in Colombia (such as coffee or electronics) where they fetched higher prices. This included a burgeoning trade in petrol, given the highly subsidised Venezuelan price, where the cost of refining is as much as ten times greater than the retail amount. The borders are porous precisely because they are controlled by the military, which has been behind much of the smuggling – illustrating that state weakness or failure is often by deliberate design because of such interests. This applies also to the exchange rate differential, where in Venezuela (as with Zimbabwe in the 2000s before the scrapping of the local dollar) this differential has been used and 'flipped' by those with access to government foreign exchange, making extraordinary profits in the process. This is inevitably a short-term game, with the government inserting itself at the centre of every transaction.

As one coffee producer put it, 'You can't sell to whom you want. You can't buy from whom you want, and you cannot set the price.'[23] Rentals were also set at peppercorn levels, sometimes as little as the cost of a roll of toilet paper, offering little inducement to home ownership. And as shortages kicked in, the crime rate multiplied – Caracas is now the sixth most dangerous city in the world, with 98.7 homicides per 100 000 people compared to 55.2 per 100 000 inhabitants countrywide.[24] The government's response was to put the National Guard onto the streets. Yet violent criminality, poor governance and corruption go hand-in-hand: Venezuela ranked at 160 of 175 on Transparency International's 2013 Corruption Perception's Index;[25] and 181st (from 189 countries, ahead only of Myanmar, the Democratic Republic of Congo, Eritrea, Congo-Brazzaville, South Sudan, Libya, Central African Republic and Chad) on the 2014 World Bank's Ease of Doing Business rankings.[26]

These problems have been of the government's own making, Venezuela matching high levels of social spending and foreign aid with a costly price and labour regime, kept afloat solely by oil revenues. Contradictions have become the norm. Under the Bolivarian Revolution, it has been impossible to fire anybody. Yet businesses could be appropriated on a whim. While businesses were expected to operate within the law, including the exchange rate regime, it has become hostage to government dispensing dollars or paying its bills timeously.

The government has, in turn, blamed 'corrupt capitalists' and 'parasites' for the troubles, drawing a link between right-wing politicians, corruption, criminality, smuggling and capitalism. Restaurants have been forced to display their prices outside, an attempt to prevent charging at market (that is, black market) rates, to avoid being issued with an *infractor* notice, essentially a final warning. But the problem has not resided with businesses trying to stay alive, but with government's cocktail of currency controls, price caps and import controls. The problem comes when everybody owns everything but nobody owns anything, making it very difficult to contemplate even trading let alone investing in this business environment.

Short-termism and patronage

The bad economic lessons from Venezuela include how not to squander today's wealth for short-term political popularity. While redistribution might offer an alluring simplicity and prospect for the marginalised, it is a short-term bet.

Chávez died in March 2013 after a very public two-year battle with cancer. Some believed that he had been poisoned by the US, given his nationalisation of its oil companies' assets and constant baiting of the White House. But like others, Venezuela's primary foe does not, no matter the political expediency of this belief, lie outside, but rather within in the form of its own government policies.

The inability to get to grips with the huge wealth divides and the related challenges of moving beyond redistribution of oil income as the only method of wealth creation has plagued this rich – on paper at least – nation. These challenges are epitomised by the attitude of an elite, which, for years, presided over the misery of the bulk of the population, rotating power between two similar-minded political parties.

Poorer Venezuelans have certainly got a fairer slice of the cake than they used to get from what Chávez referred to as the 'rotten elites' who presided over a blatantly corrupt two-party political and economic system. Venezuela had, by the time of his death, the fairest income distribution in Latin America, as measured by the Gini co-efficient, at 0.39 compared to Brazil's 0.52. But Venezuela's economy has not been growing fast enough to create wealth beyond redistribution. In fact, during the 'noughties', the economy was the worst performer in terms of GDP growth in Latin America.

Miguel Ontero, the proprietor of *El Nacional*, maintains that 'while the government has given people a lot of products they would not have been able to buy, the quality of life has not changed. They are living in the same rancho [house] they were fifteen years ago, perhaps with a plasma TV, but their prospects, their education and health are worse than before.' In part, this is down to corruption. Then Central Bank governor Edmée Betancourt reportedly estimated in 2013 that as much as 40 per cent of public sector imports never arrived, while 'ghost firms' exported money but never received imports in return.

'Imagine,' as one oil executive put it, 'if Venezuela had adopted a Norwegian model back in the mid-1990s, investing its oil reserves prudently in a sovereign fund, investing in new production, giving confidence to the private sector to play its part.'

But the country is obviously not Norway with a small conservative-minded population, a deeply rooted social contract, high levels of education and finely developed systems of democracy and justice – not to mention freezing weather. Instead, it is Venezuela, once a US sphere of influence and all that entails, with a history of social and economic exclusion, elitism, militarism and a correspondingly weak democratic and justice record – and a steamy Caribbean climate. It has been the scene of a struggle of extremes: for rapid political and economic inclusion, with instant gratification offered by oil at one end, opposed by those at the other end of the political and economic spectrum who have resented their loss of privilege. In the middle, as always, is the bulk of citizenry, muddling their way through increasingly tempestuous economic waters.

Chávez not only focused on consumption rather than investment, but created a parallel government, where he increasingly centralised powers rather than distributing them to local authorities. Rather than improving existing institutions such as schools, universities and hospitals, he created new ones; he built militias rather than strengthening the police and army; and created 'communes' (neighbourhoods) rather than empowering municipal government. Checks and balances were deliberately eroded. For example, the president of the PDVSA, Rafael Darío Ramírez, has also served as the minister of energy and mines. And through this all has run a strong thread of patronage.

The troubles experienced by Chávez's socialist experiment, given spiralling inflation, shortages of basic goods, corruption and widespread criminality and violence, does not, however, mean that there should not have been political change in Venezuela back in 1998. To the contrary, the country was long run for the benefit of an entrenched and exceptionally corrupt elite at great cost to the majority. Chávez brought change. But while this fresh start was necessary and despite his energy and charisma, the supreme commander took the country in the wrong direction – there is no short cut to prosperity as he had advocated. There were too many excesses and too little market. And the cost of his actions went beyond economic folly to the use, as highlighted above, of instruments to deliberately subvert opposition to government.

Good night at the mausoleum

It took Venezuela some time to acknowledge its debt to the man to whom it owed its freedom. In 1842, Simón Bolivar's remains were brought from Colombia to Caracas and entombed in the cathedral. In 1876 they were transferred to the Panteón Nacional in Caracas, where they now rest in a sarcophagus initialled with SB inside a modern annex to the original museum, the design a swooping clash of white, mirror-like marble and steel – post-modernism meets neo-classical.

Chávez's remains were similarly interred across town in the Cuartel de la Montana, in the midst of the barrio of Vente Tres de Enero. The symbolism is powerful. Like Bolivar's final resting place, four guards stand, rotated every two hours, resplendent in nineteenth-century red-and-gold tunics. Water surrounds the marble sarcophagus, flanked by photoshopped images of Bolivar, several pots of flowers denoting earth, the scene cooled by a breeze funnelling down the corridor from the entrance where sits an eternal flame. Outside, under the flags of all the 35 members of the Organisation for American States, next to a small 'Plaza of Eternal Motion', the 100-year cannon is ceremonially fired after four peals of the nearby bronze bell at 4 p.m. each day, its muzzle aimed in the direction of the white Miraflores presidential palace below. Red flags emblazoned with '4F' fly overhead the entrance, symbolising 4 February 1992, when Lieutenant Colonel Chávez's men assaulted Miraflores in an attempted coup. Although Chávez went to jail, he was elected six years later and never looked back.

Chávez's impact verges on the crypto-religious. His successor, Nicolas Maduro, has admitted that he sometimes sleeps next to the comandante's casket, seeking inspiration. In April 2013, he also said that Chávez's spirit had spoken to him through a bird. Other aspects of the revolution are less romantic, however, and perhaps more menacing and destabilising in the long term.

'Bolivarian revolution kits,' says Nelson Bocaranda, 'have been widely distributed, comprising a pistol, Chinese motorcycle, mobile phone and the usual red hat and T-shirt.' It is estimated that as many as one million Venezuelan Chávistas have received rudimentary military training and are armed. How they might react to a loss of power is a concern for both Venezuelans and their neighbours. Moreover, the campaign of blatant political vilification can have violent consequences, as, for example, occurred with Yitzhak Rabin's assassination in Israel in November 1997.

On the positive side of the ledger, the extent of the comandante's impact could be judged by the direction of opposition policies: no one would attempt to offer a sea change to Chávez since they would be unelectable. Opposition successors would need to be what Tony Blair was to Thatcher: similar polices with a different face. 'The tendency is irreversible. The old days will never return,' says Milos Alcalay. 'The colours of Chávez are today both in the government and in the opposition.'

Indeed, Chávez injected the variable of poverty into the debate in Venezuela, which will be difficult to remove. But eliminating poverty from the economy will require a complete change of policy tack to that which he adopted, predicated as it was on redistribution, weak institutions, centralised power, eroding accountability and rampant corruption.

The success or failure of Chávez's socialism will ultimately be measured in terms of sustainability: if it were able to allow the economy to diversify from oil, to be more than just a (rather inefficient) redistributor of oil wealth, and if it can uphold the democratic ideals and systems it accused the rightist opposition of subverting before 1999. The problem with this Venezuelan regime in economic terms is akin to that of a family living beyond its means, not unlike Argentina. It has constantly spent more than it earned, and then has sought reasons and scapegoats for its own excesses. Ultimately there are few ways to remedy this. These include spending less and/or earning more.

The spending less option is difficult where expectations are high; the earning more alternative is unlikely given the lack of investment in the oil sector and the emasculation of the non-oil economy.

Getting out of this trap is technically easy. As a start, it would require letting the exchange rate slide and removing exchange controls, thus removing the source of the greatest short-term distortions. It would be difficult to achieve this in political terms, not least since the currency, the new bolivar (created by a 2008 rebasing), is overtly connected to the Bolivarian Revolution, the symbols of which have been appropriated by Chávez as Libertador del Siglio XXI (Liberator of the 21st Century), and his successor Maduro. And it would be difficult to achieve since the government is, at its heart, less democratic than authoritarian.

Indeed, the rapid descent into authoritarianism has been the most negative development in Bolivarian Venezuela. It is politically retrograde and personally risky for some. Opposition leader Machado's foreign policy coordinator, Maria Teresa Belandria, describes the situation as extremely dangerous. 'While government might not do something itself, this incites others.' Famed local radio journalist Nelson Bocaranda had to flee to Miami for six months after the April 2013 election after being accused by the government of inciting violence. 'I have been harassed for fifteen years,' he said in November 2013, but 'this is our worst moment.'

In this environment, political activity is sometimes less a matter of conviction than outright bravery. Civil society activists and university professors have spoken of both widespread and personal intimidation and threats.

Benigno Alarcon, a specialist in conflict resolution, says that understanding the role of the military, which is so invested in politics and the economy, is critical in assessing how the country will escape its plight. In such a weak and unstable government, dependent on a mix of elections and repression, economic redistribution and growth, and of authoritarianism and democracy, attempts to find a negotiated solution depend on the costs of both tolerance and repression. If the costs of tolerating change are low (such as the military keeping its businesses without being prosecuted) and the costs of repression are high (such as the threat of international sanctions), then peaceful change is possible. But the problem with Venezuela, he says, 'is that the costs of tolerance are very high (that the government believes it will be prosecuted if they lose power) and repression very low (few have any appetite for imposing sanctions on the regime, and the chance of widespread civil unrest is low)'.

A key variable in this is the role of the international community, particularly the American market and its administration, given its primacy as the main market for Venezuela's oil exports.

*

One of the many lessons from Chávez's revolution is that it is very difficult to build a country (and an economy) based on conflict, without social peace. Polarisation, while a useful ploy to gain and retain power, is ultimately costly for all – opposition and government alike. Other lessons follow. While a redistributor of first resort of social goods, a state-run economy is no more an efficient long-term answer to poverty as it was in the Soviet Union, or a substitute for the private sector. In this, natural resources are a very helpful endowment towards success; but it is how these proceeds are used (spent or invested) that is critical. Finally, while redistributive spending might be a means of ensuring political support and power, the revolution ultimately eats itself as a mix of raised expectations, state capture and lack of long-term private sector investment turns ugly.

Just up from the Assembly, near the large mural where Chávez, Castro, Che Guevara, Bolivar and José Martí, the father of the Cuban Revolution, were depicted playing draughts, was a small wiry man in a Chávista red T-shirt with a bullhorn, constantly berating the opposition and the church and singing the praises of Maduro and Chávez. When we stopped to listen, he held out his hand: 'Nada para mi?' he asked (Nothing for me?). Railing radicalism tinged with expectations of a handout summed up the inheritance and challenge facing Chávez's successors, whatever their political affiliation. This is a lesson for others who seek to emulate the comandante, too, beyond Venezuela.

9

ZIMBABWE

Backwards to Beit Bridge?

✳

Bulawayo's architecture is impressive. Cecil John Rhodes, the man behind its twentieth-century incarnation, ordered that streets 'should be wide enough to allow a wagon with a full span of oxen to turn'. The extension of the railway through Botswana from South Africa in 1897, coupled with a flourishing mining and ranching industry and Bulawayo's strategic positioning on the crossroads of the Cape-to-Cairo and Botswana-Mozambique routes, gave birth to a substantial industrial sector.[1]

Now, however, this is broken.

While the facade remains, much of the inner stuffings have gone. Empty shops and buildings hint at a deeper malaise. The railway yards and workshops lie as still as the railways – in 2000, the country carried 20 million tonnes of cargo annually and 100 trains daily on the network; a decade on, it was eight trains and 1.7 million tonnes. In 2000, there were 350 manufacturing enterprises in Bulawayo employing 100 000 workers; twelve years later, at the peak of the recovery under the 'unity' government, there were 250 nominally operating, with 50 000 employees on their books. Most of these businesses were shells of their former glory. Bulawayo's textile and clothing sector, for example, employed no more than 3 000 workers, 10 per cent of its once peak, shuttered factories and sad, faded, tilting signage testament to its sorry decline.

Where factories once worked 24/7, now seldom, if ever, smoke rises from their chimney stacks. A city of manufacturers has become a city of pedlars of the goods made by others. Where once steel was forged and shaped, now wire-twisting sculptors eke out a living hawking their wares. Where, too, once thousands of workers thronged the streets at the 5 p.m. *shayela*, today a trickle of lucky ones make the journey home. It is not as if they are terribly appreciative of their plight, however. Everywhere is the same refrain. 'It's hard here.' 'We have nothing.' 'South Africa has everything, good infrastructure, jobs.' 'The economy is stagnant.' If the longest queue in Harare is at the passport office, Bulawayo's is outside the Western Union city branch to collect money sent by relatives and friends from outside the country.[2]

It is a city hunkered down in survival mode, all pretentions having been stripped away. Where once stood Rhodes' statue looking out over the city at the intersection of Main Street and Eighth Avenue, sits an empty plinth, reserved for the likeness of the late Joshua Nkomo, opposition leader and later deputy president under Robert Mugabe. Its erection has been delayed by his family's apparent unhappiness about the statue's small size and North Korean origins, particularly given the Asian country's link to the 1980s' Matabeleland Gukurahundi in which an estimated 20 000 of the Zimbabwe African People Union's leader's kinsmen and women were killed by forces loyal to Mugabe's ruling Zimbabwe African National Union (ZANU) in a post-liberation pogrom designed to rid Mugabe of likely military and political threats and send a strong message to any opponents. Such violence has, along with declining formal employment, dissuaded people to rise up against the regime, says Elton Mangoma, the economic planning minister in the unity ZANU-Movement for Democratic Change (MDC) government (in operation between 2009–13), since people were both scared of losing their lives or their jobs, or they 'could not resort to industrial action and strike from jobs they did not have'.[3]

Outside the city centre, across from the bus stop known as Ascot, the horse-racing track has been consumed by bush, the rails that once guided the punters' favourites slowly collapsing and disappearing in the undergrowth. The importance of maintaining the once-rich foliage of Bulawayo's Central Park and the illuminated fountain constructed on the city's 75th anniversary have similarly been overtaken by the primacy of personal survival. On the road to Harare, the scaffold over the road carrying the words 'Zimbabwe Independence 1980' was broken and bent in the middle.

This is not a romantic Rhodesiana retrospective. Bulawayo was built on imperial ambition, subterfuge and conquest, the region invaded by Rhodes' British South Africa Company in November 1893 in pursuit of one of his 'big ideas' and dreams of power,[4] schemes hatched from his chair on the stoep of the Kimberley Club, 1 100 kilometres away, a steel arrow set in the Club's front pathway reminding the magnate of his direction in life. Likewise, industry in Bulawayo, and elsewhere in the country, thrived on a combination of protectionism, sanctions and import substitution. Rhodesia's Unilateral Declaration of Independence of November 1965 and the translation of this isolationism into the post-1980 anti-apartheid struggle may have had vastly different political origins and intent, but the aim and effect was the same: protect and support local industry and interests.

What are the reasons behind Zimbabwe's industrial decline? And what does this say about the prospects and method for its recovery?

What causes economies to get stuck and collapse?

In the early 1960s, Supersonic exported car and portable radios from its factory in Bulawayo to the US. By the 1980s, Zimbabwe was reputed to be one of the most industrialised economies per capita in the world, the sector accounting for one-quarter of national production.

A half-century later and Zimbabwe is a commodity exporter, reliant on sending unrefined gold, tobacco, diamonds, platinum and people abroad to keep itself going.

The 'story' of Zimbabwe's decline is well known and documented: a bitter liberation war, which ended in 1980, was followed by a period of political reconciliation and economic progress, marred by the violent suppression of political opponents in the eastern Matabeleland region, the abovementioned Gukurahundi (meaning, in the local Shona dialect, 'the early rain which washes away the chaff before the spring rains'). In the mid-1990s, however, faced with the option of continuing with painful structural economic reforms or taking another route, the government chose the latter. And so began the seizure of land from 4 000 white commercial farmers and their redistribution, in part, to political lackeys of Mugabe's ZANU-PF (Patriotic Front), along with an attempt to force through a new constitution cementing the party's rule. The rejection of Mugabe's preferred constitution in a national referendum in February 2000 saw ZANU accelerate the land seizures and the economy tumble as agriculture outputs and exports fell, investor confidence eroded, and the politics hardened with the emergence, around the referendum, of a union-based opposition in the MDC.

Leopold Takawira, one of the early Zimbabwean nationalists, wrote before independence: 'Racial politics poison the mind and poison good taste, a racial politician only has to appeal to man at his worst.' That has been true, too, after independence.[5]

Analysis that suggests that Mugabe and ZANU are responsible for all of Zimbabwe's problems is incorrect, however, even though they have undoubtedly made them far worse with reckless management, not least of the budget. As hard as it may be to stomach, the country's overall trajectory has been downward since the mid-1980s in terms of the provision of basic services and infrastructure, and the availability of opportunities for widespread prosperity, as measured by a whole gamut of statistics and governance indicators. Instead of creating opportunities through production, wealth creation has increasingly depended on redistribution of existing assets through political connections and trading on the margins.

Although it does not place it above politics as the main cause of Zimbabwe's woes, a problem is that few Zimbabweans, white or black, have ever believed in market forces. White racial socialism in an isolated, import-substitution economy gave way in 1980 to black socialism. Neither could work; or work well enough to provide for a rapidly increasing population (up from 7.3 million in 1980 to 12.5 million by 2000) with high expectations. There is, moreover, little surprise that things changed so dramatically for the worse in the mid-1990s. Not only did the Cold War end and with it the ability to play one side off against the other and allow Zimbabwe to appear to be, at least, the moderately good regional guy in southern Africa, the then model non-racial state, but it coincided with the emergence of a democratic South Africa. Appearing to be the best regional non-racial example and being able to play the global race card for aid and sympathy suddenly lost its currency.

Playing on historical economic and racial resentments, Mugabe's brand of redistributive political economy has promised a short cut to prosperity for many, even though it delivered that only to a select few, and destroys the prospect of broad-based wealth creation. Liberation ideology has morphed into mythology; and ideals of democracy and prosperity into vulture capitalism.

This post-liberation trajectory is not unique; in other cases before and in South Africa after, economic management and delivery has failed to keep pace with expectations and, when the political crunch has come, and the ruling party is threatened by a viable opposition, it reaches for the standard cheap shots: identity politics (hitting the whites) and international capital. Given the hurts of the past and the hardships of the present, there is more than latent sympathy for this view in spite of the criminal and violent aspects, where a liberation brotherhood is apparently as firm in its anti-Western outlook as its neo-colonial conspiracies. Zimbabwe's dangers have spread beyond its borders, too, in less ideological ways. In spite of its quasi-failed state status, its intelligence services remain coherent as they have turned their hand to criminal activities.[6]

Fast forward a turbulent decade, and the MDC had become ZANU's government partner after a disputed election in March 2008 saw the creation, through South African mediation, of a 'unity' government installed in February 2009. Under MDC stewardship, the Zimbabwe dollar was scrapped amidst record hyper-inflation, and the economy stabilised.

By 2013, tobacco production, once the export mainstay, had recovered to about two-thirds of its previous levels, mainly through the efforts of smallholder farmers, driven in turn by Western companies, not the government, and the remaining 200 or so white commercial farmers. Quality, however, remained low, as did prices. Still, half of the required 2 million tonnes annually of maize, the staple, was dependent on imports. Gold production, which fell from 27 tonnes in 1999 to 3.5 tonnes in 2003, had also recovered on the back of higher prices and the lifting of price controls, operating in 2012 at about 50 per cent capacity. The MDC finance team had managed to increase monthly revenue income from $4 million in 2009 to $350 million in just two years, and diversify the sources from solely customs and excise to include VAT and direct taxes.

Without certainty of title, whether through lease or freehold ownership, the system of investment through borrowing against ownership that underpins commercial farming had fundamentally been negatively altered by ZANU's land redistribution project, if not entirely broken. The cost of the land-grabs cannot only be measured in terms of outputs. Not only could

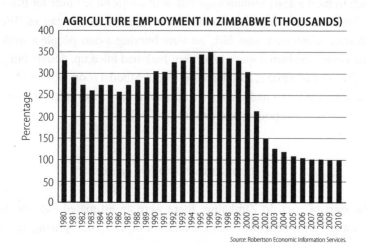

AGRICULTURE EMPLOYMENT IN ZIMBABWE (THOUSANDS)

Source: Robertson Economic Information Services.

ZANU then spread land among its cronies, but there was an additional bonus in driving several hundred thousand opposition-supporting farm workers off the land and away from the constituencies in which they were registered as voters.

Mugabe went back to creating a feudal system, where the elite were kept on-side through patronage and the remainder poverty-stricken and dependent on handouts in the rural areas. In this he has adroitly used a combination of land distribution, diamonds and threat and practice of indigenisation of foreign assets. This has had the impact of obliterating confidence on the part of those investors who could have made substantial commitments to the country, of the sort that would be interested less in externalising wealth than reinvesting their profits and building bigger businesses. To the contrary, a hostile investment climate, where government acts less as a facilitator than predator and parasite, has led to an investor retreat or, at best, attempts to make very quick fortunes leveraged by privileges and political influence. This kind of opportunistic conduct does not generate engineering firms or manufacturing enterprises, or success over generations.[7]

In so doing, this environment has kept Zimbabweans pitifully poor; poorer than they were, on average, at independence in 1980. Male life expectancy has declined since 1990 from 60 to 42 years. The infant mortality rate climbed sharply from 53 to 81 deaths per 1 000 live births over the same period.

Tendai Biti, the finance minister under the coalition ZANU-MDC government, said that on taking office there was less than a million US dollars in the coffers to meet salaries and all other foreign exchange requirements. By the time he left amidst the disputed election in July 2013, his team was bringing in enough to meet a $250-million wage bill 'with a little bit left over for this and that'. But there was a more human dimension to these circumstances. 'When I took over as minister,' says Biti, 'we were burying 4 000 people a week in Harare alone. The burial space in Warren Park had filled up, despite burying more than one to a grave, and the newer site in Mbudzi soon followed.'[8]

The financial crisis had spawned a humanitarian catastrophe. The reason behind this was bad policy; and behind that, politics.

Elections as war by other means

At the start of 2013, in Zimbabwe there were an estimated 850 000 full-time, formal jobs, little over half the amount of 2000, comprising 245 000

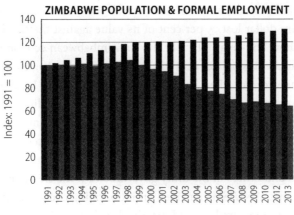

ZIMBABWE POPULATION & FORMAL EMPLOYMENT

Index: 1991 = 100

Source: Robertson Economic Information Services.

government employees (not including 70 000 ghost workers), 140 000 in industry (which had lost 80 000 since its 1998 peak), 100 000 in agriculture (250 000 down) and 220 000 in the services sector (where construction had declined from 90 000 in the early 1990s to 20 000). As a result, only about 12 per cent of the adult population had regular employment, 85 per cent of the population lived below the Poverty Datum Line and 57 per cent had incomes below the Food Datum Line.

Assuming a population growth rate of 2.5 per cent, Zimbabwe should double its population in little under 30 years. At the same time, to achieve a goal of middle-income status by 2040, Zimbabwe will have to lift its per capita income ten times from $300 in 2011 to $3 000, in effect doubling every 7.5 years. This assumes, in turn, a *real* economic growth rate constantly over 10 per cent per annum for three decades.

The advent of the unity government in 2009 offered some hope in meeting these ambitious targets. It stabilised a rapidly deteriorating economic environment that was epitomised by hyper-inflation, a collapse of basic services, human rights abuses and widespread institutionalised corruption. Until that point, the violence, farm seizures and pattern of enrichment revealed starkly the intent of the ruling elite to retain power at any cost, with party interests and power maintained at its core through the armed forces. Since the period for recovery from failure is usually at least as long as the period of decline, Zimbabwe clawed four years back in the twelve that had elapsed between the advent of the unity government in 2009 and August 1997, the moment when an embattled ZANU-PF government made a payment of $2 500 each and a monthly pension promise of $100 to some 60 000 war veterans, triggering the downward political and economic spiral. As a result, on 14 November 1997, the Zim dollar lost 75 per cent of its value against the US dollar on a single day, now known as 'Black Friday' in Zimbabwean economic history. The stock market lost 46 per cent the same day from its August levels.[9]

Biti is quite correct when he says that for Zimbabwe to break out of the cyclical crises that have characterised its economy and politics for the past 100 years, it has to be 'liberated from politics'. The 2009 unity government was a false dawn. The July 2013 election result, which resulted in a resounding official victory for Mugabe's ZANU-PF, quickly undid much of the good done by Biti and others in the unity government. If the elections were anything to go by, ZANUISM remained an intoxicating cocktail that appealed not only to an unscrupulous and greedy elite, but a misinformed and increasingly desperate populace inside and also outside of Zimbabwe's borders – perhaps more so since Zimbabweans have had to live the consequences of ZANUISM while others can only see the promises of El Dorado. Not for nothing has President Mugabe been roundly cheered at public events in South Africa since his radical policies took hold, whether this be the World Conference on Sustainable Development in 2002 or the 2013 memorial service for Nelson Mandela.

ZANU has consistently shown that elections are not the essence of democracy, but a means of political legitimacy. They have never intended to lose and give up power and privilege in the process. It has illustrated Samuel Huntington's thesis that what matters if a democracy survives is not the size of the problems it faces nor the manner in which it does so, but how its leaders respond to their inability to solve the problems facing their country.[10] Come the economic and political crisis of the mid-1990s, ZANU responded by unleashing force, fear and patronage. Elections became war by other means. Zimbabwe is not alone in this respect. As William Dobson has put it in *The Dictators*, there is a group of 'modern dictatorships' that seek to 'gain most from the global political system without jeopardising their grip on power'. Many of these countries look democratic. 'Their constitutions will often provide for a division of powers among the executive, the legislature and the judiciary.' But from Russia to Venezuela, Rwanda to Zimbabwe, they are 'modern authoritarians', with highly centralised power structures designed only to permit sufficient freedoms to stay in power.[11] Similarly, James A. Robinson and Daron Acemoğlu argue in their best-selling *Why Nations Fail*[12] that prosperity rests upon political foundations. Prosperity is generated by investment and innovation, and investors and innovators must have credible reasons to think that, if successful, they will not be plundered by the powerful. If the institutions of power (termed 'extractive institutions') serve only elite interests, then prosperity for the masses is unlikely. But inclusive institutions, they argue, are only likely to come about when it is in the elite's interest to cede power and privilege, without which they could risk revolutionary overthrow. Thus, change is less down to best practice than domestic politics and bottom-up and bottom-driven reforms.

Altering Zimbabwe's downward development trajectory will, therefore, involve more than improving governance or shoring up the productive assets of the economy. It will require a strategic commitment to the concept of wealth creation through investment, property rights and the rule of law: in sum, providing an enabling environment for business, including political stability. More especially, attracting investments in the export-oriented industrial sector will require generally being at least as competitive in Zimbabwe's investor offerings as others worldwide to attract those countries that have no special reason to want to be in a country with a turbulent political history, inefficient soft and faltering hard infrastructure, and which is landlocked.

A further, compounding reason for the decline is that Zimbabweans have voted with their feet. One Zimbabwean industrialist wistfully commented as he looked out of his window at a neighbouring secondary school: 'We have become an exporter of raw materials and raw talent.' Once so burnt, emigrants are unlikely to hurry home. The means have to be found, thus, to ensure the retention of existing and/or creation and attraction of fresh talent. Yet, as he added, 'the government wants us to eat politics, even though we are tired of it. But it's the only thing on its menu – power and politics.'[13]

This did not improve the chances for change at the polls. Dobson notes, 'What dictators and authoritarians fear most is their own people.'[14] Ensuring that the democratic process is not subverted depends on skills and organisation, 'the skills of a regime versus the skills of its opponents. The side,' says Dobson, 'that engages in the best preparation and demonstrates the most unity and discipline is likely to win out.'[15]

The primacy of politics over economic common sense is reflected in the strategies both that ZANU has used to hang onto power, and the assets that have kept them there. The use of violence, hate speech, control of media agencies, intimidation, extraordinary patronage and related elite cohesion, a setting of a strongly anti-Western rhetorical agenda and no small measure of political talent have all played their part. Undergirding this, as is intimated above, is the intent to hang onto power whatever the circumstances or cost. As the then ZANU-PF minister of justice, Patrick Chinamasa, vowed in a 2012 interview with the BBC, a Tsvangirai and MDC victory in the planned 2013 election would be 'unacceptable because of his links to the West'. Chinamasa then castigated Tsvangirai for 'campaigning and mobilising against the interests of Zimbabweans on many issues, whether talking about land, [or] seeking to reverse the gains of the liberation struggle'.[16] By publically supporting the opposition and ridiculing President Mugabe, the West, no doubt with an eye to its own political constituencies, has unwittingly cemented ZANU's core support, both within Zimbabwe's borders and certainly in the southern African region.

And Mugabe has enjoyed it both ways. While he has regularly thumbed his nose at the West's response (via sanctions and public criticism) over his (lack of) democracy, his people – and indirectly, his government – have relied on humanitarian assistance from Western partners. A quarter of Zimbabwe's population are regular recipients of emergency global food aid,[17] while Zimbabwe's share of aid as a percentage of GDP has regularly exceeded 12 per cent.[18] The Department for International Development of the United Kingdom, ZANU-PF's public arch-enemy, will spend more than £100 million in Zimbabwe in 2014 alone in providing essential services, including health care and sanitation, this money might have been better spent in even the short term, bolstering civil society and the political opposition to Mugabe. If not, rather than provide a soft landing for Mugabe through their humanitarian spending cushioning his governance failures, Western partners might be better off taking themselves out of the domestic debate and development scene altogether.

Backwards or ... forwards to Beit Bridge?

The battered yellow minibus taxi accelerated backwards in the direction of Beit Bridge, away from the roadblock near Esigodini (until 1982, Essexvale) on the road to Bulawayo.

He had little chance. Not only was the wild, wide-eyed driver up against the police's BMW, which had done a U-turn to go after him, but he had a full load of passengers and only one (slow) speed in reverse.

It is an apt metaphor for Zimbabwe's plight. Travelling through the Beit

Bridge border post is as intimidating as its reputation suggests, especially so for first-timers, uncertain of the various procedures and steps. The South African side was a nine-minute glide through, at least for a national passport holder. The Zimbabwean half more than made up for this efficiency by being chaotic and bureaucratic, with no fewer than ten different, stupefying steps for those travellers in cars.

First, queue to buy the vehicle exit pass. With no indication that the queue out of the door is not the right one for the pass, waiting in it presents a bad start. Second, get the passports stamped, this time in the aforesaid long queue. Third, obtain the temporary vehicle import permit, with the car's original registration document in hand (and bank clearance letter if they still own a chunk of it). Fourth, queue again to purchase the vehicle carbon tax, the rate being dependent on the engine capacity.

Fifth, if you have not obtained the Southern Africa Development Community third-party insurance before arriving in Zimbabwe, this step looms. Then sixth, obtain a police clearance certificate around the back of a small building set off across the road. At least there was a friendly man in there, unlike the officials behind the other counters who were displays in studied unhelpfulness.

Seventh, proceed to the customs queue for inspection, there being two lines, red and green, with apparently little distinction between the two processes, not least since they both depended on the energy level and ability of the single customs official, armed with a large stamp bouncing from car to truck, bakkie to bus. With no queue to stand in, we had to bid and plead for his attention, in the company of many Zimbabweans trying similar, though apparently more successful, techniques. If and when successful, he will attempt to calculate the value of the goods in your possession, whereupon you proceed back inside the border post building to pay the duty. Three queues later, yet more evidence of a lack of signage, we found the right one.

Ninth, once this is done, the customs official, by this stage knee- and elbow-deep in the possessions of three busloads of passengers, and busier than a one-armed pizza-maker, is cornered long enough to stamp the customs payment assessment on the vehicle pass. Then, tenth, you are on your way, with just two border checks to pass through where the blue pass is taken before heading up the bumpy road from Beit Bridge to Bulawayo.

The customs payment is the moment, roughly three hours into the process, where the folly of the system is most apparent. People pay duties on manufactured goods bought much more cheaply in South Africa because of the absence or inefficiencies of Zimbabwe's own industry.

The purpose of this is not strategic, even though some politicians might want it to be such: that is, to safeguard domestic jobs as part of a protectionist import substitution arrangement, which Rhodesia and then Zimbabwe has relied on for five decades to build and maintain the country's industry. And it is not as if the tariff payment is the mainstay of government revenue. In 2012, tariffs accounted for an estimated $380 million of the $3.5-billion Zimbabwean budget, the bulk being made up of 15 per cent VAT (over $1 billion) and Pay-As-You-Earn employee tax.

Rather, it is the centrepiece of a giant tariff evasion game. Zimbabwe imported an estimated $8.3 billion worth of goods in 2011, while exporting just $4.7 billion, the balance of payments difference being made up through goods that do not appear: smuggled items, mostly diamonds; perhaps as many as $1-billion worth of cigarettes for the South African market; and diaspora remittances. The bill for second-hand and new car imports into Zimbabwe amounted in 2011 to $1 billion annually, which alone should have brought in $600 million in taxes. Add to that the 640 000 cars, 370 000 trucks, 26 000 buses and 7.4 million travellers transiting yearly over Beit Bridge and customs' income of $380 million seems low, seemingly the product of tax evasion rather than application.[19]

The reason why the government does not have an efficient system at the border is the same reason for the twelve police roadblocks between Beit Bridge and Bulawayo, or the seventeen counted during the 370 kilometres between Bulawayo and Harare, or the thirteen over the 355-kilometre Harare-Chirundu route. The greater the number of steps and checks and lack of clarity over procedures, the greater the scope for bureaucratic 'manoeuvre'. It would not take a rocket scientist to devise a simple border-control system for Zimbabwean, South African and other cars and trucks, or for local and foreign foot passengers, with a single stop for each. But doing that would remove the need for touts and their backhanders to the officials.

Things happen for a reason, usually, but they also do not happen for a reason.

Beit Bridge was not alone. The Chirundu border post with Zambia has been refurbished using donor money into what is advertised as a model regional one-stop-border-shop.

The nearly 2-kilometre absolutely chaotic queue of trucks on the

Zimbabwe side on any given day suggests that things are not perfect yet, an instinct backed up by experience that involved a lot of 'shopping'.

First, the passports had to be stamped by the friendly, in this case, Zimbabwe official. Then it was around the corner to the 'Interpol Desk', two Zimbabwean officials reeking of the morning after the night before, in civvies, slouched behind a desk covered in newspapers and two A-4 textbooks for writing up crucial bits of information. When I asked what was needed to do or get, one pointed to the sign taped equally drunkenly to the wall that stipulated the need for original registration papers, passport and police clearance among other bits of paper. All fine, apart from the police clearance, the requirement for which was unclear and was a little difficult to acquire from South Africa on a Saturday afternoon on the border with Zambia. Told to 'wait at the car', which we did for 30 minutes, the two emerged shambolically into the sunlight in the company of their more helpful Zambian counterpart to check the engine and chassis number, telling us all the time that we would not get through and would have to 'go back to South Africa'. Then it was back inside – where the pair repeatedly asked, 'What are you going to do for us?' Playing dumb and making small talk, they grudgingly filled out our names in one of the textbooks (using our pen, which was not returned) and with much effort stamped two sundry pieces of paper. It was then over to the Zambian side of the room for a similar stamp, before heading out the building and over the road to acquire the $25 Zambian road insurance. Then crossing back to the main building, the $35 carbon tax was followed by the temporary customs import permit before heading to another building to pay the $10 'Siavonga District Council' charge and a $20 toll fee. By this time we had acquired two customs 'agents' replete with official badges, who approached us on behalf of 'the pair' for their payment and the costs of their apparent facilitation.

A several-stops-rather-expensive-shop as it turned out. Bureaucratic systems that efficiently benefit its functionaries: the stuff ultimately of state failure.

*

The corner of Tana and Linden roads in Johannesburg is the scene of the second Zimbabwean snapshot. There Emmanuel from Bulawayo makes biplanes out of plastic cardboard placards. An advertisement for houses or auctions now makes a great fuselage or wing, some in the distinctive swept-back style pioneered by Emmanuel and his apprentice, Edward, who is from Mozambique.

He started making the biplanes, with Coke tops for wheels and propeller spinners, 'a few months ago', learning the craft from a fellow Zimbabwean in Pretoria. Until then he was trying to scrape a living by 'pushing a trolley, looking for recycling. I was suffering,' he mumbles, looking down. The plastic plane business is going better. Now he sells 'two or three a day' for between R200 and R300.[20]

Emmanuel is one of an estimated three to four million Zimbabweans in South Africa, the presence of whom and the money they remit has, along with humanitarian food aid, been a safety valve preventing total social and political collapse back home. But there is a cost to getting out. 'Our country is rich,' he laments, 'and we all know why we are poor. It's that Mugabe. But we can't get rid of him.' Perhaps the most puzzling aspect about the relative decline of Africa during the 1970s and 1980s and dramatic decline of a number of its states, including Zimbabwe, is the lack of anger on the part of the populace to an environment where the elite prospered and the bulk fell behind. Such apathy, including those who have voted with their feet, suggests that countries get the leaders they deserve, however unpopular and politically incorrect that view may be.

PART 2

✳

INSTANCES OF INTERVENTION

*I wish sometimes you had a few bad motives,
you might understand a little more about human beings.*

— Graham Greene, *The Quiet American*

A little after 11 a.m. European time on 11 November 2012, as the autumn sun's rays sharpened across Kabul's mid-afternoon, the headquarters of the NATO-led International Security Assistance Force (ISAF) held its own Remembrance Day ceremony.

It was impossible to remain unmoved in the dramatic setting in front of the 'Yellow Building', the command headquarters of ISAF. 'Abide with Me' was followed by the 'Last Post', a moment's silence, then the 'Reveille', the bugler's clear notes reverberating around the concrete jungle of the military base.

Then a lone piper swirled 'Amazing Grace' and 'Highland Cathedral' as the wreaths were laid, nations once bitter enemies standing shoulder to shoulder among ISAF's 49 member-states – Germans and British, Austrians and Americans, Australians and Turks. To each, no doubt, the stirring notes that followed Holst's 'I Vow to Thee, My Country' meant different things, though on this day the message had a shared purpose.

The First World War, optimistically termed the 'war to end all wars', which was brought to an end by the armistice on 11 November 1918, cost the lives of 10 million military personnel. This puts the 3 000 ISAF casualties of the twenty-first-century Afghan mission into some context. No fewer than 19 240 British and Dominion soldiers died and more than 35 493 were wounded during the first day of the Battle of the Somme on 1 July 1916. The battle ultimately cost over a million military casualties on both sides in its four-and-a-half months, certainly the bloodiest in British military history.[1]

Public tolerance to military casualties has changed dramatically since the

First and Second World Wars. To take another example, of the 125 000 airmen who passed through the Royal Air Force's bomber command in the Second World War, 55 573 were killed and 8 617 aircraft lost. A further 8 403 flyers were wounded and 9 838 taken prisoner. That means that over 40 per cent of those who flew, died. If you take into account those who were training and never saw action, the figure rises to 65 per cent. The chances of death were far higher than these facing others, even the junior officers on the Western Front in 1916 who had a life expectancy of just six weeks,[2] or sailors – with the exception of the German U-boat fleets, where the casualty rate was, by the war's end, a staggering 27 000 of 40 000.[3] Or take the final onslaught on Berlin in 1945, which cost 78 291 lives and left 274 184 wounded on the Soviet side. The population of East Prussia was, in the process, reduced from 2.2 million in 1940 to 193 000 at the end of May 1945, along with perhaps as many as two million German women raped by the Soviet conquerors in a frenzy of atavistic revenge.[4]

At the same time, today large numbers of military forces can be 'asymmetrically' tied down by small numbers of irregular forces. Although this term – 'asymmetric warfare' – has been popularised in the light of events in Iraq and Afghanistan, its methods have been clear for centuries. What the Boers managed with success in the early 1900s was, for example, repeated by the irregular force of royalists and small number (little more than twenty) of mainly British and French mercenaries in Yemen between 1963 and 1967, tying down an Egyptian force of 60 000 and leaving 20 000 of them dead. Little wonder the Egyptians were desperate enough at various stages to employ the use of poison gas.[5]

Yet, military deaths from conflict have fallen steadily. During the 2000s, military deaths amounted to an annual average of 55 000; during the 1990s the figure was double this amount, and in the 1980s three times.[6] Paradoxically, civilians have increasingly borne the brunt of conflict. The ratio of civilian to military deaths in the First World War was approximately 2:3 or 40 per cent. The civilian to combatant fatality rate in the Second World War flipped to 3:2, with 70 million deaths overall. In the Korean War, the civilian-combatant death ratio was approximately 2:1, with as many as 20 per cent of the entire North Korean population wiped out. With over two million Vietnamese civilians and 1.1 million North Vietnamese military and Vietcong killed, this ratio (2:1) is about the same for the North in that conflict. In the Congo civil wars, which have raged since 1997, as many as five million civilians may have been killed, but only a handful of military.

Indeed, it is the military – both regular and irregular, the distinction mostly unclear – that has been responsible for these deaths.

Afghanistan is no different, with most estimates putting civilian deaths at around 2 000 annually since the fall of the Taliban in 2001.

Not that scale or origin should be a determinant of the value of life. But modern society appears less likely to risk life and limb to help those in need, perhaps because we are more cynical about politicians as a result of the slaughter of the First and Second World Wars, even though globalisation should have sensitised us more to the plight of others far away.

The world has moved on also in other, more positive ways. Alongside NATO's European members stood a disparate group, including soldiers from Malaysia and Singapore, Australia and New Zealand. ISAF's ranks have also included those from Bahrain, El Salvador, Tonga, Mongolia and the United Arab Emirates. Indeed, the costs of and commitment to such international missions, bilateral and multilateral, civilian and military, peace-keeping and peace-building, peacemaking and enforcement, UN-mandated or otherwise, have steadily increased during the past 70 years, and during the 2000s in particular.

Up to 25 April 2013, there have been 67 UN-mandated peacekeeping operations, with fifteen (plus the United Nations Assistance Mission in Afghanistan) operational on that date.[7] These involve 92 233 uniformed personnel (made up of 77 891 troops, 12 540 police and 1 802 military observers), and 16 791 civilian personnel plus 2 089 UN volunteers. The approved financial resources for the period 1 July 2012 to 30 June 2013 was approximately $7.33 billion, with outstanding contributions to peacekeeping (as of 31 March 2013) of $2.27 billion.[8]

UN peacekeeping missions are funded separately from the regular UN budget through so-called assessment accounts. This is done on the basis of the member-states' income levels (GDP per capita) and levels of external debt. Graded into four groups, A, B, C and D, most of the funding is met from groups A (the five permanent Security Council members) totalling 63.15 per cent and B (EU and OECD members) amounting to little over 34 per cent. In addition, individual missions are financed independently from member-states when a mandate is approved, based usually on a common scale and ability to pay. In essence, since most of the troop-contributing members are from Groups C and D, this entails essentially a 'North-South' financial transfer. The top five troop-contributing nations during the 2000s have consistently included Pakistan, Bangladesh, India, Nepal, Ghana and Nigeria, for example.

To these financial figures have to be added the cost of other bilateral or 'coalition of the willing' missions, such as in Iraq and Afghanistan, or through peace-building missions elsewhere, including those through the United States Africa Command, NATO and a variety of aid and other military training and assistance regimes. While direct spending is easier to calculate – for example the cost of the wars in Iraq and Afghanistan have been estimated to incur expenses of $1 million *per soldier per annum* – the longer-term costs are more difficult, more controversial and inevitably politicised. For example, a March 2013 study by Harvard University found that the cost to the US of the Iraq and Afghan wars could hit $6 trillion, an assessment based largely on related health care costs for veterans.[9]

The estimated total cost of UN peacekeeping operations from 1948 to 2007 is far less, some $47 billion.[10] By comparison, as of the start of 2012, an estimated $285 billion in military and other forms of assistance had been invested in Afghanistan since the 2001 invasion, including nearly $40 billion in official development assistance. The direct aid reconstruction costs for the US alone have been $61 billion in Iraq. The combined *direct* cost of the wars in Iraq and Afghanistan was estimated to have topped more than $1.2 trillion by 2013. In addition, the Libyan intervention has cost an estimated $2 billion, comprising a no-fly zone (at around $60 million per week) and the remainder in munitions and fuel.[11]

There is in this a danger of conflating conflict prevention (largely a low-profile, diplomatic initiative), peacemaking (bringing an end to hostilities by means of diplomacy and mediation), peacekeeping (traditionally, the observance of ceasefires and force separations following inter-state wars), and peace-building (providing a foundation for a lasting peace through re-integrating former combatants into civilian society, strengthening the rule of law, providing assistance for democratic development, promoting conflict resolution and reconciliation, and assisting with economic development).[12] And humanitarian assistance, including humanitarian intervention under the Responsibility to Protect premise (so-called R2P),[13] also figures in this spectrum of operations.

As noted in the Introduction, the direct costs of twenty-first-century global peacekeeping and peace-building ventures were estimated to be, by May 2013, more than $2 trillion.[14] It is not money alone, however, that makes a difference between the success and failure of such operations and the ability of collapsed states to recover. For example, while Germans received per capita $266 (in constant values) between 1946 and 1947, Haiti received $152 per person during 1995–96, Kosovars each $814 in 2000–01, Japan ($53 per person) received the same in 1946–47 as Afghans ($52 per person) in 2002–03. Another indicator is the correlation between the duration of the peacekeeping presence and successful nation-building.[15]

Many foreign conflicts have turned out badly for international forces in the twenty-first century. With the exception of Sierra Leone and to an extent Kosovo, British forces, for example, have had uphill experiences in Afghanistan, Iraq and Libya, with all turning out to be more difficult and worse than many had anticipated.[16] The answer to why this is the case lies in questions about legitimacy, resourcing, local ownership, local and regional politics, and also the role of identity within these territories – where the boundaries and frontiers set by nineteenth- and twentieth-century politics in some states, especially in Africa and the Middle East, do not match the identity and societal make-up and do not meet the governance needs of the twenty-first century.

*

Of course, peacemaking is not only about money and troops, but about deeds and diplomacy, too.

Peter Hain's comments on the failure of South Africa's policy towards Zimbabwe in 2001 raised the ire of Pretoria. South Africa's then foreign minister Nkosazana Dlamini-Zuma formally complained to Britain that comments by Hain, the UK's minister for Africa, were 'deeply offensive'.[17]

Hain spoke to several South African newspapers, radio and television programmes during a holiday in Cape Town. He said South Africa's policy of 'constructive engagement' on Zimbabwe had failed and that President Thabo Mbeki had neglected to recognise the implications of his strategy.

Hain was objectively correct. There is little doubt that South Africa's policy on Zimbabwe had failed – as evidenced by the hyperbolic defensiveness of the foreign minister – unless, of course, its aim was to keep President Robert Mugabe in power and subvert the democratic process in Zimbabwe. But while it may have made Hain, the South African-born former anti-apartheid activist, look good to his constituents and perhaps feel better about himself, his mouthing off was strategically flawed; that is, if his aim was to convince the South Africans (and even the Zimbabweans) of the error of their ways. If anything, it hardened the South African position – being told what to do by a former colonial power was always going to do that, especially if they were right. And it also gave the Zimbabweans useful ammunition to show that it was all Britain's fault, after all, why things had gone so badly wrong. As Mugabe was all too keen to point out shortly afterwards at the Johannesburg Earth Summit in September 2002: 'We have fought for our land, we have fought for our sovereignty, small as we are we have won our independence. So,' he added to loud applause, 'Blair, keep your England and let me keep my Zimbabwe.'

Hain's error of judgement is far from unique, however, and nor is Zimbabwe an isolated incidence in the failure of diplomacy and of attempts at external intervention. If the survival of regimes, for example in Zimbabwe, Eritrea, Syria, Saddam's Iraq, Burma and North Korea, have shown anything, it is that sanctions have proven to be largely ineffective, more a tool to demonstrate action to domestic constituencies than to change the view and practices in the target state. At the other end of the continuum, military intervention, while able to effect regime change as in Libya, Afghanistan and Iraq, can only provide a brief moment of stability in which locals can get on with making a fist of things themselves.

*

Countries, as has been noted, can change for the better. But what might internal and external actors improve on – both singly and in partnership – to create a positive, virtuous cycle in setting the conditions for ending state fragility, and ensuring conditions of stability and prosperity?

10

AFGHANISTAN

Cycles of War and Aid

✳

Helmand province is not usually a place associated with order.[1] Viewed from beneath the sweeping, snarling and veering Merlin helicopter, even the Dasht-e[2] in the largest of Afghanistan's 34 provinces looked, at the beginning of 2013, cultivated, carefully structured and commercial. As the insurgents and poppy growers have been squeezed out of the fertile area fed by the Nahr-e Bughra canal in the Green Zone over the course of more than a decade of war, they have moved into this desert.

It is not a perfect outcome, but a good metaphor for the problems of countering insurgencies, addressing state failure, and for Afghanistan itself. Never underestimate local systems of authority and control, and their adaptability. This was an important reminder as the imminent withdrawal of the bulk of the Western-led International Security Assistance Force (ISAF)[3] at the end of 2014 inevitably drew parallels with the Soviet retreat little more than two decades earlier.[4]

Many things have changed since the Taliban fell from power in 2001, and much of it for the better. Kabul was thriving, the result of economic growth averaging over 10 per cent annually for a decade. The capital had become, in a decade, a thriving bubble of traffic, new shops, wedding palaces and restaurants. It is estimated that the city, designed for fewer than 600 000 people, housed more than ten times this number by 2013 as homes literally climbed their way up the city's grey-brown surrounding hills in chaotic heaps.

Although capacity within the Afghan government could best be described as patchy, it had consistently been improving in the post-Taliban decade. The province of Bamyan is another positive example. In 2001 it was best known for the giant Buddha statues that the Taliban blew up in a pique of religious intolerance in March 2001. A decade later it had become a centrepiece of mining prospecting, a sector that offers as much as $1 trillion in rewards for the country – providing that long-term stability and rule of law can be assured for investors and the prospects do not fall prey to corruption and a flurry of speculators.

Even in the provinces with the worst fighting, such as in Helmand and Kandahar, the Taliban had been forced to change their tactics, just as they earlier shifted from direct attacks against foreign and Afghan government troops to more widespread use of improvised explosive devices (IEDs). The increasing prevalence of 'insider' attacks by Afghan security forces against international troops, known also as 'green-on-blue', indicated increased desperation in an attempt to drive a wedge between the government of the Islamic Republic of Afghanistan, its international supporters and, with the attacks on electoral institutions in the run-up to the April 2014 national poll, local democrats.

None of this progress is intended to excuse the mistakes made since 2001. For one, the international campaign has at times been too tactical, focusing on the military battle rather than the bigger political and developmental strategic picture, inside Afghanistan and its region. There has routinely been a lack of understanding or willingness to accept that Afghanistan, like other regional states, is different to the West. In Afghanistan, there is little internal unity and allegiance to the central state. Loyalties are instead based around tribal difference, historical allegiances and geographic remoteness, and mirror a lack of loyalty and faith in institutions.

The military battle itself has re-learnt the lessons gained bitterly by others. On the contrary, Vietnam,[5] scarcely a generation earlier, teaches that such wars are not won by firepower alone, but willpower, where the battles are seldom pitched but mostly episodic. These are usually at a time and place of the insurgents' choosing, where the guerrilla is elusive and cannot easily be separated from friend, where the counter-insurgent had the firepower to punish the enemy if only they might be found, and where the guerrilla sometimes employs modern technology and sometimes improvises. The same weapons – IEDs, mines, recycled bombs, booby traps, AK-47s and rocket-propelled grenades – have remained popular, along with the kidnapping, assassination and other 'weapons' of terror. The extent of the cruelty and determination of the insurgent keenly influences whether they prevail or not. In Vietnam the enemy sought safety behind international borders in Laos and Cambodia; in Afghanistan substitute Pakistan, in post-Saddam

Iraq and Iran. Thus, there is always a pressure for enlarging these wars, covertly or otherwise.

These lessons, as will be seen, mirror the experience of outsiders in Afghanistan.

The international approach has also been overly experimental. More than $40 billion in development assistance has been spent, yet Kabul's clogged roads had, by 2013, still not been fully renovated, nor indeed had the only national ring road, Highway 1. In part, this is because of a reliance on aid rather than private sector growth for development.

The international community can also stand accused of being too ambitious, of attempting nation-building when the appetite for international casualties and the duration of the commitment preferred was geared to the original post-9/11 counter-terrorism mission. There is, however, little advantage in these arguments, perhaps except in deciding whether and how to go about future peace-building missions.

Cycles of war and aid

Before 2001, the history of international involvement in Afghanistan over the last two centuries has been one of invasion, calamity, co-option, limited local learning, assassination and, ultimately, exit. As one Afghan detainee in Helmand observed, 'British forces are a tribe from the north who come down and fight the Afghans about every 100 years.'[6]

Over this time Afghans have learnt to play external protagonists off against each other – notably right after both the First and Second World Wars – in an attempt then to attract aid for infrastructure and social modernisation. In the 1950s, the two superpowers competed to match each other's investments in aid; the Soviets largely in the north, the Americans to the south. Periods of calm and relative prosperity, however, remained hostage to regional relations, not least in the 1960s, when the 'Pashtunistan' issue – the notion of an independent ethnic state straddling the 1893 Durand Line – flared up, to the cost of ties with Pakistan.

A hardening of domestic politics followed and the advent of a Soviet-backed regime in 1978, inaugurating contradictory impulses of reform (towards universal literacy and education of both sexes, the ending of usury and modernising of marriage customs) and ideology (such as with the redistribution of land) leading to 'immediate chaos' in the agriculture sector, for example, with the loss of one-third of cultivated land, and a welling up of widespread resentment.

By the time Mohammed Najibullah, the erstwhile Soviet-backed president, fell in March 1992, the economy was ruined and the country deeply factionalised between feuding mujahidin commanders: the Pashtun Gulbiddin Hekmatyar, the Uzbek Abdul Rachid Dostum, and Ahmed Shah Massoud and Burhanuddin Rabbani, both Tajiks. This tribal split led to a wider civil war and greater social and economic dislocation. As one measure, refugee flows to Pakistan and Iran, already high at 1.7 million and 400 000 respectively in 1991, increased rapidly over the next three years to 3.5 million and 1.5 million. Pakistan, fearing the consequences of regional conflagration and already at loggerheads with its traditional rival India over Kashmir, began to support a new faction known as the Taliban – literally, the 'students'. Led by a one-eyed village cleric in Mullah Mohammed Omar, and backed by Pakistan's Inter-Service Intelligence agency, the Taliban took Kandahar in November 1994, Herat in September 1995 and Kabul (from Massoud) in September 1996.

This occurred against the backdrop, it should be stressed, of a broken economy and extreme lawlessness, a country heavily dependent on a trickle of humanitarian relief. Yet the Taliban's version of stability through social puritanism – evident in the form of discrimination against women, the decrees against shaving and privations forbidding entertainment – only cemented Afghanistan's feudal and trading economic character. After 2002 and the fall of the Taliban, despite the promotion of representative democracy and universal suffrage, Afghanistan has had to deal with the inheritance of a political economy where the state's role was to extract rents and where the traditional sources of production and trade had, at best, been badly damaged.[7]

Afghanistan's cycle of war over centuries, and political and economic collapse, has thus created what Barnett Rubin has described as a 'pattern of regional economic activity and associated social and political networks that compete with and undermine legal economies and states'.[8] Under President Hamid Karzai's rule from the fall of the Taliban in December 2001 until April 2014,[9] the drivers behind this cycle – conflict, corruption,[10] the absence of rule of law, poor governance and politically connected elites – have appeared undiminished. It has been a government routinely described as 'corrupt' and 'inept'; one that 'has failed to build a stable and viable country despite the loss of thousands of lives and billions of dollars of assistance'.[11]

The state's dependence on international aid money has grown steadily over the past decade, culminating in aid amounting to almost half of GDP by the end of the 2000s. The distributive networks have linked mujahidin connections with business interests, localising predation through power centres and expedited through a combination of patronage, opaque governance, a lack of foreign political will and the continued gush of foreign financing.

Such mistakes are not an Afghan preserve. Many have been made by the international community, though few, including civilians and the military, are willing to admit them. In particular, too little attention has been lavished on areas of comparative stability and success in Afghanistan's north and west, for example, while the instability in the restive south and east has benefited greatly from extraordinary aid flows and foreign military attention. It has, in one sense, paid them to be troublesome. International assistance, military and civilian, has been tactical, not strategic.

As is intimated above, this is nothing new. The Afghan economy has long been reliant on rent-based incomes, from aid and from natural resources. During the 1950s, Rubin reminds us,[12] 'Urban society depended on state redistribution. After the introduction of a state-led development model ... the private sector was largely connected to trade, and the government controlled most urban employment.' It is a system described succinctly by one veteran Kabul politician as 'predatory and fragmented', one that is, however, said to be different to the immediate post-Soviet era in that 'it is more corrupt and there is little of the state capacity there was then.'[13]

During the Soviet occupation new trends emerged, including the increasing dependence on aid for maintaining allegiances, for subsistence (especially given the levels of rural destruction) and through redistribution in the cities that were swelled by displacement. At this time, 'the main economic actors were the commanders, a group mostly drawn from new elites that benefited from US, Pakistani and Saudi policies of supporting only Islamist parties rather than the nationalist former rulers'. Come the 1989 Soviet withdrawal, 'commanders pursued economic strategies to increase their power, wealth and autonomy, establishing bazaars and providing local security to traders in return for tribute'.

During the early 1990s, the fall in aid from traditional donors and a drop in income from natural resources elevated the importance of humanitarian agencies for food aid, while the government focused on printing money as its principal source, both of expenditure and income.

Come the Taliban

The advent of the Taliban saw, as Rubin puts it, a 'transition from localized predatory *warlordism* to weak *rentier* state power based on a criminalized open economy'. Traders required and the government profited from the suppression of predation. It is estimated that the Taliban derived at least $75 million in 1997 from taxing Afghanistan-Pakistan transit trade. Rubin notes that the rest of such an 'economy is hardly productive enough to recover the cost of governing it. Such a political economy would leave the power holders as accountable to most Afghan people as they were under previous regimes. Most of the population would be left to fend for themselves, perhaps in conditions of greater security, but without a development agenda, public services, or reforms, notably in the status of women.'[14]

Karzai was a compromise leadership candidate in December 2001, but was acceptable precisely because it was believed he had limited power and would not challenge the warlords. To make government work, he had to make deals, and soon he became, in the Australian counter-insurgency specialist (and US government adviser) David Kilcullen's words, the 'guy directing the traffic'.[15]

It should not be surprising that aid has not developed Afghanistan, not least given the history, the contemporary experience and that this method is not the way in which the donors themselves developed. The folly of this approach has been amplified by the general antipathy of many aid exponents towards the private sector, a lack of coordination between donors, otherwise aid 'fratricide', and it has been complicated by a desire for stabilisation over development, encouraging not only short-term spending to provide 'coin effect', countering the insurgent threat, but not upsetting the political apple cart by pursuing high-profile governance and corruption cases. As David Loyn comments in the UK's International Development Committee report of September 2012: 'Oversight mechanisms have been overwhelmed, while insecurity makes it impossible for many donors to visit the projects that they fund. Some have even institutionalized the absence of oversight. Massive inflows of aid also mean pressure to spend quickly, which has often led to parallel systems lacking in accountability, and non-participatory or discretionary decision-making.'[16]

But there is little gainsaying such policy lapses and ahistorical oversights. Much of this was acknowledged in the governance for aid pact the Afghan government and the donors entered into in Tokyo in July 2012. And there

have been novel policy responses by the aid community, focusing on ena-
blers for growth, governance and development, such as in the promising
mining sector, rather than simply throwing good money after bad.

More than anything, the difficulties in reforming Afghanistan into a private sector driven, open economy, reflects the character of its own society.

Here, levels of prosperity depend on political foundations, where power
is not only centralised but inclusive in its outlook, and in which investors
can be assured that their successes will not be plundered. It is only in the
interests of the elite to cede power to inclusive institutions if confronted by
something worse, such as the prospect of revolution. In other words, the
foundations of prosperity are political struggle against privilege. If, as noted
in the previous section, the institutions of power enable the elite to serve its
own interests – what is termed 'extractive institutions' – these interests will
collide with those of the masses. This is a choice because 'those who have
power make choices that create poverty. They get it wrong not by mistake or
ignorance but on purpose.' As Daron Acemoğlu and James Robinson argue,
for those intent on hanging onto power and privilege, reforms are preferably
piecemeal, since it 'makes sense to give in to a small demand rather than
create a major showdown'.[17]

For Afghanistan's level of corruption is not unusual by regional standards.
While it may be more sophisticated in China, Pakistan or India, corruption
abounds in these prominent regional actors, not by the standards of international NGOs, but by the admission of local actors. For example, Vinod
Rai, comptroller and auditor general of India, said at the World Economic
Forum on India on 7 November 2012 that for too long, politicians have believed they were entitled to govern without accountability. The following day,
President Hu Jintao kicked off the Eighteenth Communist Party congress,
which was to facilitate a power transfer from himself to Xi Jinping with a
warning on corruption, saying that a failure to tackle the issue 'could prove
fatal to the party'. Earlier, the Chinese government had blocked websites of
the *New York Times*, which had carried a story of alleging that Premier Wen
Jiabao's relatives had accumulated 'assets worth at least $2.7 billion'.[18] Even if
the methods across the region are increasingly sophisticated – speculative
land deals with insider knowledge of government plans, or companies held
by politicians in which businesses seeking contracts buy share value at over-
inflated prices – it is still corruption, at least by Western standards.

If Afghanistan was to create a political economy largely free from corruption it would be the regional exception. But as Kautilya reminds in

Arthashastra (The Science of Wealth), India's classic text from 300 BC, 'Just as it is impossible to know when a swimming fish is drinking water, so it is impossible to find out when a government servant is stealing money.'[19] As elsewhere, the only likely means to reduce corruption is through the political activism of a middle class that does not owe its wealth to political favours and to whom this type of corrupt behaviour is not only a personal affront, but a cost to their pockets.

*

As the date of the handover of military operations to local security forces approached at the end of 2014, tensions and concerns were running high in Afghanistan. As one measure, property prices in Kabul were down, political rhetoric up, and security remained problematic, especially in the restive south. Little wonder that spectre of the Soviet withdrawal in 1989, when the government collapsed three years later, abounded.

Whatever the challenges, as noted above, it was a different place at the time of the removal from power of the Taliban in 2001.

First, security was much improved. Al-Qaeda and its state sponsor, the Taliban, were no longer the countrywide threat they were once.

This has enabled, second, an extraordinary economic recovery, especially in Kabul. In part, this has been on the back of a gush of aid expenditure. It has, however, been propelled by other drivers, increasingly beyond government control, including widespread mobile phone and Internet usage. Some 18 million cellular SIM cards were in circulation by 2013, and about two million citizens browsed the Internet, while nearly half of the 35 million population had access to television.

Third, Afghanistan is a democratic country. However imperfect this process may be judged by Western standards, under the Karzai regime it has been much improved from the days of the Taliban or the Islamist movement's mujahidin midwife.

Much can be improved on, of course, not least the country's overall political economy, where those in government with influence and access seek to turn them into personal financial profit. Corruption, organised crime and warlords, not the private sector, have been emblematic of the local business environment. This is partly down to the country's own history, and partly it is a reflection of regional norms and relationships.

Crouching tiger, hidden dragon, frère ennemi?

As the attention of ISAF and, to some degree, the international community dwindles, the light will shine increasingly on Pakistan and the wider regional relationships, relationships that seem more based on historical primordialism than rationalism. As a landlocked country, an improved relationship with Pakistan has to be a feature of Afghanistan's critical future path.

Peace in Afghanistan depends on stability in neighbouring Pakistan, and that country's relationship with India; while international investment in Afghanistan's security has been a strategic move to ensure that it does not tip the balance between insurrection and chaos in neighbouring Pakistan. Thus, the Afghan campaign has not only, or even primarily, been about stabilising that war-torn central Asian state, no matter how noble that task. Afghanistan has been mostly about Pakistan. As the vogue shorthand suggests, 'AfPak' have become inseparable, but not in the way that most presume. In warning against short-term thinking, Robert Gates, then US secretary of defence, in June 2011, highlighted the need to think carefully about the 'costs of failure'.[20] The relative cost of stability, including the expense of maintaining a large Afghan army and police force, may prove to be a small investment in long-term stability, and pale against the cost in terms both of blood and treasure of maintaining a foreign force in Afghanistan.

And yet Pakistan's own challenges require a state-building project of their own. The relationship with Afghanistan has been complicated by the latter's refusal to recognise the border that separates them and bisects the Pashtun; yet three million Afghans and 20 million Afghan relatives live inside Pakistan. A regional solution also requires finding a formula, in Pakistan as in Afghanistan, for two societies – one a centralised, Western-styled democracy, the other localised and tribally based – to coexist, all the while ensuring sufficient economic growth to not only meet basic needs but assuage expectations.

For many years Pakistan has supported the insurgency, providing money, weapons or simply giving it space to operate,[21] in spite of the regional economic impact of such measured activity. While the central government might intimate that it maintains a hard line against the Taliban, as one senior former Indian diplomat has expressed: the military machine of Pakistan has been very good at providing support to the Taliban.[22] The need for regional influence and, above all, for strategic depth has been what has driven Pakistan's policies towards Afghanistan.

India's interests in Afghanistan, which reflect Pakistan's insecurity, have

grown during this century. Numerous road, pipeline and infrastructure programmes, and the $11-billion proposed investment at the Hajigak mine, are
testament to mutual self-interest and the strength of the relationship. This is
nothing new, however. India was one of the few alongside the Soviet Union, who
overtly supported the Soviet-sponsored Democratic Republic of Afghanistan
(DRA) in the 1980s and perhaps more pertinently became the first country, in
2011, to sign a strategic partnership agreement with Afghanistan since 1979.
India's opposition to the Taliban was far preceded by its alignment with the
country's more moderate regimes. So while some might say that India is '...
simply helping its neighbour's neighbour ...', a more realpolitik view might
suggest that it is more a case of your enemy's enemy being your friend. Among
all the investment prospects and attempts at détente, Afghanistan remains a
football between Pakistan and India in a game that is far from over.

Many have viewed America as being the only regional influence with any
ability to exert pressure on Pakistan, but there has been little evidence of
this – with declining aid, continued violent border exchanges and of course
providing refuge, perhaps unwittingly, to Osama Bin Laden in Abbottabad.
The bilateral relationship has been difficult, when many of their interests are
opposed – it has been akin to a broken marriage where the alimony is just
about enabling some degree of civility. This has been complicated by the
presence of another suitor on the scene, however, and while America may be
a significant supplier of arms to Pakistan, it has been surpassed by one other
country – China.[23] China also supplies significant amounts of aid to Pakistan
while developing commercial and political relations with Afghanistan and
the Karzai regime. As India had plans at Hajigak, China had pledged a
$4-billion investment at the $3-billion Aynak copper mine.[24] Instability in
Afghanistan has not been in China's long-term interest.

Thus, Pakistan's relations with India have been central to understanding
Islamabad's behaviour, and 'has both encouraged and limited Pakistani
help to the US in Afghanistan'. Fear of a Western tilt towards India more
than a fear of a Pakistani Taliban victory guides Islamabad's regional policy. Mass support for the Islamist rebellion against the Pakistani state has
been confined to the Pashtun areas, under 15 per cent of the overall population (and little over 40 per cent in Afghanistan). Hence, as Anatol Lieven
has put it, '[T]he Pakistani establishment's approach to Afghanistan has
long been driven by a mixture of fear and ambition. The fear is ... of
Afghanistan ... becoming an Indian client state, leading to India's encir-
clement of Pakistan ... In recent years, belief in the need for a relationship

with the Taliban has been strengthened by the growing conviction that the West is going to fail in Afghanistan ...'²⁵

The wrong analysis

The failings of the international effort in Afghanistan have their roots often in wishful thinking, superficial analysis and unrealistic objectives. While removing the Taliban may have been an attainable objective, at least in parts of Afghanistan, and certainly not an enduring one for all Afghans, nation-building was probably beyond the international community, in Afghanistan as elsewhere, at least as it was defined: liberal democracy, economic order, education for women, no poppies, no corruption.

Ironically, the latter has been fuelled with billions of dollars of misdirected aid, much of which corrupted not only Afghans but Westerners who were there to 'help'. Now, as a result, the story is being built that the intervention would have succeeded had it not been for the ungrateful, incompetent and corrupt Afghans themselves. As noted in the Introduction, that is an unfair evasion of the international community's own responsibilities and behaviour.

This failure or, at best, imperfect outcome, is partly due to a lack of understanding or willingness to accept that Afghanistan, like Pakistan or even India, is different to the West. In Afghanistan, there is little internal unity and allegiance to the state. This is not only based on tribal differences and geographic remoteness, but a lack of loyalty and faith in institutions reflecting local power relationships. As one Pakistani says about his own country, 'We Pakistanis can't unite behind a revolution because we can't unite behind anything.'²⁶

Unsurprisingly, these economies have not made the sort of breakthrough as has China, not least because in the case of Pakistan and Afghanistan not only does a large percentage of the economy live in poverty but women are mostly excluded from formal economic participation.

The language and strength of kinship, the importance of familial hierarchy and the weakness of state institutions, this a tautological result of a tiny tax base, provides social stability through the dominance of feudal elites and, as Lieven notes, 'urban bosses'. The power of these ties, bound throughout south Asia through honour, can be seen in the violence of retribution on matters of public prestige and shame. Or as one US diplomat has put it, 'Long before ISAF arrived on the scene, Helmand was a rough, basic place, where disputes were settled by violence.'

This is not necessarily a recognition of social and political weakness, but also of power. These ties have perpetuated in spite of attempts to change them through ideological or theological revolution, or through social and political reform. Local clans and local patronage continuously frustrate the attempts of modernists to build a united and unitary state.

Perhaps one answer to Afghanistan is to promote regional and ethnic diversity and difference, not unity? It is difficult for the Afghans to accept the notion of a single centralised authority from Kabul when the intervening powers themselves have challenges in managing their own diversity – from Scotland to Slovakia. Moreover, the idea, no matter how much of an illusion this may be, of a strong, consolidated Afghan state would do little to reassure Pakistan, among others.

Summarising the transitions

There are several contemporary transitional challenges faced in Afghanistan. *The Economist* identified three in 2012: the military transition from reliance on ISAF to control by the Afghans; politics in the form of elections in early 2014; and a general weaning off aid and the money made from contracting to ISAF.[27]

Within the economic domain, however, there are other shifts. There is a need to migrate economic activity from the informal untaxed sector (estimated in 2012 at 85 per cent of activity) to the formal and, in so doing, increase the tax net from around 10 per cent of GDP, half of where it needs to be. This requires more than just registering businesses, however, but making it easier to do business.

Take the example of Abdul Arzu,[28] a Kabul-based carpet manufacturer and wholesaler. His business employs 1 200 people, yet faces a daily challenge in accessing export markets due to the overbearing cost of transport and suffocating government bureaucracy. Moreover, he does not want to seek government assistance lest he come to the notice of tax authorities, further reducing his competitiveness. This explains why the official figure for carpet sales in 2012 was $150 million; and the unofficial figure was at least $500 million, since most trade moves over the border illegally to be 'exported' from Pakistan. Yet, expansion in this sector has been very important to the economy, with carpet weavers operating in no fewer than twenty provinces, employing at least three million people.

In the west of the country, around Herat, the costs of exporting remain high – \$6 500 per container of carpets to the US via Dubai – but it is the value of the carpets that needs to be increased through getting the weavers to make what the market prefers. Herat carpets obtain just \$30 per square metre, less than one-third of what Mazar weavers using more modern designs and colours receive.

Little wonder then that the economy struggles to export more than it imports. According to official government statistics, the value of its (official, *sans* narcotics) exports fell from \$403 million in 2009/10 to \$375 million two years later, while imports were nearly twenty times this figure.[29] This makes the value of the local Afghani currency especially vulnerable to a decline in foreign aid flows.

A second economic 'transition' resides in the gradual move from centralised financial control by Kabul and its militaries to decentralised provincial and local-level funding authorities, which would enable support of projects based on local needs. And the third is in the need to migrate the country from a system based on government redistribution and loyalty to independent private sector driven activity.

There are inevitably dangers in overlooking the considerable progress made and in overstating the formidable challenges in Afghanistan. But history illustrates the folly of disregarding them, too, in the eagerness to withdraw.

Déjà vu all over again?

In particular, the parallels from the Soviet experience, pre- and post-withdrawal, illustrate the difficulty, first, in modernising Afghanistan and, second, in managing retreat. As Sir Rodric Braithwaite reminds us, 'The intentions of the Soviet government [in 1979] were modest: they aimed to secure the main towns and the roads, stabilise the government, train up the Afghan army and police, and withdraw within six months or a year. Instead they found themselves in a bloody war from which it took them nine years and fifty-two days to extricate themselves.'[30] There are a whole host of reasons, as will be seen, as to why this occurred, which are important to identify in order to avoid repeating.

These include a lack of national coherence and discipline among Afghan partners in a deeply divided society, one ruled by 'fierce pride, martial valour, honour and hospitality, mediated by the institution of the blood feud',[31] where there is a related lack of interest in building up a political and economic system responsive to long-term *national* needs and desires. Into this environment aid was inserted, given for ideological reasons rather than on merit, and which was concerned with buying off the population rather than developing the economy by removing constraints to business. To cap it all, there existed a region ill-disposed to helping the nation-building process. All of this was compounded by the ruinous social, political and developmental effects of a decade of war. And as Braithwaite notes presciently about the Soviets, 'Their decisions were bedevilled by ignorance, ideological prejudice, muddled thinking, inadequate intelligence, divided counsel, and the sheer pressure of events.' Sound familiar?

The parallels with the collapse of the Najibullah government, after the Soviet Union was pushed out, have led to promises that this time will be different. Hence, the mutual commitments – governance by the Afghans and continued aid and security backstopping by the international community – made in Tokyo in July 2012. Yet it is not impossible to envisage a situation where a lack of good governance by Afghanistan, coupled with donor fatigue (and a shortage of funds in the face of domestic demands), results in a radical reduction in aid flows, similar to the situation that led to Najibullah's 1992 fall. Aid may not be an especially helpful tool for development, but it does grease the wheels of shorter-term economic prosperity and thus political stability.

Of course, the collapse and the failure of the Soviet incursion in Afghanistan was not solely down to fluctuating aid levels, though this undoubtedly hastened the government's demise. Moreover, the crude caricature of the failure of the Soviet Afghan strategy as one that was cack-handed and military-centric overlooks both the levels of commitment and relative sophistication and diversity inherent in the Russian-led approach.

Working with their Afghan allies, the Soviets developed 'a military strategy focused on controlling cities, securing major roads, and rapidly training and equipping Afghan forces'. They also 'used a transition plan that combined timelines and the phased Afghanisation of the war', along with national economic reform, dialogue and reconciliation processes, while mounting an aggressive international diplomatic campaign to expedite a ceasefire and the withdrawal. Yet, as noted, in 1992, just four months after Soviet aid stopped, the Afghan government collapsed and the mujahidin took over.[32]

Each year from when Mikhail Gorbachev took over in March 1985, until their eventual withdrawal in 1989, the Soviets were both more flexible and more strident in developing a 'comprehensive' approach.

That year the new Soviet premier conducted his own surge, increasing the strength of the 40th Army (the Soviet invading force on 25 December 1979) by 26 000 soldiers to 108 000, securing population centres and lines of communication and conducting aggressive military operations. In 1986, 1 868 Soviet soldiers were killed with 1 552 wounded, as well as 3 690 Afghans killed and 8 898 wounded. At the same time, the Soviets increased training and equipping of the Afghan military as it expanded to 252 900 troops, and increased its aid to the then DRA by 40 per cent to over $600 million.

Although this combination of aid, local forces and Soviet military strength came close to defeating the mujahidin, it was hampered by the poor performance of the Afghan army and their political masters. Soviet advisers criticised their Afghan allies for their 'poor shooting skills and discipline, weak command and control, and failure to care for equipment'. Frustrated, Gorbachev advised President Babrak Karmal to 'widen your social base. Pursue a dialogue with the tribes. Try to get support of the clergy. Give up on the leftist bent in economics. Learn to organize support of the private sector.'[33]

By May 1986, Karmal was gone, replaced by Najibullah, the head of the feared KhAD secret police. At the same time, the Soviets increased efforts to Afghanise the war, handing over much of the responsibility for combat operations to the DRA, while maintaining combat support through artillery, aviation and engineers, with 1 800 Soviet advisers divided among Afghan army units. Aid was increased by 12 per cent during 1985. The DRA also began payments to militias in exchange for ceasefires, with over 65 000 joining the payroll that year. Yet the human cost of the war remained consistent: 1 333 Soviet soldiers were killed in action and 1 552 wounded, while DRA losses increased significantly to 5 772 killed and 11 876 wounded. As Braithwaite notes succinctly of that era in *Afghantsy*, 'After a successful operation they would return to their bases and hand responsibility to their Afghan allies … In the end the Russians had good tactics but no workable strategy. They could win their fights, but they could not convincingly win the war. Their best efforts, military and political, went for nothing. They eventually had no choice but to disentangle themselves as best they could.'[34]

By 1987 Gorbachev shifted his focus again to pursuing an international diplomatic resolution, while pressuring for DRA political reform alongside continuing Soviet military and economic support. Early that year, Najibullah announced the National Reconciliation Policy, a comprehensive plan encompassing a national ceasefire, a power-sharing agreement with the opposition, amnesty for political prisoners, and an offer to local mujahidin commanders of autonomous control and payments in exchange for ceasefires. With such increased outgoings, coupled with a decline in natural gas exports, the Soviet Union increased its aid by a further 83 per cent to $1.2 billion.

Afghan forces continued to grow to over 323 000 soldiers, supported by 130 000 militias. The Afghan military 'demonstrated they could defeat the mujahidin in a conventional battle'. Losses for the Soviet 40th Army that year declined to 1 215 killed and 1 004 wounded, while they increased for the DRA to 6 229 killed and 12 786 wounded. Regardless, government forces controlled only an estimated 35 per cent of Afghanistan's districts.[35]

Between 1988 until the withdrawal of Soviet combat troops in February 1989, Gorbachev conducted a 'skilful orchestration of the diplomatic, military, and economic instruments [allowing] the USSR to depart on its terms', combining 'unilateral declarations, negotiations, a dramatic increase in military and economic aid, and a two-phased withdrawal to navigate the Soviet Union out of the "graveyard of empires"'. As Gorbachev noted at a 1987 Politburo meeting, 'It is better to pay with money than with the lives of our people.'[36]

In all, 21 000 Soviet civilian specialists served in Afghanistan to develop infrastructure and stimulate the economy. These included teachers (the Soviets had trained over 70 000 labourers, engineers and technicians by 1980 alone) and many engineers, among a variety of specialists. Also included was even a cadre from the Youth Communist League of the Soviet Union, or Komsomol, resembling the 2011 AfPak Hands[37] programme aimed at creating a cadre of American regional specialists, who were sent to Afghanistan to work with peers after a 'six-week crash course in the history, culture, traditions, and languages of Afghanistan.'[38]

Within Afghanistan, Najibullah continued to use the National Reconciliation Policy but reoriented it towards regime survival and an Islamic foundation. In the three months of Phase I (15 May – 15 August 1988), the Soviets withdrew over 50 000 troops while turning over the garrisons in Jalalabad, Ghazni, Gardez, Lashkar Gar, Kandahar and Konduz to the DRA. Following the securing of a Kabul air bridge, Phase Two (December 1988 – 5 February 1989), turned over garrisons in Kabul, Herat, Parwan, Samangan, Balkh and Baghlan provinces, while Operation Typhoon, an air and ground offensive into the Panjshir Valley, kept the mujahidin at bay. During this withdrawal phase, Soviet losses included 812 killed and 685 wounded while the DRA's losses escalated to 26 260 killed and 38 547 wounded. The Soviet Union, however, left behind 200 military and KGB advisers in Kabul to support the by then 329 000-strong DRA army – a lack of loyalty and faith in institutions that compares to the 350 000-strong Afghan National Security Forces *circa* 2012.

Weakened by the loss of Soviet air power (despite his own airforce comprising 7 000 personnel flying 240 attack aircraft, including MiG-21s, Su-7s and MiG-17s; 150 helicopters; and 40 transporters),[39] Najibullah increased ceasefire payments, adding another 30 000 militia to his payroll. Soviet aid again increased to $2.6 billion in 1989, including the transfer of fuel, military equipment and ammunition, while commencing weekly 600 truck supply convoys, though the withdrawal of technical experts and the capping of the oil and gas wells was a significant economic blow.

With the Russian exit, Najibullah 'took much more courageous steps [with the National Reconciliation Policy] in terms of opening up the government and society, establishing links with tribal leaders, and shedding its communist image – all of which helped the DRA government to survive into 1992'.[40] But when Russian aid stopped in 1992 and Najibullah was unable to pay the militias or his military, he quickly and dramatically fell from power.

Similarities

ISAF's military strategy has been similar to the Soviets in aiming to control the population, secure lines of communication, 'Afghanise' the military operation, aid stabilisation and development, and fight the insurgency, especially in the south and the east. Yet, like the Soviets, ISAF has struggled to secure the population. An estimated 36 per cent of key districts were under government control by September 2011. While the Soviet troop densities were by 1987 more than the desired 20:1 ratio, when 416 000 DRA and Soviet forces combined to fight the mujahidin, achieving a ratio of 32 soldiers per 1 000 members of the population, ISAF has had at its peak to do this with less combat coverage: 11.2 security forces per 1 000.

Afghan government officials now, as they were then, are widely viewed as foreign appointees; and the failure of the Afghan government and the inability to bring benefits to Afghans are seen as international failures. In both, too, public views about the presence of foreign forces inversely juxtapose with civilian casualties. The financial situation of the Karzai government has also been similar, and perhaps even a little worse than Najibullah's in 1989. From March 2010 to March 2011 the Afghan government collected $1.9 billion in revenue. However, expenditures were $17.6 billion, the difference being made up from the US and other donors. According to official government statistics, the value of its (official, *sans* narcotics) exports fell from $403 million in 2009/10 to $375 million two years later, while imports were nearly twenty times this figure.[41] During the Soviet era there was significant income from handicrafts (around 10 per cent of GDP) and, until the end of the war, oil and gas exports.

During both eras few have understood the depth and complexity of Afghanistan's tribal and ethnic relationships, where both international forces and some locals (for example, Tajiks and Uzbeks in Afghanistan) are seen as foreign, and where cultural and linguistic barriers and a lack of understanding of traditional Afghan values, are substantial hurdles to co-operation.[42] This parochialism is deeply rooted, and highlights a common strand across the eras and in Afghanistan's history – of the failure to build a nationalism amidst competing tribal and geographically based allegiances. An inability to address widespread corruption and widening inequalities, a relative anathema during the Soviet and communist era, may ultimately backfire badly both on the Afghan regime and its Western allies. This has been exacerbated by a contingent lack of public institutional capacity and private sector opportunities, especially among 'ordinary' Afghans.

Differences

On the positive side of the ledger, where the Taliban insurgency has been concentrated in the southern and eastern, predominantly Pashtun, areas, the anti-DRA/Soviet movement was scattered across Afghanistan. The mujahidin also enjoyed widespread international support and legitimacy, including from Western sources, making it easier to fund and recruit, than did the Taliban. However, both the mujahidin and the Taliban have accessed supply and succour via Pakistan and, to a lesser extent, Iran. Still, the contemporary insurgency's principal funding sources are from non-state actors and drugs.[43]

Whereas the jihad of the 1980s was national in character, the Taliban struggle has predominantly been tribal. Moreover, in spite of their aid expenditure, the Soviets visited considerable levels of destruction on many regions, quite different to the relatively soft-handed ISAF approach.

But this is not all positive.

Najibullah's National Reconciliation Policy was a sophisticated attempt to combine elements of 'amnesty, a ceasefire, a new constitution, land reforms, elections, and the co-optation of *mujahidin* commanders to decrease violence and increase stability'.[44] He also pursued political reforms to accommodate the mujahidin, including the establishment of a parliamentary democracy in 1987 and a multi-party system three years later.

In contrast, whatever his rhetoric towards the West, and despite the recognition by some members of ISAF of this imperative,[45] Karzai did not employ a similarly comprehensive plan early on to accommodate the Taliban politically, the greatest failing of the campaign during his thirteen years in office. Just 2 497 Taliban reconciled in 2011, while the cumulative number of ex-Taliban fighters numbered 6 000 by November 2012, the bulk, too, from the north and west. Unlike Najibullah, who by all accounts was intelligent, tough, resourceful and well educated, President Karzai has routinely been characterised as 'weak' and accommodating to corrupt practices in the interest of maintaining what one senior Afghan has portrayed as a 'false stability'.[46]

And there is one more crucial difference, seldom considered, and one that can be used to the international community's advantage: the major local power brokers were, *circa* 2014, personally wealthy, much more so than at the end of the Soviet operation. That has created a different stake and offers powerful and useful levers that are within easy reach of the international community, but which they so far have been reluctant to use.

Lessons

Flows of aid were crucial to keeping the Afghan government in power even after the Soviet withdrawal, though Najibullah's actions contributed to this period of government stability, including his policies on reconciliation, payment of militia and subsidy of key foodstuffs, notably the availability and price of naan. Only when the aid faucet was closed did Najibullah's regime topple, though this was hastened by the defection of the previously pro-regime Uzbek militia leader, General Dostum, to the opposition. Indeed, the withdrawal of the Soviets saw an immediate but not sustained decline in resistance to the DRA. This was not only because of the absence of a common foreign foe, but due to growing strains between the mujahidin and the improved effectiveness of the Afghan government army.

With the collapse of the Najibullah regime, old divisions became more pronounced, specifically between Pashtun versus non-Pashtun. Not only did these prosaic difficulties undermine complex policy plans, but attempts to modernise Afghanistan have continuously fallen foul of 'deeply held' cultural norms, alienating a government 'already seen by the bulk of the Afghan people as foreign'.[47]

In all of this, finding a sustainable way to exploit Afghans' economic self-interests has remained important. Putting an incentive structure in place that not only buys off elites but includes increasing numbers of Afghan people in the cycle of prosperity is crucial in satisfying this motivation. Aid money by itself – and the international community has promised a great deal in this regard – is never going to be enough.

What is additionally required is finding the means to empower the locals to influence their leadership as the principal – and most likely the only – means to encourage, cajole, support and instigate more dynamic authority in Kabul willing and able to pick up the baton. Here, too, there has been a tension between the short-term stabilisation imperative and the longer-term need to get Afghanistan onto a more sustainable development path, in which aid does not play such a critical role. The short-term argument has, not least for reasons of the need to counter the Taliban insurgency, won the day, hence the failure to openly challenge the Government of the Islamic Republic of Afghanistan over corruption cases, for example, or the spending on seed programmes, or the recognition that the security benefits of power brokers are more important than governance.

The short-term expediencies are persuasive. One does not want to risk upending the withdrawal. As Clare Lockhart notes, 'The speed and effectiveness with which a government can assume the functions of governance determines the rate at which assistance can "exit", handing over any function temporarily assumed.'[48]

Put differently, do not let the perfect be the enemy of the good.

Equally, the numbers have argued against risking nothing. According to the World Bank, as noted above, some 97 per cent of Afghanistan's $16-billion GDP originates from international military and development aid and spending.[49] Efforts at self-sufficiency are reportedly being sabotaged by 'corruption and poor governance' and while natural resources – including its mineral wealth of an estimated $1 trillion[50] – are held out in hope of a fresh source of income, examples abound across a range of geographic and cultural settings as to the 'rottening effect' this will have where institutions and independent oversight has been weak.

The question is thus: how soon will Afghanistan reach the limits of 'extractive growth', based on the redistribution of aid or even future mineral income? Is leadership likely to voluntarily transform its political institutions in an inclusive fashion, or will it only respond to pressures from below? In this regard, Acemoğlu and Robinson argue that change can be altered by 'critical junctures', events that can either speed the process along or set it back.[51]

How might these critical junctures – of which the 2014 pull-out is just one – be shaped positively in Afghanistan?

Working on the basics

There are generally thought to be three types of Taliban: religious students uninterested in political power; holy warriors; and those seeking political power. A fourth could be added: those interested in finding the means to survive and progress, including marriage (an expensive undertaking even for a rural Afghan, costing $10 000 at a minimum), as farmers or as guns for hire. This has been fuelled by familial connections, blood feuds, status and insider-outsider perceptions. The latter two often go together. Those protecting citizens against external influences are provided status.

Such elementalism is, however, a recognition of social strength, not weakness, and can be built on. These ties have perpetuated in spite of attempts to change them through ideological or theological revolution, or through social and political reform. Local clans and local patronage continuously frustrate the attempts of modernists to build a united and unitary state.

Thus, while there is no doubt that Afghanistan needs to build a domestic tax base to fund its own activities, including the security forces, and considerable progress has been made in this regard,[52] this has to be considered in the overall context of the Afghan state's responsibility and delivery to its people. It is difficult to force taxation when government transparency and corruption is viewed as widespread and service delivery is poor. Also, it must be weighed against the other demands made on business. While taxation under the Karzai government has only been about 40 per cent of what is needed to finance the Afghan state – some $2.5–3 billion has been collected annually – taxation without reciprocal Jeffersonian representation, accountability and government services may only force entrepreneurs underground, or out of business.

This highlights the need, again, to focus on improving the connection between leaders and populations, the only conceivable way that politicians will try to do the right thing. Breaking the mould of political behaviour is primarily a domestic task. Politicians, especially those culturally indifferent to liberal forms of democracy, have an abiding temptation to sacrifice the majority and live off extracting rents. Hence the need for mechanisms to assist populations in improving their lot: property rights, free speech, checks and balances, and that hard and soft infrastructure that makes their lives easier; all of which implicitly treat the government as a 'lurking threat to development'.[53]

Without this change, new institutions will invariably look just like the old ones. As George Orwell diagnosed in *Animal Farm*: 'The creatures outside looked from pig to man, and from man to pig, and from pig to man again; but already it was impossible to say which was which.'

Such change demands outsiders realising the defining role of politics and financial self-interest and the relationship between the two in shaping the character and dynamics of these environments. At the least, external interveners should seek to do no harm; to ensure that their actions and money do not fuel predatory behaviour; and, at best, should transform the political economy into one of greater inclusivity.

Afghanistan's aid lessons for others

More than a decade into the post-9/11 operation to remove the terrorist threat posed by the Taliban and their one-time Al-Qaeda allies from Afghanistan, the international effort was winding down. International troop numbers shrunk from a peak of over 135 000 in 2011 to 100 000 by the end of 2012. This was scheduled to reduce further to 25 000 by the end of 2014. At the same time, the Afghan National Security Forces were being built up as a 350 000-strong local lead.[54]

The international operation contains many lessons for others. And many of these lessons – while apposite for others – are not especially positive, despite (and perhaps because of) the extent of international dedication. In part, some of the reasons for failure are entirely of the interveners' own making. As will be seen, others relate more specifically to the nature of Afghanistan's own politics, the health of its civil society, its tribal ties and leadership.

Initially the centrepiece of an anti-terrorist action that morphed into a counter-insurgency and peace-building operation, Afghanistan *circa* 2013 contained elements of all three.

'Peace-building' may best define the mission, as the international community seeks to cement its security gains and craft the terms of its withdrawal.

In the Afghan context, it is one of state-building, where foreign militaries and donors acting in partnership with local actors attempt to provide the security, aid and political back-up to enable the reconstruction of the domestic physical and economic infrastructure, along with the political and social fabric. They are usually guided both by national interests (given the security and other threats these countries can pose to others), combined with a sense of charity and empathy towards those less fortunate. Peace-building is led by the notion that not only do others want to be helped, but that they can be helped.

This is not to belittle the sacrifices made. On the international side, there are many people involved with good intentions and making remarkable sacrifices of family, resources and, sadly, too, lives in these foreign pursuits. These missions are usually, however, hamstrung by a number of aspects.

The first is widespread risk aversion. The extent of the aversion means that the ratio of security providers versus development implementers, or process against projects, is skewed towards the former. The result has been a Kabul-centric international system of people keeping people busy, or of providing security for others attempting to make things happen.

Afghanistan has also been suffocated by having too many, rather than too few, foreigners trying to 'help', perhaps because of the focus on counter-insurgency density ratios of troops-to-insurgents as an article of faith. This has certainly been true of the ISAF bureaucracy, and lends itself to a focus also on process rather than outcomes, and often to overwhelming an already weak local state partner by the swarm of NGOs, intergovernmental organisations and other mostly foreign actors. There are frequently too many people dedicated to apparently the same tasks, not least in the field of development aid.

And overall, Afghanistan has been, as has been argued, characterised by a failure of aid. This applies in part to the issue again of process over implementation. The UK Department for International Development in 2012 had no fewer than 60 staff in its Kabul office to administer £180 million annually as one example. USAID had a staff of 250 in Kabul. Paradoxically, the ability of these organisations to oversee projects and scrutinise spending has been limited, not least given safety-related travel constraints.

It has also been exemplified by a widespread institutional defensiveness, though this has changed for the better in Afghanistan as the end of the ISAF mission has drawn near – probably too little too late, however. Given the volumes of aid that have flowed in since 2001, Afghanistan is a worst-case example of such 'best practice'. The fact that this is now widely recognised, including by the aid agencies themselves, illustrates how deep-rooted these practices are and yet, paradoxically, fundamentally how difficult it is to impose a new operating system from outside.

Afghanistan is not a regional exception. Pakistan has received more than $20 billion in aid since 2001 but with little improvement in social development indicators. This is partly due to skewed incentives, misplaced priorities and inappropriate project designs.[55]

Aid missions in both countries have been epitomised by a failure to understand and act to assist the private sector. This is hardly surprising since 'most bureaucrats in aid have no experience in business', as one aid administrator has reflected, 'as they have never been in business in their lives'.[56] Furthermore, aid has served to reinforce corruptive practices and distort local lines of accountability. It is tempting to go around often overwhelmed, cumbersome and slow local bureaucracies in getting things delivered and 'making things happen' – though this does little to ensure accountability and governance.

Aid missions have also typically been ideological and personalised. Nowhere more can this be seen in the issue of support for or against electrical power as an article of faith. This is exacerbated by the duration of the mission in Afghanistan. As one adviser now in Somalia put it, 'Afghanistan is so last year.' The quality of individuals involved suffered as a result, as has enthusiasm, while retaining little of the continuity between missions.

Aid also has a deleterious impact on commercial practices, diverting entrepreneurship towards the donors. Not only have the better-qualified and skilled headed for inflated donor salaries (which, as a guide, have been around twice as high in the managerial ranks in Kabul as businesses), but business people have fed off the aid economy.[57] This is not surprising where there have been few other productive alternatives. But the pestiferous impact of aid does not end there: not only does it create a culture of dependency, but the grand contracts that go with donor and foreign military expenditure can reinforce bad governance practices.

For example, the principal Host Nation Transport contract to support ISAF totalled $2.16 billion in 2010,[58] in providing 70 per cent of goods consumed by US troops in the field. The 6 000 to 8 000 truck missions per month worked out at over $25 000 per truck per mission. It offered the ultimate, lucrative protection racket, much greater in value than the estimated $300 million local worth of the opium industry. In the words of one logistics manager, 'You buy the security from the very people who will attack you if you don't.'[59] While not aid per se, this flow of foreign money has an equally distortive impact on the local political economy.

From the view of some Afghans, the international community has less improved the economic plight of Afghans than disproportionately benefited a small political dynasty. Part of this failing relates to the donor habit to identify, analyse and propose but seldom implement solutions to obvious problems. Hence the endless studies, consultancies, focus groups and wads of policy papers. And when they do, donors have spent money on projects hopelessly badly conceived from a commercial standpoint, such as the Kandahar Industrial Park (capable of housing 150 businesses across 33 acres, which remained idle for a long time because the most important of all industrial services – electricity – had not been supplied) and the Bost Airport complex in Lashkar Gar in Helmand. An amount of $52 million was expended (mostly by USAID, partly by the UK's Department for International Development) on this airport, which handled just one civilian flight a day in 2010.

A view from the trenches

Every country's development depends on its ability to sell things to others. By definition these have to be things others want to buy. On-the-ground personal interviews of traders in bazaars in 2010 in Spin Boldak, Lashkar Gar, Kabul and Kandahar provided an idea of the scale of the challenge.

Very few Afghan-produced goods were on sale, and virtually no manufactured goods save for clay pots, sweets, cooldrinks, matches, reed brushes and soap. Even seasonally adjusted, the absence of basic vegetables and staples was most notable in Helmand, the bread basket of Afghanistan. Apart from limited supplies of rice, cucumbers and melons, nearly all staples were imported: oil from the United Arab Emirates (UAE) and Tajikistan; flour from the US (and being resold) and Pakistan; sugar from the US; rice from Pakistan and India; potatoes, tomatoes, onions, apples, oranges and beans, all from Pakistan. Traders all cited their principal problems as high prices (they made on average $2 daily profit), a shortage of electricity (especially for refrigeration, the traders using ice instead) and security, in that order. Traders said that Pakistani rice, for example, was around $0.30 per kilogram cheaper than the Afghan product, and 'better quality'; and cooking oil $1 cheaper per 20 litres from outside. Staples of flour sold by vendors were sourced mostly from Pakistan, Tajikistan and Russia; rice from Pakistan and India; and oil from Dubai, Pakistan and Iran. When asked why no items were sourced from Afghanistan, the most common responses were that Afghan goods were of an inferior quality, and were both expensive and less abundant.[60]

Yet, in Kandahar, the Canadian government focused its development aid on education, health care (notably, polio shots) and the restoration of irrigation. When asked what the biggest challenges facing their communities are, Kandaharis overwhelmingly listed unemployment, an absence of stable electricity and high prices as their concerns.[61] The international community is guilty of 'fire-hosing' the population with what they *think* they need, rather than at least being seen to be acting on their concerns.

These are not just academic quibbles. Timorshah is a young metalworker in Kandahar City I interviewed in 2010, who had been making gates, burglar bars and other items for the local market. His steel was sourced from Pakistan and Iran, his welding rods from China and power was supplied by a small generator humming nearby. His profit, usually around 20–30 per cent, he said, was declining due to high cost of inputs. He was not the only one whose income was related to the supply of power. For the kebab seller near the governor's palace in Kandahar, using an electric fan to fuel his cooking fire, the harder it blew, the greater the profit.[62] We met the governor and mayor there, both soon to be assassinated.

A further survey conducted in Kandahar City in May 2010[63] of traders in agriculture equipment found normal seasonal patterns in prices and demands. The biggest constraints cited were security. The second problem was the cost of transport, due to a lack of drivers willing to go out to the rural areas. Foreign agency agreements with Pakistani traders were seen as a further impediment, especially to the quality of their product. Finally, a lot of agribusiness had been set up with donor money. Those businesses doing better pre-existed this flow of funds. The newcomers were unhappy about the lack of training that they have received from the donors, while the longstanding traders were unhappy with the market distortion this has created.

Kabul-based traders say that 95 per cent of all food consumed in Afghanistan is imported in the non-producing season. Even during the summer months Afghanistan is still heavily dependent on external supplies. In 2010, an estimated 170 trucks travelled daily into the Kabul market, including 120 from Pakistan (45 of which carried potatoes), a handful from China, Iran and Uzbekistan, and the remainder from inside Afghanistan. This reduced to 120 trucks during the summer season.[64]

Freedom of movement was thus assumed by donors to be a constraint to economic development as much as it was an indicator of stability and relative insurgent activity. Regardless, interviews with truck drivers – and route diagnostics undertaken – in April 2010 emerged with a slightly more nuanced picture.

A little extra ammo and a few other things

At the conclusion of the meeting with Spin Boldak's border police generalissimo, Abdul Razziq, his aide walked across the large room and turned on the satellite television. Up popped a programme on hair care for South Asians, known as 'Zing Hottie'. Indeed the presenters were just that; contrasting markedly with the meeting in the next-door room with Pashtun elders who looked like a scene out of Taliban Central Casting, and with the scene just down the road at the border in Weish, a dusty, busy frontier town, termed 'Razziqistan' on account of the then Afghan Border Police (ABP) chief's security and business tentacles.

Circa April 2010 and Razziq was in loose control of the border area from Nimruz province near Iran on the west to Zabul on the east. The 3 700 ABP men under his command clearly revered him. Then only 33 years old, he was anointed into the job by a combination of tribe and circumstance, a year later promoted to chief of police of Kandahar itself. A power-broker of note, dancing between our meeting and that with village elders and maliks, he provided security, of a sort, to Spin Boldak and surrounding areas. But he was clearly in on the game, without which he would not be able to access the patronage that ensures his local support and greases the wheels of local government, however wobbly that may have been.

The border at Weish, several kilometres south of Spin, is signified by a Champs-Elysées-styled 'Friendship Gate'. Apparently positioned 700 metres in the wrong place, in a fit of nationalism, it went unrecognised by the Afghans. Traffic skirted around its edges in a single lane for vehicles, only permitted to travel in one direction at a time, grouped ten at a time in and out of Afghanistan. Pedestrians moved by a separate, fenced-in lane, while donkey carts, bicycles, small boys carrying heavy sacks, tractors overladen with wood, kindling, mats and just about any other item that one can imagine, including the ubiquitous Afghan green plastic jugs, flowed chaotically in and out.

People and carts were plentiful because the rules, enthusiastically administered by Pakistani police, among others, with their snapping whips, allow them to avoid tariffs and taxes because of their (small) size. A plethora of rules and procedures allowed officials an opportunity for discretionary institutionalised and individual 'taxation'.

Interviews[65] with jingly truck (commercial) drivers (so named because of the elaborate decorations on their vehicles) at Weish highlighted the problems they faced. Pakistani truckers complained mostly about road conditions in their own country, and about the number of bribes they had to pay to police and 'militants'. Drivers from Quetta, for example, just eight hours' driving away, were paying up to 5 000 Pakistani rupees ($60). This apparently took away much of their profit. For those moving potatoes from Quetta, for example, the 25 000-rupee ($300) payment for the journey had to include fuel (6 000 rupees), tolls (2 000 rupees) and bribes (5 000 rupees), leaving just 12 000-rupee profit. As one driver put it while gesticulating with his trigger finger, 'I have to pay because they have a rifle.' Militants would break their windscreens if they did not pay up, while fuel theft was also not uncommon.

Their other complaints centred around the small size of the trans-loading area on the Afghan side of the border. The trucks from Karachi took around five to seven days for the journey on average, though some of the fuel trucks could take as long as sixteen days.

Afghani drivers universally reported that while the Afghan National Army did not solicit bribes, the Afghan National Police (ANP) did, between 400–600 Afghani (roughly $8–12) at each of the checkpoints en route to Kandahar. They all complained about ISAF traffic and patrols forcing them off the road, and delays through customs. Most of them returned empty to the border, reinforcing the view of the traders as to how little Afghanistan produced and exported.

These problems are not just interesting from an academic or even anecdotal standpoint. They directly affect the ability of Afghanistan to develop, to get rich by selling things across its borders. According to the United Nations Development Programme, landlocked countries like Afghanistan account for half of the twenty countries with the lowest level of human development. In 2010, the world's 31 landlocked developing countries accounted for less than 1 per cent of global trade. In some landlocked developing countries, transport costs can exceed 70 per cent of the export value. This is, according to the UN secretary general, a bigger barrier to trade than tariffs.[66]

To delve more deeply into the route, two of us travelled on Saturday

24 April 2010 on a truck among a convoy of nineteen, carrying 45 000 litres of fuel from Spin to Kandahar. Leaving Kandahar base at 2.30 a.m. we drove the 50 kilometres down from the trucking compound to the Vehicle Holding Area just north of Spin in one of sixteen Toyota 'Surf' security trucks, all manned by Afghans. Reassuring their presence may have been, but there was a cost to such large security details to other traffic on the road (and the road was, by the time of the return journey at midday, very busy), because of the 'magnetic attraction' they have on insurgents, and the image they projected of insecurity, at best a double-edged sword.

As the sun rose, we picked out a truck. Both of us were dressed in an Afghan dishdasha flowing over flak jackets, and ill-fitting turbans, trying (pretty unsuccessfully) not to draw obvious attention to our presence. My companion, a burly US Green Beret, also Greg, and I selected at random a petrol tanker in the security park. Our Pakistani interlocutor introduced us to the drivers, busy prodding a scorpion in the dust with their fingers, with a roll of the head, as the 'Department of Gregs'. When I went to lift his ruck-sack from the Surf vehicle it nearly popped my shoulder out of joint.' What you have got in there?' I asked. 'Some extra ammo and a few other things,' drawled the non-committal reply.

The petrol bowser averaged the journey at just 18.8 kilometres per hour. The fact that the truck moved faster downhill than up was an indication of its mechanical state, despite the best efforts of its driver Sherafzal and his assistant Zamidor. That Zamidor was able to run alongside the truck for much of the way gave an idea of its condition, the slowest (flat-out) speed uphill being 5 kilometres per hour, even though the road surface was reasonable throughout.

Pakistani music crackling on the cheap stereo, our load was never far from the mind, heightened by the cigarette always dangling from Sherafzal's lips, and the *gloep-gloep* sloshing noises behind us. We went through ten Afghan police (ABP and ANP) checkpoints en route. While there was no open bribe-taking, just north of Spin Boldak we passed a group of 113 trucks, all carrying containers, queuing at a post. The ISAF contractor's fixer explained that they were paying an informal toll at that point of 5 000 Afghanis ($100). The translator explained that this was to 'pay the commander', a form of taxation common where each post had a price tag attached to it, given the relationship between authority and income.[67]

Further driver interviews at Kandahar indicated that the major problems were not security, but rather the road conditions, though this view altered significantly among the drivers we spoke to in Lashkar Gar, who put security problems high on their list of troubles.

A further route diagnosis was later carried out from Spin Boldak to Lashkar Gar in Helmand on a jingly truck, highlighting a number of similar issues in a journey averaging twice the speed. Notable were the bribes to mainly ABP between Pakistan and Kandahar and security from there to Lash, in particular driving into unfilled IED holes or getting caught in the crossfire.

These trips taught that the freedom of movement constraint that the international community could most easily 'fix' was in terms of the tactics of its own and private contractor patrols. This could not only have eased travel but simultaneously reduced the level of threat perception. For Afghan drivers and business, the next challenge related to the load factors. For every ten loads into Afghanistan only one full one was taken out. An agreement between Pakistan and Afghanistan allowing trucks to carry goods over the borders regardless of nationality would have helped to balance this lopsidedness, mindful, as noted, that Afghanistan's development and thus security trajectory would, as with every other country, depend on what it could make and sell to a greater extent than possible today.

A good future outcome

Afghanistan was never, a decade after the fall of the Taliban, going to be Western Europe. That outcome was, never mind who was in charge or the resources offered, going to take generations, perhaps centuries. It was never going to be as good as people hoped, nor as bad as the pessimists predicted.

A good future for Afghanistan at large then looks something like Kabul *circa* 2014, or, to the north, Mazar, and, in the west, Herat.

Herat's tree-lined avenues, paved roads and regular electricity supply illustrate the advantage of its situation: a conducive regional setting and local leadership that sets it apart from much of the rest of Afghanistan.

Astride the western reaches of Afghanistan on the border with Iran, Herat has historically been viewed as the bread basket of central Asia. But it has not always been this way. The city achieved fame as the site where, in March 1979, the Afghan national army, under a disaffected then captain Ismail Khan, mutinied and murdered the garrison of 250 Soviet advisers and their families in the process and paraded their decapitated heads through the city on sticks.

As many as 25 000 civilians died in a bloody reprisal, with the city being repeatedly shelled before being retaken with tanks and airborne troops. Khan escaped to the countryside and became a leading regional mujahidin. After the departure of the Soviets, he ascended to the provincial governorship until being forced to flee to Iran in September 1995 when the city fell to the Taliban.

These were dark days. Journalist Christina Lamb, who as a 21-year-old spent two years following the mujahidin victory over the Soviets, returned to Afghanistan after 9/11 to discover the results of twenty years of war. Among the victims were the women writers of Herat who risked their lives to carry on a literary tradition under the guise of sewing circles.[68] During this era, the 'cyclets', the three-wheel, powered rickshaws notable in the region, obtained a certain notoriety as a place where couples could court. As a result, the rear canopies of cyclets were no longer allowed to be closed, preventing such conjugal congregation.

A decade on, and Herat was one of the first seven areas that transitioned security responsibility from NATO to Afghanistan in July 2011. While the ongoing search for security has defined areas in Afghanistan's south and east, Herat has been different.

It is the difference between Pakistan and Iran, the latter a relatively benign regional hegemon. 'The reason why things are so good,' said a foreign diplomat, 'is due to Iran. As much as the US has negative relations with Tehran, Iran plays a positive role here – through transport, remittances, cultural links – including funding for schools, mosques, clinics, university education and hospitals – and goods.'

Three-quarters of the goods in Herat are from Iran, transported through the border at Islam Qilla just 120 kilometres away on a road paid for by Tehran. In an irony of war, where despite Western sanctions against Iran by the West, 25 per cent of all the fuel of a key Western ally, Afghanistan, was sourced from the Islamic republic. And perhaps most importantly, there were 2.5 million Afghans working in Iran, their remittances amounting to $750 per person (or over $1 billion) in 2010, although Iran's economic woes (including the decline in the value of the rial and domestic changes in subsidy policy) saw this plummet to an estimated $300 million in 2012.[69]

The volume of border trade has ensured that Herat is a net contributor to the country, collecting the highest amount of customs revenue for Afghanistan, customs being the source of about one-third of the county's tax income. This may be a source of tension if times get tough, with Herat, according to foreign calculations, sending nearly $400 million in receipts to Kabul, but getting back one-third of this amount.

Iran's influence has been only one aspect of Herat's progress. The other is local leadership, the difference, as one observer notes 'between extractive and redistributive corruption'.[70] Whereas aid-driven business parks in Helmand, Kabul and Kandahar struggle for custom, more than 180 entities had set up shop in Herat, which quickly expanded to three phases. The reason for its growth and relative success has been simple: 'Transport, power, water and local ownership,' said one business adviser. 'It is a bottom-up initiative.' Ismail Khan managed the creation of the park, the former mujahid having a hand in much of what has happened in the province, despite also being water and energy minister in Kabul.

The popular Khan-type redistributive corruption can be contrasted, Kilcullen argues, with that of Governor Gul Agha Sherzai, who has controlled the Torkham Gate border crossing between Afghanistan and Pakistan. 'He does not distribute this money – estimated at $120 000 daily – among the general population, but among specific local tribes and warlords to buy their support', since the governor was from Kandahar. As another observer notes, 'Sherzai is practically a caricature of the Afghan warlord: a former Muj against the Russians, he combines ruthlessness with Machiavellian political skills and a convenient comfort with corruption or worse. He would be easy to dislike if not for the fact that he keeps Nangarhar safe and increasingly prosperous while being staunchly pro-American.'[71]

Then there has been a third type, says Kilcullen, of that exemplified by Ahmed Wali Karzai, the half-brother of the president and former kingmaker of Kandahar, who was assassinated by one of his bodyguards in July 2011. 'Highly corrupt but not distributive, intent on sending the money offshore into things like property in the UAE.'[72] This practice also reduces their stake in a successful Afghanistan. So they do not really care what happens to it.

There has been another reason for Herat's relative stability. In a positive cycle, this has created the space for a middle entrepreneurial class to emerge. The business park is evidence of this, where pipe and window manufacturing companies exist side by side with a carpet 'wash-and-trim' facility, which pounds and washes the dust out of rugs, the Shabab cyclet manufacturer, Herat ice cream, and SuperCola, among many others. Power to the park is supplied by Iran.

It is easy to imagine the circumstances under which such a 'good' outcome unravels. A combination of widespread corruption leads to the donors refusing to continue to fund Kabul under the Mutual Accountability

Framework, and emirs or less benign warlords emerge in various regions. The flow of donor funding would already have declined with the closure or shift in control of the more than 1 400 bases made up of forwards operating bases, combat outposts and various larger bases. In Herat this could be sparked, or worsened, by a tightening economic environment, perhaps due to Iran's own difficulties.

If such 'bad' outcomes are to be avoided and rather the 'good' one of contemporary Herat spread, it would be necessary for the international community to learn to reinforce success, especially in Afghanistan's north and west. There was a pressing need to ensure, however, a sound and acceptable political transition: from President Karzai to his successor, from the international community's form of proto-government to an entirely Afghan-directed and administered one, and from foreign aid to domestically generated revenue.

This would have to aim to strengthen private sector growth, led by credible personalities independent of the patronage networks. These would have to include establishing good but not overbearing regulations; providing affordable finance; political impartiality; reducing any panic in the market, which could not only upset gains, but encourage economic gouging; and strengthening civil society. The opportunities created would have to alter the strategic 'operating system' of government by forcing change from underneath, in the manner that the spread of mobile phones and related technologies (including banking) or the Internet or a free media has and might have.

Failure to fully understand – and to press for reform – of the local political economies explains, in large measure, why external intervention at peace-building is so problematic. The blueprint for a better society has to come from within; the role of the outsider is to provide the security guarantees and space necessary for that to evolve, to urge and, if necessary, to shame local partners into moving in the right direction but not to do the job for them and always to avoid the governance practices that led to conflict in the first instance.

With the above in mind, what is required in Afghanistan is to encourage practices and events that put people more in control of their own lives, making them less dependent on government and its inadequacies, and more likely, in the process, to pressure – from beneath – political leadership. These initiatives should complement trends of democratisation, regionalisation and good governance.

For the international military to exit, funding would have to be maintained to the Afghan security forces. It may, at just over $4.1 billion, seem expensive, but against the cost of failure or of further international intervention, it is probably cheap at the price. Even so, the inadequacies and risks associated with the military transition are considerable, as the Russian experience indicates. 'As a military man,' said one participant, 'I can say that the Afghan armed forces have everything required to defend themselves against the opposition. Of course, this is not an ideal army, and there are things they need to work on. But they are ready for combat. They have enough manpower to fight back, they have modern equipment and arms, and they have great combat experience.' This was not, however, an ISAF spokesperson, but Major General Lev B. Serebrov, the head of the political department of the Soviet command in Kabul, speaking in November 1988.[73] Moreover, the capabilities the Soviets left behind, particularly air and aviation, were significant. ISAF does not intend to leave anything near that. Moreover, it is unlikely that the US Congress will support $4.1 billion a year to the military without proper oversight.

And finally, support for civil society, especially the media and anti-corruption bodies, can only improve government responsiveness and positively shape the groundswell of public opinion. Corruption is a societal epidemic, not one of just a few individuals, and it requires a public campaign. Squeezing the warlords by following their money – and letting them know this is happening – is a complementary strategy, and one backed up with the personal pain of travel bans. Everyone wants to go places and be loved, even warlords.

One lesson from Afghanistan is the imperative to cultivate relationships with key Afghans. Such individuals should be selected on account of the influence, current and possible future roles in government and civil society. They could also be a source of Afghan comment for the international media on issues of controversy, in so doing potentially providing a source of pressure on the government. This could extend to support for the creation of a local strategic studies' community, as a source for further public commentary on issues, for example, on security, governance, elections and 'green-on-blue' attacks. After all, by 2013 the US government had spent $166 million[74] over a decade on supporting the development of media in Afghanistan. Supporting content, and not just method, would ensure improved checks and balances: governance, in a word.

If all this can be done and the international military exit managed in partnership with the Afghans, and the region can be persuaded to play its positive part, a catastrophic Soviet redux is not preordained across the Hindu Kush. But it remains a long list of things to get right.

*

The Soviet experience in Afghanistan is the natural analogue when contemplating ISAF's withdrawal. But the American experience in Vietnam offers equally salient lessons about the extent to which permanent change is possible through external intervention.

By the mid-1960s, three million people lived in Saigon, a city designed as a graceful colony for just 500 000, swelled by refugees from the war. 'Hundreds of babies are born each day' in the city, observed CBS newsperson Charles Kuralt,[75] 'but one in ten dies in infancy. Millions of people manage to live but one in six lives with tuberculosis. That it is not at all like Toledo,' he said, referring to the American visitors, 'or Jersey City so the Americans are appalled and with the best will in the world get about raising the standard of living. But then they are baffled when the Vietnamese who ought to be glad to be like people in Toledo, are not necessarily.' This explains why aid, too, is a failure.

By 1967, a time of escalation of the war, when American troops in Vietnam totalled 400 000, the US was spending $20 billion a year on 'planes, guns and bombs' and $525 million in aid amounting to 'more than $1 000' per Vietnamese, worth $150 billion in 2013 terms. But as To Tuk Tien, the managing editor of the Vietnamese *Guardian* newspaper, reflected at the time about the paradox of American assistance and influence: 'We cannot afford what you want to give us – televisions, motor cars, air conditioners, our own houses and all that – we don't have the means to have these things,' he said. 'So what do people do? Where do they get the money? They steal from their government and from our own people and buy from the Americans; so we become a nation of thieves and beggars.' This system lent itself, as veteran CBS newsman Walter Cronkite noted, to 'a clash of cultures with thousands of Americans and millions of American dollars, reweaving the texture of life ...' Yet, as in other subsequent conflicts, he puzzled, it is ironic that 'the people in Saigon who take the money do not entirely welcome it'.

Unlike the Japanese 'swaggering conquerors' during the Second World War or the 'confident colonialist' French, the Americans in Vietnam, says Kuralt, were 'uncomfortable ... strangers in a strange land' failing, as a Vietnamese put it, to recognise the 'futility of trying to change the Vietnamese into a little America'. To the Americans, Kuralt says, the Vietnamese appeared 'mostly inscrutable, corrupt and lazy, a curious lot'. And to the locals, the Americans seemed 'preoccupied travellers with some business to attend to and not much time for the natives …' Each of these groups, he notes, 'has picked up a few words of language from each other, but almost no understanding'.

This gulf of perception, he observed, was epitomised by the statue of two soldiers that burnished the constituent assembly in the centre of Saigon. 'The Vietnamese say the soldier in front is one of theirs; the one hiding behind is an American. The Americans say the one behind isn't hiding, he's pushing.'

When Major General Samuel Koster left his command of the Americal Division in Vietnam in 1968, a division that was later disbanded in the wake of its role in the My Lai massacre, he wrote: 'Among the major subordinate areas in which the Americal Division has extended unique services are public health, commodities/resources control, transportation and movement of supplies, refugee assistance, civil employment, claims and indemnities, mobile training teams, and measures to minimise the effects upon the civilian population caused or which would be caused by the VC/NVA [Vietcong/North Vietnamese Army] initiated actions.'[76]

Names aside, this could have been written for Afghanistan or Iraq. Equally, the concern expressed by the high (six-monthly) rotation of officers, was another lesson re-learnt in Afghanistan, though not by the Americans who initiated twelve-month tours.

Even so, two other lessons stand out from Vietnam: the necessity to avoid panic, such as over the Tete offensive, at a time when by the North Vietnamese Army's own admission, the war was turning in the favour of the Americans and their allies. Not only had Tete been a tremendous cost for the communist side, but most of the South Vietnamese countryside had slipped, by their own admission, from their control as a result of the pacification programme. 'The enemy's horrible, insidious pacification program and his acts of destruction created immeasurable difficulties and complications for our armed forces and civilian population,' recorded the North's official history.[77] Second was the importance of politics and strategy over tactics both in terms of retaining domestic support and legitimacy, a war that, especially with Iraq, the American public was suspicious of from the start, and also in their choice of ally.

At the end of it all, said Cronkite ten years after the fall of the city to the communist forces: 'Saigon, or what used to be Saigon, remains. It is different, in some ways a great deal different, but nonetheless it is there. That's the way of history. Wars are won and wars are lost, governments come and go, brave men die, and grave injustices are committed in the name of justice. But in the end, there are survivors; in the end, life goes on.'

For Vietnam, see Afghanistan; and there, for Russia, read America.

11

THE DEMOCRATIC REPUBLIC OF CONGO

The Invisible State

*

The little blue Suzuki 4x4 slithered, bounced and squirmed its way up the thick, muddy forest track, moving up through the rain and mist into green meadows dotted with grazing cattle. We could have been in the English countryside, save for the ubiquitous camouflage-bedecked, gum-booted, stoic-faced troops standing by the roadside en route, AKs handled as second nature; the small, shoeless, snotty-nosed, pot-bellied children splashing in puddles; and men and women, young and old, hauling enormous loads carried by rope slung around their foreheads. As we progressed, avoiding 4-tonne trucks heaving with charcoal bags and sheltering human bodies slipping and sliding their way down the mountainsides, the slush gave way to a corrugated volcanic topping bisecting bright-green jungle.

We were on our way to meet Laurent Nkunda, the leader of the National Congress for the Defence of the Congolese People (CNDP), an anti-government front operating in North and South Kivu provinces in the Congo's eastern reaches.[1] A temporary ceasefire was in place between the government and Nkunda's troops, enabling our passage.

Our journey started in Goma, the capital of restive North Kivu, where the UN had stationed the bulk of its 20 000 troops. It looked exactly as one might expect of a city with its history. Not only did it wear badly the years of war but it had suffered two devastating volcanic eruptions in living memory. The last, in January 2002, destroyed one-fifth of the city's surface, a stream of lava essentially cutting it in half, including shortening the local airport's runway by 1 kilometre. Combined with the state of the Congolese airlines, it had been the site of regular disasters – a Hewa Bora Airways

DC-9 overshooting and killing 40 just months before our trip. Goma's basic services were strained beyond breaking point, state neglect and incapacity compounded by an estimated 800 000 internally displaced persons milling around the Masisi and Rutshuru districts to the north of the city. The roads were mostly volcanic ash, the city resting under the shadows cast and spewed by the giant Nyiragongo crater.

Mother Nature's hand was on top of the steady decay caused by regimes whose inability to govern the whole territory had made a lie of the notion of the Congo as a country controlled by Kinshasa. The Congo had none of the things that make a state: interconnectedness, government beyond one person, a shared culture or a common language.

On the city's outskirts, AK-47-toting government troops would not allow us through the *péage* (a single poll across the road) in Sake, outside Goma. After much haggling with their rheumy commander and several phone calls to *mon general* in Kinshasa and *mon colonel* in nearby Goma, our 4x4 was able to break free of the gathering crowd, their bloodshot eyes habitually flicking over the vehicle's contents. We headed off through the demilitarised buffer zone and up into the hills.

Nkunda was to be found in the town of Kitchanga in the wild Masisi territory of North Kivu, at the end of a four-hour back-breaking ride. We waited for the rebel leader to arrive in a nondescript, functional wooden house, replete with an Oxfam-sponsored outhouse. The pink-draped wooden furniture and concrete floor spoke of a certain (if humble) privilege in a town where ramshackle reed huts were de rigeur. His arrival was announced by the entry of a tall, rail-thin soldier carrying a grenade launcher. He snapped a quick salute, presumably not at me. His smart appearance and professional manner contrasted with the earlier Congolese army encounter. Outside were two unsmiling types carrying belt-fed machine guns, and looking a little more than purposeful and distinctly edgy.

In 1994, the remnants of those responsible for the Rwandan genocide fled into what was then Zaire. About 6 000 remain there twenty years later, grouped into the Democratic Forces for the Liberation of Rwanda (FDLR), occupying a chunk of the Walikale territory in North Kivu where Congolese Tutsi, among others, had become a proxy target for their far-fetched schemes to one day again capture Kigali. This was only part of the reason, however, why war continued to rage in the Congo. It was an example of the wars that never end, otherwise termed the 'forever wars',[2] wars not fought over national interests, grievances or even over resources and greed, but those that have their own tautology, where groups fight as a way of life, exactly because there is no state, where they become conflict entrepreneurs, rather making money than aiming to seek power from fighting.

A native of North Kivu where he was born in 1967, Nkunda had abandoned his psychology studies to join the Rwandan Patriotic Front (RPF) in 1990. After the RPF seized power and stopped the genocide in Rwanda in July 1994, Nkunda was part of the invading Alliance for Democratic Forces for the Liberation of Congo force, which quickly toppled the Zairian dictator Mobutu Sese Seko in 1997. Mobutu had among other things made the unfortunate error of supporting the *genocidaire* elements. By 2003, Nkunda was a Congolese brigadier general, the regional commander based in Goma. Five years later, however, the time of our meeting, Nkunda was viewed by many as an international outlaw. Controlling an area claimed to be 'half the size of Uganda', the CNDP had refused to disarm and integrate its 8 000 (or so) troops into the government's (on paper at least) 145 000-strong Forces Armées de la République Democratique du Congo (FARDC). The Congolese government had, in turn, issued an arrest warrant for Nkunda on charges of insurrection, war crimes and crimes against humanity relating to his role in the suppression of an army mutiny in Kisangani in May 2002, and another violent incident in Bukavu two years later.

Enter the general. Dressed in a dark three-piece suit and carrying a large cane with a silver eagle as its handle, Nkunda was less Fidel Castro than Wesley Snipes. His personal and physical affectations displayed the wear and tear of his being at war for nearly two decades. We chatted for several hours before holding hands and praying before a meal of chicken and rice, Nkunda being an ordained Pentecostal minister. But when the flagon of brandy appeared, I knew it was time to run, mindful, too, of the difficult journey ahead in fading light. Although he professed to be fighting for his (Tutsi) people, and certainly there was some truth to that as there was evidence of his profiting from the export of minerals, Nkunda was ostensibly fighting due to the Congo's dysfunctionality, because of its invisible state, where a lack of government and its ability to control all forms of organised violence becomes exactly the rationale to assemble armed groups. Lawlessness begets lawlessness.

*

'Going up that river was like travelling back to the earliest beginnings of the world, when vegetation rioted on the earth and the big trees were kings. An empty stream, a great silence, an impenetrable forest,' writes Joseph Conrad in *Heart of Darkness*, 'and this stillness of life did not in the least resemble a peace. It was the stillness of an implacable force brooding over an inscrutable intention. It looked at you with a vengeful aspect.'

Quoting Conrad on the Congo has become as clichéd as journalists citing a taxi driver. But inasmuch as it is a powerful indictment of the racism of man and the impact of imperialism, it is repeated seemingly in response to the perplexing problems of systemic governance and other failures of that giant territory at the heart of Africa. There is no other logic, it seems, to explain Congo's collapse.

Yet, in the rejection of racial simile, Conrad's writing was a reaction to the stories of conquest and barbarity coming out of the Congo, hence the bravery of the shipping clerk, Marlow, who goes in search of the fabled agent-turned-evil genius, Kurtz. Conrad made it clear that, in his view, colonists were there to exploit the weakness of others. The bitter irony of his tale is of the illusion that those who appeared and professed to be the most civilised, were the most savage. Conrad referred to the institution of colonialism as a 'flabby, pretending, weak-eyed devil' and its proponents as racist, with the chief accountant, for example, dismissing the cries of a dying black man as being merely irritating.

The metaphoric paradox does not end there. The penetration of the hinterland, and colonialism per se, was permitted by improvements in transport technology and weaponry, and was carried out in the name of Christian enlightenment and commerce. Indeed, darkness is initially referenced, not in the context of race, but of maps and geography, where places of darkness are those yet to have been explored, defined and settled by colonists. And Conrad viewed colonialism as not only paternalistic (Africans were excluded from discussions about their own continent at the Berlin Conference in 1889) and ambitious (Belgium's King Leopold sought, in the Congo, to control a territory 78 times the size of his own), but rapacious in its commerce and vicious in its methods.

The Congo's challenges have not only remained over the intervening century, but proliferated. Once outwardly orderly and both the centrepiece of colonial ambition and pretence of national order, now Kinshasa is awash with people yet without order and direction. It is the epitome of scratching urban subsistence.

This is the city where army convoys race around, their methods a caricature of over-reaction and heavy-handedness against the locals. It is where the grandeur of the main arterial, the eight-lane Boulevard du 30 Juinso renamed from main Boulevard Albert I after independence from Belgium on 30 June 1960, contrasts with the poor health of the smaller transport veins. Running 7 kilometres from the Gare Centrale to Rond Point Socimat, parallel with the Congo River, the Boulevard connects the eastern and western communes of the city and services the central business district and main government offices. It cuts a grand, imperial swathe, a notice of conquest and intention. Where waving limba trees once stood, the road is dotted with the yellow shirts and steel helmets of the frantically waving and whistling traffic police, the Police de Roulage.

Their colourful pedestals, elevating them to some safety above the whizzing traffic, contrast with the empty granite plinth at the Boulevard's conclusion around the Place de la Gare, where the monarch's statue once stood. The Boulevard's refurbishment in 2010 creates an illusion of comparative order and prosperity, since most other roads are not only inadequate, but hardly maintained. The pretence of function or such grand, *poseur* illusions are of little help to most of Kinshasa's estimated eight million people. Great numbers drift in and out of the sprawling city, looking for work each day, on foot or jammed into fula fula taxis, hoping against hope. And things are likely to get worse before they improve. By 2025, Kinshasa's population is predicted to be second only to that of Lagos in Africa, expanding a staggering 70 per cent to 15 million people.[3]

Even so, it is outside Kinshasa that the true mythology of the Congolese state has been laid bare for all to observe. In November 2012, the M23 rebel group, the successor to Nkunda's rebels, seemingly walked past MONUSCO (United Nations Organization Stabilization Mission in the Democratic Republic of the Congo) peacekeepers to occupy Goma. They left after ten days and melted into the forest. The central government had little answer to their threat. The M23 was full of commanders and troops who committed awful crimes. These were no freedom fighters responding to the threat of ethnic genocide against their ranks, as they claimed. Regardless, they were highly motivated, unlike the Congolese army. It required the deployment of a fresh UN 'intervention brigade', comprising 3 000 South African, Malawian and Tanzanian troops supported by armed attack helicopters, to defeat the M23, many of whom fled over the border into Uganda.

Since 1999, with an annual budget of $1.5 billion, the UN peacekeeping force in the Congo is the largest mission in the world body's history. Originally started in 1999 as an observer mission, known as MONUC, its mandate and size were strengthened following the signing of the agreement on 19 April 2002 after the conclusion of the Inter-Congolese Dialogue held at Sun City in South Africa under the leadership of Thabo Mbeki. This formally ended the Second Congo War, a conflict also known as 'Africa's World War' in which nine countries and even more rebel groups fought out control and influence of chunks of the giant territory, measuring over 2.3 million square kilometres, one-quarter of the size of the US, two-thirds that of Western Europe.

Despite the success of Congo's first democratic elections in 2006, UN troops have remained to keep the peace, especially in the restive east where the FDLR still roamed twenty years after the Rwandan genocide. Despite having over 20 000 troops and police, and almost 1 000 international civil servants and 2 800 local staff within the 'stabilisation' mission, MONUSCO has regularly not proven to be up to the task.[4]

The UN ultimately only reflects the limits of the extent of international will; and that, in turn, is a function as to how serious UN members think Congo is about getting to grips with its own problems. As Kinshasa pretends to govern, the world pretends to help. In this environment, the UN has become the whipping boy for problems it cannot solve.

Furthermore, MONUSCO has not been an expeditionary war-fighting force, unlike, for example, the African Union's AMISOM in Somalia. As the former UN Special Representative of the Secretary General in the Congo, Alan Doss, notes, 'It is not resourced politically or materially to become one. UN forces have acted robustly on occasion, but they are not there to substitute for the Congolese army, which is part of the problem.'[5]

One can hardly blame the peacekeepers, given that those with the greatest stake, the Congolese, are apparently so disinclined to do anything for themselves, world champions at blaming others for their misfortune and failings. It is also an impossibly inaccessible and vast territory to police, even with 20 000 troops. At best, MONUSCO has been able to respond to crises rather than pre-empting them. Equally, the challenge for the African-led UN intervention brigade, despite its initial successes, is less about what happens when it is there, but rather about what happens when that force eventually leaves. Then matters would be up to Kinshasa, and the record in this regard has not been especially encouraging.

It is not just the eastern Congo that is troublesome. In March 2013, the occupation of Lubumbashi – Congo's second-largest city – by fighters of the Mai-Mai Bakata Katanga group demonstrated the profound loss of control of the rich province of Katanga. Indeed, the fighters (whose name in Kiswahili translates as 'dividers of Katanga') raised the flag of Katanga in the central square, harking back to old fears of secession by the province that in the past led to two wars, when the nominal Congolese or Zairian government only managed to keep the country whole by convincing outsiders to intervene. Similarly, Kinshasa has failed to repel the activities of various armed groups operating in different parts of the country: the Mai-Mai Morgan in Province Orientale; the Ituri Resistance Patriotic Front and the Mai-Mai Yakutumba in South Kivu; Rayia Mutomboki in North and South Kivu; as well as the Mai-Mai Gédéon in Katanga.

Sustainable solutions to these conflicts and peace will depend on dealing with the root causes of conflict in the Congo, otherwise international troops will be required to be there for a very long time.[6] What are the chances of this happening?

Systemic governance failure

If the government can scarcely impose order and governance on Kinshasa, what hope then for its outlying centres of Goma to the east and the mining town of Lubumbashi to the south, both more than 1 000 miles away as the crow flies over territory where the absence of roads can turn travel there into a journey of weeks not days? In North Kivu, for example, where Goma is situated, the state has virtually disappeared, to be supplanted instead by institutionalised rent-seeking and corruption, a tendency in which some elements of the UN force have also engaged.[7] One local, for example, applied for a licence to open a hardware shop in Goma, for which he paid a fee of US$1 500 to the General Tax Directorate, the whole process taking a year. He complained, 'Every time I went to the [tax] office, they denied I ever paid the money, yet I had an official receipt from the General Tax Directorate. I had to pay a bribe to get the licence.' He has had to contend with people claiming to be government officials asking him to pay additional taxes. 'Here nothing works because all the time people come to you saying they are from the General Tax Directorate but they have no identification at all. You just have to pay them. The tax they ask for is never uniform and depends on the mood of the person who comes to collect it.'[8]

Where power and authority exists, at least in health and education, it is in the hands of international NGOs. Not only does Kinshasa lack the wherewithal to impose its authority beyond (and sometimes within) its own city limits, but has apparently found it impossible to do so farther afield, at least without international assistance. And the latter inevitably comes at a price – of sovereignty, through business deals and by reinforcing a feeling of helplessness. Moreover, these regions have in the process understandably formed more in common with Congo's neighbouring countries, given shared economic interests and security concerns.

It follows, too, that Rwanda and Uganda have regularly been accused by the UN of fomenting instability and supporting rebels, including Nkunda's CNDP and the M23, intent on maintaining Kigali's and Kampala's security and financial interests at the expense of the Congolese. The level of involvement is exemplified by Nkunda's 'house arrest' in Gisenyi, the Rwandan town on the border with Goma, since January 2009, when called to a meeting to discuss joint Rwandan-Congo military collaboration.

Although vehemently denied, the engagement of regional actors should not be surprising. They have more at stake there than do a bunch of foreign peacekeepers. Rwanda and Uganda have been more than willing (and able) to fish in troubled waters, often for rather shady commercial reasons. They will continue to do so until the Congo puts its own house in order. And governance starts with representative government.

Election deficits and myths

On 28 November 2011, the Congo held its second democratic election in 45 years. The first, in July 2006, followed a decade of conflict, the eviction of Mobutu from power in May 1997, and a peace agreement between the regional and domestic warring parties.

The first election, costing the Congo's international sponsors a further $500 million, was won by the incumbent, Joseph Kabila. His main rival, Jean-Pierre Bemba, who disputed the results, was later arraigned in The Hague on war crimes charges.

Over the next five years Kabila and his cabal reportedly consolidated their financial position. Such deal-making centred around the mining sector, and included the 'revisitation' of extant licences and both stake-taking and percentage-making by a small number of local and foreign personalities. According to the British MP Eric Joyce who chaired the House of Commons all-party parliamentary group on the Great Lakes region, such deals are part of what he describes as a 'startling pattern of corruption' in the Congo.[9] This helps to explain why, although Congo's mineral wealth is estimated at over $20 trillion dollars, the country ranked 186th out of 187 (it beat Niger) in the 2013 Human Development Index designed to measure overall well-being of populations.[10]

In the 2011 election Kabila faced his toughest challenge yet in the form of the veteran politician Etienne Tshisekedi, then 79, a man whose personal poverty illustrates perfectly his political principles, breaking the mould of the Congo 'big man'. Not for nothing was he one of the few who stood up to Mobutu. He also refused to participate in the 2006 election, citing concerns about fraud.

Five years on, having decided to participate, Tshisekedi and his party, the Union for Democracy and Social Progress, alleged widespread electoral swindle, including ballot-stuffing, vote tallying 'adjustments' and flights from South Africa of three million pre-endorsed ballot papers.[11] If the allegations were to be believed, Congo had become an example of modern authoritarianism, where the facade of a democratic process exists, where the sophistication of election processes and tampering contrasted with the absence of the inner substance of the state of governance and the rule of law.

There were others less partisan with similar concerns. The respected Carter Center said that the election results lacked credibility,[12] while the EU election observer team joined others in citing 'serious irregularities' at the polls.[13] After some delay in announcing the results, officially Kabila won 49 per cent of the vote and Tshisekedi 32 per cent. The Union for Democracy and Social Progress claimed their man won 52 per cent of the vote, compared to Kabila's 24 per cent. The Archbishop of Kinshasa, Cardinal Laurent Monsengwo Pasinya, has observed that 'after analysing the results … it is indeed normal to conclude that they do not conform to the truth or justice. How, for example, is it possible that on Dec. 6, Mr Tshisekedi had 5 927 728 votes out of 17 329 137 votes cast, but on Dec. 9, he was credited with 5 863 745 votes out 18 144 154 votes cast? He lost 64 000 votes, even though the results from 34 000 more polling stations had been added,' he said.[14]

The 2011 election served to maintain three fictions: that the international community would put democracy first over the threat of instability; second, that President Kabila is interested in placing his people's interests over his own; and third, most importantly, that the Democratic Republic of the Congo exists.[15]

The empirical foundations for this stance are clear. Congo has been at war incessantly. It is home to some of the worst violence in the world. Probably over five million people have died (no one really can say with any certainty given the conditions in the country) in the last fifteen years, with endemic violence that *The Economist* describes as 'children murdering in gangs, civilians massacred by the thousand, rape as common as petty thievery'.[16] Construed as the 'rape capital of the world', where abuse against women is used 'as a weapon of war', it is estimated that 48 women are raped every hour in the Congo.[17]

The country rated 229th and last in the CIA's 'listing of national per capita incomes' (behind even Somalia and South Sudan),[18] 160th out of 176 in Transparency International's Corruption Perception Index,[19] and 171st out of 177 nations in the Heritage Foundation's Index of Economic Freedom.[20] There are other qualitative measures. Journalist Tim Butcher, who in the 2000s followed the footsteps of Grahame Greene's 1936 *Journey Without Maps* traipse through Liberia and Sierra Leone and Henry Morton Stanley's 1874–77 Trans-Africa Expedition into the Congo, says of the comparative infrastructure state, 'Sierra Leone's was much better than DRC. The body and bones have rotted away completely in the Congo. In Salone [Sierra Leone], the colonial soft tissue has gone but the skeleton remains.'[21]

Unfortunately, the international community's response to the Congo myth has been deliberate avoidance and the hope that, somehow and

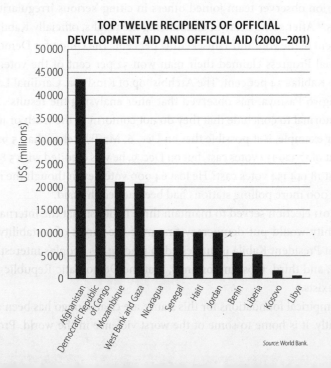

TOP TWELVE RECIPIENTS OF OFFICIAL DEVELOPMENT AID AND OFFICIAL AID (2000–2011)

Source: World Bank.

despite all evidence to the contrary, Congo could be a unitary state ruled from Kinshasa. The Central African nation has been one of the largest recipients of development assistance in the world year in and out. Between 2000 and 2011, for instance, it was second only to Afghanistan in receiving international largesse.

The Congo myth has continued for several reasons.

African leaders dislike any questioning of state sovereignty, given that many of them do not have full control of their own territory. The international community, reluctant to devote anything like the diplomatic energy and political capital that would be necessarily to think about a real solution to Congo, is happy to oblige. Despite all the protestations about war, violence against women and regional instability, Congo does not get the attention that Israel/Palestine or even Kosovo (to take two areas where there is real thinking about changing the nature of sovereignty) get from Washington, London, Paris or Turtle Bay. Finally, there are a great many inside and outside Congo who profit immensely from a large territory full of minerals and opportunities for extortion, trafficking and smuggling and who therefore have a profound interest against any sovereign power ever developing in Congo.

The inevitable result of trying to foster a fiction is that the dysfunctionality keeps popping out. At the diplomatic level, the contortions become ever more painful to observe. For instance, the 2012 State Department's Country Reports on Human Rights notes of Congo, 'The Democratic Republic of the Congo … is a nominally centralized, constitutional republic … There were many instances in which state security forces … acted independently of civilian control and of military command.'[22] Of course, if the government cannot control its own security forces, it is neither centralised nor constitutional.

The logic of pretending that a state exists leads inevitably to pathologies that do the most harm to the defenceless. At some point, countries will have to recognise that trying to aid the notional government of Congo in the hope that something will change in the future is a bad play.

Few innocents

'There are few innocents in the eastern Congo,' Alan Doss observes, 'except those who are the perpetual victims – the poor and defenceless.'

In Somalia, as in Congo, ultimately peace is not dependent on foreigners creating or keeping it, but the locals seizing the opportunity for peace and doing themselves what is necessary to keep it permanently. The failure of the Congolese to do so explains why its eastern neighbours, Uganda and Rwanda, are so engaged; and not that the Congo is damaged because of their intervention.

The Kinshasa government (and local politicians) are very much part of the problem. President Joseph Kabila has little legitimacy and credibility. The government is engaged not in management of crisis but rather their perpetuation. The resolution of fundamental problems – cleaning up the army and dealing with corruption – have been either delayed or deferred, in favour of quick fixes that survive only until the next crisis arrives.

Since the end of the transition of the 2000s, there has been no serious, coherent national political dialogue within the Congo or between the government and its external partners. Such a 'fix it as we go' approach has suited various parties just fine, including some foreign business interests, but at the cost of governance and national unity.

With close to 30 different armed militia groups in the east, and with no national cohesion and consensus on how to deal with pressing economic, social and developmental problems, the notion of a single Congo appears more fictional than ever. To change this reality, Kabila, lacking sufficient authority in Kinshasa let alone countrywide, seems to have little choice but to devolve power, both to the regions and within his government to those with a plan. The colonial legacy did not help, but the Congo's subsequent choices have also not helped.

As a lieutenant, former Nigerian president Olusegun Obasanjo saw action with UN forces in the Congo in 1960. 'It shocked me how badly prepared it was for independence by the Belgians. I have no doubt that the British did a better job in this regard than the Belgians, and believe that the French did better than the Brits. We are still paying this price today. That was the first time,' he recalls, 'I went outside of West Africa. I saw many similarities. They respected the same things, notably age and authority.'[23]

But he is critical, too, on other aspects of the inheritance. 'Congo is too large to be a unitary state. There should be a devolution of power and authority. The DRC is also crying out for infrastructure, and for institutions that can sustain democracy, development and good governance. There the rules, regulations and laws that govern government – which should be closely obeyed – are not observed, for example, over the exploitation of minerals, where they are ignored by Congolese and foreigners alike. Congolese are seldom properly trained and led, while the international community has not paid adequate attention and given adequate resources to the areas where it most needed: for example they spent $1 billion on elections for legitimacy,' says Obasanjo, 'but can't spend $100 million on institution-building.

'In 1960 I would go from Kindu to Kasongo [both in the central Maniema province] by train or by road. Fifty years later, in 2010, when I went to be the Special Envoy of the UN Secretary General, I could not make this same trip by road or rail. They told me then in Goma: what do we have to do with Kinshasa? Our food, soap and salt – it all comes from the east.'

Fixing these problems will also require regional political solutions. The lead will have to come from the Congolese but Rwanda and Uganda will, too, have to be part of it. There will be no peace in the eastern Congo otherwise. Only a stronger Congo, where power is devolved from the centre, can make that possible. That is the core of the dilemma, not UN peacekeepers.

There can be no easy or quick solutions. If, as in other cases of state salvage, the period of recovery is to be at least as long as that of decline, there is a long road ahead. It is, moreover, a fact that almost all Congolese want their country to remain a unitary state. That is largely because the international community has not provided any incentives to think about solutions other than a unitary, dysfunctional Congo. Simply bowing to the facts on the ground and admitting that there is no central power in Congo, that President Kabila can accurately be described, at best, as the mayor of Kinshasa, and that the politics of the war-ridden east cannot be solved without a new national architecture would change the debate fundamentally and lead, most importantly, Congo and those nominally trying to help it onto a path that might eventually be productive. The alternative is to continue to lie about one of the great humanitarian problems of our age.

*

The estimated total number of human souls forcibly wrenched from their homes in Africa and turned into slaves across the Atlantic is reckoned at 11 million. It was a huge business, a triangular trade of textiles and guns to Africa, slaves to the New World, and sugar, rum and tobacco back to Europe. They may not have been the first, but the British soon became the leaders, moving 200 000 women, men and children annually in the 1740s, a trade only abolished by Britain 90 years later – and as late as 1981 in Mauritania.[24] This undoubtedly did huge damage to Africa, inflicting a trauma beyond human scale. Yet, mention of Conrad's Africa reinforces the notion that

Africans were passive respondents to colonial ambition and the actions of European swindlers and pretenders. The reality is different. The European colonisers, like contemporary aid agencies and international organisations, created indigenous allies and elites and not just victims. Locals were co-opted and became agents, where the scramble for control and commerce in Africa was not only – or even predominantly – about European exploitation, but a far more dynamic process. Locals used the opportunity to seize control, appropriate territory and set up systems of government often defined less by the niceties of European democracy than the utility of indirect control through local authoritarianism. Elite co-option and creation was part of this history, no matter the extent to which Africans did not choose to be colonised by outsiders. Africans were often complicit colonialists, even though many prefer to write the history otherwise. And they remain complicit in perpetuating the contemporary illusion of the Congo.

12

IRAQ TO SYRIA

Matching Legitimacy, Strategy and Resources

✳

Probably no one in recent history ruled his people more violently than Saddam Hussein. He was a brutal man in a tough region and one who knew all the tricks.

One South African diplomat tells a story about a time he was in Baghdad in November 2000 on a routine visit. 'The Foreign Ministry called and said that all diplomatic representatives must report there immediately. We went there and were told to leave our cars and get on a bus with blacked-out windows, which freaked out some people. We were driven around for a while and then ended up at the back of the "pavilion" that is in the middle of the famous parade ground where the crossed swords were. The protocol guy walked us up the stairs of the pavilion and when we got to the top Saddam was standing in front of us in all his glory, holding that big rifle and firing it every time a column of soldiers marched past. We were seated to the back of him and to the right. I think that this was the first time that he appeared in public, for that long, since the first Gulf War. He sat on a big chair and stood up every time a column marched past and shot the rifle. We arrived there in the morning at about 11 o'clock and this continued throughout the day. He was flanked by his cronies, the short, stocky deputy president with the gangster face, Taha Yassin Ramadan, and the very *zef*-looking, red-haired, Izzar Ibrahim al-Douri, who was in charge of the Revolutionary Command Council. Really nice guys,' he added with just a hint of irony. 'The parade was the passing-out parade of the Al Quds volunteers. This was also the day that the famous picture of him with the rifle was taken. We were seated at the back to the right of him.

'After a while, it got a bit boring watching him and some diplomats requested to leave, but they were told in no uncertain terms that we were there for the long haul. They took us down for lunch at some point and then right back to our seats. It only dawned on us then that we were actually there for his protection as nobody would dare to bomb him together with a bunch of diplomats. I suspect,' he smiled, 'that we might have had too high a value of our own importance.

'It was quite cold in Baghdad at the time and most of us did not take our coats, thinking that it will only be for a short time, and were shivering. At some point Saddam turns around to us and asked in English, "Are you cold?" We all nodded our heads and he called one of his bodyguards over and gave him an instruction. Thirty minutes later the guy returned with black leather jackets for everyone. Minutes later the protocol guy returned with a box of fat Cuban cigars and, of course, everyone took a cigar and lit up, whether you smoked or not. I could always picture what it would have looked like if the international media took a photo of Saddam at that moment with twenty diplomats behind him dressed in black leather jackets, smoking big Cuban cigars! We looked like a gang of *mafiosi* …

'The parade ended late in the afternoon when it was already dark and we went downstairs for a buffet dinner and after the dinner, we were taken to a room in this complex where we shook hands with "da man" and photos were taken. I requested the protocol section several times for the photos, but the excuse was that the *ballas* (palace) took the photos and they were waiting for the palace. I am sure those photos are now on a file somewhere in another country …'[1]

No matter that Saddam was at times thuggishly comical in nature, this was a horrendous regime, responsible for a war against Iran that cost perhaps as many as one million lives on both sides and for gassing Iraq's own Kurdish people, among many other repressive acts and atrocities during his 23 years of rule. Even so, his removal by force and the chaos that ensued was an indication not only of the need for legitimacy before attempting such an action and of how badly the international community is aligned to carrying this out in a modern era, but also that success depends, fundamentally, on what the locals want. Legality does not always equate with legitimacy, and neither does power with authority. These lessons were learnt early in the reaction to the Syrian crisis ten years after Saddam's departure.

*

In December 2013, two years after US troops returned from Iraq, the Barack Obama administration committed Hellfire rockets and ScanEagle surveillance drones to help government forces fight affiliates of Al-Qaeda. A US State Department spokesperson noted that terrorists were 'seeking to gain control of territory inside the borders of Iraq' as increasing violence highlighted the security challenges facing the country. 'The recent delivery of Hellfire missiles and an upcoming delivery of ScanEagles are standard FMS [foreign military sales] cases that we have with Iraq to strengthen their capabilities to combat this threat,' another State Department official said anonymously. 'We remain committed to supporting the government of Iraq in meeting its defense needs in the face of these challenges.' Underlying this uptick in violence were pressures between the disaffected minority Sunni community and the Shiites who control the government.[2]

The removal of Saddam Hussein from power by an invasion in March 2003 led by the US and Britain not only lifted a lid on all manner of repressed tensions and violence in Iraq, but provided opportunity for other regional mischief makers. Two debates in the British House of Commons, a decade apart, summed up the political impact of the war and its aftermath.[3]

The first was held on 18 March 2003, just 27 hours before the ultimatum made by President George W. Bush for Saddam and his sons, Uday and Qusay, to leave Iraq within 48 hours or to suffer the military consequences, in which Prime Minister Tony Blair made the case to confront Saddam militarily:[4] 'So: why does it matter so much? Because the outcome of this issue will now determine more than the fate of the Iraqi regime and more than the future of the Iraqi people, for so long brutalised by Saddam. It will determine the way Britain and the world confront the central security threat of the 21st century; the development of the UN; the relationship between Europe and the US; the relations within the EU and the way the US engages with the rest of the world. It will determine the pattern of international politics for the next generation.'

He added emotively at its conclusion: 'Tell our allies that at the very moment of action, at the very moment when they need our determination that Britain faltered. I will not be party to such a course. This is not the time to falter. This is the time for this House, not just this government or indeed this prime minister, but for this house to give a lead, to show that we will stand up for what we know to be right, to show that we will confront the tyrannies and dictatorships and terrorists who put our way of life at risk, to show at the moment of decision that we have the courage to do the right thing.'

The government's motion was carried by 412 votes to 149.

Fast forward to 29 August 2013. In pleading the case in the House for action against Syria on account of its alleged use of chemical weapons against its own population eight days earlier, British Prime Minister David Cameron implored: 'Interfering in another country's affairs should not be undertaken except in the most exceptional circumstances. There must be ... a humanitarian catastrophe, and the action must be a last resort. By any standards, this is a humanitarian catastrophe and if there are no consequences for it, there will be nothing to stop [Bashar al-] Assad and other dictators using these weapons again and again. As I have said, doing nothing is a choice – it is a choice with consequences. These consequences would not just be about President Assad and his future use of chemical weapons; [but] decades of painstaking work to construct an international system.'[5]

But the Conservative politician admitted: 'The well of public opinion was well and truly poisoned by the Iraq episode and we need to understand the public scepticism.' But he noted, 'this situation is not like Iraq. What we are seeing in Syria is fundamentally different. We are not invading a country. We are not searching for chemical or biological weapons.' The world was also, he argued, as divided in 2003 over Saddam as it was united over holding Assad to account a decade on.

In spite of his eloquence and pleadings, and the clear evidence that weapons of mass destruction (WMD) had been employed in Syria against civilians, even if it was still doubtful by whom, the government motion, which said the response to the chemical weapons attack 'may, if necessary, require military action', was defeated in the House by 285 votes to 272. The fallacious WMD pretext to invade Iraq in 2003 and the violent sectarian instability that ensued in its aftermath had cast doubt on such foreign forays even among Cameron's own party – and despite the proof of WMD usage and the large number of civilian deaths in Syria.

Cameron's is a world more sceptical over the value of military intervention and regime change, despite its member-states unanimously signing up to the responsibility to protect civilian populations in the intervening years, in 2005, at the UN. If countries defaulted on their responsibility to defend their own citizens, the international community as a whole committed to a responsibility to do so. Cameron's post-Afghanistan, post-Iraq and post-Libya world is deeply sceptical about the instrumentalisation of human rights and humanitarian issues to effect regime change, especially where the outcome of this change – notably in Iraq and Libya – appears chaotic and apparently as costly in terms of the very rights it was designed to uphold and populations it was expected to protect.

Human rights are, indeed, the most frequently used justification for the war to remove Saddam. Paul Wolfowitz is seen as one of the architects of the Iraq invasion in 2003. Although ten years later he admitted that 'it may be many years before we have a clear picture on the future of Iraq, we do,' he says, 'know two important things. An evil dictator is gone, along with his two equally brutal sons, giving the Iraqi people a chance to build a representative government that treats its people as citizens and not as subjects. And we also know that Americans did not come to Iraq to take away its oil or to subjugate the country.'[6]

The former US deputy defence secretary, however, admits that the '[t]he price of removing Saddam was high, in both military and civilian blood and in treasure. But,' he says, 'he was clearly a danger to the Iraqi people and to the region; and his rule was not going to end peacefully, or even with his own death, as his sons could have carried on for another generation.'

Wolfowitz has the humility to accept that '[t]here are many things that one could wish had been done differently in Iraq. Even supporters of the war can make a long list. My own list starts with the US decision to establish an occupation government instead of handing sovereignty to Iraqis at the outset, and with the four-year delay in implementing a counter-insurgency strategy. It was already clear, soon after we got to Baghdad, that the enemy was pursuing an urban guerrilla strategy – in order to prevent a new Iraqi government from succeeding and so that the US would give up and leave – and an appropriate counter-insurgency strategy should have been developed much sooner.'

There were other unacknowledged, apparently colossal errors. Although the initial invasion was brilliantly executed, the force was insufficient and wholly ill prepared for 'the long-term occupation of a hostile country that was logarithmically more volatile, culturally and ethnically diverse, economically weak and politically complex' than any political leader realised. This was compounded by the difficulties experienced in reconstruction and the decision to disband 375 000 Iraqi soldiers – instantaneously contributing 'to a mushrooming insurgency and sectarian conflict', worsening the already difficult challenges faced in trying to stabilise the country.[7]

Strategically, the overall wisdom of regime change in Iraq, heightened by the failings of post-conflict political and socio-economic reconstruction, should inform the value of such intervention. Iraq after Saddam is a bloody reminder that, where interventions occur, it is important to set guidelines for exit to avoid turning a liberation into a conquest, an environment where resentment against foreigners can more easily be sparked into a wider revolt. With the intervener, moral authority – and legitimacy – can be more important than military might.

What are the lessons from Iraq – and have they been learnt?[8]

The shadow of war

For President Bush, the premise to invade Iraq and remove Saddam Hussein from power was based on a simple premise – the threat posed by the Iraqi dictator's possession of WMD: 'For more than a year, I had tried to address the threat from Saddam Hussein without war. We had rallied an international coalition to pressure him to come clean about his weapons of mass destruction programs. We had obtained a unanimous US Security Council resolution making clear there could be serious consequences for continued defiance. We had reached out to Arab nations about taking Saddam into exile. I had given Saddam and his sons a final forty-eight hours to avoid war. The dictator rejected every opportunity. The only logical conclusion was that he had something to hide, something so important that he was willing to go to war for it.'[9]

This threat was heightened by the events of September 11, 2001. 'Before 9/11,' says the 43rd US president, 'Saddam was a problem America might have been able to manage. Through the lens of the post-9/11 world, my view changed ... I could only imagine the destruction possible if an enemy dictator passed his WMD to terrorists.'[10] As Bush's vice president, Dick Cheney, reflected: 'After 9/11 no American president could responsibly ignore the steady stream of reporting we were getting about the threat posed by Saddam Hussein.' Cheney warned, 'The terrorists of 9/11 were armed with airplane tickets and box cutters. The next wave might bring chemical, biological or nuclear weapons.'[11]

Immediately after the attacks on New York and Washington, Cheney recalls, '[E]verybody was convinced there would be a follow-on ... The place where we thought the biggest threat lay was Saddam Hussein and Iraq.' He added, 'Anybody was basically better than Saddam Hussein.' Or as Wolfowitz put it, 'Iraq had developed chemical weapons and used them. It had developed biological weapons. It had almost gone to a nuclear weapon before the first Gulf War began. So Iraq was a known quantity when it came to having weapons of mass destruction.'[12]

That Saddam was an evil and violent man should be beyond dispute. It is sometimes overlooked in the violent aftermath of his removal that he was responsible for between 70 and 125 civilian deaths per day for each of his 8 000-odd days in power.[13] After seizing power in July 1979, Saddam was personally involved in executing 22 comrades who had dared to oppose his ascent. The toll from the war between Iraq and Iran between 1980 and 1988, launched by Saddam, was 500 000 on the Iraqi side and upwards of 300 000 Iranians. Thousands of Iraqi soldiers and civilians were killed in the American campaign to oust Iraqi's forces from Kuwait in 1991. As many as 600 000 Iraqis died, too, in his prisons and other domestic actions. Mass executions, sometimes of more than twenty at a time, occurred at Abu Ghraib, notorious long before inane US warders demeaned Iraqi prisoners. Saddam's reign of terror was reinforced by stories of torture: fingernail-extracting, eye-gouging, genital-shocking and bucket-drowning, the rape of prisoners' wives and daughters, the firing squads, shots to the head, and the sale of temporary stays from execution to families, bribing with money, furniture, cars and even property.[14] And then there was the use of chemical weapons against the Kurds in Halabja on 16 March 1988, which killed more than 3 000, the forced removal of the southern Marsh Arabs by draining their lands, and the military attacks on the Shia after 1991.

The Americans were worried after 9/11 that such weapons could find their way into terrorist hands. Thus, as President Bush put it in April 2002 at a press conference in Crawford, Texas, with Blair, then British prime minister and closest American ally, 'the policy of my government is the removal of Saddam – and … all options are on the table'.[15]

The Republican team was not alone in the US, and outside, in the belief that Saddam possessed WMD, even though partisan attempts have been made to rewrite that bit of history since 2003. President Bill Clinton explained the reasons behind his decision to strike Saddam in 1998: 'The hard fact is that so long as Saddam remains in power, he threatens the well-being of his people, the peace of his region, the security of the world … The costs of action must be weighed against the costs of inaction … Saddam will strike again at his neighbours. He will make war on his own people. And mark my words, he will develop weapons of mass destruction. He will deploy them, and he will use them.'[16]

Indeed, the US Senate, including Democrat opposition figures, such as

John Kerry, Hillary Clinton, Joe Biden and John Edwards, voted in favour of military action to remove Saddam. Hans Blix, who led the UN inspections team of Iraqi WMD, described Baghdad's response to the UN Security Resolution 1441 (of November 2002) calling for a complete declaration as 'rich in volume but poor in information'. He said in January 2003 that 'Iraq appears not to have come to a genuine acceptance – not even today – of the disarmament, which was demanded of it and which it needs to carry out to win the confidence of the world and to live in peace'.[17] Egyptian president, Hosni Mubarak, had told the US that 'Iraq had biological weapons', writes President Bush, 'and was certain to use them on our troops' but refused to make public the allegation for fear of 'inciting the Arab street'.[18] The CIA director, George Tenet, famously called the evidence against Saddam a 'slam dunk'. As Bush notes: 'My conclusion that Saddam had WMD was nearly a universal consensus. My predecessor believed it. Republicans and Democrats on Capitol Hill believed it. Intelligence agencies in Germany, France, Great Britain, Russia, China and Egypt believed it … *If Saddam doesn't actually have WMD, I asked myself, why on earth would he subject himself to a war he will almost certainly lose?*'[19]

Or as the president also asked, 'If he cared so much about staying in power, why would he gamble his regime by pretending to have WMD?' The difference in international opinion was how to deal with him and then with the French government, Germany and Russia, notable dissenters against military action.

Bush later recognised the intelligence failure that had led to the war. 'Almost a decade later,' he writes, 'it is hard to describe how widespread an assumption it was that Saddam had WMD. Supporters of the war believed it; opponents of the war believed it; even members of Saddam's own regime believed it,' he muses in his 2010 biography.[20] 'I knew the failure to find WMD would transform public perception of the war. While the world was undoubtedly safer with Saddam gone, the reality was that I had sent American troops into combat based in large part on intelligence that proved false. That was a massive blow to our credibility – my credibility – that would shake the confidence of the American people. No one was more shocked or angry than I was when we didn't find the weapons. I had a sickening feeling every time I thought about it. I still do.'

Donald Rumsfeld served as the 13th and 21st secretary of defence under presidents Nixon and George W. Bush. On the claims that his colleagues were 'somehow innocently misled' into making false declarations about

WMD, he states: 'Powell was not duped or misled by anyone, nor did he lie about Saddam's suspected WMD stockpiles. The President did not lie. The Vice President did not lie. Tenet did not lie. [National Security Adviser Condoleezza] Rice did not lie. I did not lie. The Congress did not lie. The far less dramatic truth is that we were wrong.'[21]

Or, as Charles Duelfer, head of the Iraq Survey Group,[22] put it in echoing his predecessor David Kay's words on the Group's hunt for WMD: 'We were almost all wrong.'[23] Such revelations undermined the invasion's legitimacy, no matter how bad and nasty Saddam was.[24] The lack of legitimacy and what was viewed as feckless management of the aftermath of the war also, para-doxically, served to undermine the popularity of the Republican cause in the US, especially when compounded by the 2008 financial crisis. Similarly, the apparent preference of the military option – rather than diplomatic tactics – to remove Saddam served to undermine American global leadership since Iraq, unlike Afghanistan, became viewed as a war of 'choice', not necessity. The doubts as to the steamrollering of the US towards war were expressed by members of his own team, notably Secretary of State Colin Powell, and by others, in returning the issue to the UN as the principal 'aggrieved party' – a strategy dismissed by Vice President Cheney, who cited Saddam's skilled 'cheat and retreat' history.[25]

Yet the US administration was deeply involved in the pre-war scrutiny of Iraqi WMD, not least through their own input into the post-1991 UN inspection team headed by Australian diplomat Richard Butler, which, in the words of a senior South African diplomat, an expert on the region, 'did a truly magnificent job based on excellent intelligence provided by the CIA and Israelis, and really cleaned Iraq out of WMD capability. The Americans,' he recalls, 'were deeply involved in the whole Butler-led UN WMD pro-gramme, and if they had believed what the outcome of that process was, which they should have done as they drove it, they would have known that Saddam had nothing left.' The 'final proof' for him came during a 'very bib-ulous evening with Nizar Hamdoon' (the former Iraqi deputy minister of foreign affairs – regarded as a highly competent and skilful diplomat, and former ambassador to Washington), acting as host for his South African counterpart Aziz Pahad and a 'few hangers on at a Baghdad nightclub he was a member of'. The Iraqi became 'more and more loquacious as the booze flowed'. At one point Nizar, 'by that stage totally pie-faced, during a discus-sion with Aziz about why they should get South Africa to verify and decom-mission anything they still had available – as South Africa would be widely believed at that time given that we had dismantled our nuclear and chemical WMD – leaned over to Aziz and slurring his words said, "We can't afford to say this, as it will make us vulnerable to attack by any one of our many enemies – the USA, Israel, Iran – but truthfully we do not have anything left. The UN destroyed everything but we have to posture and at least create the impression of uncertainty about whether we have or don't have, as that is part of our defence posture. We have to persist with the uncertainty over whether we have or not, because it keeps our enemies afraid to attack us.'"

The South African team shared these insights with both the Americans and British. It sent a senior official to Washington and to the UK and France to brief them. 'Our inputs were dismissed contemptuously on the basis that we had no "own" capacity even though we had compiled an extraordinary dossier of identified munitions that had been eliminated and had this confirmed to us by our people (irregularly, however) working in the UN WMD programme,' recalled the former South African official who maintains that Washington and Whitehall preferred to believe the Iraqi bluff simply because they wanted to use the deception as a pretext to attack Iraq and remove Saddam.[26]

There were also signs that the war was about more than just Iraq's WMD, the idea being, in Blair's words, a staunch US and Bush ally, to 'remake the Middle East'. The British prime minister added, '[I]n the end you are going to have go through I am afraid this long and drawn out and sometimes bloody process of transition.'[27]

And there were, perhaps inevitably, suspicions about US intentions to control the world's oil wealth, and to remake the region in Israel's favour by removing Saddam. Ron Suskind, the Pulitzer Prize-winning author inter alia of the *One Percent Doctrine* (on the Bush presidency) and *The Confidence Men* (on Obama's) had access to many of the members present in Bush's first national security meeting in January 2001, just ten days after the Texan took office. It was clear at that meeting, according to Suskind, that the Israel-Palestine issue was taken off the table by the president, and replaced by Iraq at the carefully choreographed intervention of Rice.[28] President Bush has refuted this: 'Others alleged that America's real intent was to control Iraq's oil or satisfy Israel. Those theories were false. I was sending our troops into combat to protect the American people.'[29]

There was, instead, a widespread view among the leadership that regime change, human rights, regional relations and WMD could not practically be separated. As Blair argued: '[T]he issue was undoubtedly the proliferation of chemical, biological and nuclear weapons, but obviously the nature of the regime is of some importance when you consider the threat of such a regime having WMD, so the separation of the two has always been a little unreal.'[30] And as Bush has agonised, it is not as if Saddam helped his own cause. Just after 9/11, the Iraqi regime reportedly received a letter from the US government asking for support in the war on terror. Iraq's prime minister, Tariq Aziz, gave the order to reply positively, that Iraq would help in the war against Al-Qaeda, but this direction was countermanded by Saddam. Instead, Saddam's formal reply pointed out sanctions against Iraq had killed far more than had died in 9/11, that America was not the only country to suffer terrorism, that sanctions were a form of this terrorism.[31]

Such hubris was perplexing to even his closest allies. Lieutenant General Ra'ad al-Hamdani, the commander of an elite Iraqi Republican Guard armoured corps, had boldly told the Iraqi president that the country was in the 'shadow of a war', one 'that would determine our fate' and was 'approaching fast'. Al-Hamdani warned their weapons were 'obsolete', lacking modern air defence systems, only providing 'target practice for American pilots', a brave move given Saddam's record of executing those for telling him things he did not want to hear.

In response, however, Saddam, attempting to light a damp Cuban cigar, asked 'what war?' recalled the general, keeping 'those sharp eyes fixed on me'. At the end of the meeting, Al Hamdani was called to one side, and laughed at in asking one of Saddam's favourite commanders: 'Just who are you trying to frighten?'[32] Then, on the eve of war, Sadddam summoned his top brass, and attempted to fortify them. 'War,' said Saddam, 'is coming to Iraq. We should not be on the defensive. We will not submit to the tactics of the aggressors.' Al-Hamdani was present at the meeting and recalled Saddam's message: 'The President ... said, "the Americans will attack Iraq. They will cross the desert and reach the outskirts of Baghdad. We will bring them to their knees and destroy them." He pointed to us and said: "Republican Guard. After destroying the American forces your mission is to go to Palestine and liberate Jerusalem from Israel." This was a fantasy, a dream. I will never forget that moment. This was the end of Iraq,' said the general, 'as we knew it.'[33]

Under the bellicosity, Saddam faced his own dilemmas. He could not appear weak to his own domestic and regional (read Iran) opponents. For these reasons he was perplexed about just why Washington would want him removed from power: 'Will anyone in humanity benefit if America defeats Iraq?' he asked. 'Who will benefit if Iraq's enemies defeat us? Will the American people benefit?'[34] He was confident that his regime, one opposed to religious extremism, would survive. As one of Saddam's top intelligence officials, Salam al-Jamani put it, 'The leadership believed America was not serious about regime change. Our regime was opposed to religious extremism. We kept Iran in check and in our Iraq, not one person belonged to Al-Qaeda.'[35]

Regardless, the war started at 5.34 a.m. on 20 March 2003. By 9 April Baghdad, within three weeks, had fallen to coalition forces, ending Saddam's 24 years of rule, and by 30 April, the 'invasion phase' of the war was over. This phase had cost the lives of 9 200 Iraqi military, 7 299 civilians, and 139 US and 33 British military personnel.[36]

But that proved to be the easy bit. US forces finally withdrew in December 2011, eight years and eight months later. By then, nearly 4 500 American servicemen and women had been killed, along with twice the number of Iraqi security forces, and over 100 000 Iraqi civilians, all of this with an estimated $2.2-trillion price tag.[37] Yet this terrible and oft-quoted figure actually compares favourably with the statistic, above, that over 100 civilians died each day under Saddam. Under US control, the death figure in Iraq comes to just over 30. This is not to be a Bush apologist, but it is an interesting counterpoint.

Winning the war, losing the peace

President Bush recalls that the two biggest post-war challenges were seen as 'starvation and refugees'. Sixty per cent of Iraqis were estimated to be dependent on state sources for food and as many as two million could be displaced by the war. Hence the short-term plans for food and shelter. Also, before the war, plans were developed for long-term reconstruction in ten areas: education, health, water and sanitation, electricity, shelter, transportation, governance and rule of law, agriculture, communications and economic policy. 'For each,' recalls Bush, 'we gathered data, formulated a strategy, and set precise goals.'[38] To this end, Washington created a new Office of Reconstruction and Humanitarian Assistance in January 2004, charged with 'turning our conceptual plans into concrete action'. It was headed by a retired three-star general, Jay Garner, who had coordinated the relief effort in northern Iraq in 1991. But as the president acknowledges, in recalling the old military adage, despite the preparation, 'no plan survives contact with the enemy'.[39]

President Bush also recognises other 'consequences we did not intend', most notably that 'we did not respond more quickly or aggressively when the security situation started to deteriorate after Saddam's regime fell'. Worried that they could create 'resentment by looking like occupiers', troop numbers were quickly cut from a peak of 192 000 to 109 000 within the first ten months after the invasion.[40]

Early on, in Kurdistan, it was 'like being in Paris in 1944', according to Garner's deputy, British General Tim Cross, given the warmth of the reception shown to the liberators.[41] This hinted at what might be possible in the whole of Iraq. Though Cross later criticised the post-war planning as 'woefully thin', saying 'a lot of senior generals were frustrated that they didn't have sufficient resources', singling out Blair and his International Development Secretary Claire Short in this regard, while also being critical of the system by which funding was allocated for the campaign.[42] Having already enjoyed twelve years of self-rule between the end of the Gulf War of 1991 and the invasion of 2003, and long been a target of Saddam's oppression, Kurdistan was also a different prospect to the rest of the country. There were far more power and governance holes to be filled to Kurdistan's south.

'We've really got to get this thing moving, I said, *cause* we're losing it. There are too many vacuums there and I can't fill all these vacuums, I don't have enough people.' Such was the early recollection of Garner, who was concerned immediately on his arrival in Baghdad about the sorry state of the country's infrastructure. In the capital, Garner 'went to the hospital and spent a couple of hours there and talked to doctors. They did not have anything, any electricity or anything. I went to the sewerage facility and there was nobody there. I thought we've got to get this thing working otherwise we're going to have an epidemic.'[43]

Outside the reconstruction problems, there was disagreement about whether there should be a provisional interim government or an elected one – the former would allow a quicker exit by the US. President Bush soon realised that he had to act to fill these security and political vacuums. Just two months after the invasion and having been in office for little over a month, in May 2003 Garner and the Office of Reconstruction and Humanitarian Assistance were supplanted by a freshly minted Coalition Provisional Authority (CPA), headed by L. Paul 'Jerry' Bremer. Before Bremer left for Iraq, the president reportedly told him, according to Deputy US National Security Adviser Steven Hadley, 'to establish authority and bring some law and order to that place'. Or as Wolfowitz remarked, the president told Bremer, you 'may have to call *audibles* – an American football term for when the quarterback changes the play at the last moment'.[44]

Bremer had to do just that in establishing a political process, ensuring the Shia stayed on board in attempting to reduce the divisions among Iraq's then 25 million people, to draft a constitution and, following that process, stage an election, and hand over power in June 2004. His vision to restore 'full sovereignty' to the Iraqi people included improving basic services and creating a welfare net. The pace of this process was contrary to the interests and advice of others, including, for example, Defence Secretary Rumsfeld, who favoured an expedited solution as Garner had originally intended to undertake – an election within 90 days of the fall of Baghdad.

Secretary Rumsfeld writes that 'Bremer's ambitions went far beyond the limited role for the US that the Department of Defence and the interagency process had planned for and well beyond the role that had been resourced'. He says, 'Bremer's arrival marked an unfortunate psychological change in Iraq – from a sense of liberation, with gratitude owed to the American military and our allies, to a growing sense of frustration and resentment that Iraq had come under the rule of an American occupation authority'.[45] Rumsfeld writes that Bremer seemed to embrace the media's characterisation of him as America's 'viceroy' in Iraq 'with relish'. 'He believed,' writes the secretary, 'that his assignment "combine[d] some of the vice-regal responsibilities of General Douglas MacArthur, de facto ruler of Imperial Japan after World War II, and of General Lucian Clay, who led the occupation of defeated Nazi Germany"'.[46] Such sentiment reflected the tensions between the Department of Defence and the State Department, which 'had prevented any real pre-war coordination on a blueprint for establishing a functioning infrastructure and civil administration in Iraq'.[47] The office of the vice president operated in this national security mix. When asked whether a different National Security Council would have made a difference, Powell, the 'incrementalist' secretary of state who sought change through cautious navigation rather than grand strategy, shrugged: 'I don't know. Probably not.' And when asked 'Why not?' he replied, 'Cheney'.[48]

CPA Order Number One concerned the policy of de-Ba'athification, the removal from public office of those officials who had served in the top echelon of Saddam's Ba'ath Party. Despite involving only 25 000 of an estimated 1.5 million party members, it was seen as an act of vengeance by the Sunnis against them, and embittered relations. CPA Order Number Two was to disband Saddam's army, one that was to have far-reaching consequences. Indeed, on taking over, Bremer's immediate challenge was to deal with unhappiness among the hundreds of thousands of former Iraqi military who were upset by their exclusion from the emergency payment of $20 to all Iraqi state employees, equivalent to six months' salary, as authorised by the CPA head. This antagonised Saddam's former troops, setting the stage for the surge in violence that was to follow. Originally President Bush had said that the old army was to be redeployed as a national reconstruction force. The US had also reportedly promised Iraqi soldiers if they laid down their arms they would be looked after. Even though the $20 payment decision was later reversed, ignoring this at the outset and saying that the old army 'needed to be replaced by an organization more suited to a democratic nation',[49] meant they became among America's first enemies. This was not a good idea given their training and absence of employment options. This, together with the recruitment of Al-Qaeda and other radicals to the cause, saw the resistance rise every week thereafter, worsened by the unexpected involvement of the Shia majority in the fighting. In July 2003, 88 American soldiers were killed by improvised explosive devices, a weapon that would ultimately claim two-thirds of American combat deaths.

By dismantling the army and civil service and sacking all members of the Ba'ath Party from positions of authority, Bremer both destroyed and poisoned his capacity to govern. A parallel would be in South Africa *circa* 1994: if the African National Congress had done the same to the country's governance structures when they took over, it would have caused chaos. Like the Nazis after the Second World War, many Iraqis were only nominally Ba'athist so they could have a job. Others were ideologically committed and they could have been purged. 'The Bremer administration in Iraq,' says one experienced regional diplomat, 'wrote the book on how not to deal with reconstruction in a post-conflict society.'[50]

Little wonder then that in a December 2002 study on 'Planning for a Self-Inflicted Wound', Anthony Cordesman warned that the Pentagon's post-war planning was 'uncoordinated and faltering, based as it was on ignorance about Iraq and the region with "far too many experts"', he warned, having 'never been to Iraq to the point of having practical knowledge of the country'.[51] The situation in Iraq quickly deteriorated, contrary to Wolfowitz's testimony to Congress in February 2003 that 'I am reasonably certain that they will greet us as liberators, and that will help us to keep [troop] requirements down'.[52]

From the perspective of commanders on the ground,[53] the priorities in Iraq were foremost to establish law and order. This required both a 'quality and quantity of manpower to generate real local security, within a functioning legal and penal system'. The most effective method was to employ local but accountable groups and convert them *over time* into uniformed forces or other employment training.

A related aspect was the ability to control borders. Putting more money and manpower in early to establish the right security and economic/infrastructure would have been infinitely cheaper in the long run than maintaining a constant and inadequate level of resource. There were additionally 'potential multiple wins if young unemployed men can be given uniformed high status jobs for a period until the economy has the ability to employ them. Without the ability to control the borders it is extremely difficult to prevent the sort of foreign interventions that bedevilled Iraq and, internally, to credibly present the country as sovereign.' This would have been cheap at the price, since, as one general reflected, 'A million dollars a mile for a berm and ditch is cheap against the cost of an international presence. Even the threat of fortifying the northern pipeline substantially reduced attacks on it, increased flow and paid for itself within months.'

The second priority was to get electrical power flowing. 'No power,' one officer observed, 'and no water equalled no life.' While there may be a conflict between speed and long-term sustainability, speed in generating sufficient power to meet an exponential rise in demand was critical to restoring a sense of normality. The use of military units to re-erect power lines offered one such means, on reflection, as is the institution of household and business billing 'at a very low level that undercuts generators but restores a system of accountability'. Mobile phone systems are one possible tool for billing.

A third priority was water and sewage, since it is 'difficult to feel that life is getting better if you are still drawing water from a truck and up to your knees in muck every time it rains'. Again, restoration and improvement of this sector would potentially have been 'a good employer'. Equally, associating better security with improvements to the quality of life could have helped to change behaviour, not least since 'envy is a powerful lever'.

Despite President Bush's initial bullishness on this score, the US government's own assessment on its reconstruction efforts, published in February 2009, highlighted that the programme generally did not meet the goals it set for itself on infrastructure, although it did on the development of Iraq's security forces. It was 'grossly burdened' by waste, including 'the over-use of cost-plus contracts, high contractor overhead expenses, excessive contractor award fees, and unacceptable program and project delays'. The key reason, it concludes, why reconstruction efforts so often failed to meet their mark was, in a word, 'security'. For this reason, it warns against 'an overarching hard lesson from Iraq: beware of pursuing large-scale reconstruction programs while significant conflict continues'. It also notes another 'unavoidable and compelling truth': that the US government 'had neither the established structure nor the necessary resources to carry out the reconstruction mission it took on in mid-2003'.[54]

Fourth and fifth, there was a need to resource the local health system according to the local estimate of their own needs; while 'getting kids back into school, even if on double shifts in temporary accommodation' as another 'key normality indicator'. The success of General David Petraeus in stabilising the situation in the city of Mosul in Iraq in 2003–04, where he joked he became 'a combination of both the president and the pope', was in large part down to his spending considerable time on political and social development, rather than carrying out indiscriminate sweeps.[55] 'Petraeus went in seeing his job as a delivery system of government, not primarily in military terms,' says Kilcullen, who served as adviser to the US general in 2007 and 2008 during the surge, and as special adviser for counter-insurgency to Rice.[56]

However, again, given that General Petraeus had an Airborne Division under his command, it is little wonder he could create his own 'atmosphere' while there, and Mosul slipped back to a state of instability after his departure. Petraeus relied extensively on the collaboration of local Iraqis who were technocrats to continue doing what they were employed to do in the civilian sphere. He facilitated their work and most importantly *paid* them. An estimated 10 000 Sunni insurgents were turned to the American side – or at least not against the American side – in return for being on the US payroll.[57]

Finally, from Iraq it was all important to quickly 'restore a sound currency, ensure the flow of physical cash and budget execution, and enable microcredit'. All of this has to be placed within a local political context, where the interveners enjoyed little prior understanding. This was essential in enabling 'the right Iraqis to make the running'. Knowledge of the political system and actors, old and new, was fragmented at best, especially of political parties, their motives, resources, ability to attract support, and to deliver based on manpower or money or both. This was difficult, given the dynamic nature of a post-conflict situation in which many were new players or old ones in a new situation. But understanding who the power holders were, and how they could be drawn or pushed into a better future, was key. This was a crucial aspect that the CPA got completely wrong.

Although new governance and legal structures were in place, working within rather than against the grain of the country's systems improved local understanding of foreign actions and reduced friction. Equally on health, education and social security, 'We knew, apparently, very little about what was in fact a relatively sophisticated system,' said one general. Equally, knowing 'who is paying what to whom for what, is critical intelligence'. And in all of this, the interveners were expected to balance the need and carry out immediate actions to create a long-term plan to build sustainable, domestic capacity.

But the bigger question concerns the political economy context in which foreign intervention occurred and foreign reconstruction efforts were attempted. Under Saddam, the economy was based on oil and the proceeds were redistributed principally through government jobs and state-owned enterprises, although there was an ethnic element: Saddam's Tikrit tribe were in, Kurds to the north and Shia to the south were mostly out. Oil accounted for 95 per cent of foreign earnings and two-thirds of government revenue. In the 1980s, the expenditures and destruction of the eight-year war with Iran forced the government to borrow heavily, increasing debt to $125 billion. Following the end of hostilities in 1988, oil exports gradually increased, though the system unwound as sanctions against the regime began to bite in the late 1990s, with oil production falling to 1.3 million barrels per day.

Given the size and diversity of the economy, intervention created a set of competitive patronage networks. Saddam's departure and the removal of sanctions allowed oil production to double by 2011, though attempts at diversification have been stifled by a blend of lack of competitiveness, geography, insecurity, difficult business conditions and poor infrastructure. Iraq ranks at 151st on the World Bank's 2014 Doing Business indicators, including 169th on Starting a Business, 179th on Trading Across Borders, 180th in Getting Credit and, in 189th and last place, on Resolving Insolvency.[58] An estimated 90 per cent of Iraq's power-generating and distribution systems were destroyed in the 1991 Gulf War. By 2004, Iraq had approximately 5 000 MW of power-generating capacity, and 7 500 MW of demand. By 2013 unemployment among Iraq's 32 million people (and 8.9 million workforce) was around 15 per cent, with one-quarter living below the poverty line.

Iraq to Syria: Knowing then, knowing now

To be successful, interventions require a minimum of domestic and, preferably, international legitimacy. As Jeremy Greenstock, Britain's UN ambassador at the time of the 2003 invasion, pithily summed up the debate:

'I regarded our invasion of Iraq as legal but of questionable legitimacy in that it didn't have the democratically observable backing of the great majority of member states or even, perhaps, of a majority of people inside the UK.'[59] Legitimacy depends on the backing of a majority of states, not (just) legal argument.

Additionally, care has to be taken to ensure that the state does not collapse even though the intervention may be designed to rid it of its worst elements. In this regard, any post-intervention order has to ensure sufficient widespread support through building capacity at a local level to sustain governance and service delivery. Thus, care has to be taken not to favour one group (for example, exiles, or an ethnic or sectarian group) over another. This can lead to greater violence. Here, too, elections can exacerbate inter-group tensions as differences of identity (religion, race and ethnicity) can be used to build support.

Of course, the somewhat self-righteous, post-facto justification of 'the world is a better place without Saddam' does not deal with either the medium-term instability posed by a disintegrating Iraq riven by sectarianism or the failure of the original motivation – to rid the country of the threat posed by WMD.

The absence of legitimacy made an impact at the tactical level, too. There was a lack of real political commitment to getting things right, driven in part by domestic politics. In the south of Iraq, for example, the UK probably had the chance to make a difference if its government had been prepared to spend much more money and commit many more troops to defeating the Mahdi Army, various militia and others. Yet, the multinational division based there never, in the words of one commander, 'had the troops to take them on properly even if we had been prepared to accept the casualties'.[60] This came down to two things: first, trying to do it on the cheap with not enough troops and not enough money. This prompted one commander in Iraq to note that 'unless a long-term commitment with the necessary resources is made, avoid post-conflict operations until the conflict has ended is my major lesson learnt'.

Second, political will was always lacking given that international legitimacy was questionable. Winning the hearts and minds of the population by improving their lot through restoring basic utilities and infrastructure demanded, at the outset, providing a secure environment. This would have required a much stronger and more ruthless approach to all the factions. It would also have needed a more effective military force rather than the hotchpotch coalition in the south, possessing different rules of engagement and levels of commitment. Yet, such an approach was not likely or sustainable given the lack of legitimacy.

Outside, in wars of choice like Iraq, domestic politics will always trump national survival, particularly when democratic nations are concerned. Thus, it will be difficult to have a single strategy agreed by all, even in a coalition such as NATO. And this has an impact, too, on the way in which the message about the conflict is organised and managed. Anyone who thinks that a strategic communications plan is possible needs to think again, given the huge number of Iraqi (the Shia, the Sunni, the political parties, the militia, the tribes – all of whom needed a different message), the wider Middle East, Iran, and then one's own domestic audiences at the national level and the local level. These messages have to be deconflicted; again a difficult, nay impossible, task, especially when legitimacy is fragmented.

In the absence of the purported WMD, the argument for and against Saddam's removal hinged on whether the Iraqi dictator had the intention to acquire them, which there seems to be little disagreement about, not least since such an admission would have made Baghdad appear weak to its regional foes. Whatever the trouble caused by the removal of Saddam and the cost of the ensuing sectarian conflict, Wolfowitz says the difference before and after Saddam is a 'night and day' improvement over how Iraqis were suffering.[61] For this reason he was among those calling for greater US engagement with Syria's rebels ten years on. As he put it, '[W]hen they need our help and we could provide help at very little risk to ourselves, we're letting them be slaughtered, 70 000 now. We're going to pay a price for a long time to come in Syria for that abandonment.'[62]

There is a link between Syria and Iraq's future. The likelihood of Iraqi fragmentation along sectarian and ethnic lines between its three major communities, the majority Shia, the Sunnis and the Kurds, weighs on the outcome of the Syria conflict and Iran's influence over Iraq's ruling Shia. For this and other reasons, Wolfowitz has not been not alone on Syria, though on post-Iraq and Afghanistan, he was among a minority of Americans. The conservative pundit and columnist William Kristol, for example, described President Obama's policy on Syria as 'totally irresponsible',[63] questioning what is worth intervening and fighting for if it is not ending Bashar al-Assad's rule. 'And a failure to intervene,' the *Weekly Standard* editor argues, 'makes [the US] looks weak and emboldens our enemies.'[64]

With US public opinion approval ratings on Afghanistan as a war 'worth fighting' running at below 40 per cent by April 2013,[65] Kristol was in a minority, no matter the strategic advantage in getting rid of Assad, as he pointed out, of weakening Iran and also Hezbollah, which, by then, had more than 40 000 fighters estimated to be bolstering the regime in Damascus.

This partly explains why there was so little appetite to become involved, and the regular, hollow warnings, such as those issued by Washington from December 2012 against Assad about the possible use of chemical weapons against the rebels fighting his regime. As Robert Gates, the US secretary of defence under both Bush and Obama, reminded, 'Haven't Iraq, Afghanistan and Libya taught us something about the unintended consequences of military action once it's launched?'[66]

Strategy not politics

On 13 June 2013, President Obama declared that his Syrian counterpart Assad had crossed a 'red line' by the use of chemical weapons against his domestic enemies, and America would, as a consequence, send arms and ammunition to assist the Free Syrian Army attempting to overthrow Assad. Then, following the use of sarin nerve agent in the Ghouta district of the Syrian capital, Damascus, on 21 August 2013, killing 1 400 people, the US president declared on the twelfth anniversary of 9/11 that '[o]ur ideals and principles, as well as our national security, are at stake in Syria, along with our leadership of a world where we seek to ensure that the worst weapons will never be used'. He made the case that the US must act when dictators such as the Syrian president 'brazenly' violate international treaties intended to protect humanity.[67]

The red lines, it seemed, had been criss-crossed as the US administration sought to cobble together an international response, ultimately taking the form of a joint plan with the Russians to destroy the estimated 1 000-tonne Syrian chemical weapons stockpile.

Western policy towards Syria had exemplified the primacy of narrow domestic political constituencies over policy, on the one hand, and the disjuncture between pronouncements and policy, on the other hand – put differently, between 'ends, ways and means', where domestic politics has trumped strategy. While the West rhetorically has routinely condemned the Assad regime since the outbreak of civil war in 2011 and recognised the National Coalition for Syrian Revolutionary and Opposition Forces (once the Syrian National Council), they did not provide the support necessary for its military victory. Nor, indeed, did they provide the means to ensure their more liberal interests pervaded over less enlightened strains within the rebels. If the 'end' was to remove Assad, the 'ways' and 'means' would have to reflect that goal. And if the objective was further to ensure a better type of regime came to power, the West would need to not only support those 'better' elements where they existed, but ensure their ascendancy.

The 'means' would have to be more – much more – than simply the supply of weapons, not least since the rebels had no shortage of these, but rather a dearth of the tactical and technical skills to employ them properly and effectively. It would have to involve influence through training beforehand, over a lengthy duration. It would involve air *supremacy* – on the ground and in the air – rather than only air *superiority* over the relatively sophisticated Syrian armed forces. A no-fly zone would be insufficient; one would have to be able to hit group targets in order to have a material impact on the regime's calculations.[68]

Above all, such a strategy would demand foresight and vision, where actions could match rhetoric.

The political objectives have to be clear before military and security effort is committed. These objectives have to take into consideration the lack of coherence among opposition groups and equally have to reflect a consensus among allies capable of taking this forward.

The aim of removing Assad was premised on the hope for a better society. But in whose judgement was that assessment being made – Western media, regional actors and rivals, sectarian interests, the Syrian opposition, Syrian Sunnis, minorities? This is not to say that Assad should not have been removed from power. Certainly the regime in Damascus had perpetrated horrific crimes against the civilian population. But were the alternatives to his bloody rule any better in the shape of Jabhat al-Nusra, which is affiliated with Al-Qaeda, and Ahrar al-Sham?[69] For sure the Syrian opposition was not, as Russian President Vladimir Putin tartly put it in response to Obama's June 2013 red line, men 'who kill their enemies and eat their organs', but it encompassed a full spectrum of disparate causes, from moderates fighting to topple the regime to sectarian extremists. If humanitarianism and human rights are the key considerations for intervention, then would the extremist elements observe these niceties any better than Assad? The record in Iraq suggests not.

Nor should the clamour for Assad's removal have been allowed to drown out a cold (and preferably empirical) assessment of the status of his domestic support base – rather than the volume level of his critics. Such realpolitik was described by Zbigniew Brzezinski, President Jimmy Carter's national security adviser. Saying he was 'baffled' by Mr Obama's June 2013 decision to become more deeply involved, he asked: 'What exactly is our objective? It's not clear to me that every non-democratic government in the world has to be removed by force. The Syria war is a struggle for power, not democracy,' he said. 'Is that something we should be engaged in?'

President Obama had, on his assumption to office, vowed to close the Guantanamo detention facility and get out of Iraq and Afghanistan. Going to war in Syria has run against his personal grain and America's mood. The very notion of a 'red line' supported the primacy of domestic, political calculations in this decision. But it was a wholly ambiguous criterion. Setting a red line over the killing of 150 people with chemical weapons in June 2013 after more than 90 000 had died in the civil war, smacked of polemic, not policy. This is why, while President Obama was willing to support the rebels post-red line, he was not willing to establish a no-fly zone over Syria, the White House calling it 'dramatically more difficult and dangerous and costly' than it had been in Libya in 2011.[70] The same dilemma remained, if exaggerated, after the August 2013 chemical weapon attack in Damascus.

The problem is, however, that far-away problems usually do not stay there. The Syria conflict had, by mid-2013, already drawn in Lebanon and Iran on the side of Assad, and Saudi Arabia, Qatar and Turkey in support of the rebels, while it threatened to destabilise an already wobbly Iraq and vulnerable Jordan. The latter had accepted over 500 000 Syrian refugees by the time of President Obama's June 2013 declaration, or one-tenth of its population, akin to the US accepting the entire Canadian population. There are other important implications, not least in letting the use of chemical weapons go unpunished as they are against international law. And the criss-crossing of the red lines may also have had an impact on the perceptions of American resolve, as evidenced by the Russian actions on Ukraine in March 2014, and more directly still by the rapid advance of the fighters of the Islamic State in Iraq and the Levant (ISIS) in Iraq in June 2014. This is what comes of a doctrinaire foreign policy; simply saying things do not change the facts on the ground.

Politicians willing to pronounce on problems are two a penny. Finding those politicians with the courage, constancy and integrity to not only follow their principled instinct but offer both the determination and necessary means to see them to fruition, indifferent to public opinion, is apparently much more difficult.

Heed the past

Iraq and the absence of WMD have become a stick with which to beat the Republican Party in the US, and the presidency of George W. Bush in particular. But was the WMD deception, if that is what it was, any worse than the deception over the Gulf of Tonkin incident in August 1964?[71] This incident was used as the pretext for a ramping up of involvement in Vietnam, a war that cost more than 58 000 American dead and 300 000 wounded, and an estimated 3.4 million Vietnamese lives (equivalent then pro rata to 27 million Americans),[72] against which the costs of Iraq pale. Few beat up the Democrats today over that dubious pretext for action.

Regardless of the political cynicism, whatever the justification for Saddam's removal, understanding why Iraqis from north to south never greeted the invaders with flowers back in 2003, as the optimists had cheerily hoped, demands learning from losses and mistakes.

In summary, these include the need to work to realistic timelines agreed with as many parties – domestic, international and local – as possible and not simply to try to get out as quickly as possible. It is better to be clear on what the aims and time frames are, preferably within a long-term framework of international partnership and support.

Iraq is, in this regard, emblematic of peace-building missions: a difficult and complicated socio-economic and political milieu where the knowledge of divisions, alliances and personalities were critical, as was the need for consistency of policy and personnel. Six-month tours were 'ludicrously inadequate', one general put it, for those in command positions – even if ample for the rank and file. Staying in one place longer is a useful, general rule for external missions. Such commitment should be used to drive credible local and international narratives.

This links to the need to establish local political vision and enable local action. This should not obscure difficult balances and choices. It should include the local wish for independence against rushing to failure; or the wish for early elections against the risk of having to start all over again with fresh partners. Fundamentally, the failures of Iraq should not mean that these things were not understood at the time. Some things were done badly, no doubt, and some things were learnt only after a time. Some of the right things were known from the outset, and the right things were done but with inadequate resources. Success requires doing the right things with the right resources and for a long time, probably a generation. If the great strategic mistake of the Bush administration was to invade Iraq in 2003, the great subsequent mistake has been to get out too soon.

That Saddam was undoubtedly an evil and violent dictator is indisputable. But it is less certain, to use Wolfowitz's words, that the 2003 invasion to remove the dictator offered 'the Iraqi people a chance to build a representative government that treats its people as citizens and not as subjects', or that it, as was intended by the Bush administration, offered the catalyst for improved regional stability. On the positive side of the ledger, it almost certainly frightened Muammar Gaddafi's Libya into ending its WMD programme. Yet, it also fed regional sectarianism through a surgent Shia, and popularised radical tactics, religious militancy and tribal politics from Lebanon to Yemen. Regional use of suicide bombings as part of inter-Muslim rivalries was a peculiarity before 2003; they are now viewed as a reasonable and popular instrument of the weak.

The absence of legitimacy in Iraq harmed America's global standing, undermining the honesty of its brokerage. The aspirant empire, as it was seen by some, undermined the prospect of the impartial umpire. More than all of this, the invasion was unnecessary. Military means were preferred to evict Saddam; they were not an option, as it should always be, of last resort. In the absence of a clear and imminent threat from Saddam, other means, from aid to covert operations should have been prioritised. What would Saddam's Iraq be today if several hundred billion dollars in fresh investment had been lavished on it? He would have felt less need to posture towards Tehran over his possession, intended or otherwise, of WMD, thereby emboldening regional modernisers, not militarists. Security would have come through inclusive domestic development and improved global relations, not domestic divide-and-rule tactics, and rule of law by fear. Nearly 5 000 coalition lives and countless more Iraqi lives would most likely have been saved. The region, and the world, would be a safer place.

The greater cost was to Afghanistan – the war of comparative necessity, not of choice – whose legitimacy, motives and sacrifices quickly became conflated with the Bush administration's failings in Iraq.

In this and other regards, the strategic lesson of Iraq boils down to the need for careful consideration of the options and implications of actions before resorting to war.

13

KOSOVO

Fifteen Years of Building Peace

*

War memorials, monuments and cemeteries dot Kosovo's towns and countryside. In the village of Prekaz in Skenderaj is the largest of them, to Adem Jashari, a founder and commander of the Kosovo Liberation Army (KLA), killed along with 52 members of his family in March 1998.

The site, set among the potato and wheat fields of rural Kosovo, 35 kilometres from the capital Prishtina, is a shrine, a pilgrimage for countless visiting Albanians. Designed as a Kosovar Vietnam Memorial equivalent, across the way from the semi-destroyed Jashari compound, held up by scaffolding, is a white marble expanse, dotted poignantly by raised tombstones, their inscriptions reminding of their youth.

As with all wars of liberation, Kosovars need their heroes. Jashari, who was killed in a brutal Serb operation, involving shelling of his family compound for 36 hours, has become a symbol both of resistance to Serb hegemony and Kosovo independence. His image adorns T-shirts with the Albanian slogan *'Bac U Kry!'* (Uncle, It's Done!). Awarded the status 'Hero of Kosovo' in 2008, Prishtina's airport was named after him two years later.

In reality he seems less of the good guy. Jashari, a bear of a man, having imbibed, reportedly liked to chase and shoot at Serbs. He is a controversial figure even among Albanians, at least of the thinking variety, described as a 'problematic guy' who vacillated between 'fighting and working with the Serb police, and terrorising the local Albanian population.'[1]

More important is what this celebration says about Kosovar society and attitudes towards human rights in that Jashari decided, observes one Albanian activist, 'that his family should die with him. They were never given a choice.' This relates to concerns about the KLA's wider role and tactics – that 'its members deliberately provoked [Serb leader Slobodan] Milosevic to go after the only Albanians they could, women, children and the elderly, and so deliberately got what they [the KLA] wanted: the attention of the international community'.

Celebrating Jashari's role, while understandable from an Albanian perspective, does not help to placate Serb minority insecurities and sensitivities. Put differently, it does little to nation-build. But such mythology points to still deeper challenges in Kosovo's transition.

The challenge before Kosovo and the international community

UN Secretary General Kofi Annan said in 1999 that the '[t]he task before the international community is to help the people in Kosovo to rebuild their lives and heal the wounds of conflict'.[2] It is a region with lots of deep-rooted history and enmity, which explains the bitter struggles over a small, apparently bleak territory. Landlocked and just under 11 000 square kilometres, it is smaller than Qatar and the Gambia, but slightly bigger than Lebanon or Bahrain. As Churchill once observed, the Balkans produce more history than they might consume.

Prishtina is on the site of the 1389 battle in which Prince Lazar's joint Serbian, Albanian and Bosnian force was defeated by the Ottomans, setting the stage for contemporary religious and ethnic fault lines. Although Albanians had replaced the Serbs as the dominant ethnic group in Kosovo by the end of the nineteenth century, Serbia reacquired control during the Balkan War of 1912. After the Second World War, Kosovo became an autonomous province of Serbia in Marshal Tito's Socialist Federal Republic of Yugoslavia. Despite (or perhaps because of) growing Albanian nationalism, Serbia instituted a new constitution in 1989, 600 years after the founding battle, that revoked Kosovo's status as an autonomous province of Serbia.

The tensions ratcheted up during the 1990s in the face of Yugoslavia's fragmentation. Under Milosevic, the Serbs conducted a brutal counter-insurgency campaign that led to 800 000 Kosovar Albanians fleeing from their homes.

Then, with the failure of international mediation, from 24 March until 11 June 1999, NATO bombed Kosovo for 78 days to, in the words of its spokesman, 'get the Serbs out, peacekeepers in, refugees back'[3] – to convince

Milosevic to agree to the restoration of local autonomy in the one-time Yugoslav region. Involving 1 000 aircraft operating mainly from bases in Italy and from aircraft carriers, NATO flew over 38 000 combat missions,[4] an extraordinary commitment that ended at least the twentieth-century phase of the Balkan wars. By then 13 500 people had been killed, of which 2 000 were Serbs and Romans. Some 1 754 Kosovars were still, by 2013, missing.

A NATO-led peacekeeping force, KFOR, came in behind the departing Serb forces in June 1999. The territory was placed under the United Nations Interim Administration Mission in Kosovo (UNMIK). Most of UNMIK's roles were assumed in December 2008 by the European Union Rule of Law Mission (EULEX).

In February 2008, in the midst of disagreements in the UN about the way forward over the plan proposed by then UN Special Envoy Martti Ahtisaari, Kosovo unilaterally declared its independence as the Republic of Kosovo. By 16 March 2013, the Republic of Kosovo was recognised by 101 countries, excluding (Serb-ally) Russia or fellow UN Security Council permanent member, China. Chasing diplomatic ties has become, since 2008, something of a national obsession, given the need to get above the UN General Assembly two-thirds voting mark.[5] By May 2013, the number of states recognising Kosovo stood at 100, a process clouded by controversy. In 2009, government officials in the Maldives were accused of accepting a $2-million bribe in exchange for recognising Prishtina.[6]

Kosovo is a case study of international action to prevent a humanitarian catastrophe. For a time it was held up as an exemplar of 'humanitarian intervention', thus displaying the 'responsibility to protect' civilian populations under threat. Peacekeeping and other missions, included, by 2013, 400 members of UNMIK, 2 250 of EULEX, 5 500 KFOR troops, the 600 local and international staff of the Organisation for Security and Co-operation in Europe spread across five regional centres and 30 field teams, the gamut of aid agencies, NGOs and even a smattering, too, of proselytising missionary organisations.

Shitet: What has intervention achieved?

Per capita, Kosovo is the biggest recipient of EU aid in the world. From 1999 to 2007, Kosovo received $4.5 billion in donor assistance, two-thirds of which came from the European Commission and EU governments. From 2007 to 2011, EU assistance alone for the rule of law in Kosovo totalled about

$1.6 billion, per capita aid amounting to an average of $385 during these years.[7]

While there are nit-pickers aplenty, one will search hard to find a Kosovar Albanian who views the international intervention in an overall negative light. First Deputy Prime Minister (and former president) Behgjet Pacholi says that while some aspects of this international effort failed, 'their intention was always good'. He describes KFOR as 'one the finest international institutions. It offered us security, free of charge.'

Nora Ahmetaj, director of the Centre for Research, Documentation and Publication, echoes this view: 'The international community has made mistakes, but when I think of Kosovo on 12 June 1999, it was a state of nature: no law, no institutions, where violence and revenge were our lives.' Abit Hoxha, a local journalist and analyst, seconds this view. 'KFOR has been a tremendous help in securing the environment and in rebuilding. However, there is a need,' he says, 'to distinguish KFOR from international civilian missions, where they constantly fail to recognise Kosovo's achievements though they constantly see the failures.'

Since then peaceful elections have been held regularly. Also on the positive side, Albanians and Serbs are no longer killing each other, in spite of ongoing tensions between the remaining 200 000 or so Serbs and the two million Albanian majority.[8]

But there have been two major, inter-related failings: to use aid to develop the economy, and to ensure policy choices and economic benefits are delinked from the opaque politics, influences and relationships of the liberation movement.

On the surface, much has improved since even 2008. With a per capita GDP of $7 400, Kosovo is officially a middle-income country. Wealth has grown visibly, the rise in the number and size of the cars on Prishtina's fast-improving roads being one indicator. With more than half of its generally hard-working people under 25, a minimum salary of just €170 offering possibilities for those industrialists looking for labour to access in nearby Europe, and richly endowed in a range of minerals from gold to chrome,[9] Kosovo is poised for a more prosperous, better future.

Yet, critically, unemployment remains pegged at 40 per cent of the adult population. Nearly half of the 1.5 million Kosovars live below the poverty line, with just under one-fifth being regarded by the World Bank as 'extremely poor'.[10]

The proliferation of fast-food outlets, the ubiquitous 'Auto Larje' car wash,

'Auto Polir' car polish and 'Auto Saloni' used-car lots are in part an indicator of desperation, given the lack of alternative means of income, as is the number of items from concrete blocks to property, vegetables to old tractors and trucks displaying '*Shitet*' (For Sale) signs.

This is both in spite and because of a regional safety net. Remittances from the diaspora (located mainly in Germany, Switzerland and the Nordic countries) account for nearly one-fifth of GDP, and donor-financed activities and aid for approximately 10 per cent.[11] While it might make some Kosovars too comfortable, this is also a good thing not least since the international community is, as elsewhere, not very good at delivering aid there.

Armies of expats

Donor coordination in Kosovo was the 'worst' those involved have seen, including post-conflict developing countries. In particular, coordination between European and American donors has been, in effect, non-existent, in the process affording the Kosovars plenty of opportunity for dividing-and-ruling donors. Kosovo exemplifies the problem – also seen widely elsewhere – of 'armies of expats' on fat tax-free salaries brought in, who eventually start to orient their advice towards preserving their own jobs or securing follow-up consultancies. Rather than 'achieving and leaving', they tend to foster dependency in their own interests. Kosovo suffered especially from this as it had the reputation for being as tough as Afghanistan, Iraq or Sudan, without being anything of the sort. It was, in the words of an observer, 'a good racket'.

Donor projects can be divided between 'bad' and 'good' spend.

With regard to the former, the constitutional process 'took years, armies of experts and a lot of money', but it still left areas for controversy: as EULEX found in 2010/11 over the question of how far the immunity of MPs extended. The same could be said of the Criminal Code. This was an area where numbers of consultants – from the US and the European Community, as well as bilateral – were engaged in a process of cancelling each other out and squabbling. As a result, more than four years after independence, Kosovars did not have an agreed text. On the one hand, US experts insisted on American practices that came from the US version of common law; on the other hand, Kosovo had adopted the Napoleonic civil law system under the UN, the most common in Europe. The insistence on US systems where they clashed with EU ones was also not consistent with the overarching US policy that was to get Kosovo into the EU. From an EU perspective, a 'lot' of US in-country action, from 2010–12 at least, seemed aimed at protecting the Kosovars from attempts by the EU to hold their feet to the fire on engagement with Serbia, governance, and so on. The EU, however, also undermined itself. Despite the wording of EULEX's mandate, there are no European standards in the rule of law (apart from general principles such as the separation of powers and the presumption of innocence) because some EU countries have common law and some civil law. The fact that EULEX contained a mixture of personnel from both traditions also undermined EULEX's internal cohesion and efficiency.

Border control systems were another area of stand-off between the US and the EC. The EC was trying to insist on EU standard systems that did not 'talk' to American ones. The US twisted Kosovar arms to take the US system because they wanted access to the data as part of their regional monitoring of movements for counter-terrorism purposes.

European nations also spent a lot of money trying to improve local structures for government decision-making. Yet, there were few signs that the various consultants engaged made any great difference. A key problem in this regard was that 'the prime minister exercises power through a mafioso patronage system, and transparent appointment procedures or devolved decision-making on anything touching finance simply don't happen'.

Similar problems existed with procurement reform and police reform. Again, the political will to change was not present. With the benefit of hindsight, donors believe that the police should have 'been allowed to fly solo after ten years of UNMIK partnership/mentoring, uneven in quality though that was'. Overall, it is not viewed as very good use of tens of millions of EU money, which 'would have been better spent on prisons and more prison officer mentors/trainers'.

Five hundred million euros of external assistance has also gone into the power sector, without much apparent success. Regular power cuts still occur despite the country sitting on the fifth-largest reserves of lignite worldwide. In fact, in Yugoslav times, Kosovo was a net exporter of electricity. The generation units are old, maintenance is sporadic, necessary expertise left with the Serbs, and many people simply do not like to pay their bills.

Instead of the international community accelerating the introduction of a third Kosovo C power generation plant to meet rapidly rising demand, these plans have, as one sector specialist put it, become a 'battleground'. As soon as the World Bank became involved, 'international NGOs followed suit like mercenaries, making a fortune for themselves by criticising everyone else's plans and with no interest in having a dialogue'. But 'not only do they have impractical plans, with no reasonable and practical power mix, their sole focus is reducing emissions, and promoting renewable energy, not developing Kosovo. The biggest problem is that no one is facing up to the elephant in the room. If you're going to have long-term economic growth, you need energy', she says. 'And if you are going to have energy in Kosovo, it's going to be lignite, like it or not.'

Rather than the country becoming an 'energy hub', the process is thus being hamstrung by the focus on renewables, an 'expensive luxury', which is 'symptomatic of the confusion', reflects another donor specialist, 'caused by us. This is despite everyone saying at the outset that "this time it would be different" and all of us being aware that the solution lies in the need for one institution or country to take responsibility for one sector – for there to be a lead nation.' What has been 'a victory for the NGOs' means that Kosovo, which will need at least 3 500 MW of power by 2030 by some estimates, will be lucky to have 1 500 MW.

Problems in the power sector also reflect concerns about the privatisation process overall. Confused by a distinction between public-owned and state-owned enterprises (where the former were owned, at least in part, by the workers), there has been unhappiness over the transparency and pricing of these processes, though this reflects mainly local interests rather than foreign intentions.

And then there are the areas of 'good' spend.

The programme to turn the KLA first into the Kosovo Protection Corps (for civil assistance and disaster relief) then into a slimmed-down 2 500-strong Kosovo Security Force, or embryo army, by way of demobilisation for many former combatants has been a success. However, there is controversy about the exact numbers of the KLA, with more than 35 000 claiming such status and the related benefits.

It did a lot to prevent the demobilised freedom fighters from turning into discontented, destabilising and anti-social elements. As a result, while the 'embryo army is still in the process of turning from the KLA's Che Guevara-style *bandilleros* into disciplined troops … they will get there'.

The establishment of the Kosovo Property Agency is also viewed as a success, and for a relatively small $15 million annual outlay. A multi-donor-funded agency founded by UNMIK and then adopted by 'recognising donors' after independence under a Kosovo government umbrella, the agency's aim was to restore legal title to the rightful landowners of private land and property after so many had fled their homes in 1999, but without clogging up already overburdened and inadequate civil courts. Most beneficiaries in the 40 000 caseloads were Serbs. Although the sponsoring of organised returns by Serbs to their Kosovar towns and villages were seen to be expensive and 'uneven' in terms of results, maintaining a trickle of returns importantly preserved the hope that a multi-ethnic Kosovo with a thriving Serb minority might not be an impossible dream, at least in a generation or so.

The creation of Kosovo customs is also viewed as a success, despite constant political interference over appointments. Revenues from customs receipts are totally vital to a functioning Kosovo government, given the country's lamentable economic dependence on imports. *Circa* 2013 and Kosovo customs delivers around three-quarters of all local revenue for the budget.

Scholarships have been a good investment in the future and its leaders. It is puzzling why these are not more prevalent in Kosovo as elsewhere, given the long-term educational, political and networking benefits on offer to both the recipient and provider. It is also spent in the country, valuable especially in times of relative economic hardship among donors.

Finally, the 'overwhelming' extent of international technical assistance to Kosovo has meant that, in the words of one consultant, 'the country has the best laws but much less ability to follow through on them. Kosovo has legislation without implementation.' While overall, as Hoxha says, 'Kosovo would be in a far worse position without international assistance, this does not mean that things could not have been better'. In particular, 'while we need advice, we don't need people doing the job of locals. Rather than supplementing local hotels and restaurants, the money should be steered into more productive aspects, including education. And rather than trying to teach Albanians how to live, how to brush their teeth, help them find the means to live better.'

True grit

The economic and development challenges faced by Kosovo are, of course, not unique, given the overall hurdles faced by all from globalisation and the need to ensure global competitiveness, especially among those transitioning from centrally planned economies as in the former Yugoslavia. On paper, Macedonia, 100 kilometres to the south, is wealthier than Kosovo, with a GDP per capita of over $10 000. In reality, however, from the gritty border at Tanusevci, covered in a film of cement dust, to the capital of Skopje 20 kilometres away, it is depressingly shabby, an exporter of tomatoes, tobacco, paprika, some steel and wine, and its best talent. Like Kosovo, around 15 per cent of its two million citizens live abroad, mostly in the EU, remitting money to their poorer relatives. But in other more important respects, also like Kosovo, it is landlocked and locked out of the global economy; not because both do not possess trade preferences to the giant trade bloc, which they do, but since they do not produce and trade enough.

For all the glitzy statues of Alexander the Great and other colossuses adorning Skopje's central square, times are tough. 'My father had five children,' says Farouk, 61, a local jeweller. 'Yet he could afford to send us all to school and take us on four holidays a year on one salary. Then we had more than twenty large factories and many smaller ones in Skopje alone, including a steel factory employing 18 000 people. Today,' he muses, 'my four children are unemployed. I work twelve hours a day, and never take home more than €300 a month. I struggle to meet my electricity bill even. The textile factories are all closed, and the big steel one is now run by Indians and employs just 500. And,' he snorts, as if in confirmation of the desperation of Macedonians, 'they tell us there is a 1 per cent chance of joining the European Union in the next ten years.'

Kosovo has not done so badly in comparison. It also has the advantage that most of its people, unlike Farouk, were not alive during the heyday of Tito and the former Yugoslavia. There is no golden era to look fondly back to, only a recent memory of Serb domination. 'We should not forget,' says Hoxha, a research associate at the Centre for Security Studies in Prishtina, 'that there was in 1999 a sign at the Grand Hotel that said: Dogs or Albanians forbidden.'

Despite its location on the busy Mother Teresa pedestrian walkway, the Grand Hotel is a somewhat forlorn reminder of those best-forgotten times, superseded by others that have sprung up since 2008, their standards shaped by the market and not by the state. This market is not always politically benign, however.

The rule of law link

There are wider, insidious problems in Kosovo, less developmental than linked intrinsically with the political economy.

These concern the emergence of Kosovo as a 'mafia state' – a European enclave for drugs (about 40 per cent of the continental and North American heroin is estimated to transit the territory), pirated goods, and organ and human trafficking. Money laundering and the absence of wider economic opportunity explain why there are countless motels, hotels and coffee bars, Auto Larjes, and more than 1 000 petrol stations countrywide. Although the Albanian population likes to pump up the military folklore of their KLA at every opportunity, their recent history is less full metal than fake leather jacket.

It is this aspect – delinking politics from this black economy – that both donors and local civil society have found difficult to encourage, let alone ensure. Breaking such habits is difficult to achieve where policemen earn €200 a month, a magistrate perhaps €300, and the prime minister and president of the supreme court €1 000. Flaunting the system is a badge of honour and profoundly political. Local power brokers quickly understood the priority of the international community was to prevent an explosion of conflict, and they have used that fear of destabilisation as a 'tool for political and criminal impunity', says one anonymous local activist.

There is a governance 'mindset', critics say, 'to do everything through nepotism and corruption' in Kosovo. Smuggling and other forms of criminality are one aspect, but they are linked to other, political issues, including immunity from prosecution for war crimes. Carla del Ponte, who served as the chief prosecutor of the International Criminal Tribunal for the former Yugoslavia (ICTY), has noted that 'impunity shrouds powerful political and military figures' in Kosovo, where the international community has displayed a 'fear-driven reluctance to apply the law'.[12] At the centre of these concerns is the KLA, the liberation movement once described by Bill Clinton's Balkan envoy Robert Gelbard as a 'terrorist group'.

When Kadri Veseli, a leading ruling party politician (and former head of the domestic intelligence agency known by the Bondesque acronym SHIK), reportedly threatened the international community at a 2013 political rally in Malisheva 'for putting on trial the values of the KLA through fake trials', he was tapping into a rich vein of discontent and entitlement. He was referring to the retrial ordered against a leading member of his party, Fatmir

Limaj. A 2011 war crimes case against Limaj, the former transport minis-
ter and KLA commander, and three other KLA members collapsed after
Agim Zogaj, known as 'Witness X',[13] died in Germany in an apparent suicide.
Limaj and his co-defendants were accused of torturing and killing Serbian
detainees at a prison in the southern Kosovo village of Klecka in 1999.[14] In
November 2012, Limaj, deputy president of the ruling Democratic Party of
Kosovo, and six others were also indicted by EULEX on charges of corruption, organised crime and money laundering.[15] This was not the first time he
had been in the spotlight. Arrested in February 2003 while vacationing with
Hashim Thaci in Slovenia, two years later the ICTY acquitted him of war
crimes charges. According to an internal 2004 ICTY document, there had
been a campaign of 'serious intimidation of and interference with potential
witnesses'.[16]

And he is not alone. In April 2008 the ICTY cleared the former Kosovo
prime minister (and one-time bouncer), Ramush Haradinaj, and two others of charges of abusing detainees, noting, however, their 'strong impression that the trial was being held in an atmosphere where witnesses felt
unsafe'.[17] At the centre of allegations about the link between organised
crime, the KLA and politics is two-time prime minister, Thaci, a man hailed
by US Vice President Joe Biden as the 'George Washington of Kosovo'.[18] He
has stood accused in the media as having 'established influence on local
criminal organizations, which control [a] large part of Kosovo'.[19] A 2005
German intelligence document has claimed that, after the war, Thaci, who
had served as the KLA's political chief, presided over an organised crime
empire whose leaders came from Kosovo's Drenica Valley. The Drenica
group allegedly engaged in money laundering, maintaining links to arms
and drug smugglers and Albanian criminal groups.[20] Thaci has deflected
the accusations. 'Until the war broke out, the Serbs wanted to imprison
me. In wartime, they tried to kill me. After the war, they tried to compromise me, to destroy my reputation.'[21]

The pressing need for stability can trump, in the short term, concerns for
governance and human rights; in the longer term, such expediency usually
returns to haunt international partners and locals alike, undermining the
prospects for development and stability.[22]

Little wonder that the European Court of Auditors reported in October
2012 that EU aid 'has not been sufficiently effective' in boosting democratic
standards and battling crime and corruption. 'Although the EU helped to
build capacity, notably in the area of customs, assistance to the police and

the judiciary has had only modest success.' It added that 'levels of organised crime and corruption in Kosovo remain high'. This is of little surprise when the freedom struggle was financed through organised crime.

Yet, Pacholi complains that international supervision has killed Kosovo through the 'personalisation of the agenda' and by 'trying to solve by force local political problems. Rather,' he says, 'the solution has to be through economic prosperity and by financing projects, to ensure that people have a job that will reduce political tensions.'

Reflecting on intervention

Kosovo is in some respects a bit of Africa in Europe. With the UN, EU, International Civilian Office, KFOR and government all apparently with some degree of control, plus the all-powerful US Embassy as the arbiter of last resort, like Africa there are a multitude of international actors in the game, with little coordination, and many destructive clashes and wasteful overlap.

No wonder then that Kosovo has had to resort to importing coal for its energy sector in addition to energy itself. Known for its rich soils, it imports 95 per cent of its food and other basic requirements. It consumes and hardly produces. It makes little that the rest of the world wants to buy – and there is not much inducement to do so when so much is provided by outsiders. This is exacerbated by international elements intent on hindering the development and export of two of its key resources: coal and power. With the skills picked up in a war of liberation, it is little wonder in the circumstances that these are easily adapted to criminality.

More revealing is another externally linked dimension in that such a large chunk of the constitution is devoted to protecting minorities. Human rights are not seen as intrinsic national, societal values, but rather having to be imported from outside.

Here Kosovo illustrates a recurring theme in this book – of the importance of migrating quickly from the mythology of liberation and identity-based political choices to those where such choices are based rather on issues and safeguarded not by warlords and ethnic allegiances, but by civil and public institutions, from media to parliament. International support for NGO watchdogs and parliamentary capacity-building is a good investment in this future.

14

LIBERIA

Mission with a Long Tail?

*

M any things have changed dramatically for the better in Liberia, at least from the vantage point of the visitor.[1]

James Spriggs Payne airport, for one, the secondary airfield in the centre of Monrovia, by 2013 accepted scheduled flights. Five years before it was a depot for UN helicopters and transport aircraft, its then leaky and dilapidated hangars filled with broken aircraft and other relics. The facilities have been transformed, with several civilian helicopters and light aircraft signalling a change in fortunes. A smart Liberian fire-fighting force stands by where once there were UN peacekeepers.

Equally, the main airport at Roberts has changed from a rugby scrum on arrival to a more orderly experience. Heathrow Terminal Five both are not, but the signs of war have faded, physically and organisationally. The ride into the city, a potholed nightmare at the start of the democratic era with the first administration of President Ellen Johnson Sirleaf in 2006, is much improved. A Chinese-built highway is only part of the story: solar-powered traffic lights, centre-line road markings, cat's eyes and even pedestrian crossings hint at the vast improvements in governance and expanding presence of government.

Monrovia itself has vastly changed, too. In 2006, when Johnson Sirleaf took office as Africa's first elected female president, both physical institutions and the necessary skills that were supposed to go with them were virtually non-existent. Ministries might have been lucky enough to have a competent head, which was not true in all cases, but they were usually bereft of staff, computers, financial resources and modern bureaucratic systems. The first budget of the Johnson Sirleaf administration was just $80 million, this for a country of 3.5 million people. 'There were no systems, no computers, and no capacity back then,' recalls the president, with money changing hands via an antiquated cheque system.

Then the business climate attracted just a hardy few pioneers. Among them, however, were mobile phone operators, their presence reflected in the rise of telephony from under 10 per cent of the population in 2006 to over 50 per cent within six years. With stability came fresh international investment in mining in particular, but also in a range of new hotels, restaurants and other services. The port, where a vessel lay on its side until 2010 blocking access to the main quay, is functioning again, its customs receipts the most important source of revenue to the state outside of aid.

This recovery has not been easy. Much infrastructure was badly fractured by conflict, asset stripping and years of maintenance-free abuse. Many government buildings were, in 2006, just ransacked shells. Even the Executive Mansions were unoccupied and uninhabitable, nearly all roads were in a terrible state inside the capital and especially outside, and there was no central production and distribution of electricity power. The turbines at the Mount Coffee hydro plant had disappeared altogether after its destruction by Charles Taylor's rebel forces in their assault on the capital in 1992. In Monrovia, the lamp posts on the Gabriel Johnson Tucker Bridge, linking the port to the city centre, are still peppered with bullet holes, the Mesurado waterway underneath representing the final front for various rebel onslaughts.

Getting access to the port of Buchanan or to plantations at Guthrie and the Bumi iron ore mine back then required back-breaking efforts. Places farther afield, such as Maryland, were reachable only by boat or by helicopter. Liberia's borders were largely ungoverned, at least without the help of the UN.

The UN has long held the security ring against domestic spoilers. Yet, as another indicator of returning normality, the organisation is now winding down its operations. From an authorised strength of 15 250 troops in 2006, the numbers have declined to 8 000 in 2010 to 6 000 by September 2013.[2] It will drop to 3 750 by July 2014. The 2012–13 budget started at $672 million but was cut sharply in March 2013 to some $544 million. The 2013–14 budget is approximately $583 million. There are few countries where the UN presence 'has been so broadly appreciated by the population, where relations with government are so good', notes a senior UN official, 'and where the UN Security Council remains so supportive even ten years after its advent'.[3] And the continued success of the mission hints at the need for the maintenance of a long-term commitment. At the end of Broad Street, the city's main street, the 300-room Ducor Hotel stands atop the city's highest point. Taken over by refugees during the war and totally stripped of any valuable fittings, it has been declared structurally unsafe and condemned. It had played host once to many of the great, good and the bad. The pool in which Idi Amin once swam, lies empty, its diving board pointing at a famous, more prosperous past.

Outside the looted, derelict hotel was a four-wheel drive with 'Concern Worldwide' emblazoned on its door. Forgiving the patronising label of this no doubt worthy body, its presence reinforced how far Liberia had fallen from the heady days of the Ducor. With its reserves of iron, diamonds, timber and rubber, Liberia had been among the top five, fastest growing economies worldwide in the 1950s, when it averaged an 11.5 per cent growth rate, and when the Ducor was built by the Intercontinental Group.[4]

In 2006 there were no reasonable options for the visiting traveller, apart from the legendary Mamba Point Hotel. Now the punter is spoilt for choice, with US, Lebanese and Chinese investors opening new sites.

Thus, on the face of things, Liberia's transition is a fairy tale, a shining success story, a testament to international cooperation and UN staying power. Yet, underneath the skin lie deeper problems, which can only be resolved by local action.

Some things stay the same

On the one hand, a key lesson of the international engagement from Liberia is the need to assist local leadership over the 'hump' of low capacity, fractious politics, insecurity and institutional frailty, where international partners are often 'waiting and seeing' with respect to the disbursement of funds. Leadership is all important at the inception of a post-conflict era, given that there is a greater premium in such individuals where capacity is low, systems weak and a return to conflict continuously threatens. Thus, the UN approach at the beginning to go into Liberia with relatively large numbers, spread across the country to establish centres in all of the fifteen counties nationwide and to focus on monitoring and better management of its borders was the right one.

On the other hand, some things remain the same. These relate less to the external image but the inner stuffings of the state.

As one indicator of the challenge of changing the mindset, Monrovia is dotted with signs for evangelical churches: 'City Hope – Wonder's Land', 'Winner's Chapel', 'Remedy Chapel', 'Beauty Chapel Praise Ministries', 'First Era Free Church', 'Bethal Cathedral of Hope – Win the Lord at all Costs', 'Trumpet of God Institute'. These are among the many calling for redemption and redeemers.

Why? In the opinion of Ghanaian Cardinal Peter Turkson, who sat next to me on a flight to Liberia from Ghana, such churches have filled the gap left by the fading influence and role of traditional healers in African societies. But they play the same role. For the apparently *papabile* cardinal, this also explains the increasing prominence of Islam, more than the considerable proselytising effort. Instead of forcing people to take responsibility, such religions pass this onto someone else – where it once was ancestors or other spirits, it is now some other party's responsibility.[5] It is a reaction also to what has happened to old-fashioned 'secret societies' in Liberia, but above all, it reflects the conviction that a spirit world exists.[6]

Certainly, growth of religious evangelism in Liberia, as in other African countries, speaks to the desperate difficulties faced by citizens in these societies, despite recent improvements. It illustrates just how, for all of the improving empirical indicators, life remains gruelling to the point of desperation for many people. This is one of the reasons why liberation theology in its modern form – the so-called 'prosperity gospel' – is huge in Africa, from Cape Town to Lagos. The notion that God is there to make you rich has very little to do with New Testament Christianity but everything to do with poor people who have nothing (or the 'blessed' rich who want to justify conspicuous consumption amid poverty).[7]

While GDP growth has been impressive, nearly tripling to $1.5 billion between 2006 and 2011, Liberia remains very poor. Per capita GDP was under $400 in 2012. Electricity generation, to take another indicator, was sparse and expensive, with just 22 MW of thermal (diesel) power at $0.54c kW/h feeding Monrovia, while the promised extra 80 MW of the Mount Coffee Scheme at $0.14c kW/h seemed a tantalisingly long way off. More than half of the $672 million 2012 Liberian budget was met by donors. An estimated 64 per cent of the population still lives below the international poverty line, despite the high rate of economic growth. This accounts for Liberia's low ranking on the UN's Human Development Index, for example: ranking 162 out of 169 countries in 2010.

It is said that the Liberian civil war was less a civil war in terms of a contest of ideologies than it was about looting and mayhem, the opportunities for plunder that it afforded.[8] Its GDP, as a consequence, fell by an estimated 90 per cent between 1987 and 1995.[9]

Perhaps reflecting this aspect, action on issues of reconciliation and justice for past occurrences has lagged behind 'harder' concerns about debt relief, public administration and infrastructure building in the recovery and reconstruction process. Yet, there remain deep-rooted issues of economic exclusion that have long pervaded Liberia's political economy.

From war to peace

As the motto on the national coat of arms – 'The Love of Liberty Brought us Here' – intimates, Liberia has its origins in the efforts of an oligarchy of 3 000 freed slaves assisted by the American Colonization Society to create a new home. This hints at the 150 subsequent years of tension between locals and America-Liberians (under 5 per cent of the population), which has blighted Liberian politics. This group ruled almost unchallenged from the nation's founding in 1847 until April 1980 when the America-Liberian leadership of President William Tolbert was ended by a violent military coup led by Master Sergeant Samuel Doe, from the local Krahn ethnic group. 'An uneducated "car-boy"', says Winston Tubman, UN ambassador under Tolbert, of Doe, whom he later served as justice minister. But he tapped into this sense of ethnic exclusion. 'The rice riots of the previous year had made Tolbert very unpopular when he tried to increase the price to stimulate self-sufficiency,' reminds Tubman, nephew of William Tubman, Liberia's president from 1944 to 1971, and himself a presidential contender in 2011 against Johnson Sirleaf. By the time of Tubman Snr's death in a London clinic from a prostate operation gone wrong, Liberia had the largest shipping fleet in the world, the world's biggest rubber industry, and it was the third-largest exporter of iron ore. The success, in its own way, of Tubman's Liberia was due partly to the creation of a US business lobby seeking their own private offshore destination for banking and shipping registration.

Doe's coup signalled the beginning of two successive civil wars, resulting in the 250 000 deaths and devastating the country's economy. A peace agreement in 2003 led to democratic elections in 2005. Liberia is recovering from the lingering effects of the civil wars and their consequent economic upheaval.

The coup story has become legendary for its violence. Doe and the other plotters pulled Tolbert from his bed in his Israeli-built Executive Mansion and disembowelled him, on account of a belief that 'he was immune to being killed by a bullet', says Tubman.[10] He was called that evening and told of the coup, remembering that 'many African Americans were quite pleased at Tolbert's demise, considering us Liberians are quite uppity given our success'. Most of Tolbert's cabinet were also killed, along with other government officials and members of his True Whig Party. But Doe inadvertently set the stage for his own, equally brutal and bloody end.

The National Patriotic Front of Liberia, a rebel group led by Charles Taylor, who Tubman describes as a 'clever man, but one with a criminal mind', launched an insurrection in December 1989 against Doe's government with the backing of neighbouring countries such as Burkina Faso and Côte d'Ivoire, triggering the First Liberian Civil War. By September 1990, Doe's forces controlled only a small area just outside the capital. Doe was captured by Taylor's sometime ally and rival Prince Johnson of the Independent National Patriotic Front of Liberia. Doe's ears were cut off and he bled to death, the grisly scenes videotaped for posterity. Any war that featured the likes of Johnson and Taylor, as well as Generals Peanut Butter (the *nom de guerre* of Nimba senator, Adolphus Dolo) and Butt Naked (that of Joshua Milton Blahyi, now a preacher), was never likely to be fought according to the Geneva Convention.

A peace deal between various warring parties was reached in 1995 and led to Taylor's election as president in 1997. This only temporarily paused the fighting.

A Second Liberian Civil War began two years later when Liberians United for Reconciliation and Democracy, a rebel group based in the north-west of the country, launched an armed insurrection. Together with a second group, the Ivorian-based Movement for Democracy in Liberia, the rebels launched an assault on Monrovia in July 2003. By that August Taylor had resigned and by September the UN had arrived. Things have been more or less peaceful ever since.

With Taylor in temporary exile in Nigeria, the August 2003 Comprehensive Peace Agreement accords brokered in Accra, Ghana, formed the blueprint for Liberia's two-year transition from conflict to presidential and legislative elections slated for October 2005. Johnson Sirleaf, representing the Unity Party, won 59 per cent of the vote in a run-off against George Weah, the former international soccer star.

272 — WHY STATES RECOVER

Tackling the challenges

The way Johnson Sirleaf and her government dealt with the country's myriad challenges was, first, by creating short-term momentum. Under a 150-day programme, electricity was promised and delivered to key parts of Monrovia, and refugees returned and were resettled in the city. This programme was repeated again at the start of her second term in 2012 when a further 150-day plan delivered the renovation of over 250 kilometres of road and other major infrastructure projects, such as the dredging of the ports at Monrovia and Greenville and the launch of vocational and technical training for 3 000 youths.

President Johnson Sirleaf admits that 'we did not have a 150-day plan on day one. It was developed in successive weeks between the time I was elected and the time of the inauguration, when I had teams that worked on every sector. This work was not harmonised or coherent, but it made the 150-day plan easier. Beyond 150 days, we entered into the Heavily Indebted Poor Countries (HIPC) plan and our Poverty Reduction Strategy around which our strategy was formed.'

'Our real long-term plan,' she adds, 'that was based on considerable consultation and analysis, was the Agenda for Transformation, which was three years in the making, though its roll-out was delayed by the 2011 election.'

As for best practice, the president says, 'The one country that I had wanted to follow was Rwanda, but it was quite a different environment. President Kagame was invited here and he met with us. I had also worked with Rwanda when I was at the UNDP [United Nations Development Programme], so I knew where he had started from. We had the advantage of natural resources. But we did not have the advantages they had of capacity, work ethic and discipline. We also departed from Rwanda in terms of the implementation of democracy; I am not sure,' she smiles, 'whether that was an advantage.'[11]

Government capacity was also catalysed by the installation of the Transfer of Knowledge Through Expatriate Nationals (TOKTEN) and the Senior Executive Service (SES) programmes. In 2000, it was estimated that 45 per cent of Liberia's skilled workers (defined as those with post-secondary education), or about 21 000 people, lived outside the country. Most of these were among the 500 000 people of Liberian descent who lived in the US. The common aim of these programmes was to attract these skills back home, creating a surge of excellence within the civil service, while gradually training others from the bottom up. TOKTEN aimed to recruit professional expatriates for relatively short-term contracts of 6–18 months to help build systems or train others. The SES sought to attract 100 skilled Liberians on longer, three-year renewable contracts and retain them for the long term, focusing their activities on Liberia's Poverty Reduction Strategy.[12] Antoinette Sayeh, a one-time World Bank country director for Benin, Niger and Togo and country economist for Pakistan and Afghanistan, was the minister of finance from 2006 to 2009 (thereafter head of the IMF's Africa Department) and, together with Charles Allen, the head of the civil service, a key mover behind these schemes.

High on the agenda was naturally reinstating the traditional drivers of economic growth. By 2013, Liberia had the highest ratio of foreign direct investment to GDP in the world, with $18 billion in earmarked investment since 2006. The Johnson Sirleaf government renegotiated its deals on iron ore and signed several mining and palm oil concessions. It also commenced exploration for offshore oil and gas. And it has retained its status as a flag of convenience with the second-largest maritime registry in the world behind Panama, with 3 500 vessels or 11 per cent of those worldwide registered.

There have been setbacks. Beyond palm oil and some rice planting in the north, there has been little success in getting agriculture going. Some 90 per cent of rice remains imported, the cost cancelling out the income from rubber exports, the second-largest item after iron ore. This reflects political interests in the import business but, more importantly, little interest by producers in the tough back-breaking work of rice production. If donor alternatives exist, in other words, why not take them?

The government also immediately had to deal with its $4.9-billion debt overhang. It went early along the path of HIPC debt relief, a process starting in March 2008, when it reached the 'decision point' under the HIPC initiative and embarked on a three-year IMF-supported financial programme that concluded in June 2010 with the granting of relief from being one of the most heavily indebted countries in the world in terms of its GDP-to-debt ratio.[13] This involved some tricky financial footwork. In late 2007 the World Bank cancelled $400 million and the African Development Bank $250 million in debt. After the 2008 HIPC decision point and the Paris Club debt decision shortly thereafter, a commercial buy-back of $1.2 billion at $0.03c on the dollar followed in April 2009. The fall of total debt to just $200 million was the biggest percentage debt write-down in history.[14]

Liberia also signed up to the Kimberley Process[15] in May 2007, certifying the source of its export of diamonds as conflict-free. Uncontrolled export of the gems had, during the rule of Charles Taylor and his Revolutionary United Front bedfellows in neighbouring Sierra Leone, helped to fuel the conflict in both countries. Liberia had been subject to UN sanctions on export trade in diamonds from 2001 until April 2007.

All along, Monrovia had to maintain its global security umbrella, building a small local army of just 2 000 troops under (largely) American tutelage[16] and 4 000 police under United Nations Police (UNPOL) auspices, and expanding its range of donors, governmental and non-governmental, and international advisers. The role of external advisers has been notable and in some specific cases effective, reflecting both the government's receptiveness to advice and expertise, and the relatively executive-centric nature of the administration. Under the old True Whig party system, corruption and patronage centred on a president who has to ensure resources from outside, or from foreign collaborators such as mining companies. Although this political economy has, to an extent, changed under President Johnson Sirleaf from its traditional Americo-Liberian 'ownership', some of the same problems of them-and-us elitism still pervade, even if they are now comprised, as one international official put it, 'of Americo-Liberians, returning diaspora, former warlords and politicians'.

Certainly, the inclusive nature of the political settlement – the psychotic Prince Johnson became a senator for Nimba County – illustrates the Liberian imperative to avoid creating a constituency of losers who might feel a need to resort to violence. Back in the mid-2000s, it was important to display immediate short-term benefits from stability, whether these losers are from urban or rural groups, have particular ethnic or religious origins or orientation, or whether these opportunities are shaped by gender or even race. However, there is an underlying resentment among ordinary Liberians that many of those who committed terrible crimes are not only free, but in some cases in government.

But other losers still exist, evidenced by the disparity between the monthly salaries of parliamentarians (between $10 000 and $20 000, including a 500-gallon fuel and other myriad monthly allowances), the estimated $700 000 received annually by the speaker of parliament and the $100 monthly pay of a police officer. And there is a tension always between the urge to deliver something immediately and work for the longer term. The legislature is berated in this regard as a scheme for short-term enrichment, with members being bought off on critical votes. A March 2013 USAID evaluation on financial support to the Liberian legislature, for example, concluded: 'Some key *strengths* include the fact that the Legislature is able to say no to the Executive; it is no longer simply considered a rubber stamp. Legislative feedback is increasingly being taken into consideration by the Executive.' However, it added that '*weakness* is demonstrated by the reality that leadership and direction on legislative modernization is intermittent and passive. There is little discipline in legislative functions. There are widespread perceptions of corruption. There is limited constituency outreach.'[17]

Fundamentally, in this regard, 'Liberians themselves,' says a foreign diplomat, 'have to tackle the issue of whether their country is American or Liberian, whether they themselves want to commit and live in Liberia or not. Bizarrely,' he adds, 'half the government has families and interests in the US.' Having the diaspora fill the skills gap has been expensive; it has consumed the budget on recurrent (salary) expenditures, and has fuelled the above-mentioned them-and-us perception, which was an original driver behind the conflict in the 1980s. It is a country where 'half live on the Liberian dollar and the other half the US one and off foreign donors', says one such donor.

This is compounded by the absence of job prospects outside of the government. 'There are essentially three economies here,' says another donor: 'the government, the Lebanese enclave, and the rest subsisting. There is no private sector. And until you get a private sector going more robustly and people have more reliable livelihoods, it is always going to be tough.' Corruption is related to the shortage of opportunity as well as the weakness of government oversight. 'On the one hand, many Liberians had, before 2006, never known government. This has demanded much more than re-building, but creating a whole new country and culture,' she says, 'complete with a new government system.' On the other hand, corruption 'is rooted in an idea of "it is my turn" – and positioning in the government system in this regard, worsened by poor management of natural resources.' Liberia has historically evolved in such a way that it is in 'existential need' of a patron or a sugar daddy.[18] Historically, this was first an NGO (the American Colonization Society), then for a period it was the British government, then especially after Firestone came in in the 1920s, it was the US. When the war started in December 1989, the Cold War was effectively over, so Washington did not intervene. Nigeria tried the role of godfather (1990–97) but could not make it work. From 1997 to 2003, Charles Taylor sought, as Stephen Ellis notes, 'all sorts of shady alliances, and Libya was a godfather of sorts'.

These issues are more pronounced in considering the question asked of Liberia: what happens when Ellen goes? President Johnson Sirleaf has been able to leverage her international ties developed during her time at the

World Bank, Citibank and the UN,[19] and relationships from Hillary Clinton to George Soros, to bring aid and sympathetic attention to Liberia, increased by her status as a Nobel laureate. Still the US has little strategic interest, save a humanitarian dimension in not wishing to see the country collapse again.

'When Johnson Sirleaf goes,' Ellis agues, 'there will be no such external godfather unless a future Liberian president can interest China or someone else. Even if there is an external patron, much depends on commodity prices, including aid flows. In the 1950s, Liberian growth rates were second only to Japan, for a period. The True Whig regime collapsed when it did partly because of a slump in prices for iron ore and rubber, plus high oil prices.' Moreover, there remains a schism between the Americo-Liberian Whig tendency and its structures, which President Johnson Sirleaf has, to an extent, been able to resuscitate and rely upon, and the interests of other, local ethnic groups.[20]

This all combines into an overall challenge, says a UN member, 'to get people thinking and working collectively for the greater good over generations'. Given Liberia's history of marginalisation, exclusion and weak government, 'this is still work in progress'.

Signs of success or failure?

In 2013 not one of the 25 000 applicants passed the admissions exam to the University of Liberia. Not one received a passing grade, and prospective students scored particularly poorly in English. The university quickly announced that it would adjust initial benchmark requirements to accept a portion of the applicants.[21]

This reflects other, deeper 'software' issues. For one, the literacy rate of Liberia is estimated at just 60 per cent. As is highlighted above, corruption also remains problematic, and endemic. In another 2013 report, President Johnson Sirleaf's longstanding minister of defence, Brownie Samukai, was caught on tape berating the levels of corruption in government over a proposed airport runway deal.[22]

Are these revelations indicators of deep-rooted problems, or of relative success? The answer is both. They would seem to hint at an attempt to set higher standards and a degree of transparency, at least of the fourth estate.

They also hint at a bigger challenge, especially for Liberia's international partners. There are evident dangers in the UN, in particular, withdrawing too soon – or, indeed, of leaving it too long. With the relatively effective army geared to territorial (sovereign) defence, the police are supposed to step up to the domestic plate. Yet, it is debatable whether they can manage this – the different policing cultures of various UNPOL advisers, including the Filipinos and Brazilians, have not created a coherent force but one where 'quality is terrible and corruption rife', according to one diplomat.

This highlights the key lesson from Liberia, for an 'exit strategy at the start. Liberians have become too dependent,' he says, 'too lazy, and lean too much on the UN. There is a need to get them to stand up much sooner, certainly before the 2017 election.' This, of course, has to be balanced against both the greater psychological impact of withdrawal, and the (lesser) reality of the security void. 'By not addressing early on an exit strategy, a culture of dependency on the UN and others,' says a major donor, 'has been allowed to perpetuate, and it has made it ultimately much harder for Liberians. This reflects,' she says, 'a major donor challenge in moving from their own culture of emergency response – more vehicles if you need them, for example – to sustainable development. Liberia needs to maintain its vehicles and budget for this and their replacement if you will. Yet, it is too easy for donors to simply supply new items.'

'While this is supposed to be a transition,' says a UN official, 'rather than a withdrawal, it is uncertain that the Liberians have the elements to fill the void that will be created.' This ability goes to the heart of the soft elements of systems and training. Keeping the UN presence, as with the token British force in neighbouring Sierra Leone, is seen by many as a crucial security guarantee for foreign investors and locals alike in the run-up to the 2017 election and beyond, especially given that Johnson Sirleaf will then pass on the presidential baton.

Mission with a long tail?

About 150 kilometres south from Monrovia, down the newly constructed Buchanan Road, is the Port of Buchanan. The road itself represents much of the transformation that Liberia has experienced over the last seven years.

The pothole-free tarmac surface has, for the population of Buchanan, provided easy means to access the country's capital city all year round. Previously, the seemingly interminable wet season that saturates the land for almost half the year, made the journey too difficult for most. As the road passes the airport on the outskirts of Monrovia, a UN Mi-26, the largest production helicopter in the world, is parked. Such were the means for visitors to get to Buchanan before. It is also a good metaphor for the attention that the country continues to receive from the United Nations Mission in Liberia (UNMIL) operation.

Further down the Chinese-built road are new bridges and galvanised barriers. 'Madame built this for us,' says the driver, referring to the president. A few miles further and the road hits Harbel, where the global brand Bridgestone/Firestone operates the largest rubber plantation in the world. It is a stark reminder of the West's reliance on both nature and Africa's resources, in support of its gas-guzzling ways.

The port sits on the mouth of the Saint John River. It was established in the 1950s for the export of iron ore from the mines in Nimba and Yekepa counties, to which it is linked by rail. The two sides of the port are split between the operations of ArcelorMittal and the National Ports Authority (NPA), a split that happened shortly after the port was founded. ArcelorMittal, however, was a relatively recent partner taking over the concession from the Liberian-American-Swedish Minerals Company (LAMCO), a casualty of the First Liberian Civil War. ArcelorMittal has been responsible for the majority of freight through the port – 2.1 million tonnes of iron ore annually, versus 351 000 tonnes of other freight processed by the NPA.

This is a success story in itself. In 2010 the NPA recorded only eighteen vessels for the entire year; by September 2013 there had already been 98. This flow has been built from nothing. In 2006 the port was not operating at all, a graveyard for a few rusted hulks.

Plans are afoot for the significant development of both sides of the port. ArcelorMittal has pledged $75 million to double the port's annual output to 4 million tonnes, all of which will take the 42-day journey to China. On the NPA side, there are plans to double the number of berths to six, allowing for as much as 9 million tonnes to be exported yearly, and to build facilities to offload fuel as well as to regenerate port buildings. 'I am confident this it will happen,' states a senior local politician, 'but I cannot say when.'

The port manager was eager to point out that it should include a trade-free zone, incorporating packing and storage facilities. 'It is most important that value is added,' he says hopefully.

While the plans seem impressive, and as far as ArcelorMittal's side go, both feasible and funded, what was not clear is from where the 30-fold increase in freight – mainly timber and wood chippings to heat wintery European homes – will originate. The rail is operated purely for the extraction of iron ore. The road may offer some improved access, but with the ports of Harbel and the Freeport in Monrovia within two hours' drive, such significant increases in freight are hard to envisage.

This, too, is a metaphor for the struggle to create jobs and add more value to natural resources in Liberia and other states clawing their way back up after years of conflict. Mohammed, a Guinean who came to Liberia to find work, says that the country is at peace since 'tey ah tied arr faht'in, an tey neva hah e sah gud'. But this will not necessarily remain so, especially with large numbers of listless, frustrated, unemployed youth. Sixty-five per cent of the population is under the age of 35, and about half are estimated to have only basic education.[23] Continued growth and development is a priority.

*

Liberia illustrates that stabilisation missions have a greater chance of success if they could focus on the following aspects.

The first is the need to provide a clear strategic narrative. The rationale behind interventions must be described in detail to host populations and donor constituencies. There is no substitute for explaining why they are there, what they hope to achieve, how they will do it, what choices they will have to make along the way, and how and when the exit will occur.

A second goes to the primacy of politics and statesmanship. Military-led security can provide the conditions for growth, while economic prosperity can, in turn, provide security. But at the tip of the spear is the need for political deal-making at every level. Populations must inspire politicians to become states people, emphasising what is possible and frightening them about the consequences of inaction. And these challenges to global security should be looked at in holistic terms. Contributions to peace-building in Afghanistan should inspire commitment to Africa, for example, and vice versa.

The third is to understand local motives. Foreigners need to put themselves in the minds of those they are trying to help. There is a need here to be inherently sceptical of 'heroic assumptions', that somehow a silver bullet for stabilising these states might be found. Great care must be taken to legitimise local authority whatever the possible delay in delivery.

Authority, aid and the private sector is the fourth aspect. At the outset of any mission, it is essential to expedite local decision-making around critical areas and invest heavily in law and order regimes and institutions, and to meet private sector needs. To achieve this, there is a need to devolve power from the capitals of contributing nations to the theatre level, and create systems for integrated civilian and military effort. This also demands a better aid methodology, tying expenditure to private sector requirements, stressing power, roads and efficient bureaucracy beyond much else.

The minister of finance of Liberia, Amara Konneh, and President Johnson Sirleaf are both crystal clear about the need for greater attention to infrastructure at the outset. 'If we had our time over again,' reflects the president, 'we would have given better attention to infrastructure in the very early years. We spent too much time on multiple donors with their multiple requirements and wasted too much time in the process, given that too many of them had different views. I will give you an example. John McCain made a proposal back in 2007 on a biofuel plant, which would have delivered power at $24c kW/h. The donors said that it was too high. We negotiated more, over the course of a year, and got the price down to $17c kW/h. The donors still said it was too high. Now we live with power at $54c in 2013. We could have had power in 2010 30c cheaper if we had gone with it at the outset. And instead of focusing on these issues, we have spent too much time,' she muses, 'trying to respond to individual needs and different groups, entitlement groups.'

Outsiders agree: 'Liberia should have focused more on a smaller number of issues,' reflects a foreign adviser. 'My list would be: the police, power and access to markets through roads. Trying to "do poverty" including addressing everything from health to education has spread the government and donors thin.'[24]

A final aspect is to invest in prevention and best practice. Think, in other words, in generational terms, of the next conflict, not the current one. And ensure that the lessons from stabilisation are fully digested, locally and internationally, and applied.

Speak to a Liberian or a Cambodian today and they are more likely than not to say that their future prospects have been radically improved by stabilisation missions. Could things have moved faster? Yes, but they have moved at the pace that the Liberians and their politics and systems could bear. The UN or, for that matter, other donors, could not in Liberia, as elsewhere, push on things that could not be supported by the local system. But, critically, the blue helmets have been there from the outset to provide a basis for reassurance, a warning to potential spoilers and stability.

15

LIBYA AFTER REGIME CHANGE

A Michael Jackson State?

✳

A 2013 advert on Libyan national television had three armed revolutionaries place their weapons on a metal detector and they emerge on the other side transformed into an airline pilot, doctor and engineer. It is a metaphor for the challenges facing the country in moving from the peculiar, oil-fuelled dictatorship of Muammar Gaddafi to a parliamentary, capitalist democracy.

Mustafa Abdul Jalil served as justice minister under Gaddafi. He resigned his office in February 2011 after being sent to Benghazi to negotiate the release of hostages taken by rebels, the first senior Libyan official to do so. He became chairman of the National Transitional Council from 5 March 2011 until its dissolution on 8 August 2012 and handover of power to the General National Congress (GNC), effectively the president of the country. Jalil said in June 2013 that 'the security issue is the most important issue facing Libya. It is the beginning,' he says, 'of any stability in Libya.' There is a relationship, he observes, between personal security, weapons proliferation and justice. 'Libyans get weapons to defend themselves. You cannot have justice if people are afraid of their lives.' The stationary cranes exemplifying a once-booming construction industry, are now still, suspended in time and evidence of his point that 'development can only follow security and justice.'[1]

Since the violent end to Gaddafi's rule, the militias have operated sometimes imperiously, ruling the streets of Benghazi in defiance of the central government in Tripoli, 650 kilometres away to the east, and its special forces sent to control them. The militias have said they do not trust the state with their security, and want to hang onto their weapons. But their control of the city has led to widespread insecurity and fear among the population.[2]

More than two years after the fall of the regime, government legitimacy was underpinned by a commitment to Islam – 'which we all share' emphasises Jalil – and the stress on liberation mythology: the photos of dead martyrs adorned Libyan highways. Such attachments were all the more necessary where the government had battled to get major development projects back up and where there remained pervasive tribal, geographic and ideological divisions, most notable between moderate nationalists, on the one hand, and radical Islamists, on the other.

This tendency has been compounded by the divide between those who were beneficiaries of the old regime and the new. For example, on 28 May 2013, the president of Libya's parliament, Mohammed al-Megarif, who had served under Gaddafi as an ambassador before becoming an opposition leader in exile, resigned. Three weeks earlier, under much pressure from militias that had besieged government departments, including the Justice Ministry, the government adopted the controversial Political Isolation Law, banning former Gaddafi officials from senior government posts for ten years. Earlier, on 5 March, a meeting of the ruling GNC was besieged by protestors who insisted that the GNC debate the Political Isolation Law. When one of the GNC members tried to leave, he was beaten by protestors. Al-Megarif attempted to leave through a back door and his armoured vehicle was shot at. Had the vehicle not been armoured, the president of the GNC might have been assassinated.

The remainder of March saw further protests and armed clashes at different oil and gas facilities around the country, including the Mellitah Oil and Gas facility, the Zawiya refinery, a Sirte Oil Company facility and Waha Oil Company field. Then, two-and-a-half weeks later, a car bomb exploded in front of the French Embassy in Tripoli. Five days later on 28 April, militias urging the passage of the Political Isolation Law ransacked the Interior Ministry and blockaded the Foreign Ministry and the Justice Ministry. They then moved on to the Electricity Ministry. The blockades lasted a week until the GNC ultimately voted on the Political Isolation Law on 5 May. These events paralleled other subsequent acts of violence. Two police stations in Benghazi were bombed on 10 May.[3] This was just a snapshot of two months in the life of Libya after Gaddafi.

His regime was highly personalised, centralised and eccentric, a man self-styled 'Guide of the First of September Great Revolution of the Socialist People's Libyan Arab Jamahiriya', 'King of Kings of Africa' and 'Brotherly Leader and Guide of the Revolution'. Gaddafi's Libya was one where every room, nook and cranny was adorned with bizarre teardrop Rayban-bedecked images of the brother leader. Gaddafi had systematically disman-tled and personalised even the rudimentary institutions he had inherited on his *coup d'état* in 1969.

It is little surprise then that even two years after Gaddafi's departure, Libya would not classify as a failed state. It had gone from a cult to a moribund state, floating uneasily and increasingly violently on oil. As Libya awakes from 40 years of Gaddafi's rule, does the nightmare lie behind or in front of it?

The backdrop

Libya's 6.4 million people are almost all Muslim, indeed Sunni Muslim, and predominantly Arab. Perhaps, in the long term, this relative homogeneity may provide opportunities for reconciliation.

But there are significant longstanding tribal and regional divisions that play out in contemporary politics. These relate to and are worsened by the difficulty in achieving national reconciliation and cohesion. On 6 March 2012, for example, authorities in Benghazi declared the semi-autonomy of their Cyrenaica eastern region, from Tripolitania. The roots of regional en-mity go back 2 000 years, or more.

Given that it resides on the path of invading powers, Libya's history and political cultures have been shaped by the presence of great civilisations, from the Phoenicians who from 700 BC based themselves in Lebdah (Leptis Magna), Oea (Tripoli and Sabratha), the Greeks, who, from 631 BC, moved in to establish the city of Cyrene in the east of Libya, and the Romans. The fall of the Punic capital at Carthage in Tunisia prompted Julius Caesar to formally annex Tripolitania in 46 BC. Their development of great trading entrepôts at Sabratha and Leptis Magna to Tripoli's west and east, are testa-ment to Libyan wealth and Roman extravagance.

Six hundred years later, Tripoli and Cyrenaica fell to the armies of Islam. The subsequent mass migration of two tribes – the Bani Salim and Bani Hilal – from the Arabian Peninsula forever altered Libya's demographics and poli-tics. The Berbers were displaced from their traditional lands, while the Arab settlers cemented their cultural and linguistic presence. Another 900 years passed before the Ottomans occupied Tripoli. Then, on 3 October 1911, the Italians attacked, claiming to be liberating Libya from Ottoman rule: déjà Roma all over again. Italy maintained the two traditional provinces, with separate colonial administrations until 1929 when Tripoli and Cyrenaica were united as one colonial entity. In 1934 the name 'Libya' was added, the territory split into four provinces of Tripoli, Misrata, Benghazi and Derna, with the restive Fezzan area, to the south, known as 'Territorio Sahara Libico', administered militarily.[4] During almost three decades of Italian rule, a quarter of Libya's population died as a result of the fighting, starvation or displacement, an era ended by British forces in pushing Axis forces west out of North Africa. By January 1943, Tripoli was in British hands and, by February, the last German and Italian soldiers were driven from the kingdom. Independence followed in 1951. Shortly afterwards, the fortunes of Libya, known mostly as an exporter of Second World War scrap metal, were transformed by the discovery of oil in Cyrenaica.

The country declared independence in December 1951 as the United Kingdom of Libya, a monarchy under King Idris, who swiftly set about centralising wealth and power. With the discovery of oil in 1959, this tendency saw growing resentment among various factions, culminating in the seizure of power from the monarchy on 1 September 1969 by a 27-year-old army captain, Muammar Gaddafi, who had been partially educated in UK military institutions as a signals officer.[5] British and American military bases were shut, all newspapers, churches and political parties closed and 30 000 Italian settlers deported.[6]

Gaddafi's attempts at nation-building were constant if sometimes extreme and always eccentric, from regular name changes to personality-based ideological cultism. The few institutions that survived Idris' concentration of wealth were, as noted above, dismantled by Gaddafi, aside from the Central Bank, given its role in processing personal wealth and national oil income. 'The state did not essentially exist under Gaddafi,' says an African Development Bank specialist. 'It was personalised and deeply corrupted, with perhaps as much as one quarter of oil production syphoned to his personal account. There was no health care system, for example, apart from basic treatment. Thus, when people refer to the need to *rebuild* the Libyan state after Gaddafi,' he says, 'what they are really referring to is the need to *build* the state from scratch.'[7]

The Libyan Arab Republic was changed in 1977 to Socialist People's Libyan Arab Jamahiriya (the latter meaning 'state of the masses') and, again in 1986, to the Great Socialist People's Libyan Arab Jamahiriya. Hence, too, Gaddafi's little green book, in which, following the announcement of the start of a popular revolution in 1973 with the formation of General People's Committees, a system of direct democracy, he outlined his 'Third International Theory'. Such bizarre behaviour, including his attempts to create the 'United States of Africa', was apparently exaggerated by a debilitating drug addiction by the end of his rule. Those who met him at the end of his life describe an effete physicality, sweating under layers of make-up, wearing Michael Jackson-like military uniforms more sandy stage than Sandhurst. His human rights record, however, and willingness to sponsor conflict elsewhere, made him less thriller than killer.

Still, Libya's cultural, geographic and colonial differences and influences remained, however, no matter the *deinsitutionalising* impact of Gaddafi's personalised rule. Under King Senussi, deposed by Gaddafi in September 1969, Benghazi was the capital city of Libya. Moreover, Benghazi is also known to be a city of dissent and of opposition movements. Under Senussi's reign, Libya comprised a confederation composed of three autonomous regions: Cyrenaica, Tripolitania and Fezzan. Despite possessing 80 per cent of the country's oil reserves, Benghazi and the Cyranaica region are significantly poorer – and perceive themselves as such – than Tripolitania.

These tensions have been overlaid with ideological divides, including between moderates and jihadists. Tensions among these entities are reflected in the various divergent visions of a new post-Gaddafi order, the nature of the transition to a democratic system, and the relative regional success or failure of rebuilding attempts. The country has suffered an estimated $5 billion in (civil) war damages, along with the costs of more than a decade of international sanctions and isolation from the mid-1980s. After Libyan agents were charged with the 1988 bombing of Pan Am flight 103 and the 1989 explosion of a French UTA airliner over the Sahara, UN sanctions came into effect, and were only lifted when the chief suspects in the Pan Am Lockerbie bombing were handed over to a Scottish court. These sanctions cost Libya an estimated $30 billion in lost oil and other revenues. Its rehabilitation was cemented with the payment of compensation to victims of the Lockerbie bombing, and Tripoli's announcement on 19 December 2003 that it would abandon its chemical and nuclear weapons programmes in the wake of the invasion in Iraq and toppling of Saddam Hussein.

But this was not enough. On the tail of Tunisia's 2010 Jasmine Revolution, protests against Gaddafi's rule began in Benghazi in February 2011. This quickly escalated into a countrywide rebellion, with opposition forces establishing the abovementioned National Transitional Council.

The international response quickly ratcheted up as Gaddafi turned his military against the civilian-based opposition. The UN Security Council passed an initial resolution on 26 February, freezing the assets of Gaddafi, the proclaimed leader of the Great Al-Fatah Revolution, and his inner circle, and restricting their travel. When, in early March, Gaddafi's forces pushed the rebels back and reached Benghazi, UN Security Council Resolution 1973 authorised the creation of a no-fly zone and permitted the use of 'all necessary measures' to prevent attacks on civilians. Just hours after the Resolution passed, UK Prime Minister David Cameron said, 'It is almost impossible to envisage a future for Libya that includes him. Gaddafi must go, he has no legitimacy.'[8]

Such 'necessary measures' included a substantial NATO-led air operation from 19 March 2011, the initial coalition of Belgium, Canada, Denmark, France, Italy, Norway, Qatar, Spain, the UK and US expanding to nineteen states. By the time the NATO mission finished seven months later on 31 October 2011, NATO had flown 26 500 sorties, the air campaign strengthened by NATO and other special forces operating on the ground.

By August 2011, the rebels had taken Tripoli. Gaddafi, who had evaded capture, and was reportedly intent on fighting a rearguard campaign, was captured and killed out of hand near Sirte on 20 October 2011. With his death, the National Transitional Council declared the 'liberation of Libya', the war officially ending three days later.

Challenges and advantages

However, a low-level insurgency continued between local militia and tribes, reflecting all manner of fault lines and challenges: political, bureaucratic, criminal and social.

For one, the country's criminal justice system is dysfunctional. 'The severe deficiencies of the current judicial system are rooted, first and foremost, in the failings of the one that, in principle, it has replaced,' observed Claudia Gazzini of the International Crisis Group. 'Four decades of arbitrary justice under the Gaddafi regime served as a burdensome backdrop to the new government's efforts.'[9]

There have been difficulties, too, around the role and control of various militia and the spoils of conquest in terms of government appointments and funding, and the settling of old scores. The Warriors Affairs Commission has processed an estimated 145 000 former militia members as part of a Disarmament, Demobilisation and Reintegration scheme to both place them in civilian employment and simultaneously boost private sector growth.[10] But progress has been slow, not least because control of militias equals power and an insurance policy against political disfavour.

The costs have been high. Former president Jalil sums up this challenge. 'The traditional army belonged to Gaddafi. The new revolutionaries do not trust the old system; they want a new army. But the people of the old army say that the revolutionaries do not have enough discipline. It is difficult,' he acknowledges, 'to allow the revolutionaries to control the army, as every military needs to be subject to the law of a country. The solution,' he proposes, 'is to send the revolutionaries for training abroad to get them to settle down and to gain the mentality of a conventional army.'

The role of the militias has been exacerbated and prolonged by the proliferation of weapons. Andrew Shapiro, the US assistant secretary of state for political-military affairs, said in October 2011 that Libya had about 20 000 man-portable surface-to-air missiles at the war's outset. NATO's top military officer, Admiral Giampaolo Di Paola, said in September 2011 that the alliance had lost track of at least 10 000 surface-to-air missiles from Libyan military depots.[11]

One UN official has described the weapons 'strewn all over Libya' as a 'smorgasbord' of arms and ammunition, a tempting target for 'all manner of criminal gangs, cross-border opportunists, and local militias'. It is estimated that, *circa* 2013, there were 3.5 weapons per Libyan countrywide; and the scale of the proliferation problem is '100 times worse than Iraq, and 30 times worse than Afghanistan'. In part, this is due to the NATO bombing campaign and the alliance's failure to 'clean up' immediately after itself, and partly because of the way in which Gaddafi organised his military units and deployed his weaponry.

With at least six known coup attempts against him, Gaddafi kept the formal armed forces (about 30 000-strong) weak, divided, deployed in out-of-the-way places, and usually separated from key equipment, including ammunition. As part of a strategy to 'coup proof' his regime, Gaddafi's security was instead provided by his presidential guard, explaining largely why this force and not the army fought against the rebels. At Hun, for example, in the centre of Libya, Gaddafi established a new Ministry of Defence. But he kept the explosives under separate lock and key elsewhere, complicating more recent attempts by de-miners to destroy existing stocks. Attempts to clean up weaponry have been complicated by government 'wanting its slice of the cake', with various ministries from foreign affairs to agriculture establishing de-mining/

unexploded ordnance units in anticipation of incoming contracts.

The geographic size and ungoverned nature of Libya is challenging. The world's seventeenth largest country (Africa's fourth) with 80 per cent of the population living in urban, mainly littoral, centres, it has lengthy (and largely unpoliced) borders with Algeria (982 kilometres), Chad (1 055 kilometres), Egypt (1 150 kilometres), Niger (354 kilometres), Sudan (383 kilometres) and Tunisia (459 kilometres), plus a coastline of 1 170 kilometres. This enables smugglers and other miscreants virtually free reign and raises questions about the most practical means of governing these vast, sparsely populated areas.

The problems created by a lack of government control, political tensions and high expectations have been compounded by the absence of a shared vision and strategic planning and decision-making capacity. The ruling GNC is a heterogeneous group, whose members apparently shared the purpose only of ridding the country of Gaddafi. The resultant policy inertia is worsened by a stovepipe bureaucracy – one has only to attempt to acquire a visa for Libya to appreciate this – and deeply autocratic culture. This will take a generation to erase, but in the meanwhile will exert a degree of paralysis and inactivity across government. Under the strongman, decision-making was centralised, not delegated, and discretion discouraged. It was also highly corrupt, rent-seeking in the extreme.

Economic rent-seeking and redistribution

On the positive side of the ledger, Libya is potentially very rich, possessing the world's fifth-largest reserves of oil, and the largest in Africa with an estimated 44.3 billion barrels in 2010.[12] Oil production was, *circa* June 2013, 1.5 million barrels per day, about half of its 1969 peak, however, due to the Organization of the Petroleum Exporting Countries (OPEC) quotas. The costs of production are among the lowest in the world, at little more than $1 per barrel in some fields. The relative proximity to European markets is also a plus, the destination of 85 per cent of Libyan oil, making it the third-largest exporter to the EU (behind Norway and Russia). This combination of oil and its relatively small population have given Libya the highest nominal per capita GDP in Africa, at over $12 000, and a GDP of $80 billion. But this points to a much greater, deeper problem as the economy strives to diversify and create employment for its population, where literacy is over 90 per cent even if market-related skills are reputedly low.

Oil provides some 95 per cent of Libya's exports. It is a tremendous developmental source, but its dominance is indicative of the challenge the country faces – like all natural resource-dominated economies – in diversifying. Government revenue is a function of oil sales, and subject to the vicissitudes in the market price. The oil curse has also left Libya without any effective tax authority, with a tax/GDP ratio of just 2.7 per cent in 2012,[13] compared to an EU average of 38.8 per cent in 2011.[14] Libya's wage bill for its customs department is estimated to be 'two to three times higher' than the tax take of $100 million.[15]

And more than all of that, the problem with an economy such as Libya's, where the state redistributes oil wealth through public sector jobs (estimated at 85 per cent of formal employment) and food and fuel subsidies, is that it operates counter to the capitalist model, based on individual choice and personal freedoms. For example, subsidies constitute $16 billion or over 15 per cent of the total budget – one of the highest as a proportion of GDP in the world.[16] Fuel, as one measure, costs just $10c per litre. Little wonder that smuggling of fuel is a profitable business, especially to neighbouring Tunisia.

The subsidy imperative has been strengthened by the increase in militia numbers on the state payroll, reputedly numbering 120 000 (for the policing Supreme Security Council) and 140 000 (Libya Shield paramilitary) by mid-2013, earning supposedly twice as much as the regular government units. Demobilisation was necessary but these men would need to have somewhere else to go.

Oil economies are seldom capitalistic, but rather rent-seeking, crowding

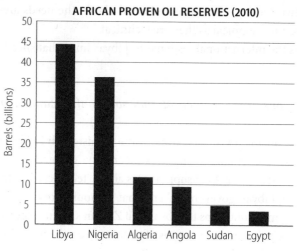

AFRICAN PROVEN OIL RESERVES (2010)

Source: Global Resources News.

out the private sector through an overvalued currency, personalised and politicised contracting, and the operations of state-run monopolies. Private enterprise is also impossible where the financial market is immature and where there is collateralisation of property foreign. In essence, economic freedoms cannot be extracted from wider personal freedoms and rights. Until now, it has not been in the interests of Libya's elite to create such a system, and they do not possess the institutional and legal mechanisms to do so. One way of getting off the oil addiction, one specialist offers, is to 'do a Norway – put half of the income aside in a sovereign fund, forcing belt-tightening'. But this is obviously politically risky.

It is also compounded by the fact that, in the view of an international expert working with the Central Bank and various other economy-related ministries, 'Libyans see themselves not as poor Arabs, but as an elite, as part of a rich country. The problem is that the government also views itself as rich. But they are not, at least not for the next ten years. Oil production is limited to between 1.5 million barrels per day and 2 million barrels per day, and this defines the limits of the GDP.' And this dependence remains very vulnerable to a 'downdraft' in global oil prices, as the national budget is predicated on oil at $90 per barrel.

International efforts to get the economy on track since the revolution have focused on the basics: understanding the level of liquidity, and establishing systems and institutions for more effective forecasting. This much is required. As another technical specialist noted, 'The Central Bank is like that of Dubai in 1970. Everything is done on paper, the exchange rate being published twice a day.'[17] But, as is indicated above, the needs are as much political and philosophical as they are technical.

What was the international response to Libya's immediate needs?

Lessons from the international post-conflict campaign

In May 2013, during a visit of Libya's Prime Minister Ali Zeidan to NATO headquarters, the Atlantic Alliance's Secretary General Anders Fogh Rasmussen stated that NATO support was about 'technical assistance upon request of the Libyan government' and that it should not be considered as NATO deployment of troops to Libya.[18] Ali Zeidan said in response, 'NATO will give us technical advice in terms of training, we will have technical support and we will be helped in training if we need so.'[19]

This was quite different to the aid onslaught in Iraq, to take a contemporary analogue.

In fact, the international community's support to get rid of Gaddafi has been different to that which removed Saddam, literally from start to finish, and in volume, scale, control and focus.

First, there was legitimacy in the form of UN Security Council Resolution 1973. Second, rather than a large ground attack, Libyans did the fighting on the ground, supported by NATO from the air. No NATO soldier was lost in the process. Third, in heeding the lessons of the post-conflict failure in Iraq, the post-conflict international effort has been coordinated by the UN but led by local government, not an Iraqi-style external authority. And fourth, in sharp contrast to the surfeit of resources available to the Coalition Provisional Authority in Iraq, the level of assistance has been tiny – reflecting a lack of American leadership in the engagement. Fifth, it has also reflected Libya's middle-income status, that it can fund its own recovery from its own considerable cash resources.

By June 2013, international assistance had taken various forms. At the centre was the United Nations Support Mission in Libya (UNSMIL), comprising of 159 staff, with an annual budget of US$33 million in 2012 and continuing to increase in 2013. Its activities have been focused in four main areas: democratic transition, rule of law and human rights, security sector reform and international assistance coordination.[20]

Immediately post-revolution, the EU collectively donated €150 million,[21] five times the initial donation from the US. Under the European Neighbourhood and Partnership Instrument initially agreed in 2008, the level of funding is €30 million split over two years, as at May 2013. The EU's interest, and position as the largest donor, is perhaps unsurprising given that Tripoli sits only 600 kilometres away from the Italian coast. Much of the focus of the European effort has been on the European Union Border Assistance Mission with its 165 staff (and €30-million budget).

The international community has approached this particular problem with short arms and deep pockets. Not only is there a serious fatigue evident on the back of a decade of interventions, but Libya is not a country of great poverty and disease – its massive mineral wealth means that it is not short of money, just skills and experience. This may be why the private sector could offer a pragmatic solution to many of the state's problems; just as soon as the government's capacity can expand to a point of being able to manage the private sector – there is a legacy of some 13 200 stalled contracts worth $180 billion.

It would appear that everything is on the table, from training the military to educating its population. Despite the differences in approach between Libya and Iraq, the international community has apparently not been able to convince the Libyans to learn from their experiences. The biggest failing in Iraq was perhaps the aforementioned de-Ba'athification process, essentially forcing Saddam's soldiers and officials out of a job. Unlike Nazi Germany and Imperial Japan, rather than culling officials only to a certain level, the state was purged of almost everyone with a link to the previous regime, giving them little stake in stability and curbing the insurgency in the process. In Libya, the Political Isolation Law of 2013 threatened to replicate this gross strategic error.

While the UK may have played centre stage in the campaign to remove the colonel, and its military advice on the restructuring of the armed forces was, in particular, requited by the regime, many of its allies have not matched this contribution: which, by comparison to the efforts in Iraq and Afghanistan, is modest. Even though it has an active Defence Advisory and Training Team and a significant development team with embedded advisers in the ministries of interior, defence, justice, planning and finance (including funding IMF and World Bank experts), the UK has been slow to backfill financial resources behind its initial military commitment in removing Gaddafi, and has been overshadowed by others, including Italy, Libya's main trade partner, which reportedly offered €350 million in aid in 2011,[22] possibly to assist in shoring up its open-ended contractual relationships, and Turkey, which had pledged over $300 million.[23] The UK had good intentions but, as with much of the rest of the international community, they were slow to match this with resources: words with fewer deeds.

In contrast, the US did not made these empty pledges, with a total of $1.5 million comprising the total Department of State and USAID spend in 2013 – 0.1 per cent of their contributions to Egypt over the same period; a clear message that this was not their problem,[24] and a signal to those in Europe with whom it has a special relationship: you started it, you finish it.

There have also been methodological problems that relate to influence. It takes time for external actors to get to understand how things work in Libya, as elsewhere, and to make the personal connections necessary to influence local parties. This is especially important, technical experts on the ground argue, 'in the absence of developed institutions, where getting anything done depends on the trust of people'.[25]

The relative lack of international presence relative to domestic resources will inevitably reduce foreign leverage, making it more difficult for technical missions to hold Libyan feet to the fire on policy matters. This is exacerbated by poor donor coordination: 'They coordinate nominally, with regular monthly meetings,' says one foreign analyst. 'But behind doors there are expenditure rivalries.' This is apparently amplified by the donors subcontracting tasks to private sector agencies, such as the EU to the International Management Group, bringing in a private sector, competitive ethos and imperative.[26]

Certainly on paper, two years after the removal of Gaddafi, the situation in Libya looked worrying. Parallel policing (Supreme Security Council) and military (Libya Shield) structures, comprising militia members, were considerably more numerous than corresponding state agencies, yet were not under government control. The government did not even possess a majority let alone a monopoly of violent means. But there were countervailing trends and tendencies. The militias were made up of different groups, as is Libya per se: federalists, nationalists, tribalists, criminal groups, Salafists and secularists, old and new guard, urban and rural groups, and those from the marginalised east and those from the more prosperous west.

And the vast majority of Libyans are Muslim and Arab, offering some social glue nationally, and consensus as to what the country should look like: a conservative Islamic state and society.

Not a failed state, but ...

Keith Simpson, British Foreign Secretary William Hague's aide, has argued that the historical parallel for the Arab Spring is not the collapse of the Soviet bloc in 1989, it is in the European revolutions of 1848–51. These saw, in some cases, regimes being overthrown and in other cases reactionary forces were able to hold on to power. 'I think it is the same with the Arab Spring,' Simpson has noted. 'It is mixed.'[27] Or as Frederic Wehrey has observed more explicitly concerning Libya, 'As in any post-conflict situation, Libya's transition will not be clean or linear and is likely to be marked by leaps of progress and heartbreaking setbacks.'[28]

The cost of the chaos that ensued after Gaddafi's demise has justifiably raised concerns about the primary goal of international action and instrumentalisation of norms such as R2P: was it to safeguard civilians, or was the responsibility simply to protect on humanitarian grounds the pretext for regime change? Either way, the chaotic and violent outcome has illustrated, again, no matter how bizarre Gaddafi's leadership style and nasty his regime, the outcome may be at least as bad. No doubt, this awareness and the outcome of post-Saddam Iraq figured in the calculations about Assad and Syria.[29]

Yet, for all of the perceptions of a country wobbling between anarchy and democracy, the capture of the state, not its destruction, as much as it exists, has been the key prize for various parties.[30] Whether the militias and jihadists can be convinced to do this through politics and not the barrel of the gun has been the key question; and if they lose, whether they were similarly willing to remain part of Libya and not attempt to hive off different fiefdoms of control or even geographic portions of the country. A failure to elevate politics, not violence, as the principal dispute mechanism and to ensure its corollary in disarmament, is crucial, without which Libya could easily and rapidly descend into a retaliatory cycle of violence.

Outsiders have only a limited role to play in helping Libya help itself. It has been hand-holding that Libya has needed rather than handouts. But international partners would have to stay the course and display some steel. Unless the international community was to return to Benghazi (from where it had retreated following the attack on the US mission on 11 September 2012, which killed the ambassador, Christopher Stevens, and another diplomat) especially, the heart of the revolution, it would likely not be able to influence – to assist – Libya. If it failed to do so, said one UN official, 'It sends a message: target a few individuals and they will leave. We should instead be sitting down with the government to work out how to reclaim Benghazi. We need to stand and deliver, and not be gun-shy.'[31]

The operation to remove Gaddafi was seen as 'cost-effective',[32] costing about $1 billion, or about 0.1 per cent of what was spent in Iraq. Given both the comparative savings in foreign and Libyan lives and the production of detailed plans for the post-war phase, Libya was seen, in the months following Gaddafi's overthrow, as a place where 'the lessons of Iraq [had] paid off'.

But this has been less by design than neglect.

International apathy since 2011 has been palpable. But this in itself has presented an opportunity. In Libya, unlike other interventions, the principal metric for the interveners cannot be about the money they are spending – because they are spending very little. Success in Libya will thus have to be measured by the reduction in levels of violence, extent of disarmament or absorption of militias into government, cantonment and security of weapons, establishment of capable institutional decision-making and management structures and mindset, and the inclusiveness of the constitutional-writing and acceptance process. Such criteria should be the key indicators of government capacity-building and development, in Libya as elsewhere.

16

MALAWI

A Different Sort of Leadership

*

At around 9 a.m. on 5 April 2012, Malawi's President Bingu wa Mutharika suffered a heart attack in the capital Lilongwe. As far as the public knew, his life hovered in the balance in a South African hospital where he succumbed officially a day later.

The reality was quite different.

It emerged later that the president, who was meeting a young female MP at State House, was admitted by 10 a.m. to nearby Kamuzu Hospital. With no suitable facilities there, including life support, a request was put in to the South African government to evacuate Bingu, 78, 'down south'. In the interim, in trying to keep a lid on things, the staff was all but cleared out and a minimal police presence established at the hospital.

Even so, already by 10.10 a.m. news of his plight began to leak out to locally based ambassadors. Vice President Joyce Banda, who was packing her car and preparing to leave for her house on the lake over the holiday weekend, also heard the news about this time. She decided immediately to stay put in Lilongwe. Despite a fraught relationship with Bingu, which had seen her expelled from the ruling party, she called his wife, former minister of tourism, Callista Chimombo, to offer her best wishes for a speedy recovery.

By the time the emergency air ambulance from South Africa arrived and was ready at 6 p.m. to accept the president, whose condition was officially described as 'critical', he was dead.

Chaotic scenes at the airport ensued. Bingu's corpse was smuggled through Lilongwe's cargo section. But the crew refused to load a cadaver. One can only imagine what Monty Python would have made of this episode.

Then his family, led by his wife, boarded and refused to leave the plane. It took an intervention, reputedly by South African President Jacob Zuma, to fly the body to a military base in Pretoria. It was in the interests of a small clique around the president's brother, Peter Mutharika, to maintain the public illusion of a life-and-death struggle to provide the space to plan his succession.

The 'Good Friday Gang' as they became known in Lilongwe – including then information minister, Patricia Kaliati; sport minister, Symon Vuwa Kaunda; health minister, Jean Kalilani; local government minister, Henry Mussa; deputy minister in the office of the president, Nicholas Dausi; and the deputy foreign affairs minister, Kondwani Nakhumwa – apparently decided among themselves on Friday to seek a court order barring Joyce Banda from stepping up to the presidency, as constitutionally ordained, and putting Peter in her place.

The South African government, unwittingly or not, nearly became party to a coup. That would have made it a very bad Friday beyond Malawi.

However, the Gang did not reckon with Joyce Banda and other good Malawians. 'The people of Malawi have the right to know the state of health of President Bingu wa Mutharika,' she said at the time. 'I am appealing to the people of Malawi that we must abide by the rules. The laws say if the president is incapacitated, the vice president takes over. It's my hope that Malawians shall adhere to the Constitution.'[1]

She also phoned around donors to reassure them, and then called the army commander, General Henry Odillo, who stationed troops around her house. With the constitution and the army on her side, the die was cast.

This was not lost on the 'crowd'. Fifteen ministers threw their lot in with JB, as she is popularly known, at this point along with one-third of the ruling Democratic Progressive Party's 147 MPs. Despite an attempt at further delay by the chief justice on account of leaving his robes 240 kilometres away in Blantyre, she was sworn in as president on the Saturday afternoon, among the guests the diplomatic corps, chief of the police and General Odillo.

But a few other things happened behind the scenes, which illustrate the value of quiet diplomacy, but not necessarily that practised by diplomats. Indeed, this had an effect perhaps precisely because it did not involve governments alone, permitting greater latitude by those who had through other channels become friends first and partners second.

I invited then Vice President Banda to attend the Tswalu Dialogue in the Kalahari, along with General Odillo and another Malawian army officer on 2–4 March 2012. Remarkably, she had never previously met her army commander, and was somewhat anxious at the prospect, given her deteriorating relationship with her president. At the Kalahari meeting she spoke openly about the risk to her personal well-being. At her urging, I intervened in the margins of the meeting with General Odillo to ask him to ensure 'that no harm came to her'. This he promised to do. Also present at the Tswalu meeting, attended by 50 military officers, diplomats, politicians, policy analysts and journalists and held on the topic of the 'economic dimension to peace-building', was the then UK chief of defence staff, General Sir David Richards.

When news was received of President Bingu's demise, in alighting from a transatlantic flight, I was called several times by Vice President Banda's office to ask for advice. The immediate response was the preparation of a memo outlining several options for Joyce Banda depending on the 'Gang's' actions. The UK chief of defence staff contacted General Odillo to reassure him of his personal support at this difficult time, and to stress the importance of 'doing the right thing' by the constitution, a failure to do so which might have led Malawi down a path of international isolation, in addition to the obvious consequences and costs to its domestic economy, politics and the populace. The rest is history. Though there was little doubt that General Odillo was always going to do the right thing anyway, the moral support and counsel likely helped.

Speaking in Blantyre on 26 February 2013, President Banda recalled the impact of the dialogue at Tswalu on the outcome of these tumultuous events. 'Then we got there [to Tswalu] and found Sir David Richards ... and found Richard Myers of the US military and found other generals from Africa, including my own. I had never met [General Odillo] close before. It provided an opportunity for us, first time to meet ... at that time, I was going through a very difficult time.

'And four weeks later, here ... on 5 April, the president died, and because of the circumstances around that death and the *coup d'etat* when they could have taken over, the constitution called upon the general [Odillo] to make a decision. And the general is the one that came over to me to make a decision that day, with that full network at Tswalu gathered around him and supporting him to say just make the right decision, we are all standing behind you. Unbelievable,' she added. 'No one believes this story, because people did not know what happened over those two days. So, me and Tswalu and Brenthurst ... Yes, because there is no way I should talk about my position without talking about Tswalu, without these people and Odillo there.

'Because when I called [Odillo] the first day, I said he must come. This is when the president died [on 5 April], they didn't tell me, while they were trying to manoeuvre the takeover. They were trying to take the body out. There were two days when they could take over ... without me knowing. So, the 5th, I went to bed without knowing a thing.

'The 6th, it was on CNN and BBC, but here they were refusing to announce [his death], they were saying no, he is just ... So, at that point I called [Odillo] and he said, "Yes, I will come." I said I was going to be making a press statement and "You must come". He said, "I will come." But he didn't come. He sent his number 2 and 3. [On the] 7th of April, in the morning, the death was announced. So I called him back and said I wanted [him] to come. He said, "Yes, I am coming." I said, "No, because yesterday you told me you were coming, and you didn't. I want you to come." Because at that point I was clear that they had chosen another president and they were going to go to court to bar me from challenging that decision. So while papers were being prepared and people were waiting for the swearing in of another president, I am in the middle and I am looking for the general to support me to come to me and stand with me according to the constitution.

'This relationship of five weeks ago [formed at Tswalu] and the network that stood around [Odillo] and with him throughout the night of 6th is what gave him the confidence to stand on the right side, because the constitution was on his side ... Yah ... somebody has said,' she laughed, '"Write a book about it."'

So ended 60 hours of confusion and a near coup. But getting into power was one thing for Joyce Banda. Changing Malawi for the better demanded transforming a political economy defined by middlemen and systemic public sector-led corruption, and that was another thing.

A pernicious political economy getting worse?

Still, half a century after its independence in 1964, Malawi is one of the poorest countries on earth.

The $320 annual per capita income of the Central African nation places it above only Burundi and the Congo in global rankings, the more remarkable since it has never, unlike most of those states at the bottom, experienced a civil war. And the pressures on limited resources is steadily increasing as population numbers swell and the productive side of the economy fails to keep pace. From under four million people at independence in 1964 and

16 million in 2014, the population is predicted to reach 50 million by 2050. This is a reality inasmuch as the parents of the 50 millionth Malawian have likely already been born. And the economy has not, so far, kept up with these demographic changes.

There is an annual demand of $2.4 billion by Malawians for foreign exchange, yet the sources of supply hardly match: $800 million in donor support (in 2013); $360 million from tobacco; $300 million other exports (sugar, tea, coffee, mining, tourism, legumes); and some remittances, mainly from its gardeners, housekeepers and nurses, among others, working in South Africa. Put differently, 40 per cent of the government budget of $1.5 billion is funded by donors.

Where the British imperial period in Malawi was dominated by the commercialisation of agriculture and the role of missionaries, the first post-independence government was a 'corporatist state'. With Hastings Kamuzu Banda installed as the post-colonial president (he hoped in 1971, 'for life' – he was wrong) of a one-party state with his Malawi Congress Party at the centre, Malawi's economy to an extent defied its landlocked and resource-poor status, achieving notable progress in both agriculture and industrial development. Paul Theroux, who spent time working in the Central African country as a Peace Corps volunteer, remembers that in the early 1960s the 'defining song' was '*Zonze Zimene za Kamuzu Banda*' (Everything Belongs to Kamuzu Banda).[2] An autocrat he may have been, but Banda also used his foreign ties adroitly in the Cold War context, securing development money from apartheid South Africa; had security ties with Israel; a railway from Canada; intelligence from Romania and Korea; and sought investment from the UK, especially in the form of Lonrho and the man described by Edward Heath as the 'unacceptable face of capitalism',[3] Tiny Rowland. The army was Western-trained; the police and paramilitary Young Pioneers looked East for support. Parastatals ran great chunks of the economy, led by the shadowy Press Corporation business empire, hidden behind high tariffs and

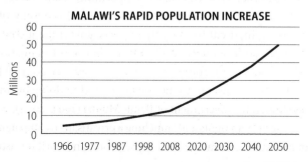

MALAWI'S RAPID POPULATION INCREASE

Millions

60
50
40
30
20
10
0

1966 1977 1987 1998 2008 2020 2030 2040 2050

Source: World Bank.

fiercely monopolistic, which produced one-third of the country's GDP and employed 10 per cent of the workforce.

During the 1960s, Malawi built pockets of domestic industry and diversified from agriculture into other areas, including tourism, with support from white South Africans who were prevented from travelling to most other places in what was then termed 'black' Africa. Banda's was, however, an easier task than that facing contemporary Malawian governments, not least since demand for tobacco was relatively high (if production 40 per cent smaller) and there were far fewer mouths to feed, in fact four times fewer, than 50 years on. There was corruption, but 'at the highest levels only', says one senior government official. Banda's iron fist kept dishonesty in check and long-haired miscreants in jail. (The government infamously did not allow in visitors whose hair touched their collar – this was my experience as a wild and woolly haired student on my first visit, driving all the way from South Africa in December 1983.)

Crowding out

The advent of democracy in 1994 saw liberal change, some of it not for the better. This is not a problem with democracy per se, but the rent-seeking that has accompanied a combination of factors: improved human rights without a corresponding advancement in institutional capacity, increased reliance on donors, the shrivelling of local industry with liberalisation and diminished protectionism, increased consumer expectations, swelling population numbers and weak governance – coupled with the need for political parties to find funds and patronise their supporters. 'The transition was badly handled, no doubt,' says one donor. 'There was no transparency at the start, and coupled with the need to fund political parties, it set the stage for things going wrong absent the discipline and fear that Kamuzu instilled. Opportunity made thieves.'

It is this system we call corruption. It is a political economy of middlemen, those taking their cut from costly imports, government contracts and tobacco auctions, adding no value apart from their reinforcing political influence and personal connections. Personal tax avoidance is an art form, not only at a cost to the fiscus, but to the consumer and to doing business.

The first democratic government of Bakili Muluzi (1994–2004), while massively improving human rights and launching a privatisation campaign, oversaw a period of industrial contraction, a collapse of soft and hard infrastructure, a weakening of the bureaucracy and an increase in corruption. Decision-making and planning was no longer institutionalised, but 'made on the podium'.

Bingu's first term restored confidence in the public sector and saw greater spending on education. But, like Muluzi, the levels of corruption and favouritism of his Lomwe ethnic group intensified as he headed into a terrible, if abbreviated, second term. Whereas Muluzi, a Muslim, improved ties with the Arab world and Bingu with China (at the expense, inter alia, of the country's longstanding diplomatic ties with Taiwan), neither was able, Hastings Banda-like, to diplomatically manipulate these links to Malawi's advantage. Without charismatic leadership, the incentives – and disincentives – did not exist to encourage ethnic elites to give up their preferences for the benefit of all, to build an inclusive Malawian state. This reflected a failure to provide abundant resources for national development, given the overwhelming focus on subsistence or 'survival' production, the erosion of a strong central authority, the relative absence of individual property rights and the lack of checks and balances in encouraging another system other than distribution to preferred elites.

The 50-year trend in Malawi has thus seen increasing rent-seeking – self-enrichment and cronyism – by politicians, declining industrialisation, a focus on increasingly problematic primary exports (notably tobacco), a lack of strategic nuance in its diplomatic relationships, the rise of politically connected business elites, and the presidential personalisation of planning decisions and Malawi's economic choices.

Around one-third of government revenues are sourced, in a perverse tautology, from customs receipts. Yet the cost of moving imports is staggeringly high, as much as 65 per cent of the value of goods, says Joyce Banda's minister of trade and industry (and 2014 election running mate), Seston Gwengwe. It costs an astounding $7 800 to move a 40-foot container from Durban, the route of three-quarters of goods. There is, according to some, a transport cartel, where individuals in government have interests. This also helps to explain why the cost of fuel touches nearly $2 per litre, and the cost of doing business reflects this essential input. The trading sector and the political class thrive on this model.

Malawi imports what it consumes and exports what it produces. Corruption is institutionalised in other ways, where government officials flout conflicts of interest, infamously not only receiving backhanders for procurement contracts, but being engaged in setting up their own businesses to do so.

With the public sector by 2014 50 per cent larger at over 170 000 people than 30 years ago, and responsible for consuming 40 per cent of GDP, it is the buyer, partner, funder and borrower of first resort, crowding out the private sector, making the cost of borrowing prohibitively high in an environment where funds are scarce and inflation rates consequently high. 'Government is,' says Reserve Bank Governor Charles Chuka, 'the business.' The impact of such crowding out in a market short of foreign exchange saw interest rates at 37 per cent and inflation nearly 25 per cent at the end of 2013.

This system inevitably leads to scandal.

Eighteen months into her unexpected presidency, President Banda's government was embroiled in 'cash-gate', a scandal implicating government officials in syphoning perhaps as much as $250 million from the budget. Matters came to a head with the the attempted assassination in September 2013 of the Ministry of Finance budget director, opening a can of worms on corruption, which impacted on every aspect of government operations and its relations with donors.

Everyone appeared to have their fingers in the public cookie jar, partly because it is the only jar on the shelf. The central allegation is that the ruling People's Party was siphoning off money to pay for the May 2014 general election. Thirty-three bank accounts were frozen and 68 people were arrested in the first two months of the investigation, including private individuals and government officials from the departments of tourism, finance and the office of the president and cabinet.

This was the final straw for some donors, a number cutting off aid in response, rocking the regime and raising questions about President Banda's survival and suitability. As she put it, 'theft is a national tragedy, but it's my problem and my fight and I will sort this out with or without the donors' help. But for those who think that we have only woken up to this on hearing these cash-gate revelations, they are wrong. Why after all,' she asks, 'did we appoint the man, Paul Mphwiyo, to investigate this, who was shot? He was appointed to fight corruption.'

But the extent of the rot surprised her. 'I knew when I took over for sure that we needed to recover the economy,' she says. 'But what I had not realised was the extent of the theft, that we had the same people stealing, jumping from one party to another. The reason why Malawi has remained stagnant and poor is because we built up and they siphoned off, we built up, they siphoned off, and so on. We estimated that one-third of our resources have been stolen in this way.'

Tut-tutting donors

Tut-tut as they might, donors have been complicit in the system for a long time, not least during Bingu wa Mutharika's regime, when the $140-million annual government subsidy for seeds and fertiliser (the so-called Farm Input Subsidy Programme), endorsed and funded by some donors in the interests of food security, became little more than a giant political and personal feeding scheme. As Governor Chuka put it, 'How otherwise can you explain why we get 1 per cent increase in maize outputs in a year despite spending this sum?'

It is all too easy to finger Joyce Banda's regime of corruption. Yet, through the Malawi Government Action Plan, she aimed to undertake the most far-reaching governance reforms of any Malawian leader in the last twenty years, which offer the governance conditions necessary for sustainable, long-term growth. Of course, there are problems, as befits the world's third-poorest country. It is not Denmark, after all. Government agencies lack the capacity and the will to clean up their act. The government has said it will cut back on unnecessary travel, but the need for political campaigning is relentless.

President Banda found the job tough going. 'If I had known, I would not have wanted to be in this job,' she smiles.[4] 'I was able before to do all the things I enjoy through my activism, and I was better off doing that. There are many things that you can do more easily outside that you cannot do in government.' She found the biggest challenge to change 'entrenched interests. I did not know that we had such cartels, so desperate that they would, in Malawi of all places, resort to shooting each other. But,' she adds, 'I have placed this fight before my political career – and if we can succeed, we will grow, and be rejuvenated.' And she was angered by her international critics who are supporters only if she does what they want. 'They told me that we should not have bought arms for our peacekeeping or the [seven patrol] boats for the Lake,' she states. 'But we needed them to ensure security on immigration, to provide a rescue capability, to protect our interests and to live up to our international obligations. Sometimes I think,' she mused, 'all they want is a trophy that can be paraded around.'

Joyce Banda's short-lived government faltered in the tumultuous May 2014 election, which she then declared null and void, ironically attempting an unconstitutional move of the sort that she had to parry just two years earlier to get to State House in the first instance. Regardless of who is in power, however, something more than political regimes will have to change in Malawi, otherwise donor assistance and fragility will be forever, along with a pestiferous cycle of state contracts, corruption, imports, backhanders, public sector procurement and vested interests.

In the short term, the government will have to convince the donors to turn the taps back on, and leave them there, otherwise the future looks bleak, with a likelihood of rampant inflation, political turmoil, bureaucratic paralysis and social unrest. For their part, the donors realise that the withdrawal of budget support could throw the country into a tailspin. In the medium term, the government says that it needs to reduce its dependence on donors, and points to the need to increase revenues. But at 25 per cent of GDP, the tax take is already high, threatening to strangle investment in the economy. The key to the revenue answer lies both in the need to reduce government expenditure and to grow the economic pie, not just try to increase the size of government's slice.

The governance agenda has to include party funding reform, and the means whereby public officials are remunerated. 'Salaries,' it is said, 'are poor, but income is okay.' Civil servants and politicians top up their salaries through travel allowances, as much as $800 per day for overseas travel. Little wonder there was dissent when, under donor pressure, Banda slashed all non-essential travel. From an economic perspective, reforms are imperative, but are trickier politically. There is a need, in carrying them out, to identify those who have no interest in reforms because of their rent-seeking activities, 'who', says one donor, 'don't care if the country does not move one inch, so long as their interests are safe'. All of this is more difficult in what is acknowledged as a 'deeply jealous society', one where 'people trust outsiders more than each other'. On his departure from office in 1994 at the age of 96, Malawians, said an unrepentant Kamuzu Banda, were 'children in politics', saying that they would miss his rule.[5] Human rights groups estimate that at least 6 000 people were killed, tortured or jailed without trial during his quixotic, if violent, reign.[6]

Over the past 50 years Malawi has become more dependent on donors as its domestic sources have stagnated and its population increased. During the next 50 years it should look to a future beyond aid, not least since that is a way that Malawians, not others, will own the development process and the choices that go with it. The danger of donor conditionality is always that recipients take the money on offer not because they are convinced of the policy requirements that go with it, but because they need the money.

In this, Malawi has to position itself through policy into a good news development story, not an aid and NGO crusade.

System change

Malawi's pending population explosion means that it is going to be easier to carry out the necessary reforms – to mindset, customs, culture and elite-focused politics, along with policy on key economic sectors of tourism, agriculture and mining – sooner rather than later. Things are possible, in other words, for Malawi's government at 16 million that are not available at 50 million. To parody Denis Healey, the former UK chancellor of the exchequer and foreign secretary, 'Governments come and go, but the rules of arithmetic and geography remain the same.'[7] The history of successful reformers is that they used a crisis – and Malawi's changing demographic picture is a crisis – to institute necessary changes, but they are more successful when they act fast, tough and do not spare their own people in the process, that they share the pain. The Arab Spring along with Mali reminds of the consequences of such inaction, too.

At its core, Malawi requires changing the political economy from being centred on government to one centred on the private sector. Cutting out the middleman is an imperative in all of the above, the intermediary who costs the producer and adds a costly premium to goods coming in and going out. But to emphasise: simply developing better policy on the above areas is not enough – the solution is not better infrastructure (even though that will make a difference), or a better price for tobacco farmers (though that, too), or value addition to basic crops (even if this might reduce imports and possibly help exports), but rather all of the above and more: the entire regime of policy, governance and growth.

Yet, ask any government minister about their plans, in Africa and not just Malawi, and they will say their strategy is 'jobs, jobs, jobs'. Nothing wrong with that, except that jobs are an output of better policy, improved governance and higher growth, not a strategy in themselves. As important as short-term governance actions is a change in the philosophy of development, whichever government or president is in office. There will, as above, need to be a stress on growth and civil service reform, not just revenue collection. And this means, fundamentally, moving away from the donors as the most important constituency to be consulted and accommodated – as tough a challenge but as liberating an opportunity for them, likely, as Malawians.

17

SIERRA LEONE

Shrugging off Legacy

*

During Sierra Leone's decade-long year civil war, Aberdeen Bridge in the capital, Freetown, gained brutal notoriety.[1] It was the scene of the high point of the advance by the rebel Revolutionary United Front (RUF) into and through Freetown in January 1999. The fighting for and around the bridge was vicious and no quarter was given or expected. A combination of the Nigerian army (a component of the Economic Community for West African States Monitoring Group force, ECOMOG), the Sierra Leone Army (SLA) and Kamajor militia (also known as the Civil Defence Force or CDF) pushed the RUF off the bridge as they were beaten out of the city, temporarily as it turned out. As Sierra Leone moved from coup to coup from 1991 and rebel forces grew as the government faltered despite Nigerian army backing, there were 'scores' of reported executions by ECOMOG on the bridge. During the rebel incursion, the bridge was under the command of an ECOMOG captain who earned the name of Captain Evil Spirit among the local population.[2]

The decade of civil war in Sierra Leone consisted of immensely complex and fluid forming and reforming of alliances as different parties strove to control the spoils of the state. By the time of the British intervention in aid of President Ahmad Tejan Kabbah in May 2000, state functions had practically collapsed, with ministries in confusion and officials lacking any direction. The Ministry of Defence staff, for example, comprised three officials. Most businesses and government offices had been looted and vandalised during the RUF's attacks. There was no water, electricity or any other public services operating in Freetown. Large numbers of armed military, paramilitary, ex-SLA, civilians and CDF roamed the city, occupying buildings, manning checkpoints throughout the town and extorting money from the populace to permit passage. The Sierra Leone Police Force was totally ineffective, untrusted and seemingly corrupt at every level. There was no communication to towns outside Freetown other than via radio and satellite telephone, and no safe road access to the interior. To quote Eeben Barlow, the head of Executive Outcomes, the South African-based private security company invited in by then head of state Valentine Strasser to stabilise what seemed to be a lost situation and secure the diamond areas: 'With its untold mineral reserves, immense forests of great beauty, magnificent beaches and a warm climate, the belief that Sierra Leone would become a model state and blossom into a flower of great African beauty was fast become [*sic*] a pipe dream. The rich diamond areas in the east had become a bloody curse and the magnificent jungles were a haven to the RUF and whatever horrors they could dream up. With the rebels and the Sobels [soldiers by day, rebels by night] vying for power and the ruling elite up to its neck in corruption, Strasser realised that he had to do something.'[3]

These horrors almost defy description. Barlow relates the upshot of a RUF attack on a village called Wordu, which the rebels had turned into a 'living hell': 'They had repeatedly raped the females, regardless of their ages. Seven-year-old girls were gang-raped in front of their fathers who were forced at gunpoint to watch. Adolescent boys were forced to rape their own mothers. What followed was even worse. After being raped the women and girls had burning stakes rammed up their vaginas. After that the village boys were forced to shoot their own parents, or face death themselves ... Still not satisfied with their orgy of torture and butchery, the rebels chopped off hands, arms, noses, ears and other body parts with their machetes. Several villagers had their eyes gouged out with red hot coals.'[4]

It was an extreme but not untypical example of a state with all the epiphenomena and none of the institutions of government. It was unusual only in its brutality: rape, cannibalism and amputation were common, with children often among the victims.[5] The life expectancy of the population was only 49 years, the per capita income little more than $120. That population was desperate for peace and, albeit cautiously and with a scepticism born of previous failure, was prepared to give the RUF and its leader, Foday Sankoh, a chance.

Since then Sierra Leone has come a long way, its positive change in fortunes in large part the result initially of forward-leaning external military action along with subsequent, continuous embedded technical assistance, notably in the security sector. It shows what can be achieved by a mixture of a political will and a few good people. It is an important example of where overseas military intervention was not only justified, but was also successful and, equally importantly, relatively inexpensive.

But it will require more than outsiders for the country to transition successfully from failed state to development success.

Today the Aberdeen part of Freetown is a peaceful tourist spot, Man O'War Bay servicing water taxis from Lungi International Airport across the bay and host to a scuba diving school. A derelict yellow hovercraft lies beached where fishing boats bob constantly in the chop. Just down from Arsenal Chicken Take-Aways and the garish orange Chinese-run Good Leone Spa Massage Beauty Salon Guest House, which doubles as a casino, at the turn-off to Alex's somewhat seedy bar, wooden stalls sell brightly coloured tourist clothes and beads. Women do the trade there, touting basins of groundnuts and other foods while clumps of young men loiter, hinting at a wider social malaise. The nearby Cape Sierra Leone Lighthouse, built in 1827, alongside the fenced-off hotel by the same name, offers views of the Atlantic Ocean. The lighthouse keeper radios passing ships, including those ferrying iron ore from the port of Pepel down-river off Tasso Island to larger carriers moored 5 miles offshore. Such activity, evidence of stability and normality, offers hope of a better future. Yet, the lighthouse itself has not worked for a long time, despite the installation of solar power. The roads around Aberdeen, like most in Freetown, are badly rutted and potholed, testament to the relentlessly tough climate and generations of zero investment and maintenance – put differently, a lack of governance.

All this points to the challenge of taking Sierra Leone, like other post-conflict states, from the phase of relatively short-term stabilisation to the longer-term phase of development.

Background

Sierra Leone (literally, 'Lion Mountain', the Italian rendering of the name given by the Portuguese explorer Pedro de Sintra after the hills surrounding what is now Freetown Harbour), founded on 11 March 1792, was Britain's oldest colony in West Africa. Five years earlier the once major slave shipment point had been ceded to the British. With 400 freed slaves settled the same year, the area became known as the Province of Freedom and their first settlement as Freetown, even though local slavery, ironically, continued in the rural areas until the 1970s.[6] Despite several revolts by the indigenous groups against the newcomers, it developed into a small but relatively prosperous territory, with a distinguished educated elite and even a university, Fourah Bay College, was even established in 1827. At independence in 1961, the country seemed set for a stable future as a democratic and developing state, perhaps even a model one given the negotiated independence process and peaceful twentieth-century history.

What went wrong?

One factor was that diamonds, source of much of the country's wealth, and over two-thirds of its (official and unofficial) exports by 1990, undermined its social and political stability.[7] Annual export estimates of these gems range between $70-250 million, though much of this has avoided formal channels, which in 2000 accounted for just $25 million, for example.[8] As farmers abandoned their fields to flock to the diamond areas, so these tiny but fabulously valuable stones provided enough cash to corrupt anyone who needed to be bought off, from top politicians to local police officers. This corrosion both infected and was accelerated by wider political events and a collapse in the provision of basic services and governance.

The immediate post-colonial leadership of Sir Milton Margai was, on his death in 1964, succeeded by his stepbrother Albert, who focused his efforts on positioning members of his Mende tribe. (The population comprises sixteen major ethnic groups, the two largest and most influential being the Temne, predominantly in the north, and the Mende in the south-east.) When the prime minister refused to step down after losing an election in 1967, the military stepped in, only to be overthrown by a further coup led by non-commissioned officers a year later: the spectacle of the entire officer corps, dressed only in their underpants, being marched off to jail vividly symbolised the collapse of the only national institution capable of maintaining public order. Though the new president, Siaka Stevens (aka 'Shaking' Stevens in his dotage) succeeded in restoring a semblance of stability. This was achieved only at the price of a thoroughly corrupt body politic, increasingly alienated from the people it governed and centred on personal patronage.

State structures were, in this environment, geared to keeping the president in power and in pocket. Marketing boards, for example, were set up supposedly to gain farmers better access to markets and, in the process, to prices. In Sierra Leone these rents increased, however, and the share of the farmer quickly reduced: in the mid-1960s, palm kernel farmers were getting

56 per cent of the world price, cocoa farmers 48 per cent and coffee farmers 49 per cent. At the height of Stevens' nearly two decades in power, farmers were getting just 10 per cent.[9] The remainder was divvied up between his supporters and, as anyone who knows Sierra Leone's infrastructure, not re-invested back into the country.

Stevens left office in 1985 at the age of 80 following riots in Freetown with a personal fortune estimated at $500 million, having cut deals on diamonds and even entered into negotiations for an American company to use Sierra Leone as a toxic waste dump. Little wonder his seventeen years of office were compared to a 'plague of locusts'.[10]

From 1985, Sierra Leone's government was run by the former head of the military, President Joseph Momoh. Viewed as a 'well-meaning drunken wom-aniser with few political skills or leadership qualities', Momoh later acquired the nickname 'Dandago', meaning 'idiot' in the local Limba language.[11]

The civil war began in March 1991 when the RUF, then a small armed group, accompanied by Liberian fighters and Burkinabé mercenaries, en-tered south-eastern Sierra Leone from Liberia. Their stated aim was to over-throw Momoh's corrupt government. They claimed their larger goal was a radical, pan-African revolution based on the Libyan Gaddafi model. Sankoh and other leading figures in the RUF were heavily dependent on Charles Taylor of Liberia. They had all met in the mid-1980s while undergoing guer-rilla training in Burkina Faso and Libya at al-Mathab al-Thauriya al-Alamiya, Gaddafi's World Revolutionary Headquarters in Benghazi. Taylor launched his own attack on Liberia in 1989 but was thwarted in part by ECOMOG, which, despite its reputation – 'Every Car or Movable Object Gone' as the prevailing parody – for a long time was all that stood between the rebels and government capitulation and chaos. Taylor aimed to prevent Sierra Leone from being used as a base by his Liberian opponents, the United Liberation Movement for Democracy, as well as to acquire diamonds and other plun-der to finance his own campaign and subsequent regime.

Momoh was deposed on 29 April l992 when junior officers led by the abovementioned 25-year-old Captain Valentine Essegrabo Melvin Strasser delivered a démarche to Momoh's office in Freetown complaining about sinking army morale, not having been paid for several months. Strasser, in his twenties, became the world's youngest (at the time) head of state on 1 May 1992. He had been wounded in action on that day at Kailahun and it was this experience, together with the lack of equipment, pay and support to fight the rebels that prompted his putsch, code named 'Operation Daybreak'. Strasser's junta styled themselves on the National Provisional Ruling Council. With the RUF cutting off state revenue by attacking Sierra Rutile, a titanium mining entity, and the security situation deteriorating, Strasser turned to foreign mercenaries for support. Executive Outcomes, comprising battle-hardened former South African Defence Force special forces operatives, achieved through its involvement 'what thousands of UN peacekeepers five years later were unable to do: they stopped the war' at a cost of $35 million, just one-third of the government's annual defence budget.[12]

Sonny Janeke spent a year flying helicopters for Executive Outcomes in Angola against UNITA forces and thereafter nine months in Sierra Leone. 'The RUF were not at all like UNITA, who the South Africans had trained well. We only had one real, big contact in Sierra Leone, compared to ongoing fighting in Angola, where we would come back with bullet holes in the choppers all the time. Freetown was run-down when we arrived, with the rebels on the outskirts of the city, but we quickly got things organised. Within months things started working well. This allowed the elections to take place [in February 1996]. But perhaps it went too well, since the contract was cancelled. Within a month of our departure things went bad again.'[13]

The cost of the Executive Outcomes mission was some $50 million, although $20 million of that remained unpaid, compared, Barlow points out, 'to the hundreds of millions spent by the UN'. After eleven months, under what Barlow says was pressure from vested interests in the UN precisely for this reason of Executive Outcomes's cost-effectiveness and from corporate rivals, the company left Sierra Leone, amid much disinformation about how much it was being paid. 'The negative media pressure had become too intense and we had no way of resisting that front,' he reflects.[14] But as with the British intervention in 2000, Executive Outcomes' 250-strong force showed what could be done with the right organisation, skills, limited air support[15] and concentration of firepower.

Before the election, however, on 16 January 1996 Brigadier General Julius Maada Bio overthrew Strasser who, he claimed, was clinging to power. Strasser, who had gone to a meeting in the Defence Ministry at Cockerill in Freetown, was overpowered, handcuffed, bundled into a helicopter and flown, like his predecessor, to Guinea. He was just 29.

After a second round of voting on 15 March 1996, the former UN diplomat Kabbah, leader of the southern-based Sierra Leonean People's Party (SLPP), was elected president. Soon after, the country was plunged back into war. In May 1997, 33-year-old Major Johnny Paul Koroma led a successful *coup d'état* against the Kabbah government. Dressed in a T-shirt and baseball cap, 'barely articulate, he made an unprepossessing head of state'.

An attempt three days later by ECOMOG to oust the junta ended in a violent fiasco when Nigerian troops, among others, were trapped in the Mammy Yoko Hotel in Freetown and surrounded by government forces. In June, Koroma invited the RUF to join his junta and created a merged 'People's Army'. But, in February 1998, a Nigerian-led ECOMOG force had put Koroma to flight after just a week of fighting. The fighting continued, reaching its peak in January 1999, when the RUF sacked Freetown in the menacingly titled 'Operation Leave Nothing Behind', leaving 5 000 dead.

The UN's involvement and British engagement

The Lomé Peace Accord, signed on 27 March 1999, gave Sankoh the vice presidency and access to diamond wealth in exchange for the RUF ending fighting, their disarmament and deployment of a UN peacekeeping force. Although criticised over the amnesty offered to the RUF, it was welcomed by the international community on the assumption that it would stopped the fighting, one that soon proved wrong. On 3 October 1999, Sankoh and Koroma returned to Freetown and held a joint press conference with President Kabbah. They apologised for the atrocities carried out during the eight years of the civil war and promised to strive for a speedy implementation of the Lomé Accord. On 22 October, the Security Council unanimously adopted Resolution 1270 to establish a 6 000-member peacekeeping force to be known as the United Nations Mission in Sierra Leone (UNAMSIL) with a six-month mandate to oversee the implementation of Lomé. The wider international community at last appeared to be paying serious attention to Sierra Leone.

Then, in February 2000, as it became apparent that there would be a security vacuum with the phasing out of ECOMOG, the UN Security Council voted to increase the force from 6 000 to 11 000. But UNAMSIL forces (made up of forces from Bangladesh, Ghana, Guinea, India, Jordan, Kenya, Nigeria and Zambia) encountered difficulty as soon as they entered Sierra Leone; the RUF prevented Indian and Ghanaian elements from deploying to the eastern Bendu region. Furthermore UNAMSIL, despite a Chapter VII mandate,[16] interpreted its brief in a traditional UN peacekeeping manner, as one of neutrality between the parties. This seriously impeded the development of close relations with the democratically elected Kabbah government it had been sent to help, and ensured little cooperation between the latter's army and the UN.

Matters did not improve for UNAMSIL. On the very day that ECOMOG officially transferred its duties to the international force, the RUF attacked Kenyan UN soldiers. On 4 May 2000, 208 Zambians who had been sent to relieve the Kenyans were taken hostage and their thirteen armoured personnel carriers were captured. On 6 May, 226 Zambians surrendered to the RUF, bringing the total number of hostages now held by them to over 500. The same day the secretary general of the UN requested that the UK and other countries act to improve the situation. On 6 May the RUF, using the captured armoured personnel carriers, began to advance on Freetown. Lunsar, on the approach road, fell to them and on 7 May the RUF were only 40 kilometres away from the capital.

The UN appeared powerless to stop the RUF and indeed started to evacuate their civilian staff from the country. The government and UNAMSIL seemed, and indeed believed themselves to be, on the verge of collapse. Into this deteriorating situation, on 5 May 2000, a British military team was ordered to assess the situation and to recommend whether or not to respond to Secretary General Kofi Annan's request.

The RUF's advance on the capital at Freetown prompted the British government to dispatch an operational reconnaissance and liaison team to prepare for the evacuation of foreign citizens. The operation, code named Palliser, was, after Kosovo in 1999, the second most significant deployment undertaken by Britain's Tony Blair. Following the Kosovo mission, Blair outlined his 'Doctrine of the International Community', advocating a greater use of humanitarian intervention, where armed force is deployed to protect civilian populations, rather than exclusively to protect national interests.[17] There was an unusual personal link too. Blair's father, Leo, a barrister, had taught law at Fourah Bay College in the early 1970s.

Within 36 hours a sizeable British military force, that at its height grew to 5 000 people and included an aircraft carrier and Harrier jets, started to arrive. It became clear that such a force could achieve much more than an extraction operation if it was able to stiffen the resolve of the better UN contingents and turn the loyal rump of the SLA and the Kamajor militia into an effective fighting force.

On 6 May, the RUF blocked the road connecting Freetown to the country's main airport at Lungi. The next day, British soldiers began to secure the airport and other areas essential to an evacuation. After the completion of the evacuation of some 500 people over the course of a week from 8 May, the mandate of the British forces began to expand. They assisted with the evacuation of besieged peacekeepers – including several British ceasefire observers – and began to assist UNAMSIL. Only on 17 May did British soldiers come into direct contact with the RUF, when the rebels unsuccessfully attacked a British position at Lungi Lol, near the airport, withdrawing with some 30 casualties. Although Lungi Lol was much further east than Whitehall was comfortable with, 1 PARA's Pathfinder Platoon established a defensive outpost there. It was designed to lure the RUF to attack it, enabling the British troops to give them a salutary and damaging drubbing, thereby irrevocably establishing their psychological superiority. The aim was achieved.

That clash also provided a deterrent against further attacks. With its vital ground intact, UNAMSIL was given a chance to regroup and reorganise.[18] The evacuation was curtailed and confidence slowly started to return.

What UNAMSIL could not, and would not, do was push the RUF back from its positions close to Freetown. To do this, the British coordinated and sustained the efforts of a disparate grouping of Sierra Leoneans, largely CDF and ex-SLA, who remained loyal to their president. Guided at every level by British officers and non-commissioned officers, over the next few weeks they succeeded in securing much of the inland road route between Freetown and Lungi Lol, relieving the military and political pressure on Freetown and its beleaguered government. The RUF started to splinter into different factions and Taylor began to lose his grip. This at first ad hoc twin-track operation by the British, giving support to the UN on the one hand and assistance to the government of Sierra Leone on the other, soon became official strategy. To give it further effect, the UK deployed additional troops, including a sizeable amphibious force.[19]

The result was total psychological ascendancy over the RUF that bought the government and the UN the time they needed to reassert themselves. And perhaps more important, in a different psychological sense, was the impact of the UK's role on the mood of the people. They at last felt the glimmerings of genuine hope for the future, a feeling reinforced when many RUF leaders were detained, including Sankoh himself, who was taken into custody on 17 May while trying to escape from Freetown.

By mid-June 2000, the security situation had stabilised sufficiently to allow the British operation to be terminated, although the UK agreed to provide additional military support in the form of financial and training assistance to the new SLA, now renamed the Republic of Sierra Leone Armed

Forces (RSLAF). The British and UNAMSIL intervention in Sierra Leone demonstrated that given the right conditions, leadership and mandate, the military can be a force for good. This positive contribution continued well into the next decade.

The sequel

For a while, the security situation continued to improve as UNAMSIL finally began to deploy troops outside Freetown. But it soon became clear that they had neither the will nor the capability to push home their advantage. Nor, at that stage, was the fledgling RSLAF in a position to do better.

In early October 2000, the situation started deteriorating again. UNAMSIL, far from gaining strength and authority, appeared to be in danger of moving backwards, especially when India announced the withdrawal of its contingent. The RUF remained in control of over half the country and was strengthening its grip on some key areas, including the diamond-producing regions needed to finance its operations. It showed no sign of returning to negotiations, and was beginning to expand its operations into Guinea. Taylor continued actively to support the RUF and seemed impervious to ill-coordinated attempts by the international community to bring him into line. The UK's efforts with the RSLAF were beginning to bear fruit but lacked a powerful coordinating headquarters to bring coherence to the work and to develop a plan to defeat the RUF, harnessing and informing other work at the strategic level.

The same team that had succeeded in May returned, this time explicitly charged with the development of a coherent plan that would ensure the RUF's defeat, while devising a long-term solution that would ensure future stability. The work, combined with some bold initiatives by UNAMSIL's civilian and new military leadership, forced the RUF to sign a ceasefire agreement at Abuja on 10 November 2000. The RUF's new leader, Issa Sesay, publicly conceded that the British commitment to Sierra Leone, and the opportunity it had provided the UN, was the distinguishing factor in its decision to seek a peaceful outcome. The rebels had succumbed to the British aim of 'persuading the RUF of the inevitability of defeat'.[20] Although too much time was taken exploiting the agreement, this was a conspicuous success for the UN, the Sierra Leonean government and the UK. It signalled the end of the conflict and an opportunity to start improving the lives of the country's long-suffering people.

The RUF began to disarm after political pressure, and later economic sanctions were exerted on Liberia. The Sierra Leonean government eventually signed a ceasefire with the RUF that obliged the latter to enter the Disarmament, Demobilisation and Reintegration (DDR) process. By September 2001, when the British training teams were replaced by an international force, the International Military Advisory and Training Team (IMATT), the DDR process was almost complete.

An ongoing process

That process was still, to some extent, in train thirteen years after the end of the war.

Some 18 000 UN peacekeeping troops were on the ground in Sierra Leone from October 1999 to December 2005 at a cost of $2.3 billion. During that period the country made vital progress in a number of areas with the help of the international community, in particular Britain. It saw the disbandment and rehabilitation of former combatants; the complete overhaul, retraining and equipping of the armed forces by the British-led IMATT; the establishment and training of a new police force; a massive influx of international aid and assistance, plus foreign expertise embedded within key government ministries; the demobilisation and reintegration of child soldiers into their communities; the revival of the minerals sector and the clamping down on illicit smuggling of diamonds; the introduction of various measures to promote investment and tackle corruption and money laundering; and the September 2007 elections – won by the opposition leader Ernest Bai Koroma's All People's Congress (APC) with 54.6 per cent of the final vote against then Vice President Solomon Berewa's 45.4 per cent in a run-off. Thereafter, Koroma led a peaceful transition to a new democratic government. This election marked an important step forward in Sierra Leone's democratic development, and reflected, in particular, the progress made in security. The various militias, which had, in 2000, numbered over 18 500, had, by 2007, been downsized to 10 700 and melded into the SLA. By 2013, the numbers had been further reduced to the optimum defence force size of 8 500. Palo Conteh, a London-educated barrister, former soldier and now defence minister, says, 'Previously citizens did not trust the army. They were in fact fighting them. They would have put a tyre around the neck of a government soldier once, and lit the match. Yet at the 50th anniversary of our independence,' he paused, 'it brought tears to my eyes to hear the crowds chanting "SOLDIER, SOLDIER, SOLDIER" in support of the army that they had once so hated.' The security guarantee provided by IMATT has been crucial in this regard, characterised by a belief (however misplaced) that 'a British battleship would appear at the first sign of trouble'. Even though IMATT was, in April 2013, replaced by the International Security Assistance Team, and the numbers cycled down from more than 100 trainers and mentors in 2007 to just twelve in 2013, this perception of an external guarantor remained largely intact.

Disconcertingly, however, at the time of the 2007 election Sierra Leone was, according to the UNDP Human Development Index, the poorest country in the world. In the same report released in October 2009, only Niger and Afghanistan ranked lower. Although it had moved up ten places from the bottom by 2013 and life expectancy had risen between 2001–10 from 41 to 48 years, endemic youth unemployment at about 70 per cent and acute income inequalities mean that it has remained volatile and vulnerable. Part of the challenge relates to the pressures of people and to the absence of investment in infrastructure, recurring themes throughout this book. Sierra Leone's population, just two million at independence on 27 April 1961, was four million at the war's end. By 2013, it hovered around six million, its numbers swollen by the return of refugees who had fled the region during the 2000s.

While its economy has bounced back, with a growth rate averaging 9.3 per cent for the thirteen years from 2000, this reflects a period of acute recovery post-2000, when growth was as high as 18 per cent in 2001 and 27 per cent in 2002. While there have also been impressive declines in poverty, from 66.4 per cent to 52.9 per cent of the population between 2003 and 2011, its people remain poor.[21] While GDP per capita is, on average, three times greater than the figure in 2000, when overall GDP was under $700 million, GDP per capita is still at just $350.[22] By the government's own admission, 'The average income of Sierra Leoneans ... is scarcely enough to fulfil their wide range of modern needs for a good quality of life.'[23]

There are a number of impediments to development, including its poor infrastructure base, low skills levels, reliance on two sectors for employment and export income – mining as well as subsistence agriculture in which two-thirds of the population are engaged – governance and, critically, underneath the recovery iceberg, mindset. Even with the first phase of the Bumbuna hydro scheme on line, Sierra Leone produces just 76 MW of energy, little more than an English village. Despite improvements, such as being one of the world's top ten business reformers and fastest movers in the index, the country still ranked 142/189 on the World Bank's 2014 Ease of Doing Business indicators,[24] reflecting concerns about corruption, weak personal and institutional government capacity, and poor governance. While its dependence on minerals – notably iron, gold, diamonds and rutile – is cited as a hindrance, it is the management of these assets and the way in which governments and elites have responded to them that are regarded as the key problem, given the opacity of deals being struck. With transparency, these resources could be a considerable development asset. For example, iron ore production grew significantly at the start of the second decade of the twentieth century to over $500 million in exports (or 5.5 million tonnes) in 2012. Still, commercial agriculture has been neglected, partly as a result of a reliance on donors and minerals and partly because of a failure to conduct land reform. Two-thirds of the population remains locked into subsistence agriculture. The country is heavily dependent on aid flows – its GDP in 2012 was $2.4 billion,[25] while aid figures amounted to perhaps as much as $500 million annually. The relative importance of the donors can be gauged from the next largest source of income – mining – which brought in less than $50 million in royalties and taxes in 2012 compared to export receipts of $165 million from peak recorded production levels of iron and diamonds.[26]

Sierra Leone illustrates the axiom: the period of recovery from conflict is at least as long as the period of decline. It has been characterised as a country working its way out of a deficit. By 2013, its 'country balance sheet' was definitely no longer in the red, but at zero. Thus, it sits at what the African Development Bank describes as a process from 'transition' to 'resilience'; put differently, from stabilisation dependent on foreign donors to development through the mobilisation of national resources.

Several transitions are implicit: firstly, from the belief that salvation and opportunity will come from outside to what Sierra Leoneans themselves do (or don't do). Secondly, that government and donors have been clear about what is required to take the country from stability to development, from the status of a 'fragile' to a 'least-developed' and then onto a 'middle-income' country, and this is reflected in the government's own 'Agenda for Prosperity'.

Thirdly, that exiting fragility is not 'simply', as Sierra Leone's finance minister, Dr Kaifala Marah, has put it, 'about fixing and returning to the point of decline, but about rebuilding in a different way. It is more than having security on the streets of Freetown, or having kids in school. It is about the quality of education and the presence of opportunity.'[27] There is little point in getting back to the place at which the precipitous decline began. Something different, politically and economically, has to be created. In Sierra Leone, as in other similar circumstances, such 'system change' requires government setting priorities that are matched by available resources, and which are increasingly funded by domestic (tax) resources. For this, Sierra Leone would need to focus on: good policy, especially on tourism, agriculture and infrastructure (roads, ports and energy); ensuring transparency, especially in big mining deals; and by maintaining good regional relations through the Mano River Union to ensure harmonisation of border and policy, including taxation to prevent smuggling.

Fundamentally, this demands that countries 'do' the right thing without pressure from external donors, and 'own' these solutions. Historically, donors have had a poor experience with imposing conditions on recipient states because this has reduced local ownership, inflamed paternalistic sensitivities and provided an 'out' for local responsibility. Such conditions can, on the contrary, encourage and excuse more radical political and policy shifts. Donors, in this scenario, also risk being undermined by the activities of others outside of the traditional donor compact, epitomised by the Chinese with their easy cash and mining interests, not only willing to cut side deals with the government free from governance conditions, but deliberately seeking to undermine such stipulations and standards. It is a fine balance, though, given that the same or worse could be said for the unconditional approach, such as that taken by the US with Mobutu in Zaire.

Two possible scenarios, good and bad

A good outcome for Sierra Leone is one where not only does the political settlement of the 2000s stick, but it amounts to more than a box ticked simply for holding elections. This would be a scenario where mining and other revenues are equally and transparently collected and distributed on the basis of need rather than ethnicity or geography, for example between the Mende-dominated south and east or Temne north and west, or between the urban and rural areas. The National Minerals Agency, set up in 2013, is in this outcome a transparent and technocratically minded prototype for other government departments. In this, too, the professionalism of the security forces, including the police, is enhanced, and necessary attention is paid to addressing regional Mano River Union border issues, such as logging, mining and people flows. It is one where the commercial and smallholder agriculture sector booms, respectable mining companies are attracted and where, finally, the government's setting of priorities is matched by its allocation of resources spread increasingly throughout the country's nineteen local government councils, along with a large dollop of political will, improving stability. The costs of doing business would be reduced through better governance, policy and well-maintained infrastructure.

A bad outcome is one, by contrast, where urban tensions rise over a lack of jobs and presence of foreign workers, where the rural sector (from where the RUF drew much of its support) feels marginalised, and where illegal regional flows of people, goods, money, diamonds and arms continue. It is where the police remain corrupt and poorly trained, and where the armed forces prefer to spend time on UN peacekeeping duty (where they earn $800 per month) rather than dedicating themselves to domestic issues (where they earn $80). It is where, as now, the president's security detail reflects a wider disquiet, being made up of regular police, paramilitary presidential guard members and 'boys from his village'. It is conceivably a picture in which Islam (followed by 80 per cent of the population) becomes radicalised or where previously unimportant Sunni and Shia tensions rise. In this scenario, the economy remains dependent on donors and natural resources, and fails to diversify around other traditional export crops such as cocoa and coffee. And also in this scenario, in the absence of transparency and a domestically founded good governance regime, Sierra Leone shifts in international orientation from a British quasi-protectorate to a Chinese take-away, with scant regard for labour standards, the environment, legal niceties and contracts.

Responsiveness is crucial in this sensitive and volatile environment. Often when solutions are eventually agreed, they are applied far too slowly, sometimes because of lengthy donor lead times (which is one reason why the Chinese become preferred partners). In the military, the concept of tempo – acting relatively quicker than one's opponent – is recognised as vital to success. When this is not achieved, the initiative is lost and the enemy will surely win. In Sierra Leone it became clear too often that well-intentioned solutions were being overtaken by events. Applied too late, they would become irrelevant, often aggravating the new problem.

Here bureaucratic inertia and incompetence are endemic and positively inimical to progress. Lungi was the scene of some of the toughest fighting during the civil war. Yet, more than a decade later, the functioning of the international airport was still subject to the most elementary of challenges. In March 2014 more than 100 passengers were left stranded after British

Airways and Kenya Airways, the top two international carriers to Sierra Leone, cancelled flights after the airport's status was downgraded after discovering that the only functioning fire engine there was broken. 'We are working very hard to fix the faulty gearbox system of the fire engine and to add to the fleet,' said the general manager of the local airports authority.[28]

Worse, it is clear that sometimes those responsible for solving problems deliberately take longer than they might have because the problem they are charged with solving is their working life, income and even *raison d'être*. This is a recurring criticism of many UN workers. Also NGOs are often less effective than they should be because they suffer from the same institutional rivalry and bureaucratic inefficiency as government agencies. They also pull in too many directions, undermining each other and failing to see the big picture.

What about the next generation after the British and other partners have taken a back seat?

As is highlighted above, a good solution for Sierra Leone in the next 25 years is, by the government's own description, contained in its 'Agenda for Prosperity'; of a middle-income country with a per capita GDP equivalent to $1 000, or three times more than in 2013. This will require an economic growth rate little over 7 per cent per annum for 30 years, not an impossible target given Sierra Leone's natural resource endowment and relatively low per capita starting point. More than anything, such a sustained strategy will, at its heart, demand that locals, not foreigners, own the growth agenda and its policy and governance specifics and that these are market friendly.

Helping countries to help themselves

Whatever the relative weight of donors, outsiders should be wary of continuously attempting to hold local feet to the fire of good governance, the rule of law and sound policy, in Sierra Leone as elsewhere. Instead, as Jerry Maguire,[29] in a 1996 blockbuster of the same name, starring Tom Cruise, might have put it, 'How do you help countries to help themselves?' The long-term answer lies in incentivising local actors to make these decisions on good policy for themselves. The difficulties in this regard cannot be understated: for instance, the annual Ibrahim prize for African leadership – which provides $5 million over ten years and $200 000 per year for life thereafter to a former head of state displaying exceptional qualities – has proven to be an insufficient incentive, with just three winners awarded in the first seven years since its inception in 2007.[30] The incentives for bad decisions are great, not least as these decisions are seldom penalised at the polls by those electorates that are apathetic, distracted or vote on the grounds of identity rather than the basis of issues and record.

Sierra Leone, like other losers, needs to change the way in which it is seen as a recipient of international charity. To do so, it would not only have to brand itself but start to think of its policy choices 'beyond aid' – and in so doing distinguish its promise by aligning its strategies to the post-charity world.

Yet, Richard Konteh, the president's chief of staff, admits, 'Sierra Leone should own its solutions, but does not yet.' Foreigners also have a poor history of keeping local politicians on track. Presidential advisers have a better record at improving processes in Sierra Leone (as elsewhere in Africa) within government and in terms of their messaging to the outside world, than they have a permanently and positively changing policy. Indeed, outside policy influence appears to depend less on process management than on the warmth and trust inherent in personal relationships, in getting local actors to see choices – and their advantages – less in terms of patronage and 'spreading the love', but the logic of national development. Unfortunately in this regard war distorts not only what is right and wrong, but the belief of what is due to its actors from the state and from the peace; as Konteh puts it, 'naked greed'.

In the transition from stabilisation to longer-term development, the solution in Sierra Leone, as elsewhere, thus resides in changing the style and substance of politics, the very reasoning on which policy and governance choices are made.

More than downsides, shrugging off legacy

There is little gainsaying the fact that Sierra Leone is scarcely recognisable as the country that featured in the 2006 *Blood Diamond* blockbuster. It is politically stable, has enjoyed several peaceful ballots, and is slowly restoring the infrastructure and governance regimes necessary to run a state. The government is putting in hard yards to develop institutions such as the all-important National Minerals Agency, sometimes against the odds of available human and financial capital. It is another country from that which could not control its sources of wealth and even its capital, and *in extremis* resorted to mercenaries to assist in shoring up the situation.

But it is a long, hard road to recovery.

Much work remains to be done to recover a society that suffered over 50 000 deaths and many more rapes and mutilations during its civil war. As Barlow graphically reminds us, it was a 1990's *Lords of War* archetype: guerrilla forces and militias rampaging through the countryside and towns, raping, pillaging and destroying property and people's lives and hopes. The lopping off of hands and arms – 'short sleeves' or 'long sleeves' was the 'choice' offered to the unfortunate victims – is an abiding physical legacy, though the damage to people and ways of life is perhaps more profound, if harder to discern.

There is a danger, however, of seeing only the challenges and downsides. There are many reasons to remain optimistic about Sierra Leone, even though there are thousands of reasons also given for pending failure.

For there are other important signs of normality. In April 2012, the UN-backed Sierra Leone war crimes court in The Hague concluded its work with Taylor's conviction for aiding and abetting crimes in the civil war. Six months later, in the November 2012 elections, the first held since the end of the civil war without UN oversight, President Koroma won a second term, signalling and reinforcing Sierra Leone's democratic progress. And the wheel has come full circle. In April 2013, Sierra Leone deployed a battalion of troops to Somalia to join the African Union peacekeeping mission in that once fellow 'failed state'.

And there are more personal measures of maturity and stability by which one might judge the progress made since the end of the civil war. Take, for example, one political figure from the 1990s.

After his overthrow in January 1996, Valentine Strasser left Sierra Leone via Guinea for the UK to study law at Warwick but dropped out after a year, citing pressure from fellow students who were unhappy about having the former generalissimo in their midst. Denied entry into the Gambia in 2000, he moved back to Sierra Leone where he lives in Grafton, east of Freetown, in reduced circumstances. That is where I found him during a 2013 visit.

Getting there is a 90-minute road journey through traffic along the Kissy and then the Bai Burah roads, worsened by the number of street vendors touting everything from Sierra Leone to Manchester United flags, surplus American clothes and biscuits. At the Jui turn-off, marked by more stalls and star-signed bars, we headed towards the hills, past the Church of the Latter Day Saints ('Visitors Welcome' apparently), over the old bridge, next to which Chinese contractors were laying the concrete-and-steel foundations for a twenty-first-century replacement. Underneath women were washing their clothes and themselves, while others sat cross-legged under a hoarding up the hill, smashing rocks into sub-base for the Chinese. Then we turned down another road to Grafton where the former 'head of state' ('not president', he admonished) was waiting in stone-washed jeans, new sneakers and a striped golf shirt, just past the mechanic and 25 metres from the Goodyear sign. He looked older than his 46 years, perhaps a reflection of a lifestyle described by his detractors as one of playing draughts and drinking palm wine under the trees.

In the reed-roofed, wooden lean-to, Strasser explained the drivers of conflict that had led to his 1992 coup. 'We wanted to see a representative government that would end the war, which was eating the economy. We had then a one-party state. If we could do that, huge savings would have been possible [to allow] spending in the social sectors – hospitals, homes and schools. Widespread poverty, rising illiteracy, youth unemployment, corruption and ethnicity,' he added, 'were all related. A vicious cycle,' he says. And the state 'was also taking a lot of the mining wealth, since it was a state company then that was running things – they should be blamed'.

Strasser believes that the key problem has now been resolved, permitting stability and progress. 'We were a one-party dictatorship, which dominated things. The only choice that people had was to organise themselves into armed groups. And the military, in turn, had to intervene. Now we have a democracy. Most of the cabinet is, of course, from the north,' he admitted, 'but the south is evenly represented in parliament, which is a counterbalance. It is not a perfect ethnic outcome,' says Strasser, an ethnic Krio, the immigrant group of freed slaves who were repatriated to Sierra Leone. 'The north votes APC and the south SLPP, but a multi-party democracy is not nearly as pernicious as what we once had.' Strasser points to the improved level of foreign investment, especially into mining, which he said was providing new job opportunities and improved living standards. And, he adds, 'the rails and road infrastructure have been remarkably improved', no doubt mindful of the road construction just beyond the Grafton turn-off.

Strasser was something of a radio talking-head during the 2012 election. Ideally, he would like to go into politics 'but for that', he smiles, 'I need money'. For the moment he is setting up a small computer school to make his contribution to his community. That the former strongman is living openly in Sierra Leone, free to express his views, is a positive sign of political maturity, light years from the RUF he fought against and the military regime he once headed.

18

SOMALIA

The World's 'Most Failed' State

*

In *Vanguard of Victory*, a review of South African military victories in East Africa in 1940–41, Conrad Norton and Uys Krige write of the 'White City of Mogadiscio, Capital of Italian Somaliland, [a] town won by man from the desert … Literally without a tree, a shrub or a bush, Mogadiscio clings to the edge of the desert, strikingly picturesque with its snow-white buildings, many of great antiquity, its slender white towers, minarets and cupolas, and its rose-red Arab mosque. Towards evening, the town is invested with the most delicate pastel colours, and the encircling red sand-dunes glow like rubies lit by an inner fire.'[1]

Seventy years on the picture was very different.[2]

As one measure, the language associated with this Horn of Africa country is almost uniformly negative. It is usually deemed to have 'failed', been 'destroyed' or 'ravaged', become 'a territory without a state' or 'stateless'. Mogadishu is 'Africa's most wounded city', the capital of a country where 'descriptions of chaos, hunger and anarchy' abound, with problems ranging from 'religionist authoritarianism' to 'clans' to 'foreign interests'.[3]

To take a somewhat more quantitative benchmark, by 2013 Somalia had been listed for six straight years at the bottom of the Failed States Index.[4] Indeed, it has become the archetypal failed state,[5] a caricature of misery, death and excess to which photojournalists travel in search of images of destruction, collapse, human suffering and helplessness. It is not hard to find them.

Parts of Mogadishu looked like those pictures one sees in sepia of Ypres, Amiens, Stalingrad or Berlin. In the old part of town, in the area around the once-prestigious Lido Beach, the shells of buildings, pockmarked carcasses of war, formed monuments to more than two decades of fighting since 2007 between the African Union's peacekeepers (known widely as AMISOM – the African Union Mission in Somalia) and the militant jihadist Al-Shabab movement. Five years later the roads were still mostly unpaved, less a path in places than bucking bronco, testament to decades of no investment, while there was rubbish all over the place, smouldering underneath the human and goat scavengers, with plastic bags flying and lying everywhere. The grandstand at Tarabunka where the former dictator Mohamed Siad Barre took the salute of his armed forces, was a tangled mess of concrete and reinforced steel, discarded car chassis and panels, and pathetic refugee shelters and shops.

And the locals told me things had really improved.

On the western outskirts of the city were thousands of refugees crammed into Zona K and Camp 77, enveloping the once-proud but run-down Gaheyr University facilities. We turned off towards the old stadium (a camp for some of the 350 000 internally displaced people in Mogadishu,[6] from more than 1.2 million countrywide), past Village Restaurant where two suicide bombers killed themselves and a dozen civilians in an attack shortly after the election by parliament of a new president in September 2012. Beyond, the Bakara market complex beckoned, a site for occasional Al-Shabab suicide bombings and assassinations. Regardless, it remained a hive of commercial activity, people going about their business on foot and donkey carts, peddling petrol and fussing outside brightly decorated premises advertising building material and auto spares. Women constantly moved in radiantly coloured scarfs and veils like flares in the dusty gloom.

Somalia is sometimes said to be a 'place of great promise', one of those 'opportunities in a lifetime', as a Mogadishu business person put it, 'when you can start at the bottom, all over again'. It has bountiful fisheries, as befits a country with a 3 300-kilometre coastline, the longest in continental Africa, not least given that pirates have forced those fishing illegally to think again. It has a great Dubai-like location, a 'portal' between the Gulf, Arabia and Africa. It is remarkable how, for all the outward destruction, much of the economy has survived.

In fact, the failed state of Somalia has actually served some segments of the population rather well. Failure for some is good business for others. This is one reason that Somalia cannot be rebuilt unless Somalis change their attitudes toward each other, whatever the African Union or the wider international community offers and does. While the territory was described as the 'most failed state' by the UK's foreign secretary, William Hague, during his visit to Mogadishu in February 2012, in some respects it works, for a few. It is estimated, for example, that piracy originating from Somalia netted $400 million between 2005 and 2012. A World Bank and UN report highlighted the cooperation that lay behind this trade, between externally based financiers and the local Somali community, which 'provides goods and services to pirates', including food, repair services and the supply of *qat*. The proceeds, which have been used both to invest in legitimate business and criminal activities, were 'typically moved by cross-border cash smuggling, trade-based money laundering, bank-wire transfer and the abuse of the Money of Value Transfer Services'.[7]

Though the pirates were largely out of business by 2014, partly as a result of international patrols on the high seas, they still held some 49 hostages. Still, the majority of the country was very dependent on external assistance for both security and the institutions of central government. Since the collapse of the Siad Barre regime in 1991, there have been several international efforts to stabilise Somalia, most recently by AMISOM. By March 2014, under UN Security Council Resolution 2125, more than 22 000 African Union troops and police were fighting on behalf of the Somali government with this aim. Equally, under the Busan New Deal Compact for Somalia signed in Brussels in September 2013, donors were, more or less, singing from the same peace-building hymn sheet.[8]

AMISOM: An African success story in Somalia

From controlling just the airport at Mogadishu and a small area around the presidential compound in 2007, within six years AMISOM was instrumental in driving Al-Shabab from the capital and large parts of the countryside. This ushered in the longest sustained period of relative peace and governance that the Somali capital has had since the 1991 collapse of Siad Barre's rule by a coalition of opposing clans formed into the United Somali Congress.

But AMISOM is not the first attempt to re-establish order in Somalia – and nor has its experience been plain sailing. That was hardly expected, given the history of conflict in the region.

Somalia was created in July 1960 with the merger of British Somaliland

and the former Italian Somaliland to the south. A military junta led by Siad Barre in 1969[9] quickly formed a socialist regime, borrowing heavily from China in employing volunteer agriculture labour, nationalising industry along with banks and businesses, and forbidding clan membership as an attempt to stress loyalty to the central government. Already poor relations with its neighbours, soured by Mogadishu's territorial claims on Somali-inhabited areas of Ethiopia, Kenya and Djibouti, came to a head in 1977 when Somali forces attempted to seize the Ogaden region of Ethiopia. Siad Barre's military defeat by Addis Ababa's Soviet- and Cuban-backed forces spelt the beginning of the end for his regime.

Since the ousting by clan-based forces by the Siad Barre regime in 1991, various international attempts to re-establish government control have interspersed periods of warlord supremacy, widespread famine and Islamic radicalism. Soon after Siad Barre's overthrow, the coalition divided into two groups: one led by Ali Mahdi, who was chosen as president by an internationally sponsored conference in Djibouti – the first of many such outside attempts to impose a government on the country – and the other by Mohamed Farrah Aidid. However, four opposing groups – the United Somali Congress, Somali Salvation Democratic Front, Somali Patriotic Movement and Somali Democratic Movement – continued to fight. A fifth group, the Somali National Movement, broke away in June 1991 and established the Somaliland Republic in the north.

A recent history of collapse

Despite ongoing attempts to broker a peace, in September 1991 severe fighting broke out in Mogadishu and spread throughout the country, with more than 20 000 casualties, and leading to much destruction, especially to Somalia's agriculture base. The international community's endeavours to deliver food supplies were subject to hijacking by clan leaders and warlords, and used to barter for weapons. An estimated 80 per cent of the food delivered was stolen, and the resulting conflict and famine caused the deaths of another 300 000 people between 1991 and 1992. In July 1992, after a ceasefire between the opposing clan factions, the UN sent 50 military observers to monitor the distribution of the food assistance.

In August 1992, the US government initiated Operation Provide Relief under UNOSOM I to guarantee, by military force, the delivery of humanitarian relief. However, most of the food was looted as soon as the planes carrying it landed. In response to a UN request for assistance, in December 1992, as he was preparing to leave office, President George W. Bush, offered help under the proviso that US troops would lead the operation. About 25 000 international troops (mostly US Marines from 1 Marine Expeditionary Force, Australian light infantry from the Royal Australian Regiment, and French and Italian forces) were deployed to Somalia in a mission renamed Operation Restore Hope.

Under the UN-approved Operation Restore Hope, from 3 December 1992 to 4 May 1993, the US-led coalition provided humanitarian assistance. After President Bill Clinton was inaugurated in January 1993, he decided to hand over leadership of the mission to the UN. In May 1993, most international combat troops withdrew, and the UN officially took over under a peace enforcement mandate. The leaders of Somalia's armed factions agreed on a federalist government based on eighteen autonomous regions. The UN renamed the mission UNOSOM II; its mission was to initiate 'nation-building' in Somalia, disarm the various factions, restore law and order and help the people set up a representative government. UNOSOM II possessed a strength of 28 000 drawn from 26 countries, including about 1 800 US troops, who continued to operate under Operation Continue Hope from May 1993 to March 1994.

Then, on 5 June 1993, 24 Pakistani troops were ambushed and killed by Somali militia while inspecting an arms depot. Aidid was suspected of being responsible. Two weeks later, a $25 000 warrant was issued for information leading to his arrest. Given a deteriorating security situation, in early August, the US deployed Task Force Ranger, comprising Delta Force operators, special operations aviation assets and Ranger light infantry forces. Task Force Ranger was not under UN control, and was thus able to conduct combat operations aimed at removing the perceived threat to UNOSOM from Aidid, his United Somali Congress militia and his Habr Gidr clan.

The battle for Mogadishu and Black Hawk Down

The hunt for Aidid and his lieutenants resulted in an escalating series of poorly targeted raids, and culminated in the Battle of Mogadishu on 3 October 1993, which ended with eighteen US soldiers and one Malaysian dead, 73 Americans wounded and between 500 and 1 000 Somali militia and civilians killed. Task Force Ranger was withdrawn within weeks, and the remaining US troops pulled out a few months afterwards, the event being made famous by the Mark Bowden novel and subsequent Hollywood blockbuster *Black Hawk Down*.

Thomas Pickering was the US ambassador to the UN at the time of the Somalia mission in 1992. He recalls the motivation for the intervention: 'In the post-Cold War world, we were in a state of euphoria about our success, and we thought we should try the same formula in other parts of the world. The US was willing to take the lead in using its political and military power, with the belief that this might translate into the UN Security Council becoming the centrepiece of similar actions.' Even at the outset, he says, there were 'questions about whether we should use force, how big the force should be, how long it should stay there and the likely degree of difficulty the mission might encounter'.[10]

Pickering sums it up by observing that if you 'want such a mission to be done correctly, then you need to have an idea of what you want to see emerge ... you need a political vision and a set of measures and institutions and policies through which this political vision and conditions of stability can be achieved, along with a force to allow you the space for development and the building of institutions. You also need to define the force on the basis of the role ahead and not the size of the expected conflict.'

Since that time there have been no fewer than fourteen attempts to establish a government in Somalia. In 2000, for example, clan elders and other senior figures appointed Abdulkassim Salat Hassan president of Somalia at a conference held in Djibouti, setting up a transitional government at the same time. In 2004, following protracted talks in Kenya, a new deal was cemented in order to create the Transitional Federal Government, but this government faced 'a formidable task in bringing reconciliation to a country divided into clan fiefdoms', an effort complicated by the rise of the Union of Islamic Courts in 2006, which gained control of the capital and much of the southern part of the country.[11]

The rise of the Union of Islamic Courts in 2006 underlined the desire of many ordinary Somalis for predictability and order, after more than a decade of near anarchy, with local control exercised by clan-based militia who fought each other in a loose and shifting series of temporary alliances of convenience. This created a lethally complex environment for ordinary Somalis, who had to negotiate an extremely complicated series of decisions about which faction to support, on an almost daily basis, in order to be safe.

The Union's appeal rested less on its military capability than on its Islamic authority and, thus, its association in the minds of many Somalis with a cleaner, less corrupt, less abusive, more consistent form of government. The desire for rule of law, public order and predictability was a key element here. The very strictness and severity of the courts' judgments was reassuring for local business and community leaders who expected greater consistency and certainty, creating a more predictable environment for them to protect their families, homes and business interests. As in many similar cases, the predictability and security that the courts' union provided was reassuring to the local population, causing many in the community to support them irrespective of the appeal of their ideology. Over time, however, their ferocious strictness and the emergence of patterns of corruption and abuse disillusioned the population, emboldened challengers to attempt to retake power and led to a collapse of the Union of Islamic Courts' control over Mogadishu.

As Somalia continued to disintegrate again, US-backed Ethiopian troops intervened to support the Transitional Federal Government against the Union. Ethiopian troops successfully strengthened Transitional Federal Government control of the western city of Baidoa in September 2006, and moved into Mogadishu that December. Two years later, in January 2009, Ethiopian troops pulled out of Somalia. The Islamists, headed by the more radical Al-Qaeda-influenced Al-Shabab movement – a younger, more militant offshoot of the defeated Union of Islamic Courts, with a similar theological appeal but a more aggressive and expansionist political and military posture – quickly advanced, retaking Baidoa and moving on Mogadishu.

By this time, AMISOM had been created. Set up in January 2007, AMISOM superseded the Inter-Governmental Authority on Development (IGAD) Peace Support Mission in Somalia, which was established the previous September. In March 2007, Ugandan military personnel arrived in Somalia. By July 2010, soon after deadly bombings by Al-Shabab at Kampala in Uganda, the African Union agreed to widen AMISOM's mandate from peacekeeping to peace enforcement in order to engage Al-Shabab.

Pushing out Al-Shabab

UN Security Council Resolution 1964 of 22 December 2010 took AMISOM from 7 650 troops to 12 000, and Security Council Resolution 2035 of

22 February 2012 to 17 731. As AMISOM slowly expanded its area of control and pushed Al-Shabab out of key areas within Mogadishu, in October 2011 Kenyan troops commenced operations against the group in southern Somalia, integrating its troops with AMISOM the following month. By 2014 AMISOM comprised troops from Uganda (6 363), Burundi (5 432), Kenya (4 651), Djibouti (960), Nigeria (140) and Sierra Leone (850) plus an African Union headquarters element, while AMISOM had increased the area under its 'control' to encompass most of the middle third of the country. In 2014 this expanded further with the incorporation of 4 500 Ethiopian troops already operating independently in the west to be under nominal AMISOM command, not least for reasons of funding. By 2014 this made AMISOM the largest UN-mandated peacekeeping mission in the world.

While African nations provided the troops, Western donors have coughed up the money. Humanitarian assistance amounted to $1 billion in 2011,[12] and development aid was estimated at $200 million in 2013, the EU was alone spending €25 million per month, and over the previous seven years had spent over $2 billion.[13] The Turkish government has been among other key donors, seeing the country as a strategic African and Muslim partner, providing reconstruction assistance in Mogadishu, including refurbishment of the airport, the running of which was taken over by a Turkish company in 2013. UN agencies, primarily based in Kenya, have also increased significant funding for humanitarian relief.[14]

These figures exclude financing for the African Union mission, which is estimated at $500 million annually. Additionally, as of 2014, the American and Italian governments footed the bill for a $100 monthly stipend paid to 9 061 of the 20 000 Somali National Army (SNA), with Italy stumping up for another 3 274. The government additionally paid a further $100 salary plus a $60 food supplement. This force includes lightly equipped troops, along with the Somali Police Force that operates mainly in Mogadishu and surrounding towns, and (under separate funding arrangements) a much more capable and better equipped paramilitary force that operates under the Somali National Security Agency, the local government's intelligence service.

AMISOM's bill has to be put into some context. Compare this to the $1.5 billion annual expenditure (and the $10 billion spent since 2000 by 2013) for 19 000 UN troops in the Congo, or the international attempt to 'sort out' Afghanistan, which has cost an average of $30 billion annually over the past decade. AMISOM has been, in the words of one foreign adviser, 'an incredible success story ... for very little money' – presuming it delivers, of course, on what it has begun to do.[15] AMISOM's mission has been to support the Somali government, meaning fighting on its behalf while integrating Somali troops into a single national army with the assistance of an extremely small but highly capable group of Western mentors and advisers. In so doing, AMISOM has managed to achieve what no other foreign force could – stabilising the capital and other key centres including Kismayo, expanding the reach of the Somali government beyond Mogadishu, pushing back Al-Shabab, establishing rudimentary but increasingly effective rule of law, and giving Somalia another chance. AMISOM's new mandate under UN Security Council Resolution 2124 allows, for the first time, support to 10 000 SNA when conducting joint operations with AMISOM.[16] Additionally, the inclusion of Ethiopian troops under AMISOM permits improved coordination and thereby higher concentrations of AMISOM forces to be used in Al-Shabab-held areas.

Parallel politics

To be sustainable, any military action has to be led or, at least, paralleled by local political developments.

On 10 September 2012, the 57-year-old educator and civil society activist Hassan Sheikh Mohamud was elected as president by MPs, the first leader to be chosen inside Somalia since the overthrow of the Siad Barre regime more than twenty years before. This was hardly a transparent process: the new president was elected by MPs who were themselves selected by tribal elders, some of whose status was vehemently contested by the members of the very clans they supposedly led. Parliamentary seats were bought and sold for as much as $25 000 cash.[17] In the process, Hassan Sheikh defeated the incumbent Sheikh Sharif Ahmed, whose UN-backed Transitional Federal Government was accused of the corrupt diversion of as much as 90 per cent of aid.[18] The report by the UN Monitoring Group was rejected by the Mogadishu government, the prime minister's office describing the allegations as 'absolutely and demonstrably false'.[19] Other donors agreed, pointing to the fact that government never received aid direction along with the UN's own inefficiencies and predilection to use subcontractors without the necessary controls.[20]

Two days after his election Hassan Sheikh survived an assassination attempt. Little wonder that he was moved to say: 'Security is my number one, number two and number three priority.'[21] Lauded as the head of a 'constructive elite' coalition (one that built 'universities, hospitals, charities and businesses in the country during the long civil war'), which 'defeated a parasitic elite coalition' of 'warlords and moneylords' and which had 'devoted all its energies to diverting public funds,'[22] he offered Somalia its best chance in twenty years of emerging from devastating civil conflict. But he would have his work cut out to ensure success – removing, in the process, the reasons for collapse in the first instance.

Causes of conflict

Somalis, like Congolese, are quick to point to external reasons for failure: the role of regional actors (Ethiopia, France and Kenya) intent on destabilising a country that has historically coveted those chunks of their own territory that are dominated by ethnic Somalis (Ogaden, Djibouti and Kenya's North Eastern province respectively – the five points of the star on Somalia's national flag represent these areas, along with Somaliland and South-Central Somalia). The ethnic Somali population in these overseas territories amounts to nearly as many as the population of Somalia itself: with Ethiopia (4–6 million), Djibouti (500 000), and Kenya (900 000), along with what may be as many as one million or so in Yemen.

Somalis frequently refer to the Cold War and its superpower manipulations. They also talk about how Siad Barre dramatically altered their fortunes as a result of the war with Ethiopia, which Somalia lost so badly, back in 1977. A few might go even further back and speak about the injustices of colonialism, though these memories pale against recent scars.

On paper, Somalis would seem to have a point. They are fiercely nationalistic, despite the little central government has given them, and, unlike most Africans, share a common language, culture, ethnicity and religion. Even though they have faced expansionist threats from Portugal, Ethiopia, France, England and Italy, they have always resisted. As one British officer remarked after bombing and finally subduing Muhammed Abdullah Hassan, the so-called 'Mad Mullah', in 1920, 'It is wonderful how little we have managed to impress the Somalis with our superior power.'[23]

In practice, however, the 'fierce nationalism' failed against the clan differences. As Henry Kissinger observed on the reasons for the failure of the Somali state: 'Unfortunately, the effort to set up a central authority in

Somalia, much less a democracy, comes up against historical reality. Somalia was not a country but a collection of warring tribes, half of which had been governed by Italy before independence, the other half Britain, so that the new country lacked even a common colonial history.'[24]

The contemporary threats to Somali security can be grouped into three different but related clusters, all of which are internally generated: first, that of Al-Shabab, the Al-Qaeda-inspired Islamist movement that has fed off a cocktail of lawlessness, religious ideology and youth frustration.

A second has been the absence of government and governance, which allows private militias to go relatively unchecked at the local level. This has been a vicious cycle. As the speaker of the house, the veteran politician Mohamed Osman Jawari, observed: 'How can we gain the taxes to build the necessary institutions and provide services when the shopkeeper has a bigger gun than the tax collector?'

This situation is, third, related to the most intractable problem in contemporary Somali history: the clan system. Once a basis of social stability and consensus, it is now a basis of power and control outside of government.

The central problem of Somalia is the virtual impossibility of governing Somalis, from without and also within.[25] The nineteenth-century traveller Richard Burton's famed relayed comment on the Somalis, 'every man his own sultan',[26] perfectly expressed that difficulty. Where individual Somali leaders have gained authority, this was derived from their wisdom, piety or ability to articulate some project of broad appeal, and was personal to themselves. 'Somalis don't like to be dominated, to be a minority,' says Liban Egal, one of the '50 or so' prominent Somali diaspora who returned in 2012. Though clans are often cited as the 'building blocks' of Somali society, they are united only against outsiders, and liable to splinter to the lowest level internally. Siad Barre managed to govern Somalia after a fashion for over twenty years through a mixture of ruthless repression and manipulation of clan alliances, but his regime ultimately fell as a result of military defeat, the eventual counter-productivity of repression (especially in Somaliland), and a domino effect when clan militias changed sides as his fall became inevitable. In the process, he flooded the country with weapons.

This legacy is still visible. By 2013, 20 000 SNA and 6 500 Somali Police Force members loosely associated with the central federal government were under arms, plus a further 9 000 militia members around the country (excluding Somaliland and Puntland). The plan was to expand the police by a further 2 300 in 2014, though 'it is difficult to get figures on the police',

AMISOM has said. 'People put on a uniform in order to be paid, even though it seems some of them joined in 1948.' When asked about numbers, one Somali police major responded, 'It is difficult to say. There are no statistics.' Siad Barre had, at the time of the Ogaden invasion in 1977, about 550 000 troops. In that era, military service represented a medium of patronage and also a lever for ensuring central government control in this fractious country. 'We should not expect them to keep things together with just 10 000 or even 20 000 troops,' reflected a Ugandan officer based in Mogadishu in 2012. 'Somalis are quick to change sides and revert to the bad ways at the first sign of trouble and government weakness. The pickup truck can revert to being a technical truck once more overnight.'

The ingrained clan system

The clan-based system of power has long been institutionally ingrained within the political system. 'They talk in one language and have one religion,' one AMISOM officer has noted, 'but in truth, it is very complicated.' Until late 2012, political power was shared among the clans according to a 4.5 formula: each of the major clans (Darod, Dir, Hawiye and Rahanweyn) had an equal share, while the remainder made up the 0.5 (the Isaaq, who predominate in Somaliland, absented themselves from the internationally sponsored conferences in 2000 and 2002–04, which developed the formula and were consequently not included). According to the 4.5 formula, since President Hassan Sheikh is Hawiye, the prime minister would have to be from the Darod group,[27] the two deputy prime ministers Dir and Hawiye, and the speaker Rahanweyn and his deputy from the 0.5.

This formula, though it still applies in the Somali parliament, was broken in November 2012 when then Prime Minister Farah Shirdon Saaid appointed a ten-man cabinet that defied the long-standing arrangement. Under the Transitional Federal Government, the council of ministers had been a huge and unwieldy group of up to 42 members, a group that was optimised for clan representation rather than effective governance. The November 2012 decision represented the first time in recent memory that Somalia has had a small, executive cabinet focused on governance rather than a large clan-based council, even though this was later expanded, given the extent of each ministers' portfolios.

Historically, Siad Barre's attempts to suppress the clans resulted, in the words of one Mogadishu-based adviser to the presidency, 'in clanism'.[28] Thus, the decision to move away from the 4.5 system exposes a paradox: absent clan representation, political consensus would be difficult and there is a risk that excluded clans may resort to violence. Yet, assigning political representation based on a clan formula simply links political identity more and more tightly to clan identity, reinforcing the very clan identity-based power politics that the formula was intended to defuse. The resultant clanism is manipulated for political and economic ends, with one consequence, for example, that in addition to Somaliland (an Isaaq clan-dominated territory) and Puntland (where the Darod predominate) 'there is potential for 20 mini-states in Somalia' along the lines of the self-declared autonomous state (under the stewardship of the Sacad sub-clan of the Hawiye) of Galmudug to Mogadishu's north, a confederation of Galguduud and Mudug provinces. Similarly, the Sool and Sanaag regions declared themselves to be autonomous states within Somaliland in 2008 and 2007 respectively.

Unlike the vast majority of post-independence African states where the immediate, principal challenge was the formation of a viable transcendent nationalism capable of uniting widely divergent ethnic groups who found themselves grouped together in 'states' created by the colonial enterprise, the Somali consisted of a single ethnic group. Their members, in the judgement of British anthropologist I.M. Lewis, arguably the foremost living authority on all things Somali, 'considered themselves bound together by a common language, by an essentially nomadic pastoral culture, and by the shared profession of Islam'.[29] This cultural unity, however, had never historically resulted in the emergence of a single polity because Somali identity is traditionally rooted in paternal descent, meticulously memorialised in genealogies that determine each individual's exact place in society.

In modern times, the advent of instantaneous mass communications has, ironically, rendered these traditional divisions an even more significant factor in Somali national politics, as it has enabled both geographically separated members of the same groups, including those in the far-flung diaspora, to interact with each other and organise themselves to pursue common political objectives. Thus, despite the efforts of the Siad Barre regime to impose 'scientific socialism' with the professed goal of uniting the nation by eliminating its ancient clan-based political culture (although even he eventually fell into a pattern of relying primarily upon his own clan and those of his mother and his son-in-law), after the dictator's fall, the country fragmented into cantons controlled by different clan (or sub-clan, or sub-sub-clan) militias. Mobilised by powerful figures and sustained by the spoils of conflict, these armed factions vied with each other for control of territory and such economic assets as could be found amidst the ruins of a collapsed state, including everything from incoming flows of international assistance to charcoal and bananas for export. No single leader or organisation was able to build any countrywide constituency; instead, each group sought to hold onto what it could and, especially in Mogadishu and other cities, engaged in turf wars with its rivals to try to wrest away some of what the latter had. And they never seemed to tire of the fighting.

No surprise then that foreign attempts to help rebuild a Somali state, from Operation Restore Hope in the early 1990s through to support for the Transitional Federal Government in the late 2000s, have likewise proved counter-productive: first, they divided Somalis between those supporting foreign engagement and those opposing it (General Aidid, Al-Shabab); second and probably more important, they provided endlessly squabbling Somali politicians with continuous pay-offs, and little incentive to reach any settlement, which in any case they could not deliver because they had lost the support of the clan constituencies that they nominally represented. The denial of food to starving compatriots in order to gain cash and control power for themselves, at the time both of Operation Restore Hope and again during the 2012 famine, shows the depths to which Somali community leaders have been prepared to sink. Somali society is sufficiently resilient, and endowed with support mechanisms outside the state (for example, through the remittance nexus offered by a remarkably effective cellphone network, and the large Somali diaspora) that enable people to survive without a state far better than many other peoples can manage with one?

In fact, as noted above, some have prospered precisely because of its absence.

Failed, not entirely broken

The combination of entrepreneurialism, aid and remittance flows, and survival tactics has ensured survival if not prosperity for a small elite. The civil war created a 'second economy' based on cross-border smuggling, or arbitrage, fed by a traditional nomadic pastoralism, informal financing, a kinship-based support network and the *hawala* remittance system.[30] In this, warlord control of major urban centres like Mogadishu and Kismayo was aimed at the lucrative pickings of foreign aid and a concentrated market.

The livestock industry is another case of how this parallel economy survived, even prospered, without a central state, in part because it is rural and dependent on external demand for live animal exports to regional countries. As Peter D. Little concludes in an examination of this sector, this is the 'ultimate paradox ... that some sectors of Somali economy and society are doing quite fine – as well as, if not better than during the pre-war (pre-1991) years'. Although he acknowledges that the 'Somalia based on arms and urban warlords is markedly different from the Somalia based on livestock and skilled herders'.[31] Still, the shift from Siad Barre's command economy to a more open, unrestricted, if ultimately anarchical, one, has had its advantages.

Yet, there are urban examples, too. The Somali shilling is fully convertible and floating, adjusting constantly to the market, the rate being set throughout the day by traders at Bakara market. Somalia may be a country without a central bank and functioning Ministry of Finance, but monetary policy and supply works quite well regardless, even though many of the local notes are filthy and raggedly threadbare. Although international institutions require local bodies through which to operate, the Somalis have managed without.

The *qat* trade, controlled by politically connected individuals, is a further example. Each morning, for example, at least two flights carrying the amphetamine-like leaf, the chewing of which causes excitement and euphoria, are the first to make it into Aden Abdulle International Airport in Mogadishu from Kenya, where the cargo is carefully unpacked, counted and whisked off to the capital's markets. Fresher is better in this trade. Arriving usually on Dash 8 aircraft from Wilson Airport in Nairobi,[32] each flight carries an average of 5 tonnes of the leaves. With a constant street value of $20 per kilogram, this amounts (at least) to a $750-million annual trade in Mogadishu alone, and this only from that portion of the *qat* that is flown in. The entrepreneurship and distribution system efficiencies of the *qat* trade are impressive, but its social and development effects are paralysing: while families in Mogadishu are living on less than $1 per person per day, an adult male will, anecdotally, spend $10 a day on *qat* – also known locally as *miraa*). The effects of *qat* go beyond direct finances: 'It creates a nation of promises in the afternoon, and amnesia in the morning,' reflected more than one expatriate. 'But even if it allows Somalis to forget temporarily the hardships that they experience daily, it destroys the social fabric and work ethic.'

While roadblocks and informal taxes provide local sustenance, Al-Shabab has enjoyed its own organised sources of income, notably from charcoal exports, mainly to Arabian Gulf states. Centred on the area around the port of Kismayo, these increased from an estimated 80 000 tonnes in 2000 to 120 000 tonnes ten years later, with a further 20 000 tonnes for domestic use. The Kenyan-led seizure by AMISOM of Kismayo in late 2012 was a severe blow to this trade.

Charcoal is the ultimate extractive economy: low calorific value, benefiting a tiny elite and with virtually zero environmental sustainability. Ironically, until it imposed a ban on this trade in early 2012, the UN was purchasing over 50 tonnes of charcoal a week for troops in Mogadishu, a contract worth $1 million annually.[33] Under UN Security Council Resolution 2036, in February 2012 the world body banned the purchase of charcoal from Somalia, shutting down a trade estimated to be worth as much as $15 million annually to the rebels, or 20 per cent of Al-Shabab's income.[34]

This is not a new or a unique phenomenon. As Little noted in 2003: 'Since the collapse of the government, there has been a massive increase in deforestation motivated by a growth in charcoal exports to the Middle East. In northeastern Somalia alone, it is estimated that charcoal production and trade results in deforestation rates as high as 35 000 hectares per year. Charcoal is commonly referred to as Somalia's "black gold" and much of it is exported to Saudi Arabia, where it fetches $5 per bag or about 300 per cent more than local prices. Conflicts between charcoal makers and camel herders who need trees for their herds, and between the former and militia factions who control the trade have resulted in several armed skirmishes. Clan elders attempt to control the trade and extraction of trees, but have been only minimally successful.'[35]

The extent to which Somalis have prospered in spite of war has led some to question if this was not their preference all along. Michael van Notten (writing as Graham Green), for example, notes the advances made by business since the Siad Barre era: 'Business is booming in this unusual country where taxation and government regulation used to destroy almost all private business ventures ... its sin is that it defeated the UN army that came to restore the central government that the Somali nation had abolished in 1991.'[36]

However, finding the means for survival, says Liban Egal, should not be confused with prosperity. Corruption, he argues, 'is part of that survival process'. Moreover, the elite, no matter how 'parasitic', at least publically recognises the need for change. As Little has argued, 'the "ungoverned" nature of Somalia and its economy, heralded by some as a triumph of the free market, are currently the country's own worst enemies'.[37]

Whereas once there was a thriving, if small, manufacturing sector, with Somalia producing sugar (1 000 tonnes monthly from Kismayo), cigarettes, cooldrinks, spaghetti/pasta, fish, clothing and auto spares, by 2012 there was little more than livestock trade, local fishing, bananas and other produce, small home-based pasta factories, foam for bedding, Caafi water bottling and a mothballed Coca-Cola factory. (Coca-Cola is much sought after by *qat* chewers.) Official imports were $800 million in 2012, and exports just $300 million, dominated by the livestock trade and a small related business in animal skins, and camel meat along with dry lemon.[38] Mobile phones have also taken off, partly because of the lack of local infrastructure and the importance of the diaspora and their remittances, telephony being key in ensuring the flow of external money.

The president of the Somalia Chamber of Commerce and Industry, Mohamoud Abdi Ali Gabiere, has said that 'while we have differences and difficulties in politics, we are united in business'. The Chamber was restarted in March 2012 after a 21-year hiatus, and within six months had more than 70 members. Gabiere points to the tremendous opportunities available in reconstruction and natural resources. 'We have a climate like California! Also one of the largest coastlines in Africa, over 8 million hectares of agriculture land, and many ports on the Indian Ocean.' Or as Liban Egal notes, 'You only see opportunities like this once in a lifetime, when a country is totally rebuilt from the ground up, with roads, schools, electricity, etc.'

But Gabiere admitted that the lack of security, skills and investment, all of which are related to the war, have been debilitating. 'It is impossible to rebuild,' he said, 'without justice', and that is 'below zero'. He observed that '20 years is enough. We need to re-engineer the society here. We now need a government and to move away from a clan-based society and change the mind of the people.' He added, 'People are tired. They know that there is no benefit from [the civil war].' Or as the speaker of parliament emphasised: 'This time will be different. People are tired. They are very much in need of good governance and law and order. But their expectations are also very high – and government lacks a sound and competent civil service to deliver the services they expect.'

There is a steep path to climb if Somalila is to attract more than traders to its economy. The country ranked, in 2013, 175th and last place on Transparency International's Corruption Perception Index with North

Korea and Afghanistan, and did not even merit a ranking among the 189 countries on the World Bank's 2014 Ease of Doing Business listing.[39]

Even if in the absence of a government Somalia has enabled a few to prosper, it has not been good for the whole – far from it. Not only is it personally threatening, the lack of security radically increases transaction costs for business. This is a lesson that Somaliland learnt quickly two decades ago, when its population put in place a local political solution to address instability.

Success depends on Somalis

The reasons why AMISOM has been a comparative success are, principally, that it is prepared to go where others have feared to tread, is willing to accept international assistance and advice (for example, around fire control to reduce civilian casualties), to suffer casualties itself in pursuit of its objectives, and, above all else, not to deceive itself about the extent of the Somali problem.

Another reason for AMISOM's success has been what its commanders have described as the 'human face' of the mission. No doubt in Uganda's case this has been shaped by the country's own experience in fighting against Milton Obote's regime in the 1980s and, then, against the Lord's Resistance Army in the north thereafter. The Ugandan People's Defence Force (UPDF) has the benefit of extensive combat experience and a well-developed doctrine for guerrilla warfare and counter-insurgency, making it one of the most capable military forces on the continent.

As Lieutenant General Andrew Gutti, AMISOM's force commander from May 2012 until December 2013, who also earlier led the UPDF's operations against the Lord's Resistance Army, has observed, there is 'no difference' between these operations. In both 'we have to provide security and operate among the population, winning them over'. One of his predecessors, General Katumba Wamala, who was to become chief of the UPDF, has stressed, 'A reason for AMISOM's success had been its approach of respecting Somalis and extending to them services like medical care. To many it was strange for soldiers in uniform to treat people in our hospitals including injured Al-Shababs. The human face put on the mission has been a great contributor to its success.'

This does not mean the operation has been without its surprises or setbacks. As AMISOM's commander, Gutti noted, 'Logistical support has been very challenging given our rate of expansion, and UNSOA [United Nations Support Office for the African Union] has found it very difficult to keep up, which has created a lot of gaps and overstretched our communications at times.' Another surprise related to what the Mission found in Somalia. 'There are no administrative set-ups,' said the general in September 2012, 'where we go. The population was not being administered, and it is difficult to locate who is the leader. We usually look around for a man with grey hair, and then work with him in putting the process together.'

There is an explicit recognition that after a generation of violent anarchy, what Somalis most want is predictability and a rules-based order, and that the side that best delivers this to the population is most likely to prevail.

Despite their small number, Al-Shabab's fighting prowess has also surprised some observers. By the start of 2014, Al-Shabab, which, in AMISOM's words, 'recruits where they are [*in situ*]', comprised probably little more than 6 000 fighters. Although the Islamist movement is virtually bereft of supplies, 'they are very tough', says one Ugandan private who served three months on the frontline, 'because they are not frightened of dying'. The insurgents have continually ceded territory to AMISOM but have avoided being pinned down, trading space for time. They have sought to avoid a decisive battle, withdrawing the bulk of their combat forces so as to preserve their political negotiating strength and maintain the possibility of a comeback. As AMISOM has expanded, Al-Shabab has also sought to reinfiltrate into previously cleared areas and has attacked convoys on the limited number of road routes between government-held towns. When cornered, Al-Shabab has also engaged in intense fighting: although AMISOM's deaths officially numbered around 500, for example, unofficially the figure was put at five times this number by 2014, and especially high among the Burundian and Ugandan detachments. Few Western governments would be able to justify this casualty rate in a foreign peacekeeping mission, least of all in Somalia.

AMISOM has also been guilty of over-reaching. Instead of consolidating control in Mogadishu, political pressures in the troop-contributing nations pushed operations out in the rural areas and along the coast. One result was a decline in security in the capital, as Al-Shabab changed its own tactics to take advantage of and to compensate for its own losses. Controlling Mogadishu has been critical to establishing order in Somalia, and a failure to do so would endanger the AMISOM mission. In part, however, these hiccups recognise the challenge, too, in moving from war-fighting to asymmetric warfare (suicide terrorism by another name), and reflect the importance of intelligence gathering assets, both within AMISOM and the Transitional Federal Government.

There have also been other challenges. There is a risk that a combination of low empathy with the local (non-Bantu) culture, military overstretch and fatigue, and Somali chauvinism towards outsiders could see AMISOM come under increasing attack both within Somalia and in their home countries. AMISOM's ultimate fate and judgement on its effectiveness thus has to be reserved. Its success depends partly on providing the stability so that Somalis can extend the reach and effectiveness of their government. It depends also on whether Somalis will take responsibility for their own destiny. 'Everything we do must be about enfranchising them,' says one Ugandan officer. 'When people own the security themselves,' reflected General Gutti, 'they are in a position to say *enough is enough*.' If Somalis revert to playing their age-old games of clanship and corruption, then AMISOM's blood and treasure will have been spent in vain. While foreigners can provide the space to sort things out, Somalis have to deal with the underlying causes of conflict themselves.

Changing the incentives

Given the levels of destruction, if Somalia – the archetypal failed state – can be 'fixed', anywhere can. Until now, foreign interventions in Somalia have ultimately failed for a variety of reasons, not least since they only temporarily altered the local balance of power, where the intervener became a temporary, if very powerful, warlord, who needed to be factored in and engaged by other power brokers. As soon as the foreign intervener left, the place collapsed around feuding local parties. This is one reason why it is difficult to imagine an exit strategy for AMISOM, whether as an African Union or UN blue beret mission – or at least an exit strategy whereby Somalia remains stable.

There is always going to be a limited window of opportunity for effective governance and mounting problems in circumstances like Somalia's. Any leadership has to make a difference quickly, raise taxes to do so (including building infrastructure and paying salaries) and stay alive. All three things may not be simultaneously possible. Getting the politics right has to take precedence. In the case of Somalia, as in others elsewhere, there is a need to address 'conflict entrepreneurs',[40] those who profit from the continuance of fighting and a lack of governance. They need to be given a stake in stability, in the system of governance and 'normal' commerce, at least as much as they need to be pressured by military means to cease their pernicious actions. As Adrian Leftwich writes in *States of Development*,[41] 'Politics matters because politics shapes states and states shape development.' Development was thus fundamentally about politics, rather than financing and technical solutions, and this reflected the power of local leadership and the value of conflict negotiation and compromise.[42]

There is also a need in this regard to address the age-old tension between 'centralists' versus 'regionalists', those who favour a concentration of power in Mogadishu versus those who prefer a devolution of authority and, with it, resources. Many have felt that the Transitional Federal Government, in attempting to introduce institutional structures, has been too centralist in its thinking.

＊

Dr Abdiweli Mohamed Ali, also known as Abdiweli Mohamed Ali Gas, served as prime minister of Somalia between 2011 and 2012. Gas beat the incumbent Abdirahman Muhammad Mahmud 'Farole' by one vote in the 66-strong parliament to become president of the Puntland semi-autonomous Somali region in January 2014.

Although Gas had stood unsuccessfully for the presidency of Somalia in 2012, as prime minister he oversaw the first big military push against Al-Shabab. He argues that the contemporary Somali peace will be unlike earlier, failed attempts given that 'people have said enough: enough of lawlessness, violence and instability. We are sick and tired, and sick and tired of being sick and tired.' This difference, says the Harvard-educated economist, who holds joint US-Somali citizenship, is largely down to an honest recognition of the problems behind state collapse, and Somalis' own related understanding of past failures to create the conditions for peace.

'The first problem,' he says, 'has been in the collapse of state institutions. It's like a broken glass – very difficult to get back together again. A second is in failed leadership, not offering Somalis what they, like people elsewhere, want, namely peace, stability, food for their kids, shelter for their family, health care and education.

'We have also learnt that since governance is a social contract with individuals, we cannot live separate lives, as small communities, religious bodies or clans, outside the nation. We have experienced the whole gamut of dictatorship, warlordism, piracy to terrorism, all of the bad things and options imaginable.'

Such lessons should also, he notes, be learnt from previous attempts to establish peace. 'Without local ownership, peace will be elusive. Somaliland and Puntland managed to create peace easier given that they have strong traditional leaders around which to create a cohesive state, by employing the Somali custom of resolving differences under the acacia tree, and just talking and talking and talking.' This is why, he remarks, 'holding peace conferences outside, which Somalia did for so long, does not work, and why until now we always failed.'

But, he says, the list of things to be done before success can be declared is long and formidable. 'Liberation' from Al-Shabab, he observes, has to be followed by 'stabilisation', then 'reconciliation to deal with spoilers'. This has to be backed up, in turn, by the 'delivery of services better than Al-Shabab can manage' to create an alternative to the Islamists. The conclusion to this peace process, he says, is the creation of an effective administration. This must include the 'building of a Somali National Army capable enough to take over from AMISOM', an effort that he views 'with mixed feelings. On the one hand,' he says, 'AMISOM has contributed a lot in coming to save Somalia from itself. On the other, it has created a feeling of dependency, which cannot last forever.'[43]

A solution to Somalia's challenges, or those of any other failed state, will also not ultimately come from a person who is more acceptable to foreigners. Although that will help turn on the international aid faucet, a form of governance can be constructed only by allowing locals to build it from the base themselves, however precarious and chaotic this may be. The steps that Somalia has taken towards reasserting statehood in the form of a nominated parliament and, through that body, an elected executive, will have to be paralleled by political dialogues at a local level and with traditional leaders, and will have to be followed through by development actions. The latter has to start with the basics: cleaning up Mogadishu; fixing the transport infrastructure, especially roads and ports; offering at least the prospect of improved basic services, including hospitals, schools, sewerage and electricity; and building the institutions of governance, prioritising the security sector (integrating the various militias, and paying and training them), implementing transparent financial controls, and conducting a national census and issuing of identification cards. Of course, there is a tension – a chicken-and-egg situation – here. As the speaker of the Somali parliament has observed, 'Public institutions are important to reduce the power of the clan.' A tall but not an impossible order; one that will require forging a hitherto absent degree of political consensus and collaboration across clans and interest groups. Only then will it be different in Somalia this time.

The Atlantic Council scholar Peter Pham has suggested with respect to the failings of the Mogadishu regime, noting its 'rampant corruption … as well as its repression of press and other freedoms' and the evidence uncovered by the UN that senior Somali officials were delivering weapons to both Al-Shabab and clan militants, that the US, for one, 'should roll back its recognition and adopt a policy requiring all Somali actors to earn such engagement as might be accorded them through real performance.'[44] Should the externally directed attempts at stabilisation fail, an alternative would see foreigners withdrawing from the process, and removing support for essentially externally fostered regimes, while imposing as strict a 'quarantine' as circumstances demand on activities (for example, piracy and external terrorism, in the case of Somalia) that threaten the international community as a whole.

Yet, such a quarantine is difficult to effect in a region where the borders are notoriously porous and communities interspersed. Instead, as Somalia's northern neighbour Somaliland's comparatively successful recovery has shown elsewhere in this volume, transiting from conflict to peace requires changing local incentives for conflict, instituting apparently endless domestic dialogue, political rapprochement, and, above all else, reconciliation. In this regard, as Somaliland's President Ahmed Silanyo has emphasised: 'Our lessons are about the importance of reconciliation, of many meetings and no miracles, just hard work. We recognised that we are all in this together, that we are one big group, and acted on that.'[45]

PART 3

*

ILLUSTRATIONS OF RECOVERY

Democracy ... contains within itself the means of orderly change through choice and consent. Clash of opinion is the stuff of which democracy is composed.

— Margaret Thatcher, *Daily Telegraph*, 17 March 1969

Zambia's first 27 years of independence from Britain under President Kenneth Kaunda was a two-act play: an initial period of euphoric expectations and nation-building tinged, from the early 1970s, by the reality of uncompetitive one-party politics and, from the early 1970s, continuous economic difficulties.

At independence in October 1964, the Central African nation had 300 000 full-time jobs for its then three million people. Fifty years later there were little more than 400 000 formal sector jobs for over 14 million people. From the 1960s to the 1980s, Kaunda's government attempted to catalyse employment and modernisation through protectionism and subsidies. The various industrial efforts – from car assembly plants to textile facilities – failed, not least because these fledgling enterprises could not survive without government intervention and the domestic market was ultimately too small and discerning.

Kaunda's political legacy of one-partyism was in the end rejected wholesale by discerning Zambian voters; his economic legacy was similarly disappointing given the near-destruction of the advantages at independence of the country's natural resource endowment.[1]

With the advent of multi-partyism in 1991, the economy slowly recovered as investors were attracted back into the all-important copper mines and related services sectors. Today, as a result, Zambia is on the move, though there are some serious speed bumps, literally and figuratively.

The drive north from Ndola towards the Congo through the towns of Kitwe and Chingola and past the great mining facilities at Luanshya, Nkana,

Chambishi, Konkola and Nchanga, illustrates both the positive changes in the Central African country, but also a number of the key challenges.[2] The pantechnicons ploughing the rutted road with their valuable loads contrast markedly with the pitiful sight of vendors plying their paltry wares on the roadsides. Piles of tomatoes in plastic packets vie for customers along with overstuffed purple couches in a giant open-air factory-cum-parking-lot outside Kitwe, live chickens held out by their feet, the occasional metalworker banging away turning scrap into something useful. The notable feature is the lack of diversity in goods, and the youth of the sellers and the conditions in which they operate. The Kitwe-Kasumbalesa road through Zambia's Copperbelt has taken a pounding in recent years, ironically because the volumes of trade have improved.

The long lines of trucks ferrying concentrate and copper cathode, supplies and mining equipment make a welcome change from the somnolence of just two decades before. In 2000, Zambia's copper output fell to a low of 257 000 tonnes, the consequence of nationalisation, stultifying statism and a linked lack of skills and knowledge, technology and investment.

In 2010, Zambia managed to reproduce its 1972 record production of 720 000 tonnes of copper. It took the industry that long to recover after Kaunda's ruinous nationalisation policies. After 1991, the government had little choice but to privatise the mines and close other ailing parastatals in an attempt to rescue the moribund economy. The reforms also focused on ending price controls, removing subsidies on foodstuffs (fiercely resisted as it was politically sensitive), the devaluation of the kwacha (which as a result slid rapidly from parity with the dollar to an effective 6 000 kwacha in 2014, though the government had in the interim rebased the currency by lopping off three zeroes), and cutting back government expenditure.

Getting the mining industry back on its feet has been a long, slow process, reflecting the years of decay and underinvestment. During the late 1980s, keeping the main mining operation, Zambian Consolidated Copper Mines (ZCCM), afloat cost the government $1 million a day. As the copper price picked up in the 2000s on the back of Chinese demand, the industry not only righted itself, but drove Zambia's growth to average more than 5 per cent in the twenty-first century.

As welcome as this turnaround has been, Zambia has consistently failed to diversify its economy away from mining into other sectors, notably tourism, industry and services, the sectors where new jobs could be found.

In 2010, the Brenthurst Foundation[3] worked with President Banda's government, at its request, to establish a path for a fast-track development strategy, to be known as 'Enterprise Zambia'. This focused on the changes that government could make to encourage investment and bring growth, for example: in government services, the creation of 24/7 customs posts at key crossing areas; with agriculture, the establishment of a private sector-linked extension service; in encouraging diversification, the targeting of value addition in tourism and agriculture; and with mining, the establishment of a practical regime for retaining existing investment, beneficiation and expansion.

Little was implemented. Despite President Banda being an affable and likeable person, his government was not a high-energy organisation. It seemed too easy to cruise on the improving proceeds of copper.

In September 2011, Zambians voted out Banda and brought in Michael Sata and his Patriotic Front party, the aim presumably being to bring relief from crushing poverty (in which two-thirds live) and endemic unemployment by sparkling policy reform. Sata managed a narrow election victory, his Patriotic Front winning 60 seats over the incumbent Movement for Multiparty Democracy's (MMD) 55, a difference of 180 000 votes. The third-placed United Party for National Development won 28.

Known as 'King Cobra' on account of his political venom and abrasive style, the 74-year-old Sata had worked his way up the political totem pole the hard way, via stints as a police officer, trade unionist, British Rail station sweeper and, eventually, as the governor of Lusaka in the mid-1980s under Kaunda. He served as cabinet minister in Frederick Chiluba's government, until he fell out with the ruling MMD and formed the Patriotic Front in 2001.

Sata offered a new start. But rather than make a fresh start and enable new investment in both mining and other, different business sectors, his government's answer to its development dilemmas has been to return to the statist past. Little has been done to remove the impediments to attracting new investment outside of mining, which provides for $8 billion (or 80 per cent) of Zambia's export proceeds.[4]

Instead, the mining sector was squeezed for more revenue and new hurdles were created for other business sectors. Progress in tourism, a key area for new jobs, has historically been stifled by over-regulation. Not fewer than 33 permits and licences were, for example, required to establish a lodge during the Banda years.

The answer of the Sata government to improving the tourism sector has not, however, been to remove unnecessary government, but to attempt to buck the global market trend and create a national airline. Zambia's experience with a flag carrier has historically been poor (the national airline going bankrupt in 1994 once government subsidies were withdrawn) and littered with bankruptcies. This was predictable, an easier gesture than improving, for example, the experience at its airports, not least Ndola, the gateway to the Copperbelt, where baggage handling was still, in the twenty-first century, a hole in the wall. Visa regulations add another hurdle of expense and uncertainty to foreigners: why, after all, charge people for the pleasure of spending money in your country? When I suggested this to a Zambian minister in 2013, he lectured me on why Zambia had to impose visas on those 'rich' countries that had similar restrictions on Zambians in place – colonialism still stung bitterly it seemed. The country is among many that would do well to take a leaf out of the Georgian reform book by removing visa requirements on citizens of all countries with a higher per capita GDP.

This took place against a backdrop of worsening fiscal conditions. Government external debt increased from $1.8 billion at the time of Sata taking over to $4 billion by 2014, and was anticipated to ramp up again to $6 billion before the next election in 2016. Although Lusaka issued its first ever international debt offering in the former of a $750-million Eurobond in 2012,[5] much of this income had been directed to recurrent budget (salary) expenditure, rather than on infrastructure as originally intended. At the start of 2014 it was planning a second bond issue, this time for $1 billion, in order to meet a projected 8.5 per cent fiscal deficit, though the downgrading of Zambia's credit rating was likely to make this a considerably more expensive venture to the government, up from a 5.625 per cent yield on the 2012 offering likely over 8 per cent.[6]

There have been some positive changes, not least in Zambia's power production, which should nearly double in output between 2014 and 2020.[7] This increase is critical for improving living conditions in a country where less than 20 per cent of households have access to energy, and in increasing smelter capacity for the mines. Zambia was at 152nd position (out of 189 countries surveyed) on the ease of 'getting electricity' indicator on the World Bank's 2013 Doing Business rankings.[8] Regardless, overall, the business environment remains difficult. Ratcheting taxation and other bureaucratic controls, along with the use of rampant government spending to buoy political support, raises questions about the extent of commitment overall of Zambians to reform; whether these only take place under extreme pressure and, once this is relieved, there is a reversion to old, statist ways. This also relates to the overall challenge of institutionalising a growth agenda beyond party politics, politics that have got messier in Zambia.

As president, Sata lost little time in increasing his majority. According to the MMD, eleven of its MPs were 'encouraged' to cross the floor by the lure of deputy ministerships and a reputed $50 000 cash payment.[9] Pressure was ratcheted up in other ways. The former president, Rupiah Banda, was stripped of immunity over a corruption charge and put on trial. His successor, Nevers Mumba, the former vice president, was arrested for causing a breach of the peace,[10] while the leader of the United Party for National Development, Hakainde Hichalema, widely known as 'HH', was also detained on charges of incitement and the death of a Patriotic Front cadre respectively.[11]

Speed bumps are a Zambian obsession. Every town seems to have them, some small and jagged, others long and flat, often in the form of rumble strips. Their location and frequency leaves the traveller as puzzled as to their purpose as Zambian politicians are apparently about the speed bumps in the economy.

Vice President Guy Scott told me in August 2012 that the high costs of borrowing and an overvalued exchange rate lie at the root of addressing Zambia's overall challenge in creating jobs for its burgeoning youth population. He has a point. Local bank lending rates have consistently been over 25 per cent, hence the government's attempts to cap them in 2013.[12]

Others thus argue that the costs of borrowing and slow rate of job creation are symptoms of a wider malaise. The high expense of doing business and the uncertainty of the political environment, says HH, are closely related and far more constraining.

He, too, has a point. Take the Chirundu border to the south with Zimbabwe through which much of the country's traffic flows, its extraordinarily opaque bureaucracy described in Chapter 9. Though this border post has been refurbished using donor money into what is advertised as a model regional one-stop-border-shop, the nearly 2-kilometre absolutely chaotic queue of trucks on the Zimbabwe side suggest that things are not quite that perfect yet. Again, little wonder that Zambia ranked 163/189 on the 'trading across borders' indicator on the Doing Business listings.

The 67 per cent rise in the minimum salary in 2012 further raised the premium of doing business. This was not helped by a 51 per cent local ownership stipulation in the then mooted Companies Act. With an effective tax rate touching 50 per cent (even more if one considers the 'free carry' of the state-owned ZCCM in ventures), Zambia is already one of the highest cost mining investment destinations. But instead of aiming to bring these costs down and lessening policy uncertainties to encourage new business and capital inflows, the Sata government quickly fell into the trap of targeting those already there.

On the road out south of Lusaka is a symphony of speed bumps before, during and after the cement factory. Having to accelerate to overtake a drunken, semi-dressed pedestrian weaving her way down the middle of the road, I was pulled over by a white-gloved police officer 'for speeding'. Told to get out of the car and sit down on a chair next to the patrol car in which four officers sat eating (or at least badly mauling) roast chicken, I was informed of my fate.

'Now you must pay,' said the policewoman sucking on a chicken bone. 'It is 270 000 kwacha [then $45] for your crime.' I protested that they said I was only 3 kilometres per hour over the limit and that I did so only to swerve into the other lane to avoid hitting the drunken woman. 'Yes, we saw her. Okay, then its only 180 000.' I still protested. 'Okay, then how much do you think is reasonable?' I got back in the car 100 000 kwacha lighter and, despite my asking, with no receipt to show for this donation, I am sure, to the Zambian exchequer.

No, it is not the costs of borrowing that are principally at fault. It is the costs of doing business and the vagaries of the rule of law and policy environment that make job creation so difficult in Africa.

Such challenges are, as elsewhere on the continent, likely only to get more severe than easier with the projected rate of population increase. The UN has it tripling by 2050. Even its most cautious projection has it at 100 million by 2100, with the best estimate being 140 million.[13] The Zambian government's primary task is the same as in many other African countries: to create jobs by attracting the businesses that do not have to be there because of resource endowments, but can go anywhere else in the world. Only by going this route will Zambia be able to grow its middle class. At least that is what experience from the rest of the world teaches. Finding the right answers to this over-riding development challenge requires asking some awkward questions: what does business want? What did not work in the past, and why? What might others teach us – and what might others do in this regard? Such questions apply in many other cases of recovery.

19

ANGOLA

Giving War a Chance

*

General Abílio Kamalata Numa was one of thirteen people present in Dr Jonas Savimbi's party when the rebel leader was killed in action near Lucusse in Angola's Moxico province on 22 February 2002.[1]

The general's biography reads like Angola's political history. Like Savimbi, Numa was born in Moxico in the highlands of central Angola, and joined the National Union for the Total Independence of Angola (UNITA) movement in 1974 at the age of nineteen, immediately after his seven years of high schooling. Initially based in Benguela as a political secretary, he was integrated into the guerrilla army after independence from Portugal in November 1975 and the outbreak of civil war between the liberation movements – UNITA, the National Front for the Liberation of Angola (FNLA) and the ruling Popular Movement for the Liberation of Angola (MPLA). By 1979 he had been elevated to the role of political commissar for communications, and the following year was made the commander of this section.

In 1982 he was the chief of staff to Savimbi's government, and the next year was appointed political commissar of UNITA's armed wing, FALA, the Armed Forces of the Liberation of Angola, replacing General Geraldo Sachipengo Nunda (today chief of the general staff of the Angolan Armed Forces, known as the FAA). Thereafter, Numa took charge of the central south front, overseeing the fierce battles of Cuito Cuanavale, Cassambo and Kaombo. In 1988 he was sent to command the northern front until the end of the war. With the signing of the 1991 ceasefire, Numa joined the Joint Military and Political Commission (JMPC) as second in command to the then Angolan army chief, General Joao de Matos.

With the collapse of the September 1992 election and the ensuing violence, Numa fled back to the northern front. By 1997, he was second in command of a rebuilt FALA to General Altino Bango Sapalala, Savimbi's son-in-law, who went under the *nom de guerre* 'Bock', with General 'Kanhali Vatuva' (Mário Vasco Miguel) as the political commissar. Before the civil war resumed in 1998, negotiations continued between Savimbi, based in Andulo, and the government in Luanda, facilitated by the UN envoy Alioune Blondin Beye. This process, however, collapsed amidst mistrust and the death of the Malian Beye in a plane crash in June 1998 as he flew from Togo to Côte d'Ivoire, two countries close to Savimbi.

By then, too, Savimbi's paranoia was starting to show – Bock and Numa were arrested along with top generals Tarzan, Anteiro and Asubidabala (literally 'The Whistle of the Bullet'), reflecting both Savimbi's insecurities and MPLA mischief. In one of the meetings of the JMPC, MPLA General Higino Carneiro reportedly asked Savimbi to send General Bock to Luanda for a weekend, undermining the relationship between the leader and his chief general. From then on, according to Numa, UNITA became very fragile in terms of command experience, with mid-level officers such as Arlindo Samuel Kapinala ('Samy'), Geraldo Abreu Muhengu Ukwachitembo 'Kamorteiro' (who took over as FALA chief of staff from Bock), Elias Malungo Pedro Bravo da Costa 'Kalias' (who died in an aircraft crash in Huambo in 2011), and others taking over, leading UNITA into the last phase of the conflict. This inexperience showed in the strategic choice made by UNITA to seize regional cities such as Huambo and Cuito, which was Savimbi's idea. Numa was among those who rather favoured controlling 'useful' areas, as opposed to cities that were difficult to defend, especially those in the diamond-rich Cuango in the province of Lunda Norte. In the end, Savimbi's ideas prevailed. That decision 'trapped' UNITA into the central area, placing a premium on logistics and air supply. When UNITA lost its main airbase at Andulo, the die was cast.

Numa was rehabilitated in 2000 at the time that Bock, Tarzan, Anteiro and others were killed by Savimbi, and made chief of operations. From 2000 and, especially after the events of September 11, 'Dr Savimbi', recalls Numa, 'started telling us that there would be trouble ahead'. Even though the sanctions against UNITA had been imposed in 1993, from 2001 especially, the Americans, he says, 'saw UNITA as a danger'. Starved of his principal source of external income through diamonds, UNITA's movements were increasingly constrained. Savimbi realised then that he would not last long, 'his remaining cause being the survival of the party', according to Numa. Manoeuvres were conducted on a limited basis in Savimbi's home area of Moxico, which he knew well, and had the hope of finding food. 'People by then were dying of hunger, and troops were leaving, going home and defecting. We had no fuel and had to walk everywhere', remembers Numa.

'Dr Savimbi started to manage only at the time of his end', says Numa. 'He was very clear: he said goodbye to us. He gave very clear orientation to some of his leaders, including General Samuel Chiwale, the senior general. He said that General Dembo should direct the party after his death, but he died from his diabetes and exhaustion just after Savimbi.' Chiwale is now an MP.

And then, the inevitable end.

'Our column, numbering between 300 and 400 men, was being pursued by a very strong FAA offensive. It attacked on 18 February [2002] and our column divided. Dr Savimbi, and Generals Sammy and Dembo and their families grouped into one, General Kamorteiro into another, and myself into another to guard the rear', remembers Numa. 'The same day, Dr Savimbi's commando was captured. My group of five met up with Dr Savimbi on 20 February. He told me that his group separated again in the jungle into a group of eight people, including his wife Valentine. On 21 February I left the place we met at to look for the main column. On the evening of the 21st we slept in a small clearing. On the 22nd, very early in the morning, we began our march to the east. At around 7 or 8 o'clock, on the right corner of the Luo River, we felt an attack. It was an attack on the column of General Big Joe. We were obligated to change our path to the north-east. Around 12 we spotted a drone circling, doing recognition, an Israeli plane.'

Contrary to legend about Savimbi recklessly using his satellite phone as he had given up the fight and expected to be captured, 'he was very careful', says Numa. 'All the time we used the phone, we had to be 40 kilometres from him. But it was always easy to see where we were from the air, due to desertification.'

'We stayed seated until about 1 o'clock when we started moving again. I was in the front when I detected footprints. There was a lot of moss there as it had been raining, so we could not exactly work out where it was from, but we could see that it was from military boots. Dr Savimbi said it could be their military or UNITA, and gave orders to go on into the depths of the forest. When we were in a safe place Dr Savimbi told us to camp, and I sent out a mission to scout for the enemy. I stood always in the same tent as Dr Savimbi. From 20–22 February, I always stood in the same tent as him.

I asked him if I could use the solar panel to charge my batteries as we wanted to watch the football that night. When I left the tent, I heard screaming and shots, and I saw Dr Savimbi running. We all ran in different directions into the forest. I saw that Valentine, Dr Savimbi's wife, was wounded in the leg. After twenty minutes of shooting I heard a helicopter coming. I then realised certainly that Dr Savimbi had died. Also when we were running, we heard a fusillade of shooting, presumably the shots that were directed into the body of Dr Savimbi. That was it, the 22nd of February.'

Savimbi's bloody corpse had at least fifteen bullet wounds. It was displayed on state television to confirm his demise, and he was later interred in a tomb in Luena in Mexico. Numa was chased for another two weeks. By then General Paulo Lukambo 'Gato', then UNITA secretary general, who had been captured, was negotiating with the government. 'I managed to reach a place to contact him [Gato] by radio – to let him know that I was still alive. After the Luena peace agreements were signed, I went to Mexico on 2 April, and arrived thereafter in Luanda on 2 May. I knew that I was being chased to be executed,' he smiles, 'as I was once part of the FAA, and they did not want to see me again.'

*

Little over ten years after Savimbi's death, on 31 August 2012 Angola staged its first presidential election since the abortive 1992 attempt, with President Eduardo dos Santos winning a comfortable victory. The same October, the country launched a $5 billion sovereign wealth fund to channel the country's oil wealth into infrastructure and other investment projects. This was on the back of an 11 per cent annual growth in the 2000s, which peaked at a salivating 22.7 per cent in 2007.

What might Savimbi's death and the subsequent economic boom tell us about methods and benefits of conflict resolution? Is war a means of securing political transition – as is suggested both by the failure of UN-brokered efforts in the 1990s – and long-term stability? For Angola seems to run against the conventional grain in this regard, especially in the context of its time.

Peacemaking in the 1990s

During the latter half of the 1980s there occurred, on average at any moment, five ethnic and other forms of political conflict worldwide, which required massive humanitarian assistance and which were classified as 'complex emergencies'. That number quadrupled to twenty in 1990, and peaked at 26 in 1995,[2] many of them in Africa. In fact, the first modern 'complex humanitarian emergency' occurred in the 1967–70 Nigerian Civil War over Biafran secession. Overall, United Nations High Commissioner for Refugees expenditures, one reflection of the increase in the management of complex emergencies, grew rapidly from the late 1970s, from US$70 million to US$1.3 billion in 1996, for example. This was then more than the core budget of the UN or the development funding of the United Nations Development Program.

Paradoxically, while the money for assisting complex emergencies grew significantly, by the latter half of the 1990s it was proving difficult to mobilise international support for African crises – what the former UN secretary general, Boutros Boutros-Ghali, described as 'orphan crises',[3] meaning those largely ignored and neglected by the world. In part, this was because of the absence of a clear-cut situation where intervention may provide a workable solution; and in part uncertainty about whether the protagonists actually want to solve the conflict. There is, after all, a fundamental difference between a durable peace and an armistice. Somalia was a case in point in the early 1990s, where a massive effort to prevent its bleeding could not be sustained and eventually did not seem to be worthwhile. Geography and national interests have also played their part in justifying intervention, as does the sheer scale of the problem. For example, Kosovo involved a relatively small and accessible territory and a single army largely responsible for perpetrating the abuse. The Congo *circa* 2000, by comparison, absorbed two main opposition forces plus eleven different rebel groups. And while military force could pressure Serbian President Slobodan Milosevic into pulling out of Kosovo by destroying Serbia's infrastructure, there was no such infrastructure to leverage in the Congo.

Do no harm

It could also be argued that the presence of international forces actually makes it less, rather than more, attractive for parties to generate internal solutions – as in the case of the Cyprus stand-off between Greek and Turk, for example, given that local communities have to accept responsibility before the outside intervening forces can help to guarantee it. In this regard, British columnist Simon Jenkins has claimed that the interventions made by the international community in the post-Cold War period, apparently in support of human rights, have simply replaced 'one wrong with another', providing an open invitation to any separatist movement, with the guarantee of a 'very expensive internationally protected statehood'. Although NATO's action in Kosovo was presented in terms of a moral crusade, this act did not, he has argued, represent a 'new standard' of international behaviour. Multilateral military interventions lead only to what he terms 'frozen societies' under the imperialistic protection and tutelage of the UN and of NATO.[4]

Jenkins' view aligns with that of the American military strategist and historian Edward Luttwak. In 'Give War a Chance', he contends that 'although war is a great evil, it does have a great virtue: it can resolve political conflicts and lead to peace. This can happen when all belligerents become exhausted or when one wins decisively. Either way the key is that the fighting must continue until a resolution is reached. War brings peace only after passing a culminating phase of violence. Hopes of military success must fade for accommodation to become more attractive than further combat.'[5]

There is perhaps some clarity as to whether the international community does 'enough' to end conflicts. For most of the time it apparently does not. Conversely, there is little consensus as to what 'doing more' entails. When there is no clear enemy, principles of intervention are indistinct and decisions much more complicated – all of this frequently in geographical areas where there is no direct national interest at stake and where the threats to peace come not from easily identifiable states but from non-state or sub-state actors and units. At the same time, while it is easier to assess the risk of doing something, and that is enough to put most governments off, the risk of not engaging is uncertain if no less real.

This dilemma of intervention is not new. The search for peace and collective action has always been, as historian A.J.P. Taylor noted, subject to the 'cleavage between principle and expediency' or, as the former British foreign secretary, Douglas Hurd, has argued, 'getting the balance right' between the forces of idealism and realism.[6] The competing forces of idealism and realism suggest we still live in an imperfect world with inconsistent rules, in spite of widening concern about human rights and humanitarian issues. This dilemma has bedevilled global states people. The failure of the 1990s' New World Order was only the latest in a long series of similar endeavours: among them were the ideas of Woodrow Wilson, the Nazis (the Neuerung), the Allied wartime planners (Atlantic Charter), Third World thinkers in the fostering of post-colonial self-reliance during the 1960s or the New International Economic Order of the 1970s.[7] The pact proposed at the 2005 Gleneagles G8 summit to double international aid and slash debt to developing countries in return for better governance, can be seen in this vein.

In each of these, reality scarcely matched the high ideals. As Wilson, the proponent of so-called open diplomacy (with more popular appeal and participation), noted optimistically in February 1918: 'We believe that our [the US's] own desire for a new international order, under which reason and justice and the common interests of mankind shall prevail, is the desire of enlightened men everywhere.'[8] His doctrine of idealism, of a peace based on democracy and justice rather than the balance of power and frontiers was, however, not to be, either in 1918 or in the early twenty-first century for that matter.

The UN option

Angola is an example of a country once besieged by UN peacemakers, peacekeepers, NGOs and fellow travellers, but which found its own path to peace, however sustainable or unsustainable that may ultimately prove to be.

As noted above, the civil war had raged from the chaotic Portuguese pull-out and Angolan independence on 11 November 1975. The two main protagonists – the MPLA and UNITA – were fuelled and directly supported by outsiders, the US and South Africa for UNITA and the Soviet bloc and Cuba in the case of the MPLA. A total of more than 400 000 Cubans served in Angola over seventeen years from 1975. For a while, in 1987/88, the 60 000-strong Cuban garrison was, for the MPLA, the difference between stalemate and defeat at the hands of the formidable South African Defence Force-backed UNITA.

Then, with an agreement for Namibia's independence struck in the late 1980s, came, falteringly, a peace process in Angola itself, culminating in the May 1991 Lisbon Accord. Peace in Namibia enabled the South Africans to get out of the former German colony they had ruled since acquiring it under a League of Nations mandate after the First World War. This meant curtailing, after a time, South African military support for UNITA, the Cubans leaving and the MPLA officially ending its sanctuary of South Africa's African National Congress liberation movement in return.

Malcolm Ferguson was one of the South African negotiating team for the Angola-Namibia accords. He remembers the moment at which his colleagues realised the MPLA would never leave power willingly. 'We were meeting with an Angola delegation at a dreadful airport hotel in New York. One of their team, a general, said to us, "The MPLA will never give up power. We control the capital, and in Africa, if you control the capital, you control the country." The penny dropped at that moment for our side. Afterwards General Jannie Geldenhuys [chief of the South African Defence Force] said to us: "*Jy het hom gehoor. Manne, ons moet nou vrede maak*" [You heard him. Men, we must now make peace].'[9]

In spite of the presence of a substantial United Nations Verification Mission (UNAVEM) through three phases from January 1989 until July 1997, numbering over 7 000 troops and observers at its peak and at a total cost of nearly half a billion dollars, things went badly wrong in the 1992 election. The parliamentary elections gave the MPLA an absolute majority, but the presidential elections were supposed to go to a second round, with neither Dos Santos (49 per cent) and Savimbi (40 per cent) gaining a first-round majority.

The conventional wisdom is that Savimbi badly misjudged matters in a fit of pique, and opted to go back to war, so prolonging the conflict by another decade and, ultimately, denying himself a place in history as a potential future president of Angola. 'The mistake that Savimbi made, the historical, big mistake he made, was to reject [the election] and go back to war,' has observed Alex Vines, head of Chatham House's Africa programme.[10] While the victors usually write history, the reality is somewhat more complex, in which all protagonists are guilty. Indeed, there is little evidence to suggest that the MPLA had any intent in handing over power through the ballot box, and would retain it just as it had seized it in 1975.

Savimbi fled Luanda, being smuggled out in FAA uniform, according to senior members of UNITA, because he 'was suspicious of being killed'. This was founded on a lack of trust, especially on issues for UNITA of security and the economy, underpinned by their belief that the MPLA would refuse to accept electoral defeat. General Carneiro, again, reportedly told a meeting of the JMPC that 'if the victory is not the MPLA's, then their tanks would come and drive on the winners'. Already in the build-up to the September election the mood was said to have become 'absolutely impossible' despite the visit by Pope John Paul II in June and a summit with Savimbi and Dos Santos in August to try to resolve the impasse, at which the decision was taken to integrate all the generals into the military.

By the time the results were published on 6 October 1992, according to

UNITA, 'they realised there had been a fraud'. Although a special electoral commission within the JMPC attempted to work through the problems, on 31 October the shooting began in Luanda, initially at the airport, but quickly spreading around the city. Savimbi had dispatched UNITA's vice president, Jeremias Chitunda, and General Elias Salupeto Pena 'Mango' to Luanda to negotiate the run-off election. Chitunda and Pena's convoy was attacked by government forces on 2 November in Luanda. They were both pulled from their car and shot dead. UNITA's parliamentary leader, Abel Chivukuvuku, was seriously wounded in a separate incident. UNITA believes the MPLA offensive, known as the Halloween Massacre, was pre-planned since its attempts to stop the fighting through contacting the high command came to naught. A total of 10 000 UNITA supporters were said to have been killed countrywide, with more than 3 000 in Luanda alone.

Numa, who, like other former UNITA generals Gato, Alcides Sekeolo, Demóstenes Amós Chilingutila and Gongederial Garcia Victor, had become an MP by 2013, says that the mistake was made not by UNITA, but by the MPLA. 'We were used to them never keeping to their agreements. We believed that Dr Savimbi would be killed if he did not leave Luanda.' The depths of this mistrust have, from UNITA's vantage, their origins in the failure of the parties to stick to their pre-independence agreement in 1975. 'After the [January 1975] Alvor Agreements [setting out the terms for the peaceful transfer and sharing of power from Portugal and between the liberation movements],' observes Numa, 'the MPLA had a clear agenda for the control of power and UNITA and the FNLA reacted to that. From the time I joined in 1974,' he says, 'UNITA always planned democracy in Angola.'

'The lesson,' says another UNITA cadre, 'twenty years on, is that if money and security is not top of the agenda, the prospects for a peaceful settlement are useless.'

The UN was powerless to stop the war and, in the end, had very little to do with its conclusion, despite much effort. A UN-brokered peace deal had been signed in 1994 in Lusaka, and two years later Dos Santos and Savimbi agreed to form a unity government and join forces into a national army. In April 1997, the unity government was inaugurated, though Savimbi declined a post, failing to attend the inauguration ceremony. The successor to UNAVEM, the United Nations Mission of Observers in Angola (MONUA), was unsurprisingly wound up in 1999.

UNITA regrouped military at Huambo. Once the war proper kicked off again in 1998, the rebels got the upper hand initially until a combination of the abovementioned sanctions, poor strategy choices and improved capacity within the FAA turned the tide, to the relief of a war-weary population. The arrival in Luanda of the former UNITA general, Nunda, who had fled Savimbi's wrath, is deemed to have tipped the military balance. Working in tandem with General de Matos, Nunda is seen to have 'turned' the advantage the way of the FAA. Contrary to popular opinion, UNITA does not believe that foreign mercenaries made 'much difference', save the operations conducted by Executive Outcomes in protecting the oil areas around Soyo in 1993/94, and in providing 'some training to the FAA'.

Political choices

What does the death of this rebel leader explain about the nature of conflict and of political choices?

In an age when the public 'default stop' is towards conflict resolution and negotiation, military solutions can play their part in settling conflicts, just as the death of one person can make a substantial difference. The number of senior UNITA generals who came in from the bush after Savimbi's death, in spite of many expecting them to carry the fight on, is testimony to the hold *mais velho* (old man) had over them and the error of his ways.

Savimbi's decision to go back to war confined him to a life on the run, a short period of military ascendancy in the mid-1990s being overturned by his rapidly narrowing international support base (itself a function both of his increasing illegitimacy following the 1992 election and the politics of oil) and the stiffening of the military resolve of the Angolan government. His poor choices are borne out by his uncertain legacy for UNITA. Following his death the party has, perhaps inevitably, struggled to redefine its character out of the shadow of its 'big man', to rebuild its leadership and institutional structures and normalise its funding sources outside of the diamond booty favoured by Savimbi. Many of its former fighters continue to face uncertainty, with endemic unemployment in their rural home areas in spite of Luanda's post-2002 demobilisation, demilitarisation and reintegration programme. This has affected even those closest to him. Valentine, the wife (Savimbi had several and apparently fathered some 30 children) who was with him at his death, is today a nurse in Luanda. But she is 'struggling' financially in the opinion of her colleagues, since her welfare and of people like her 'is not on the agenda of the government'.

Stability, however, requires more than just a military victory, even if that is a good place to start. It demands inclusive development to avoid building a constituency of losers who have little option but to resort to violence as a means of survival, and a political opposition as a critical check and balance on untrammelled power. Thus, if the path to peace was eventually locally owned, funded, led and organised, what of the path to prosperity?

A short economic history

Between 1963 and 1974, the Angolan economy grew at an extraordinary 25 per cent per annum, doubling almost every four years. This went hand in hand with burgeoning employment. Angola was once the world's fourth-largest coffee and sisal producer, most of it farmed in colonial-style large plantations. Yet as the war began to bite, the population moved away, and with the exodus of farming capital and skills, from a peak of $180 million in coffee exports in 1974, in 2010 the figure was just $250 000. Rural employment has suffered at the same time as the population has trebled from about six million at independence to 20 million by 2013.

However, the growth has been poorly distributed. It is a great irony that an avowedly Marxist-Leninist party in the MPLA has presided over a period of highly unequal economic growth. Despite an average per capita income of nearly $9 000 and enormous mineral riches, over two-thirds of Angolans live under the $2 per day poverty line, with one-third reliant on subsistence agriculture for their income. There is little formal sector employment apart from the government. Its Gini co-efficient – a measure of inequality – stands at 58.6, according to the World Bank, behind only the Seychelles, Comoros, Namibia, South Africa, Botswana and Haiti, and just above Honduras, Bolivia and the Central African Republic in the bottom (worst) ten.[11] Yet an estimated one million each Chinese and Portuguese are in Angola to find work, the former hustling on their new economic frontier, the latter on the back foot, pushed to return by poor economic prospects back home in the wake of the global economic crisis.

With squalor steps away from the beachfront Marginal and its five-star hotels, Luanda is officially the world's most expensive city. A quality hotel room costs $800, a bottle of water $6, and a ham and cheese sandwich a gagging $40. Perhaps nowhere better illustrates the unfortunate axiom: Africa's poor because it is expensive, and expensive because it is poor. Paradoxically,

Angola remains stubbornly near the bottom of the UN's human development index: life expectancy was just 46 in 2010, for example, and one-third of adults are illiterate.

A combination of oil and war also explains why traditional employment sectors such as coffee have been neglected, there being little incentive to diversify with such a resource endowment. Oil reserves are estimated at 13 billion barrels, and by 2013 production was at just under two million barrels per day, placing it on a par with sub-Saharan Africa's biggest producer, Nigeria. As one Angolan investment executive put it, 'Without oil we can expect no development. It gives us a chance. But with oil there is no guarantee of development. That depends on choices.'

Oil has, however, helped to stabilise a terrible inheritance. Out of a population of seven million in the 1980s, by the end of the war, an estimated 1.5 million people had been killed and four million refugees created. Hard and soft infrastructure, from roads, ports and railways to education and health systems, have had to be rebuilt, in many cases from scratch. The number of cars, the endless roadworks along with the cranes and skyscrapers now dotting the capital's skyline all illustrate that progress is being made. As one indicator, the national budget was, for 2011/12, at an effective $60 billion – ten times the figure of a decade earlier. Diversification has also been very difficult in a country where, in spite of the hydro-carbon dividend, long-term electricity blackouts are now a regular feature and where the traffic chaos is world class, clogging the streets and commerce alike.

Like any political party, the MPLA would like to dominate, to control the political and economic environment, in part for reasons of power and wealth, and in part since the sentiment of Marxist-Leninist centralisation and triumphalism over UNITA remains. Not for nothing are there still avenues named after iconic left-wing figures, from Freddie Engels to Vladimir Lenin. 'Comrade,' says one local observer, 'is in the MPLA's blood. It sees the world in terms of competitors and threats, not as potential partners.'

Opposition politician Chivukuvuku left UNITA after unsuccessfully challenging Isais Samakuva for the leadership in 2007. His CASA-CE (Broad Convergence for the Salvation of Angola-Electoral Coalition) party received 6 per cent of the vote and eight seats in the 2012 election, the MPLA winning with 72 per cent and 175 seats, with UNITA, the official opposition, taking 19 per cent of the vote and 32 seats of a total of 220.[12] Chivukuvuku argues that reforms must prioritise 'remoralising society' by ensuring transparency along with basic services and getting government out of business. That will require the elite giving up on some of its privileges, something African leaders – with few exceptions – have historically been reluctant to do.

Oil has fuelled chronic rent-seeking. Despite President dos Santos' 21 November 2009 call for a zero-tolerance policy against corruption, the presidency is seen as the 'epicentre of corruption', engaged in a variety of enterprises encompassing petroleum, telecommunications, banking, media and diamonds. When describing their state, the words 'rent-seeking', 'clientalism', 'patronage', 'elite interests' and 'party control' are routinely invoked by Angolans. It is the land of stark contrasts, of swish luxury cars moving in a sea of street sellers, hawking everything from imported fruit to toilet seats, car deodorants and second-hand mobile phones. Dr Onofre Santos, one of seven Constitutional Court judges, noted in 2011, 'Angola is like Russia. The people who are millionaires got the money via the state, where the party is like a monarchy, and remains both hegemonic and a distributor of wealth. Yet', he says, 'we don't discuss this. There is a conspiracy of silence.'

The Russian analogy is moot. A 2013 report by Corruption Watch in the UK focuses on a particular past deal in Angola that exemplifies the 'old way' that Angola's elite initially got wealthy, and set themselves up with enough capital to launch into any new business opportunity that their hold on state power opened for them.[13] In 1996 Angola signed a deal with Russia to re-structure its $5 billion Soviet-era debt, to reduce it to $1.5 billion; Angola would pay off the debt over fifteen years beginning in 2001 (together with $1.39 billion interest for the period through 2016). Russia then engaged an intermediary, Abalone Investments, which was based on the Isle of Man and set up purely to service this deal. Abalone arranged to buy the debt from Russia for only $750 million (with no interest payment), but to complete purchase of the debt by 2006. However, Angola – through the state oil company Sonangol – reportedly paid Abalone the full $1.5 billion to write off the debt, with the extra funds being corruptly siphoned off to the people involved in Abalone, senior Angolan officials and others. Abalone was set up by Arcadi Gaydamak and Pierre Falcone, two well-connected and controversial business people who had close links with Angolan officials, thanks to their involvement in what would become the separate Angolagate arms and oil scandal. In this single deal, some $700 million was apparently lost from the state into private hands. Angola, as one analyst put it, has 'legalised corruption'.[14]

Much has changed

It is wrong to suggest, however, that little has changed for the good in Angola over the past two decades.

First and foremost, the war has ended. The international community could not achieve what a small number of mercenaries started by stopping Savimbi, emboldening the government to get its own campaign moving.

The corruption environment in Angola has altered dramatically from the era when Sonangol was little more than a piggy bank for the elites. As Andrew Feinstein, the director of Corruption Watch, has acknowledged, 'Angola is trying to clean its image up especially regarding fiscal management.' Corruption has not disappeared in Angola of course; rather, it has morphed into a far more sophisticated system of cronyism and abuse of power, covered with a veneer of apparent reform and intolerance of abuse. There has also been a shift in the source of the funds and where they are being directed. Ironically, the export of a large slice of Angola's wealth into property and banking ventures outside the country, notably in Portugal, is indicative both of the absence of local opportunity and the lack of faith that Angolans have in their own systems, including the protection of property and rule of law, and the ease of doing business.

Vice President Manuel Domingos Vicente has said, 'The main objective of the Angolan government is to strengthen the economy … and not only in diamond and oil production. With this intention the Angolan government intends to renovate basic infrastructure … improve agriculture production … and modernise and extend the telecommunications network.'[15] The government, he emphasises, has allocated nearly $5 billion to this end annually. But more than money will be required. As Santos has argued, 'If there is no diversification in the economy, poverty will continue. The government cannot be the only source of wealth or the agent of development.'

To grow and to create employment, the ruling party and its elite will inevitably have to allow space for the private sector to operate, and permit UNITA and others the political and media space to act as a proper opposition, providing a check and balance on untrammelled power, which is also a means of ensuring greater competitiveness. As one former UNITA soldier has noted with a tinge of sadness, 'It is not a matter of the shortage of money, but of mindset, of education, and of vision for all politicians. We should not invoke so intensely the history of winners and losers in the battlefield, since we all lost something. We need,' he says, 'to move on.'

20

BURKINA FASO

The Mobylette African Capital

*

'The country we are trying to copy,' says François Compaoré, agricultural economist, the president of Burkina Faso's brother and his close adviser, 'is Israel. We have only few resources; only some agricultural products, more recently some mining, and hard workers. The most important asset we have is in opening the country and being willing to compete.'[1]

The streets of Ougadougou, Burkina Faso's capital, resemble, however, more Vietnam than the Holy Land, the roadways buzzing with mopeds and motorbikes. Not for nothing has it been described as the 'Mobylette capital of Africa', this French inheritance being overtaken by cheaper Chinese imports, facilitated by a fast-growing banking system. Financing arrangements for these $1 000 mopeds work at a cost of 200 CFA francs per day, or $40c. Unusually for a country so conservative in many respects and where two-thirds of the 17 million population is Muslim, many of the riders are women, models of unflustered poise and precision in Ouga's traffic. 'The moped is a symbol of the independence of the Burkinabé, their desire to do things their own way,' says one regional observer. 'The character of the Burkinabé is to reach autonomy. That's why you will not find human trafficking here, this is why we will take a bike, not a bus,' says one official.

In the 1980s, every Vietnamese ambition, it was said somewhat patronisingly, was to own a washing machine and Honda Dream motorcycle. Through a combination of better government, hard work and appetite for self-improvement and consumerism, there were more than four million motorcycles for Saigon's seven million people alone within a decade. Far from the image of Vietnam as a country ravaged by war and its subsequent command-economy foolery, it quickly became an analogy for stability and development.

Ditto Ougadougou. Its wide, well-maintained and relatively clean streets even have bicycle lanes. But this is not the only respect in which the country has cut its own path.

The road less travelled

There are not many African countries that would state their intent to emulate Israel. Likewise Burkina Faso is also one of just four African countries that, by 2013, still maintained diplomatic ties with Taiwan in preference to mainland China – the others being the Gambia, São Tomé and Príncipe, and Swaziland. This pays Ouga handsomely in terms of grants, especially towards its ambitious agriculture development schemes.

It is a country that does not appear to mind swimming against the tide, which has made it different to the rest of its region. Situated at the crossroads between West Africa and the Sahel, Burkinabé think of themselves as a gateway to both, roughly equidistant from most regional capitals. They speak not of a series of disadvantages, but rather a set of 'unique strengths' in the combination of their landlockedness. These include a strong sense of national identity based on respect for traditional rulers, despite the presence of more than 60 tribes; a formidable 'Swiss-type' of work ethic as one Western ambassador described it; a refreshing modesty and concern for detail and punctuality; the relatively late blessing of natural resources, and 'poverty for a very long time', which has forced the population to find ways to work together. 'If three of us are from the same ethnic group,' says a Burkinabé business person, 'it would be a surprise. But this does not affect the functioning of the state; to the contrary, it's a special cultural heritage.'

Burkina Faso grew its economy at over 5.5 per cent from 2002 to 2010, with low annual inflation of under 2.5 per cent during this time. This, in part, relates to a recent mining boom: seven gold (and one zinc) mines were opened in five years from 2008. Burkina is the fourth-largest gold producer in Africa, after South Africa, Mali and Ghana.

By 2012 gold mining accounted for around 25 per cent of government revenue, or $400 million, exports rising to 32 tonnes in 2012 from just 12.5 tonnes three years earlier. This is expected to increase again to 40 tonnes in 2013. No fewer than 941 concessions had been 'delivered to the private sector', Pascal Diendere, the director general in the mining ministry, said in April 2013.

But this is not the sole asset base of the economy. Agriculture still contributes officially at least 20 per cent to GDP (though some have this as high as 35 per cent), the main source of income for most Burkinabé, with 80 per cent living in the rural areas. Burkina is Africa's number one cotton producer, and the government is actively pursuing plans to expand production of a range of products including vegetables, fruits, sesame, shea butter and cashews. There have been other improvements, including in livestock production, which has also been lifted from little over 60 000 tonnes in 2004 to 150 000 in 2012, although just one-third of farmland is, by the government's own estimates, farmed. Just 14 per cent of potentially irrigable land is exploited.[2]

It has undertaken the privatisation of some 50 parastatals, virtually all save for water and electricity, the deregulation of price controls (except on petrol, although the cost remains high, standing at over $1.30 per litre for diesel in 2013), and has instituted a reform programme throughout the public service. Labour costs are low, averaging $70 per month, about half of an equivalent position in Côte d'Ivoire, for example, says one regional banker, or 25 per cent of a comparable Nigerian.

A regional escape act

Having got out early enough from the patronage umbrella of Colonel Gaddafi, not only has Burkina avoided going the way of neighbouring Mali, but by 2013 it was a significant contributor to African Union peacekeeping missions in that country and elsewhere. Ouga had committed 800 troops each to its neighbour and to Darfur, plus 140 police each in Darfur and Guinea-Bissau.

Such progress both is a result of and is reflected in the country's listing in the World Bank's 2014 Doing Business rankings at 154th of 189 countries.[3] This is not impressive in itself, as Ghana (67), Sierra Leone (142), Liberia (144), Nigeria (147) and the Gambia (150) rank above it among the countries of West Africa. (It is questionable to the outsider at least how all of these countries, including Sierra Leone, can have a better record – if anything this undermines the validity of such indicators as a measure of the cost and difficulty of doing business.) Still, Mali (155), Togo (157), Gabon (163), Côte d'Ivoire (167), Cameroon (168), Benin (174), Guinea (175), Niger (176),

Senegal (178) and Guinea-Bissau (180) are among those below. More than that, in the 2000s Burkina ranked consistently among the top ten governance and business reformers.

The government has set up a performance monitoring unit, known as the SCADD, led by the Ministry of Finance and deployed within every government department – with the exception of the Ministry of Defence. As Compaoré observes, Burkina's success and competitiveness will depend on 'improved public administration, to ensure that corners are not cut. We have to practice a "win-win" business model,' he says. A 30-strong Presidential Advisory Council, made up of equal numbers of locals and foreigners, has been established, with working groups on legal, fiscal, productive and organisational aspects of government and reform. As a result of such reforms, at least among the higher ranks, Burkina's senior civil servants are not only knowledgeable and punctual, itself a rare trait in the region, but possess strategic insight into the government's vision and limits.

Burkina is also in the top half of all nations in Transparency International's Corruption Perception Index and ranks 83rd of 175 placings.[4] Of continental African countries, only Botswana (30), Rwanda (49), Lesotho (55), Namibia (57), Ghana (63), South Africa (72), Tunisia and Senegal (both 77) and Swaziland (82) rank above Burkina in the 2013 listing. As one foreign diplomat put it bluntly about the expectations of government officials in this regard, 'They are satisfied with just 2 per cent ...'

Little wonder the country is something of a 'donor darling', one of nine US Millennium Challenge countries in Africa (and 23 worldwide) in 2013, a status that is worth $481 million in development assistance over five years. Throw in the World Bank, the EU, the Swedes, the French, African Development Bank and the Taiwanese, and the annual aid figure is around $1 billion – at least – or $70 for every Burkinabé.

This has enabled the government to plan and actually implement ambitious agro-infrastructure projects, including at Bagré, Vallée de Sourou, Kompienga and Samandéni. Also on the stocks is an ambitious scheme for a new, $600-million public-private-partnership international airport at Donsin, the next stage beyond an immediate plan to double the number of visitors to one million by 2015. And in all of this, it aims to become the strategic hub for West Africa, leveraging its location and membership of the CFA franc zone along with Benin, Côte d'Ivoire, Guinea-Bissau, Mali, Niger, Senegal and Togo.

It was not always this way.

Only up from Upper Volta

The circular staircase in the headquarters of the secretary general of Burkina's armed forces is studded with pictures of successive ministers of defence. A long line of civilians comes to an abrupt end in 1983 when a picture of Captain Jean-Baptiste Lingani Boukary appears in fatigues in the place of the unsmiling men in suits. He is followed by a youthful then-Captain Blaise Compaoré, who served as both minister and president from 21 September 1989 to 25 July 1991.

During the 1980s, Burkina Faso was far from a donor darling, rather a poster child for the excesses of African militaries, illustrating how long it takes and how difficult it is to repair the damage of excessive militarism and its conniving civilian counterpart, especially amidst the challenges of nation-building, high post-colonial expectations, a rapidly expanding population, and in spite of rich natural resource endowment. In part, this troubled history had its origins in a particularly egregious colonial history.

Even if most Africans, in contrast to some Asians, universally regard colonialism as a bad thing, it was worse for some than others. A territory contested by Britain and France, the tussle was ultimately resolved in favour of the latter, the Mossi kingdom of Ougadougou becoming a French protectorate in 1896.

Initially, the former Mossi states were assimilated into the Colonie du Haut Sénégal-Niger. Then, in 1919, the colony was dismantled and the territory of Upper Volta – as contemporary Burkina was known – established. Unlike neighbouring Senegal and Ivory Coast, however, Upper Volta was considered little more than a labour reservoir, and scarcely developed.

Independence from France in 1960 brought little change.

Maurice Yaméogo, Upper Volta's first president, was interested mainly in consolidating his power and feathering his own nest. He banned all political parties save his own, while his attempts at economic management and direction brought little relief to a population then numbering five million.

In the spirit of the times in that region, coup then followed coup. The first, in 1966, was led by Lieutenant Colonel Sangoulé Lamizana and followed mass popular demonstrations. A brief civilian interregnum was reinstated in 1970 until Lamizana took it upon himself to again intervene in 1974, suspending all opposition. This meant tackling the trade unions, however, and they brought the economy to its knees with a nationwide strike in 1975, mobilising for a new constitution and elections.

Regardless, three more putsches followed over the next five years until, in November 1982, Captain Thomas Sankara staged a particularly bloody coup and seized power in the name of his People's Salvation Council, heading up a Marxist-dominated National Council for the Revolution.

Within two years, Sankara had set about reforming the country, renaming it 'Burkina Faso' (literally, the Country of Honest Men). Focusing on self-reliance in rural areas, things slowly improved, despite its radical rhetoric, the regime sticking to its budget and balancing its books. Suspicions abounded, however, and there were tensions between the military leaders. Sankara thought there were traitors behind every tree, lurking in the barracks. As it turned out, even the paranoid have enemies.

Burkina Faso was one of few countries in Africa to enjoy per capita GNP growth during the 1980s. But this did not save Sankara. In October 1987, a group of fellow junior officers seized power. Sankara and twelve others were rounded up and shot, the new regime citing the deterioration in regional relations as a key reason for the need for a 'correction' to the 'revolution'.

With Sankara's dismembered body buried in an unmarked grave outside Ougadougou, Compaoré, who had assumed leadership after the 'revindication', as this grubby episode became known, set about consolidating his power base, reversing his predecessor's nationalisations, returning the country to the Bretton Woods fold, and patching up relations with the West. He has continued assiduously in the way in which he started, though at his own pace and in his own way.

In 2013 Compaoré entered his 26th year in power, having seemingly learnt a trick or two from his once father-in-law, Félix Houphouet-Boigny, Côte d'Ivoire's longstanding leader. Democracy has developed slowly but, again, steadily. Presidential elections were held in 1991, and again in 1998. These were both won handsomely, but not surprisingly, by Compaoré. In 2000, the constitution was amended to reduce the presidential term to five years.

The amendment, which took effect during the 2005 elections, would have prevented him from running again. With a constitutional council ruling allowing him to stand, Compaoré won landslides again in the 2005 and 2010 elections. Only 1.6 million bothered to vote on the latter occasion.

Yet success is deeper than statistics and elections.[5]

The average Burkinabé possesses an unusual sense of pride, industry and modesty. Government offices are smart, efficient and highly focused, unusually so for the developing world; and they house educated, articulate and business-like ministers. This ethos seems to pervade most of the society, where the different ethnic groups pride themselves on coexisting peace-fully. Indeed, one Christian government minister remarked that he and his Muslim wife would offer the first cuts of their Christmas dinner (presumably the turkey, not the ham) to their Muslim neighbours, and that this was common practice across the country – and vice versa. Bishops and imams are reported sometimes to have a better dialogue between each other than they do among factions of their own faiths. It must be especially reassuring for a government in a region that is seeing the progressive radicalisation and militarisation of Islam. Indeed, the few signs of radicalisation that have appeared have been dealt with in a typically understated Burkinabé way, with the quiet closure of the offending mosques and without further incident. This tolerance extends beyond ethnicity; views on gender, for example, also seem unusually developed. A country permitting its women to work, is a country that unleashes a significantly larger workforce – and on the surface, at least, it seems as though Burkina Faso is reaping the rewards of such relatively progressive thinking. For a predominantly Muslim country with conservative social norms, remarkably there is barely a niqaab or burqa to be seen; far more common is the sight of women commuting to work and taking their children to school on a scooter. If there are fault lines that exist, then they are smoothing over them well.

Some locals base their progress on the historical roots in the Mossi kingdoms, one of the strongest in Africa, around which a sense of common, national identity has been constructed. Of course, Burkina's recent impressive record should not obscure ongoing problems of poverty.

Not everything is rosy

Despite the surface colour and visual vibrancy, it remains a very poor place, with GDP per capita under $600. Nearly half of the country lives under the $1 per day global poverty benchmark. Average life expectancy at birth is little over 55. With just ten doctors per 100 000 people, infant and maternal mortality remains staggeringly high, with a rate of seventeen deaths per 1 000 children under five, ranking it the ninth worst worldwide (behind, with the highest/worst first: Chad, Afghanistan, Congo, Guinea-Bissau, Sierra Leone, Mali, Somalia and the Central African Republic).

There are other negative social indicators. Three-quarters of girls and women are reported to have suffered female genital mutilation. Though this oft-repeated statistic may be overstating the extent, this practice regardless speaks to gender inequalities, and is a focus also of the First Lady's social concern. At over six births per woman amounting to a population growth rate over 3 per cent per annum, it is firmly in the top ten fastest growing populations worldwide and expected to double every 23 years. The extent of urbanisation is expected, by the government's own admission, to reach 35 per cent by 2026.

The government is faced, thus, with the matter of youth unemployment. It is a subject that comes up in every conversation; 'our biggest challenge, and the biggest challenge of the region' as one official reflected. Two-thirds of Burkinabé are under the age of 25.

There is also rising criminality and widening banditry, especially in the Tuareg north-east, on the border junction with Niger and Mali. Already blisteringly hot and dry much of the year, the country remains hyper-vulnerable to climate change. Even though the government has plans to increase power via investments in solar, Burkina remains short of energy, producing a meagre 250 MW, with just 14 per cent electricity coverage in 2010. There is a scarcity of human capital, too, in this country without universal primary school coverage, and with just a two-thirds completion rate of those who do attend. While political freedoms and human rights are considered 'severely restricted', opposition activists point to the immense wealth of the president and his entourage.

One result is that the Sankara name is still revered among some Burkinabés.

But that is about as far as the mythology goes. While Compaoré might get some human rights flak, many fear what will happen when Blaise (63 in 2014) goes, in 2015, or whenever, given his status as the father of Burkina's reforms. There is little doubt among foreign diplomats that he is the driver of the reforms, an unlikely Lee Kuan Yew perhaps, but nonetheless a committed one – brave enough to pay a visit to Israel in 2008, for example. Officials have followed this trail to learn from the Jewish state in turning its own desert into, first, an agricultural success and, later, a high-tech oasis. President Blaise, as he is widely known, is apparently not one to pay lip-service to the rhetoric of reform.

Yet, the minister of mines, Salif Lamouossa Kaboré, who has overseen enormous growth in his portfolio, says that he, like his colleagues, is unconcerned about post-Blaise Burkina. 'Stability,' he argues, 'is reflected in the law.' And his brother François says that while 'I am close to the president, and he is my friend', here 'law is law. If I do something wrong, he won't protect me. The strength of our success is in our institutions and in the sophisticated debates today in our parliament. Our institutions are not dependent on one person.' But the president's brother is himself seen as an exception to this general rule, with characters around him being implicated in a number of scandals, a cause of some political controversy and even unrest.

But maybe, as in Israel, it is the population who will make the difference, and not the leadership. Only time will tell, but in the meantime, things are moving, like the swarms of Mobylettes, in the right direction.

21

BURUNDI AND RWANDA

Getting Beyond Tribalism

*

Burundi and Rwanda emphasise the stark costs and challenge of overcoming the politics and, sometimes, violence of identity. As they attempt to do so, they illustrate, too, the difficulty in getting beyond people and personalities as a way of defining progress to, instead, systems and institutions of government.

At first glance, these East African neighbours appear to be two sides of the same coin. They are roughly of equal size, Rwanda's population at 11 million, Burundi's touching 10 million. Both have exactly the same ethnic make-up: Hutu 84 per cent, Tutsi 15 per cent and Twa 1 per cent.[1] Both have been sites of regular inter-ethnic pogroms and in the case of Rwanda, the 1994 genocide that saw nearly 10 per cent of its population, around 800 000 people, hacked to death over 100 horrifying days from April to July.

There are deeper differences, however, than this superficial analysis, illustrated by Rwanda's place (32nd out of 189 economies for 2014) on the World Bank's Doing Business rankings, compared to Burundi's 140th ranking. Rwanda's per capita GDP, while still low at $570, is more than twice that of Burundi's ($250).[2] Rwanda's score in Transparency International's Corruption Perception Index jumped from 31 in 2005 (where 100 = no corruption) to 53 in 2013, while Burundi regressed from 23 points in 2005 to 21 points in 2013, with a low of 18 in 2009.[3]

There are other differences, not least the role of international actors and institutions in helping to bring stability. They are also ethnic inversions as to how politics has played out.

While the minority Tutsi are generally seen as the victims in Rwanda, to its immediate south in Burundi the Tutsi-controlled army was responsible for perpetrating regular atrocities against the majority Hutu. Tutsis effectively ruled Burundi from independence until the election of a Hutu government in 2005. Governments espousing a Hutu-majoritarian ideology dominated politics in Rwanda from independence in 1962, conducting regular massacres of the Tutsi, culminating in the 1994 genocide.

Indeed, against the pale of Rwanda's 1994 event, it is sometimes forgotten that Burundi suffered a massive trauma just the previous year. Indeed, the mass killings of Hutus by the largely Tutsi army in 1972 and the 1993 slaughter of Tutsis by the Hutu populace are both described as genocide. In 1972, martial law was proclaimed by a Tutsi officer, Michel Micombero, whose bewhiskered face sported a set of lamb chops that would not look out of place under a pith helmet on the set of *Zulu Dawn*, and whose sepia photo still hangs among the cast of leaders in the entrance hall of the presidency in Bujumbura. Lists of Hutu targets were carefully drawn up, including the elite and those with a military background. The government claimed 15 000 were killed while Hutu opponents purported some 300 000. Just over twenty years later, in June 1993, the Hutu-led Front for Democracy in Burundi won the election. But tension grew quickly between the new government and the army and its political backers, and President Melchior Ndadaye was assassinated on 21 October 1993 by Tutsi officers. Possibly as many as 300 000 Tutsi and Hutu were massacred as reprisal followed reprisal in the following months.[4]

Does this history preordain the future for these two former German (from 1916, Belgian) colonies, or is it principally shaped by what they do? What is the relationship between democracy and stability in both, and how might they migrate from ethnic-based to issue-based politics? And what can they teach us about the role of economic growth as a conflict mitigator?

Swallowing Burundi's bitter pill of ethnicity

Burundi has made strides in the twenty-first century in spite of the post-independence history of tribal persecution and conflict, not fewer than nine coups and, ultimately, civil war. Indeed, the challenges it faces now – a very poor country with extremely limited government capacity – have to be viewed in this context. The social and institutional inheritance of the current regime reflects the mistrust, lack of dialogue and violence that has long been part and parcel of the political landscape and the upbringing of its politicians. Accountability and transparency based on good governance and incentivising officials has been a largely foreign concept for both a government and a society locked in a survival mode.

Nevertheless, the country has been largely at peace since the mid-2000s. A new, integrated military has been created. Ongoing political compromise is being made on the basis of ethnic power-sharing. The government has provided free health care for children and pregnant mothers, free primary schooling, and Burundi, once a security drag, is now a contributor to international peacekeeping missions, including in Somalia and Haiti.

Yet, by the government's own admission, much more needs to be done, assiduously and urgently, without which Burundi not only will fail to make progress at the pace its citizens hope for, but could slide back into fragility and even failure.

*

Around the table at the Hôtel Club du Lac Tanganyika in Bujumbura in 2011 were two Congolese, one a successful educator with his own NGO, another a mining executive living in Pretoria, a Burundian working in the beer industry in Angola, a Burundian business person running a courier company, an eminent local advocate, and myself. Spot the odd one out. The conversation ranged during the evening over the usual topics: politics, family, business and the economy. It was only after several hours that something struck me – any sense of being an outsider related only to my poor French, not skin colour.

Refreshing for a white South African, perhaps, but politics in Burundi has long been defined by identity. Over 50 years ago, on 13 October 1961, Prince Louis Rwagasore, Burundi's prime minister, was shot and killed on the hotel's porch only metres from where we were drinking. The country's national and independence hero, a member of the (Tutsi) royal family[5] married to a Hutu, Rwagasore was seen as someone who could bridge the divide between the two groups. He was shot by a Greek resident, Georges Karagiorgis, acting apparently in cahoots with the pro-Belgian Christian Democratic Party (PDC). Belgium had allowed for the creation of political parties after 1948, out of which grew two main entities: the Union for National Progress (UPRONA) led by Rwagasore, and the PDC led by Belgian loyalists. UPRONA had won legislative elections the same month of the prince's assassination. 'It was a bit like what could have happened in

South Africa if Nelson Mandela was murdered before assuming the presidency in 1994,' reflected one politician.[6] Karagiorgis, allegedly paid by Belgian settlers who thought the country better under Hutu rule, was tried and executed in Bujumbura (then known as Usumbura) the following June. But the impact of his action lasted much longer, the country descending into a spiral of violence.

At the time the Hôtel Club du Lac Tanganyika was owned by another Greek, Kratsonis Papadopolos, who also ran the nearby Kapa Bakery. After the lake unexpectedly rose and flooded the hotel in the late 1960s, Papadopolos got out of the kitchen and sold both businesses, though there were few takers for the hotel given the water damage and gruesome history. Enter the Iserentant family, Belgian settlers who had fled (barely) with their lives in 1964 from their coffee, timber and essence smallholding across the lake at Fizi in the Congo, overlooking the then Burton Bay. The hotel was reopened in 1973 after four years of hard restorative work, though Papa Iserentant died shortly thereafter, and his wife took over, supporting five small children on the proceeds. With Belgian restaurant training behind him, her son Marc has run the establishment since 1983 through thick and thin, coups, wars, economic collapse, destruction, a ground-out peace and hesitant recovery. Out of despair came at least one family's salvation.

Was Prince Rwagasore's murder a symptom of underlying tensions or a cause of the violence that was to follow over half a century in Burundi?

Burundi's vicious cycle

When, upon Burundi's independence in July 1962, the constitutional monarch King Mwambutsa IV appointed a Tutsi prime minister, the Hutus, comprising the parliamentary majority, felt hard done by. An attempted coup by the Hutu-dominated police was brutally put down by the army, led by the aforementioned Captain Micombero, who was a Hima Tutsi from Bururi province. Mwambutsa was eventually deposed in 1966 by his son, Prince Charles Ndizeye (who took the royal name Ntare V), but Micombero soon returned to the political fold to topple Ntare and abolish the monarchy. By 1972, violence escalated with the launch of systematic attacks by the extremist Hutu organisation Umugambwe wa'Bakozi Uburundi (Burundi Workers' Party), with the intention of exterminating all Tutsis. Amidst ongoing violence in 1976, another Hima Tutsi, Colonel Jean-Baptiste Bagaza, led a bloodless coup and promoted various reforms. In August 1984, Bagaza was elected as head of state of a single-party regime.

In defence of his regime, Bagaza says, 'There was confusion everywhere. There was civil war. We had to find a solution to this and we also needed to transform our country, end chaos, and put us back on our feet.'[7] He added, 'There was no electricity, no water, and no roads, so we had to create industry and improve the transport system.' Then in 1987, at the instigation, he claims, of France and Belgium in alliance with the Catholic Church, Major Pierre Buyoya, yet another Hima Tutsi, staged a coup, suspended the constitution and reinstated military rule. 'He was just an instrument of others,' recalled Bagaza, 'at a time when things were different, where we had Mobutu on one side, [Rwandan Hutu president] Juvénal Habyarimana on the other, and the US and Russians were providing the Cold War context.'

Following the appointment by Buyoya of an ethnically mixed government, in June 1993 Ndadaye's Hutu-dominated party won the first democratic election. Following his assassination and still more violence, the next president, Cyprien Ntaryamira, also a Hutu, had the misfortune to hitch a ride with President Habyarimana in April 1994, and was killed together with his Rwandan counterpart when their Falcon aircraft was shot down on its approach to Kigali International Airport. Amidst further waves of fighting, violence and refugee flows, Buyoya seized power again in a second *coup d'état* in 1996. The regional and international community played a key role in brokering a power-sharing agreement between a Tutsi-dominated government and Hutu rebels in 2003, leading to a new constitution in 2005, and the election of a majority Hutu government of President Pierre Nkurunziza of the National Council for the Defence of Democracy-Forces for the Defence of Democracy in 2005 and, again, in 2010.

Burundi has been the site of a comprehensive UN mission since 2004 when the Security Council established the United Nations Operation in Burundi (ONUB) 'in order to support and help to implement the efforts undertaken by Burundians to restore lasting peace and bring about national reconciliation, as provided under the Arusha Agreement'. It was succeeded by the United Nations Integrated Office in Burundi (BINUB), established by Security Council Resolution 1719 of 25 October 2006; its mission to monitor the ceasefire, support the political process and ensure the Disarmament, Demobilisation and Reintegration of former combatants.[8] ONUB peaked in 2005 at 5 665 total uniformed personnel, including 5 400 troops, 168 military observers and 97 police. BINUB's strength was approved at 450 personnel.

When Burundi's minister of finance, Tabu Abdallah Manirakiza, in 2013 described his country's development conundrum as a 'vicious cycle', as portrayed below, it is not surprising that the solution he and others postulated is based on an increase in external support. This vicious cycle, he says, has its roots in the weakness of the institutions inherited at his country's independence, compounded by subsequent attitudes and events. Institutional weakness fed off and exacerbated political and ethnic differences, discouraging long-term investors and instead attracting 'opportunistic investment', which, he says, 'cannot develop the country or reduce poverty'.

And if poverty prevails, there are limited resources and fighting inevitably ensues over their control. Hence, the ongoing violence, coups and civil war, which then weaken these already frail institutions further. So starts, ends and continues Burundi's vicious cycle of fragility and underdevelopment.

Members of Bujumbura's government have, in response to this cycle of violence and underdevelopment, consistently argued that the next step in Burundi's recovery has to be a Marshall Plan in order to break this vicious cycle once and for all. In the finance minister's analysis, a trebling of per

THE CONFLICT
DEVELOPMENT
VICIOUS CYCLE

Institutional weakness
Poverty and rapid population growth
Short-termist policies, actions and investment
Failure to invest in infrastructure, people and systems
Identities politics, political rupture
Widening corruption
Isolation of private sector
Politicisation of institutions
Judicial system collapse
Democratic failure
Serial coups and rampant militarism
Skills haemorrhage
Humanitarian relief, not donor development
Violence, collapse
No local ownership of the problem or solution

capita annual aid to $90 would provide the necessary injection of finance 'to remove the pressure from those who are trying to control resources for their own purposes' and, in so doing, to increase investment for private production. 'There is a very fragile balance. If we do not generate more resources, we could find ourselves in a civil war once again,' he says.

Others disagree on the need, foremost, for funding. As Charles Nihangaza, a former minister of finance, has argued, 'It's not money that's the problem; much more so is the lack of human capacity.' In an environment, he adds, 'where there is corruption and bad governance along with this low capacity, it is not surprising that investors are not coming'. He lamented, 'We should have been able to take off in terms of investment after the war, but the notion of the state,' he says, 'is not understood in the same way by everyone – some see it as a source of personal interest, working for just a few people.'

Indeed, the Marshall Plan argument for Africa forgets important aspects of the flows of funds to Europe at the end of the Second World War. First, the amount provided over a four-year period from 1947 was equivalent to $150 billion in today's money;[9] second, the Plan was for *rebuilding* Europe, not building it from scratch. The absorptive capacity of European countries, their skills base, was such that even though there was acute physical destruction, they were easily able to efficiently deploy the money and get back on their feet. This is why the Plan also never exceeded 2.5 per cent of GDP; whereas in Burundi aid already amounts to nearly 20 per cent.[10] Aid transfers to Africa have historically been high as a percentage of overall income, as the graph below illustrates.

Even so, the extent of such disagreements, and the fact that they are

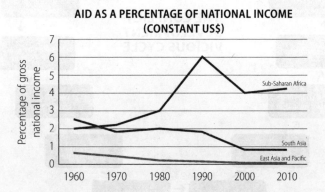

AID AS A PERCENTAGE OF NATIONAL INCOME (CONSTANT US$)

Percentage of gross national income

Sub-Saharan Africa

South Asia

East Asia and Pacific

1960 1970 1980 1990 2000 2010

Source: World Development Indicators (2012) from Ines Ferreira and Marta Simoes, 'Aid and Growth: A Comparative Study between Sub-Saharan Africa and Asia', *Applied Econometrics and International Development* 13(1), 2013.

expressed openly, is testament, again, to Burundi's progress. But responsibility for the vicious cycle does not start and finish at independence and its solution does not rest with the donors alone, even though this is understandably the Burundian preference. Nor does atrophy and apathy explain all; there are more sinister, potentially malignant actions.

The cost of progress

The second most densely populated African country after neighbouring Rwanda, Burundi can be split into two parts. The great Imbo plain stretching north to south enveloping Lake Tanganyika, which covers nearly one-tenth of the territory, and bordering also on Tanzania, Congo and Zambia. The second comprises the mountainous highlands, quickly rising from the lake, where the capital Bujumbura sits at its northernmost tip, to over 2 000 metres, the site of the agricultural export backbone of coffee and tea. It is here, too, that large mineral reserves are to be found, notably of nickel, but including cobalt, copper, platinum, tantalum, tungsten and a range of rare earths.

This is not all. One hundred kilometres south of Bujumbura near Rotovu, on the road to Tanzania, is 'the southernmost source of the Nile'. Every East African country claims to possess the great river's origins, but at least the Burundians are specific about their fame.

Yet, for all its natural resources, Burundi's people are in the bottom ten worldwide in per capita income terms, earning an average of $200 annually, 70 per cent of its 10 million people mired below the poverty line. Part of the reason for this is a birth rate touching 3.5 per cent, meaning that the country doubles its population every twenty years or so.

Despite abundant water resources, Burundi faces chronic energy shortages. It is one of the most energy-scarce economies in Africa, with just 40 MW for the whole country. As one government official put it, 'There is not a single product that Burundi can make that is competitive, even in the region, because of energy [shortages].'

The underlying reasons for Burundi's challenges are partly bureaucratic, partly geographic, partly educational, partly cultural and partly political. Landlocked and over 1 000 kilometres away from the nearest seaport, Dar-es-Salaam, Burundi is expensive to operate in and to get to. Globalisation, save for aid, is pretty much one-way traffic for Burundi.

388 — WHY STATES RECOVER

The port on Lake Tanganyika in Bujumbura is a testament to both of these challenges and to how regional integration has failed Burundi. Port volumes had fallen by around one half in 2013 over 2012 (110 000 versus 230 000 tonnes) due to the closure of the Tanzanian rail-link between Dar and the port of Kigoma, from where goods were shipped up the lake to Bujumbura. As a result, the costs of trucking directly from Dar to Burundi have added $3 000 to the costs of a 40-foot container, totalling an astonishingly high $6 500. Whereas lake traffic to the Burundi capital was previously split 50:50 between the Zambian port of Mpulungu in the lake's south and Kigoma, now Zambia (to where goods have to be trucked) comprises '95 per cent' of the source traffic. Unsurprisingly, virtually all trucks reaching Bujumbura are reportedly from Tanzania. And '95 per cent' comprises imports rather than exports.

Such difficulties are compounded by widespread corruption. Not for nothing has the government number plate suffix 'AGB' become parodied as Association des Grands Bandits. One of the reasons for this, says a senior Burundi defence force officer, 'is that the government came into power with nothing, nothing in their pockets. This was a big mistake. They are trying to make up for lost time.' Others disagree. Foreign business people point to a decline in corruption, even though many have a concern about apathy.

Despite the government spending over 8 per cent of GDP on education, only 60 per cent of Burundians are functionally literate, the result of years of exclusion and underinvestment. In a vicious cycle, agriculture continues to support 90 per cent of the labour force, comprising also nearly half of economic output. Children are a labour asset, their work in the fields keeping many from already inadequate schooling institutions.

The overall challenge facing Burundi is in moving from the short term to a longer-term development road, from donor-led stability to private sector-led growth and development. While the government rhetorically realises the need to open up space for the private sector to grow the economy, it is too easy to remain addicted to donor sources.

To achieve this it would be necessary to maintain the fragile political compact. Proposed constitutional amendments – which would allow President Nkurunziza to run for a third term in elections scheduled for 2015 and whereby a single prime minister from the ruling party would replace two vice president posts currently shared between Hutu and Tutsi – in early 2014 stirred the worst political crisis since the end of the civil war. Out of such negatives there has, however, been progress. The Hutu-Tutsi struggle no longer entirely defines Burundi. 'We spent 40 years fearing genocide,' said one Tutsi officer. 'That is now over. The army is integrated 50:50, to insure against this threat reoccurring,' while in other branches of government the quotas are pegged at 40 per cent Tutsi, 60 per cent Hutu. Government has a handle on where the problems lie, even though they seem to have misplaced the solution.

Indeed, as the former head of UNOB, Karin Landgren, put it in her final dispatch to the Security Council in July 2012, Burundi looked 'immeasurably different' from the conflict-ravaged country of a few years before, although 'decisive and confident leadership' was required to consolidate governance that allowed dissent, and shunned corruption and spurred development. 'This fragile, beautiful and courageous country has travelled a long and difficult distance along the road of peace consolidation in a little over a decade,' she said to the Council. She added, 'It should no longer surprise us that war-torn countries do not put away their weapons and blossom instantly as plural and stable democracies.'[11]

Whereas Burundi has sought to address, for the moment, much of the undergrowth of its ethnic tensions, Rwanda has taken an opposite path, where no quarter is asked for nor given to its enemies in the belief that the country can bury the ethnic question through development.

Rwanda: Hell in a small place

The same month that South Africa emerged from apartheid to enjoy its first democratic election in April 1994, Rwanda descended into genocide. As South Africans queued patiently and in generally good humour in the April sun to choose their leaders, Rwandans slaughtered each other in a cauldron of tribal-political violence, pitting Hutu against Tutsi, radical against moderate, village against village, neighbour against neighbour, friend against friend, and even, at its bestial climax, in 'mixed' marriages, fathers against wives and even their own children. A 30 000-strong Hutu Interahamwe ('Those who attack together') militia affiliated with the dominant political party spearheaded the attacks and fed hate ideology that denigrated the Tutsi as *inyenzi* – cockroaches. The violence was carefully planned and implemented by a cabal of ethnic Hutu extremist elites in the context of civil war, with the intention of eliminating political opponents in naming an ethnic other in the Tutsi. Not only were 800 000 killed in this premeditated

onslaught, but the 100 days left more than 300 0000 orphans and two million refugees, among them the remnants of the génocidaires who fled mostly to Zaire and Tanzania.[12]

Rwanda was hell in a small place,[13] an unadulterated illustration of the
cost of getting things radically wrong, of playing the politics of racial identity at the expense not only of national unity, but liberty and security. As the
Genocide Memorial Centre reminds us, 'The country smelt of the stench of
death ... Rwanda was dead.' It was the consequence, the memorial contends,
of 'a highly centralised, repressive state with a single party system', catalysed
by economic slump with the fall of the global coffee price in the mid-1980s.

Little wonder then that Paul Kagame, de facto Rwandan president since the
Rwandan Patriotic Army he led took power from the fleeing interim government in July 1994,[14] strictly does not permit politicians to mobilise on ethnic
grounds. The official line is that there are no Tutsis or Hutus, only Rwandans.
This is in his self-interest, of course, where power and privilege are held predominantly by Tutsis like Kagame, and not the Hutu. This has predominantly
been driven by a sense of an imperative for a *national* project, of the need
to prevent the genocide from ever reoccurring. The intention of the Kagame
and the ruling Rwandan Patriotic Front (RPF), which have held the view on
ethnicity since before taking power, has been, simply put, that tribal ties will
become irrelevant if there is enough prosperity to go around.

This may have been at the cost of democracy, however, at least as the
West knows it, and good governance, contrary to external perceptions. In
the 2010 election the 53-year-old sitting president was declared the winner
with over 93 per cent of the vote, with the second-placed candidate, Jean
Damascene Ntawukuriryayo, a former minister in Kagame's government,
polling a shade over 5 per cent. One Hutu candidate, Victoire Ingabire, who
had been living abroad, created controversy following her return to Rwanda
with comments relating to the genocide. Accused of breaking the country's
laws regarding genocide denial and 'divisionism',[15] she was arrested in April
2010 and, though released on bail, was prohibited from running. In response
to opposition claims that the election was tainted by repression, murder and
lack of credible competition, Kagame said of the result: 'I see no problems,
but there are some people who choose to see problems where there are not.'[16]

Kagame is an enigmatic figure, his outspoken tough-mindedness a light-
ning rod for international criticism, but with an impressive record in driving Rwanda's transition. He is impatient and focused. For him 'development
is a marathon that must be run at a sprint'.[17] Steven Kinzer, his biographer,

credits him with fostering Rwanda's rebirth. But he also cautions against a personality of 'chronic impatience, barely suppressed anger, and impulsive scorn for critics'.[18] Others are even less charitable, seeing him as autocratic at home and fomenting and profiting financially (by trading in minerals) from instability in the neighbouring Congo.

He is tapping into a rich vein of disenchantment, democracy being described by some as a Western 'imposition' on Africa;[19] crudely put, a cost to be endured if African countries want to pick up aid. The contemporary Rwandan choice is rooted in a less ideological perspective, however. While keenly aware of their democratic shortcomings, Rwandan officials puzzle over how to balance representative government against the spectre of their recent, bloody ethnic rivalry. Their history reminds this is no place for academic experimentation or simply trusting in God, people, democracy and institutions.

Rwanda is a monument to policy paradoxes. Kagame supported the removal of the Libyan dictator Muammar Gaddafi in 2011. 'Given the overriding mandate of Operation Odyssey Dawn to protect Libyan civilians from state-sponsored attacks,' wrote Kagame in the local *New Times*, 'Rwanda can only stand in support of it. Our responsibility to protect is unquestionable – this is the right thing to do, and this view is backed up with the authority of having witnessed and suffered the terrible consequences of international inaction.'[20] Kigali has also committed 3 500 troops to the UN peacekeeping mission in Darfur in Sudan.

Kagame has shown no sign at all of changing course in the face of international advice, scorn or threats – whether these are over democracy at home or on the Congo. Contrary to accepted contemporary donor norms and niceties, Kagame has publically questioned the relationship between democracy and development. 'Genuine democracy,' he has remarked, 'can never be equated to election cycles.' The emphasis, he has said, on such 'cycles' is often done at the expense of sustainable socio-economic development. 'Those who disagree with or criticise our development and governance options,' he said in 2013, 'do not provide any suitable or better alternatives. All they do is repeat abstract concepts like freedom and democracy as if doing that alone would improve the human condition. Yet for us, the evidence of results from our choices is the most significant thing.'[21]

Perhaps he is referring to the type of criticism from his erstwhile biographer Kinzer.[22] 'The central task of his second seven-year term,' wrote Kinzer shortly after Kagame won the election in August 2010, 'which by law must be his last, is to add broader democracy to this security and prosperity.' Kinzer warned of his literary subject: Kagame 'still has the chance to enter history as one of the greatest modern African leaders. There is also the chance, however, that he will be remembered as another failed African big-man, a tragic figure who built the foundations of a spectacular future for his country, but saw his achievements collapse because he could not take his country from one-man rule toward democracy.'[23]

Might Rwanda have done better?

The criticism boils down to a single question: in the light of the genocide and its limited economic options, given how countries with a similar history such as Burundi have performed, and given, too, its turbulent region, could Rwanda have done things differently – and in so doing, done better?

It has certainly marshalled scant resources phenomenally well and made significant development progress. In fact, its rate of household poverty decrease illustrates both how well it has done with few resources, and also how badly other better-endowed states perform in this regard.[24] It has actively and diligently, and on its own terms, attracted a stream of international well-wishers and fellow travellers. Nearly always their engagement has been on Rwandan terms, one legacy of the genocide.

Rwanda had a United Nations Assistance Mission (UNAMIR) *in situ* during the horrors. The events were graphically described by its commander, Roméo Dallaire. 'I know there is a God,' said the lieutenant general and later Canadian senator, 'because in Rwanda I shook hands with the devil. I have seen him, I have smelled him and I have touched him. I know the devil exists and therefore I know there is a God.'[25] Although the UN Security Council reinforced UNAMIR in the midst of the genocide on 17 May 1994 with an extra 5 500 soldiers and 50 armoured vehicles, not one additional peacekeeper arrived in Rwanda before the RPF victory in July. 'The world,' recalls the official Rwandan history, 'withdrew ... and watched as a million people were slaughtered.' Or as UN Secretary General Kofi Annan, who had headed the world body's peacekeeping division in 1994, put it ten years on, 'The international community is guilty of sins of omission.'[26]

Understandably, in the circumstances, Kigali has preferred to get on with things in its own way and create the conditions for international engagement, not wait for assistance.

As Kagame noted in a meeting of foreign military and other officials in Kigali in July 2007, even though the success to peace-building is deemed to involve local hearts and minds, 'there is a tendency to formulate a plan externally and impose it on a failed state. If we had not resisted, Rwanda would still be governed by the UN. If [an imposed solution] works, it can only be temporary and in the end it is disastrous. UN officials outside Rwanda tried to convince the world that Rwanda needed UN administration.' Yet, he said, a 'first [UN] mistake is to look at a situation as if all sides [génocidaires, RPF and victims] are the same. Dallaire tried to get me to talk on the same level as the génocidaire government. I could not convince him that one party was wrong and I was right. I'm not sure the UN attitude has changed.' He also added, 'We must decide the priorities for the international community, or at least there must be discussion. NGOs cannot replace governments: they must work with governments. Without coordination, I'd rather not have NGOs.'[27]

This president palpably has limited tolerance for outsiders who believe they know better than his government, who he says present themselves as the 'only saviours', and who especially disdain those who are critical. 'We can't be seen as the ones behind the good story', he says, since the view is 'nothing good can come from us'.[28] Kagame has repeated many times that he is less interested in the perception of himself and his country than 'results', since 'if you have a good perception but nothing is real, it will be exposed',[29] and that freedom involves more than democratic choice, but freedom from want and the need for security. Such a stance has invariably led to some tension with donors and attracted criticism. Kagame is portrayed as 'the global elite's favourite strongman', for example, an 'international hero for reforming Rwanda', a role that 'doesn't come without moral hazards'.[30]

The prevalence of foreign, especially North American, accents in the lobbies of Kigali's burgeoning number of hotels is but one indicator of the predominantly positive external image of the country and its leadership. The Rwandan has built and stoked a personality cult – carefully nurturing influential international friends, and assiduously carving out an image as a benevolent dictator, a leader who delivers. Politicians and other celebrities have found it hard to stay away, both for reasons of conscience and charity, but sometimes just employment. The former British prime minister, Tony Blair, has been a vocal supporter and regular visitor, as has Bill Clinton. The former US president who was in office at the time of the genocide, has said that Rwandans 'rallying around their national pride, have built predictable systems that reward enterprise and hard work, and created an exceptional blueprint for other developing countries';[31] the country is a 'disciplined ... forward-looking place'.[32] In 2010, Blair described Kagame as 'visionary' at a time when others were distancing themselves from the Rwandan leader. Blair, whose African Governance Initiative had established a presence inside the Rwandan presidency two years earlier, added, 'I'm a believer in and a supporter of Paul Kagame. I don't ignore all those criticisms, having said that. But I do think you've got to recognise that Rwanda is an immensely special case because of the genocide. Secondly, you can't argue with the fact that Rwanda has gone on a remarkable path of development. Every time I visit Kigali and the surrounding areas you can just see the changes being made in the country.'[33]

Despite the relative absence of democracy, public sector donors have equally been keenly supportive of Kagame, even twenty years after the genocide contributing half of Kigali's budget. This illustrates a tension for outsiders: on the one hand, between supporting a leader of a government that gets things done, and wanting to make amends for doing too little during the genocide and wishing to prevent another similar event; and on the other hand, insisting on a representative, accountable and open system of government. Rwanda is not the only place where there is such a tension, of course: Ethiopia is another example.

Despite his innate scepticism, Kagame has understandably seen the financial and diplomatic value in opening the country to outsiders keen to help and be part of a success story. Led from the outset by church groups, public and private donors have given handsomely to the Rwandan cause. Private supporters have given to schools, sent cows and malaria nets, and even funded puff publications endorsing the president and his vision.

It is a morality play, a polarised and polarising world for the critic, both outside and in. It is virtually impossible to avoid alienating someone when narrating Rwanda, if not only because of who is doing the telling.

Outside one is either a Kagame apologist or credible critic. Kigali has an equally bifurcated view: friends and supporters on the one hand; and those on the other hand intent on bringing the regime down, destructively tarnishing Rwanda's hard-earned reputation with clichéd, shallow analysis, stooges, unwitting or otherwise, for those who find the RPF victory and rule hard to accept. This aversion to criticism reflects a famous national stoicism and sensitivity to public censure, the latter exacerbated by the schism still around the genocide and its aftermath, possibly to the extent of political

space, and to the injured pride, too, that goes with the years of Western conquest, appropriation and being told by others what to do. The deep-rooted
hurt and insecurity emanating from this latter period is succinctly summed
up by the memorial museum's words: 'We did not choose to be colonised.'

Whatever the reasoning, the world of the Rwandan critic is impossible to
inhabit free from often personalised counter-attacks.

Filip Reyntjens is a well-known opponent of Rwanda's (lack of) political space. He has argued that Rwandan elections are not really exercises in
democracy; they are highly managed affairs in which the result (in the form
of overwhelming victory for the RPF) is guaranteed. The counter-argument
is that Rwanda has developed a 'consensual' model of politics as a necessary
antidote to its recent and explosive political history.[34] That the world is not
so Manichean and uncomplicated is difficult to accept, of course, especially
when the regime is convinced that the stakes are so high and fears, with historical justification, that if their position was undermined, the results may
be deadly. Such fears are compounded by living next to a 'non-state' in the
shape of the Congo, where elements not only profit from the lack of order,
but use it as a base to maintain their resistance to Kigali. None of this excuses the way in which some in Rwanda have made money on the back of a
post-Habyarimana *tabula rasa* and their regime contacts. Nor does it justify
violence as a preventive strategy. But it does highlight the dilemma facing
Kagame and the RPF.

Less controversially, few who have visited Kigali fail to be impressed by
the outwardly orderliness and cleanliness of the hilly capital (even though
the same was said about the Habyarimana regime). Under his leadership,
Kigali has vigorously pursued reforms with great purpose and extraordinary efficiency. By 2008, as highlighted above, Rwanda was among the top
twenty reformers globally in the World Bank's Doing Business indicators. In
2014 it ranked the best performing country in the East African region as well
as second easiest place to do business in sub-Saharan Africa, behind only
Mauritius and ahead of third-ranked South Africa. For the second year running, Rwanda also ranked third in the World Economic Forum's regional
competitiveness tables. Even though this performance tends to gloss over
critical areas of weakness, for example its 160th place ranking in 2014 in 'trading across borders',[35] this illustrates an extraordinary commitment to technocratic reform – in essence, of Rwanda using its scant resources to best effect.

This has translated into improved economic growth. During the 2000s,
Rwanda was among the top ten fastest growing economies worldwide, at

over 7.5 per cent per annum. It has been lauded for its efforts to move from reliance on subsistence agriculture to a technology driven society, 'with an emphasis on home-grown entrepreneurship and foreign direct investment'.[36]

To the outsider, at least, it is a country constantly striving for improvement.

Pitchette Kampeta Sayingoza is the permanent secretary, the principal civil servant, in the Ministry of Finance and Economic Planning. Obviously bright and committed, she speaks passionately about the need for innovation and changing direction.

Until 2000, she says, the focus was on stabilisation, security and conflict resolution, with the government rebuilding around the pillars of providing health care (where nineteen years later there was 93 per cent coverage) and primary education (96 per cent). This required wholesale overhauling of government systems and the courting of donors and foreign investors alike. Donor inflows peaked at 81 per cent of government budget in 1996.

Then, in 'the mid-2000s', she says, Rwanda 'found the missing piece. Up until that time agriculture had been growing at 2 per cent per year.' Given that more than two-thirds of the population lived in the rural area, 'increasing productivity was to have a tremendous impact on poverty'. Since then a growth in agricultural output of more than 8 per cent annually through land reform, including the consolidation of small plots, improved inputs such as seed and fertiliser, and 'massive extension' has 'not only improved food security but improved cash flow for farmers as they moved from subsistence to cash crops'.

Following this progress, the government has turned its attention 'from supply to demand', to 'building markets' for both fresh produce and processed goods – as she terms it, 'from tomatoes to ketchup, from potatoes to chips'. In support of this strategy, she pointed out that the year-on-year export of flour to Congo has expanded by 30 per cent.

Building these markets relates to the biggest contemporary economic challenge faced by Rwanda, which is to balance its books between the import-driven surge in construction and consumer goods with increasing exports. 'The big opportunity', she says, 'is in urbanisation: Rwanda is the second-fastest urbanising country in Africa, but we are also one of the least urbanised. The concentration of cities offers much lower costs of doing business and economies of scale in the provision of infrastructure.' Six major cities are targeted for expansion. The country is looking ahead, too, to building on its relative regional information and communication technology prowess, and to develop further its tourism and conference sectors. Countries with much more have done far worse.

The Kigali of 2014 is, in this regard, unrecognisable from the capital of even five years earlier. 'Imagine if Habyarimana came back today,' exclaimed one Congolese, 'he'll think he has landed in New York!' Forget the burgeoning number of glassy high-rises, rather it is the growth of housing in the outlying suburbs and the matching road network that is more impressive. Where, for example, in Gisozi, there was little more than a bumpy mud track outside the age-old timber yards, five years later there were a series of tarred roads leading to pharmacies and shops advertising the three mobile phone providers between restaurants and other outlets. It is now a different world – but not in every respect.

In getting ahead, Kigali and Kagame have at times allowed spin and ambition to cloud the operational reality and obscure the pursuit of narrower interests. The attempts to create a system that would drive both telemedicine and the One Laptop Per Child programme of Internet-based learning, for example, contrasts with the country's lack of electricity. Rwanda possesses a total installed energy capacity of 110 MW for 11 million people, much of it delivered to Kigali, an amount that would comparatively supply electricity for just 370 000 Brazilians. For all of the talk of broadband connecting every home, most Rwandans still cook with charcoal, wood or dung. There are other issues stifling growth, less to do with hardware than political software. Some of Rwanda's challenges are unlikely to be met by the state alone, yet Kigali's relationship with the private sector is ambivalent. The economy is dominated by the RPF's own business conglomerate, Crystal Ventures (formerly Tri-Star), originally set up to fund the party in exile, today a reputed $500-million enterprise and the largest employer after the Rwanda government. Conflicts of interest that have inexorably arisen have been 'solved' in favour of the RPF's interests, unsurprisingly, which goes some way to explain the challenges that some foreign firms have experienced in accessing and prospering in the Rwandan market. Such crony capitalism contrasts with Rwanda's image of aesthetic incorruptibility and efficiency.

Still, despite its rejection of public criticism, the government does apparently listen and take advice. Crystal Ventures was, in 2013, said to be getting out of its milk and water bottling venture, had sold many of its shares in mobile phone service provider MTN and, Kampeta said, was withdrawing from the NPD-Contraco construction entity. 'Although we are accused of "crowding out" the private sector, we have rather tried to "crowd them in"; remarked Kampeta, 'by using government and party money to build businesses, like the Serena Hotel or the Bank of Kigali, that either did not exist or were doing badly, and then quickly exited.'

The dangers of crowding out and the imperative to crowd in have seemingly been learnt from others, including Singapore, displaying a willingness to learn from others that has not always been the case. Whatever the critics might say, Rwanda has in external public minds quickly moved from an example to be avoided to one to be emulated. A model post-conflict peacebuilder in many respects, determined, single-minded, focused – all of these have been labels used to describe Kagame's intention and policies.

Thus, it has been especially puzzling why the government has stumbled into a series of disasters in the Congo, especially given the economic potential for Rwanda to act as that giant, ungoverned, Central African country's provider of services and much else. This involvement has also been surprising given, in Kampeta's words that, in the wake of the 2008 global financial crisis, the Rwandan government's acute awareness of 'a stricter convergence between foreign policy and foreign aid'.[37]

The Congo domestication

Predictably perhaps, given a leader with strong views, by the start of the second decade of the twenty-first century, sympathy and assistance for Rwanda was looking shaky, with aid being made conditional on Kigali's international relations in particular. The influential *Economist* magazine, for example, described Kagame as 'increasingly ruthless'.[38] The key catalyst was not the state of democracy at home, however, but rather Rwandan support for anti-government forces in the neighbouring Congo, not the first time Kigali had been accused of so doing. Granted, neighbours are like family; you do not choose them. But it would have been betting against Kagame's indubitable diplomatic nous to suggest he was unaware of the risks of long-term engagement in a state that famously has consumed those who have attempted to establish order from outside, from King Leopold on.

Since 1994, Rwanda's international and domestic relations have become inextricably and increasingly negatively linked to the Congo. At the time of the Lusaka Agreement in July 1999, ending the Second Congo War, Kagame reputedly told his troops that they should pull back from the Congo and adhere to the deal, given the risks of being 'domesticated' by the giant Central African country.

At first, Kigali's Congo presence was motivated by the need for security, in crude terms to chase the remaining genocidaire element away or kill them. As part and parcel of this imperative, given that he no longer ruled the territory, it was Kigali that organised and sponsored the removal of Mobutu Sese Seko in a short campaign ending in May 1997, and installed Laurent Kabila in his place, thereby controlling the army and essentially Kinshasa itself. A year later, with relations worsening, Kabila asked the Rwandans to depart, and Kigali attempted to do the same to him, which ended in failure, with Rwandan forces overstretched and Angolans and Zimbabweans more heavily involved on Kinshasa's side.

During this time, Rwanda also got embroiled in a series of deadly skirmishes with its one-time sponsor and ally, Uganda, ostensibly over control of the airport at Kisangani. According to some, this had everything to do with the control over resources; for others, it was about enmity between the former allies, of the perception by the Rwandans that the Ugandans, in whose army many Rwandans including Kagame once fought, looked down on them.[39]

Since then Kigali has stood accused of supporting Laurent Nkunda's Congolese rebel movement, and, more recently, of sponsoring a new variant. A UN report released in October 2012 said the country was running an armed rebellion in the form of the M23 group, which stood accused of human rights abuses in the Congo. According to (largely circumstantial) evidence in the report, the mainly Congolese Tutsi M23 were directly commanded by Rwanda's defence minister, General James Kaberebe, once upon a time the chief of staff of the Congolese army under Laurent Kabila, and the military mentor of his son and successor, Joseph.[40]

Unsurprisingly, Kigali and Kampala (which was also implicated) angrily rejected the accusations. Then, in October 2013, the US, a long-time Kagame ally, imposed sanctions on the Rwandan military in the wake of the allegations that Kigali was sponsoring M23, which was said to have child soldiers in its ranks.[41] In early November 2013, M23 collapsed after a joint assault by the Armed Forces of the Democratic Republic of Congo and UN forces, and both its leaders and foot soldiers sought exile in Uganda.

In part, this shift in fortunes reflected realpolitik, at least the Congolese part. It was wholly naive to expect Rwanda to act differently in securing its own security interests and or to remain indifferent to the fate of Congolese

Tutsi-inhabiting eastern Congo when the UN was apparently so powerless and the Congolese government at best disinterested to act against the remnants of the forces that committed the genocide. There have also been economic interests at stake. But the Congo's instability could not be Rwanda's fault alone. As the finance secretary rails, 'It's hypocritical. When was the Congo apparently better before?' she asked rhetorically. 'The international community accuses us of interfering when they want Congo to be fixed, even though they don't know how to fix it.'

But it was puzzling why Kagame, the arch-strategist, would allow himself to be drawn into a country so deeply that the Congo has at once both, in the words of one Rwandan military officer, 'domesticated' (in Congolese political and economic terms) and negatively internationalised Kigali.

Finding a better way?

'One of the asymmetries of history,' wrote Henry Kissinger of Singapore's Lee Kuan Yew, 'is the lack of correspondence between the abilities of some leaders and the power of their countries.'[42] Kissinger's one-time boss, Richard Nixon, was even more flattering. He speculated that, had Lee lived in another time and another place, he might have 'attained the world stature of a Churchill, a Disraeli, or a Gladstone'. In other words: it was a shame Lee had a small country.

For Lee made great strides. By the 1990s, Singapore's per capita GDP was higher than that of its erstwhile colonial master Britain. It had assiduously targeted multinational companies to use the island as their base, both to supply capital, but also necessary technology and know-how. Today Singapore has the world's busiest port and is the third-largest oil refiner. Lee managed this extraordinary transformation within a generation. The corollary of the tough decisions he had to make was the maintenance of an authoritarian regime. In his own words, he did not believe that 'democracy necessarily leads to development. I believe,' said Lee, 'what a country needs to develop is discipline more than democracy'.[43] Lee's approach was founded in the painful separation of Singapore from Malaya, and the racial tensions inherent in a crowded, multi-ethnic society. As he reflected on his country's independence on 9 August 1965, 'Some countries are born independent. Some achieve independence. Singapore had independence thrust upon it.' In a referendum three years before, his government had 'persuaded' 70 per cent of the electorate to vote in favour of a merger with Malaya. 'Nothing had changed – except that we were out,' recalled Lee. 'We had said that an independent Singapore was simply not viable. Now it was our unenviable task to make it work. How were we to create,' he asked, 'a nation out of a polyglot collection of migrants from China, India, Malaysia, Indonesia and several other parts of Asia? … We were a Chinese island in a Malay sea. How could we survive in such a hostile environment?'[44]

The same might be asked of Burundi and Rwanda.

Will economic growth without acknowledging ethnicity – the Rwandan way under Kagame – ultimately deliver? Or is the Burundi method to openly manage ethnic differences better in the long run, though in the short term it has complicated governance, worsened rent-seeking and compounded low economic growth? Or what potentially of a hybrid: Kagame's intense, technocratic, impatient development model matched with Burundi's relative democratic and ethnic openness? The latter is at least an option for the RPF in Rwanda given their status as a victor, where they have the power to choose the type and extent of political freedoms, but less so for Burundi.

Why bother with such a question? There is a concern that in Rwanda, ethnicity is artificially suppressed, that one day, instead of withering away it will explode, again, in the face of the Tutsi population, especially as the original RPF generation age and their grip loosens. According to such logic, contrary to Kagame's intent that economic progress will suppress tribal ties, Rwanda's economic progress is, for some, at the root of opposition to Kagame. 'Economically he is doing really well, but like most despots, he is doing that at the expense of political openness,' says Thomas Tieku, a conflict-mediation specialist based at the University of Toronto. 'Those who are benefiting from the economy will quietly support him. But others absolutely can't stand him.'[45]

A more full-fledged democracy would, according to this argument, offer a built-in conflict resolution mechanism. In South Africa, to take another example where identity pervades, the race card is routinely played by politicians already in power to their advantage because they are the majority. In Rwanda, this is forbidden, because the government is the minority and also because they know the terrible cost of doing so. However, there is a shared challenge between South Africa and both Burundi and Rwanda. Progress in all is always going to be difficult if significant chunks of the population see themselves as victims of, rather than partners in, change. Kagame has to avoid being hoisted by his own petard, given his dismissal of foreign 'imposed solutions', as above, yet standing accused of imposing his own Tutsi dictatorship. The sense of exclusion that drove the hate of the first post-independence Hutu government and of the extremists under Habyarimana is unlikely to be ameliorated in this environment.[46]

For it is unclear also what the longer-term effect will be of the accrual of the country's economic gains largely to the RPF's core (although increasingly fractured) constituency as income inequality grows. While the current government uses its genocide credit to assert its carte blanche in remaking the country in its vision, this is exclusive rather than inclusive, and not only on ethnic lines, even though such politics, whether of inclusion or exclusion, is a strategy of political and military elites (in Burundi, too). Such discourse determines who is included (good, hard-working citizens who work towards the vision of the government) and who is not (broadly speaking, government critics and dissenters).[47]

Kagame would like to achieve for his country what Lee and his successors have done for Singapore. Certainly, Rwanda has learnt some lessons from the island state, not least the establishment of an overarching Rwanda Development Board to attract foreign investment and coordinate government. Yet, there are important differences. As Lee has observed, 'social cohesion through sharing the benefits of progress' and 'equal opportunities for all and meritocracy, with the best man or woman for the job, especially in leaders in government' were his 'basic principles that have helped us progress'.[48] Whereas Singapore has incomparable location and could feed into and off other nearby high-growth economies, Rwanda is landlocked in a difficult neighbourhood.

The global context is also different. Democracies were an exception, not the rule, in the 1960s and 1970s. Today the opposite holds. While ongoing instability in the Congo might be akin to the insecurity faced by the East Asian periphery during the American-Vietnam war, the threats to Rwanda are more direct on its western border, and there is no superpower providing an overall security guarantee as a first and last resort as the US did for Asia. And while Singapore received considerable aid, especially from Britain (£50 million in 1968, 75 per cent of which was in the form of loans, and all to be spent on British goods and services) to make up for the loss of British military expenditure between 1968 and 1971,[49] this pales by comparison to Rwanda's and, especially, Burundi's annual aid tranche as a percentage of government income. Despite Kagame's trenchant criticism of donors, Rwanda's progress has been more aid driven than he would like to admit.

More than any of this, however, is Rwanda's challenge in its need to bring along the majority of the population, where the principal beneficiaries are ethnically aligned to the person in charge. Here the official tagline of the genocide commemoration, 'genocide against the Tutsi', is far from aligned to the nation-building mantra of government.[50] At some point, the Tutsi in Rwanda will have to stop wanting to appear the victim of those terrible days and see the Hutu, by deed and words, equally so. The response, like the problem, cannot be solely technocratic, but political. As Kagame has put it, 'Sustainable socio-economic development gives rise to greater democracy.'[51]

This will take time, perhaps a generation, or more. As Burundi's President Nkurunziza reminds us, 'We spent 20 years killing each other ... and changing that mentality takes years.'[52] It has to happen, however, as the fundamental costs of identity over issue politics are high, where the government is held accountable only by one social group, and its actions and interests are therefore geared to this elite. Such *extractive*, to use the terminology of Daron Acemoğlu and James Robinson, rather than *inclusive* societies are unsustainable in the long run, given their lack of 'agencies of restraint', including a vibrant opposition and the institutions that go with it. The ultimate antidote for identity politics – the extraction environment – revolves around instituting a 'high level of political rights'.[53] Not breaking this cycle of extractive government and predicating change entirely on control and economic growth is a huge gamble, one that risks further violent reaction, whatever labels are put on it.

22

CHILE TO ZAMBIA

Natural Resources – During and After the Rush

*

'There is *naaahting* here,' implored the driver about job prospects in Kimberley in South Africa's depressed Northern Cape region. 'But we still have good security. And we are hoping,' he emphasised the last word in a northern *Kaaaap* twang, 'that the university will come and create jobs.' As we headed out of the city he pointed to the area on the left-hand side of the road and instantly contradicted himself: 'Greenpoint, that's one of the worst areas for crime. You must not go there.'

Things get worse the further out you go. Jan Kempdorp, 100 kilometres to the north, once the site of a concentration camp for German sympathis-ers during the Second World War, depended on income from farming and labour on Kimberley's and Kuruman's mines. 'Now there is nothing,' shrugs Gladys, 51, who came to Johannesburg to look for a job. 'There is no work, and many have been forced to go off the white farmers' land because they also have no money. People sit by the side of the road,' she says gesticulating with her finger pointed up, 'like this, waiting for work, all day, for nothing. The best is that you get R280 per child a month from welfare, or R1 200 if you are over 60. If you live that long,' she added shyly. South Africa's unem-ployment rate (including those who were no longer looking for work) was touching 40 per cent in 2013; in Jan Kempdorp it is much higher. Although democracy in 1994 brought political equality in South Africa, cities were laid out by apartheid, and economic inequality persists. The dispossession of African land and the enforcement of racial segregation went hand in hand with the 'opening up' of South Africa's interior and the development of its mineral booty.[1]

Kimberley, the city that is globally synonymous with diamonds and riches, and has even given its name to the geological pipe that bears diamonds and the global regulatory regime for the gems, highlights all the post-boom problems and the dilemma facing many resource-rich countries in Africa and weak states elsewhere – how to get more out of natural resources while they are still coming out of the ground?

The Kimberley story

The story of Barney Barnato, Cecil Rhodes, Kimberley and the mining of diamonds is inextricably linked to the story of South Africa's development, warts and all.

Rhodes is now commonly caricatured as an arch-imperialist, racist and capitalist, an image not helped by ambitious Cape-to-Cairo schemes, a ruthless character, with visions of Africa (and elsewhere) dominated by Anglo-Saxons, and the existence of the once-eponymous white-ruled republic immediately to South Africa's north. 'It is redundant to wonder whether Rhodes was a racist,' writes Jeremy Paxman, 'as to question whether he wore a moustache on his self-satisfied face, for the evidence is overwhelming. When he plotted his Cape-to-Cairo railway or, as prime minister of the Cape, cast lustful eyes on the lands beyond the Limpopo and Zambezi rivers he was not thinking of the welfare of anyone but the Anglo-Saxon race.' Yet his impact was unmistakeable. Mark Twain was one who, unable to decide on Rhodes as 'a lofty patriot or the devil incarnate', observed that 'when he stands on the Cape of Good Hope, his shadow falls to the Zambezi'.[2] And focusing on his racism and imperialist ambition alone does not do justice to the entrepreneurship that necessarily lies behind economic development and progress, or of Rhodes' strategic guile and steel, evident in the risks he took in wagering a fortune and the manner in which he outmanoeuvred his opponents. Never was this more apparent than in the way he dealt over Kimberley with his greatest business challenger – and pretender.

Barney Barnato, born Barnet Isaacs in London's East End in 1851, became a prize-fighter and music-hall turn before he and his brother Harry joined his cousin David Harris in the Cape in 1873, four years into the 'diamond rush', the athletic Barnato walking from the Cape to Kimberley and carrying a box of cigars as the means to start a business. From humble beginnings as a 'kopje-walloper' – an itinerant diamond buyer scouring the mines in search of spot purchases of cheap diamonds – within a decade, the Barnato Diamond Mining Company was competing with Rhodes over the amalgamation of the untold diggings.

The rivalry ended when Rhodes bought him out for a shade under £5.4 million in March 1888, an amount equivalent 120 years later to more than £2 billion, the biggest private cheque ever cut at that time. Rhodes claimed to have learnt early on in Kimberley in his efforts to convince a farmer to sell a water pump that would start him on his business fortune that 'every man has his price'. So Barnato had his, if a rather large one.

Thus emerged De Beers Consolidated Mines, grew the reach of the British colony into the interior, deepened and formalised the segregation of races, and proceeded South Africa's industrialisation. In the process, diamond mining and marketing was transformed from an idealistic scramble centring on the wild and woolly activities of frontiersmen (and a few women) to a (more) stable industry around bankers, financiers and romantic consumers. But wild it was.

The rush can be traced back to 1866 when Erasmus Jacobs found a small brilliant pebble – later known as the 'Eureka', a 21.5-carat diamond – on the banks of the Orange River, on the De Kalk farm. There years later the larger 'Star of South Africa' (47.69 carats) was also found there, and in 1869, an even larger 83.50-carat stone was found on the slopes of Colesberg Kopje on the farm Vooruitzigt belonging to the De Beer brothers. What followed was less a rush, however, as the historian Brian Roberts has noted, than a 'stampede'.[3] Within a month 800 claims were cut into the Colesberg hillock, worked by as many as 3 000 men. As the land was lowered so the hillock became a mine – first the New Rush and later the Kimberley Mine or Big Hole.

Nearly two years after colonial commissioners had arrived in the town of New Rush in November 1871 to exercise authority over the territory on behalf of the Cape government, the town changed its name to Kimberley. Annexation to the Cape Colony followed inevitably in 1877. By then it was the second-largest town in South Africa after Cape Town, with a permanent population of 13 000 whites and 30 000 blacks. An estimated additional 50 000 black labourers migrated to the town annually on short-term contracts to work for the 5 000 independent diggers. Inevitably, there was soon controversy about the rights of black landowners and diggers, the latter complaining about the high pay that black labour was able to command given the demand. The Mining Act of 1883 formally turned the tables, decreeing that 'no native' was allowed to handle explosives and work on a mine except under the charge of a white man. From 1885, mine owners decided to house black mine workers in Kimberley in closed compounds. To access the town, 'African workers passed through a guarded gate, along a fenced walkway to the mine they worked at, and returned the same way. The only difference was that they were searched for diamonds on their return. They could only leave these compounds to go down the mine or to return home at the end of their contracts.'[4]

It was also a frontier den of iniquity, amidst the heat, dust, high prices and barren landscape,[5] a mix of drinking saloons, 'mean-looking' corrugated-iron houses and canteens 'bereft of comfort', gambling dens, the tents of diamond *kopers* (buyers) and hosts of prostitutes, all aiming to take the fortune off the men as quickly as it had been found. Rhodes and Alfred Beit, his banker and a partner in De Beers, would start their day with a customary Black Velvet at the Kimberley Club, a mixture of champagne and stout that Rhodes claimed 'makes a man of you'.[6] Although there was no alcohol officially sold on Sundays, 'it was common for men to buy several bottles of alcohol before the bars closed on Saturday night and to sell their contents on Sundays. The result was that as many as 50 per cent of the men failed to report for work on a Monday.'[7] A Scottish doctor, Josiah Matthews, estimated that two-thirds of his caseload could be traced to alcohol, the most popular drink being Cape Smoke, 'a powerful brandy, never matured and frequently adulterated by unscrupulous canteen keepers and illicit liquor dealers'.[8]

As miners arrived in their thousands, the Colesberg Hill disappeared and was replaced by the Big Hole – the largest man-dug hole in the world, 463 metres wide, with a perimeter of 1.6 kilometres, and 240 metres deep. Underneath the Big Hole, the rest of the mine's Kimberlite pipe was mined to a depth of 1 097 metres, excavating 22.5 million tonnes of earth in the process.

In partnership with Charles Rudd, Rhodes built up a large holding in the De Beer's mine, and on 1 April 1880, they launched a joint stock company as the De Beers Mining Company. Others were doing the same. By 1879 just twelve companies controlled 75 per cent of Kimberley. Consolidation of the diggings ultimately brought improved safety standards, but at a terrible cost: by 1886, in the rush to increase production to wipe out smaller miners, the death rate at the De Beers mine had reached 150 per 1 000 employed.[9] The disease and danger saw, by 1888, the death rate among Africans rise to almost 100 per 1 000, making Kimberley one of the deadliest towns in the world.[10]

The hub of early industrialisation in South Africa, the city also housed South Africa's first bourse, the Kimberley Royal Stock Exchange, which opened on 2 February 1881. It became the first town in the southern hemisphere to install electric street lighting in September 1882. South Africa's first school of mines was opened here in 1896, though it relocated to Johannesburg. Less salubriously, Kimberley was the start, also, of South Africa's migrant labour and compound system, later copied on Johannesburg's Gold Fields. Blacks quickly became a subordinate labour force only, and legislation followed, including the 1913 Natives Land Act, which drove scores of peasant farmers off their land. African writer Sol Plaatje, a leading member of the African National Congress and after whom the Kimberley municipality is today named (and the envisaged Kimberley university will be an eponymous tribute), records how he found bands of African peasants travelling all over the Orange Free State from farmer to farmer in the hope of finding shelter. 'It was heartrending,' he wrote, 'to listen to the tales of their cruel experiences derived from the rigour of the Natives Land Act. Some of their cattle had perished on the journey, from poverty and lack of fodder, and the native owners ran a serious risk of imprisonment for travelling with dying stock. The experience of one of these evicted tenants is typical of the rest, and illustrates the cases of several we met in other parts of the country.'[11] In his account in *Native Life in South Africa*, he noted, 'It looks as if these people were so many fugitives escaping from a war.'[12]

The 1911 South African Census recorded a 'native' population of 4 019 006 in the Union of South Africa, 67.3 per cent of the total population of 5 973 394, of which whites made up 1 276 242 (or 21.4 per cent). According to the findings of the Beaumont Commission established in terms of the Natives Land Act, farms owned by whites constituted 74 per cent of the total at that time, native reserves and native-owned farms 8.9 per cent and Crown (state) lands some 12.4 per cent.[13] Questions of morality apart, the dangers of the Act were, even then, self-evident. John X. Merriman, MP for Victoria West, said of the Act in the debate on the second reading of the Bill, House of Assembly on 15 May 1913: 'A policy more foredoomed to failure in South Africa could not be initiated. It was a policy that would keep South Africa back, perhaps forever. What would be the effect of driving these civilised Natives back into reserves? At the present time, every civilised man – if they treated him properly – every civilised man was becoming an owner of land outside native reserve, and therefore he was an asset of strength to the country. He was a loyalist. He was not going to risk losing his property. He was on the side of the European. If they drove these people back into reserves they became our bitterest enemies.'[14] And so the stage was set for the next 80 years of racial separation, economic marginalisation and consequent political unrest.

Barnato died in 1897 in mysterious circumstances, officially lost overboard near the island of Madeira whilst on a passage home to England. His money went mostly to his two-year-old son, Joel Woolf, who proceeded to make a smaller fortune from a large one in supporting Bentley and its motorsport ambitions, including at Le Mans, where he won the 24-hour motor race three times in a row in the late 1920s.

During the consolidation negotiations, Woolf had asked Rhodes about his arguments for extending his commercial and political interests across the continent. 'Aren't those just dreams of the future? Dreams,' said Joel, 'don't pay dividends.' 'No, my friend,' replied Rhodes, 'they're not dreams, they're plans. There's a difference.'[15] But Rhodes' politics hardened and money became more important as he grew older, John X. Merriman complaining in 1891 that with few exceptions 'all his familiars are self-seekers and stuff him with adulation for their own purposes'. After a 1892 corruption scandal involving the issuing of a tender to James Logan, a former railway porter, to enable a monopoly of food services on the railway, Rhodes was exposed, in one-time friend Olive Schreiner's eyes, 'with all his gifts of genius ... below the fascinating surface, the worms of falsehood and corruption creeping.'[16]

In the Cape parliament Rhodes also led on measures to formalise racial segregation, spending money on white public schools over 'Coloured' education, supporting the imposition of curfews on Africans as Kimberley had done, leading with legislation to create a 'native' reserve in the Eastern Cape, and encouraging separation in railways and sport. Seen as increasingly rude, dictatorial, overbearing and ambitious by former friends and colleagues, his political career ended in ignominy with the infamous Jameson Raid to launch a coup in the Transvaal in December 1895. He died, seeking relief from the sea air for his respiratory condition, in his humble cottage at St James in Cape Town in March 1902 at the early age of 48. On his final day, 26 March 1902, as he lay gasping, 'purple' in the face, looking like a man deep into his seventies, his friend and biographer Lewis Mitchell heard him murmur, 'So little done, so much to do.'[17]

Kimberley's luck eventually also ran out. The original Big Hole, the old Kimberley Mine, closed in 1914 after 14 million carats had been officially mined, though with smuggling by the early myriad diggers the unofficial figure is perhaps several times this number. Although De Beers is still searching for gems in the tailings from the mine dumps, all its other underground mines nearby had closed by the end of the first decade of the twenty-first century.

A combination of 'alcohol abuse, unemployment and zero prospects' have made the Northern Cape, of which Kimberley is the capital, South Africa's 'most violent province', with the highest rape and assault rates countrywide. As one Cuban doctor working in Kimberley said in patching up yet another stab victim, 'Know what's your country's national sport? Stabbing.' With assault and rape bunched as 'social fabric crimes', a 2000 study showed a 'disturbingly close link' between attackers and their victims, 'indicating a widespread breakdown in families and personal relationships. One in five violent attacks were by a family member, partner or ex-partner, while more than half the perpetrators were a friend or acquaintance.'[18] Since then, officially the unemployment rate for the province has declined from 35.7 per cent in 2001 to 27.4 per cent in 2011, and the government claims the average household income had 'more than doubled' over the same period.[19] But it is not clear where these improvements come from, apart from definitional tinkering. With a number of high-profile corruption cases, the opposition Democratic Alliance has described the region's governance as mired in 'ineptness'.[20] And the authorities are largely bereft of plans for development save for building the aforementioned university and strengthening the conference and tourist attractions of the now 100 000-strong city. Like the 1870s, it is a big black hole of governance and social maladies but absent of the nineteenth-century entrepreneurial zeal.

Namibia's forbidden areas

Inside the Namdeb building in Windhoek are two diamond-sorting floors. Eighteen men and women peer through magnifying glasses each year at 1.5 million carats of annual Namibian production, worth some $850 million in exports. Small, less valuable yellow or darker stones are graded in lots; the bigger stones, two carats or more, are individually sorted. It is a high-security environment, with one of the diamonds, at over 80 carats, touching $3 million in value. Namibia's Diamond Trading Centre is at the heart both of the country's commercial sector and the city itself.[21]

For all of the construction happening around its outskirts, erecting shopping malls and townhouses, Windhoek's city centre is sleepy, if tidy. Perhaps it is the heat. Perhaps also it is the fact that government employs 100 000 of Namibia's two million people – that private enterprise is the smaller player. It is estimated that the ratio of government employees to dependants is not less than 1:17.

The next largest employer is Namdeb, the government-De Beers joint venture, and its related businesses, with little over 2 500 workers. Such imbalance between the public and private sectors is not a long-term bet for prosperity. The public sector wage bill is ultimately paid for by the taxes generated by the private sector, in Namibia as elsewhere.

Diamonds were discovered in the Namib Desert in April 1908 near Lüderitz on the coast, when Zacharias Lewala, a former worker from the Kimberley diamond fields, found a diamond near the railway. Shortly after he handed it to his supervisor, a diamond rush to the desert sands resulted in the mining of seven million carats for colonial Germany until the start of the First World War in 1914, following the declaration of the 350-kilometre Sperrgebiet (Forbidden Territory) of coastline in 1908.[22] The deposits were so rich that diamonds could simply be scooped from the valley floors and, later, vacuumed from the seabed.

After the war, the territory of German South-West Africa (SWA) was placed under South African control in the form of a League of Nations trusteeship. Disputes over this process and the desire for local self-government resulted ultimately in the formation of the South-West African People's Organisation (SWAPO) in April 1960, and the guerrilla war that ensued against South African control. But there were also disputes right from the start: British Prime Minister David Lloyd George was unimpressed by his South African counterpart General Jan Smuts' arguments for annexation on the grounds that SWA was 'only a small country'. Lloyd George said in reply, 'But, General, that reminds me of the unmarried Welsh girl who was asked if she was pregnant and replied: "It's only a small baby".'[23]

Shortly after the war, the various colonial mining companies were combined into the Consolidated Diamond Mines of South West Africa, later renamed CDM, by Ernest Oppenheimer, and which was granted the rights to the Sperrgebiet. The diamondiferous beaches near Oranjemund yielded 65 million carats of high-quality gems over the next 80 years, with a further 12 million sucked out of the sea, an area first exploited in the 1950s.

Following independence from South Africa in March 1990, CDM was transformed into the 50:50 Namdeb venture. But it is not as if the government does not get its chunk. Under the terms of a 2011 agreement, the state keeps about 93 cents in value of each dollar mined by Namdeb.[24] Of course, government would like to see even more value retained locally in the form of polishing and sales facilities. About 10 per cent of diamonds are traded and cut locally, though expanding this percentage is challenging, given the relative costs with other polishing centres. At upwards of $75 per carat, the cost of doing so in Namibia is at least three times higher than India, for example.

As for other options for economic growth, with two-thirds of the population living in the rural sector,[25] half of the population depends on agriculture, even though Namibia still relies on food imports. It enjoys good fishing on the rich Atlantic coast, and there is potential in other mining areas, particularly uranium.

In tourism, Namibia hosts a million visitors a year, ranked by *Lonely Planet* in 2010 as the fifth-best tourist destination worldwide for value. However, only a quarter of the million visitors are estimated to be genuine tourists as opposed to shoppers across the northern border with Angola. Regardless, the sector brings in an estimated $750 million annually, or 15 per cent of GDP.

But there are other unrealised development prospects, and the most exciting ones will depend on government doing things differently. These are not the sometimes mooted schemes to build a nuclear power station by 2018 or to resettle the land owned by 4 000 mainly white commercial farmers. Indeed, the government has shown little appetite to go down that route, so far, not least since the bulk of its voters, the Oshivambo, comprising half of Namibians, were the least affected of all Namibia's tribes by the colonial land-grab.

Rather, they hinge around developing the offshore Kudu gas field and dams on the Angolan border, both of which offer the prospect of energy self-sufficiency. Namibia imports 70 per cent of its electricity. It could, with refurbishment of the Atlantic port of Walvis Bay, including improved transport links, offer an alternative outlet to landlocked neighbours Zambia, Zimbabwe and Botswana, and even the southern Democratic Republic of Congo. And its relatively developed logistics and other service sectors could provide a nearby solution to northern neighbour Angola's needs in this regard.

None of this is going to be easy. The challenges experienced by Namibia Breweries, purveyors of the Windhoek Lager brand, in breaking into the South African and Angolan markets are illustrative. Challenges in penetrating the latter market – 'selling beer to a thirsty neighbour' as one observer put it – speaks to issues of protectionism and corruption in Angola and its paternalism towards Namibia. More encouragingly, from virtually no market share twenty years earlier, the Brewery has today a 10 per cent slice of South Africa's 28-million hectolitre annual beer consumption, and is aggressively targeting the Botswana, Zambia, Mozambique and Tanzania markets.

Indeed, there is much to be positive about in Namibia. Human rights have been entrenched and the era of impunity under white rule has ended. Elections are staged regularly, two presidents have left at the end of their mandatory two terms, and the media is very lively. It has come a long way in the generation since the end of apartheid.

South African business people also acknowledge their Namibian counterparts as 'good at getting things done, in executing against a strategy' and as 'easier to get things done'. Labour is passive compared to South Africa, with strikes 'unheard of' outside the mining sector. But at the same time, growing corruption and slow decision-making in government and the 'stagnant policy terrain' are all cited as impediments. Corruption is seen as having worsened with the arrival of Chinese businesses, especially dominant in the construction sector, which are seen as having 'scant respect for labour standards'. Education and skills are problematic, too, despite the dedication of one-fifth of the government budget to this sector.

Unsurprisingly, there are huge wealth divides, skewing Namibia's 'upper middle-income status' of $4 700 per capita: a case of 'extreme wealth of Windhoek's big cars versus', in the words of one Namibian executive, 'the vast majority struggling to survive'. Though unemployment is officially under 30 per cent, unofficial estimates all put joblessness 'north of half the population'.[26]

More than anything, however, the greatest hindrance to economic growth and employment is the lack of experience of senior government people in business. In part, this is induced by their generation's fascination with politics. 'Where people were in the struggle determines who runs the show and how they view others'. In part, such stagnation is additionally determined by the 'extent to which the energy of the older guys has petered out'. And, in part, this is driven by the party's need to 'spend money, create jobs and win votes'.

What it amounts to is the dominance of a single party and the state in the economy: young people aim at that sector for employment and 'define their state of living by their relationship with government'. The country has stagnated in terms of ideas and competitiveness. It slipped eighteen places between 2012–14 in the World Bank's Doing Business rankings to 98/189,[27] and similarly dropped on the World Economic Forum's competitiveness listings from 74th out of 139 states surveyed in 2010/11 to 83/142 in 2011/12 to 92/144 a year later. According to the 2013 report, an inadequately educated workforce was the main factor hampering Namibia's competitiveness, followed by the access to financing.[28]

Certainly the cost and access to finance for entrepreneurs are a constraint. The financial markets are poorly developed. Micro-loan businesses' monthly interest charges to borrowers range from 26 per cent (for payroll-deducted loans) up to 100 per cent (for unsecured loans), yet this had grown to be a R1-billion business in Namibia by 2013.

Behind stagnation is politics. The dominance of SWAPO[29] – the party routinely takes two-thirds of the parliamentary seats – means there is little political pressure to 'do anything' or 'have new ideas' or 'make any changes'. Though a National Planning Commission turns out the obligatory five-year national plans, these remain vague goals and are seldom debated – a new forbidden area if you will. There is a need, says one civil society analyst, 'for a more energetic, enlightened political leadership'. It is a country living, as one business person noted, 'on past profitability' of diamonds and other sectors, fine for now, but flagging a plausible cocktail of widening wealth divides, increasing political tensions and populist policy radicalisation in the future.

Botswana's challenge beyond diamonds

On each new visit to Botswana one cannot but be impressed by the former British protectorate's progress. New buildings, new roads, new enterprises (including the diamond-sorting plant just outside the airport), new hotels, a plethora of Chinese restaurants, new shopping malls and even a new airport terminal.

It is easy to forget the situation at independence in 1966. Possessing then just 10 kilometres of tarmac road, Botswana was one of the least developed and poorest nations in the world, with a per capita income little over US$70. The majority of the population was dependent on subsistence agriculture.

There were just under 30 000 people in salaried employment and little over the same number of migrant workers, mostly employed in South

Africa's mines. Their remittances totalled around one-fifth of Botswana's total exports. There were fewer than 50 university graduates, literacy was scandalously low, and there was scant access to health, sanitation, water, telephones, electricity, public transportation and other services.

Botswana depended then on British foreign aid not only to develop, but to survive.

By the turn of the twenty-first century, Botswana's per capita GDP was more than South Africa's, at over $14 000 in purchasing-power terms. Botswana learnt quickly how to gain maximum value from its natural resources, in this case diamonds, establishing a productive relationship with De Beers.

Diamonds were first discovered in appreciable quantities in Botswana in 1967. The De Beers Botswana Mining Company, later rebranded as Debswana, a 50:50 government-De Beers venture, was launched originally in 1969. The Orapa mine and the Jwaneng pipe, the richest diamond mine in the world, followed. Diamonds, partnership and governance have been at the core of the Botswanan success story. Botswana produces 35 million carats a year, more than a quarter of global diamond production.

But this success has created other problems. Diamonds account for 35 per cent of GDP and around 85 per cent of exports. As much of the rest of the economy lives off the diamond industry, Botswana's dependence on diamonds is almost total.

This has not been lost on successive governments.

In 2005, a colleague and I assembled a group of international specialists at the invitation of the government of Botswana to help devise a strategy for economic diversification. This was a great opportunity of work in a country that had done all of the hard work. Atypical of much of our work in Africa, this did not involve recovering a traumatic period of collapse. The foundation of diamonds was already in place; the 40th anniversary of independence in 2006 offered a moment to take this to the next level.

Out of these preliminary discussions emerged the Botswana Economic Advisory Committee, which was to oversee this strategy. But very little happened. In part, this may have been down to not having the right people leading the Committee; in part bad timing given the temporary collapse of the diamond market in 2009; but in part something else.

This was not, of course, the first time that Botswana had attempted to diversify, though various efforts have consistently been costly failures. The Financial Assistance Policy, terminated in 1999, provided labour and capital subsidies. Very few of the 3 000 operations started under this programme survive. The Citizen Entrepreneurial Development Agency policy that replaced the Financial Assistance Policy offered low-interest loans along with mentoring and support programmes, but met with very limited success.

These failures ask whether government would have been better off passing these grants as savings to businesses and citizens alike in the form of lower tax rates? Instead of creating permanent jobs, these schemes institutionalised inefficiencies and high operating costs, even though to Botswana's credit, it closed them down, a rarity in the developing world, given powerful political constituencies usually quickly gather around subsidy programmes.

Regardless, the underlying structural challenges of the economy persist.

The reason that these efforts failed, like the twenty-first-century endeavour, is largely because of apathy and the wrong choices. Little other than the former explains why the new, Chinese-built airport in Gaborone remained, two years later, only partially completed. Life on diamonds is too easy. 'When they wake up in the morning,' reminded a Costa Rican colleague of this phenomenon, 'they know they have only to work half a day since half their income is guaranteed. We on the other hand,' he reflected, 'have to work from the moment we wake up – there is no natural resource dividend.'[30]

Bad choices are easier to remedy than bad mindset, even though both actions are necessary to get beyond diamonds in Botswana's case.

A first thing for Gaborone to do in this regard would be to reduce the costs of doing business to below that of its nearest and greatest competitor – South Africa. This does not demand subsidies, but a general improvement of the competitiveness environment. This includes addressing the high value of its currency, the pula, one of the effects of natural resource dependency and inflows, and the costs of banking and telecommunications.

More than anything, however, success at diversification requires making growth and development the central objective of government policy, the issue that every president should concentrate on from morning to night, every day, every week, month and year. This would make Botswana, poised as it has been for a while on the cusp of a new, 'second' stage of development, really different, developing from assets other than resources.

Such a laser focus on development is, after all, what set much of East Asia and parts of Latin America on a different trajectory, but is uncommon in Africa. Chile is a case study in using natural resources to full advantage in spite of a recent, violent political history.

The Chile transformation

'He may have been a son-of-a-bitch, but he was our son-of-a-bitch.' This is the description that Vernon Walters, former deputy director of the CIA under Richard Nixon, offered of General Augusto Pinochet Ugarte of Chile. The coup that deposed President Salvador Allende and brought Pinochet to power on 11 September 1973 remains a defining point in Chile's economic fortunes, as much as it is a sticking point politically.

Walters' paraphrasing of Franklin Roosevelt's remarks allegedly made about the Nicaraguan dictator, Anastasio Somoza, in 1939, reminds of the differences in the manner in which the former Chilean strongman is viewed in the international community – between respect for his economic reforms and extreme distaste over his human rights record. At least 3 000 people were murdered or 'disappeared' in the wake of the 1973 coup, and the remains of more than 1 000 have never been located. These divergent positions are reflected inside his country as well.

Yet Chile's economic growth since then has been nothing short of remarkable, particularly during the 1990s when it averaged an annual rate of over 7 per cent. In 1972, Chile was recorded to have the 'second worst economy in Latin America'. Inflation had reached 500 per cent, there were frequent strikes and 'nationalisation, price controls and high tariffs were the order of the day'. The state controlled more than two-thirds of economic output.[31] From a low of $4 000 per capita in 1975 in the wake of political instability, real income per person more than tripled over the next 30 years.

This transformation has been built on two pillars.[32]

The first was the institution of free market economic reforms in the mid-1980s by Pinochet's team of bright young economists – the so-called Chicago Boys,[33] predominantly (but certainly not exclusively) trained at the University of Chicago, some of whom later continued their work at the Instituto Liberdad y Desarrollo (Institute for Liberty and Development), which was established in 1990. These reforms were not, contrary to some impressions, based on purely market-driven behaviour.

There were a number of different phases and polices, each with varying success.[34] In 1973, the junta dealt with its socialist inheritance from Allende (which had included widespread nationalisation), by implementing market-driven liberalisation. This involved the privatisation of banks, the freeing of interest rates and tariff reductions. However, these moves resulted, by 1982, in very high interest rates (touching 40 per cent), high unemployment (over

30 per cent) and a 15 per cent economic *contraction* as dollar-denominated borrowings threatened to cripple the economy as the peso fell. Pinochet's rule from 1982 until his stepping down in 1989, was characterised by different policies, inter alia by the introduction of price controls and subsidies on exports, and the strict regulation of interest rates.

The second pillar of economic transformation rested on a massive increase in domestic copper production. Copper, of which Chile supplies nearly a third of the world's annual consumption, accounts for some two-thirds of export revenue.

The transformation of this sector, however, over of a quarter century has been spectacular. In 1990, the private sector accounted for less than one-quarter of Chilean copper mining output. The two largest private sector mines – Mantos Blancos (owned by Anglo American) and Disputada (then owned by Exxon)[35] – accounted for around 150 000 tonnes mined annually, while the four mines owned by the state company, Corporación Nacional del Cobre de Chile (CODELCO or National Copper Corporation of Chile), Chuquicamata, El Teniente, Salvador and Andina – produced approximately 750 000 tonnes annually.[36] This public-to-private sector ratio reflected the two earlier stages of nationalisation of the mines in Chile: the first in the late 1960s under Eduardo Frei[37] when the state acquired 50 per cent of the above four CODELCO mines from the private sector, with compensation. The second was in the early 1970s, when President Allende nationalised the remainder without compensation (although this was later reversed by Pinochet). After the coup, Pinochet did not seek to grow CODELCO, even though the generals sat on its board and the military then received 10 per cent of the sales income. Instead, with the input of the Chicago Boys, foreign investment was facilitated by low and stable income tax and non-discriminatory treatment of foreign and local companies under Chilean tax laws contractually agreed between the state and investors mostly under Decree Law 600 (DL600)[38] of 1974, which provided for a 'contract' between the investor and the state of Chile, the establishment of free trade zones, the introduction of policies guaranteeing the remittance of profits and capital, free choice as to the percentage of foreign ownership and non-discrimination with local investors, and tariff liberalisation.

By 2011, foreign investment totalling almost US$82 billion had been attracted through DL600, representing 56.5 per cent of the foreign capital entering Chile since 1974.[39] Byzantine labour policies inherited from the Allende and earlier days were unwound through a series of measures instituted in 1979 that were designed to decentralise collective bargaining, improve transparency in union voting and allow greater choice in union membership. Employment became a much simplified matter. Reform of the pension system in 1980 also allowed workers to opt out of the government-run pension system and instead put the formerly mandatory payroll tax (10 per cent of wages) in a privately managed Personal Retirement Account. This had a major positive impact on Chile's economy and society. By 2011, 8.8 million Chileans possessed private pensions. This change helped to improve the sustainability of Chile's pension system, promote the development of capital markets and domestic investment, and remove some labour market distortions by allowing personal choice in pension allocation, which had the effect of encouraging people to work in the formal sector. Instead of seeing pension contributions as a tax over which they had no control, the Personal Retirement Account became viewed as a defined deduction and future benefit.[40] Overall, this system improved the competitiveness of the pension system by taking its management to the market.

And in all this, critically, Chile has kept corruption down, and not just by Latin American standards. It has consistently ranked in the top twenty better performing countries in Transparency International's Corruption Perception Index, ahead of many developed countries.[41] Its police force, while accused of human rights abuses, is still regarded as the best in Latin America.

The results were instant and positive, despite the low copper price in the 1990s of under $1 per pound (which, by contrast, averaged $3.50 per pound in the 2000s). In 1992, Escondida, the largest copper mine in the world, was built by a consortium involving BHP, Rio Tinto and Japanese companies. By 2013 it was producing around 1.4 million tonnes annually. Alongside new CODELCO investments (notably Radomiro Tomic, which was started in 1997), Cypress Amax bought El Abra mine from the state in the early 1990s. Then, in 2002, Anglo American concluded the purchase of Disputado for an effective $1.4 billion. By the turn of that decade, Disputado (encompassing two mines, Los Bronces and Soldado, with a smelter known as Chagres) had quadrupled its output to 400 000 tonnes and the value had increased, based on the sale price of a quarter of its stake in the mine to Mitsubishi in November 2011 (for $5.4 billion) to over $20 billion.[42] Overall, by the end of the 2000s, CODELCO was producing more than twice as much copper as it had done twenty years before; yet the private sector was producing two-thirds of the annual national output of six million tonnes.[43] With the right policies in place, the state (and thus Chile's population) was able to attract private sector players to develop what they could not afford to do. All were winners.

In sum: Chile's transformation has been policy and not personality led. Predictability of policy, the 'financeability' of projects (given that banks now put up more than half of the requisite capital), which reflects a belief in the security and profitability of the investments, and long-term purchasing agreements of copper were all key to using Chile's natural resources more effectively for development. The results are all the more notable when compared to the record of others. In stark contrast to Chile, Zambians are poorer today, after two generations, than they were at independence.

The Zambian comparison

One 2013 study[44] shows that mine nationalisation in the early 1970s cost Zambia an estimated $45 billion in revenue. The study points out that Zambia would have generated mineral rents totalling $65 billion if it had continued to produce at an annual rate of 700 000 tonnes over the 40-year period from 1970. Instead, it managed only $15 billion. The 'opportunity loss' exceeded the international aid it received over the period. The challenge for then, as now, is to find a formula, as Chile has done, which allows the sharing of resource rents and, at the same time, allows for increased investment and production. The revenue can then be used (wisely) by the government for the purposes of improving the infrastructure and overall 'efficiency context'; thus allowing diversification.

Certainly, the decline in the copper price after 1973 and the simultaneous rise in the oil price did not help, but Chile, which produced less copper than Zambia in 1970, by comparison rapidly increased its production over these four decades, nudging 6 million tonnes today. In so doing, it positioned itself to take full advantage of the doubling of world copper production and demand from 1990. By 2013 Chile comprised more than one-third of global production; yet Zambia shrunk to under 5 per cent from 14 per cent in 1970. The counter-argument, that by *not* producing, Zambia has saved its resources for later, is cynical if not nihilistic: a generation of Zambians has lost opportunities that they did not have to. Subsistence mining and subsistence extraction, if you like. It might keep you alive but you will never be able to grow it into greater wealth or increased standards of living.

In a twist of history, Anglo American's nationalisation payout from Zambia government in January 1970 provided the seed capital (through Minorco) for its stake in Chile's mines. By the mid-1990s, Anglo was perhaps the largest foreign investor in Chile, attracted by a combination of resource deposits, sound macroeconomic policy and a welcoming policy environment. Even though Chile had (and has) significant state involvement in the mines, policy was stable and predictable for private investors. Indeed, by having the state, in the form of CODELCO, as a major copper producer itself means that legislators have a deeper understanding of what mining means, of the returns, of the complexities and of what it can and cannot reasonably be expected to deliver in society. It has also focused, in the process, on what it does well (producing copper) rather than getting hung up on the need to add more value to this product through beneficiation – essentially by adding more value through processing or conversion into manufactured goods. In recognising that India and China among others have surplus smelting capacity, Chile has not built a major new smelter in a quarter of a century.[45]

Chile's experience suggests that parastatals are not all bad; but that beneficiation is not always good. Its experience suggests, too, that in mono-resource type countries government needs to play a much stronger role than in more diversified economies. But the Chilean state has used the proceeds wisely, whereas in many other mono-economies, governments can end up in a symbiotic and predatory partnership with the private sector.[46]

There is a human dimension to these mining statistics. As highlighted above, Chile's per capita income has risen dramatically over the last two decades to (in purchasing-power parity terms) $15 000, while Zambia's, after reaching $2 000 in the mid-1960s, fell to under $800 in the early 1990s, recovering to just $1 600 by 2013.

Whatever his political critics may say, Pinochet's lasting contribution to Chile's development was to establish a functioning market-driven economy, control over which he was prepared to cede to professionals. In stark contrast to the Latin American experience, the military under Pinochet was also comparatively (though certainly not entirely) corruption-free. Moreover, he was ultimately prepared to hand over power to a civilian government in 1989 – again, hardly typical of military leadership in the region – through a democratic process.

Pinochet's role in Chile's economic reform and experiences elsewhere, notably in East Asia, raises inevitably questions about the widespread belief that economic reform is more, not less, successful and likely in authoritarian states. Although this is dealt with more explicitly in the next chapter, it suffices to say that the evidence is mixed. Pinochet's early years were very poor; and only in the 1980s did the junta start to get policies right once it reached out to others, including the technocrats. And growth really took off in the democratic 1990s. Responsive democratic government is arguably more necessary to the development and the implementation of sustainable reforms. Authoritarianism is more often than not used to excuse poor or autocratic leadership, to obscure poor management and to restrict accountability and transparency. Moreover, notions of democracy have to be carefully scrutinised, because the nature and 'culture' of the democratic system and the relationships of key sectors (such as the ruling party, legislature, executive and civil society) are crucial to the success of economic reforms. And, as will be argued below, business has a wider role in inspiring such a long-term view and policy behaviour.

From big holes to better fortunes

Kimberley's Stockdale Street is synonymous with the diamond industry. It has remained a site for De Beers' activities even after the shift in diamond mining from the Northern Cape to Botswana. Inside the neat terraced double-storey row is the boardroom, its walls bedecked with venerable members – only portraits of the dead hang there – including the rich and famous: from Cecil Rhodes to Barney Barnato, David Harris, Ernest Oppenheimer and Alfred Beit, and even some unusual bedfellows such as Field Marshall Archibald Percival Wavell, once viceroy of India but better known for his military prowess in eastern Africa and the Western Desert in the Second World War, who served as a De Beers director from 1947 until his death in May 1950. A step outside the entrance, however, and Kimberley is struggling. De Beers have generously sponsored the R50-million rehabilitation of the museum replicating Kimberley's corrugated-iron shops, banks and hostelries around the Big Hole, into a world-class site, as well as the refurbishment and conversion of the Kimberley Club, which Rhodes and other 'big men' used as their local lair, into a boutique hotel. But in the city where diggers and fortune-hunters once flocked in their thousands, government is now the main employer. For all of the money and rich history, as indicated, Kimberley is one of the more impoverished parts of South Africa, beset with problems of gangs and rampant alcoholism, in part consequences of unemployment. While diamonds have dried up, drink has flowed apparently unabated for nearly 150 years.

Of course, this does not mean that diamonds should not be mined and cannot bring wealth; to the contrary, Botswana and South Africa show how they can be a catalyst for extraordinary development and wealth creation. But they are finite: each gem mined, as Nicky Oppenheimer, Sir Ernest's grandson, has reminded, is one gem less. For the stones to make a development difference, as he has also put it, governments and their citizens and business all have to 'live up to diamonds'.

Part of the answer is in technology and capital. Ecuadorian Professor Orazio Belletini has identified three factors that enable resource-rich countries to develop the technology to take full advantage of their endowments.[47] First, the presence of sufficient capital and private sector expertise. Second, the need for a level of education and skills, capable of technical progress and managerial proficiency. And third, this is made more difficult where there is wide inequality (such as that measured by the Gini co-efficient) and the presence of a small elite. Indeed, the latter may encourage the very sort of political extremism that undermines attempts to diversify.

In great part, the answer is about policy and the strength of public institutions. Governments have to be wise about the policies they employ that look beyond mining. And if entrepreneurs are in this process of extraction unaware, deliberately or otherwise, of their wider responsibilities, especially when the mining has stopped, towns become museums to fortunes that were once made, but not left behind. The old nineteenth-century extractive elite did not behave in this regard that differently to the more obviously rapacious contemporary rent-seeking governmental variants so often roundly and justifiably criticised for their self-service, corruption and bad governance.

There are big differences, of course, between these eras, but it is possible to see why, as a consequence, the current political crop often see fit to behave the way they do, both to their own people and with sneering disdain (if not a little envy) towards the old white elite. It helps to explain why those politically popular yet developmentally short-termist policies implicit in the populist version of 'resource nationalism', which can be about nation-making and institution-building but tend to involve the looting and dilapidating of resources,[48] appeal. They have learnt well Rhodes' observation that 'money is power, and what can one accomplish without power? That is why I must have money. Ideas are no good without money,' he said, 'For its own sake I do not care for money. I never tried it for its own sake but it is a power and I like power.'[49]

It is all too easy for critics to point to the extremes of poor governance on minerals. The terrain is not – and should not – be defined by the 'non-state'[50] of the Central African Republic, for example, where rebels and government compete to plunder diamond, gold and other spoils through violent control, the archetype 'Blood Diamond' exaggeration. Or even the manner in which the political elite in Zimbabwe has prospered from the mining of diamonds at Marange near Mutare in the east of the beleaguered country, while at the same time impoverishing their subjects through radical redistributive land seizures. Yet, it is the less extreme development circumstances, thus off the radar of activist NGOs, that are more common and more difficult to chart in terms of the policy regimes necessary for economic growth and job creation – the Namibias, Botswanas and Zambias of this world.

In these, government has to give the private sector space to operate, otherwise countries are doomed ultimately to economic and development failure. A reciprocal sense of irony and humility is thus imperative on the part of entrepreneurs. Government has to ensure that it retains and uses well as much of the profits of these enterprises through taxation as can be derived, while ensuring they remain commercially sustainable, and distributes them into education and infrastructure especially. It should not get hung up on areas of activity where the country does not possess a comparative advantage, including polishing of gems and the smelting of ore, especially since the value addition to the later process is electricity, a commodity in short supply in most fragile states and best used on providing domestic lighting and refrigeration than Soviet-style heavy industrialisation.

Equally, business has to make money in a way that goes beyond profits if it wants to be an agent of social and political change, in providing an example to government, and in making its preaching for the long term on the rule of law and sustainable development that much more believable. And the contractual interface between the two parties of government and business has to be transparent along the lines of the Extractive Industries Transparency Initiative,[51] so citizens know who is getting what.

Responsible capitalism involves much more than profits; responsible government demands using its share of those profits wisely.

23

COLOMBIA

Attention to Detail

＊

Picture the scene. A swelling crowd under a hot tin roof in one of the densest jungle areas in the world, gathered to hear a senior minister explain what the government had done and was going to do for them, and asking what they might do in return.

One of the poorest of Colombia's 32 'departments', Norte de Santander, nestling in the north-east on the border with Venezuela, has historically been host to virtually everything among its 1.2 million people apart from good government: left-wing guerrillas, right-wing paramilitaries, coca growing, illegal gold and coltan mining and narco-trafficking. Drugs and insurgency have become inextricably integrated with the region and each other during the past 50 years of trouble. Two years from 2011 to 2012, for example, saw more than 400 drug laboratories and nearly 80 tonnes of cocaine destroyed in Norte de Santander alone.[1]

This region is sparsely populated in terms of both people and infrastructure. The jungles, frequently bisected by curving, wide, mud-brown rivers, occasionally make way for parcels of palm oil trees, although farming is defined more by random cattle, smallholdings and secret coca plantations. It is, says the defence minister, Juan Carlos Pinzón, 'the heart of Timochenko country', referring to the *nom de guerre* of the head of the Fuerzas Armadas Revolucionarias de Colombia (FARC, or the Revolutionary Armed Forces of Colombia), Rodrigo Londono Echeverri.

The bridge over the sweeping Catatumbo River would not be out of place on the set of David Lean's 1957 *Bridge Over the River Kwai* classic. The

426 — WHY STATES RECOVER

structure's age and design tells its own story of government's paucity of resources and an earlier age of ignorance and neglect. 'These are people that the country forgot,' reflects the deputy defence minister, Jorge Bedoya. The absence of roads, extreme topography and the levels of insecurity demanded we fly by Black Hawk from the airfield at Tibú to the town of La Gabarra just 60 kilometres away.

But these citizens were no longer being ignored. La Gabarra and the surrounding region has become the epicentre of the government's strategy to win control of the countryside, deal with the narco and insurgent threat and, in so doing, extend governance to all.

The security and governance campaign was started by the two-term administration of President Álvaro Uribe Vélez in 2002, when the FARC guerrillas had control of most Colombian roads and milled in groups as many as 500-strong, including just 30 kilometres from the capital at Bogotá. The campaign has been accelerated under the subsequent presidency of Juan Manuel Santos Calderón.

Once Colombia was known for its murder rate, drug cartels and figures such as Pablo Escobar, the Medillin drug lord. At its peak in the mid-1990s, Colombia experienced 36 000 murders annually (fifteen times the level of the US), ten kidnappings daily, and 75 weekly political assassinations[2] as the military, police, guerrillas, drug lords and paramilitaries all wrestled for control. Some 3 000 police were killed during 1997–2001.[3]

Something had to change. By the end of the twentieth century, by the army's admission, 'We were about to lose it. The guerrillas had almost moved from their first two stages of warfare [guerrilla warfare and "movement"] to the third, conventional war. We were losing a lot of guys, with bases being overrun. We did not have the numbers or equipment to take them on, with C-47 [Dakota] gunships, Mirage [fighters], which made a wonderful noise but little else, and very few helicopters. There was also a big disconnect between the different arms of the service. And,' the retired former chief of the army reminded, 'we were being spread very thin in the jungle, making ourselves very vulnerable big time.' By 2000, the guerrillas had 'deployed from Ecuador to Venezuela, had built themselves considerable infrastructure in the south-east around Caquetá and Meta, and not only had Bogotá surrounded, but had deployed guerrillas to its outskirts. Road transport between the major cities was very difficult, if not impossible. A change of strategy was necessary' he recalls.[4]

Just half of Colombia's countryside, dominated by difficult-to-access mountains and dense jungles, was under government control in 2002; ten years later the government figure was over 90 per cent. Homicides more than halved from 28 837 (or 70 per 100 000 population) in 2002 to 14 746 (or 30.8 per 100 000) by 2012, placing Colombia in tenth position worldwide, below Honduras in first (or worst) place at 90.4 per 100 000, Venezuela (53.7), Belize (44.7), El Salvador (41.2), Guatemala (39.9), Jamaica (39.3), Swaziland (33.8), Saint Kitts and Nevis (33.6) and South Africa (31.0).[5] Kidnappings dropped over the same ten-year period from 2 882 to 305; and car robberies, as another measure, from 17 303 to 7 926.[6] The improvement in security has enabled the Colombian economy to develop, creating a positive cycle of governance and growth that reinforces stability. Economic growth averaged 5 per cent during the ten years from 2002, enabling fresh public investment in infrastructure and further funding to an expanded armed forces and police.

Ending violence has, however, demanded undoing not just recent but more ancient history.

A brief history of violence

Although the drug trade has helped to stoke criminal violence and, since the end of the Cold War, lubricate the contemporary insurgency, Colombia's political history has been a continuously violent one. From the time of the sixteenth century, colonial conquest through the period of increased resistance to Spanish rule in the eighteenth century to the liberation wars led by Simón Bolivar between 1812 and 1819, the state experienced widespread violence. During the nineteenth century, Colombia suffered no fewer than nine civil wars, and more than 50 anti-government insurrections. The 1899 War of a Thousand Days left 100 000 dead and led to the loss of control over Panama as a result of Washington's fomenting of a Panamanian secessionist movement in a step to safeguard US control over the envisaged canal. In 1856, in 1860, in 1873, in 1885, in 1901 and again in 1902, sailors and marines from US warships were forced to land in order to patrol the Isthmus. This was not always at its own bidding. In 1861, in 1862, in 1885 and in 1900, the Colombian government asked that Washington protect its interests and maintain order on the Isthmus with troops.[7]

It is said, as a result, that not only does Colombia have the longest-standing record of democratic rule in Latin America, but also more than 150 years of war. Colombians have had to learn to deal with 'democratic insecurity'.

Much of this violence traditionally centred on political differences between the two major Colombian factions: the liberals (with federalist tendencies) and conservatives (with centrist leanings). These political distinctions also, however, aligned with rural and urban divides, the system of landlords and peasants, of elite wealth and grinding poverty: of oligarchs, unequal land distribution and an indigenous Indian and Afro-Caribbean underclasses.

Official figures show that nearly half (46 per cent) of Colombians live below the poverty line and one-third of this number (17 per cent) in 'extreme poverty'. Yet, the high Gini co-efficient, at 0.587 in 2009, one of the highest in Latin America behind only Haiti, Bolivia and Honduras, illustrates the dangers of measuring prosperity by average per capita incomes, which in Colombia is nearly $4 000 (or $10 000 in purchasing-power parity terms). This poverty gap is starkest between rural and urban areas where 62 per cent of the rural population are poor compared to 39 per cent in urban areas (where 75 per cent of Colombians reside).[8] This divide stokes socio-political unrest and feeds conflict. Land has also been a point of friction: less than half of 1 per cent of landowners own nearly two-thirds of rural land.[9] It is a nation of haves and have-nots, a highly stratified society where the traditionally rich families of Spanish descent have benefited to a far greater degree than the majority, mixed-race Afro-Colombian and Indian population.

The scarcity of avenues for social mobility provides a constituency for radical insurgents – and those making a living by illegal means.

Such historical divisions and political differences peaked in 1948 with La Violencia, the most destructive of Colombia's wars, which left 300 000 dead. The spark was the assassination of Jorge Eliécer Gaitán, a populist liberal leader, followed by urban riots in Bogotá, popularly known as El Bogotazo. The end result was a 1953 military coup, the only twentieth-century Colombian military intervention in politics, and a 1957 pact between liberals and conservatives to share power for the following sixteen years. However, this set the stage for the next violent episode as disillusioned liberals established their own independent rural communities, while wealthy landowners (and later the drug lords) raised their own paramilitaries. Fuelled by an influx of weaponry, ideology and money, this quickly morphed into armed conflict.

By the 1960s, armed self-defence groups of communists had, by then, established their own local government – the Marquetalia Republic – in a remote region, in addition to the enclave of Sumapaz outside Bogotá. An attack on this area by the Colombian army led to the formation of the Bloque

Sur (or Southern Bloc), which, in 1964, renamed itself the FARC. Fuerzas Armadas Revolucionarias de Colombia-Ejército del Pueblo (FARC-EP, or the Armed Revolutionary Forces of Colombia-People's Army), came about in 1982 at the Seventh Guerrilla Conference. This saw a major shift in strategy from rural areas and small-scale confrontations to wider areas and even into urban areas.

Also on the anti-government side was the Ejército de Liberacón Nacional (ELN, or the National Liberation Army) founded in 1965, and the Movimiento 19 de April (M-19) urban guerrilla movement, also created in 1965. The army was in turn supported by a variety of paramilitaries including, most prominently, the Autodefensas Unidas de Colombia (United Self-Defence Forces of Colombia), established in 1997. A 1984 ceasefire led to a successful peace process with the M-19 movement (which was, with the ELN and FARC, a member of the umbrella Guerrilla Coordinating Board), although the FARC and ELN decided to continue the struggle. With the tailing off of support from the Soviet Union and Cuba, the guerrillas turned to the narco-trade as their principal means of finance. This funding, which initially took the form of a revolutionary *gramaje* tax, bolstered by profits from kidnappings, bank robberies and other criminal activities, brought in what the Colombian police estimated at $3.5 billion annually by 2005, or 45 per cent of FARC funding.[10] Their right-wing *paramilitares* opposition similarly received as much as three-quarters of their income from the drug cartels.

Such a violent history does not have to be destiny, however. It has its roots in poor political leadership and bad choices – and consequently, as the 2000s have shown, can be significantly altered by better policies and leaders. Longer-term, sustained change is dependent on more than the energy and intentions of political leadership, but a deeper adjustment to ensure a less unequal and polarised society. Economic growth is a key part of this formula, as is establishing the state and its attributes from infrastructure to the rule of law in the rural areas.

The governments of Uribe (2002–10) and, from August 2010, Santos, have put Colombia into a better position in the twenty-first century to confront the violent threat posed, in particular, by an entwined scourge of drugs, widespread criminality, the leftist insurgency and rightist paramilitaries. The way it has been tackled, from the outset of Uribe's presidency and into that of Santos', has been through the concept of 'democratic security' – until the early 2000s a Colombian oxymoron.

The elements of democratic security

Uribe's predecessor President Andrés Pastrana (1998–2002) broke off three years of peace talks with the FARC after the group hijacked an airliner and kidnapped a Colombian senator who was aboard. Pastrana formulated Plan Colombia, a $10.6-billion initiative partly funded by the US and launched in 2000 to take the guerrillas on.

Things progressed slowly at first. At the time of Uribe's inauguration under the sound of distant mortar fire on 17 August 2002, 120 (of 1 099) mayors could not govern from their municipal offices and there were no police stations in 158 of these municipalities.[11] As his vice president, Francisco Santos Calderón, put it: 'The security situation was like the parable of the frog which is slowly heated up in warm water, never realising that he is being cooked alive. Well, the population was the frog, and we did not realise how bad things had become as a society.'

With Uribe's arrival, Colombia underwent a dramatic transformation from widespread insecurity to increasing normality. Born in 1952, the staunchly Roman Catholic Uribe was formerly mayor of Medillin and governor of the coffee-producing region of Antioquia. Despite the death of his father at the hands of FARC rebels in a botched kidnapping in 1983, Uribe, who himself survived a number of assassination attempts, has said that his anger did not influence his policies. But he seized the security problem in a manner unlike any of his recent predecessors, creating a wave of national political support and an unprecedented degree of consensus. Despite an ongoing national risk of terrorism, the dramatic improvements in security and strong economic performance saw Uribe's approval rating at 85 per cent, even after leaving office.[12] By then the FARC's approval rating was just 2 per cent.

Uribe's administration spoke of three missions: protect the population; control national territory; and take the fight to the guerrillas and paramilitaries – or, as one member of his government observed less scientifically, 'kick the bad guys up the arse so hard that they negotiate, but we negotiate not from a position of weakness but force'.

In so doing, he did not reinvent the wheel, but capitalised on the start made by Pastrana, including his improvement in international relations, especially the relationship with Washington, taking the fight to the guerrillas and paramilitary groups. To do so, he had to not only change tactics but also, more significantly, deliver the means necessary to establish a modern, stable Colombia. Through 'Democratic Security', he effectively turned the guerrillas' own *combinación* strategy[13] against them.[14]

Colombia's success in turning the tide, however, shows that weak states demand more than a change of policies, but a building of state institutions. It also illustrates the extent to which strategy and leadership can make a difference. The first step in the new policy was being able to take the fight to the guerrillas.

Tactically, this was reliant on a more aggressive approach in the security sector – on more money, soldiers and police, a more powerful justice system, the spraying of coca fields, better intelligence and more aggressive government tactics. As one measure, the security forces have grown in number from just under 200 000 in 2002 to touch 500 000 by 2013, while the number of full-time professional (as opposed to conscripts who serve a mandatory two-year period) soldiers went up from just over 55 000 in 2002 to 90 000 by 2010. The defence budget was increased to accommodate these measures, from 4 per cent of GDP to over 5 per cent during the 2000s, the increase partly financed through a 1.3 per cent 'Wealth Tax' earmarked for national security issues.

Quality and not just quantity has, however, been another measure of transformation of the armed forces. New equipment – including Black Hawks, Super Tucano aircraft from Brazil, unmanned aerial vehicles, and the latest communication, surveillance and command and control technology – has paralleled the creation of a dedicated special operations command and greater investment in troops and their training.

The security forces (and, indeed, the entire government) have pursued a counter-guerrilla strategy based on 'Clear, Hold and Build'. While the military and police together have undertaken the lion's share of actions in the first phase, the follow-up actions have been integrated with other government departments through the Centro de Coordinación de Acción Integral (Co-ordination Centre for Integral Action), though backfilling the space created as the security forces have pushed the FARC back with infrastructure and socio-economic activities has been slower than desirable, a problem common to similar campaigns such as in Afghanistan.

Someone's in charge

For many, Uribe was elected with 'very anti-Colombian ideas and speech' of establishing national authority with a mandate of law and order.

He played, by his own admission, both psychiatrist and strategist in dealing with the security problems beyond Bogotá's suburbs – getting the elite to recognise that the state could not be weak when it came to taxes but also strong on security. These two components, he successfully argued, were related. He also tackled long-held fears about the primacy of the security forces over the civilian government. As Pinzón said when deputy defence minister in 2006, the war had to be '20 per cent military and 80 per cent state-building and political'.

The FARC was put on the back foot through targeted military action. The nexus between the insurgency, paramilitaries and drugs has also been tackled successfully, one measure being the fall in criminal violence. The positive cycle was reinforced as foreign investment rose to $19 billion by 2012. Uribe's campaign to counter the FARC also involved a targeted reintegration of guerrillas into society, political talks, infrastructure expenditure (especially on roads since they 'move the guerrillas out and business in') and extensive dialogue throughout the countryside.

Uribe led the way in the latter regard, staging day-long, televised consultations known as *consejos comunitarios* (community councils) each Saturday across the country, where the audience could pose questions to him and ministers. This way he covered most of the thousand-plus municipalities and 32 departments in his eight years, many more than once, creating not just positive public relations, but a genuine feedback loop.

This illustrates perhaps the most seminal aspect of Colombia's reforms, and most salient lesson of all.

'Some aspects of management and leadership,' says Uribe, 'cannot be delegated and have to be led by your own example. This demands a combination of macro-vision and micro-management to ensure,' he emphasises, 'the long-term vision but the personal appetite to intervene in every detail.' And this, too, requires 'a sincere permanent dialogue with the population, keeping them informed of what is possible and what is not'.

As Uribe put it in January 2013, Colombia still had certain advantages, which he sought to play to. 'It had never defaulted on its debt. It had never had hyper-inflation. It always respected international contracts. But,' he added, 'the country was in very bad shape because of narco-violence. I had to recognise that the moment to do something had arrived, and that previous options had not worked. We had to understand why, even though we had good, hardworking people and good economic management, we had such low levels of economic investment, just $2 billion in 2002. The answer was violence, where narco-trafficking had invaded politics and undermined the rule of law.'

Hence, says Uribe, his three pillars of reform and action. 'Security with democratic values, and investment with social responsibility' as the first two. Both these were aimed at improving a third, social cohesion 'by improving education, health care, and micro-lending, all reducing income inequality'. But such a plan and rhetoric, he acknowledges, had fundamentally to be backed up by action, and not just by more meetings and additional words.

'We tried to have a connection between our speeches and the facts on the ground, since it was important to convince the population based on facts.' Recognising also that one or two government terms were not enough to change everything, 'we focused on short-term victories, realising that progress was dependent on the accumulation of small victories that created momentum and synergies'.

Both Uribe and Santos recognised that a combination of geography, topography and colonial history had left the Colombian state too weak to govern an inhospitable and inaccessible territory, little over twice the size of Texas or of France. By the turn of the twentieth century and into the twenty-first, Colombia was not so much a failed state as an 'insufficient' one. Uribe had to not only change tactics, but the strategic circumstances of the Colombian state.

The weakness of the state and the vested financial interest of certain paramilitaries and political factions in keeping it that way helps to explain why Colombia has battled so long with its drugs problem, and why tactical military offensives will, ultimately, only prove part of the solution in changing this situation.

Reflections of the man: Álvaro Uribe

The Colombian city of Pereira was the scene of a roadshow on 8 November 2013 as Uribe led a rally for his former finance minister Dr Óscar Iván Zuluaga to take on the incumbent (once Uribe's defence minister) President Juan Manuel Santos in the May 2014 election.

A crowd of several thousand thronged inside the exhibition hall in this city of 550 000. Situated in a small valley in the midst of the western Andean mountain chain, the terrain is akin to a tropical Somme, a landscape pockmarked by nature, covered in a bright green felt, the city clinging onto the mountainous topography, the range running down the region like a giant's spine, its vertebrae smoothing out on the way to the Pacific coast 300 kilometres away.

Pereira is best known for its outsized football stadium and as the heartland of the country's coffee-producing region, the so-called Eje Cafetero (Coffee Axis), famed for its rich soils.

On this Friday it was an evening for another national sport – politics.

The crowd sat attentively and patiently through speeches by the party chairperson, clutching their balloons in the national colours of yellow, red and blue. He was the trailer for the main event.

Then it was Uribe's turn, there officially to bolster Oscar's campaign, but clearly the main man.

Dressed like his politics, conservatively in an open-necked shirt, dark slacks and blue sports jacket, he was totally at home on the podium. He drew laughs from the audience, despite his outwardly serious, studious demeanour, his technique no doubt honed from all those weekends spent on his presidential consultations. Then, as now, he displayed enormous staying power, a man on a mission.

Off the stage the crowd gathered around, eager to have their photo taken alongside the man who had brought stability and prosperity to his country, while overhead giant helicopter-blade fans cooled the faithful as the evening wound on. It was clear who they had come to listen to, Uribe's speech drawing cheers, applause, shouts of encouragement, oohs, aahs and laughter.

Under Uribe's leadership, as a consequence of economic growth, improved prosperity and security, poverty reduced from over 54 per cent to 45 per cent of the 48 million population. Homicide and kidnapping levels also fell by more than 70 per cent over the course of his two terms.

Security was very much in attendance at the event, heavies behind, left and right of the podium, and soldiers and armed policemen outside. This is hardly surprising given the ongoing, if diminished, threat from drug lords, right-wing paramilitaries and left-wing FARC guerrillas, the three at times scarcely discernible in terms of their aims and methods.

Apologising profusely for bringing me to Pereira, a 45-minute flight west of Bogotá, on account of his punishing election schedule, later, as we journeyed through the city in his Land Cruiser, I asked Uribe whether he had any role models, for himself and for Colombia when he started his political odyssey.

'I was born in 1952,' he stated, 'right in the middle of a political crisis, when violence took hold of the coffee region where we were from. At the same time, my mother was very active in politics, in securing the right of women to vote. My political career was formed at her hand, accompanying her to political events. The same year that women received the vote in Colombia, 1958, coincided with the start of the Cuban Revolution. Fidel Castro selected Bolivia and Colombia as the two countries where he wanted to replicate his revolution. We saw the rise from that time of communist-directed guerrillas, and from then until now, I was outspoken against this development, when at times it was not popular to be so, such as when I was at university. I remain as committed today to fighting terrorism as I was then.'

As for international role models, 'I only have one – President Lincoln. He was a person who aimed to improve the life of the ordinary person. More than staying in his office, he went out into the streets to do this. I have tried to have the same ideal in Colombia, to live in contact with ordinary people.'

As for country models, 'Spain is of course our mother nation. The United States is the benchmark of democratic values, of ethics. And Germany has an excellent education system, especially its vocational training that has made it very competitive.'

And what might he do differently if he had his time again – what does he identify as his principal mistakes?

'Perhaps I would be a bit more calm at certain times,' he smiles. 'I am working my way through my checklist of mistakes. For instance, I am often criticised for interfering in the details, of not having the right balance between global vision and micro-management. But the history of Colombia is one of having excellent vision and poor execution. If I had to be truthful, the areas we made mistakes were areas where I did not intervene and micromanage. For example, I am asked why I did not disapprove of the efforts to extend my term.'

The constitution was altered to allow him to stand for a second term and his supporters introduced, unsuccessfully as it turned out, an amendment that would have permitted a third. 'It was a crossroads for me – on the one hand, I wanted to complete what we had started, and not risk a setback; on the other, I did not want to perpetuate the presidency.'

And why would he seek to come back into politics, pitting his Uribe Centro Democratico party and his preferred candidate Óscar Iván against the man who had succeeded him, President Santos, his former defence minister?

'Ask, my wife, Lina, and she will tell you I never stopped campaigning. I

436 — WHY STATES RECOVER

never quit. I am now running for senator,' he says, 'because my intention at the start, when I was a mayor and then a governor and a senator, was never to run for president. I wanted all the time to fight for a better place for a new generation of Colombians. Given all my privileges, I will,' he emphasises, 'fight until my last day.'

But there is more. 'I am running because [President Santos] promised he was going to continue with our policies. Everyone will recognise that he was elected because of his commitment to our main policies. Yet since then we have suffered a deterioration in security. Our social progress has slowed. Our economy should be stronger. I also disagree with the idea of impunity for terrorist groups, the FARC, which kills and kidnaps, and constitutes the greatest cocaine cartel worldwide.' Then he was out of the car into a crowd at a local hotel. At the time, it was later revealed, the FARC were putting together an assassination operation against Uribe, to be carried out by a rebel unit – Teofilo Forero Mobile Column – operating in central Colombia.[15] Presumably, this accounted for the extra security that we picked up from the airport, and the jammer for improvised explosive devices (IEDs) we carried in the car. He must have known this at the venue, and in the car, but it did not seem to intimidate him or slow him down.

Colombian political rallies are energising. No dour speeches making tendentious over-intellectualised arguments about colonialism, race or history; indeed, no speaking notes at all were visibly present. Óscar Iván was on the balls of his feet as his voice rose and fell, his hands outstretched at key moments as he stressed what he could do as president. But in the end, it proved insufficient, Santos winning the vote for another four years on 15 June 2014, his victory a destiny choice by Colombians for peace talks over Zuluaga's and Uribe's preference to fight on.

Back to La Gabarra – and the future

As Huey helicopters thump-thumped their way about overhead in La Gabarra and our other stops in this restive region, providing top cover, the relentless heat, jungle and this noise offered plenty of opportunity for Vietnam flashbacks – but not in terms of the positive record for the government over the insurgent.

For Uribe's 'democratic security' programme there is now a 'Sword of Honour' campaign, aiming to take the fight further to the FARC while consolidating control in 140 of the more troublesome municipalities such as Tibú.

This has demanded keeping the pressure on the FARC. But this has had its limits, especially among populations caught between the violence and promises of the guerrillas and the reality of few economic opportunities. Poverty is widespread, and opportunities few and far between. In La Gabarra, a one-horse town if ever there was, the same scruffy, cheap restaurants and fashion shops line the main dirt road, one after another.

This much is recognised by government, having allocated $150 million over three years for the military to carry out projects with a quick socio-economic impact, from water reticulation, sewers, bridges and roads, to community sports centres.

The government is also continually puzzling over how to innovate further in taking the fight to the FARC and the smaller ELN and Ejército Popular de Liberación movements.

We were in La Gabarra in November 2013 for Minister Pinzón to open one of eighteen new sports centres built countrywide by the army in 2013, this one by the 30th engineering battalion, 'Jose A Salazar'. In dripping humidity and 35-degree-celsius heat exacerbated by the tin-roof complex, the whole town seemed to turn out for the occasion, with even the local talent-for-hire lining up and leering from their balcony as the soldiers patrolled by.

Pinzón's message was clear. The government has built the sport facilities and is building the road to Tibú, and the FARC is not. If any of you, he said to the crowd, by then spilling out of the complex, know someone in the FARC, a friend or a relative, let them know that they can demobilise.

There has been a steady increase in the volume of demobilised and re-integrated guerrillas, 1 100 in the first ten months of 2013 alone, and 12 000 since 2002. A further 6 000 are estimated to have been killed by the army, the Ejército Nacional. As a result, estimates of FARC numbers have them declining from 25 000 frontline fighters in 2002 to little more than 7 200 a decade on, and the ELN, to around 2 500.

The Princeton-educated Pinzón is out there giving these messages 'two or three days a week'; his deputy Jorge Enrique Bedoya, who went to Harvard, 'most weekends'. High-energy and quality people always make a difference. The conscious care taken by senior commanders over especially the lowest ranking soldier was notable, perhaps aware of the risks for them in this war zone. Or as Karl Lippert, the head of SABMiller in Latin America puts it, 'Colombians are smart, educated and work like hell.' He should know. His employer is the largest investor in the country with a stake of $7 billion, and Colombia now the source of the largest profits for SABMiller, the second-largest brewer worldwide.[16]

At the same time that Bogotá has offered guerrillas a way out individually, it is doing the same with their movements. During 2013, peace talks were under way in Havana, Cuba. These talks have been a source of some disagreement between Uribe (who believes you cannot negotiate with terrorists) and his successor. The government has also endeavoured to consolidate both its legitimacy and moral authority in stressing its adherence to international humanitarian law and due process, not least through the deployment of representatives of the attorney general's office in far-flung areas.

This progress is not without challenges. The FARC, while under tremendous military pressure, has not stood still. The chief of the army, General Juan Pablo Rodriguez, admitted in 2013 that 'the FARC is not stupid. They adapt and change, and every day is more difficult for us.'

As it has lost territorial control, the FARC has shifted its strategy from semi-conventional war once more to terrorism.

Rodriguez, who spearheaded taking the fight to the FARC with two years in command of special forces, highlights three innovations the army needs to undertake to meet this new threat. First, how to improve intelligence 'in all its forms' – human, technology, historical and what he terms 'combat'. This demands, especially, he says, penetration of the enemy's structures. His second imperative is to improve 'operational techniques and methods'. And third, to ensure the support of the civilian population, which will assist also, he points out, in a positive cycle with intelligence.

Training is part of this, as is technology. As Rodriguez put it, 'In asymmetric warfare every day you should change, every day you should innovate in the combat field, otherwise you will fail.'

Instead of full-frontal attacks of a decade ago, FARC has resorted to melding among the population, using its militia, referred to by the military as 'FARC in civilian clothes', as a first line of attack, sniping on soldiers and employing IEDs. The presence of the GCOEX tactical electronic warfare soldiers with us in Norte de Santander told about the need to jam remote detonation devices. An IED was discovered at our remote helicopter landing site just hours before we got there, the fresh record of the detonation a brown smear on the bright-green hillside.

When the mayor got up to speak, the questions from the crowd in La Gabarra spoke volumes of the intersection between governance, security and economic opportunity. Residents asked for a bank to be established (there wasn't one) so they could pay their debts, another wanted a garbage service for the town. The chief of the armed forces, General Leonardo Barrero, empathised with their plight, referring to his past experience in managing coca eradication elsewhere, encouraging the farmers to get into other crops and become part of the solution.

This is a tough sell, given the economic and farming conditions. And it was going to be a hard slog to bring the region into a normal governance regime, given the years of neglect and given, too, the proximity of the border with Venezuela, long a sanctuary for the FARC and others, and a conduit for drugs.

Herein lies another core challenge of fighting an insurgency – establishing the means for wealth creation that offers today's narco-insurgent a legitimate alternative that goes beyond scratching a living from small-scale farming. Without such an alternative, a political settlement cannot address the narco dimension, since FARC fighters will simply become conflict entrepreneurs rather than fighting for political power. This is more difficult when, after 50 years, generations of people – known generically as Familias Farianas (FARC Families) have become deeply inculcated in this way of life and means of living.

Breaking the conflict-poverty cycle

No doubt the improvement in security has enabled the economy to develop. Pro-market economic policies helped Colombia reduce poverty by 20 per cent and cut unemployment by 25 per cent (from 15.7 per cent in 2002 to about 8 per cent in 2013). A reduction in public debt levels to below 1.5 per cent of GDP, and an export-led growth strategy, together facilitated growth, with improvements in the security situation establishing a positive cycle.

Colombia has the fourth-largest economy in Latin America, behind Brazil, Argentina and Mexico. Foreign investment more than doubled between 2000 and 2010. The government's economic policy and democratic security strategy engendered a growing sense of confidence in the economy, particularly within the business sector, a confidence encouraged by fiscal incentives (essentially tax holidays) worth as much as 1 per cent of the country's GDP of $250 billion.

But change is not only about financial figures and riches. According to public figures, recipients of public health care surged from less than 400 000 in 2002 to a shade under eight million in Uribe's first (2002–06) term, and 'basic and medium' education coverage from 7.8 million to 9.3 million scholars during the same period.

Democratic security's critics argue that while the violence has mainly affected poor people, decisions have been taken largely in the cities by members of the rich elite. They have argued, furthermore, that the influence of the drug barons remains strong, extending over the borders in terms of trafficking routes and money laundering schemes, and into government and the Congress. Although there have been substantial improvements in social conditions, there is still widespread poverty, especially in the rural areas. This helps to explain the example of the drug lord Escobar's popularity. His funding of low-income communities led to El Patrón acquiring a Robin Hood status in Medillin where there is still, today, a suburb named after him.

This has required improving the aspect of counter-insurgency that most campaigns struggle with – linking security with sustainable employment creation, especially in the rural areas. The government has a role to play in finding new ways of wealth creation, by assisting with the necessary physical infrastructure that will help create the markets, and with farming inputs. However, it has always had to walk a fine line between rewarding success and 'good behaviour' while recognising the need, also, to arrest outright failure.

There is a need for the law to be extended, too, and to allow it to take its course. And the government has recognised it will have to keep up the military pressure on the FARC. This requires not only doing many things at once but continuity of effort, as local military commanders have been quick to acknowledge.

If this can be achieved, the region might become known for something other than drugs and trouble. Politicians and business people, local and national, have grasped this nettle through regular, weekly security town hall meetings. As we flew on to Cúcuta, the capital of Norte de Santander, at the end of a full day, the locals made it clear that better policing had succeeded in bringing down the crime rate, especially by tackling the drug gangs.

But business there also faced a new challenge, making it more difficult to prosper. The decline in the value of neighbouring Venezuela's currency, the new bolivar, has encouraged flooding of the Colombian market with cheaper, subsidised Venezuelan goods, including palm oil. Businesses urged the government to take action at the town hall meeting. Bring in the army, they demanded, as if Bogotá did not already have enough on its plate.

*

Sustained success in countering Colombia's complex insurgency will be down to the country's ability to maintain a high enough economic growth rate, and generate employment, all the while extending the state outwards into the ungoverned jungles and mountains. This may not make the insurgency disappear altogether, but it will assist in dissipating much of the sense of grievance that has historically fuelled it.

The need for balance between force and reconciliation and in creating alternative livelihoods to drugs, not only the maintenance but strengthening of justice systems, and above all else, commitment to detail, good people and need for a long view are all sound lessons. This holds true for fighting the FARC in Colombia as it does Boko Haram in Nigeria or Al-Shabab in East Africa.

24

MYANMAR

The Roots of Reform

*

There is no denying Myanmar's[1] poverty and backwardness compared to its region.

In the rural areas, where two-thirds of the country's 53 million people live,[2] it is of a back-breaking sort, women and men waist-deep in paddy and other fields, planting and harvesting in an apparently endless cycle of production and survival.

Then there is a type of poverty visible from the circular railway in Yangon (Rangoon), a bustling, sprawling city of over five million people. This is of the heartbreaking plastic-bag variety, children and people living in wrenching squalor, not helped by the extreme climate, playing, cooking and trading in among heaps of rubbish and green putrescent rivers and puddles clogged with litter.

Myanmar is best described as a Vietnam of twenty years ago, poised at economic take-off. Yes, per capita income is the lowest in Southeast Asia at about $870 (in nominal terms), but this represents a staggering rise since the early 2000s when it was just $150. Average growth during the 2000s has been 12 per cent annually, at least according to official figures. There are all manner of infrastructure challenges, and dependence on just three exports – logs, gas and vegetables – but the government has plans (if not the money) in place to address these, while the garment and shoe sectors are growing fast.[3]

Things are changing in a way that resembles other Southeast Asian experiences. Near the railway depot at Insein in Yangon, once also the location of Rangoon's main jail, men and women sit trackside tortuously tearing and recycling plastic. Ninety minutes north of the city, cycling in the rural community of Ngasutang through the eggplants, rubber plantations and cashew trees, we were astonished to find a cottage industry weaving hospital bandages on machines that would have done Charles Dickens proud, their *clackity-clacking* more of a giveaway than the nondescript location. These were packed and labelled *in situ* as 'Y2K' bandaging for Yangon's hospitals, providing a fresh source of income for the farming community. Not too far away workers processed the sap from the rubber trees into flat mats, hand-rolling these sheets before hanging them out to dry. Government remains a price setter and determinant of who farms what, but its influence can only decline.

It is from these small acorns of value addition that a diversification and jobs will grow, in Myanmar as it has done elsewhere in Southeast Asia.

Myanmar's relative backwardness is a result of 50 years of military rule from 1962. Despite the devastation of the Second World War, in 1960 its per capita income was $670, more than twice that of neighbouring Thailand and three times that of Indonesia.[4] Equally, change has been on the back of political reforms, which saw press freedoms return soon after the first election in twenty years held in 2010, Nobel laureate Aung San Suu Kyi's once-banned National League for Democracy (NLD) contesting April 2012 by-elections, and Western sanctions being lifted. International re-acceptance happened at a fast pace. President Barack Obama popped in for a six-hour tour as a stamp of approval shortly after his own re-election in November 2012.[5]

McKinsey, the consultancy, speaks of a 'Myanmar Moment', of the potential inherent in developing a country from one where per capita income is low, where people enjoy an average of four years of schooling, and where $650 billion in investment is required by 2030 to 'support growth potential'. If it can get things right, the report says, there could be a fourfold increase in GDP by 2030 to $200 billion, expanding a 'consumer' class from 2.5 million to 19 million over this time, with a potential to create 10 million non-agricultural jobs to help service the needs of a 500-million-strong regional market.[6]

By the start of the second decade of the twenty-first century, there were reformers on both sides of the political divide, government and the opposition. Why did the country change direction after half a century of self-imposed isolation?

The backdrop to change

The Taukkyan Commonwealth War Cemetery near Yangon is grim evidence of the brutality of the war with the Japanese between 1941 and 1945 and a reminder, too, of the costs of colonialism, some more cerebral than visceral. Just off the main Yangon-Bago highway, 35 kilometres north of Yangon, it holds the graves of 6 374 Allied and Commonwealth servicemen and remembers another 28 000 whose bodies were cremated or not found or identified, many from India and including some from Nigeria and Ghana. Today, the men of the Gold Coast Regiment, the West African Electrical and Mechanical Engineers, the 6th Rajputana Rifles, the 5th Mahratta Light Infantry and 4th Bombay Grenadiers lie side by side in the baking heat under bronze tombstones with their, in local parlance, 'Britisher' soldiers in arms from Worcestershire, Lincolnshire, Bedfordshire, Ulster and Devonshire regiments among others – a testament to the integrating effect of colonialism if nothing else.

The oval stone memorial and the immaculately tended gardens with their thick buffalo grass and frangipani trees combine in a serene tribute. They serve also as a reminder of the costs of that campaign, especially to the locals. Thant Myint-U, the grandson of the former UN secretary general, U Thant, jarringly reminds that 'the Burmese had nothing to do with the war, but it destroyed their country'.[7]

The war started before 1941 as a staging post for combat flights by US General Claire Lee Chennault's Flying Tigers, who were paid a bounty for each Japanese plane shot down, along with resupply flights over the 'Hump' for the Nationalist Chinese forces fighting the Japanese. So dangerous were these peaks and high the losses (more than 600 planes and 1 000 men) over the outlying Himalayan ranges, the Naga Hills and Santsung Mountains, that collectively they became known by the dark-humoured aircrews as the 'Aluminium Plated Mountain'.

Within four months from their landings in Lower Burma in December 1941, the Japanese drove the British out of Rangoon. With British and Commonwealth armies forced to withdraw into India, Burma became a war of guerrilla tactics led by men such as British generals William Slim and Orde Wingate, along with their American counterparts 'Vinegar Joe' Stilwell and Frank Merrill. The latter gave his name to Merrill's Marauders, while the unconventional Wingate (who would wear an alarm clock around his wrist, subject to going off at times, and a raw onion around his neck, which he would occasionally bite into; a man described by Lord Moran, Winston Churchill's personal physician, as 'hardly sane – in medical jargon, a borderline case')[8] established the Chindits, a corrupted form of the Burmese mythical lion Chinthe, the statues of which guarded Buddhist temples. The costs of the Burma campaign were terrible. Of the Commonwealth force of 606 000, 14 326 died in battle, the rest from tropical disease, with 47 000 wounded. Japanese casualties were much greater, with 144 000 dead and 56 000 wounded, though the toll of the Burmese civilian population topped one million, principally from the effects of war, including famine and disease, forced labour and war crimes.[9] Wingate, seen by some as the father of modern guerrilla warfare, did not live to see the war's end, another casualty of the frailty of air operations, the B-25 bomber in which he was travelling crashing into the jungle near Manipur in India after a recce in Burma in March 1944.

Annexed as a province of British India on 1 January 1886, the pre-independence political history of Burma is one of divide and rule by the colonial authorities, used to maintain their political grip and pursue strategic economic interests. The colonists relied extensively on indirect rule where minorities predominated. The population has constantly suffered racial tensions among its 135 recognised ethnic groups with their 250 spoken dialects. Relations between ethnic Burmans (also known as the Bamar, comprising 68 per cent of the population), Shans (9 per cent), Karens (or Kayins, 7 per cent) and hill tribesmen including the Kachins, Nagas, Mons and Chins have 'rarely advanced beyond animosity'. It is the site of the world's longest-running guerrilla struggle between the central government and the Karen National Liberation Army (KNLA).

The KNLA, formed in 1949, is the military branch of the Karen National Union, which has campaigned for the self-determination of the Karen people. Disputed territory overlaps with ungoverned badlands, most notoriously the Golden Triangle opium production centre at the intersection of the borders of Myanmar, Laos and Thailand, the trade itself a consequence not only of demand but of the end of the Chinese civil war when remnants of the Kuomintang fled to the territory and established themselves in Shan State with a need to finance their continued struggles. As General Tuan Shi-wen, commander of the Kuomintang's Fifth Army, admitted, 'Necessity knows no law.'[10]

The majority Bamar were marginalised and prevented from serving in the military and other government arms, even as their own social and economic structures shifted. They were to get their own back. During the peak of the British colonial period between 1914 and 1942, Chinese traders and Indian rice farmers, moneylenders (*chettyars*) and artisans arrived in their hundreds of thousands to service expanding imperial investments in oil, timber, mining and rubber. At the start of the Second World War, Indians comprised an estimated 60 per cent of Rangoon's population. This restricted local social mobility, the result being inflamed racial tension, occasionally leading to riots (as in 1930–31) and increased criminality.[11]

By the 1930s, despite a degree of self-government in neighbouring India after the end of the First World War, Burma's retention of direct colonial rule saw the rise of student resistance, led by Thakin Aung San and Thakin Nu, two leaders who were to feature further in the struggle for independence. Aung San fought with the Japanese to dethrone the British, until switching sides in March 1945, just before the Japanese surrender in Yangon in August. A general strike in 1946 saw the ascendancy of Aung San's Anti-Fascist People's Freedom League, and led to Burma's independence on 4 January 1948.

Aung San did not live to see this moment, having been assassinated along with six cabinet ministers at the Government Secretariat buildings in Yangon in July 1947. Thakin Nu, known by then as U Nu, became the first prime minister.[12]

From colonialism to isolation

From being one of the least-known countries, stuck in the economic doldrums and politically autarkic, Myanmar has quickly been put on the twenty-first-century tourist map. Whether it be cruising the mighty Ayeyarwady River, taking in the majesty of the 99-metre-high Shwedagon Pagoda (described by Rudyard Kipling as a 'winking wonder', and by Somerset Maugham as a 'sudden hope in the dark night of the soul'), walking the floating gardens and market on Inle Lake or temple counting, Myanmar is rich in sights and comparatively low in cost. The Mandalay Division at Bagan, which contains 2 200 ancient shrines, is regarded as one of the greatest archaeological sites in Southeast Asia. Buddhas abound: reclining, standing, sitting, in gold, brass, plaster, jade and marble; as do their earthly disciples, there being no fewer than 1.4 million monks padding along in their rich red-brown robes countrywide.

By the start of the 2010s, it had become one of the hottest tourist destinations worldwide, with offerings routinely described as 'fabulous', 'unique' and 'amazing'. More than a million tourists visited Myanmar in 2012, up from 816 000 the previous year, with earnings rising nearly 70 per cent in one year, to over half a billion dollars from $320 million.

It also has some of the finest colonial architecture in the region. The Pegu

Club, which has given its name to the world-famous cocktail, was a British-only exclusive colonial club, built almost entirely of teak in 1882. Today it is dilapidated, abandoned by its last tenants, the army audit corps, its swimming pool a mass of bush, the eaves falling down, the ballroom empty save for overhead fans and a few stray dogs, and the parquet flooring pilfered, with the urinal, where Kipling might have taken a pee on his visit en route to San Francisco in 1889, being one of the few items not stripped out.

It is a brash reminder of the arrogance and paternalism that lay behind colonialism. Kipling recalled the club was 'full of men on their way up or down'. What stood out most for the literary genius was the morbid chatter about 'battle, murder and sudden death', the wars waged in the name of empire: 'that jungle-fighting is the deuce and all. More ice please.'

It is no surprise that, at least in the immediate post-colonial era, Burmese were keen to see its ilk disappear. Although membership was open to 'all gentlemen interested in general society', as the regulations stipulated, in practice that meant 'whites only'. Before he became a writer, George Orwell – the pen name of Eric Blair – arrived in Burma in 1922 to join the Indian Imperial Police. In *Burmese Days*, he provides insight into the way of such clubs, and the type of Englishman 'common, unfortunately – who should never be allowed to set foot in the East' in satirising through his character Westfield, who 'shrugged his thin shoulders philosophically … sat down at the table and lighted a black, stinking Burma cheroot' before saying: 'B—s of natives are getting into all the Clubs nowadays. Even the Pegu Club, I'm told. Way this country's going, you know. We're about the last Club in Burma to hold out against 'em.' Westfield added: 'We are; and what's more, we're damn well going to go on holding out. I'll die in a ditch before I'll see a nigger in here.'[13]

Old Etonian Blair never fitted in with the colonial scene, unlike his contemporaries who took pride in being *pukka sahibs*.[14] He survived five years in a variety of postings across the country, before leaving for England in 1927 after he contracted dengue fever. He later wrote that he felt guilty about his role in the work of empire and 'began to look more closely at his own country and saw that England also had its oppressed masses in the working class', who became 'symbolic victims' of what he had seen in his Burma stint. Through the eyes of his character John Flory, Orwell sketched the underbelly of the empire, the community of the Katha Club, which 'whiled away interminable evenings with tepid gins and tonics and inane club chatter about dogs, gramophones, tennis racquets, the infernal heat and, inevitably, the insolence of the Burmese'.[15] Burma had helped to transform him 'from a snobbish public-school boy to a writer of social conscience who sought out the underdogs of society.'[16]

The Pegu Club served as a Japanese officers' brothel between 1942 and 1945 and then was requisitioned by the Royal Air Force immediately after the war, presumably for different purposes.

The club is just one of 189 public buildings constructed before 1930 with a 'distinctive architectural style' on a heritage list, including the Government Secretariat, the red-brick headquarters of the Burma Railway company and the original home of the Rowe & Co. department store. Known as the 'Harrods of the East' before the nationalisation of all of its 12 200 branches throughout Myanmar in 1964, Rowe & Co. would issue a 300-page catalogue four times a year featuring 'ladies and gentlemen's outfitting, millinery, boots and shoes, crockery and glassware, brassware, trunks, cutlery, watches and clocks, and saddlery.'[17]

The sights and history do not end with buildings, temples and Buddhas. At the appropriately named Insein, where Blair once ran the jail, there is a collection of steam engines that would send trainspotters into a tremble. Peeking over the walled perimeter is a sign on one of the ancient examples: 'Cowans, Sheldon and Co. Ltd, Carlisle, England'. All the more remarkable then that a country that was once so globalised in colonial terms and the centrepiece of an extractive empire in East Asia then cut itself off from the world for half a century.

In part, this related to colonial racial exclusion. 'The core of Burmese politicians,' reflects Thant Myint-U, 'started from the notion that globalisation was against the Burmese. They were the bottom of the class structure, exploited by the foreigners, the Brits and the Indians. And then the vacuum created by their departure was filled by extremists on the right and the left, who shared a disdain for institutions and for history.'[18] This was also in measure due to internal struggles and the need to focus on nation-building, denoted by the single white star in the middle of the Burmese flag.

A regular pattern was soon established after independence of nationalist insurgencies of various minorities (notably the Karen), totalling not fewer than fifteen separate ethnic insurgencies at one point, and chronic economic problems from its independence start. Attempts at resuscitation through an eight-year plan of 1953 devised by US experts known as Pyidawtha (or Happy Land) delivered little as squabbling and fighting intensified, leading, in March 1962, to a coup led by General Ne Win. Thereafter, all businesses, including banks, were nationalised, and the country moved into a period of self-imposed isolationism. Ne Win, who had ruled by decree for twelve years, established the Socialist Republic of the Union of Burma in 1974, though this move and his formal stepping down from power in 1981 did little to improve matters. International relations were in little better shape, as the Socialist Republic of the Union of Burma withdrew from the Non-Aligned Movement in September 1979, less non-aligned than introverted and isolated. Despite the socialism moniker, this was a fiercely nationalist regime, with one of its targets being Chinese communist-supported Maoist rebels.

Circumstances worsened with the crushing of student protests in August 1988 by the *tatmadaw* (military). Although multi-party elections were announced and Aung San Suu Kyi, the daughter of the independence hero, proposed the formation of an interim government, on 18 September that year the military instead re-established its authority and set up the State Law and Order Restoration Council, known by the sinister Blofeld-like acronym SLORC. With thousands fleeing to neighbouring countries and the National League for Democracy under Aung San Suu Kyi's leadership barred from participation in elections, Burma was renamed Myanmar the following year. Although GDP grew steadily during the 1990s at over 4 per cent per annum, by the early 2000s the situation had once more descended into recession, hastened by the construction of a new capital at Naypydaw (Abode of Kings), 320 kilometres up the Sittaung valley from Yangon at a cost of $4 billion.

Seeding the Saffron Revolution

A series of non-violent demonstrations led, again, by students followed the removal of fuel subsidies in 2007, which doubled the price of petrol. By September, the campaign had escalated to a mass movement, headed by Buddhist monks, hence the popular term Saffron Revolution. Although this was put down by the regime, with the imprisonment of 6 000 monks, a combination of Cyclone Nargis, which raged through the Ayerwady Delta at a cost of 200 000 lives, peace agreements ending armed rebellions in the Mon-Shan and Chin regions and the rise of President Thein Sein saw Aung San Suu Kyi released from prison in 2010 in the run-up to national elections. Despite criticism of the election process and results, won by the military-backed Union Solidarity and Development Party, the reform process gained momentum. Press censorship was relaxed and some 1 000 political prisoners were released. By-elections in 2012 saw 43 seats (of a total of 664)[19] of the 46 available won by NLD candidates, including Aung San Suu Kyi, who took the contest in Kawhmu, a poverty-stricken rural area.

The speed and extent of the change have surprised pretty much every Burma watcher. The changes in policy towards a 'disciplined democracy' since the 2010 elections 'stem largely from internal factors, and the government's interest in modernising Burma, not as a result of economic sanctions or foreign threats'.[20] Such sentiments were heightened by tough economic times, principally the result of widespread corruption and lack of investment, and a feeling that the country was being left behind by its own region.

Three key factors are cited for change: first the change of leadership. Matters started with Senior General Than Shwe and his decision to bow out from public influence by encouraging reform and the reform-minded Thein Sein, the somewhat obscure 'number five' general in terms of seniority, who promoted a seven-step reform plan.

General Than moved for the sake of his legacy and his interests. He faced an uphill fight to bring other senior generals on board, which required him to move fast for the 'project' to work. Some believe he was prompted by the need to secure the military's wealth; that the generals needed to change in order to remain in control of the transition process (à la China and Vietnam). As Sean Turnell of Macquarie University explains, 'The cynical view is that the best way for the military to ensure it could retain its wealth was by increasing the limits on untrammelled power.'[21] In so doing, successors to Than Shwe would not go after him and his associates in the same way he had turned on Ne Win's family.

There was the related aspect of personal agency. There are those who believe that Thein Sein had been biding his time for twenty years, waiting for the moment, F.W. de Klerk-style, to reform. When it came, he seized it, recognising, too, that the survival of the military and security of its considerable commercial interests ultimately depended on political and economic reform.

Second, there are external drivers: the pressures of international opinion and economic sanctions, and the twin fears of being left behind and dominated by China.

Regular contacts with China, its patron-in-chief, highlighted that greater openness to foreign trade and investment was not in conflict with regime stability and the retention of power. But China also produced other catalytic tensions. While Beijing's increasing influence was essential to circumvent sanctions, it was seen as increasingly exploitative and arrogant, such as over its interference regarding the Kachin tensions in the north and its aggressive business people, as well as the importation of its own workforce.[22] A dose of 'Burmese xenophobia, hyper-nationalism and the fact that the old guard in the military had cut their teeth', recalls Turnell, 'fighting Chinese-supported guerrillas' played a role, too. Matters peaked with the Chinese-funded $6-billion Myitsone Dam scheme, from which the Chinese would take the bulk of the power. Suspension of that project in 2011, when 25 per cent complete, along with the granting of telecom licences to Norway's Telenor and the Ooredoo Qatari over China Mobile, signalled a new era.

Concerns about China were coupled with a desire to get Myanmar to become a 'normal' country, 'a country with problems à la Thailand, but nothing outlandish', says Turnell, and not to be left behind by a region that had made huge progress while Myanmar had fallen behind. Exposure to the premier regional body, the Association of Southeast Asian Nations, brought home this point to Myanmar's leadership, especially in comparison to its historical rival Thailand. Myanmar exports one-third of the rice volume it exported in 1937, notes Turnell, a function not only of a 250 per cent population increase over the past 50 years, 'but lack of productivity related to the absence of credit for seed and labour inputs in the rural areas'. This highlights the importance of targeting growth early on in the agricultural sector.

All this relates to the choice of economic model, the third critical factor influencing change. 'There was a "Damascene" moment that they needed to do something', reflects Turnell, 'despite their lack of exposure to the world. This imperative was strengthened by an early influx of émigrés, and their latching onto a regional model they could emulate in Vietnam'. Key individuals stand out: Winston Set Aung, who had gained experience at the Asian Development Bank, the US-educated economist Zaw Oo and U Myint, who all congregated in the Myanmar Development Resource Institute. Along with the economic planning minister Kan Zaw and finance minister U Win Shein, there were quickly enough people with sufficient at stake to overcome old vested interests, even though there remain potential spoilers, notably Shwe Mann, the former 'number three' general and subsequently the Speaker of the House.

*

Whatever the exact impulses, it is a mistake to see the Burmese solely as responding to outside pressures rather than having any agency of their own.[23]

There is no evidence to support a view that international sanctions prompted political change, even if only by the admission of those applying them. In

2009, for example, then US Assistant Secretary of State Kurt Campbell informed a congressional committee that sanctions might pose only some 'modest inconveniences' for the regime. Former French Foreign Minister Bernard Kouchner told the Foreign Affairs Committee of the French National Assembly in the same month that such sanctions 'serve no useful purpose'. Or as Turnell has explained, 'If we look into Burma's economy, sanctions are really a marginal issue in terms of the overall economic performance.'[24] To the contrary, the pressure applied by foreign governments and organisations, and their strong rhetoric, were in some ways counter-productive, encouraging a 'bunker mentality and the development of a garrison state'.

'Western sanctions had minimal impact on changing Myanmar's domestic policy,' notes Barry Desker of Singapore's prestigious Rajaratnam School of International Studies.[25] 'Such sanctions may have slowed the process of change as the leadership did not have the opportunity of learning from Western nations who cut off contact.' Not only were sanctions hardly likely to influence a country that had self-imposed sanctions for 50 years, they also exacerbated racial and cultural sensitivities.

Nor, says Burma expert Andrew Selth, were incentives to reform any more successful. As Foreign Minister Win Aung put it in 2002, 'For us, giving a banana to the monkey and then asking it to dance is not the way. We are not monkeys.'[26] This, Selth notes, 'made the intensely nationalistic military leadership even more determined to resist external pressures and set their own agenda for a managed transition to a new system of government'.

The financial and visa sanctions variants introduced from 2003 may have been more effective than generally believed, at least in increasing the sense of isolation and reducing the options for travel and 'escape'. Sanctions may also have tipped the scales in convincing the military leadership that the cost of remaining as is was much greater than the cost of reforming, just as the liberation war 70 years earlier had convinced the British that the 'cost of staying was much greater than the cost of leaving'.[27] And the sanctions issue was also linked to the realisation that sanctions were blocking American influence in a strategically important country between India and China.

Three signposts for the future

Myanmar International Terminal at Thilawa just south of Yangon is the country's largest seaport, handling the majority of Myanmar's imports and exports. One terminal deals with oil and gas exports. Further south are long lines of trucks stacked with huge logs of teak, waiting their turn to disgorge their loads. And further still is the car terminal, with new and second-hand imports lined up, the result of a relaxation of import regulations, which are likely to exacerbate traffic congestion. While the country remains dependent, for now, on much the same raw material exports as 50 years ago, if the rest of the region is anything to go by, it is only a matter of time before Myanmar is making vehicles for export. The area around the port has been prioritised as a Special Economic Zone, the first of three such areas in Myanmar.

This is not going to be easy. Mynamar's problems remain formidable. It is a land of extremes: scorching heat and drenching monsoons, rice and rivers, and elites and poverty.

Its infrastructure is among the weakest in the region.[28] The Asian Development Bank observes that only about one-quarter of Myanmar's population had access to electricity in 2011, versus all of Malaysia's and some 90 per cent in the Philippines and Vietnam. Only 1.26 people out of every 100 in Myanmar have fixed telephone lines, versus roughly sixteen in Indonesia, while only 0.03 out of 100 have broadband Internet subscriptions, compared to about eight in Malaysia. One-third of Myanmar does not have access to safe water. And while it has 40 kilometres of roads for every 1 000 square kilometres, Vietnam has 480. Myanmar has eighteen vehicles per 1 000 people, while Thailand has 370.

The constraints go beyond statistics.

At the Golden Myint shoe factory outside Yangon, owner Aung Min complains about the high cost of electricity and land. 'It is more expensive to buy land here than in Hollywood,' he smiles. His business is subject to regular blackouts and is reliant on his own generator to keep production going. National electricity production is 1 655 MW, while peak demand is estimated at 2 370 MW.[29]

Even so, his business produces 4 800 pairs of shoes daily, of which 15 per cent are for export, and he employs 500 workers at the smallest of eighteen such factories registered countrywide. Garment production is also growing, with 200 major factories registered in this sector. This growth reflects low labour rates, Myanmar's competitive advantage. While comparative wage rates in China are now $300 per month, and whereas Thailand and Cambodia 'in the margins of $10 per day', and Bangladesh 'about $60', Myanmar's rates are just $90 per month. This is partly because of supply. Aung Min gets between 'seven to ten' people looking for work each day. And low rates and menial work also reflect the paltry state of Myanmar's education system, where only half of children complete five years of schooling.

The pace at which it is moving explains why one foreign embassy, which 'received five commercial enquiries from its companies in all of 2011', by 2013 'received not less than one new enquiry each day for those wanting to do business in Myanmar'.[30]

There are other challenges. Corruption is endemic, the country ranking 172nd out of 174 places on Transparency International's 2012 Corruption Perception Index, above only Sudan, Afghanistan, North Korea and Somalia. Much of this is tied to military and other crony involvement throughout the economy. As Thant Myint-U has noted, 'In Burma by the 1990s, the military was the state. Army officers did everything. Normal government had withered away'.[31]

The political economy is, moreover, structured to accommodate and, for now, maintain vested interests across the country. In addition to its two major corporate interests in the Myanmar Economic Corporation and the Myanmar Economic Holdings Limited, the military has traditionally controlled customs and licensing among other areas – one reason that cars used to appreciate in value or that SIM cards once cost $1 000.

Equally, the war economy in the north is related to the control of natural resources, from drugs to jade. Sanctions also encouraged and fostered such illegality.[32] But things are changing: the budget was made public for the first time in 2012–13, if only partially so, not least given the extent of off-budget expenditure by the military, which accounts, in total, for around half of the budget, with resultant fiscal stresses, especially where the tax system is so weak.

As a result, while the government has a plan to diversify and reform the state, the details of this programme are seen as 'hugely challenging', given that the 'system is so stretched' with 'a handful of people doing everything'. This is amplified by the refusal to devolve authority and tendency to micromanage, not least given the small number of reformists.

After 50 years of misrule, there is hardly a sector of government and the economy that does not require reform and, sometimes, total overhaul. This will take time and resources. Managing popular expectations will be important, as will be handling tensions between ethnic groups in a society where discrimination and economic exploitation has defined government, although the armed forces remain steadfastly committed to national unity.

And strains between ethnic groups are overlaid with Buddhist-Muslim frictions. In all of this politics is becoming more competitive, not just for the government. Aung Sang Suu Kyi and her NLD, their red-and-white signs and T-shirts now in open view, also has to transition from political icon and prophet with a powerful international constituency to local politician. Regardless, Myanmar is moving in the right direction. Herein is a lesson, or two, for those seeking to encourage other countries along a reform path.

Teachings

To ensure reform in one of their number, regional actors have to be similarly arrayed, pushing more or less in the same direction for change. Without this dimension, reforms are unlikely. The international community has similarly to avoid giving any policy or political wiggle room.

Here the increasing economic differentiation of East Asian states is an important motivation. The Asian Tigers (Taiwan, South Korea, Singapore and Hong Kong) followed Japan's transformational example, and were in turn followed by the next generation of reformers, including Malaysia, Thailand, Vietnam, Indonesia and the Philippines, and later still, Cambodia and Laos. The success of each created the opportunities and regional example for the next. Myanmar, put simply, did not want to be left out, especially since it was once richer than those who have since moved ahead.

Self-respect and pride should not be underestimated as a force and barrier for change. Burmese society is characterised by *onana*, the need to avoid causing offence or for someone to lose face. Equally, not unlike in Africa, age earns respect, and the wisdom of elders is much venerated. No wonder the vestiges of, let alone the underlying assumptions behind, the colonial era grated.

Another lesson concerns those countries seeking to manage better their natural resources, to handle crony capitalism and rent-seeking, and deliver the conditions for diversification, economic growth and job creation. This diversification path is well trodden, at least in Asia, though others in Africa and to an extent in Latin America have found this difficult to emulate, in part because of a lack of political and policy discipline, and in part because of the challenge of managing high expectations often inflated by political developments.

All of this takes time. 'We were cave dwellers in economic terms,' said one Yangon government official, 'until just recently. Democratic economic development is going to take time to implement.' This is exacerbated where the country lacks an education system to support the reform process.

This relates to the importance of keeping things moving. As noted above, there are high expectations. There have been positive changes in Yangon, yet these are largely to be felt in the rural areas. 'In fact,' says Turnell, 'for many of those working the paddy fields, things have got harder in the last few years with higher inflation, ever more creaky infrastructure and continued poor education.' If the reformers can keep growth up, they will find the political process easier, especially the management of minorities by meeting aspirations.

Ensuring the fruits of reform are felt relates to the importance of creating a coalition for growth, both inside and outside government, which is in turn necessary to keep the process moving. There is only a limited cohort of those in favour of reform. The corollary is the importance of managing spoilers – in the case of Myanmar, populists who might use short-term redistributive measures to gain power, whatever the longer-term political and economic costs. Equally, there is a need to keep the military on-side while slowly undoing its stranglehold on the economy.

Finally, perhaps the most important lesson of all from Myanmar, as in many similar situations elsewhere, is that its people have been held back by the state. They should take heart that, even though the challenges appear formidable, they are not the first to pad this path. And when the circumstances change, people are quick to take advantage.

*

From Myanmar to Mali, successful engagement by outsiders in the domestic affairs of states requires a combination of domestic desperation (that the outsiders represent one of the few options), regional and international pressure on the various conflicting parties to settle, and a clear mandate and method. The latter requires leadership – or at least leadership that can seize the moment and appreciate the timing. From the perspective of the external intervener, whether this be in terms of engagement in conflict mediation or in encouraging economic reforms, the logic of the benefits of reform, while argumentatively clear to domestic and foreign audiences alike, sometimes has limited practical effect. Rather, the focus of intervention has to be on changing incentives – to increase the stake of those in power in the success of reforms.

25

SINGAPORE

Choices Behind Change

∗

A round the table in the meeting room at Temasek, the Singaporean investment company, were six executives from Brazil, Pakistan, Russia,
India, Zimbabwe and the US. Their diversity was illustrative of the meritocratic impetus that has driven the island-state for five decades. Temasek, the
original name of the fourteenth-century settlement in modern Singapore,
itself is emblematic of the island-state's tenets of growth. The $250-billion
company was founded in 1974 out of a need to separate government ownership of assets, including the ports and airline,[1] from their management. Even
though it is '100 per cent owned by government', Temasek's now international strategy and role is based fundamentally on commercial rather than
political rationale, very different to most developing countries, where government's economic choices are made overwhelmingly on political and not
commercial grounds.

∗

Singapore may indeed no longer be a useful example of success for other
developing nations to follow, at least for those states emerging from failure
in the twenty-first century. With a per capita GDP of over $51 000 ranking it
in the top ten worldwide according to the IMF, the Singapore story probably
seems a long way off for those countries stuck at levels around $1 000 – most
of the countries covered in this volume. It is a lesson in leadership, planning,
continuous innovation, commercial logic and using its only natural resource
– its people and minds – to best effect. It is, one African finance minister has
put it, 'less a salient lesson than an inspiration' of what is possible.[2]

Regardless, the Singapore story is relevant. It has come a long way in 50 years, and even further in 70, when, at the end of the Second World War, things looked very bleak. Kranji War Cemetery is there as a reminder of a brutal and destructive past. Sitting atop a slight hill 22 kilometres north of the city of Singapore, overlooking the Straits of Jahor, it is the resting place of 4 461 Commonwealth war graves and a memorial to another 24 000 who have no known final resting place.

It tells a story of colonial history, imperial ambition, failure and conquest. This much is evident from the variety of nationalities resting at Kranji, Rupert Brooke's 'corner of a foreign field' – Australian, British, Kiwi, Indian, Nepalese, Dutch, Sri Lankan and, of course, Chinese, Malay, Indian and other Singaporeans. Faced with the apparently unstoppable Japanese advance down the Malay Peninsula, on 30 January 1942 the British-led Commonwealth forces cut the Jahor causeway. Despite this move, a week later the Japanese crossed near Kranji. Running out of ammunition and faced with water shortages and a disintegrating force, Lieutenant General Arthur Percival had little option but to surrender to General Tomoyuki Yamashita, the 'Tiger of Malaya', on 15 February. It was the largest capitulation of British-led military personnel in history. During the Malaya and Singapore campaign, 30 000 Japanese troops had faced down nearly 140 000 Allied personnel, of which number some 30 000 died in combat or in captivity, many perishing in building the infamous Thai-Burma 'Death Railway'.

Three and a half years of bitter occupation commenced until Lord Mountbatten accepted the surrender of all Japanese forces in Southeast Asia at Singapore's municipal (city) hall in September 1945. The process of recovery was initially slow. Even twenty years later, at the time of Singapore's unexpected exit from the Federation of Malaya, the country was a 'Third World trading power, an entrepôt centre choked by polluted rivers',[3] where the bulk of the population did not have access to electricity, running water or other basic services, and per capita income was just $500.

Today, of course, the former colony is another country. Kranji, which had been a central ammunition depot, became a POW camp. The tops of the cranes of the former British Naval Dockyard at nearby Sembawang are just visible from the Commonwealth Memorial, the location now of a world-class ship-repair facility, one of the few useful bits of infrastructure the newly independent Singaporean government inherited and turned into a commercial asset. The main POW camp and hospital at Changi to the south-east of the island was transformed into the airport known today as *the* regional hub. The island, which has increased its size by 20 per cent, or 17 000 football fields, through land reclamation, is a sparkling high-tech metropolis.

Outlining contemporary lessons

There is much else to learn from Singapore's transition from a malaria-ridden swamp to innovation and technology leader. The closure of British bases from 1967 meant the loss of one-fifth of the economy. These problems were compounded by ethnic tensions, strikes, communist agitation and more than 10 per cent unemployment. But in just one generation Singapore transformed itself to a high-income country. By 1970, in just five years from independence, Singapore's per capita GDP had increased to $950, and unemployment was under 3 per cent. By the turn of the century, per capita GDP was $25 000; in the five decades since independence, per capita GDP has increased thirteenfold in real terms.

The importation of talent has been one key aspect. From little over one million people at independence, of the 2013 population of 5.3 million, around 1.5 million are expatriates, permanent residents or migrant workers, the latter mainly from South Asia and the Philippines. The injection of immigrants is part of a strategy to maintain GDP targets – and one that is much criticised by the opposition Workers' Party, which fears a dilution of national identity and the risk of unsustainable population injections as the country attempts to make up for a low (1.16 per cent in 2011)[4] total fertility rate (well below the replacement rate of 2.1 per cent) as the result of an ageing population, arguing that 'such trade-offs should be made in favour of the well-being of Singaporeans and not GDP targets.'[5]

There is, inevitably, a flip-side to this choice: rapid growth facilitated by a sharp increase in the inflow of foreign labour has created social tensions, as seen in the riots on 8 December 2013 (the same day as the start of the Japanese attack on Malaya in 1942 and preceding Pearl Harbour because of the time difference). The riots involved Indian migrant workers after an Indian worker was killed when he was knocked down by a bus.

Even so, along with skills, the use of its (limited) natural assets and acquisition of cutting-edge technology has kept Singapore at the forefront of a global service economy. As one example, some 30 million (TEU – twenty-foot equivalent unit) containers were offloaded at the ports in 2008, making it the second busiest worldwide, with the target of 45 million TEUs by 2013. Some 85 per cent of these are transhipped, with connectivity to 600 ports worldwide and more than 60 vessels sailing daily. Around 90 per cent of containers are cleared by customs within eight minutes, 100 per cent within just thirteen.

And its policies – rather than its rhetoric – have reflected its intention to capitalise on its nineteenth-century advantage as a crossroads between goods and people.

There is a zero tariff on imported goods, while personal and corporate tax rates were by 2009 capped at 20 per cent and 18 per cent respectively. Its trade equals over three times its GDP, facilitated by a network of fourteen free trade area agreements (with nine more under negotiation in 2009), coupled with its regional relationships in the Association of Southeast Asian Nations. Singapore is the gateway to the world of free trade.

While the government's International Enterprise agency is used to promote Singaporean business outside, Singapore's Economic Development Board (EDB) has, since its inception in 1961, aimed to create jobs and business opportunities by attracting ideas, technology and capital and by enhancing the business environment. Through its 22 offices worldwide, the EDB has been central in asking of government: what is the next big thing that the island should be planning for?

This requires forward thinking since such strategies take around a decade to take effect. Very little use has been made of fiscal incentives to attract companies, since projects need to be sustainable in their own right. Increasing resources are spent on research and development, which rose threefold in twenty years to 3 per cent of GDP by 2010.

Given that in the mind of its policy-planners Singapore 'cannot survive without globalising', trade is not the only aspect of globalisation that has been embraced. By 2013, there were nearly 40 000 international corporations on the island, 7 000 of which were multinationals and 60 per cent based their headquarters there. The EDB recognises that it is engaged in a 'global war' on talent, contrary to many countries under study in this volume, which are instinctively protectionist. Indeed, the EDB's 'future strategies' aim to position Singapore as a 'home' for business, talent and innovation. These three aspects are, by contrast, foreign concepts to many fragile states, despite their rhetoric to the contrary, with tension-filled relations between business and government, identify-based politics that dissuades rather than attracts foreign talent, and an educational environment that fails to accommodate youth aspirations and development needs.

This underpinning philosophy has seen Singapore continuously change focus: in the 1960s this was on labour-intensive industries; in the 1970s on more skills-intensive industry; the following decade saw a shift to more capital-intensive business, notably the petro-chemical sector; services and technology provided the focus in the 1990s; and in the 2000s, it was knowledge and innovation. During the 2010s, there has again been a shift to laser optics, robotics and 3D printing as part of a $500-million 'future of manufacturing' government-sponsored programme that seeks synergy between such 'disruptive technologies' and aims to ensure that Singapore's economy maintains the manufacturing sector's one-quarter share of its $276 billion (by 2012) GDP.

A very flexible labour market helps companies to withstand external shocks, changes and challenges, driven by a philosophy that 'it is better to have a low-paying job than no job at all'. A symbiotic relationship is enjoyed between government, the unions and business. As senior minister (and former prime minister), Goh Chok Tong, put it, 'Singapore Inc. is a metaphor for the private sector, government and the unions all working as one.'[6] This institutional arrangement helped to resolve the stand-off between the unions, government and business early on in Singapore's independence. This type of thinking was necessary given the circumstances the new country had been born into in August 1965: the unpleasant and unexpected divorce from the Malaysian Federation, regional conflict in the form of Konfrontasi between Malaysia and Indonesia, pressing problems of high unemployment, housing and education, and the threat of civil unrest. Instead of being overwhelmed by the challenges before government, Singapore did not let a good crisis go to waste.

All of this is a reflection of the need to institutionalise the principles of growth. In Singapore's case (as in any other), these were: fiscal prudence, a stable and competitive exchange rate, low interest rates, price stability, outside orientation, a focus on growth engines (such as manufacturing, services and the necessary soft and hard infrastructure) and improving factor competitiveness. This has demanded discipline from government over the entire post-independence-year period, as well as attention to detail and sound, prescient leadership. Singapore has filled, through hands-on management, the gaps prevalent in other developing regions between vision, planning and execution. It has also relied on novel policy ideas, for example the public Housing Development Board (HDB), which provides 80 per cent of the overall housing requirements, or over 900 000 apartments, for Singaporeans from just 23 per cent in 1964. Apartments are funded, in turn, through a combination of home-owner grants and loans, the latter both commercial and from the Central Provident Fund, a mandatory savings scheme, in which employers and employees contribute respectively (a maximum of) 16 per cent and 20 per cent of salary. This scheme was not only necessary to clean up Singapore's 'squatter colonies and slums', says the HDB's Sng Cheng Keh, but home ownership gave the population a 'stake in their society, building a strong work ethic, a store of value to be monetised, and a sense of belonging'.[7] The philosophical origins of the HDB go back 100 years, when the tale of Singapore was one of two cities and societies: one driven by international finance, steam and the telegraph (Singapore's trade increasing eight times between 1873 and 1913, for example), rich and living it up; the other, a rickshaw society, marginalised, overcrowded, violent, poor, disease- and drug-ridden, and where laws and justice did not apply equally.

The key Singapore lesson is of the need for assiduous and innovative planning to move from vision to actuality, a process rooted in the realities of meeting the population's principal needs – jobs and housing were the priorities in the 1960s, better infrastructure and urban renewal those of the 1970s, for example – by generating economic growth and mobilising financial resources, among other methods through forced savings and targeting local and foreign direct investment. Indeed, a striking aspect of Singapore's development is the continuous, driving reinvention and fast-paced expansion of its model; one year a scheme, the next a Singapore Flyer, Marina Bay Sands, ArtScience Museum, underground oil storage tanks, $1-billion Gardens by the Bay, and so on. 'It is because we don't want to be fail,' reflected one official. 'We also have no natural resources to fall back on,' she added.

The need to keep ahead and the earlier social pressures combined to sacrifice a few sacred cows along the way, such as in the development of Singapore International Airlines (SAI). Founded from the dissolution of the air partnership with Malaysia in 1972, SIA was the first to acquire a 747 in Southeast Asia, busting the European and North American dominance of the skies along the way. But to get ahead, it had to challenge the International Air Transport Association's (IATA's) stranglehold, which regulated everything from sandwich sizes to the costs of tickets, headphones and drinks. Under J.Y. Pillay, who had previously headed the economic conversion of the former British bases, SIA left IATA and revolutionised customer service, paving the way for the development of an airline, by the 2010s, seen as the second-largest worldwide by market capitalisation, with a value of $14 billion. The same sort of carefully adjudged risk taking, under Singapore's first finance minister, Goh Keng Swee, had led to the earlier development of the Jurong Industrial Estate, what he described as 'an act of faith in the people of Singapore', but a decision seen at the time as little more than 'folly'.[8]

Bucking the trend did not mean that Singapore sought to buck the markets or the needs and sensitivities of multinational companies and international finance: to the contrary, it acted to strengthen regulatory institutions to shore up early on any perception of developing country risk. It is also important not to take the wrong political lessons from Singapore: that an authoritarian government is necessary for growth or for difficult decisions to be made. Yes, the island like others in the region – including South Korea, China, Turkey, Indonesia and Taiwan – has modernised economically under authoritarian rule. But Singapore is hardly the Soviet Union when it comes to freedom of individual choice and the type of economic system followed. And, yes, sometimes democracy may not be conducive to political stability, especially in low-income settings.

But what does this say about those countries that have not developed in spite of – or because of – possessing authoritarian systems, of which there were many in Africa, for example, up until the end of the Cold War? While some might like the 'big-man' image, the reality of Singapore is more nuanced, as will be seen, in involving much more than one person and fundamentally being reliant on institutions in the pursuit of development. The arguments that purport for a separation of democratic and economic reforms presume, too, that elites preside over passive populations, whereas in most cases democracy has been a bitterly fought for contest led by activist civil populations against these elites, not least in Africa. The most remarkable aspect in Singapore's transition is in its unwillingness to look back – something it shares with others in the region. Whereas most, if not all, African nations berate colonialism at every turn (not least since it offers the prospect of aid and of externalising their problems and excusing regime inadequacies), Singaporeans or, for that matter, Vietnamese seldom mention this history. It is not that they do not have things to complain about: on 18 February 1942, large numbers of Chinese were assembled by their Japanese occupiers at mass screening areas. Many were accused of anti-Japanese activities, and summarily executed. It is estimated that 50 000 lost their lives in such Sook Ching (literally, to purge/eliminate) operations. They are commemorated in the Civilian War Memorial near Raffles Hotel, with four 70-metre vertical pillars symbolising the ethnic Chinese, Malays, Indians and other races who perished.

Remarkably, even this pales against the Vietnamese suffering during the Indochina War. An estimated three million Vietnamese (around 7 per cent of its population) perished along with 58 183 US troops, though the war still remains defined by American fears and losses. Regardless, the language of the region remains transfixed on competitiveness, not colonialism, where increased productivity and not the state is viewed as the key to job creation.

Singaporean officials speak with some frustration about the many study trips they endure from other regions and even countries within their own region, which translate into nothing 'other than the fact they want us', says one Ministry of Foreign Affairs official 'to supply ready-made solutions, free-of-charge to fix their problems'. Harvard's Matt Andrews has noted in this context that 'many African governments are pursuing reforms as signals to ensure continued external support and not as real solutions to the problems they face'.[9] While external support may continue as a result, these reforms are often inappropriate, not implemented and do not yield the expected results. Where more successful, reforms tend to be 'problem driven', meaning that 'they don't start with someone identifying a "best practice" reform that looks good on paper'. They also emerge 'through a step-by-step process of experimentation and learning'. And they are also 'the product of broad engagement by a myriad players, not just presidents and ministers, who ensure that the emergent solutions actually work and who ultimately own the results'. More than anything, writes Andrews, the kind of processes that 'generate real change and improved functionality require hard work, not easy reforms'.

The experience of leadership

Born in July 1924, S.R. Nathan was the sixth president of the Republic of Singapore between 1999 and 2011, in the process becoming the island-state's longest-serving president.[10]

This was a fitting climax to a long and distinguished civil service career, which had started much earlier as a medical social worker in the mid-1950s. After a stint at the Ministry of Foreign Affairs, he was appointed deputy secretary of the Ministry of Home Affairs, before moving to the Ministry of Defence where he served as director of the Security and Intelligence Division. In this role, he was among a group of officials who volunteered to be held hostage by the Japanese Red Army during the Laju Incident on

31 January 1974, when members of the Red Army bombed petroleum tanks on Pulau Bukom off the Singaporean coast. He was later decorated for his role in this event.

Nathan has also successfully mixed public with private experience, as is often the Singapore way with its officials. After a second stint at the Ministry of Foreign Affairs for three years until February 1982, he left to become the executive chairmperson of the Straits Times Press. He has held a variety of directorships, including that of chairperson of Mitsubishi Heavy Industries Singapore. He was posted as Singapore's high commissioner to Malaysia, and from July 1990 until June 1996 as ambassador to the US. He was made ambassador-at-large on his return and concurrently served as director of the Institute of Defence and Strategic Studies at the Nanyang Technological University. He resigned both posts upon being elected, unopposed, as president for the first time on 18 August 1999 and re-elected in 2005.

'Things,' he recalls, 'did not seem hopeless back at Singapore's independence from the [Malayan] Federation in 1965; they were. Independence came overnight. There was no gestation period, hardly any time to prepare at all. We did not have time, experience, precedent or the practices of independence. We had our entrepôt market cut and our economic hinterland removed. We were also under threat. We broke off from a federation that possessed all the guns – they could have imposed their rule on us, and the only reason why they didn't was because we had Australian, New Zealand and UK troops here to fight the communist insurgency.'

There was no magic, he insists, in Singapore's transformation. 'We had to decide what to do, in order of priority, and what the impediments were and how we should overcome these. When I was asked as head of state, "What is Singapore's magic?", I always replied: "There is no magic. It's a question only of whether you have the will to do something else." Usually those that asked me the question then changed the subject, presumably because that's not the magic answer they want to hear.'

Although Nathan emphasises the role of leadership as a means of setting and articulating a vision to people 'who might not even have fully understood this even though they stood listening to them', this team was made up of more than just one man in Lee Kuan Yew, however. Lee was the man who presented the public face and managed the politics between the players, but there was a team. 'From the start, when we were fighting for internal self-government in the 1950s, there was always a team, among them: an economist (the no-nonsense Dr Goh Keng Swee),[11] another a journalist (S.

Rajaratnam, later foreign minister) who had learnt his politics as a pamphleteer in the anti-colonial movement in London, the lawyer Eddie Barker who was the intellectual, and Devon Nair from the communist camp, which helped us understand the other side's ideals and techniques. They had their differences, of course, but these were never articulated in public. For example, there were disagreements on whether to enter the federation and its risks, or on fighting the communists, or over the implementation of laws that were repressive, differences on how to treat organised labour, and the contradiction between protecting the interests of labour and ensuring the interests of the unemployed.'

Lee's memoirs[12] are testament to how the former prime minister regarded the opinion of his colleagues and how often there were differences of outlook within government on key issues, including notable developments such as Changi Airport, when there was some disagreement about whether to develop the existing field at Paya Lebar or proceed with a new and very expensive site at Changi. International consultants and a committee of senior officials had recommended a second runway at Paya Lebar, at an extra S$400 million compared to S$1.5 billion for Changi. Lee successfully motivated for Changi. As one of his senior civil servants puts it: '[Lee] did not get everything his own way as there were senior cabinet ministers like Goh Keng Swee who were just as influential on policy. The difference is that Lee was the most articulate and shaped public perceptions.'[13] Additionally, Singapore made sure that the best and brightest were attracted, that they paid them properly, and they were given full support by leadership to do their job. With delegated power and authority went responsibility, of course.

While Lee was something of a one-man band in terms of the use of his time abroad to promote Singapore, he used his time strategically. He never seemed to grow fond of being out the country and used to the trappings, something African leadership would do well to heed.

Nathan emphasises the value of growth as the essential glue and moderator of extremism. 'In our case, when the economy was depressed, race became a very important factor, as each person sought advantage through his race – Indian, English origin, Malay and so on – in trying to get a job. It's only prosperity,' he reminds, 'which has diluted that trend.'

In all of this he maintains that the Singapore 'model' does not exist per se. 'But there are key building blocks,' he says, 'along the way' that should be followed by every state in their own way: 'security, labour relations, economic policy, the need for foreign investment promotion'.

Some things are unavoidable. 'Low-income countries cannot escape the low-wage model in creating jobs. Politicians cannot afford,' he says, 'to be moralistic about this. They must accept that investors will come where they will make a profit, otherwise they won't come at all. You cannot have Western-style trade unionism in such countries if you want to progress.' This may be surprising advice from a man who cut his public service teeth in the 1960s in the Labour Movement, but as he puts it, 'You cannot protect the employed at the expense of the unemployed.' He reminds that 'as demand goes up, so pay goes up'.

Here he blames the West for creating such an unrealistic set of expectations in this regard on the part of developing countries, including in Singapore at independence and in contemporary Africa. 'If you look at the founding fathers in the United States, they did not prioritise the kind of democracy that they have today. There was a common faith in this regard, but there were many injustices along the way, not least those caused to the Indian population and through slavery. When I was ambassador to the United States I used to say to them, "We have done nothing of this sort, so give us time" [to develop our democracy]. Democracy is a process of development – where progress is made one step at a time.'

And in all of this, he comes back over again to the unavoidable importance of setting priorities to match resources and specific circumstances, and of leadership in not only possessing the will to make these choices but the personality to explain and justify these to their citizens.

*

Singapore thus still matters, like Vietnam and other rapid developers, as an example not only of best policy practice, but principally as an illustration of what is possible over a generation, as tough as these lessons might be for those wishing to find a short cut to success. Singapore itself learnt from others. 'We will one day make the TV sets,' said Lee Kuan Yew after a trip to Egypt in the late 1950s. 'They make 50 000 annually with RCA, an American company ... We can do that here. Our workers are as skilful and hardworking as the Egyptians or any other countries who make the tyres, the TV sets, the air-conditioning units ... why must we always be buying and selling other people's goods?' he asked.[14] Fifty years on and 'there is nothing wrong', says Singapore's Deputy Prime Minister and Minister of Finance Tharman Shanmugaratnam 'with starting off with low skills and getting into the game'.[15] It offers an opportunity 'to move into the manufacturing value chain; that's what we did'. As was noted also in the context of Myanmar, too, the intermediaries translating one experience to another are important to determining success.

While Singapore might, in the twenty-first century, then, apparently hold few lessons for fragile states, the basics today are no different to the basics then: leadership, vision, planning, execution, attention to detail, responsibility, accountability, skills and education, and innovation and continuous reinvention.

26

SOMALILAND

The Power of Local Ownership

*

'Supreme' fuel bowsers shuffled their load between the parked aircraft. 'The happy way to fly', proclaimed the airline poster. 'Dubai, Jeddah, Nairobi, Kampala, Djibouti, Mogadishu, Hargeisa, Berbera, Bassaso and Galkaio' were its stated destinations. Most seemed like holidays in hell, except if you were, like me, getting out of Mogadishu.

Behind the departure hall's doors was a sweaty scrum of burkas, screaming children, hennaed beards and plastic chairs. The overworked air conditioners were, as the stickers on them subtly reminded, a gift of the International Organisation for Migration and the Government of Japan. Ditto the scanners enabling access to the area, and as the signs proudly announced, just about every notable building project in the city.

This was a state getting to its feet very wobbly. Little wonder that the slogan of the airport handling company was 'Doing difficult jobs in difficult places'.

Outside the *qat* team had nearly finished unpacking the Dash-8, one of two regular morning flights from Nairobi carrying the leaf amphetamine, a $750-million annual fly-in trade to Mogadishu alone. Chew on that.

The *qat* express was later joined by an ancient DC-9 and a number of plain white EU and other charters, all with Kenyan registrations. Then in waffles the grandmother of them all, an Ilyushin Il-18, a four-engined turboprop built more than 50 years ago. It looked totally knackered, though, and seemed out of sorts, taking the whole runway to stop.

Never mind, I thought, it is a cargo plane, another *qat* runner or something bringing in supplies for the then 17 000 African Union AMISOM troops.

No such luck. The Boeing 737 denoted on my e-ticket was about to be gazumped by the Soviet Union's finest. This nice surprise, however, was still in the future as we lined up at the gate two hours late for departure, still not sure where the bus was going to take us.

When it dumped us at the steps of the dinosaur, I asked myself, orphans and widow in mind, in the words of the Clash, 'Should I stay or should I go?' I had to get to Hargeisa in adjacent Somaliland, but this plane might prove to be the parody of the airline, an 'unhappy way to die'.

But, as they say in parts of Johannesburg, '*vok voort*'. Against my better judgement I stepped aboard, eyeing the pools of fluid forming beneath the engines and the corrosion eating away at the top of the tailplane.

Inside was worse.

Things were very tired. The oversized porthole windows, replete with hand-painted surrounds, were totally opaque with frosting of the Perspex, condensation and grime, some sort of frothy liquid bubbling continuously between the double-glazing on pressurisation cycles. The seats bent over forwards and backwards like a spineless academic. The tables were hewn by a Siberian blacksmith, but they, too, had succumbed to the ravages of Somali maintenance, as had the lights, air swivels and everything else in sight. In fact, the only things that seemed to work were the engines and presumably the pilots.

Whatever they were paying them, it was not enough. Gauging from the number of *Allahu Akbars* and *Inshallahs* on the intercom, they were also seeking a little outside assistance. They were not the only ones. 'Why are you on this plane?' asked the man next to me to the only obviously non-Somali person on board. I could only swallow audibly in reply.

After an endless takeoff, we clawed our way skywards. Ninety minutes later we were descending into Berbera in Somaliland, much to the relief of the passenger of little faith and the woman across the aisle praying openly while gently thudding her head into the slumped seat in front.

Berbera has one of the longest runways on the continent. Built by the Soviet Union in the mid-1970s to counter the US's military presence in the region, it was used to launch patrols over the Indian Ocean and Gulf by Tupolev Tu-95 'Bear' long-range maritime patrol aircraft. The Ilyushin was coming home, sort of.

In fact, the hot-as-hell coastal town of Berbera is something of a Soviet aerospace graveyard, with three Il-8s and a dead Antonov lying derelict where it had veered off the runway after a heavy landing, which destroyed the undercarriage.

When Somalia's dictator Siad Barre switched sides from the Soviets to the US in 1977, the facility was passed over for Washington's use, being surveyed by the US Army Corps of Engineers as an emergency landing site for the Space Shuttle in 1987. They also built a swimming pool, of course, though that lies forlornly empty, with the strains of Credence Clearwater Revival seldom heard around these parts now.

When the Somalilanders gained control over their territory with the fall of the Siad Barre regime in 1991 and declared their independence from Somalia, the airport and nearby port were among the territory's few assets, and were quickly stripped by looters as Mogadishu's control relaxed. Briefly taken by the rebel Somaliland National Movement and then bombed by Siad Barre's airforce in 1988, the capital Hargeisa, 160 kilometres inland, was also in ruins.

Yet there is more to its recovery and relative stability than miles of tarmac or the absence of industry. Somaliland's relative calm compared to its southern neighbour reflects twenty-something years of consensual politics, hammered out in the aftermath of the civil war. The former British protectorate has developed a stable system of politics, blending modern and traditional elements, including an elected president and House of Representatives as well as an Upper House of Elders (*guurti*), securing the support of clan-based power structures. The commitment to representative democracy can be seen in the staging of local elections in 2002, presidential elections in 2003 and again in June 2010, and parliamentary elections in 2005.

Critics say that Somaliland's democracy was facilitated by the dominance of a single clan, the Isaaq, unlike Somalia, which has to balance the competing interests and ambitions of four major clans and several smaller ones. But this understates the differences between the Isaaq's sub-clans and sub-sub-clans, ignores the internal violence that accompanied the birth process, which had to be resolved, and overlooks the tremendous hard work that went into it.

Out and in then out again

The nineteenth-century traveller Richard Burton's famed comment on the Somalis, 'every man his own sultan', perfectly expressed the rejection of that obligation to obey that underlies the institutions of governance. Where individuals did gain authority, this was derived from their wisdom, piety or ability to articulate some project of broad appeal, and was personal to themselves. What passed for the colonial state in British-ruled Somaliland involved little more than the supervision, with the lightest of touches, of existing conflict management mechanisms; while in Italian Somalia, to the south, colonial statehood remained almost entirely alien to the indigenous population. Somalis had – and have – their own mechanisms, including the form of customary law known as Xeer, for managing the often fractious relationships between themselves, to which the colonial state was generally an irrelevance, at worst positively damaging.

In June 1960, the protectorate of Somaliland achieved independence from Britain. Five days later, it elected to join Italian Somalia in a union. (French Somalia – now Djibouti – only acquired independence from Paris in 1977.) The marriage did not work, with Somalia descending not into military dictatorship, civil war and chaos, but with Mogadishu repressing its northern Somaliland constituent in good measure throughout.[1]

In the centre of the capital, Hargeisa, is the 18 May independence memorial, comprising a MiG-17 fighter-bomber erected on a plinth. This commemorates the event when, having lost control of the province, Siad Barre ordered his air force, operating from the local airport, to bomb the city, which was briefly captured by Somali National Movement (SNM) fighters in May 1988, resulting in many thousands of civilian casualties. As Mark Bradbury notes, by the time of Siad Barre's fall three years later, the main cities of Hargeisa and Burso 'had been reduced to rubble and all public utilities and services had been destroyed. Hargeisa from the air,' he writes, 'resembled a city of dry swimming pools, which on closer inspection were shells of houses whose roofs had been systematically looted during the war. Many villages had suffered similar fates and both urban and rural areas were littered with landmines and unexploded ordnance. Landing at Hargeisa airport in 1991, one had to gamble on surviving the drive into the centre of town without losing one's luggage or car to armed men.'[2] Not for nothing was Hargeisa known as the 'roofless city' after systemic looting by Siad Barre's forces had stripped it of roof sheeting and even doors and their frames.

Somaliland's democracy was built on five major internal conferences, starting with the Grand Conference of the Northern Peoples in Burao, held over six weeks and concluding with the declaration of Somaliland's independence on 18 May 1991. The capital of British Somaliland, Buroa was then, in the words of Mohamud Jama, then a UN official, 'a mess – the stench and flies forced us to wear masks over our mouths. The refugee population and the militias had defecated in the buildings, and there were no services.' The declaration was signed in an octangular tin-roofed building near the colonial governor's building, without electricity and running water, the white walls outside still pockmarked by bullet holes, the blue inside smeared with dirt and graffiti.

Today children play on its porch, swinging on its pillars, darting around the sandy streets. The city is determined to leave the building just as it was, says the deputy mayor, Mohamed Mahmoud (known widely as 'Ubax leh' – the flower seller) as a memorial to the heady events of 1991. And Burao, the capital of the Togdheer province, five hours' bumpy driving from Hargeisa, is now stable and prospering, the site of reputedly the largest livestock market in eastern Africa, commerce further fuelled by remittances, urbanisation and its status as the second-largest city in Somaliland, the population having swelled from 70 000 in 1991 to 450 000 in just 23 years.

Back in the early 1990s, however, efforts were focused on resolving deep-seated tribal and other enmities. These conferences, unlike the peace process in Somalia to the south, were largely managed and financed without foreign support. Somaliland's events were 'bottom-up, not top-down', emphasised the then minister of foreign affairs, Birmingham University-educated Mohamed Omar, in 2012, 'unlike Somalia's, which has been top-down, driven by donors through leadership and taking place outside the country'. Somalilanders concentrated on achieving peace, not on acquiring financial rents for delegates from the process, a feature continually blighting Somalia's attempts.

The last peace conference in Boroma, a town of 40 000 on the road to Djibouti, in 1993 was held in the region of then governor (and later vice president) Abdirahman Ahmed Ali, taking place over five months 'under the trees' where people brought their own food and their own shelter. 'This type of dialogue was not new to us, as from time immemorial, from before the colonial period, Somalilanders,' says Ali, 'had their own reconciliation process, and when government institutions failed, these traditional measures took over once more.' More than anything, he stresses, 'its strength lay in the fact it was home-grown, indigenous and not alien. Foreign help was absent, which was a blessing, which is why it was successful.'

After Boroma, the future direction was set. But it also took sound leadership to keep the process on track. It has been a long slog rather than a single event, re-establishing law and order and local authorities, and deciding on and then building government institutions. There were differences to be settled between three groups outside of the complex clan and sub-clan structures: *mana-gaaho* (referring to a road in Ethiopia in which the SNM had its bases, denoting those who fought in the insurgency); *mana-festo* (those who stayed in Mogadishu, and tried to negotiate a political settlement with Siad Barre); and *mana-seer* (those who lived the comfortable life outside and drank sweet – *aseer* – drinks).[3]

There were also early differences between those who wanted the territory to remain part of greater Somalia, those who wanted increased autonomy and those who sought outright independence, resolved in favour of the latter. But once this had been agreed, it provided a common goal around which to unite. More intractably, there was a clash of cultures of governance, between those intent on enriching themselves from their control of militias and continued instability perpetrated by those who did not, says Omar, 'have the security of the country in mind but only their own interests and power'. This mood has pervaded in Somalia to the south since 1991. Slowly, and again through adroit leadership, reconciliation and the building of institutions, the warlords in Somaliland eventually gave in to a longer-term governance vision.

This was not without violence. The process had to survive several bouts of internal conflict related to control of revenues around key facilities, notably the port in Berbera in 1992, Hargeisa's airport in November 1994 and road checkpoints near Burao in March 1995. Similarly, and more recently, the secessionist movements in the areas of Sool, Sanaag and Cayn, which decided to band together into a new independent state within Somalia called Khaatumo, were partly fuelled by clan differences. Yet, it is weak governance institutions, the effects of the drought and lack of jobs and economic opportunities, says Abdullahi Mohammed Odawa, director of Hargeisa University's Observatory of Conflict and Violence Prevention, that are the common denominators for most instances of violence, whatever the clan differences.

Disarmament and demobilisation followed reconciliation. Militias were disarmed and some of their members brought into the 7 500-strong national army and 10 000 police force. This happened, says the former vice president, 'through a combination of reconciliation and family support to take this step'. There was little by way of finances to sweeten their decision. Ali recalls the day that Admiral Jonathan Howe, the special representative for Somalia to UN Secretary General Boutros Boutros-Ghali (from March 1993 to February 1994) came to Hargeisa. 'In Mogadishu, he had a big office doing all the Ds – demobilisation, demining and disarmament – with millions of dollars in its budget. He asked me: "What do you need?" I said we would accept assistance with our efforts given its vital importance to our process. He said "yes", but nothing ever materialised. Instead, we did it by ourselves with very little ... but perhaps,' he notes, 'that is why it worked.'

Local civil society quickly also took off, keeping politicians honest. As one measure, there are no fewer than four English weekly newspapers, and eight Somali language versions in Somaliland today. This has helped to keep the conflict resolution process constantly on track, including at tense times, such as the presidential contest in 2003, which was won by just 80 votes.

Finally, the need to construct a domestic revenue base has firmed local ownership of the process. Somaliland's success has been in spite of the lack of diplomatic recognition and the donor volumes that would inevitably accompany that status. No country formally recognises Somaliland: outside of Africa, the world is waiting for Africans to make the first move; inside the continent, Somaliland's uncertain status favours those neighbours who want to keep it dependent on their patronage and those who fear secessionist tendencies within their own borders.

No honey, no swarm

While there is an international humanitarian organisation and considerable NGO presence in Somaliland, the absence of international recognition has dampened aid flows and, consequently, and more positively, the extent of the 'swarm' of external players.[4] Rather than waiting on change, Somaliland has had, again, to make a plan. In a tough, dry region, hampered by diplomatic isolation, revenues have been hard to come by. Inflows are reliant on diaspora remittances and the trade in livestock, especially with nearby Yemen and Saudi Arabia.

The minister of mining, energy and water resources, once a US oil executive, is exercised on the role played in this regard by international agencies. 'The international system,' he reflects, 'is geared not to getting out of a crisis, but keeping you there by responding only to war, refugees, internally displaced persons and other aspects of collapse. While such "flies in your face" might appeal to the system and to those giving money,' he says, 'it only makes the system purveyors of poverty, rather than being one geared to supporting the organic solution required.'

Aid flows have been steady rather than spectacular, one side effect of a lack of international recognition. This is a source of great frustration among Somalilanders. The head of the English-language *Republican* newspaper says: 'It keeps people out. It keeps the state fragile. It keeps investors out. It shuts the door on international monetary organisations. It limits the progress of the country, trade, and travel. It keeps us an isolated island. Our recognition,' he added, 'is our right.' Or as another official put it, 'The Somali state had given us so little for 30 years, it was necessary to do it differently. That the Somaliland state has given us so much in the last twenty shows us this was the correct decision.' As the deputy head of the Academy for Peace and Development, Abdirahman Yusuf Duale, reflected, 'In 1991, there was no water, no electricity, nothing ... Its change has come about today through an organic process, where the public own the government.' And there are wider aspects. As Mohamed Omar argues, 'We offer an alternative to Somalia – a credible, stable, peaceful, transparent and democratic system.'

'Peace is a critical first step in recovery and development,' reminds Ignatius Takawira, the head of the United Nations Development Program (UNDP) in Hargeisa in 2011.[5] But getting beyond it is more difficult, and demands local ownership of development. And this has proven much more easily said than done in Somaliland, since non-recognition has not only limited the range of funding sources (including notably the African Development Bank and World Bank) but has compromised the need for the government to be in the driver's seat. As a result, NGOs have become a channel for donor funds, carrying out projects on a contractual basis rather than having government take control through budget support. Donor funding is estimated at $120 million annually, around half of this, by 2014, channelled into the Somaliland Development Fund. Most of this Fund goes into roads and water infrastructure, and much of the rest into boosting agriculture. By comparison, the EU alone was spending €25 million each month in Somalia to the south.

The absence of formal international acknowledgment stings, but Somalilanders still see little alternative to the path they have chosen, recognition or not.

'It is almost 20 years,' said President Ahmed Mohamed Mohamoud 'Silanyo' in June 2011, 'since Somaliland has reclaimed its independence. Before that it was fighting for a very long time to reclaim that independence. Like many other countries, as part of the Somali people as a whole, during the time when we were part of the British protectorate, Somalis were divided in many parts, between French Somaliland in Djibouti, and between Kenya and Ethiopia. There was at one time a desire to unite all Somalis as one.'

Known to Somalis by his nickname Silanyo, born in 1936 in Burao and educated at the universities of London and Manchester, where he received a Master's degree in economics, Somaliland's fourth president[6] served as an official at the Ministry of Planning and Coordination in Mogadishu before becoming national minister of planning and coordination between 1969 and 1973, minister of commerce (1973–78 and 1980–82) and the chairperson of the National Economic Board (1978–80), before serving as the chairman of the rebel Somali National Movement from 1982 to 1990. A member of Somaliland's House of Representatives from 1993 to 1997, he was the minister of finance from 1997 to 1999, and minister of planning and coordination from 1999 to 2001. He won the 2010 election against the incumbent Dahir Riyale by 49.59 per cent to 33.23 per cent, taking office on 27 July 2010.

He remembers the period leading up to Somaliland's independence on 26 June 1960. 'In the succeeding I was young at the time, at that time our nationalism was growing everywhere. That led to many, many wars, with Ethiopia so many times … but unfortunately this was not supported by the international community, and led to disasters everywhere. Eventually we had no choice as Somalis but to give up … and to remain separate [communities] in Kenya and Ethiopia … eventually also the people of Somaliland after a very long struggle decided to re-establish their independence on 18 May 1991.

'During this period, there is no doubt about it, it is no secret, that Somaliland has been peaceful … what some have described as an "oasis of peace" in the Horn of Africa, compared to other parts of Somali-speaking territory where stability has become very elusive. Now we developed a constitution, a democratic system of government, and established peace and security, and despite the fact that we have not had international support, in the sense of international recognition. This does not mean that the international community does not engage with us. It does and governments help us … in various fields, in health, in development and education, in many areas. All the same, we are not entitled to certain institutions such as the World Bank and the IMF, institutions that were set up to assist developing countries, to push their development.

'If we were to wait for Somalia to settle down, it would mean that we would not even exist. Since we have established our constitution and a democratisation process and security and development, we feel that we are entitled from the international community not just to engage with us, but to recognise us.

'The basic issue that borders could not be changed as they were from the time of independence has worked against us. But that principle does not work in two ways ... On 26 June 1960 when we became independent, we were not part of Somalia, we joined Somalia days later. So the fact that borders should remain as they are at the time of independence, that principle of Africa breaking up does not apply to Somaliland. Secondly, but even if you accept that principle ... it has been changed by realities like South Sudan ... We feel that the people of Somaliland are entitled to recognition and support and assistance. No matter what happens, we have waited, and we have struggled for a very long time. Even if we have to wait for 100 years, we will continue exercising our independence, our stability and our development ...'

He added, 'The advantage of recognition for Somaliland is everything, it is a lot. We would be a full member of the international community. There would be much more confidence by business people to invest in Somaliland. We would be part of the programmes of the World Bank and other institutions.'

Silanyo believes that the success of Somaliland was dependent on local ownership. 'If ever there is an example of a country in our region that has built its own institutions, it is Somaliland. The Council of Elders has been built up entirely by Somaliland ... These institutions developed during our long struggle for independence. It is not directly elected, but represents all the communities of Somaliland, based on a traditional system, a just form of government, to represent all communities in Somaliland. The existence of this house is an example of the system that Somaliland has developed to maintain its unity.'

Paradoxically, while contemporary isolation impedes the consolidation of its development, Somaliland's home-built steadiness so far exemplifies the limits of external intervention in stabilising countries and the necessity of local ownership.[7] The irony does not end there. The route to reclaiming Somaliland's independence lies through Mogadishu, in getting its southern neighbour to agree to a divorce; but the Mogadishu government is barely functional, little more than a Western-supported and African military-controlled client state. As Jama remarked in 2014, 'We have had 23 years of peace and no recognition. Mogadishu has had 23 years of recognition and no peace.'

Still, there is little gainsaying Somaliland's challenges.

The economy is stable, if poor, based on livestock farming and exports (about $100 million annually, more than half of all exports), remittances (about $800 million annually, or more than $4 000 per family) and telecommunications. The Somaliland government budget was just $152 million in 2014, much of it sourced from customs charges in Berbera and tax on the *qat* industry. GDP is estimated at $350 per capita annually for its 3.5 million people.

Economic growth rates have not, however, been rising fast enough to deal with the backlog in development and the devastation caused by the civil war, along with the expectations of Somaliland's increasingly globalised, youthful population. The speaker of the house, Abdirahman Abdillahi, noted in 2011 that 60–70 per cent of the population is unemployed, with more than half of the youth without opportunities to 'go further in their studies or in finding a job'. He says that this 'could be a time bomb' for radicalisation, where the veil is, university professors agree, more on view than ever before. Without such action, the likely scenario for Somaliland shifts from consolidating democracy and improving stability and prosperity to increasing radicalisation and instability along the lines of Mogadishu. 'Either we develop our model,' observes academic Abdirahman Yusuf Duale in reference to Somalia, 'or they [the youth] spread.'

One of these challenges is also the national addiction to *qat*, being chewed by an estimated 20 per cent of the population. Not only does this divert as much as $450 000 daily (though traders' figures put this as high as $3 million) into a consumptive habit, but it results in laziness, contributing to an already low rate of productivity. 'It is a chronic social, health and economic problem,' said the minister of development and planning in 2011, 'one of the most important that we need to address.' It has also created an exceptionally powerful *qat*-trading elite.

The infrastructure is rickety. The 60 kilometres of freshly paved road from Jijiga in Ethiopia's Somali-populated Ogaden region, commonly known today as 'Region Five', eastwards towards the Somali border at Tog Waajale contrasts with what lies ahead. Tog Waajale's dirt streets are festooned with the Somali 'national flower', the plastic bag, while goats feed on mounds of rubbish and wide-eyed children and idle youth hustle for a handout. Once through the ropes slung across the track denoting the border, the next 20 kilometres in Somaliland is tough going, a series of mud roads crisscrossing their way through a multitude of dongas over the flat, bleak terrain, scarcely a knee-high tree in sight before the tarred, if bumpy, road to Berbera is reached. This road, and Ethiopia's connection with the port of Berbera on the Gulf of Aden, could do with some planning and finance, though given Somaliland's limited means, this is likely to come only from development assistance. And such aid is unlikely without the international recognition Somaliland lacks. Only when one intersects with the Boroma road does the going get easier over the 90 kilometres from Ethiopia to Hargeisa, although it is a journey interspersed with frequent security checkpoints, *qat*-stoned soldiers, their stained teeth a giveaway to their habit, peering out of make-shift shelters on the side of the road.

While Somaliland has myriad social and developmental challenges, it has shown the way forward, warts and all. It owns its recovery. That is the key lesson for its southern neighbour, Somalia, as it is for anyone else building peace after war.

27

SOUTH AFRICA

Components for Resolving Conflict

*

South Africa shows that countries can change for the better, and that outside assistance and pressure can be important in setting the stage, but that locals have to get on with things themselves. No matter our emotional desire for heroes, it also shows that peace processes require more than the efforts and leadership of just one person, and that the success of such processes is determined not just by elections or the return of stability, but longer-term questions of prosperity and social cohesion.

On Nelson Mandela's death on 5 December 2013, the world mourned the passing of a leadership icon. In a remarkable if, at times, gushing display of global outpouring of grief and respect amidst quite a lot of 'doughnutting' on the obsequies by VIPs who should have the decency to behave better, Mandela was lionised as a man 'who by his courage saved his country; and by his example inspires the world'.[1] As Senegalese President Macky Sall observed on the event, Mandela was a 'role model for Africans and also for humanity', giving Africans 'pride in being black – a dignity in being a black man'. He was South Africa's 'greatest son', said President Jacob Zuma. 'We have lost one of the most influential, courageous and profoundly good human beings that any of us will share time with on this earth,' said US President Barack Obama. 'Through his fierce dignity and unbending will to sacrifice his own freedom for the freedom of others, Madiba transformed South Africa and moved all of us,' he added. Or as David Cameron put it, Mandela was 'not just a hero of our time, but a hero of all time'.[2]

Mandela's special qualities

Mandela ushered in a new era for South Africa, a country viewed until the advent of democracy in April 1994 on the cusp of revolution and collapse. His lack of bitterness and brand of extraordinary humility and a human touch offered a path to South Africans out of the political mire, and acted as an example, too, for others farther afield. As Tony Blair put it, it was not just about the content, but about the 'way he did it'.[3] He also not only made racism just 'morally wrong and misguided', Blair noted, but 'just stupid and irrelevant'. The former British prime minister also notes that without a Mandela-like figure, things in South Africa 'could have been catastrophic'. Certainly there were moments this was true, and he could be a calming and inspiring presence, such as in April 1993 when South African Communist Party head Chris Hani was assassinated by a white immigrant. 'Tonight I am reaching out to every single South African, black and white, from the very depths of my being', he said then on national television, warning that 'our whole nation now teeters on the brink of disaster.'[4]

James Robinson, a BBC correspondent in South Africa in 1990, recalled the first press conference after Mandela came out of prison on 11 February, which was held at Archbishop Desmond Tutu's house. Asked what had surprised him the most on his release, Mandela said, 'The number of white people who were there to meet him.'[5] Reconciliation, politics and a sense of timing oozed out of every pore. It went beyond just knowing what to do. As Blair has remarked of Mandela, 'it was not just what he did, but the way he did it … He would make an immediate connection with people.' He was not always this way. As Tutu, who housed him on that first night of freedom, has written. 'Some have said Mandela's 27 years in jail were a waste, suggesting that if he had been released earlier he would have had more time to weave his charm of forgiveness and reconciliation. I beg to differ. He went to jail an angry young man, incensed by the miscarriage of justice in the travesty of the Rivonia Trial. He was no peacemaker … The 27 years were absolutely crucial in his spiritual development. The suffering was the crucible that removed considerable dross, giving him empathy for his opponents. It helped to ennoble him, imbuing him with magnanimity difficult to gain in other ways. It gave him an authority and credibility that otherwise would have been difficult to attain.'[6]

Yet, it took more than the 27 years in prison to mellow him. When he emerged that February from Victor Verster prison, he gave a speech to those massed at the Grand Parade in Cape Town infused with the party line of class struggle and armed insurrection. Whatever his ideological convictions, however, he was also quick-witted and expedient, realising that his party needed to move with the (post-Cold War) economic and political times, and to take adversaries along with him to achieve power, even if negotiations were only a peaceful means to that end. The African National Congress's (ANC's) opposition to an infamous racist and brutal government, and a recognition of the desire of (most) whites to change, enabled the ANC to overcome its obvious organisational and institutional weaknesses into an unbeatable strength, answering the question posed by Howard Barrell, the author of a doctoral thesis on the ANC's military wing, Umkhonto we Sizwe (Spear of the Nation): 'How did the ANC succeed when it so evidently failed?'[7]

To these political aspects could be added an innate sense of timing. The wearing of a Springbok captain's rugby jersey at the 1995 World Cup won over even the most hardened white South African, and that was before the team won the cup. He was a tough political opponent, but even his apartheid opponents were struck by 'gravitas, his dignity, his regal bearing and his apparent willingness to be reasonable'.[8]

Needing a dance partner

Still, he could not have played transition politics alone. During the negotiation phase Mandela needed someone to dance with, to be able to determine the transfer of power to marshal in the new, post-apartheid era. His great legacy was not the negotiations, since many were involved in that process, and talks had in fact started without him four years before he walked out of prison, but reconciliation between South Africans. Through force of personality and morality, he provided an example to unite not just black and white, but those among his own ranks who sought retribution and favoured extremism. His predecessor as president, F.W. de Klerk, has noted in this regard the lack of bitterness by Mandela, which allowed 'a remarkable degree of consensus, embodied in our constitution', enabling the building of a bridge between the conflict of the past and the peace of today.[9]

Mandela was also not alone on the ANC side, but was the moral giant, especially once O.R. Tambo had been incapacitated by a stroke; De Klerk shocked even the most optimistic of South Africa-watchers, given his conservative roots and apparent instincts. He was on paper an unlikely a reformer as there could ever be. But his leadership in unbanning the ANC and other organisations and releasing Mandela and others from prison set the stage for an unexpectedly peaceful revolution in the early 1990s, in the process defusing the violent upheavals that increasingly defined and transfixed the country, and its economy and international responses during the late 1980s. He, too, possessed a sense of timing. As his friend and fellow lawyer Ignatius Vorster reminded, 'As a lawyer, F.W. always had a great sense of timing. If he had been a rugby player he would have been an excellent flyhalf.'[10]

Frederik Willem 'F.W.' de Klerk was born into a conservative Afrikaner political family. His National Party lineage was impeccable. His paternal great-grandfather was Senator Johannes Cornelis 'Jan' van Rooy. An aunt was married to National Party Prime Minister J.G. Strijdom, the so-called Lion of the North. His father, Jan, became secretary of the National Party in the Transvaal province in 1948, and later rose to a cabinet post and president of the senate, becoming interim state president in 1975.

Elected as an MP in 1969, F.W. first entered the cabinet in 1978 under Prime Minister B.J. Vorster as minister of posts and telecommunications and social welfare and pensions. Under P.W. Botha, who took over as prime minister in October 1978 and as state president in 1984, he held various ministerial posts, including sports and recreation; mines, energy and environmental planning; mineral and energy affairs; internal affairs; and, from 1984–89, national education and planning. From 1982 he was the Transvaal leader of the National Party, and in February 1989 was elected as the national head of the National Party. Within six months he was state president, replacing the incapacitated Botha, who, in an irony of history, like Tambo had suffered a stroke. The reformer quickly came to the surface and the political pragmatist acted immediately. 'It was a measure,' says veteran journalist Ray Hartley, 'fundamentally of F.W.'s strength of character' that he moved against his political upbringing and with his political instincts.[11]

Once installed as president, after a particularly robust meeting with Botha, De Klerk lost no time in calling for a non-racist South Africa and for negotiations about the country's future. Even those closest to him expected a more cautious, controlled style of reform. Writing in March 1989, his liberal-minded brother Wimpie believed that his younger sibling would attempt to 'hold the middle ground by means of clever footwork, small compromises, drawn-out studies and planned processes, effective diplomacy and growing authority through balanced leadership and control'.[12] This was the Mikhail Gorbachev perestroika analogy. But South Africa was different. It was not possible to reform by thin slices, proving Alexis de Tocqueville's warning that 'the most perilous moment for a bad government is when it seeks to mend its way'; if nothing else, the violent reaction in the streets to Botha's Tricameral Parliament in 1983 rammed that home.

Two other aspects confirmed this: the mutual dependency of black and white South Africans and the increasing realisation by Afrikaners in particular that, ethical questions aside, apartheid was not required to enable them to prosper and be secure; in fact, to the contrary. Still, De Klerk had to go against the grain and delivered the security that none of his successors had either been able or willing to do, despite huge cost, politically and militarily. The lyrics of Bright Blue's iconic anti-apartheid song 'Weeping' remind of De Klerk's predecessor, Botha: 'I knew a man who lived in fear ...' [13]

On 2 February 1990, De Klerk announced the lifting of the ban on the ANC, Pan Africanist Congress and the South African Communist Party, releasing Mandela among other imprisoned leaders. 'The season of violence is over,' De Klerk said. 'The time for reconstruction and reconciliation has arrived.' This paved the way for open negotiations on the country's future, which had begun in secret during the Botha years.[14]

'I spelt out my agenda in the first speech I made after being elected leader of the National Party in February 1989,' recalls the former state president. 'I said, "Our goal is a new South Africa; a totally changed South Africa; a South Africa which has rid itself of the antagonism of the past; a South Africa free of domination or oppression in whatever form; a South Africa in which the democratic forces – all reasonable people – align themselves behind mutually acceptable goals and against radicalism, irrespective of where it comes from. How we reach that goal is the common challenge which all of us face." I wanted: 1) a constitutional state subject to the rule of law; 2) constitutional continuity between the past system and the future systems; 3) a Bill of Rights that would protect the rights, including property rights, of all South Africans; 4) a genuine, inclusive democratic dispensation; 5) the separation of powers and a strong and independent judiciary; 6) accommodation of cultural and linguistic diversity, including the right to education in the language of choice.'

Three necessary components

Overall, the route from apartheid to democracy teaches that three components are necessary for successful conflict resolution.

First, the parties have to have equal external pressure applied to them to get to the negotiating table. In the case of De Klerk's National Party, the ruling party that had won the election in 1948 and legislated apartheid, a combination of financial sanctions, a worsening regional security environment, the arms embargo and international isolation and opprobrium more generally all helped to push it in this direction.

'Sanctions,' De Klerk admits, 'were, of course, also a factor. By the mid-1980s our economy was increasingly isolated and we had to deal with the crisis caused by the refusal of international banks in 1985 to roll over our short-term loans. Sanctions caused enormous distortions in the economy and probably cost us 1.5 per cent growth per annum. Nevertheless, the economy actually grew at an annual rate of 2.7 per cent between April 1986 and February 1989. Sanctions were also often counter-productive. They increased opposition to foreign interference and hobbled two of the greatest forces for change: economic growth and exposure to the world.'

More encouraging for the white regime was the success of the negotiations to end the war in Angola in 1988 and ensure Namibia's independence in 1990, a prototype for what South Africa might expect. In the case of its major opponent, the ANC, the end of the Cold War and, with it, the sources of support both for itself and its major regional allies provided the push factor. As De Klerk acknowledges, 'A further factor was the successful conclusion of a tripartite agreement in 1988 between South Africa, Cuba and Angola. This resulted in the withdrawal of Cuban forces from Angola, the implementation of UN Resolution 435 and the independence of Namibia. The negotiations with the Angolans and the Cubans – and the subsequent successful implementation of the UN independence plan during 1989 – reassured the government that it could secure its core interests through negotiations with its opponents.'

The perestroika reforms led on the other side of the world by Gorbachev had another consequence, in taking 'the monkey off De Klerk's back', enabling 'him to justify to his people what would otherwise have appeared to them a suicidal course of action'.[15] As De Klerk admits in this regard, a 'critically important factor for change was the collapse of global communism in 1989. At a stroke, it removed the government's primary strategic concern relating to the influence of the SACP on the ANC. Throughout the '70s and '80s virtually all of the members of the ANC's NEC [National Executive Committee] were also members of the SACP. The demise of international-al expansionist communism and the manifest success of the free market economies also opened a window of opportunity. It meant that there was no longer any serious debate with regard to the economic policies that would be required to ensure economic growth in a future democratic South Africa.'

But as Allister Sparks has observed, despite the comparison sometimes made, in respects De Klerk was very different to the last Soviet leader. 'He stayed with the changes, he did not try to freeze the process. He came to rec-ognise that you cannot reform an oppressive system, that if you start to relax it you have to go the whole hog. There cannot,' noted Sparks, 'be perestroika, only abolition. He accepted that as it became evident. His own process of change kept pace with events ...'[16]

Second, the protagonists have to realise that there is more to be gained from ending the fighting than continuing with it – that no military victory is likely, or is affordable politically or financially. This much was clear to the National Party, who held most of the military cards, and to the ANC, which, while it subsequently has preferred to pump up the folklore around its military prowess, was overshadowed militarily by untrained and uncon-trolled youth on the streets of South Africa's townships. 'The acceptance by all sides that there could be neither a military nor a revolutionary victory and that continuing conflict would simply turn South Africa into a waste-land', was central to the success of the negotiations. 'The security forces had accepted this reality by the early 1980s. The ANC did so only after the 1986 state of emergency restored order in the country. Discreet contacts between the ANC and the government – partly initiated through Nelson Mandela while he was still in prison – enabled both sides to explore possibilities for negotiated solutions.'

De Klerk says, 'It would be a mistake to underestimate the government's awareness of the need for a satisfactory solution. It was acutely aware that the status quo was unacceptable and unsustainable. By the late '70s it had realised that "separate development" had failed and held no prospect what-soever of bringing about a just or workable solution. The partition of the country on which it was based was hopelessly inequitable; the economy – and the supposedly "white cities" – were becoming more integrated with each year that passed; whites did not constitute a majority in any geographic region of the country; and the solution was vehemently rejected by a vast majority of blacks, Coloureds and Indians.' At the same time, he says, 'A revolution was also taking place on the education front. In 1980 just under 30 000 black South Africans wrote matric – of whom about 50 per cent passed – compared with 49 000 successful white candidates. After the education reforms introduced by the De Lange Commission, black high school education expanded rapidly. By 1994 more than 410 000 black South Africans wrote matric, of whom 201 000 passed, more than three times the number of white matriculants that year. Also by 1994 there were more black South Africans at university than whites.'

He adds, 'Economic growth of the 60s and 70s was [also] a major change factor. Between 1970 and 1994 the black, Coloured and Indian share of personal disposable income increased from 29 per cent to almost 50 per cent. Millions of black South Africans moved to the cities and improved their standard of living and education. By 1989 they had begun to occupy key positions in the industrial and commercial sectors. Increasingly, they were becoming indispensable in the white-collar professions.'

And third, there needs to be leadership, ready to seize the moment, capable of sensing and realising all of the above circumstances, and establishing a methodology for the negotiation process. 'Leadership plays a key – and perhaps a crucial – role,' says De Klerk. 'Some present and past leaders simply would not have had the skills and/or the temperament to manage the process successfully. Others might have risen to the occasion if they found themselves in leadership positions. Few – if any – on the ANC side would have been able to play the role that Mandela played so consummately.'

Pierre Buyoya knows something about power and negotiations, until now the longest serving president of Burundi, having led a coup as a young major in September 1987. He ruled until the advent of a civilian government in 1993 and, when this fell apart amidst inter-ethnic violence costing some 150 000 lives, again from 1996 to 2003. During the peace negotiations in 2000, he dealt extensively with former President Mandela as the external facilitator in trying to hammer out a peace deal between the majority Hutu and minority Tutsi. With the creation of an ethnically inclusive government, the Tutsi Buyoya handed over power to his Hutu deputy in April 2003.

'In the short time I worked with him I could see Mandela was a controversial man,' recalls Buyoya. 'He was not a common mediator, but a very strong one and most of the time used pressure on the parties, very strong pressure … To move on some of the issues. I also learnt to resist him and [to do so] I went to talk to those white people who had negotiated with him in South

Africa, who told me that if you resist him, he will recognise you have a point. 'But he was also a man of great integrity, pressurising all sides equally. No side was happy with him ... we sometimes thought he was going beyond his mandate in the negotiations. But he never focused or favoured on one side or another.

'His other great characteristic was his link between the leaders and their people. He said that "you cannot take a decision against the interests of the people". He helped sell the decisions to our people, in addressing parliament, and in talking to the [Tutsi-dominated] military, both senior officers and soldiers. He spoke to church leaders and civil society, even those who were opposed to the peace process. And he also went to talk to the prisons. This was difficult for us, for you know how prisoners are treated in Africa. When he came from there our discussion was a little hard, as he had himself been a prisoner.'[17]

Back home, Mandela's role was comparatively easier than De Klerk's in at least one regard: he only had one thing on his agenda, to negotiate a democracy, while his opponents fussed over myriad issues and plans, from group rights to job protection. As De Klerk admits, 'I wanted more or less the dispensation that is included in the 1996 constitution and especially in its foundational values ... However, I also wanted "power sharing" of some kind at the executive level that would ensure the institutional inclusion of minorities in the processes by which they are governed. Initially, we wanted something along the lines of the Swiss model with a rotating presidency, without limiting the power of the majority to govern. In the end we proposed the establishment of a state council – broadly representative of our communities – that would have considered all legislation and initiatives that would affect minorities, but without a veto power. We felt that this would give all South Africans a voice in the process of government.'

Still, Mandela had to ensure that his negotiating foe – his most essential partner – had enough to sell the solution to their own side. In any negotiation it is essential, as President Obasanjo has reminded, 'for leadership to know how hard to push, and also to know what it can realistically sell to its own'. Such is mutual negotiating dependency.[18] Mutual dependency was recognised by Mandela. As he put it on Norwegian television in 1993, the day before receiving the Nobel Peace Prize jointly with De Klerk: 'It is absolutely crucial that we recognise that we should live together as a common nation with a common destiny.'[19] Then, reminding his opponents he was not a pushover (De Klerk said Mandela 'could be brutal' in negotiations),[20] he added that almost the entire South African government were 'political criminals', though there was no alternative to working with them.[21] Mandela had to overcome stern resistance within the ANC to accept the joint award in the first instance.

There was not an alternative to working together.

Avoiding mythology

Of course, mythology demands different versions of history, and time forgets. Successive ANC leadership has preferred to publically view the negotiation process as a victory and a defeat, with whites, represented by the National Party, being the vanquished.[22] But the outcome of the March 1992 whites-only referendum on political change suggests that whites had already accepted black majority rule, voting 69 to 31 per cent in favour of the question: 'Do you support continuation of the reform process which the State President began on 2 February 1990 and which is aimed at a new Constitution through negotiation?'[23] This realisation was borne out by the remarkable status enjoyed by De Klerk among politicians per se, and not just in Africa: he negotiated his party from power.

As De Klerk recalls: 'Of course, we realised that there would be no possibility of the National Party winning the 1994 election. The most that we hoped for would have been about 30 per cent – which we felt would put us in a strong bargaining position when it came to the negotiation of the final constitution. If there were no irregularities in the election of 1994 I think we came near to 28 per cent! It was calculated that ±1 000 000 irregular votes were cast for the ANC and the IFP [Inkatha Freedom Party].'

He adds: 'From 1986 onward the Bureau for Information (later the South African Communication Service) regularly conducted very large-scale national opinion surveys, which consistently indicated core support of ±62 per cent for the ANC; ±20 per cent for the National Party and ±11 per cent for the IFP.'[24]

This hints that the bigger challenge for Mandela was reconciling blacks with whites, and the ANC's broad church with white-led political parties, rather than the other way around. The recall of Mandela's successor as president, Thabo Mbeki, and the widespread booing of his bête noir, President Jacob Zuma, at Madiba's memorial service on 10 December 2013, shows just how much this reconciliation remains a work in progress.

'There were many who argued the case for tough love – don't make it easy for them,' recalls Verne Harris of the Nelson Mandela Centre of Memory, housing the former president's archives. 'Reconciliation was a beautiful fit for South Africa, but we forget that it wasn't the only approach being discussed at the time.'[25] He was a 'great unifier' within his own party, says F.W. 'He pulled black people to the middle ground just as it was my role to pull whites to the centre, too, to make negotiations and compromise possible. But,' he adds, 'Madiba also was very important in the reconciliation process between black and white and especially towards my own [Afrikaner] people.'[26]

But even after 1994, he needed, as the World Cup rugby jersey episode illustrates, to keep everyone on board. Transition would take time.

Mandela was 'indubitably', as the author Rian Malan has observed, a man of great courage, of 'unwavering resolution' and one who used 'grand charm' as the most powerful weapon in his arsenal, from winning every fight at the negotiating table to winning over South African (and global) hearts.[27] There is undoubtedly an emotional need for black South Africans, especially, to have a hero after the years of having their noses rubbed in it by white men and apartheid. The global outpouring of grief on his death and the apparent need for others, for non-South Africans, to feel they had to write or say something on his passing tells another story – perhaps the low expectations there are of politicians generally, the need, again, for heroes, or the moral, literally black-and-white clarity of the anti-apartheid struggle. Mandela could not have, in US Vice President Joe Biden's whimsical exaggeration on his passing, on his own lifted 'a nation to freedom'. Had he done so, democracy would be vulnerable in his absence. In fact, if the transition had been about one man, as many could interpret from the sentimental eulogies, then South Africa has reason to fear. There are certainly doubts if the country will attract such sympathetic attention from the world for many years. The notion, too, that South Africa's transition – like East Asia's economic transformation – was a 'miracle' belies the perspiration behind it then and necessary in the future. Mandela's death provided an opportunity for the old, related fears and media inaccuracies that he was the glue holding the country together and that a future of racial strife loomed in his absence. The reality is, of course, that it was no miracle, and that it was the work of numerous people, many of them not in government. Mandela himself was human, perhaps the reason that so many identified with him. 'He retained in his cabinet underperforming, frankly incompetent ministers,' Tutu has said of Mandela. 'This tolerance of mediocrity arguably laid the seeds for greater levels of mediocrity and corruptibility that were to come.'[28]

The truth is, too, that transition is more than just an electoral or negotiating moment or even a brief period, but a long hard slog, where recovery is, at least in economic terms, at least as long as the period of decline. As veteran *New York Times* correspondent Bill Keller says, what 'Mandela left in his wake was not yet a government, or even a genuine political party, but a liberation movement, with the mentality, customs, and culture of constant struggle'.[29] But his death also shook South Africa from its 'malaise of lethargy' and galvanised immediately a week of intense debate about the country's leadership and its future, peaking, oxymoronically, in the low point with the jeering of President Zuma at the Soweto memorial and the 'flawed selection' of a schizophrenic sign language interpreter who had faced a murder charge, not only 'permanently spoiled all visuals from the memorial for eternity' but 'smacked of the mediocrity that has entered and become so endemic in so much public service delivery in the country'.[30]

*

Twenty years after the end of apartheid South Africa is another country. This is credit to the remarkable leadership of Mandela and De Klerk, among others.

The progress made goes a long way to explain continued support for the ANC despite its failings and the country's under-achievement, at least when measured against expectations. The majority of South Africans will, it seems, for the foreseeable future maintain their support for the ruling party based, in the main, on its liberation credentials, the political movement that helped them regain their pride after years of having their noses rubbed in it by whites. 'It's like support for the Catholic Church,' reflects one business person. 'Because a few priests are caught fondling boys, it does not mean the rank and file desert the Church.'

The main opposition comparatively lacks liberation credentials, whatever its liberal values and record in running the Western Cape province.

Whatever its flaws and inefficiencies, the ANC has also delivered change to poor South Africans, especially those in the rural areas, where the bulk supports the ANC. There have been huge improvements in the 'Social Wage', with 44 per cent of South African households receiving one form or another of social grant (16.1 million citizens in 2013, compared to 2.4 million in 1996), dramatically reducing poverty levels, even though the $10-billion annual outlay to do so has placed significant pressure on the budget. There has also been a notable increase in the numbers who have access to education (though not as impressive improvements in the quality, sadly), to public health clinics, and to electricity and clean, piped water. All this is reflected in poverty levels: just 11 per cent of South Africans experienced hunger in 2011, down from a quarter of the population ten years earlier. It is impossible to be a serious, credible contender for political power in South Africa without a track record with the poor.[31]

The negative side of the ledger, however, centres the ANC's involvement – both as an organisation and its leadership – in government contracting and other business, the rising levels (or at least the grubby blatancy) of public sector corruption and the apparently imperious disregard some in the ruling elite has towards both the ethics and institutions of governance. As Mugabe's Zimbabwe next door reminds, continued success will demand respect for the very institutions spawned by the anti-apartheid struggle, especially the judiciary and parliament. Also, for all of the abovementioned progress, 85 per cent of black Africans, the group comprising nearly 80 per cent of the South African population, remain poor. Correspondingly, 87 per cent of white South Africans are in the middle-to upper-class categories. Reports suggest that the country has the highest Gini co-efficient worldwide, with 36 per cent of the labour force unemployed. And labour productivity has not kept pace with labour costs, which is reflected in the paucity of foreign direct investment inflows, averaging just $1.9 billion a year for the period 1994 to 2012.[32]

Today, writing this on the cusp of the May 2014 election, two scenarios stare out. The upside version is that the country continues to muddle through in a persistent state of policy inertia: that the high-growth, job-intensive twenty-year National Development Plan (NDP) becomes a casualty of ideological infighting and a lack of decisive leadership, political will and implementation capacity. The downside scenario is that the ANC's rule is threatened and, in response, it lurches left, attacking the easy targets: big business, whites, the mines and perhaps even the constitution itself. For many in the ANC, any substantial loss of votes could only be explained by counter-revolutionary forces and their subversion, not by the failure to deliver social services, political patronage, cadre deployment or tenderpreneurship. A third, unlikely (if desirable) scenario also exists, one of high economic growth and job creation à la the NDP. To realise this, however, the ANC will have to resolve the contradictions between, for example, cadre deployment and a development state, or between economic growth and the alienation of foreign investors. Attraction of the latter will also demand defending – preferably, championing – capitalism, rather than perpetuating an environment where it has become a dirty word and its proponents, business, a target of state opprobrium. It will also demand, as John Kane-Berman has argued, a 'cheaper, nimbler and smaller state', though this will be both ideologically contentious and politically difficult where jobs have proven so difficult to create outside the government.

The signs have been troubling.[33] Party loyalty regularly trumps that to the country or the constitution, perhaps not by the dissenting booers at Mandela's funeral, but at least by the elite. 'The ANC flows through my veins', said the former finance minister, Trevor Manuel, who oversaw the longest period of growth in South African history, and who has subsequently headed the planning commission, which produced the NDP blueprint. 'It's not a job, it's a belief system. I will always remain a loyal and disciplined member of the ANC. None of this would have happened in my life without the ANC affording me the opportunity to serve my people', he remarked on stepping down from parliamentary politics in 2014.[34] While he did a great job, this 'belief system' is a long way from Mark Twain's 'loyalty to the country always, loyalty to the government when it deserves it'. And race is employed as a tool to justify policy. As the writer Zakes Mda commented on Mandela's December 2013 passing, 'It is ironic that in today's South Africa, there is an increasingly vocal segment of black South Africans who feel that Mandela sold out the liberation struggle to white interests.'[35]

Countering this negativity rests on having a leadership and a population that are instinctively democratic, not majoritarian. It also demands a focus on some big, transformative ideas. Before 1990, South Africans were seized with the anti-apartheid struggle, a minority attempting to uphold this regime, the majority successfully overturning an odious order. After 1994 the country enjoyed the reconciliatory politics of the Mandela years and, for all of his philosopher-king idiosyncrasies over AIDS and Zimbabwe, the conservative economic policies of Mbeki, which produced solid (if unspectacular) economic growth and accelerated social transformation. What the country needs, as Hartley has sagely put it, 'are the politics of the Mandela period and the economics of the Mbeki years.'[36]

South Africa, twenty years after its first democratic election, illustrates that establishing a path to peace was but one, albeit critical, aspect of transformation; sticking to it is another.

28

VIETNAM

No Lack of Excuses

*

I have been travelling regularly to Vietnam since 1994. Back then Hanoi was emerging from the dark ages of conflict and communism. As its *doi moi* (renovation) reform programme had only just begun to take hold, most of its industries were state-owned and run, the bulk of the fleet of its national airline were Soviet Ilyushins, Antonovs, Yakovlevs and other equally risky bits of scrap (to be avoided in the interests of self-preservation), and though motorbikes were starting to make inroads, most people moved around on cart and foot, in clunky East bloc Ladas, motorised tricycles, belching buses and a steam-powered railway. The country was obviously poor, conditions invariably tough and the standard of living low.[1]

Today, twenty years later, the country is virtually unrecognisable.

Hanoi is no longer a dour administrative hollow and Saigon, as the locals still term it, has recovered once more its status as one of the great cities of Asia. Despite myriad problems including rickety infrastructure, inflation and financial overheating, Vietnam has been one of the fastest-growing economies in the world for the past two decades, averaging 8 per cent GDP growth from 1990 to 1997, 6.5 per cent from 1998 to 2003 and over 5 per cent since 2004, in spite of periodic global travails.

Yet, if there was ever a country that had an excuse not to develop, it is Vietnam. Destroyed by successive wars over hundreds of years with China, Japan, France and the US, divided by colonialism and imposed foreign administrative systems, spread out over a long border, ethnically divided and dogmatically committed to socialism, it should be one of the poorest countries in the world. Instead, starting from nothing, the moment of its transformation was the abandonment, under severe social pressure, of a rigid adherence to communism in the mid-1980s. At this point, the energies and aspirations of its people supplanted those of the state; as a result, it has placed itself on a steep growth and development trajectory.

It is not as if this difficult history is forgotten. It is just that the Vietnamese have successfully put it behind themselves, and looked forward. And its recovery, as much from its own failures as from war itself, contains many lessons for others attempting the same.

*

Move over, Alpe d'Huez. Hai Van Pass between the imperial Vietnamese capital of Hue and the port of Da Nang has its match. Not known as the 'ocean cloud pass' for nothing, the 21 switchbacks of Alpe d'Huez, where the 'real' Tour de France often transits, have an average gradient of 8 per cent over 14 kilometres. Hai Van gains 1 000 metres over some 10 kilometres, a road that BBC *Top Gear*'s Jeremy Clarkson described as a 'deserted ribbon of perfection'.

Cycling is a great way to see a country. For one, the sights are at eye level, and the sights, sounds and scents are in your face rather than behind a darkened, speeding window. And as my wife reminded me as I struggled to keep up with her as we rode 600 kilometres down the Ho Chi Minh trail, north to south, the pace (or lack of it) allows one to absorb the images rather than just view them.

Starting in Mai Chai, north-west of Hanoi, we made our way along the hill tribes on the Laotian border through the old Demilitarised Zone (DMZ) to Khe Sanh, then swung east following the Ben Hai River along the DMZ to the coast and on to Hue, Da Nang and Hội An.

It was an extraordinary experience. There are great rolling hills and wide swirling rivers everywhere: this is a land of mountains, water and agriculture. The endless shimmering rice paddies are defined by the women in conical hats working them, like markers on a great green felt board. Giant limestone carbuncles mark, too, the border with Laos; they flatten as one moves coastwards. In 30-plus-degree Celsius heat, with humidity to match, it is also a great way to shed a winter coat. The ubiquitous water buffalo were at the start giving me comely glances, their wooden bells *tunk-tunking* in apparent excitement; it had not been a kind season.

The Ho Chi Minh trail was the 5 000–13 000-kilometre (depending who you believe) route along which supplies were moved from the ports of Vinh and Ha Long to the Viet Cong and People's Army of Vietnam soldiers fighting the US-supported Army of the Republic of South Vietnam. For the Americans, this was a war of infiltration and interdiction, and pacification of Viet Cong supporters, all the while attempting to turn its South Vietnamese ally into a viable and credible military, economic and political force. This should sound familiar to anyone with knowledge of contemporary Afghanistan or, for that matter, post-Saddam Iraq.

Politically incorrect, I know, but I now have a certain sympathy for Richard Nixon as he puzzled over what to do about the North Vietnamese supply routes through neighbouring Laos. The Ho Chi Minh trail splits at Po Chau in Ha Dinh province, one trail moving into the dense forests of Laos around the DMZ into the south, the other continuing southwards.

This also explains why there was so much fighting around the area immediately south of the DMZ, which was established after the temporary 1954 peace. Names such as Khe Sanh, Hamburger Hill at Aluoi, Quang Tri province, Da Nang, Hue, the Rockpile and Lang Vay are among those that have passed into military (and some into Hollywood) legend.

A Marine stronghold, think images of red dust and aircraft landing among incoming fire, and you are probably remembering Khe Sanh, the site of a 75-day siege in 1968. Heavily reinforced by the US commander General William Westmoreland at the behest of President Lyndon Johnson, who feared Khe Sanh would be his, as the Texan termed it, 'Din Bin Foo'. It was a place best described by one Marine officer: 'When you are at Khe Sanh you're not really anywhere. You could lose it and you really haven't lost a damn thing.' US forces eventually themselves destroyed the base and moved on. Today, the site, which claimed the lives of 500 Americans from Vietnamese shellfire from the surrounding hills and at least 10 000 North Vietnamese under 100 000 tonnes of US bombs, is disturbed only by the sound of birds in the trees and the slap of corn leaves in the gentle breeze.

Hanoi maintains that Khe Sanh was really a distraction from the Tet Offensive, which boldly took the fighting into Saigon and Hue and, in doing so, illustrated the lie that the war was being won. In liberating Hue, a city of great charm and sophistication, from the Viet Cong after Tet, an American officer memorably said they had 'to destroy the city in order to save it'.

The jungle with Laos is extraordinarily dense and hilly. As we (or at least, I) struggled up endless 10, 11 and even 12 per cent climbs, it seemed like a different world – and in many respects it is. We ate lunch with the Van Kieu hill tribe, one of several prejudiced by the Hanoi government as a result of their support for the French colonial and later US forces. (Our guide book, purchased in Hanoi, had the pages on the hill tribes excised, presumably for this reason.) But at no time did we feel unsafe or unwelcome.

Indeed, quite the opposite. I am sure that we were asked, 'Helloooo, how are you' by at least half of Vietnam's children – like Africa, the country is very young, with two-thirds of 85 million under the age of 25. The naive curiosity shown towards foreigners – we had people regularly stop us in the rural areas just to stare and giggle – is all the more remarkable given the casualties in the war: just under 58 000 Americans died in the conflict (of the 3.1 million who served there), along with 224 000 South Vietnamese and one million North Vietnamese/Viet Cong soldiers. But civilians bore the brunt of the casualties – four million Vietnamese (10 per cent of the then population) were killed or wounded during the war.

No shortage of devastation

The giant cemeteries along the DMZ's Highway 9 are enduring testament to these losses, incense burning along the rows of gravestones, each with a yellow star set high on a red background. Around them are statues and reliefs depicting heroic acts of war and sacrifice. The timing of their deaths, mostly around 1971–72, illustrates the way the war was turning at the time. Their average age, mostly men born between 1945 and 1950, shows that while America has its Vietnam generation, so does Vietnam that of its 'American War'.

Not that all things are entirely safe today. Two-lane highways regularly stage four cars/scooters/water-buffalo carts/honking trucks/tooting minibuses/foreigners on bicycles abreast. Not so much a game of chicken as free-range driving.

This is a country, after all, that has gone from the water buffalo to the Lexus, at least for some, in a generation. After reunification in April 1975, the government lost a decade with crazy socialist policies, including collectivised agriculture, which resulted in famine and collapse. They got real in the mid-1980s, allowing farmers, at the start of the *doi moi* process, to keep a slice of their production.

Given half a chance, the super-industriousness and entrepreneurialism of the Vietnamese shone through, just as it does in other environments given a similar break. From 1990 to 2005, Vietnam's agricultural production nearly doubled, transforming Vietnam from a net food importer to the world's second-largest exporter of rice.[2] Although coffee had been introduced by French colonists in the mid-nineteenth century, the industry withered due to war and central planning. Following *doi moi*, the introduction of private enterprise has seen a surge of growth. By 2000, virtually from nothing Vietnam had become the world's second-largest coffee producer after Brazil, with an annual production of 900 000 tonnes. By 2010, coffee production was over 1.1 million tonnes, second only in export value to rice. Cashew nuts has seen a similar expansion, Vietnam building an industry virtually from nothing in the last decade, shifting quickly from exporting the raw nut to developing its own processing techniques.

Fish products, textiles and electronics industries are also booming. The garment sector has added a million jobs in the last five years alone.

The Number 3 Factory of the May 10 garment factory outside Hanoi is, in some respects, an epitome of a state socialist enterprise. And it is not just the name. Above the entrance of May 10 is an inscription by Ho Chi Minh. 'A clear mind makes good work' implores the veteran nationalist leader from the grave. Pictures of the bearded icon smile down on the chattering sewing machines of the 3 000-strong May 10 Number 3 working class.

May 10 – literally 'Sewing 10' – was founded in 1946 to make military uniforms. But things have really taken off since the Vietnamese *doi moi* economic reforms of the mid-1980s and especially since its partial privatisation in 2001. Since then, exports have been growing at 15 per cent per annum. The fifteen May 10 factories employ 8 000 people, exporting $40 million annually in shirts, trousers and suits, mainly to the EU and US.

This growth parallels what has happened in the sector – and elsewhere. Spurred by the end of the US embargo in 1995 and the global quota regime a decade later, along with Vietnam's accession to the World Trade Organization in November 2006, the garment industry added one million jobs in five years from 2005. Some 3 700 companies now employ some 2.5 million machinists and other workers. The sector, for example, generated $11.2 billion from exports in 2010, up 23 per cent year on year.[3]

It is not as if the industry does not face significant challenges, internal and external. China is a major competitor, despite the high productivity and low wages of Vietnamese workers. Monthly salaries average $150. However, productivity is exceptionally high, not least because May 10's workers, as an example, own 62 per cent of the company since privatisation in 2001, the state retaining a 38 per cent share. As a result, an annual dividend payment per worker averages around 20 per cent of the yearly salary.

There are advantages, too, from being so close to China. The sight of huge bundles of chopsticks, manufactured on the banks of the Black River from 10 metre-plus bamboo poles floated down, reminds, too, of the size of both the domestic and regional market. The Chinese eat a lot of chow mein.

Everywhere there was development going on, roads being paved, bridges erected, hotels going up, quarries churning and crushing, and laden trucks scurrying.

Using aid well

All of this is done by the Vietnamese – I did not, as across Africa, see any Chinese construction people around, and it is highly unlikely the notoriously xenophobic Vietnamese would welcome their once colonial master and neighbour in this or any such role. It illustrated the most important lesson of all in post-conflict reconstruction: it has to be owned locally. Some of this nationalism is undoubtedly contrived. The Soviet-style posters (more numerous interestingly in the rural than urban areas), usually featuring Ho Chi Minh, extol the feats of communism and exhort the Vietnamese to higher, socialist feats. Ho is everywhere you go, from schools to banners, posters to lamp poles.

Ownership does not mean autarchism, however. Vietnam has been the target of external aid over the past 40 years – lots of it. Under the Soviet era, from 1975 to 1989, it received an estimated $1 billion annually. Like all such centrally planned economic experiments in Vietnam and elsewhere, it was money after bad, and failed dismally, at least if the aim was to develop Vietnam (rather than keep it ideologically and strategically 'on-side'). With the advent of *doi moi*, from 1993 through 2004, Vietnam received a total of $14 billion in Official Development Assistance, mainly from Asia, the US, multilateral bodies (notably the World Bank and Asian Development Bank) and EU members, about half of that pledged. This steeply ramped up. During the 2000s, the annual amount pledged more than doubled from $2.5 billion at the start of the decade to over $6 billion by 2008. By 2010, more than $50 billion had been pledged and, again, half of this amount actually committed. Donors point out that the impact of aid has been much greater in Vietnam due to local ownership and the sectors of focus: in the fifteen years from 1993, for example, the single largest sector of expenditure was transport (28 per cent), followed by energy (22 per cent).[4]

Even so, today the focus is not on aid as the principal means of development. Pick up an English-language newspaper in Vietnam and several pages will likely include detailed listings of the scale and type of foreign direct investment by country and sector. There are also section lists of possible private sector investment schemes in public infrastructure projects. Foreign direct investment has climbed sharply, disbursed capital totalling $11 billion in 2010 alone. The same year Vietnam's exports ($71.6 billion) were up by 25 per cent.

Ho's posters of manufactured nationalism aside, there is a solid Vietnamese grounding for local ownership of the country's direction and future. These attributes, plus the inquisitive charm and hospitality of its people, have enabled Vietnam to progress from being known as little more than a war to a major tourist destination within a generation. Employment from tourism increased from 1.3 million to five million jobs between 1995 and 2010. In 2010, Vietnam received 4.4 million international visitors, up two million over the previous ten years.

Putting people first

It is possible to see some countries emerging from conflict elsewhere (Rwanda, for example) similarly following this example, with single-minded leadership and, for biking, lots of picturesque sites. There are other parallels with the Central African country – though the Vietnamese stick avidly to the unwritten rule of leadership automatically stepping down after ten years. Further afield, perhaps we will be cycling the Khyber Pass in 30 years – or perhaps not?

The Vietnamese are, if nothing else, pragmatic. A decade before the US withdrawal from Vietnam, Ho said to the Americans: 'We will spread a red carpet for you to leave Vietnam. And when the war is over, you are welcome to come back because you have technology and we will need your help.'[5]

This is a country of contradiction. Members of the ruling 2.5 million-strong Communist Party (a process of selection that involves careful scrutiny of three generations to check applicants' ideological purity) question what it means to be a contemporary Marxist. As one party member put it: 'Vietnam has a lot of bamboo. Its people, too, are very flexible, though they remain very strong. After all, Ho said that we must be flexible.' What is officially termed a 'planned market economy' is driven less by ideology than the search for margin and access to global finance and markets. In essence, do not believe (or practise) what you preach. With half of 12 000 state-owned enterprises privatised already by 1995 and a further 1 300 merged, sold or closed by 2010,[6] the private sector is, for all of the rhetoric, increasingly dominant. 'All the government had to do was to create more favourable conditions for foreign investment,' said one garment industry specialist. 'The private sector did the rest.' Of course there are challenges, not least in the absence of political space, Vietnamese prisons reportedly holding 'hundreds' of dissidents, according to Human Rights Watch. Speaking after the April 2014 releases of Nguyen Tien Trung and Vi Duc Hoi, two prominent political prisoners, Human Rights Watch Asia director Phil Robertson said that 'there is a very long way to go before we can say that Vietnam is making any sort of appreciable progress on human rights.'[7]

In his classic *The Quiet American*, Graham Greene writes, 'Vietnam can hold you like a smell does.' It is not only because of the pungent odours of the Vietnamese street markets though. It is a dizzying combination of the energy, bloody-mindedness and perspiration behind its onward progress.

*

Vietnam thus illustrates that the answer to the question of 'why' there is poverty often lies in the difference between success and failure in the world at large. This difference can be found in policy choices – the distinction, to take another example, between Vietnam before and after its own reforms. Success requires liberating people from the heavy hand of government and ideology – put differently, putting people rather than narrow-minded dogma and political interests at the heart of development. But its bloody history, rapid economic rise and no lack of excuses compared to others who have done relatively poorly, raises the question: if Vietnam, why not others?

PART 4

*

PULLING THE THREADS

Success does not consist in never making mistakes
but in never making the same one a second time.

— George Bernard Shaw

On Saleh Salem Avenue in Heliopolis, Cairo, near the 1973 war pano-
rama, was sprayed the graffiti 'Go out Mubarak'. An arrow commanded
the way for him to the airport.

He reluctantly followed the advice, though not to the letter. After eighteen
days of heaving people protests in what was known as the Lotus Revolution,
the octogenarian departed office on 11 February 2011, turning over power to
a Supreme Council of the Armed Forces. The constitution was suspended,
both houses of parliament dissolved, and an announcement made that the
military would rule for six months until elections could be held. In May,
Mubarak was ordered to stand trial on charges of murder of protestors. A
year later, found guilty of complicity, he was sentenced to life imprisonment,
an ignominious end to 30 years of once all-powerful office.

February 2011 was a month of high hopes in Cairo, and elsewhere. The
euphoria over Egypt's '25 January' movement, known as 'the day of rage'
when over 50 000 activists first occupied its epicentre in Tahrir Square,
was at its peak. Protestors and tourists alike flocked to the square, just the
other side of Qasr al-Nil Bridge, nestling alongside the Egyptian Museum,
where enterprising vendors sold patriotic headbands and flags, and fathers
snapped pictures of their children waving flags, their arms around soldiers,
some draped in flags on top of tanks. Then, in the heady weeks following
Mubarak's fall from power, grace and immunity, the focus of change shifted quickly from whence I had travelled to neighbouring Libya where the
struggle between those protesting the 42-year-old regime of Muammar Al-
Gaddafi in Benghazi soon turned violent.

The rest is now history, a bitter struggle to remove Gaddafi controversially supported, on humanitarian grounds, by Western air power and on the ground by Arab-led logistics. Elsewhere in the region, Bahraini protestors continued to battle their government. In Sanaa in Yemen and in Algiers, too, street protests simmered. The Arab Spring was approaching its zenith.

A common denominator between these countries was, as was seen in the earlier Chapter 6 on Tunisia and the various Arab Springs, a lack of democracy and economic opportunity, the existence of careless elites and a burgeoning, itinerant underclass.

In Cairo, a teeming city of maybe 20 million, maybe more, this combination of factors streamed into two worlds: one chic, secular and relatively comfortable, catered for and protected by the state system; the other ramshackle and desperate where social needs and aspirations were met, if at all, by Islamic groups, headed by the Muslim Brotherhood, an organisation founded in 1928, its political ambitions long and sophisticatedly driven through service provision among Egypt's neglected underclass.[1] In the one world, children are privately educated, their meals are taken at Western-style food emporia; in the other, it is rote learning madrassa style, chewing subsidised bread.

These worlds are the difference between life on the island of Zamalek, circled by the Nile, with its cypress trees, swish shops, apartments, run-down Edwardian mansions and tree-lined avenues separated by the river from the 'other' – the old slum of Imbaba where, clawing on its extremes, those in the shanty of Western Munira live on the edge. Roughly the same size (just 21 square kilometres) as Zamalek, Munira's population density is, however, ten times the number, at 50 000 people per square kilometers – in thumbnail terms, more than four people squeezed per room. Unlike the comforts across the river, in the 1980s Munira had no schools, hospitals, public transportation or even sewerage.[2] Little wonder that an Islamic leader, Sheikh Jaber, was then able to take over the area for three years, collecting taxes and implementing a strict code of Islamic morality. 'Extremism is grown on a good soil,' reflects one Egyptian journalist, 'and a combination of injustice, poverty and insecurity is just such a soil. Crimes come from these areas, but crimes are committed against these people all the time.'[3]

Journalist Angy Ghannam recounts the experience she had in El-Duweiqa, where many inhabitants collect garbage for a living, at the foot of Mokattam Hills, a rich area of the city. 'There was a rockfall in 2008, which killed 100 people, the poor residents believe because of the construction of a golf course, which is on top of the Mokattam Hills above them. At the foot, people live in terrible conditions, where untreated sewerage runs in the streets and children are vulnerable to the worst of things. Mothers told me that they prefer now to sleep together with their children so that if something happens, another rockfall, they "can all die together". I have seen a lot in my time, and am pretty hardened to such thing, but this was difficult to accept. And they look at the golf course with all the rich people above them, and think they caused the landslide. These are different worlds.'[4]

Such living conditions are not unusual in a city built in the early twentieth century to house just three million people. 'The paradoxes are palpable,' writes Mary Anne Weaver, 'like the poverty, the indifference and squalor, and the grotesque displays of wealth; the impression of a country with a civilization going back five thousand years but inchoate, formless, built insecurely upon the ruins of the past.'[5]

In Egypt, the Lotus Revolution brought, for a moment, these two worlds together, where indifference met, if reluctantly, indigence. But there were different motives in this congregation for these groups, splits that soon became violently evident.

For the public leadership of the Tahrir Square throng, it was largely a bourgeois revolution, one driven by the social media and middle-class values, tastes and aspirations. Symbolically, a Google executive Wael Ghonim was a prominent organiser,[6] the digital link explaining why Egyptian activists have referred to these heady days sometimes as the 'Internet Revolution' or 'Revolution 2.0'.[7]

The middle class wanted to take Egypt to the next level, to create democratic politics, to have an 'opposition that contests policy and creates options and legitimacy for government actions'. In so doing, the revolution 'showed that we are not Chinese: growth without democracy is not enough, especially where you have an internationalised middle class. And we are not India: democracy without growth won't work in Egypt.'[8]

Among this group there was anger at the way in which Egypt's ruling elite, represented by Mubarak's National Democratic Party, and Mubarak's family and coterie had profited financially, apparently believing that they were above politics and the military institution, and the longevity of life itself. Even though his health obviously was declining, Mubarak carried on regardless, presumably until his son, Gamal, took over, displaying in the process a remarkable, pharaonic degree of political contempt and personal egotism.

The protestors unknowingly have played into the hands of the most powerful institution in Egypt, the military. Recognising that Mubarak's powers were declining and intent on protecting its interests against political contamination and a pending transfer of power to Gamal, who had no personal martial pedigree, they allowed the protests to run their course in removing the president.

The military has long been seen as the institutional backbone to Egypt's social order. From the arrival of Alexander the Great in 332 BC until the abdication of King Farouk in 1952, the country was ruled without interruption by foreigners, and thereafter from 1953 until 2012 by military men. In successive regimes led by Gamal Abdel Nasser (1954–70), Anwar Sadat (1970–81) and Mubarak, the gravitas afforded by leadership during war and possession of the 'key levers of power' have made the armed forces the 'only institution able to effect change by force', enjoying a 'detached, exceptional status',[9] seen as the ultimate guardians of a secular, modern state.

But this is only part of the picture. The resultant absence of legitimacy and lack of a common touch was complicated by a legacy, which the army had introduced under Nasser and perpetuated by his successors, of socialist bureaucratic inertia, vested business interests and corruption on a grand scale. The privilege of power afforded to the armed forces both maintained and enabled an empire of commercial interests, benefiting from 'preferential customs and exchange rates, tax exemption, land ownership and confiscation rights' and 'an army of almost-free labourers' in the form of conscripted soldiers.[10] The military is deemed to control around 40 per cent of the economy, most notably in areas such as cement manufacture; for some crowding out the private sector, but for others, a pillar of the establishment without whom 'things would not work as well'.[11]

Even though the notion perpetuated that the state would, in the spirit of Nasser's Arab socialism, act to ensure a cradle-to-grave existence, the reality was different. With seven million employed (including 700 000 more between 2011 and 2013 alone) by the civil service, the heavy hand of officialdom had crushed the fiscus, increased domestic debt levels and smothered private initiative. More than that, there was a 'huge gap' between the economy and the people, evident in an absence of an economic debate more generally, and about the choices – between growth, education spending or subsidies, for example – involved. The state sector remained dominant, with more than 150 enterprises, and the incentives were badly skewed and distortive.

By 2014, Egypt was already devoting a tenth of its GDP and one-third of the government budget to subsidies for food and fuel. Around 7 per cent of GDP was spent annually subsidising the cost of fuel, at around $0.25 per litre (about three times less than cost and among the cheapest in the world). Given that few of the poor had cars, this was essentially a tax on the poor for the benefit of the wealthy, and one riddled by corruption.[12] Attempts by the government in 2013/14 to institute a smart card system for fuel requiring registration 'connecting warehouses with gas stations' and a second stage 'connecting gas stations with consumers' revealed that 300 of 2 600 gas stations did not exist, instead being conduits for fraud. Attempts to establish how many cars there are on Cairo's jammed streets have similarly proven difficult: figures varying between two and three million, given issues of registration.[13]

Those Egyptians at the bottom of the social pyramid may have shared the democratic aspirations of their middle-class Tahrir Square compatriots, but with a different outcome in the form of a more radical, Islamist government, which offered a more sympathetic alternative to those locked in the slums, with a basic education if few employable skills, and even fewer job opportunities, especially among the youth, given that three-quarters of the country's unemployed were between fifteen and 29 years of age.

Pundits argued, in the wake of the Tahrir Square uprising, that any incoming Egyptian government would have to be 'pro-development and pro-democracy as the people have demanded'. While these aspirations may have remained consistent, they were wishful thinking and have been dulled by the reality of governance and the difficulties of government.

This was a tricky reform path for any government to navigate through, complicated by worsening social circumstances. As investor and security perceptions and realities changed, the economy shrank suddenly as confidence dried up and receipts from tourism dropped. During the crisis in 2011, there was $9 billion in outflows of Treasury bills to a stock of just $200 million, and $17 billion from the stock market.[14]

Whereas annual tourist numbers peaked at 14 million before the crisis, responsible for $13 billion annually, this had at least halved within just two years. In 2010, the tourism industry comprised 13 per cent of GDP and directly or indirectly employed one in seven workers. Unemployment doubled to 14 per cent, though with 650 000 new entrants in the job market annually, these numbers look far worse if another 27 million, the same number as the current workforce who fall outside the definition and are, in the words of one economist, 'a proxy for the informal economy', are added to the calculations.[15] With money leaving and growth failing, the fiscal deficit also doubled to 14 per cent from 2011 to 2013, a blow softened by generous grants from the Gulf states. Without this, the Treasury admitted in March 2014, things could have been much worse.[16] The fiscal situation was in part tenuous because the government's low take from tax as a percentage of GDP, just 14 per cent given the local art form of tax avoidance and the relative size of informal economic activity, was conservatively estimated at 30–40 per cent of GDP.[17]

At first, the Supreme Council of the Armed Forces sought through political influence to consolidate the military's role, to put it above politics. Hence, the relatively smooth path to the elections in June 2012, which elected a government headed by the Muslim Brotherhood's Mohamed Morsi, the first-ever democratically elected president of Egypt.

Things quickly went from bad to worse with the Brotherhood. Their confrontational ineptitude worsened an already suffering Egyptian economy. In their journey from prison to the presidency, while Morsi and his men apparently had a vision of what they were fighting against, they had less so in terms of what they wanted to do apart from consolidate their financial and political power base. They also proved hopelessly inept at running the ministries they sought to dominate, more intent, from the perspective of some, at seizing power and wealth.

This put them on course for a collision with the military, whose influence Morsi personally sought to unpick.

His relationship with the armed forces may have tipped with the dismissal of the defence minister and armed forces chief, Field Marshal Mohamed Hussein Tantawi, and army chief of staff in August 2012, part of Morsi's apparent aim to reduce military influence over the new constitution specifically and politics more generally. Yet, the military were largely in control of the replacement, providing Morsi with a list of three names to choose from. Moreover, the widely unpopular Tantawi's removal was also in the armed forces' best interest, and specifically those of his successor, Field Marshal Abdul Fattah Al-Sisi.

This was followed by attempts to strip the judiciary of the right to challenge his decisions in November that year, and his appointment of Islamist allies as regional leaders in thirteen of Egypt's 27 governorships the following June. Then, on 3 July 2013, Morsi was removed by the military, headed by Al-Sisi, scarcely a year after he had taken over. Before this event, Al-Sisi had warned that the 'army is a fire ... Do not play against it and do not play with it.'[18] Amid widespread street protests against his rule, even those once politically opposed to Mubarak in the slum of Imbaba wanted the military and Al-Sisi, head of intelligence under Mubarak, back in charge.[19]

The army was not slow or too touchy-feely to assert itself. In August 2013, hundreds were killed as security forces stormed protest camps in Cairo set up by Morsi supporters, leading to the declaration of a state of emergency and the imposition of curfews. The Brotherhood put the number of dead at 6 000; independent tallies around half this figure. In a society where 'vendetta' is a way of life, there is a danger that such violence sets the stage, observers say, for ongoing cycles of counter-violence.[20]

By March 2014, some estimates had the number of detainees since the Brotherhood's departure from government at around 20 000, compared to a total of roughly 3 500 arrested during his year in power.[21] Attacks against the security forces also increased, with groups such as the Al-Qaeda-inspired 'Ansar Beit al-Maqdis (Champions of Jerusalem), which claimed responsibility for the 24 January 2014 bomb attack on Cairo's police headquarters, Ajnad Misr and Molotov Against the Coup, making their presence felt, increasing both the political temperature and rate of economic descent. Sixteen security force members were killed during Morsi's rule in an attack in the Sinai by militants; according to government estimates, 202 army and 246 police had been killed between 3 July 2012 and March 2014.[22]

Still, some opposition to the July 2013 coup was peaceful. The Brotherhood's four-fingered 'Rabaa' gesture – in reference to Rabaa al-Adawiya Square, the site of the deadly August army crackdown on pro-Morsi supporters – became one way of expressing disquiet over the military-backed regime. 'It is not certain why the military cracked down in this way,' asked one journalist. 'Why end the sit-in, and why end it this way?' The same might be asked about the verdict to condemn 529 Brotherhood members to death in March 2014; a harsh and polarising message.

Regardless, the economy has responded well to improved political certainty, helped by the Gulf inflows, totalling $16.9 billion by April 2014 – $6 billion from Saudi Arabia, $6.9 billion from the United Arab Emirates and $4 billion from Kuwait.[23] While the stock market contracted by 42 per cent in 2011, it increased again by 51 per cent the following year, and went up again 24 per cent in 2013, although in the first half it was down 14 per cent and up in the second by 42 per cent. By the end of March 2014, the market index was up 42 per cent over 2011, making it one of the top three performing bourses worldwide.[24]

Underpinning the political and developmental challenges, no matter the government in power, are the drivers of demography and geography. Although Egypt encompasses a large territory, the size of Spain and France combined, 95 per cent of the population lives on less than 5 per cent of the land, a thin 'strip of green' that follows the Nile from Aswan and the border with Sudan to the Mediterranean. The economic growth and development challenge across the region, as in sub-Saharan Africa, partly centres on the need for better governance, but it is also substantially shaped by population growth. The North African and Middle East region's population has quadrupled since 1950, and is projected to increase from 450 million over the next 35 years to 700 million by 2050, more than the estimated population of Europe. As noted elsewhere, sub-Saharan Africa's numbers have increased from 100 million in 1900 to 900 million, and should peak at around two billion inhabitants by 2040.[25]

The sheer issue of scale is confounding. Population growth remains pinned at 2.6 per cent annually in Egypt, 'the result,' says one banker, 'of the intersection of poverty and culture, a belief that you need a big family as security'. But, 'if Egypt is successful at providing for this extraordinary number there are real questions whether the environment can sustain it'.[26] Already Cairo has one of the worst air pollution records worldwide. According to the World Health Organization, the average Cairene inhales more than twenty times an acceptable level of air pollution every day, equivalent to smoking a daily pack of cigarettes.[27]

All this has left things in the balance. The long road ahead may encourage a more radical, Islamist solution to the plight of the 45 million Egyptians locked in poverty, crowded into Imbaba-style accommodation. Globalisation is a skills-premium phenomenon, and the only social mobility for those without them in Egypt, as elsewhere, is down.

Few would disagree that Egypt first has to get out of its bind by stabilising the political environment and restoring some degree of fiscal order, in part with the inflows from the Gulf states. A second part is to undertake structural reforms, including dealing with the subsidies, and rooting out the worst of the corruption by using more intelligent means of delivering these reforms to the poor (rather than the middle class). There is a need, too, to lift up the abysmal standard of education to focus less on rote learning than developing minds and imparting skills.

Private sector consumption and investment are key drivers for growth. There have been positive moves. In 2000, the public sector comprised more than half of all investments; now the private sector supplies two-thirds. Energy, health care and transport, for example, are relatively devoid of private involvement, and remain poor performers. But changing this system requires breaking with the statist past.

Egypt also shows just how difficult it is to change a way of 'doing business' overnight. As elsewhere in the region, the service 'culture', private and public, is a reflection of the absence of a meritocracy and prevalence of a paralysing combination of patronage and chauvinism. The challenge of changing the constraints of mindset, tradition and customs, the stuff that lurks under the recovery 'iceberg', is compounded by the difficulty, too, in holding entrenched leadership to account in weak democracies.

It may be that one has to accept not only the limits of an authoritarian Iraq-style security option, where the security forces are unable to institute a clampdown on violence, but that there is a prospect of a situation where there is a 'new norm': of a booming stock market and relatively high rates of growth, but high unemployment, inflation, political volatility and extent of violence. The likelihood of this outcome depends on the ability to strike a political compromise between the political poles and for leadership to carry through on tough decisions, from ending subsidies to enforcing the rule of law.

Egypt's roads, drivers and traffic are a good metaphor of the ingredients for reform. The best way, it is said, to navigate Cairo is to fly over it. The local parking and zigzag driving customs illustrate a careless 'me-first' habit, erratic tendencies worsened considerably by a terminal text, talk and drive habit. Such traits display a total disrespect for each other not to say the rule of law, one result of which turns traffic to hard-setting treacle – taking hours sometimes to move even metres. Getting this right demands a cocktail of measures: cracking down on transgressors, curbing bribe-taking by traffic officers, limiting the number of cars per se and in the city limits – and above all else, the necessary will to make this happen. What is the likelihood of this occurring; the same might be asked of wider structural economic reforms?

In announcing his candidacy for president in the 2014 election and his retirement from the military to do so, Al-Sisi said it would require a 'joint effort' to make the changes necessary for Egypt to prosper: 'It was not the politicians or the military that removed two regimes. It is you, the people … The making of the future is a joint effort. It is a contract between the ruler and the people … a ruler cannot succeed alone … it takes the joint effort of both the ruler and the people to succeed.'[28]

Al-Sisi's role has evoked parallels, inevitably, with Nasser, less in terms of his shared military background (and, indeed, there are notable differences in this regard: Nasser, as the son of an Alexandria postal worker, moved from school to school, finishing his education at the Egyptian Royal Military Academy; Al-Sisi has enjoyed an international military education in the UK, US and Saudi Arabia), but in terms both of the scale of reforms necessary and the expectation that somehow one man could magically pull off a miracle. In the 1950s, when the army first took over, there was a similar choice facing Egypt, on which the country was divided: a return to a parliamentary democracy and constitutionalism, and the army back to its barracks by one segment; another wanted a 'strong, unchecked charismatic patron who promised land and bread'. By late 1954, under Colonel Nasser, 'basic freedoms and parliamentary constitutionalism were among the casualties' with Egypt establishing 'an officers' republic: a state where the armed institutions are above any other, including the elected ones.'[29]

There are also parallels in the nature of the challenge of the Muslim Brotherhood, repressed, imprisoned and otherwise persecuted under Nasser.[30] On 26 October 1954, a Brotherhood member, Mahmoud Abdel Latif, fired eight shots at Nasser who was speaking in Alexandria's Manshiya Square. All of them missed, perhaps because the event was staged or maybe because the would-be assassin was a poor shot. Whatever the case, the 'Manshiya incident' provided Nasser and his junta with necessary support and latitude to crush the Brotherhood and especially its paramilitary wing, Al-jihaz al-Sirri (Secret Apparatus).

One of the 2 000 members incarcerated was Sayyid Qutb, a former Ministry of Education official and author of the best-seller *Social Justice in Islam*, which set out the principles of an Islamic socialism. Qutb's radical thinking was linked to the levels of state repression, including his imprisonment for nearly a decade in Tura Prison and torture by the Nasser regime, as has been argued is the Brotherhood's use of counter-violence in the 1960s and early 1970s.[31] Qutb and two other Brothers were hanged by the government in August 1966.

The campaign against the Brotherhood contained aspects of Nasser's regime at its worst, masked at times by the Arab nationalist at his charismatic best. To an assembled audience he joked: 'In the year 1953 we really wanted to compromise with the Muslim Brotherhood if they were willing to be reasonable, and I met the head of the Muslim Brotherhood and he sat with me and made his requests. The first thing he asked for was to make the wearing of a hijab mandatory in Egypt and demand that every woman walking in the street wear a tarha [scarf] ... every woman walking. And I told him if I make that law they will say that we have returned to the days of Al-Hakim bir-Amr Allah who forbade people from walking at day and only allowed walking at night, and my opinion is that every person in his own house decides for himself the rules. And he replied: "No, as the leader, you are responsible." I told him: "Sir, you have a daughter in the School of Medicine and she's not wearing a tarha. Why don't you make her wear a tarha? If you are unable to make one ... girl – who is your daughter – wear the tarha, you want me to put a tarha on ten million women, myself?'[32]

Judging from Morsi's subsequent political ascendancy, however, Nasser only succeeded in pushing the Brotherhood underground, a reality that should focus on Al-Sisi. Nasser more successfully, if not ultimately especially productively, overhauled Egypt's political system, abolishing the monarchy, sidelining the Turco-dominated political class, and institutionalised sweeping economic reforms to land ownership, the public sector and in industry. Ownership of the country's assets was transferred from a small capitalist class to the state, and industrialisation was accelerated, the economy growing at an average rate of 9 per cent per annum for a decade. By 1970, Egypt had the largest share of its labour force employed in manufacturing of 21 less-developed countries surveyed by the OECD, including Argentina and Chile.[33] But hopes of a modern future imploded on the rock of the wars with Israel, a horrible human rights record, poor use of agriculture land and a stifling Soviet-style (and sometimes trained) bureaucracy a benchmark for inefficiency, a 'deathbed of talent' and a bastion of 'sterile thinking'.[34]

While the global context has changed, where security trumped human rights as it did under the Cold War, the regional environment is still, more or less, accepting of stability over niceties, not least since this is in various autocratic monarchies' best interests. This logic is also explained by the Brotherhood's own attempts to subordinate democratic principles to its own ends.

According to this way of thinking, if Al-Sisi could deliver growth, confront corruption and keep prices down, he would stay, and Egypt would claw its way back, slowly recovering the economy and building bridges across the political divides. While an economic solution might help to create the conditions for peace, without getting the politics right, economic recovery is unlikely beyond short-term stabilisation measures, including aid transfers from various friendly Gulf states.

There is another, different future, one where the country descends into civil conflict. This is the Egypt of ultra-polarisation, of conservative nationalism at the one end, supportive of the army at all (democratic) costs, and Islamic radicalism at the other extreme. Polarisation and revenge fuels a cycle of never-ending and always descending violence, economic collapse and further bitterness, poverty and hatred, especially in a cultural context where revenge is an accepted form of justice. Syria is the model, suicide bombings the technique, and emigration and a rapidly sinking economy and shrivelling (and exiting) middle class a consequence. A security solution is not enough in the absence of a political compromise where the middle class has shrunk, left or headed for the poles. No matter the staging of a fresh election in May 2014, the removal by the military of the Muslim Brotherhood from office has closed off the democratic option for them as a route to power and sets the stage for more violence.

For the former upside to occur and the latter scenario to be avoided, however, astute political leadership is necessary, recognising that security is only part of the solution, and a temporary one at that. In this, the media would have to avoid demonising Islamists as terrorists and the '25 January' leaders as Western agents or Zionists as many, by 2014, seemed to prefer.

One other big thing has changed for Al-Sisi since Nasser's time, which will make his job tougher. The population expects change, in Egypt as elsewhere in the developing world. Coupled with rampant population growth, this factor more than anything will require a fresh start, ending 70 years of Egyptian 'business as usual'.

29

THE PRIOR QUESTION

Why Some States Fail

*

W hat do the various case studies teach about the reasons for and likeli-hood of state failure and recovery? Why does Africa house the ma-jority of fragile and failed states, whereas states in East Asia have turned fragility into extraordinary success, maintaining economic growth rates at multiples greater than anything seen previously in 200 years of European and North American development history?[1] This has, as noted, driven down the share of the global population living in poverty by more than half to around 21 per cent by 2010. The graph below illustrates the fast pace of China and India's poverty reduction over the past three decades:[2]

Between 1960 and 2010 China, Hong Kong, Malaysia, Singapore, South Korea, Taiwan and Thailand grew at more than 4 per cent per year, producing

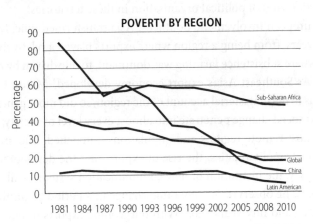

POVERTY BY REGION

Source: World Bank.

a more than sevenfold increase in income over 50 years. At the same time, the Congo, Central African Republic, Guinea, Haiti, Madagascar, Nicaragua and Niger became poorer than they were 50 years ago. To this sorry list might be added Afghanistan, Liberia, Sierra Leone and Somalia, but for which complete data is missing.[3]

Yet, despite this divergence over the past 50 years, Southeast Asia and sub-Saharan Africa enjoy prominent parallels, at least in the transition from traditional society to the colonial variant.

In their traditional pre-colonial world, the authority of Southeast Asia's various rulers (with the notable exception of Vietnam, where there was always much greater state control from the centre) was only absolute in and around the seat of power, where their control 'diminished in proportion to the distance one moved away from the capital'.[4] Equally, state borders were 'uncertain and porous', reflecting the lack of close links between these centres of authority and their outer periphery. The Southeast Asian region was as a result not made up of the eleven states that comprise the twenty-first-century version, but rather a more diverse and fragmented mosaic, of not less 'than forty states' comprising kingdoms, principalities and sultanates.[5] Their authority was delegated through a combination of alliance-making and simply allowing some regions to get on with matters in their own way.

Southeast Asia's twentieth-century economic transformation has its origins in the end of this traditional world. The spur for this was in the industrial revolution elsewhere, which accelerated the search for colonial possessions and their commodities. It also changed the focus and methods of production, and of political organisation in these territories.

With European involvement, Southeast Asia transformed quickly, in less than 100 years, from being a region where exports played a relatively minor role and where subsistence farming was dominant, to one driven by external demand. 'As Southeast Asia's export economy developed,' Milton Osborne reminds us in his magisterial account of the region, 'so did more general economic and social change penetrate into almost every level of society, leaving only the most remote regions and populations untouched. The growth of the great metropolitan cities, the rise of exports and the development of a cash economy, the institution of new communication systems – all of these are products,' he observes, 'of economic change in a period beginning only one hundred and fifty years ago.'[6] With burgeoning exports of rice, rubber and tin, among other new commodities, to fuel the industrial demands of faraway economies, came improvements to road, rail and port networks to get them to these markets. With such increased trade, changes occurred in society: instead of seeking to migrate to the cities to escape the hardships of rural life, 'peasants methodically set to work to grow more and more on what was, proportionately per capita, less and less space'.[7]

Traditional Southeast Asian societies were characterised by ethnic disunity, frail institutions and limited governance outside of the capital, weak democracy, subsistence agriculture, fragmentary external trade linkages and acute social stratification – indeed, many of the conditions prevalent in weak states today, especially those in Africa, the home to three-quarters of those classified 'fragile'. Sub-Saharan Africa underwent much of the same colonial experience as Southeast Asia, which left its states similarly globalised, at least by the standards of the time, and with new products to sell into these markets and fresh borders and state units to manage. But, as noted above, whereas much of Southeast Asia has made staggering development progress, Africa has lagged, not least in terms of per capita incomes. Instead of employing and building on the colonial inheritance, that era is seen almost entirely in negative terms in Africa, not only in terms of stripping away the dignity of its indigenous peoples, but in Sudanese Omar al-Bashir's terms, for leaving 'ticking time bombs here and there' in terms of inapposite borders and weak governance and institutions.[8]

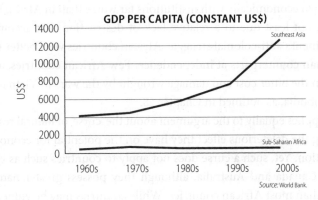

GDP PER CAPITA (CONSTANT US$)

Southeast Asia

Sub-Saharan Africa

Source: World Bank.

So where did things go wrong for Africa? What has it been about the African political economy that apparently predisposed so many of its countries to fragility and failure? And what might this tell us for their recovery?

The easy answer to this is that many African countries have, by comparison to Southeast Asia, made poor policy choices, and often because this has been a way of ensuring control, power and wealth.[9] If this is the case, the prior question is 'why' – why, when they have experienced much of the same as Southeast Asia in terms of the history of external involvement and exploitation of commodities, and even of bitter nationalist struggles, has Africa not ascended a similar high-growth development path?

The drivers of under-performance and failure

Even though around two-thirds of poverty reduction comes from growth,[10] the reasons for failure do not rest on single factors alone – GDP output, geography, leadership, the extent of fault lines, ideology, skills levels, the colonial legacy, and so on – but rather how they act in combination. Put differently, it is not one thing; it is everything.

Single-issue explanations – and their corollary, magic bullet, one-thing solutions – can easily be rebuked. African countries have, for example, not faced any peculiar structural impediments to their development.[11] Although a lack of human resources is often cited as a constraint, South Korea overcame a capacity shortage, sending bureaucrats to Pakistan and the Philippines for training in the 1970s. Though institutional capacity is similarly cited as a structural impediment, some countries (not least some in Southeast Asia) have grown economically with institutions far worse than in Africa. In some respects, not least due to a relative lack of destruction that accompanied the continent's anti-colonial struggle, African countries were better off than their Asian counterparts at independence. Few African countries, after all, can claim the bitter cost and damage wrought by the wars in Vietnam, Laos and Cambodia, as outlined in Chapter 28.

This applies equally to the argument about the 'curse' of natural resources, including the deleterious effect they have on the potential for economic diversification. Yet, such a curse does not apply to countries such as Norway, the US, Canada and Australia, although they possess greater natural resources than most African countries. While countries may be vulnerable to the management or pricing of one sector, they are not poor or weak because of a lack (take Singapore) or surfeit (Norway) of such endowments. Instead, problems arise where the systems of governance are *not inclusive* and rather fractured, fragmented or elitist, and characterised by rent-seeking, often along ethno-political or other fault lines.[12] A political economy based on hard mineral exports, most notably oil, can in these *exclusive* circumstances also fuel authoritarianism, given that so much of the country's total export revenue is captured and controlled by central government or by these elites. Such financial flows can help to support governments that would otherwise have collapsed, enabling authoritarians to maintain their rule.

Noting overall the 'structural handicap arguments' are 'confusing the cause and the symptoms', the Cambridge economist Ha-Joon Chang has concluded that these are handicaps 'only because you are underdeveloped; it is not that they cause underdevelopment'.

The culturalist arguments about work ethic are equally subjective and erroneous in the East Asian context, even though such differences have long been seen as both obstacles and assets to development. The British had false, as it turned out, cultural impressions about Germany in the nineteenth century, while the Allies had very negative (and entirely fallacious and costly) views about the fighting ability and economic sophistication of the Japanese in the early twentieth century. 'They would not make good pilots because of their poor eyesight', was the commonly held view about the Imperial Japanese Army before the Second World War. Pearl Harbour and the skilfully flown Zeros soon proved this legend untrue.

A number of multilateral organisations had equally harsh views about the growth prospects of East Asia in the 1950s on account of the region's Confucian work ethic. The 1950 UN Human Development Report noted, for example, that 'economic progress will not be desired in a community where the people do not recognize that progress is possible'.[13] And they picked the wrong winners with unnerving accuracy. Burma was said by the World Bank in 1958 to have 'made remarkable economic progress ... [its] long-run potential compares favourably with those of other countries in South East Asia'. The World Bank's 1957 economic report was optimistic about the Philippines, which it said had 'achieved a position in the Far East second only to Japan ... The prospects ... for sustained long-term growth are good'. Equally, the World Bank's chief economist in 1967 predicted that for Africa 'the economic future before the end of the century can be bright', listing seven African countries that he wrote 'clearly have the potential to reach or surpass a 7 per cent rate of growth'. All listed had negative per capita growth from 1970 to 1998.[14]

Rather than culture, Jared Diamond has emphasised the role of geography as the principal reason for success or failure.[15] This pertains to the less obvious aspects, though. While landlockedness is cited as an impediment to growth in the case of Rwanda, Burundi, Uganda or Malawi, for example, it has apparently not applied to Switzerland.

More salient is the lack throughout much of sub-Saharan Africa of a critical mass of skilled people to participate in development (especially in the cities), resulting in high labour costs and low economic growth. Africa is both sparsely and unevenly populated.[16] Less than one-third of Africans reside in countries around the average continental density. While there were, as noted in the Introduction, only 27 Africans present per square kilometre across the continent (compared to the global average of 45.21 square kilometres, or the Asian average of 119 square kilometres), there were 341 Rwandans per square kilometre (about the same as India, Israel and Belgium) and 271 square kilometres in neighbouring Burundi; yet just 25 square kilometres in the Democratic Republic of Congo.[17] Whereas the relative density of the Asian peasantry ensured a level of social organisation, Africa's sparse populations have not leant themselves to this extent of control.[18] Instead, parts of Africa were characterised by what anthropologists refer to as 'segmentary lineage' societies – those tribal units operating outside of state formations where authority is derived from lineage, not the state, where family is part of a larger 'segment' of more relatives and their families. Historically outside and frequently marginalised from the state and the formal economy, these groups were – and are, in places like South Sudan – often pastoralists and nomadic.[19]

This highlights another related, negative influence of populations and geography. The inheritance by the post-colonial state of imperial borders made local government less competitive; less inclined to govern outlying territory and invest in bureaucracies and other aspects of statehood or by raising taxes to enable territory-wide government (apart from establishing points of taxation and tariff entry and exit or ensuring rents from commodities), secure in the knowledge that no secessionist or irredentist contender to its rule could legally arise.[20] Such lackadaisical governance was enabled by the moratorium imposed by the Organisation of African Unity on alterations to colonial boundaries. This explains in turn why so little has been spent on developing national infrastructure as a means to broadcast power, and where, in cases like Mobutu's Congo, it has been a target of deliberate neglect, keeping the country together by keeping it disconnected and apart. It also explains the African axiom: control the capital and you control the country, an aspect that the ruling MPLA learnt quickly, as was seen in Chapter 19 on Angola.

The virtual absence of fighting over borders during the colonial period by European powers and the absence of external threats faced by post-colonial

African states also reduced pressure, Paul Collier notes, 'to invest in either fiscal capacity or a legal system which would have assisted private prosperity'. Given, too, that the principal threat facing regimes was from internal dissent, this invariably resulted in repression of certain groups representing this threat. In the process nationalism was discouraged, undermining the economy and state capacity, and leadership sought to deliberately weaken armies, given the threat of coups by under-resourcing them or by establishing alternative power structures. Military spending was a divisive issue, not a national public good. In this environment, it was instead one where 'the army that defends you represses me'.[21]

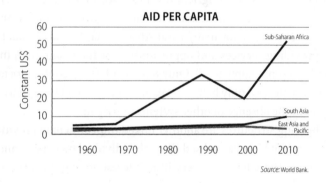

AID PER CAPITA

Source: World Bank.

Whereas the ratio of tax revenue to GDP in states was commonly around 20 per cent in developing countries, in some cases (Ghana and Uganda, for example) this shrunk to just 5 per cent in the 25 years after independence, despite donor conditionalities and technical capacity-building to try to offset this trend. The tendency towards less reliance on domestic sources of tax revenue was both an effect of and reason for increasing inflows of foreign aid, which reduced the need to rely on and invest in state capacity to raise taxes. 'Since aid commonly amounted to around half of public spending,' Collier notes, 'the effect was substantial.' Aid has helped African leaders to stay in power, assisting in circumventing indigenous channels of accountability, including parliament and fragmenting and disincentivising attempts at nation-building. The impetus to give aid is greater than the pressure in Western countries to withhold it, which is a reflection of bureaucratic inertia, personal ambition and national, colonial guilt. Hence the view among some recipients that they are helping Westerners by taking it.

Despite the contemporary fad to bash aid as the explanation for all of Africa's problems,[22] Asian countries have also received comparatively large amounts of donor assistance. During the 1960s, the values of aid per capita received by these countries were roughly the same. From the mid-1970s, the value of aid flows to sub-Saharan African countries soared. In 1972 the difference in aid received between the two regions was some $3 per capita, though this discrepancy increased to around $50 by the mid-2000s. Despite some dissenters,[23] it is generally accepted that better policies should in all probability result in more effective aid, higher growth and faster development.[24] Thus, according to this view, Asian countries have put aid to better use because of improved governance and policies and firmer local ownership of projects.

The richness of African agriculture has also, in some cases, proven a hindrance to the development and extension of government and the state. The ease of subsistence for many rural Africans has let government off the hook in providing services and opportunities for them, although this relative wealth does not apply to all. Only 8 per cent of the continent's land has a tropical climate, and only half receives adequate rainfall to support regular agriculture in the absence of other systems of irrigation.[25]

Land-holding structures are another linked impediment to growth where land value cannot be collateralised through individual ownership and mortgage schemes. There has been very little interest among the leadership for such reform; and quite the opposite in Zimbabwe, where, as was seen in Chapter 9, land has been seized and redistributed based on political allegiances. All this has perpetuated the colonial system of using land allocation for local power brokers (that is, chiefs) to allow indirect rule. By 2009, over 80 per cent of land across Africa remained in customary tenure, while in some countries, such as Mozambique or Tanzania, no private ownership of land was permitted.

Thus, in some cases, fragility has reflected the presence of too many people for the state and economy to cope with; in others too few. In some cases (say, Somalia, South Sudan, Afghanistan, Congo) this is down to a lack of social organisation – these are 'pre-market' societies, driven by ethnic and other divisions, and with few of the advantages of economies of scale, critical mass of populations, dense transport routes and access to the outside world for technology, capital and markets. In these environments, in the aforementioned 'segmentary lineage' societies, without wider economic opportunities, identity- and cultural-based grievances can quickly turn to violence. Despite differences within ethnic groups, people will generally stand with each other (and fight) against outsiders.[26]

Society and politics

Smaller country geographic size apparently lends itself to better functioning states and also to political liberalisation, partly because leaders are in touch with the electorates. Infrastructure is generally easier to provide (since the scale is smaller), governance is more straightforward, and there are often fewer and less complicated ethnic and other divisions to manage.

There appears to be a related relationship between better governance and fragility. The OECD's 2013 report on fragile states[27] is one that stresses the governance dimension to the origins of fragility, defining the condition as one where there is 'weak capacity to carry out basic governance functions' and the lack of 'ability to develop mutually constructive relations with society'. It considers a 'thick' conceptualisation to encompass 'the multiple dimensions of state-society relations' and a 'substantive understanding centred on the quality of state-society relations and with greater attention to potential stress factors, including economic vulnerability, demographic dynamics, climate change and technological innovation'. It basically says: improve governance, and things will get better.

Again, however, this says very little about the underlying socio-political dynamics that contribute to the poor governance that leads to fragility in the first instance.[28] As Seth Kaplan has put it, 'It does not mention identity in the whole report, and mentions the word sectarian once.' In so doing, this 'ignores the most fundamental question determining whether states are fragile or not: do groups of people with different identities, ideologies and interests feel enough solidarity and fraternity with their fellow citizens to work together inclusively?' Cohesion and legitimacy, thus, are critical, rather than stressing 'Western ideological conceptions of how states ought to work'. A single 'institutionalised' society does not, across the fragile states environment, exist, which explains why, as Kaplan points out, India is able to survive periodic crises despite weak governance, widespread poverty and fractious politics, whereas richer countries are not.

Despite the facade of statehood, and expensive and complex attempts to instil and encourage transparent and meritocratic governance systems and norms, tribalism, sectarianism, even male chauvinism, continue to rear their head in many fragile states, operating according to primordial distributive patterns. Getting past such clan and other primordial relationships is critical to building allegiance to the state. While religious-based institutions and law existed in most regions historically, the rise of independent legal institutions, such as in Europe, paralleled its economic and industrial emergence over the past 500 years. The establishment of a free press, free scientific inquiry, the development of banking and the spirit of Enlightenment were crucial in the European development cocktail.[29]

Religion and sectarianism is, however, just one characteristic that can be used to subvert national endeavour; ethnicity is another. From dividing the spoils between Sierra Leone's two major tribal groups, Temne and Mende, balancing presidential candidates from among Congo's 200-plus ethnic groups, keeping the peace between Tutsi and Hutu in neighbouring Burundi and Rwanda, or in undoing the legacy of racial apartheid in South Africa and Zimbabwe, the politics of identity can be used to shade questions of policy substance in politics.

This highlights the practice of zero-sum economics, where there is continuously one group or another, defined often by race, religion, ethnicity or even gender, left out from the benefits of participation – a permanent 'constituency of losers'. This encourages poor participation in institutions, sets a low threshold for violence, and can ensure that segments of society just get along, and societies remain highly fragmented politically and unequal. It is questionable, of course, whether such a physiognomy begets political instability and violence, or the other way around – whether the chicken follows the egg.

It is not the religious or multi-ethnic make-up of these states per se that are problematic, however, but rather the way in which these ties manifest politically in increasingly difficult and insecure environments, in which patrimonialism and patronage pervade. As Robert Rotberg notes: 'The typical weak or failing state descends into failure when ruler-led and ruler-designed repression and discrimination provokes – after years, even decades, of despair – a reaction on the part of disenfranchised or disadvantaged ethnic groups or coalitions. New insurgent leaders emerge. They become peaceful agitators or sometimes morph into militant warlords.'[30]

Why has identity mattered so much and in such a pernicious way, especially in Africa but also among others in our group of fragile or failed states? Why would leaders take aid, make the right noises about reform, and then change very little of substance with respect to governance and the way political systems function and are accountable? Why would they make political choices based on narrow personal or local interests without the apparent commitment to popular welfare enjoyed throughout much of East Asia? Why were they unable – or unwilling – to build growth coalitions that transcended these narrow interests and divides?

No doubt a difficult colonial history has a role, breeding conflict and leaving Africa at least largely with unnatural borders and poor terms of trade – and its people a devalued sense of their own worth, angry with outsiders yet lacking confidence in their own abilities and suspicious of their fellow country people. But the colonial legacy argument can only go so far, not least because others have prospered in spite of it. As President Barack Obama noted during his first visit to the African continent as president in July 2009,[31] colonialism does not explain the corruption, tribalism, patronage and self-destructive policies that have seen the continent's development slip so far behind its needs and its peers in other regions.

In part, the answer seems to lie in the extent and type of colonial penetration. In the Philippines, for example, long a relatively under-performing economy by Southeast Asian standards, 200 years of Spanish colonialism and the inseparable notion of church and state, as in Latin America, resulted in the pervasive spread of Christianity. This gave greater power to local-level leadership, yet beyond the village or district level power was not allowed to pass out of Spanish hands – leading to widespread resentment and sowing the seeds for the late nineteenth-century Filipino revolutionary movement. This also seems to be related to the nature, duration and extent of colonial conquest. The creation of immigrant societies, though of course not without resultant and ongoing tensions, such as in Malaysia, Burma or Singapore, has resulted in 'mixed' societies, with all the advantages of external trade and finance linkages, along with expertise that immigrants offer.

Perhaps Southeast Asia was able to overcome the legacy quicker because the myth of European superiority – and its corollary of Asian 'inferiority' – was graphically upended with the Japanese crushing of European and American forces in the early stages of the Pacific War. This 'political bombshell' shattered some of the 'most significant presumptions of the past' – of European racial and colonial dominance. 'Following their defeat the white-skinned aliens could be toppled from their privileged position in society to become no better off than the coolies who had laboured to maintain the fabric of colonial society in the years of peace,' as Osborne reflects.[32] Instead of building on the European legacy, African governments sought to reject it, due to the anger generated by alien interests and the enslaving of peoples, even though their own populations were complicit in this regard. This may help to explain why, even where there were bitter nationalist struggle for independence, such as in Kenya and Zimbabwe, these ultimately exacerbated identities rather than reconciled them in creating a sense of nationalism.

Or why these states have been hostile towards outsiders, or why they have kept institutions and governance weak, and democracy under control, given both the fear of diluting tenuous control and being held accountable. The insecurity towards outsiders may also help to explain why the tendency of many weak states in Africa has been to look to outsiders for salvation, most notably through aid.

The duration of colonialism may, conversely, be a metric of failure. The colonial experience in Africa was generally briefer than that of Asia, allowing the colonial units less time to cohere.[33]

And perhaps the most important factor of all, however, is in the relationship between government and the private sector. Yet, the economic failures in the past have been due in part to the African attitude towards business. Private sector growth has largely been an anathema, and not just in the period after independence. The colonialists – be they British, French, Portuguese or Belgian – whatever their ideologies in Europe, established highly interventionist states that actively prevented indigenous African economic enrichment, while protecting white settlers and colonial companies.

By and large, the African leaders that succeeded the colonialists after independence were comfortable with the economic systems they inherited (once stripped of racism), especially as state intervention offered many patronage opportunities for their allies. Expanding state control and intervention was one of the few levers open to them in the context of overall state weakness.

This was exaggerated by the failure of the liberators, Morgan Tsvangirai, then Zimbabwe's prime minister, lamented in August 2012, 'to have a plan beyond redistribution and no focus on production' and an environment where 'politics has been about personality cults, not policies'.[34] In Asia, like in Africa, market economics is a very recent phenomenon. They, too, had highly interventionist colonial states that were part of imperial protection schemes. As in Africa, they retained (or even increased) such intervention post-colonialism, when some transitioned to socialism or communism. The difference appears to rest in the disinterest of African elites in 'what works' for the nation but rather, overwhelmingly, they are interested in themselves, both for reasons of self-enrichment and control. This may explain why African politicians have taken quasi-capitalism on board but will not go further; they will 'open up' the system in piecemeal fashion to gain maximum personal advantage (from cellphone companies to infrastructure investments) but will not go the whole hog because they do not care and because true liberalisation might threaten their fiefdoms. And the cost at the polls of this selfish approach is diminished because of the role of patronage and identity politics, and the weakness overall of electoral systems.

The costs of this model need to be carefully assessed, including in those countries considered recent stellar growth performers.

Ethiopia is a case in point as to how the space for private enterprise has been seriously constrained as a result of such thinking, and arguably narrowed over the past twenty years less in the interests of national development than a small elite – or, for that matter, regional relations. The limited space for private enterprise within Ethiopia, whether foreign or local investors, can be illustrated by the extensive business interests of the Endowment Fund for the Rehabilitation of Tigray (EFFORT), owned by members of the ruling Tigray People's Liberation Front, and by the role of the Ethiopian military's own company, METEC, which has grown quickly from its inception in 2010 by grouping nine businesses previously owned by the Defence Ministry, including Dejen Aviation Industry and Gafat Armament Industry. Six other industries, including plastic, tractor and vehicle spares manufacturers, were transferred to METEC from the privatisation agency. Within three years it had grown to operate as many as 75 factories nationwide, overseen by a board headed by the defence minister, employing about 13 000 people, with the priority aim of 'import substitution', according to Deputy Prime Minister Debretsion Gebremichael, who was responsible for economic coordination. 'They cannot do it on their own so they look for partners, international as well as local. They're bringing many actors to the picture but at the heart of everything it's METEC.'

METEC gained the contract to provide the electro-mechanical works for the $5-billion Grand Ethiopian Renaissance Dam on the Blue Nile in partnership with the Paris-based Alstom, Europe's second-largest power-equipment producer. METEC was also commissioned to building the Coal Phosphate Fertilizer Complex Project in the region of Oromia for the Privatisation and Public Enterprises Supervising Agency, and was the main contractor for the government's Sugar Corporation, which was constructing ten cane plantations and processors nationwide at a cost also of some $5 billion.[35]

As EFFORT's presence illustrates, METEC's privileged role is not unique. And nor is the government merely a passive bystander, but actively privileges its own proxies at the expense of the private sector per se and growth and development more generally in Ethiopia, with long-term consequences for a population which, if the projections are accurate, may be as many as 120 million by 2030. As one regional specialist has noted, 'There are three sorts of companies in Ethiopia: green, which are those state-owned, some NGOs and embassies, and those with ruling party connections; yellow, some private sector, including hotels; red, the remainder. If you are in the green group, it will take a few days to two weeks to clear your goods at Djibouti. If you are yellow, it will take five weeks, and red takes anywhere between six months to a year.'[36] Ethiopia has achieved phenomenal economic growth since 2003, averaging 8.7 per cent between 2007 and 2012, for example. Yet, there is a long-term cost in crowding out the private sector, both in terms of efficiencies and foreign sources of capital. As Befekadu Wolde Gabriel has noted, 'The staggering double digit economic growth success story is accompanied with another shadow story of endemic rent seeking practices which becomes the greatest threat to the nation's steadfast economic growth and national security.'[37] It is not like the politicians are unaware.

This so-called 'developmental state' model was actively promoted by Prime Minister Meles Zenawi, who argued this was a logical response to the failure of other options: 'The fundamental nature of the neo-liberal paradigm has thus led Africa into another economic dead end and into a fragile unstable democracy that is not only incapable of evolving into a stable and mature democracy but actually hinders the development of an alternative path of democracy that leads overtime to such a mature and stable democracy.'[38] Yet, he was alert to the downsides, though the rhetoric has led the reality of countering this consequence. In delivering his last ever parliamentary report, the late prime minister declared that his government was in the middle of a critical battle between developmental officials and rent-seekers from within. 'It was them – the public thieves – or us.' His successor, Hailemariam Desalegn, has repeatedly declared rent-seeking public enemy number one.[39] Regional allies routinely express frustration at breaking into the attractively large Ethiopian market, where several areas – notably, transport, telecommunications, financial services and trading – remain closed to outsiders.[40]

In part, this relates to the domestic imperative to secure local interests first, and a suspicion of foreigners as well as a fear of being unable to control them. As Ahmed Nuru, an adviser to the Ethiopian minister for industry, put it: 'The financial sector is open only to domestic investors. In view of the past global financial crisis, I think we are taking the right path, being cautious on how to open up this sector.'[41] Others relate this choice to the presence of aid. For example, such 'authoritarian development', says the economist William Easterly, occurs 'when the international community – experts from the UN and other bodies – swoop into third world countries and offer purely technical assistance to dictatorships like Uganda or Ethiopia on how to solve poverty'. Given that the primary interest of these rulers is to stay in power, aid, like the development interests of their citizens, plays only a subordinate role. It is what Easterly terms a 'false bargain' – development promises instead of rights.[42]

Whatever the motives behind this model, the effect on crowding out the private sector is likely to make more difficult Ethiopia's stated desire to reach middle-income status by 2025. Prime Minister Desalegn estimates that this will require $150 billion in investment, mainly on infrastructure and social services, which in part will be found, he says, by checking illicit financial flows – money embezzled or leaving the country illegally or via transfer pricing. '[W]hen you consider this much-needed investment in light of the figures on illicit financial flows,' said the prime minister, 'one can get the sense of the relative ease with which countries in Africa, including Ethiopia could have saved and improved lives.' He added that 'with such outflows in check, we will also be able to adequately self-finance and strengthen regional and continental organisations and processes that play important roles in maintaining peace and security. The size of these resources that Africa is being robbed of also indicates how national development gains could easily be reversed.'

But this analysis misses a key point: that at least some of the money leaves because it has nowhere to go due to a lack of business opportunities, partly, as he stressed, due to 'rent-seeking' behaviour, but, of course, also due to crowding out by the very state- and party-led activities that the Ethiopian government has permitted. Equally high levels of domestic corruption and the absence of attractive investment terms, including around taxation, pose a further investor disincentive. It is not that there is a shortage of money, or of opportunity or of capable African partners and entrepreneurs. Money will always find somewhere to go; there is a need to encourage it to go the right way. The problems of rent-seeking, indeed, lie in over-regulation, where the state is at the centre and governance is weak, allowing scope for corrupt manoeuvre by officials. While it is politically expedient to look outside for the problem and the financial solution, the easier-to-solve reasons explaining a lack of financing and rates of development are invariably internal.[43]

Rather, such 'crowding out' is usually less about national development than securing institutional interests and roles. It is also about making money for a group closely connected with the state and ruling party. Long-term developmental interests are seemingly not a core consideration, even though they are regularly used as a justification for state-led actions; hence, for instance, the industrialisation import-substitution argument that is regularly invoked to justify bias against foreign goods and capital.

Whereas Asian leaders expressed themselves in terms of 'export or die', African leaders have not been interested – or importantly, have not been pressured by their own electorate – in explaining to their populations their development vision, and how the private sector is an essential part of the growth equation. If African countries are to develop economic systems that produce self-sustaining growth and, critically, jobs, they are going to have to remove the anti-business animus that has existed since most of their countries were birthed as colonies, and to move on with liberalisation.

When governments have allowed markets to work so that Africans could enrich themselves, the response has been spectacular, whether it be cocoa farmers in the colonial period who adopted the new crop at a furious rate or contemporary cellphone companies who have made Africa the fastest growing area for communications. Until now, entrepreneurs in weak states have made progress by circumventing their governments. To truly succeed, governments will have to be enthusiastic about creating an environment where business will prosper.[44] This places a premium on leadership, not least in promoting what the Indian information technology entrepreneur Nandan Nilekani (who has gone on to a second career in rolling out the country's identification card, no small task) describes as 'horizontal issues' – ideas related to development, education, health, employment – rather than 'vertical issues' (caste, religion, race and region).[45] It requires that people were linked more by notions of citizenship (in his case, 'Indian-ness') rather than sub-national allegiances. He reminds us that '[l]ooking at our problems through the prism of ideas helps us see how clearly ... flawed policies limit our growth'.

Indeed, development across Southeast Asia has relied on the pursuit of market reforms, setting countries and governments deliberately apart from others to attract investors. This has been based on improvements in human and policy institutions, including effective rule of law, the enforcement of contracts, openness to trade and capital and the protection of private property rights. This tells a story about the responsiveness of government.

The Asian authoritarian excuse

East Asia's development success has, for some, justified authoritarianism, given that the region's economies have managed high economic growth rates without full political rights. The benefits of this model are said to include the creation of an environment where decision-makers can enjoy relative autonomy from electorates and public opinion. Thus, they can make tough, if unpopular, decisions because these do not have to be tested immediately or regularly at the polls.[46] Such regimes are also said to be able to avoid the pressures of providing resources to their electorates through redistribution of public and private goods. In so doing, their relative autonomy prevents excessive public consumption, deflect the pressures for patronage and corruption as well as pork-barrel projects such as airports and stadiums, and avoids undermining property rights, all of this in environments where, with the emergence from colonialism, the state and political institutions are weak and the professional class small.

'The danger with democracy in a developing economy,' says Termsak Chalermpalanupap, a research fellow at the Institute of Southeast Asian Studies in Singapore, 'is that you get "money politics". That is, elections become a crude form of vote purchasing to the highest bidder, and government becomes a means to skim off money for the elites who benefit disproportionately when checks and balances don't function effectively.' For example, he says, in his native Thailand, 'it is common knowledge that between 10 and 40 per cent of public project money is skimmed off or lost, the result mostly of large-scale corruption'.

Hence, what Columbia University's renowned economist Jagdish Bhagwati[47] has argued is a 'cruel choice' between economic growth and democracy, where democracy should be deferred until economic growth had transformed society.[48] In emphasising such features, Chalmers Johnson's seminal account of Japanese development,[49] in which he coined the term 'developmental states', highlights the importance of nationalism (where economic means are seen as the principal means of ensuring national survival), state control of finance, labour relations, the role of the economic bureaucracy (especially in Japan the Ministry of International Trade and Industry), the use of incentives and the existence of giant conglomerates such as the Japanese Zaibatsu or the Korean Chaebol.

This argument – along the lines of the aforementioned 'Kigali consensus' – reduces growth and development to one single factor: authoritarianism. Even though for some aspirant totalitarians it may be the most attractive feature of the East Asian growth story, there are many other aspects of that region's relative success that are overlooked in this analysis; for example, high spending on education, bureaucratic responsiveness, attractive policy for business investment, low wages, high productivity, investment in infrastructure, raised agriculture outputs and an overwhelming focus on competitiveness. Whereas authoritarian democrats elsewhere have tended to rely on single commodities for exports (oil or minerals usually), East Asian states have been rapid industrial diversifiers and job creators. By comparison, 70 per cent of Russian exports (and 35 per cent of government revenue)[50] comprise oil and gas; in Venezuela this is 95 per cent (and 45 per cent).[51]

Moreover, the presumption is that the authoritarian ruler or system is both benevolent and efficient, and Africa's experience before the Cold War, when by the start of 1980 there were just two democracies (Botswana and Mauritius) among sub-Saharan Africa's then 47 countries, shows this to be wishful thinking. This should be unsurprising. As noted in the Introduction, there is a clear link between democratic and economic performance, and not just in Africa. Of the top 47 countries in the UN's Human Development Index, those classified as having 'Very High Human Development', 41 are deemed as 'Free', two (Singapore and Seychelles) 'Partly Free' and just four (Brunei, Hong Kong,[52] the United Arab Emirates and Qatar) 'Not Free'.

The great asset of democracy is that it enables a test of philosophies at the market place of the political consumer. It makes politics and policies more competitive. Democratic regimes also promote property rights better than authoritarian regimes by offering impartial, depersonalised institutional guarantees, while popular pressure through elections can promote better public spending.[53] Indeed, Africa's dismal average annual economic growth performance in the 1980s, in particular, of just 1.7 per cent, could be related to the authoritarian nature of most of its rulers,[54] even though other factors – from the weakness and unresponsiveness of bureaucratic regimes, low spending on infrastructure and education, the power of urban interest groups in policy-making, and the presence of ethnic and other fault lines – also played their part. Furthermore, even in an Asian context, the state-led model has its drawbacks, not least the failures inherent in picking winners in terms of different industrial projects and sectors, the slowness to develop financial markets where there is a reliance on government as a source of finance, the existence of cronyism, the lack of competitiveness and disregard for risk – secure in the knowledge that the state would bail out failing firms, and where bureaucratic interest groups are given intense power.

For example, the development record of militarised regimes – the ultimate 'big-man' government – in Africa has been poor. The graph overleaf illustrates the difference in economic performance between those governments in sub-Saharan Africa where the military has abstained from a role in politics (Botswana, Cape Verde, Cameroon, Djibouti, Gabon, Kenya, Malawi, Mauritius, Senegal, South Africa, Swaziland, Tanzania and Zambia), and those elsewhere where it has been involved since independence.

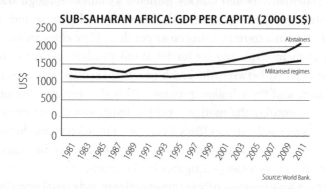

SUB-SAHARAN AFRICA: GDP PER CAPITA (2 000 US$)

Source: World Bank.

Thus accountability in Africa has demanded democratic systems; in parts of Asia, at least, this has not always been necessary, though this, too, is changing and will likely continue to change. China has, for example, averaged 9 per cent annual growth rates for three decades under authoritarianism, doubling its economy every eight years, perhaps the reason why it can afford limited freedoms.

Moreover, while there has been corruption under democracies in Africa (and undoubtedly more under dictatorships, especially of the military sort), Asia's authoritarians have been far from corruption-free either: think Imelda Marcos' world-class shopping habits and her 3 000 pairs of shoes or Suharto's Indonesia, described as a 'family business', among many examples of Southeast Asian excess and illegality.[55] Apart from Singapore, Malaysia and Brunei,[56] the rest of the Association of Southeast Asian Nations region congregates in the bottom half of Transparency International's Corruption Perception Index.[57] This, says Chalermpalanupap, reflects the lack of dedicated institutions to fight corruption, the failure in some countries to pay properly and thus incentivise public officials, and wider checks and balances on executive power – in a word, democracy.[58]

This highlights a different and deeper malaise around institutional practices in the absence of democratic controls. It is hardly surprising that lowly officialdom engages in petty corruption when the leadership has perfected the kleptocracy by which their business practices are defined. Paul Theroux's Angola, highlighted in the *Last Train to Zona Verde*, his ultimate African travelogue, is the archetype, run by a government that is simply 'predatory, tyrannical, unjust, utterly uninterested in its people ... and indifferent to their destitution and inhuman living conditions'. This explains the enormous wealth of the president's daughter Isabel, the only African female billionaire, who has systematically and quickly gathered $3 billion through stakes in Angola's strategic banking, cement, diamonds and telecom sectors, under her father's rule in a country living on $2 per day.[59] Here elites are interested primarily in themselves, and are fearful of independent sources of wealth. Hence the contrast between the lavish personal excesses and expenditure of politicians, and their hollow promises. This also explains the practice – though not entirely the motive – behind indigenisation schemes, from the subtleties of South Africa's Black Economic Empowerment, through increasingly strenuous demands for resource nationalism, to the deliberately politically obvious excesses of Mugabe's land seizures.

Rather than have business people gain experience and capital over time, the process of wealth extension has been purposely politicised for two reasons: one, to keep it among favoured friends, and two, to control it. Wealth had to be transferred with the creation of favours from the wealthy. Race and allegiance have been the key political criteria for this transfer. But when this enemy dries up, as in Zimbabwe, the foe is sought and identified in ideological and ethnic differences within, where 'liberal' equates with undoing party control, power and wealth. The result is a primitive, primordial rent-seeking, a failure by leadership to account to citizens and the latter's failure, divided and ruled by short-term spoils and identity politics, in order to hold them to account at the poll.

Such systems – where democracy is weak, and kept so deliberately – often goes hand in hand with a Mercantilist or, if expressed in earlier terminology, Malthusian view of political economy. Instead of the world being one where improving productivity through capital investment, technology, improving skills and labour specialisation leads to increases in wealth, it is rather viewed as a zero-sum environment, where wealth is possible only by securing finite resources in the face of external competition and internal demands. In this world the state becomes – or deliberately ensures it is – the principal route to securing wealth and security, either through domestic control (such as nationalisation) or external conquest. Wealth, geography, political control and power are inseparable in these minds, contrary to the twenty-first-century globalists who see the movement of capital, goods and skills as increasingly free, fluid and 'stateless'.

In sum, authoritarianism is not a reason for success – just as it can be a reason for failure. Rather, the difference between East Asia and Africa appears to lie in other factors, not least the strong attachment Asian leaders have displayed towards popular welfare of their people, acting against long-term vision, contrasted with the transactional, short-term nature of much African leadership and policy.

The political economy of state failure

The core role of the state is to provide public goods, including security and justice, in return for taxation. Efficient taxation requires, in turn, an administrative structure, fiscal capacity and a vibrant private sector to create the funds to be taxed and from which the state survives. Growth of the private sector requires the institution of appropriate policy and political commitment to a rule of law.[60] In fragile states, the threads of governance, society, politics and economics entwine in a pernicious manner to stress already limited capacity and tenuous habits and institutions of accountability.

The absence of democracy has further reduced elite sensitivity to the objectives and demands of ordinary citizens. Even where democracy has existed, at least formally, vote-buying, voter intimidation and ballot fraud have not only defrauded the process but dampened the intended democratic effect of greater competitiveness and improved accountability on both promises and governance.

Equally, identity has trumped issues in the hands of unscrupulous politicians. As Collier notes: 'If a sense of ethnic solidarity locks in votes for particular candidates regardless of their performance, then politicians

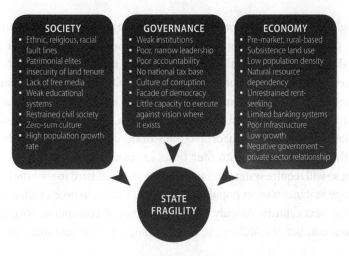

SOCIETY	GOVERNANCE	ECONOMY
• Ethnic, religious, racial fault lines	• Weak institutions	• Pre-market, rural-based
• Patrimonial elites	• Poor, narrow leadership	• Subsistence land use
• insecurity of land tenure	• Poor accountability	• Low population density
• Lack of free media	• No national tax base	• Natural resource dependency
• Weak educational systems	• Culture of corruption	• Unrestrained rent-seeking
• Restrained civil society	• Facade of democracy	• Limited banking systems
• Zero-sum culture	• Little capacity to execute against vision where it exists	• Poor infrastructure
• High population growth rate		• Low growth
		• Negative government – private sector relationship

STATE FRAGILITY

have less incentive to deliver what voters want.' It follows that ethnic and sectarian inclusivity tends to parallel the creation of an effective state.

This process has to be domestically founded. Again, as Collier notes: 'The piecemeal introduction of individual components of this system by either inheritance from colonialism or external intervention is fragile. All failing states initially inherited democratic political institutions, which rulers rapidly dismantled. Many of them also inherited fiscal and legal capacity, which they dismantled.'

Reforms happen when leaders see an opportunity for progress, and when they believe that their interests are threatened by their country's decline – the issues that, for example, motivated F.W. de Klerk to end apartheid in South Africa. In many cases, however, and especially in fragile states, leaders can keep making money regardless of whether their country goes downhill – in fact, sometimes because it is going down is the reason for them to be able to make money.[61]

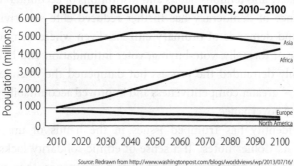

PREDICTED REGIONAL POPULATIONS, 2010–2100

Source: Redrawn from http://www.washingtonpost.com/blogs/worldviews/wp/2013/07/16/
the-amazing-surprising-africa-driven-demographic-future-of-the-earth-in-9-charts.

Might increased numbers of people help since this is what lies in store for many fragile states? Greater concentrations, as was noted in Chapter 21 on Rwanda, offer the prospect of cheaper delivery of infrastructure and social services, and better functioning labour and capital markets. The answer as to whether the pending demographic explosion is a blessing or a curse is: it depends on what states and people do. In Africa, for example, the predicted population increase will quadruple the workforce and the resource burden over the next 100 years, with four times as many mouths to feed as today. Doing so will require system change. It is, for instance, hard to see how Nigeria will cope as it increases its population from 160 million to over a billion people over the next century. Already beset by troubles of 'corruption, poverty and religious conflict', it is 'difficult to imagine how a government that can barely

URBANISATION: 1990–2012

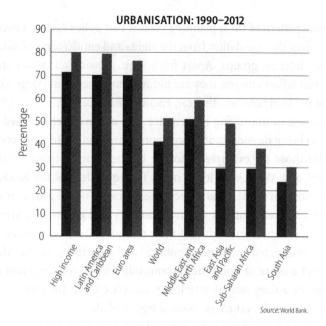

Source: World Bank.

serve its population right now will respond when the demand on resources, social services, schools and roads increases by a factor of eight'.[62]

This could create new stresses as much as it does new opportunities. While the proportion of sub-Saharan African city dwellers is slated to increase from 37 per cent of the population in 2010 to over half by 2025, in some African cities the population could swell by up to 85 per cent. By then a number of mega-cities will emerge, including Lagos with 15.8 million people and Kinshasa 15 million. Unless something dramatic happens, current food and water shortages, poor infrastructure and a lack of housing are likely to increase along with the 70 per cent of Africans who currently live in slums. Sudden changes in fertility rates or a reduction of violence in the countryside (especially in Congo and Nigeria) or improved public service are all possible, and could retard this development, but are unlikely if based on current experience and policy.[63]

The self-interest of leadership should not be underestimated in this regard, no matter how short term. As has been noted, the 'invisibility' of poor slum dwellers in Kenya is an issue that government among others in Africa – where it is estimated that as many as 62 per cent of the urban population live in slums[64] – cultivates by refusing to reform their town planning laws, with the consequence that slums remain unadopted by policy-makers and deprived of central and local government services. The outcome of the retention of an old colonial pattern of town planning rules is that policy excludes ever-larger proportions of the population from the rights and entitlements of citizenship benefiting different groups. Apart from their growing alienation from the mass of their fellow citizens, they are sliding into a deeper and larger development and political hole, one that can encourage radicalism.

The process of improving governance will, at the extremes, need to find a means to bring on-side conflict entrepreneurs who profit from continued instability; those for example, who live by the Somali saying, 'Maxaa igu jiraa?' (literally, What is in it for me?), the equivalent of the Kenyan saying, 'It is our turn to eat.' This reflects the character of the people at the top; inexperienced presidents intent on democracy and governance are seldom a match for wizened warlords and their methods. It also echoes the nature of externally directed and funded political and security processes. These not only distort a sense of domestic responsibility for actions and failures, but can reinforce a deep-seated inferiority complex about the capacity to run one's own affairs, the cruellest colonial legacy of all.

Mozambique's pointers in the political economy of recovery

Maputo's contemporary glass, steel and concrete buildings contrast with the baroque and art deco style of the colonial era. The skyline is dotted with construction cranes working on office blocks, new accommodation and perhaps unusually, for a country with a GDP per capita of just $600, parking garages.

It was not always like this. Much of this is catch-up growth. 'Locals preferred to send money out for 30 years,' said one banker, 'if they had it. Now the money is staying here, and foreigners are investing, too.' Mozambique's capital city is buzzing in anticipation of the revenue from exports from the giant 22-billion-tonne Zambezia coalfield in the central Tete province, and the even more lucrative offshore gas finds in the Ravumo Basin to the north, the fourth-largest worldwide.

This is the country that picked itself up at the end of a devastating civil war in 1992 and has then grown its economy for twenty years at an annual average of over 7 per cent. This should not be surprising, since the former Portuguese colony was once sub-Saharan Africa's sixth-largest industrial economy, with huge agricultural and mining resources, and good tourism offerings. And, in estate agent parlance, it has 'location, location, location' next to a continental economic powerhouse in South Africa, responsible for a third of Mozambique's trade and the bulk of its foreign investors, and a source of work for many Mozambican diaspora.

But underneath the shiny skin of a new airport and classy hotels are more deep-rooted socio-economic and political issues that have proven much tougher to resolve as Mozambique moves through the phases of post-civil war stability to recovery, development and transformation. While consistently one of the world's fastest growing economies, the country has ranked among the lowest in per capita income, inequality, life expectancy, poverty and human development. In part, this is a legacy of a bitter colonial history of racial exclusion, and of a decade-long civil war. Yet, better policy could put this right – if Mozambicans chose to do so.

The country's rapid and chaotic independence process, which followed the Carnation Revolution coup in Portugal on 25 April 1975, left Mozambique virtually devoid of skills. This could have been avoided, but the incoming Frelimo (Mozambique Liberation Front) government chose to get rid of as many of the 370 000 or so Portuguese colonists as possible. Armando Guebuza, then the interior minister, and from February 2005, the president, issued an order to most Portuguese residents to leave within 24 hours (though in effect they had 90 days). Ninety per cent of settlers fled under the '24-20' order, since they were restricted to 20 kilograms of luggage, and with them went the bulk of skills and capital that had created a burgeoning industrial, agriculture and mining sector. In some cases, their spite led them to sabotage or destroy their investment on departure.

Not that the government helped much. The loss of this talent was compounded by catastrophic attempts by the incoming Frelimo government at social engineering, including collective agriculture projects.[65] With Operation Production of the 1980s under Guebuza, to take another example, the government attempted to forcibly move jobless urban people to the rural areas. A one-party Marxist state, supposedly the culmination of the ten-year guerrilla struggle against the Portuguese, may have been ideological bliss, but was practically a very bad idea. 'While colonialism itself and the manner of the decolonisation process created a lot of problems,' reflects Luisa Dias Diogo, the former prime minister and minister of planning and finance, 'on balance the policies followed after independence created even more problems.' The 're-education' camps for dissidents was an extreme manifestation of this moral cul-de-sac, in which as many as 30 000 are said to have died.

Such mistakes were worsened by white mischief. A civil war between Frelimo and, at first, the Rhodesian midwifed and, later, apartheid South African-sponsored Renamo (Mozambique National Resistance) movement destroyed much of what was left. Once thriving coastal cities such as Maputo and Beira, their services already under stress due to capacity problems,

became crammed with refugees. As many as half of the then 12 million population was displaced, and a million died, mainly of starvation.

With the end of the Cold War and the political transition underway in
neighbouring South Africa, a peace agreement with Renamo followed in
October 1992. Democratic elections were held two years later, in October
1994, and have been staged regularly since.

By then Mozambique was officially among the poorest countries on
earth, with an annual per capita income of some $137, having halved from
ten years before. Despite the improvements to security and transport and
considerable social progress since then, along with rapid economic growth,
seemingly intractable problems remain.

Most notably, the number of poor has increased, from 54.1 per cent in
2003 to 54.7 per cent in 2010, according to the government's own criteria.
Tellingly, 59 per cent of Mozambicans survive at the international benchmark
of $1.25 per day, and 90 per cent exist on less than $2 per day.[66] Mozambique's
share of the global economy has crawled from a miniscule 0.02 per cent in
1980 to 0.03 per cent 30 years later, with its GDP per capita, at $600, still un-
der 10 per cent of the global average. This compares unfavourably to South
Africa's 80 per cent, a visible benchmark for Mozambicans of what could be.[67]
And while life expectancy has risen (from 45 years in 1994 to 49 in 2011), this
improvement has been a long, hard slog, and still places Mozambique below
the average for sub-Saharan Africa (56) and other low-income countries (61).

This is partly a consequence of rapid population increase – from 10 million
at independence to 25 million in 2013 – and the nature of investment. High
growth has sprung from big ticket investments, known as 'mega-projects',
including the coal projects and the $2-billion Mozal aluminium smelter
in Maputo, but these create little in the way of jobs. These types of major
investment have benefited the government rather than people in terms of
direct employment. For example, Vale employs only 1 400 workers in its
Moatize coal operation, of which 400 are from the host Tete province. For
these mega-projects, including the gas fields, to contribute to sustainable
development, policy will have to assist small businesses to flourish, most
notably around credit and more flexible labour laws.[68]

With 80 per cent of Mozambicans dependent on agriculture for income,
and the sector providing one-third of GDP and 20 per cent of exports,
and with 90 per cent of its arable land uncultivated, agriculture offers the
prospect of major returns. There is, however, disinterest in the sector, some
political resistance to large-scale commercial farming (given the historic

link with colonial plantations), and overall a suspicion about the motives of private, independent business.

Take Mozambique Leaf Tobacco as an example. MLT has been operating its $90-million Tete-based factory and business since 2004. It sources its (mainly burley) tobacco from 130 000 farmers countrywide, including 55 000 in Tete province alone. Based on a 6:1 dependency ratio, its operations have positively affected the lives of more than a third of the province's 1.8 million people. Employing 380 extension officers for these outgrowers (more than the government has countryside), MLT has provided all inputs, including seed, fertiliser, transport and technical help. The average farmer, tilling around half a hectare, now sells an average of $600 worth of tobacco per year – money that they, just years before, could only have dreamed of. In addition, MLT provides a 50 per cent subsidy for maize seed for food security.

Despite its obvious benefits to the populace, there was considerable pressure on the company, especially at a provincial level, to 'open up' to political interests. Since then the government has left it alone because it positively affects the lives of so many; but has also lent very little support and even deliberately sought to exclude its representatives from policy discussions.[69]

Major benefits would be possible for the bulk of the population if government policy was aimed at the two golden requirements of poverty alleviation and wealth creation in farming – improving yields and scale. No rocket science is needed. This requires finding the means to make finance cheaper, clarifying land title and transfer, reducing the tax and bureaucratic burden, especially on the smaller farmer, allowing the repatriation of foreign investment, and ensuring that the country remains ahead of the infrastructure game. Still, this has been a neglected aspect of policy.

A stifling and slow bureaucracy has also played its part. While investor regulations have been streamlined, trying to turn around the practices of a recalcitrant bureaucracy infused with a Lusophone zeal and Soviet manners, they remain, as one business person put it, 'half educated, living on a shoestring and thus corrupt'. With government making up half of the formal workforce, there is a danger, too, in this regard of crowding out, with the state a heavy borrower in the local market. Moreover, the national savings rate is very low, with an estimated 2 per cent of banked customers (some three million) classified as 'savers'.

The roots of these problems, however, lie in policy and, prosaically, in politics and its personalities.

The elite are served only by opening up the economy to the extent that it profits them. Hence, they were very slow to move to open skies, the deregulation of airlines, which would do much to increase the number of higher-yield fly-in tourists annually, where Mozambique enjoys just 10 per cent of the numbers landing in Kenya or one-fifth of those in neighbouring Tanzania.

There is a corresponding lack of daylight between the party, key personalities and business. Not for nothing has President Guebuza become known as 'Mr Guebusiness'.

And there is a consequent lack of transparency in procurement (such as with the controversial €850-million EMATUM – Mozambique Tuna Company – ship deal in 2013)[70] and disclosure of deals. 'It is a monopolistic, oligopolistic environment,' says one donor, 'where corruption and inefficiency are two sides of the same coin.' The problem has become so deep-seated in the psyche and the incentives are so skewed that, as one business person observes, 'if you cut out corruption, nothing works'. Instead of a national development 'project', Mozambique has, as he put it, 'rent-seeking by the elites, led by the president and his family'. It is difficult for donors, among other outsiders, to help improve this situation, where 'new donors' from the BRIC (Brazil, Russia, India and China) countries, for example, 'are offering loans without conditions', where the 'donor agenda is increasingly commercial' and where the inflows from mining are greater than budget support from aid, for example, even if donors still account for 35 per cent of the budget overall.

Brazen rent-seeking and widening wealth disparities do little to encourage a tax-paying culture. As the banker put it: 'The hospitals are a disaster, the roads potholed, the electricity and water doesn't flow, so why pay tax – save to pay for the minister's new Mercedes?'

Little wonder in this environment that Renamo went 'back into the bush' in 2013 to restart its paramilitary activities, claiming Frelimo had rigged elections and marginalised the opposition. Renamo later said it was pulling out of the 21-year-old peace deal because government forces had captured the base where its leader, Afonso Dhlakama, was staying, though he managed to escape.

This environment has an explicit link to rule by a liberation movement. In Mozambique's case, the ruling Frelimo party dominates. If you were not part of Frelimo, says one donor, you have 'no hope at all, in business or in getting a state job'. They are not interested in sharing the wealth with others, including Renamo. It is, he says, 'reverse Clausewitz', referring to the Prussian military strategist, 'where politics and the economy are war by other means'.

30

THE FRAGILITY 'INDUSTRY'

Getting Past Routine Responses

*

Since the end of the Cold War, military intervention has defined Western foreign policy. The motives and mechanics have been endlessly picked over, spawning a new lexicon across the globe: 'Chapter VII resolutions', 'the responsibility to protect', 'no-fly zones', 'regime change', 'humanitarian intervention', 'surgical air strikes', 'do no harm', 'complex operations' in meeting 'complex insurgencies', 'ungoverned spaces', 'campaign strategies', 'peace-building', 'stabilisation', 'building resilience', 'nation-building', 'external and internal stakeholders', 'counter-insurgency', and more. Specific interventions have become a metaphor for political views: those against intervention point to the humiliating mess of Iraq or the Afghan quagmire; those in favour highlight the success of operations in Bosnia and Kosovo.[1] In pursuit of some noble and sometimes inglorious goals, the American government has spent over $3 trillion in the last two decades, more than a million soldiers have been deployed on foreign operations from over 60 countries,[2] and new countries have emerged in Bosnia, Kosovo, East Timor and South Sudan.

Whatever the combination of goals that might have guided previous and subsequent state-building missions, from humanitarian instinct to more callous commercial interests, their practical consequences are on full view: they are inevitably long, difficult, messy, expensive, open-ended, violent and confusing. It is not that the downside was hidden. Even before becoming president, George W. Bush, warned in 2000. 'Let me tell you what else I'm worried about: I'm worried about an opponent who uses "nation-building" and "the military" in the same sentence.'[3]

Despite this warning, since then leaders and governments have been both toppled by intervention and because they intervened. Quickly the Bush administration, among others, moved to acknowledge this new threat. The 2002 National Security Strategy cautioned, 'America is now threatened less by conquering states than we are by failing ones. We are menaced less by fleets and armies than by catastrophic technologies in the hands of the embittered few.'[4] Or as Francis Fukuyama wrote in *State-Building* in 2004, 'Weak and failing states have arguably become the single most important problem for international order.'[5]

That there were methodological flaws to this argument, of course, was overlooked or rationalised in the search for enemies and answers, especially after 9/11. For one, the more effective terrorists were largely not impoverished products of weak, ungoverned states. Rather they have been recruits from the middle class of relatively affluent states. Stabilising failed states would also not remove the threat terrorists posed since they were both mobile and their operations preferred a degree of state functionality anyway, enabling them to move money and themselves around.

Regardless, quickly sophisticated, digital technology and new doctrines were developed to meet the failed states challenge and its corollary of state-building. Insurgents responded in more prosaic but no less effective ways, including the improvised explosive device. And so the debate about improving the formula for such interventions continues, while there is a need to protect civilians, secure external interests and an apparent lack of alternatives.

So discussion about the ethics and efficacy of intervention will continue to rage about past actions and future problems. There are some who believe that no intervention should occur, ever. Some believe, often because they do not want external scrutiny of their domestic policies, states should be free to do what they want within their own borders. Some contend that wars should be allowed to be fought out, as happened in Angola culminating in the death of Jonas Savimbi or in Sri Lanka with the military defeat of the Tamil Tigers.[6] Some even believe that violence is cultural, and well-meaning outsiders cannot stop it. For instance, Conor Cruise O'Brien, an intellectual with practical experience of the early Congo operations, said in 1992, 'There are places where a lot of men prefer war and the looting and raping and domineering that go with it, to any sort of peacetime occupation. One such place is Afghanistan. Another is Yugoslavia after the collapse.'[7]

Both intervention and non-intervention contain horrors, from Iraq to Rwanda, raising doubts about what to do. Will more lives be saved or lost in the process? Is the military footprint too light or too heavy? Which actions are of necessity and of choice? Should we be guided by what we ought to do, or what we can do? Is there a way of avoiding many of the downsides and upholding the strong moral justification for protecting others? And one question sums up the debate overall: can we get interventions right?

Answering that demands understanding, of course, why the 'international community' so often gets it wrong.

Two schools

Rory Stewart and Gerald Knaus identify two interventionist schools: one that seeks to 'plan' their way out of conflict, prescribing 'a clear strategy, metrics, and structure, backed by overwhelming resources'; and, second, 'the liberal imperialist school' that 'emphasises the importance of decisive, bold, and charismatic leadership' in rescuing countries from their own citizenry, situations regarded as 'terrifying and tragic: a rogue state, a failed state, a threat to its neighbours or a threat to our credibility … where "failure is not an option"'.

There is overlap between these two schools in terms of solutions. Both favour improving governance and strengthening (or creating) state capacity from institutions to laws as the means to state stability. This path to stability and recovery goes through 'a decisive and well-planned international intervention (with generous resources, a coherent strategy, coordination, staffing, communication, accountability, research, defined processes and clear priorities)'.

Both schools are intrinsically optimistic about the role that outsiders can play, and their corresponding ability to define, measure and solve problems. Yet, they are contrastingly (and paradoxically, given the inescapable source of success) pessimistic, Stewart and Knaus note, about local capacity, often portrayed 'as criminals or victims'. This is primarily an outsider-in project: success from the proponent's perspective depending mainly on getting the 'formula right' and resourcing the effort properly.[8]

Heroism and courage, like sincerity, are not criteria for success, however. As interveners rotate between situations, lessons are discovered only to be relearnt, the foreigners driven by the notion that, somehow, this time 'it will be different'. A lack of continuity allows projects to become personal rather than institutionalised, and perfunctory rather than specific. Given the time frames of the actors, the metrics established by interveners usually gauge the money and resources expended rather than another commonly used term, the longer-term 'effect' of this expenditure on the ground. There are many dangers in supply-side aid measures – the tail attempting to push the horse, put differently – as opposed to the demand of the target state, and their capacity to absorb and usefully employ the funds. Failing the matching of demand and supply, distortions and even more severe developmental damage can occur.

International interveners battle to operate in these environments let alone transform the political economy of the recipient states, even though this is what is required, given that simply reinstating the past is not good enough since these conditions contain the roots of failure. And forced state-building involving major social, political, economic and cultural change, cannot be managed relatively quickly, and not by outsiders. Indeed, remedying state weakness is fundamentally a political act, one where 'a social order has become maladapted to the globalizing world – when governing institutions are weak, personalized, or kleptocratic; corruption is rampant; and the rule of law is noticeable by its absence ...'[9]

Even so, it is often conceived as an apolitical exercise, one driven by technocratic imperatives, not least because these are easier to deliver. Thus, those trying to help countries from outside invariably make lists, a failing that this author could stand accused of, reflecting an impatience and time pressure to 'get the job done'. Lists become a substitute for local knowledge and the longer-term and more tedious job of understanding what lies behind local politics and engaging with its personalities. The following, the lists go, is needed to build a state and a better future: rule of law, a tax system, civil service, investor-friendly policy, police service, financial system, one-stop shops, and so on. And in the same spirit, plans would be drawn up detailing how this might be achieved, essentially another list of items, this time prioritised, funded, staffed and sequenced. But mostly, these were tautologies masquerading as plans, only fleshing out the relationship between problems – corruption, security, administration – rather than identifying how they might be eliminated. As Rory Stewart has noted, 'Our entire conceptual framework was mad. All these theories – counter-insurgency warfare, state-building – were actually complete abstract madness. They were like very weird religious systems, because they always break down into three principles, 10 functions, seven this or that. So they're reminiscent of Buddhists who say: "These are the four paths", or of Christians who say: "These are the seven deadly sins". They're sort of theologies, essentially, made by people like Buddhist monks in the eighth century – people who have a fundamental faith, which is probably, in the end, itself completely delusional.'[10]

This reflects ownership. Getting from systems where there is corruption, at least as outsiders define it, or insecurity or a lack of a civil administration is unlikely to happen, not by foreigners or those attempting to haphazardly graft on outside ideas. Locals know more about their country and its ways than foreigners. 'In the end,' says Stewart, the Tory MP who has worked as a government administrator in Iraq and run an NGO in Kabul, 'the basic problem is very, very simple. Why don't these interventions work? Because we are foreigners. If things are going wrong in a country, it's not usually that we don't have enough foreigners. It's usually that we have too many.'

This is often exacerbated by 'who' is *in situ*. One of the key problems in Western foreign and defence ministries is the pervasiveness of 'generalists' and what could be termed 'generalism'. This is not an accident but the result of deliberate policy. There is a belief that generalists are bright (and usually young) people who can quickly understand any problem. Specialists, on the other hand, are crusty dogmatists whose prejudices become ingrained and get in the way of efficiency. Specialisation is actively discouraged by a revolving-chair policy; a person will be working on the Middle East for a year or two and then be deployed to the Iceland desk or whatever. To the extent that any generalists become specialists, it is piecemeal and largely accidental (the person did two postings in Jakarta, he was in southern Africa before, etc.). Of course, the shift having taken place a couple of decades ago, it is a system that has become immune to self-criticism because everyone within it is now a bright-spark generalist with an over-inflated view of their knowledge and skills. Bright they may be, but no amount of brains can make up for the patient acquisition of specialist knowledge over decades. This approach is compounded by a failure of bureaucracies to learn lessons. Once complete, even the own files of governments are seldom reopened to better understand conflicts and circumstances past.

Hence, the inevitable pressure to 'get out' of such missions, usually around the ten-year mark, as the international community tires of failure and casualties. This usually occurs even though the moral and strategic imperatives of the original missions remain. Withdrawal, like senseless aid expenditure, is often driven by narrow short-term interests.

Despite the exact condition of 'state failure' being difficult to determine, consequent with ambition to intervene, there is regardless a plethora of literature – an industry on intervention – about how to redress the condition. Major think tanks, university departments and even global institutions from the World Economic Forum to the World Bank have failed or fragile states units, sections, centres or programmes, focusing on everything from better ways to spend aid money, apparently improved methods of encouraging reforms, lessons learnt, and on the stresses felt by vulnerable groups within these states and within their cities.[11] For example, the United Nations' 2010 World Development Report centred on fragile states, as did the 2010 European Development Report and the 2013 OECD report on fragile states and resource flows, among a wave of other more academic literature.[12]

The huge policy demand for such work has often appeared inversely proportional to the paucity of factual research on the topic and that reflected in the lack of knowledge about local systems, customs and mores – the reasons, in other words, why things work the way they do. The same could be said more generally for the amount of aid money expended, and the lack of clarity about the results. Sierra Leone, for instance, long held up as an example of what could be achieved by focused, single lead-nation intervention and embedded support in helping to get a government back on its feet, was still expected, ten years after the end of the fighting, to remain 'fragile' if not 'failed' for many years to come. There is also no one factor that unlocks success, no matter how attractive it is to distil a campaign in this way, just as there was no single reason for failure in the first instance. The installation of a market economy and democracy are, to take another example, not by themselves sufficient conditions for success, as the civil war in Iraq post-Saddam illustrates. Equally, aid is no assurance of changed local political behaviour, although signs of the limits to its role as an expeditor and incentive have long been ignored. President Lyndon Johnson famously offered a billion-dollar development programme to Ho Chi Minh in 1965, thereby misjudging Ho's determination in the fight for self-determination and unification of his country.[13]

Equally, external involvement and advice and aid expenditure is no guarantee of development and governance success or even rapid advance, as seen in the difficulty of building a stable, functioning and legitimate Afghan state more than ten years and billions of dollars after the 2001 intervention that removed the Taliban from power. To the contrary, the arrival of large numbers of outsiders, vividly portrayed as an out-of-control 'swarm',[14] can overwhelm the already weak host government.[15] Aid can instead distort accountability between leaders and their citizens, circumventing local institutions and elected leadership.

Regardless, as noted, a series of templatic responses (usually and frequently presented in the form of PowerPoint with carefully staggered and articulated pillars, actions and aims) have emerged as a 'solution' to the problems of the target states.

In the more extreme cases of collapse and violence, this has involved restoring physical security and providing emergency humanitarian assistance, generally followed by a political settlement along with the creation of new armed and police forces through demobilisation, disarmament and development and security sector reform. Elections usually follow. And as the situation becomes more peaceful, the international interveners generally become more adventurous, moving into the justice sector and gender reforms as part of a 'package' of development and stabilisation initiatives, muddling through by trying to build both the hard and soft infrastructure of states. But interveners, whoever they are, while they can have success with the early stabilisation juncture (as in Mali in 2013 through the French-led intervention) and into an election process, they have proven to be very poor at governance and development, not least because these require locals working together, often the source of the problem in the first instance.

As this book shows, and as Robert Zoellick has intimated in the Introduction, the difference between success and failure, inclusive and exclusive economic growth, stability and violence, lies in more than the efficacy or innovativeness of the approach adopted by external actors. The drivers of state creation include legitimacy, not just stability; soft systemic not just hard physical infrastructure; and the emergence of issue- rather than identity-led political and economic choices, where self-interest is subsumed by, or at least correlated with, national concerns.

As was stressed in the previous section, governance, the rule of law and ownership through democracy – the three inverse descriptors of the variants of failure – are essential preconditions for recovery, growth and prosperity. Underlying these externally directed attempts are two problems that the interveners are badly equipped and disposed to handle: solving political differences, including questions of identity and nationhood, and fixing the local economy. The former UK ambassador to the UN (and deputy to the Coalition Provisional Authority's Paul Bremer in Iraq), Jeremy Greenstock, has emphasised the dangers of intervening in such environments: 'The identity mosaic of a free world doesn't fit the national boundary setting of the twentieth century,' he explains. 'The West has to be careful about intervention to sustain a situation that no longer carries the same legitimacy.'[16]

At a minimum, this requires clear goals on the part of the intervener and a strategy to achieve them – aspects that are more frequent in their breach than observation.

The absence of strategy

For all of their often exaggerated sense of mission and moral purpose, interveners quickly and invariably become domestic players. While most local populations will offer foreigners the benefit of the doubt, there is only a limited window of local goodwill towards outsiders.

To justify the intervention at the outset, and to explain the inevitable challenges, 'Western politicians, diplomats, generals, and policy-makers' traditionally describe the countries into which they intervene as the quintessence of terror and tragedy, a unique existential threat, or an inescapable obligation.'[17] Of course, such a portrayal is as untruthful as it is self-serving: there are a whole set of interests and obligations that have to be balanced worldwide. Moreover, these situations and states are not blank slates on which the interveners can pattern their solutions, but societies with 'functioning local forms of security, administration and dispute resolution', which predate the crises and will have to offer at least some of the solution. The modern intervener does not possess 'the power, the knowledge, or the legitimacy' to fundamentally reshape these societies.

This is not to say there is no role for mediators or outsiders, or that conflicts cannot end peacefully. As *The Economist* reminds us, not only have most (all bar ten in fact) of the 150 large civil wars since 1945 been resolved, and are shorter now (averaging 3.7 rather than 4.6 years) than before 1991, but a military victory is less common today (some 13 per cent of cases) than before (58 per cent), with negotiated endings increasing fourfold to 40 per cent of cases.[18] This achievement is in spite of deep hatreds that spark such wars, which make peaceful solutions difficult and require huge energy, considerable skill and commitment, and ongoing resources.

But there are routine failures. Diplomacy often plays a poor second fiddle to military intervention as a means to ending conflict (think Mali, the Central African Republic, eastern Congo, Afghanistan, Iraq or Somalia), and is frequently behind the curve in predicting and preventing fighting (think the Arab Spring). In part, this is a reflection of a cluttered agenda, and a lack of will and focus on the part of the political principals. Certainly, diplomats are not to be entirely blamed. Ever since Thomas Jefferson, Colin Powell has noted about the role of secretaries of state (a post he occupied under George W. Bush from 2001 to 2005): 'They have been criticised at one time or another for being like diplomats, for trying to find peaceful solutions, to building friendships around the world, to creating alliances.

That is,' emphasised the former chairman of the Joint Chiefs of Staff, 'what we do.'[19]

Take Afghanistan. The post-2001 campaign has been characterised by consistent Western political failure to appreciate local dynamics and to act with necessary will. This botch was not exclusively the military's fault. Far from it. This has been the responsibility of those political leaders who sent and maintained the troops there and eventually decided to bring them home again. Their political failure exacts a terrible toll in terms of blood and treasure.

From the outset, the notion that political control could be exerted countrywide through a change of government in Kabul was a naive fallacy. It was similarly folly to believe that Afghanistan's operating system – of patronage politics run along tribal lines – would change at the same time with an antiseptic brew of aid, governance, technical assistance and improved security. Quite the opposite. Gushing foreign aid, politicised governance and a violent insurgency has helped to cement a mafia-like system and culture of impunity in Afghanistan. It followed that the fight against the insurgency would not be won by an Iraqi-style military surge,[20] but by better politics.

Predictably, President Hamid Karzai behaved like an Afghan virtuoso, playing the capitals of NATO like a violin – rising and falling in shrill volume, always one tune ahead of the West. He spent his energy holding the West accountable, playing to his domestic galleries and blaming the West and its strategy and Pakistan for his country's plight, avoiding scrutiny on his family's finances, and his record on the real stuff of development – jobs, health, education and agriculture. For example, knowing that the West was unhappy about the way in which the Afghan private security companies were profiting and the impunity of their actions, Karzai's response in 2010 was to ban all such private security companies. The first told to leave the country was the British-linked Blue Hackle, which had a key role in guarding fixed installations. In so doing, Karzai was guaranteed a reprieve from the pressure to reign in the private security companies. This was shrewd, even though it ensured competing centres of power to Kabul, but perhaps that suited him equally well.

'Karzai has seen thirteen ISAF [International Security Assistance Force] commanders, five UN special representatives, five US ambassadors and three EU special reps come and go,' said one foreign expert in 2010, less than a decade into the intervention. 'He has seen it all before. He can sit around and dictate things on his timescale.'[21] Or as the old Afghan cliché had it about the West: 'You have the watches, and we have the time.'

The real problem ISAF (and the international community more broadly) has experienced that is that it has never 'owned' the political strategy. Indeed, since the rather ham-fisted efforts by the former American UN ambassador (who later served as special representative for Afghanistan and Pakistan until his untimely death in December 2010), Richard Holbrooke, during the 2009 election to undermine Karzai, there have been rather divergent political strategies. This was compounded by the 2010 Lisbon Summit setting a withdrawal deadline of December 2014, which of course gave even more encouragement to Karzai to set his own course apart from ISAF.

Playing this great game better than their Afghan hosts demanded improved understanding on the part of Western politicians, the sort of knowledge not garnered by two-day fact-finding trips (a misnomer if ever there was) and episodic summits. Greater unity of effort between Western capitals was required for the necessary brinkmanship and showing some steel, in this case with President Karzai, in making certain things publicly conditional for continued Western assistance and the ongoing cost in lives and materiel.

In such cases, international diplomatic methods of managing and dealing with conflict have become absurdly poor in the media age, focused more on the opportunity for publicity than consistent, diligent engagement. Such a play demands expert staff with deep local knowledge and a willingness to not only employ and manage them, but leave them *in situ* for a long time. And it requires sustained engagement, of a style that Prince Klemens Wenzel von Metternich, the Austrian foreign minister, employed: blunt when he needed to be, publicity-seeking, charming and, above all else, deeply personal. As Holbrooke observed about Vietnam, the Balkans and Afghanistan: 'People sit in a room, they don't air their real differences, a false and sloppy consensus papers over those underlying differences, and they go back to their offices and continue to work at cross purposes, even actively undermining each other.'[22]

The mark of great strategists, says the historian John Lewis Gaddis,[23] is in 'the efficient use of available means to accomplish chosen ends'. And the mark of great political leadership, he notes, is that they have 'destinations in mind and maps for reaching them'. Added to this strategic vision are other desirable qualities, as with Margaret Thatcher, of 'an utter unwillingness to mince words' in speaking 'truths, not platitudes'; or with Ronald Reagan, the 'movie actor turned politician turned broadcaster', an 'ability to see beyond complexity to simplicity'. Nelson Mandela had equally, according to one of his political opponents, an almost genius-like ability to use gestures and symbols to shape his nation.[24] But it was not without steel. As the ghost writer of his autobiography (and, latterly, editor of *Time*) Richard Stengel defined 'The full Mandela':[25] 'He is a power charmer, confident that he will charm you, by whatever means possible. He is attentive, courtly, winning, and to use a word he would hate, seductive ... The charm is political as well as personal, and he regards himself not so much as the Great Communicator but as the Great Persuader ... he would always rather persuade you to do something than order you to do so ... [but] he will always stand up for what he believes is right with a stubbornness that is virtually unbending.' Finding leadership with this vision, application and long-term commitment is rare and certainly more difficult than simply blaming those on the ground as to why things are going badly.

The absence of strategy does not end with military interventions. The summit phenomenon exists, too, with other aspects of policy, where long-term strategic engagement and assiduous diplomacy has given way to the shorthand of acronyms. We live in a world continuously defined by acronyms for problems, solutions and opportunities: BRICS (Brazil, Russia, India, China and South Africa) and MINT (Mexico, Indonesia, Nigeria and Turkey) are two examples, coined by Goldman Sachs economist, Jim O'Neill, to identify new-wave markets. BRIC summits have followed, even an organisation bearing the name. The absence of content and commitment to this cause – rather than simply spelling out the potential opportunity – is manifest, giving rise to a new abbreviation: CEMENT – Country in Emerging Markets Excluded by New Terminology.[26] While new groupings might offer the promise of a short cut to prosperity, sadly no such route exists in reality.

A longer-term view

While many would like to see the solution coming externally through aid and similar forms of assistance, the blame attached to colonialism illustrates the paucity of this approach. Seldom do the international cavalry appear riding over the hill; nor is it usually a good outcome where they do. The alternative is to consider why better domestic development choices have not been made; and why domestic electorates so often fail to hold the feet of leadership to the fire, easily persuaded by identity politics over principle and issues.

Outsiders, too, can serve to deflect these domestic pressures in a number of ways: food aid can remove accountability for failed land reform, agriculture policies or extension services; aid can reduce the need to develop domestic revenue systems and the two-way responsibility that goes with this; external military support can help to stabilise a country but it can also protect bad regimes; while external policy advisers, especially the high-profile sort, can, sometimes unknowingly, deflect, if not entirely delegate, ownership of solutions.

Foreign interveners are usually weaker than either they imagine, as Stewart and Knaus contend, or they are willing to admit even though they 'are inevitably isolated from local society, ignorant of local culture and context, and prey to misleading abstract theories'.[27] Their lack of local legitimacy and support contrasts with the power and nous of domestic political leaders, which is how they got there in the first instance, and resilience of local institutions. Post-conflict societies are hardly a blank slate. Clouded by something between a patronising imperialist zeal (in bringing enlightenment to others) and humanitarian instinct (saving others from themselves), the interveners somehow believe they can do things that they cannot do at home.

Therefore, it is unsurprising that the preconceived plans and notions of interveners, as the cliché has it, seldom survive contact with the ground. These circumstances are 'intrinsically unpredictable, chaotic and uncertain', rapidly and radically confounding both these 'well-laid plans and careful predictions'. The upset of removing a leader or government has consequences to power structures far greater than just governance or rule of law. And this has to be managed within a time frame vulnerable to the election time tables and political attention span of the intervener.

From experience, in Africa and elsewhere such as in Afghanistan, economic and governance reforms and their international counterpart in aid need to be focused on an abiding understanding of a country as it is, rather than on international interests or a prejudicial image of how things should be. Regardless, much aid is based instead on personal preferences of the giver person or nation, short-term foreign interests or political correctness. In essence, it is given in the belief that the state has failed and there is a *tabula rasa* to reconstruct it, rather than in the knowledge that the state and society works in ways that are not only difficult to comprehend but to accept. As an inevitable consequence, much of this money is wasted.

These actions are also exemplified by a constant failure to understand and act to assist the private sector. This is hardly surprising since most bureaucrats in aid have little or no experience in business. Overall, they are more focused on solving or reducing problems or changing things than 'enabling' things to happen. And when such failure happens, which is often, the response is that the intervention would have succeeded had it not been for the ungrateful, incompetent and corrupt locals themselves. This is patently unfair.

But foreigners are not the only ones – or even the principal actors – to be blamed. For state failure is principally not the fault of external actors. Responsibility, as is threaded throughout this volume, is primarily a domestic issue. Yes, the post-colonial inheritance of many countries was poor; but this has not disqualified some, including Vietnam, Singapore and Botswana, to take three disparate examples, from making significant developmental progress. Comparing their forward-looking focus to the rearward fascination of many African countries, in particular, is revealing, if depressing. The Congolese, among others, will not try to explain their nation's great travails without externalising the reasons, placing responsibility at the door of the Belgians, Americans, Europeans, Rwandese and others.

The manner in which African governments, in particular, have attempted nation-building and the extent to which identity rather than issue-based politics continues to dominate affairs, sometimes deliberately, is an obstacle to domestic progress. Here local leadership is, for the most part, to be blamed. And there is a vicious and self-defeating tautology – the expectation that assistance will come from outside. This view, often born in the colonial experience, and which exists on both sides of this divide, can condition the manner in which states expect the world to come to their assistance, and the way in which the world expects and wants to do so. Africa is not alone in this regard. Haiti is, as will be seen, another illustration from another continent, though it exhibits many of the conditions prevalent across Africa.

A longer-term view is necessary for recovery. Primarily this has to be taken by their leadership rather than outsiders. Indeed, while 'buy and hold' is an investment strategy that works for companies, it can also do so for countries.

Popularised by billionaire Warren Buffet, known as the 'Sage of Omaha', the term 'buy and hold' is synonymous with taking a long-term view; not aiming to enter low and sell high, but rather to build a business over generations. This approach discourages speculative investment and promotes the practice of holding onto shares for years in the belief that the stock is undervalued, and that sound management and patience will not only add value for the investor, but create wealth and jobs in the process.

Buy and hold is also the strategy necessary to fix failed states. Local leaders need to adopt this approach, investing in the future of their countries, and not simply using their power to extract personal wealth. This is not charity. It is in their enlightened self-interest to do so, and is their responsibility. Their citizens have a role to play, too, in holding them to their responsibility, and ensuring, too, that they do not overstay their welcome. This volume highlights various leadership strategies, including those of countries that have helped to turn around a seemingly impossible dysfunctional inheritance.

It finds that countries have succeeded when, in owning their recovery and reforms, the local political economy permits individual entrepreneurs and enterprise to flourish, when policies are predictable in spite of the change in political regimes, when domestic stability allows long-term investments in education and infrastructure, and when citizens hold leaders accountable. Leadership that exhibits a commitment to popular welfare is one necessary ingredient as is a system of government that institutionalises both state responsiveness and responsibility to the needs of citizens. Indeed, as will be seen throughout this book, there is a premium on leadership, especially at the outset of recovery when state institutions and systems are weak and capacity low.

*

There is much to be gained though by getting things right – or at least better. The G7+ group of eighteen self-declared 'fragile states'[28] reminds us that about 1.5 billion people of the 2013 world population of seven billion live in such situations, and that 70 per cent of these states have seen conflict in the past 25 years. Despite 30 per cent of all aid being spent in them, these countries are furthest away from achieving the basic quality of life benchmarks, such as in education and health care, under the UN Millennium Development Goals[29] (MDGs), with 'basic governance transformations' at least a generation away.[30] As the 2011 World Development Report notes in this regard: 'No low-income fragile or conflict-affected country has yet achieved a single MDG. People in fragile and conflict-affected states are more than twice as likely to be under-nourished as those in other developing countries, more than three times as likely to be unable to send their children to school, twice as likely to see their children die before age five, and more than twice as likely to lack clean water.'[31]

State recovery and success is not an easy, foolproof or a linear, vectored exercise. It is fraught with setbacks and often danger. It is about politics and people. It demands managing and ultimately subverting identity politics, where tribe, family or religious ties rule, for more constructive issue-centred politics. And it demands identifying the exact reasons for failure in the first instance, if that is how the locals see things, and living with their solutions.

31

CONFRONTING
AUTHORITARIAN DEMOCRACY,
MANAGING IDENTITY POLITICS

✳

As he underwent another bout of relentless torture, George Orwell's hero in *1984*, George Smith, is told, 'If you want a picture of the future, imagine a boot stamping on a human face – forever.'

On 31 July 2013, Zimbabweans went to the polls. According to the official results, they voted to re-elect President Robert Mugabe with a 61 to 33 per cent majority over Prime Minister Morgan Tsvangirai. At the same time, they elected Mugabe's Zimbabwe African National Union-Patriotic Front (ZANU-PF) with a majority of more than two-thirds in parliament, the margin of victory enabling the ruling party to alter the constitution if it chose.

These results were a significant about-turn from the 2008 election when Tsvangirai beat Mugabe in the first round and where the Movement for Democratic Change (MDC) formed the parliamentary majority. Tsvangirai then pulled out of the 2008 presidential run-off in the face of violence that left 200 of his supporters dead, agreeing later that September to be part of a unity government under a Global Political Agreement facilitated by the then South African president, Thabo Mbeki.

Putting results into numbers illustrates how big this five-year shift was. In 2013 Tsvangirai got about the same number of votes, some 1.1 million, he received in 2008. In 2013 Mugabe more than doubled his vote to 2.1 million.

No doubt the MDC walked into elections it was unlikely to win, a schoolboy error if ever there was one. Despite Tsvangirai's courage, stories about his personal life and taste for the trappings of power had sullied his image.

Mugabe was unlikely to make the same mistake twice in 2008 and 2013.

Not for nothing did the president, who had ruled the country since independence in 1980, shrewdly pronounce just days before that 'if you lose you must surrender,'[1] no doubt said with all the conviction of an estate agent. Opponents believed the 89-year-old was a changed man, admitting the prospect of defeat. Of course, he was referring to the MDC.

In a report released just before the poll, the International Crisis Group noted there was little chance that the elections would be free and fair. It said that the voters' roll was in a 'shambles, security forces unreformed, the media grossly imbalanced, the electoral commission ill-prepared and allegations of rigging pervasive.'[2] Despite South Africa's President Jacob Zuma offering his 'profound congratulations' to Mugabe on his victory and the African Union observer team declaring the elections 'free, honest and credible',[3] African observer teams did not pronounce it 'fair'.[4] As Ebrahim Ebrahim, South Africa's deputy minister of international relations, put it, 'We did not say that the Zimbabwean election was fair, we said it was free ... we did not use "fair" or "credible".' Similarly, Tanzania's foreign minister, Bernard Member, told reporters that 'we did not say it [the election] was fair'.

The reaction showed the extent to which solidarity and the short-term expediency for stability had trumped human rights. It illustrated the vulnerability of high ideals to practical political realities, human rights to the politics of identity and personal morality, and to cynical opportunity. As President Barack Obama put it at Nelson Mandela's memorial on 10 December 2013, 'There are too many of us who happily embrace Madiba's legacy of racial reconciliation, but passionately resist even modest reforms that would challenge chronic poverty and growing inequality. There are too many leaders who claim solidarity with Madiba's struggle for freedom, but do not tolerate dissent from their own people. And there are too many of us who stand on the sidelines, comfortable in complacency or cynicism when our voices must be heard.'[5]

Yet, the extent of the set-up has surprised many. Some of the results were unfathomable without wholesale rigging. Take Matabeleland, where Mugabe's ZANU-PF swept all but three of 24 seats, but where his forces were responsible for the deaths of more than 20 000 civilians in the Gukurahundi military operation in the early 1980s. There is no way, given even the MDC's ineptitude, that the Ndebele would vote ZANU-PF.

Critics have claimed that, aside from intimidation, ZANU-PF clinically defrauded the process in four main ways.[6] First, it inflated the number of officially registered voters, officially up to 6.4 million from 5.2 million in 2008, with dead people and duplicate voters. There were over one million people on the voters' roll either deceased or departed, and 109 000 over 100 years old. The MDC has claimed 838 000 duplicate names. This was further manipulated to bolster key geographic areas of support. In 78 of Zimbabwe's 210 constituencies, the number of voters was greater than the number of inhabitants, even assuming an improbable 100 per cent registration rate.[7] Checking the roll was slowed by its late release (the MDC only obtained a copy six weeks before the election) and its unavailability in electronic format.

Second, there was deliberate under-registration in areas and among groups regarded as opposition strongholds. Nearly two million potential voters aged under 30 were unregistered according to the Harare-based Research and Advocacy Unit, an independent think tank. The MDC reportedly found 500 000 people had been moved out of their resident areas to other electoral districts, while 45 000 people had their identity numbers changed without their consent. Registering voters was a 'nightmare' for the MDC – while on the ZANU-PF side they simply drew up lists of people and handed them in for registration. They were also accused of moving 'hundreds of thousands of people into strategic areas in preparation for the poll'. The MDC believed that 250 000 families – over a million people – were settled on farms taken away from their owners in the peri-urban areas in exchange for supporting ZANU-PF, their numbers further enhanced by reselling small plots to homeless people on the same condition.

Third, voters were turned away in MDC areas, while ZANU-PF supporters were bused into marginal constituencies. While the number of polling stations countrywide was increased by around 5 per cent over 2008, the number in Harare was reduced despite the influx of people in the intervening five years.

Finally, an additional 35 per cent more ballot papers – two million – were printed than the number of registered voters, way above the international acceptable best practice of 5 to 10 per cent.

Regardless, the facade of democracy – the formality rather than the reality of voter registration, and the impression of the campaigning of voting itself rather than the reality of manipulation, inflation, duplication and intimidation – was enough not only to win Mugabe a seventh presidential term, but to ensure, critically, the apparent legitimacy of the process.

Certainly the election raised questions about the loss of support for the once-ascendant MDC, which appeared often as hapless as ZANU-PF was ruthless, and whether it should ever have committed to a process

horribly stacked against it. It also asks about the role of the region in failing Zimbabweans (among others), and the role of outsiders more generally.
Western policy was a dismal failure in influencing the process, at least if this
result was anything to go by. Businesses also hunkered down, preferring to
do as little as possible in supporting Mugabe and the MDC while trying to
hold onto their assets in the face of seizures and the threat of indigenisation.

Herein lies the rub about democratic control. Systems can be manipulated to rig elections. It is much more difficult to rig an economic outcome,
at least for a sustained period of time. As Zimbabwe learnt with its prolonged period of decline, culminating in 231 million per cent inflation in
2008 wiping out the savings of a generation, you cannot fool the market.
More and more Zimbabweans, of which 2.2 million would be dependent
on food aid in 2013, were crossing into neighbouring countries looking for
work. By November 2013 this figure was at 1 200 per day, with 700 of this
number into South Africa.

Orwell's *1984* was supposed to be a portent of the future, where totalitarianism had triumphed and individualism was smothered, along with ethics,
creativity, honesty about history, law and even love. Citizens were forced to
feel towards their Stalin-like dictator and his counterparts, those who prefer
and run a world permanently at war.[8]

Circa 2014 for most Zimbabweans, this was not the future, however, but
the present. And Zimbabwe was not alone.

The sophistication of authoritarian democrats

The Introduction and the various case studies illustrate another form of state
failure, of authoritarian democracy: how authoritarian governments use a
variety of techniques to maintain the illusion of democracy in spite of regular elections.

These are not necessarily Stasi-like states – the East German secret police
employing 91 015 persons full-time, including 2 000 fully employed unofficial collaborators, 13 073 soldiers and 2 232 officers of German Democratic
Republic army, along with 173 081 unofficial informants inside the GDR in
1989, in a population of just 16 million, or around 2 per cent. Rather the
methods are most subtle and sophisticated, even though the aim is the same
– to retain a monopoly on power even while (and perhaps because) individual freedoms improve.

A variety of tactics are used to retain power and the illusion of democracy: local NGOs are pressured through tax and other inspections and audits, with stringent registration procedures, and through clampdowns on foreign donor flows, while government-sponsored NGOs proliferate. The withholding of state media to opposition parties is a tried and tested technique. Even if overturned in the law, this can be used to stall opposition campaigns, as in the case of the state South African Broadcasting Corporation's refusal to run the adverts of the opposition Democratic Alliance in the run-up to the May 2014 election, contrary to constitutional provisos.[9] As a result, in the view of veteran liberal South African politician Alex Boraine, 'based on the record of the ANC [ruling African National Congress] in exile and in government, with their passion for control, their intolerance of opposition, and their stated belief that they are destined to rule "until Jesus comes", should they lose their majority they will refuse to accept the will of the people'.[10] The ANC has not been alone in such failings. With their focus on fighting colonialism and racial exclusion, most liberation movements have lacked an effective plan for wealth creation beyond redistribution, a sure way to run these economies down in the absence of the necessary skills and investment even to retain rather than expand the colonial economic pie,[11] and in the circumstances resorted to extraordinary measures to maintain control as failure fed repression and vice versa. Tanzania's Mwalimu Julius Nyerere is a case study in point. Though Africa needs its heroes, and Nyerere is undoubtedly a liberation icon, there is some mythology here, disguising the cost and consequence of his policies in search for higher ideals. The Arusha Declaration of 1967 committed Tanzania to a policy of socialism and self-reliance. The policy's cornerstone was the *Ujamaa* ('familyhood') village: an agricultural collective run along traditional African lines, whereby basic goods and tools were held in common and shared among members. The combination of crushing bureaucracy, a lack of incentives for increasing production and political repression stifled initiative and Tanzania's economy. Despite being in the forefront of the struggle against apartheid, Mwalimu ('teacher' in Kiswahili) routinely held more political prisoners than the hated South African apartheid regime.[12] He was no democrat. As recalled by (Lord) Peter Carrington, who had to deal with the Tanzanian president as Britain's foreign secretary in the Lancaster House negotiations enabling Zimbabwe's transition to independence in 1980, Nyerere 'made it plain that he would not accept any outcome – which by then meant an election – unless Mugabe won it. He would accuse us of cheating.'[13] His preference for one-party rule entrenched policy uncompetitiveness: he won 99 per cent of Tanzania's election in 1970, and 93 per cent in both 1975 and 1980. No wonder *Ujamaa* was sometimes referred to as the 'pyjama policy', since it put Tanzania to sleep', as one Kenyan business person has lamented.

These are countries where criticism is seen as treason, where diversity of views is seen mostly as a weakness and seldom a strength. Leaders who discourage the study and critical scrutiny of their own situations so obviously lack a sense of irony, given that such questioning helped not only to achieve liberation from colonial authorities but also has been at the root of innovation in developed economies.

Such regimes like party lists and appointments, not direct elections. They target media outlets and independent journalists, while again ensuring they are front and centre of the local news outlets. They play to the need for stability, while buttering up supporters with contracts, social grants, pensions and jobs – a recipe for widespread corruption and stagnation. The concept of a 'development state' or 'state as the agency for development' is the preferred language. State employment is kept high, along with loyalties: in Singapore, the ratio of state jobs to others is at 6.35 per cent, and under 10 per cent in Japan and Taiwan.[14] In South Africa, with 37.6 per cent unemployment registered in 2013, the state is now the largest employer, at just under 23 per cent of the workforce.[15] Malawi, as was noted, has some 200 000 civil servants for a population of 15 million, making up the vast bulk of those formally employed. There are seven million such public officers in Egypt, to take another example, or more than 210 000 army and police alone in South Sudan consuming 80 per cent of the budget, and a civil service of 700 000 among just five million wage-earners in Kenya, public sector salaries consuming half of the government budget. Though this presence has a suffocating effect in all these and other cases on the fiscus and the private sector alike, these posts ensure the practice of patronage linked to political support is alive and well.

And when it comes to elections, as the example of Zimbabwe illustrates, this is more sophisticated than simply beating up or imprisoning opponents, or even fiddling with election results. Techniques include gerrymandering districts, tampering with voters' rolls, inventing shadow voters, delving into voting records (most infamously through the Maisanta digital database in Venezuela),[16] redistribution of the spoils in the form of contracts and goods to supporters, strangulation of resources for opponents including through intimidation of funders, clamping down on foreign funding to NGOs and control of media assets. Elections are a necessity to maintain legitimacy, and so they become a target of the state apparatus. As William Dobson noted about Venezuela under Hugo Chávez: a 'unique paradox: with each election, the country loses more of its democracy'.[17]

Even without charismatic (if enigmatic) Chávez at the helm, the system takes some beating, as was noted in Chapter 8. On 14 April 2013, Nicolás Maduro, picked by Chávez as his chosen successor before the Venezulean leader's death from cancer on 5 March, achieved a narrow election victory, just 270 000 votes over opposition candidate (and former political prisoner of Chávez's) Henrique Capriles Radonski.

The increased sophistication of this approach can also be seen in Zimbabwe's 2013 presidential election, which, as highlighted above, equally did not rely on widespread violence, as had been the case five years earlier. To the contrary, Mugabe restrained party militia and his armed forces, ensuring that very few reports of violence reached the international press where they could trigger criticism. This did not mean that the threat of violence was removed; to the contrary, again, members of civil society and the opposition were subject to intimidation, arrest and other forms of persecution before and during the election process, including raids on the offices of civil society organisations by state security agencies and arrests of their leaders and opposition politicians on 'spurious' charges. The 2013 sophisticated variant of the Zimbabwe election playbook also relied on the state's absorption and emasculation of critical civil society organisations, including the once-doyen Zimbabwean Confederation of Industry, the Chamber of Commerce, the Farmers' Union and the Chamber of Mines, which 'like the coils of a large python ... have been gradually taken over by politically linked individuals and co-opted into the state system of patronage and loyalty to the ruling party no matter what'.[18]

Iran offers another post-digital election prototype. The Islamic Republic's 12 June 2009 elections saw the incumbent Mahmoud Ahmadinejad running against three challengers. Within 24 hours, the official news agency announced that with two-thirds of the votes counted, Ahmadinejad had won the election with 62 per cent of the votes cast, with his main opponent, Mir-Hossein Mousavi, receiving 34 per cent. The Iranian Green Movement sprung up in opposition to the results, with prominent Iranians, including film directors, actors, the Iranian national football team, scholars and religious figures, some of whom were consequently imprisoned for their protests. Much of the criticism was levelled at the pre-election violence and intimidation, including the torching of Mousavi's offices in Qum two weeks before the election. Mobile phone communications were interrupted in Tehran on election day, while earlier the Iranian government blocked access to Facebook across the country in reported response to its use by candidates running against Ahmadinejad.

The extent of the rigging by incumbents and chances of a shock election not only reflects the (lack of) commitment to norms and rights, but the vested financial and commercial interests in keeping things just the way they are, from Venezuela to Zimbabwe, and including Iran where, for example, the Islamic Revolutionary Guard Corps has grown in interest as a 'parallel military force established to protect the country's Islamic system', and also as a business entity with an estimated annual income of some $100 billion annually.[19] Reform strategies have to take such dynamics and narrow institutional interests into account.

Resisting their rise

As Thatcher reminds, 'A democratic system of government rests in some measure on the consent of the governed. But consent will never be unanimous. There will be a majority for and a minority against ... Democracy,' she said, 'therefore contains within itself the means of orderly change through choice and consent. Clash of opinion is the stuff of which democracy is composed.'[20] Put differently, the subversion of democracy is usually bad for policy options.

The rise of the oxymoronic 'authoritarian democrats' can be resisted. The history of non-violent democratic activism illustrates the importance in this process of singling out the foreign supporters of regimes, not local officials, and one or two key personalities, in attempts to fragment their facade. Targeted sanctions against these individuals may also take effect, if only as a tool of ostracism, since there is nothing a political pariah usually likes more than to be loved. Benazir Bhutto, as one example, talked about the effectiveness of financial measures on leaders given the pressure points. 'The first call they will get will come from their mistress shopping at Harrods when her credit card is stopped,' she told biographer Ron Suskind. 'And the second one from their wife complaining why little Ahmed's fees have not been paid at Georgetown. They will soon change their ways.'[21] There are counterarguments, including that sanctions externalise the reasons for a country's problems, as ZANU-PF has attempted to do with targeted measures against prominent party members in Zimbabwe. But the hostile rhetoric about these type of personalised measures suggests that they are effective – or at the very least, personally painful.

Non-violent rallies and gatherings can be useful at bringing social and political issues unobtrusively to the surface, while key slogans and symbols (the Jasmine Revolution in Tunisia, Czechoslovakia's Velvet Revolution, Georgia's Rose Revolution and the Orange Revolution in Ukraine are examples) can be powerful, politically catalysing tools. In all of this, however, there is a need to put yourself in your enemy's shoes, and to offer them a non-violent way out.

Technology can be useful in elections, but it has its limits and can be counter-productive, playing into the hands of authoritarians, not least through state procurement opportunities. Given the expense of biometric systems, in the Democratic Republic of Congo, for example, the 2010 elections cost $360 million, with $58 million spent on biometrics, and in Ghana, $124 million and $76 million respectively. Kenya's 2013 elections cost $293 million, with donors contributing $100 million.[22]

Polling is another method of resisting intimidation and attempts to play the identity card. By contacting sample groups directly, it is possible both to establish what the issues are that concern voters, and play to these, in so doing altering identity stereotypes.[23]

It is not only the ruling parties, however, that are at fault or need to be checked or change. Take the Zimbabwe example again.

Opposition ownership of the solution

Even if they might not have been technically defeated at the disputed 2013 poll itself, the opposition MDC was totally outmanoeuvred throughout the process by ZANU-PF and its leader President Mugabe.

The MDC 'lost' an election it should never have gone into, since somehow its leadership had convinced itself they would win. They should have known that Mugabe, the great survivor, would never have agreed to a poll he risked losing, at least not after his 2008 election performance. The MDC was not only naive in expecting to triumph, but thinking it could then, against all odds and prior experience, secure a transfer of power.

If only a fraction of the above allegations are to be believed, the MDC lost on 31 July 2013 because of a fraudulent voters' roll. But in the judgement of some civil society activists, it capitulated well before the time because its leadership had become estranged from its grassroots supporters, and because they had been sucked into the system by the trappings of power during the MDC's 52 months in a government of unity with ZANU-PF from February 2009.

After the 2013 election, with just 49 MPs in a 210-strong parliament, the MDC faced an uphill battle. At the core of this was not how it might engage in Zimbabwe's formal political institutions, but rather how it might reinvent and rebuild itself.

Many questioned whether the MDC – and by extension, the country – could make progress under the leadership of Tsvangirai. Despite his once undoubted personal courage, he was increasingly seen as compromised by his personal peccadilloes and professional misjudgement in going into an election he later described as a 'farce'.

Yet, changing the party and the direction of the opposition would not be easy. Activists who have complained that the MDC has lost attachment with its supporters faced the stark choice of mobilising for leadership change or giving up on him by opting out of politics or starting another party.

Even if there was a new MDC leader, a lot of rebuilding would have to take place in reconnecting grassroots constituencies with the centre, and in creating political alliances with other opposition parties and civil society movements.

But, fundamentally, it is no good hoping that when Mugabe goes, Zimbabwe's problems will disappear.

Actuarial science will eventually catch up with Mugabe, 90 years old in February 2014, probably sooner rather than later. But this might not change things for the better in Zimbabwe, or in its opposition. Mugabe's demise would likely offer once more the prospect of a coalition government under Deputy President Joyce Mujuru as a means of co-opting the elite. That formula, as the earlier government of national unity showed, might offer the facade of political stability, but, aside from the fortunes of a select few, little chance of growth, development and prosperity.

Such stability, above all else, has been the clear policy goal of southern Africa's regional actors. The sacrifice, in the process, of democratic values has, however, longer-term consequences, both for Zimbabweans and further afield since Mugabe's brand of populism and 'vulture capitalism' is unlikely to stay at home.

As one Zimbabwean opposition activist puts it, the costs of attempting to cut a deal with ZANU-PF in the hope that you might gain access to the levers of power, means of income and get on-side, reminds of a Shona saying: '*Usa ramwire munda makundo, uchifunga kuti anozonyara*' (Do not give up a field to baboons thinking they will be shy to finish off the field). It is a variant on Pastor Martin Niemöller's poem about the rise of the Nazis in Germany and the cowardice of groups in opposing them: 'First they came for the Socialists, and I did not speak out, because I was not a Socialist. Then they came for the Trade Unionists, and I did not speak out, because I was not a Trade Unionist. Then they came for the Jews, and I did not speak out, because I was not a Jew. Then they came for me – and there was no one left to speak for me.' This highlighted the dilemma facing the international community in its actions towards the Mugabe government. Sanctions have been increasingly ineffective against a regime in the face of international disunity. Mugabe did not fly to London for regular medical treatment, for example, but to East Asia. Yet while the removal of sanctions could help focus attention on domestic actors, the danger was that this might also embolden ZANU-PF and strengthen its domestic credibility. And the same precarious human rights conditions still pertained, which led to their application in the first instance.

The answer for foreigners and Zimbabweans alike concerned about the course of political developments has been to focus on ZANU-PF, to try to get it to reform. But this has not proven to be enough. If the last fifteen years has taught one thing in Zimbabwe, it is that recovery will not happen through ZANU-PF mending its ways. The MDC, too, would have to change.

∗

Ensuring free and fair elections is only one democratic challenge. Another is guarding against identity trumping issues in politics, historically a temptation, especially for liberation movements. Where there is egregious state behaviour and the limits of democracy – or the presence of identity politics – do not permit or encourage the electorate to change their government, this can only dilute confidence by private business, believing that governments have virtual impunity where race, fear, apathy or institutional weakness trumps even the worst of government excesses. A lack of such confidence leads to a failure to invest in productive assets and ensures a downward spiral of economic contraction, job losses and recrimination.

Managing the politics of liberation and identity

Marius Fransman, the leader of the ANC in South Africa's Western Cape province, and the country's deputy minister for international relations and cooperation, in 2013 claimed that 98 per cent of landowners in the city of Cape Town were white and Jewish. 'The reality is … 98 per cent … of the land owners and property owners actually is the white community and, in particular, also people in the Jewish community,' he told the Cape Town Press Club in October.[24] Some South African property records prior to 1994 list the race of owners, but never their religion. Fransman vowed that the ANC would 'reclaim' the Western Cape, and accused the provincial government led by the opposition Democratic Alliance of having a 'close' relationship with Israel.[25]

Bizarre stuff, especially from a much-touted non-racial democracy, behind which there was, however, a political logic. Given that the province was run by the Democratic Alliance, and contained 1.3 million Muslims, his comments were interpreted as 'little more than a cynical attempt to win over Muslim voters' ahead of the May 2014 elections. He was sadly not alone in the playing of the racial card. The month before the election, sports and recreation minister Fikile Mbalula said that a 40 per cent quota for whites in national and provincial sports teams would be imposed, and that those codes that did not comply would be stripped of their national colours and deprived of funding.[26]

Whatever else, a generation after the release of Mandela from prison in February 1990, racial identity politics continued to shape South African politics, as it did in Zimbabwe more than 30 years after that country's independence.

*

Thabo Mbeki, by his own admission,[27] stood accused of re-racialising South Africa politics. Yet, he has expressed concern that much of Africa has been unable to fabricate a 'common political citizenship' based not on national or tribal identities but higher ideals of 'social justice' and 'law-based order'. Failure to do so, says the former South African president, leads to the 'rapacious enrichment of a small group, the severe compromise to the integrity of the state machinery, and failure to address the fundamental socio-economic interests of the population as a whole'. Rather this serves to 'mobilise … opposed ethnic groups into bitter struggles for access to resources …'[28]

The political economy of liberation movements – where the fight for freedom has in many cases quickly transformed into an entrenched right to rule and access to the economic spoils – overlaps with the use of racial, ethnic and religious differences to ensure power. As Winston Churchill remarked,

'We shape out buildings and afterwards our building shape us.' Or, put differently, the last places to be liberated and decolonised are the liberation movements themselves.[29] Indeed, Mbeki is correct in identifying the need for an urgent reorientation to issues beyond national identity, given the drivers of change across the African continent.

Sub-Saharan Africa's population is, as noted, projected to more than double to two billion by 2040, when the region will provide more than one-quarter of the world's youth, or nearly 300 million people. Already around half of this cohort is unemployed or inactive. Political 'business as usual' is not delivering and is unlikely to deliver the jobs on the scale required.[30]

In the absence of the creation of job opportunities, as popular frustrations over a lack of delivery against expectations grind, there is a danger of populist political and economic responses, from so-called resource nationalism to outright nationalisation, populist authoritarianism and even violent terrorism. This is exacerbated by a 'disconnect' between the actions of the ruling party and expectations of the population. The relative absence of a middle class as a buffer against excess exacerbates these tendencies. This class, defined by those earning between $4–20 per day, accounted for little over 13 per cent of Africa's population in 2010, or 38 per cent if including the so-called rich class (less than $20 per day) and floating class ($2–4 per day).[31] The credit of first-generation liberation movements could evaporate as subsequent generations take over, despite all the attempts to keep this alive through a combination of mythology and patronage. Already, for example, just twenty years after its democratic transition, more than half of South Africans are under 24 years old. Moreover, keeping a brought church together, where the binding influence is to fight for a bigger aim (the end of apartheid, for example), is more difficult when that goal has been achieved. Hence, the reluctance of liberation movements to disavow the struggle and its racial, anti-colonial and other totems, and transform themselves into competitive political parties.[32]

Singapore's Lee Kuan Yew reminds us of the cost of such politics. On his third trip to Zambia, in 1979, he noted: 'Everything was in short supply. The shops were empty. Imported toiletries were absent and there was little in the way of local substitutes … They had no foreign exchange, and their currency was rapidly depreciating. President Kenneth Kaunda's major preoccupation was politics, black versus white politics, not the economics of growth for Zambia.'[33] The continued permeation and definition of politics by race, religion and ethnicity has tremendous costs, as Kenya and others remind.

Kofi Annan has referred in this regard to the dangers of a 'winner take all' approach to politics, that none of Africa's myriad minorities should be alienated by permanent exclusion. 'We must turn our backs on the "winner takes all" approach to politics which has been so damaging to our continent,' says the former UN secretary general. 'We have seen how this has led to abuses of power by the winner and encouraged losers to reject democracy as a peaceful means for change.'[34]

Lee concluded that the success of once-poor Singapore has been dependent on social cohesion through 'sharing the benefits of progress, equal opportunities for all and meritocracy, with the best man or woman for the job, especially as leaders in government'.[35] He also stressed the importance of leadership as a gel in holding society together, of the need to develop a common nationhood as a prerequisite for development and advancement, and of the related need to avoid living in two different realities: of an indifferent elite at the top of the pile with the bulk of society scraping a living at the bottom. Indeed, in Asia, it is the commitment to popular welfare by leadership that has distinguished its development trajectory.

Changing the role of identity in politics depends in part on addressing the wealth divides that can define such differences. It also requires leadership willing to give up playing games of divide and control – able to view the longer-term advantage to no longer playing the race, tribal, geographic or religious card.

It takes a remarkable politician to see this bigger picture, beyond their immediate constituency and the next election. The ultimately brief (and failed) political marriage in February 2014 between the Democratic Alliance in South Africa and the Agang SA party of the veteran anti-apartheid activist Mamphela Ramphele, could have, if it had stuck, accelerated the emergence of a non-racial opposition, offering a more politically (read, racially) palatable alternative for which more black South Africans might be prepared to vote. But its failure indicated the defining role of personalities, the depth of identity in South Africa's society and that no leapfrogs were likely; instead, a slower process of producing credible leaders from the bottom-up, from inside these parties. In the process of attempting such a bold move, mistakes were inevitably made, as the critics were eager to gleefully point out from behind the safety of their computers, such *Schadenfreude* reminding of John F. Kennedy's remark that 'victory has a thousand fathers, but defeat is an orphan'. Seldom, of course, do politicians and advisers, doers rather than debaters, have the luxury of time afforded to the armchair critics. But perhaps the biggest error was trusting that this time 'it would be different' and that egos would be subsumed in the interests of breaking South Africa's persistent and costly feature of racial, identity politics.

Progress will take courage, of course, along with a degree of far-sighted common sense. When negotiating a charter for South Africa's mining sector, one targeted from the 1950s for nationalisation, Phumzile Mlambo-Ngcuka, the country's minister of mineral and energy affairs under Mbeki, said that keeping the industry healthy was imperative for the country since, in reference to the racial division of ownership and wealth in the sector, 'whether you shoot a zebra in the black or white stripe, it dies regardless'.[36] During her tenure, finding common interests between government and business was one aspect, most constructively done through the building of relationships in private and not public slanging matches worsening already fragile egos and hurt.

Mlambo-Ngcuka's observation holds true generally in the necessity to move from a debate centring on questions of identity and wealth exclusion and redistribution between groups to one aimed at national development issues. Without such a national imperative, the focus is inevitably on internal differences and discrimination, not wealth creation, hardly a recipe for long-term recovery and prosperity.

*

A lack of political competition – whether this is a result of identity politics or a weakness of democratic systems – usually costs countries dearly in the form of corruption, lack of economic competitiveness, crony capitalism and monopolies, and a lack of innovation and fresh ideas. As Dmitry Mdvedev, then president of Russia, lamented in a speech to the Duma in November 2008: 'The result is that the state bureaucracy is the biggest employer, most active publisher, best producer, and is its own court, own political party, and ultimately its own people. This is a completely ineffective system and leads only to corruption. It gives rise to legal nihilism on a mass scale, goes counter to the Constitution, and hinders the development of innovative economic and democratic institutions.'[37]

Authoritarian democracy observes the principle rather than the practice of democracy and its institutions. These are only the nation's interest, of course, if your party is in power, while things are going well and if commodity prices, usually key to such countries, are high. The sort of rent-seeking behaviour it encourages looks more like a vicious, not virtuous, cycle of long-term stability and development.

32

THE QUIET PROFESSIONALS

Aid, Advice and the Art of Recovery

*

In the cramped and dusty village of Chabelley, a bumpy car ride west of Djibouti city, along a washed-out track strewn with garbage and the carcasses of dogs, electrical goods and old cars, local contractors were putting the finishing touches to an American-funded clinic.[1]

A nurse, doctor and midwife were to be permanently staffed here to attend to the 800-strong community, the children of which wait excitedly outside the gate for handouts from visiting military personnel. The natural human instinct to give 'them' soft drinks, water, pens and food has fuelled their perception of foreigners as providers, bringing relief in various forms from a harsh existence. Aid is seldom for nothing, however.

Military-led programmes of the Combined Joint Task Force-Horn of Africa, based in Djibouti but operating all over Africa, have successfully built clinics, wells, bridges and schools across the region with the intention both of building support for the international presence on this tiny, bleak territory and improving regional nations' civil governance and military capacity.

Its small beer, perhaps, measured in inputs: less than $10 million per year, compared to the United States Agency for International Development's (USAID's) annual expenditure in Africa of over $10 billion.[2] Yet to understand whether or not such an effort has been successful, even if as an instrument of diplomacy rather than purely of development, we need to look beyond inputs to consider what some development professionals refer to as a 'theory of change'.

It is easy to berate aid as being responsible for regime failure. But aid is only one method for stabilisation and development where a multitude of challenges require a suite of such tools, albeit one that it is often preferred by external actors, not least since they can attempt to change the incentives through conditionality and can manage perhaps the most important metric to their taxpayers – the extent of spending. Moreover, not only do donors provide a substantial proportion of government revenues in such situations, they also bring expertise critical to what are usually small and isolated economies.

Indeed, what foreigners can do usefully through aid is to strengthen the benefits of better and costs of bad choices. As Paul Collier argues, donors can 'change *incentives for government* both intentionally through the conditions they set, and unintentionally through the revenues and expertise they provide.'[3]

The enormous aid investment in Afghanistan and elsewhere over the decade has not, however, demonstrated that the clear lesson that business-driven assistance plays a key role in post-conflict peace-building has been either internalised or practised. What then might best be the role of economic development assistance in conflict and post-conflict environments, from the standpoint of both theory and practice?

Theories of change

Military strategists often consider warfare in the context of a 'theory of victory', a theoretical construct that makes sense of strategic analyses, allowing informed choices by defining military success and explaining, in some manner, how specific actions contribute to it. While there is no universal (or universally agreed) theory of victory, thinkers such as Colin Gray[4] and William Martel[5] have contributed to a vigorous strategic debate that informs the thinking of real-world practitioners in the field.

In the realm of foreign assistance, a 'theory of change' fulfils a similar function, stating 'what expected (changed) result will follow from a particular set of actions'[6] or, more elegantly, 'a theory of how and why an initiative works.'[7] Just as in military strategy, theories of change are contested, with writers such as Dambisa Moyo,[8] William Easterley[9] and Collier[10] criticising certain approaches to modernisation as practised by Western aid agencies since 1945.

As these analysts, among others, have noted, $1 trillion dollars in aid to sub-Saharan Africa over the past 50 years of independence is testimony to how much easier modernisation and development is said than done, for the continent's annual per capita GDP remains pegged at under $1 000. The extent of the failure of traditional foreign assistance, a focus on aid to the exclusion of fair trade and strategic investment, is reflected in donor defensiveness: 'things could have been much worse' is an oft-repeated but counterfactual argument.

This lack of an agreed theory of change is particularly evident for stabilisation programming in conflict-affected areas. In the past this was often referred to as post-conflict reconstruction, but as the wars in Iraq and Afghanistan have shown, much stabilisation and reconstruction programming must now, perforce, take place during conflict, and this makes it even harder than usual for aid agencies to design, monitor and evaluate their programmes in an effective manner.

One theory that often underpins stabilisation programming for conflict environments is that populations engage in violence, or support illegal armed groups, in part because they lack employment or essential services. The government fails them, they lack means of support, and so they turn to the insurgents. Providing essential services and jobs, the theory goes, takes violent young men off the street, gives them something to do, and may make people shift their allegiance away from illegal armed groups toward the legitimate government. A corollary to this theory is that foreign assistance, by making a local government more capable, can close the gaps in its service provision, build its capacity over time and thereby help it win over its population.

This theory, unfortunately, is often both unstated (indeed, it is often unconscious) and heavily disputed. There is, in fact, little hard evidence that increased development spending, or short-term stabilisation programming, actually results in a decrease in support for insurgencies. On the contrary, researchers, such as Eli Berman, Joseph Felter and Jacob Shapiro[11] and Andrew Wilder and Stuart Gordon,[12] have shown a strong correlation between increased aid spending and *higher* levels of insurgent violence in both Iraq and Afghanistan.

Even at the level of theory, as long ago as the mid-1960s, the RAND Corporation economist Charles Wolf was arguing that while development spending in insurgency environments may (or may not) have a substitution effect that might encourage populations to shift allegiance from insurgents to the government, it will definitely also have an income effect – increasing the availability of resources to everyone, including insurgents, and so strengthening an insurgency in absolute terms, even if its strength declines relative to that of the government.[13] Wolf's thesis was, and remains, controversial – yet it suggests that key questions within the economic theory underpinning stabilisation and counter-insurgency remain unsettled.

Nowhere has the task of translating money into practical effect proven more difficult than in post-conflict reconstruction. Typically, the 'post-conflict' period is characterised by an urgency to get things done on several fronts simultaneously, from restoring security to rebuilding shattered institutions. This requires a sharp influx of money. The danger is that this money serves to undermine longer-term development, even while it produces positive effects in the short term. Afghanistan is a salutary case in point. The gush of foreign aid into the country has helped fuel corruption, criminality and unaccountability. As a consequence, Afghanistan's political and economic progress has faltered.

While the military aspect of stability operations (including counter-insurgency and peace operations) has received serious scholarly attention, the role of foreign assistance (including both official development assistance – that is, traditional government-to-government aid – and a host of military, humanitarian and private interventions in the same space) has not been thoroughly analysed. This lacuna is partly born of the fact that development is not perceived in 'life or death' terms. The consequences of military failure are immediate and palpable: numbers of wounded and killed. The repercussions of mismanaged aid are less tangible and often only evident after several years or even decades. But they are no less ruinous for it. Indeed, the death and misery resulting from lack of development in recipient countries often far outweighs the lives lost through armed conflict.

The nature of the challenge

The wars in Iraq and Afghanistan along with a welter of post-conflict peace-building and peacekeeping operations, many of which are in Africa, have prompted vigorous re-examination of current practice. But this is not a new issue.

As the veteran commentator Walter Cronkite observed about Vietnam in 1968: 'We are allies. South Vietnam supplies the battlefield and we supply endless streams of young men, vast squadrons of planes, the machinery or war and the money. The money is staggering. Twenty billion dollars this year [1966] for planes and guns and bombs, and $525 million more for economic aid. That amounts to more than $1 000 for every man, woman and child, including the Viet Cong. There is more money where that came from and we keep pumping it into Saigon. Saigon is the city,' Cronkite observed, 'where we will find out if it's possible to get our money's worth in Asia. But the ironic thing is that the people in Saigon who take the money do not entirely welcome it.'[14]

Similarly, Christopher Hitchens had this to say about Pakistan: 'There's absolutely no mystery to the "Why do they hate us?" question, at least as it arises in Pakistan. They hate us because they owe us, and are dependent upon us … Our bought-and-paid-for pretense … has led to a rancid, resentful official hypocrisy, and to a state policy of revenge, large and petty, on the big, rich, dumb Americans who foot the bill.'[15]

This is the classic problem of patron-client relations – the asymmetry of interest and influence between donors and beneficiaries creates the dependency and mutual resentment that Cronkite and Hitchens describe. Economic development programmes in post-conflict environments are especially prone to this problem, because the stakes are so high for local power brokers, while the chaotic and insecure environment makes monitoring and evaluation of programme performance next to impossible.

The extent of the challenge can be seen in the difference between stabilisation programming (quick-impact spending to achieve short-term improvements in security) and longer-term development spending. For example, digging wells, building clinics and schools offers immediate, tangible results that are easy to measure in bricks and mortar. Donors are excellent at tracking inputs, such as dollars spent and buildings constructed. But they have been far less successful in measuring projects' abilities to achieve outcomes, such as improved education or better public health, upon which long-term development spending and oversight are dependent. What is more, the link between these outcomes and *sustainable* security and stability, most appropriately to be measured in the cycle of growth, jobs and social inclusion, is rarely given due consideration.

The conflict-prosperity cycle

Economic assistance, moreover, does not necessarily offer the grounds for stability that donors are looking for in post-conflict environments. Stability is not a linear but rather a cyclical phenomenon, where security begets economic development and vice versa. Thus, even successful projects with strong buy-in from locals, which actually boost the economy, may not be enough. And even if they are constructed to international standards, raising the local bar, this, too, may not be sustainable without external pressure, oversight and further largesse. The risk of relapse into bad old ways of doing things is ever-present. And local actors are not fooled for a moment. They realise that their place in the donor sun is only fleeting and thus exploit this opportunity for all its worth: donor-funded projects can simply create spoils over which local power elites compete, creating grounds for new internal conflicts or exacerbating existing ones.[16]

In Somaliland, for example, the lack of international recognition exacerbates aid expenditure failings and distortions. 'It is only visible in people coming and going,' said the minister of planning, Saad Shire, of the impact of aid. His colleague, the minister of finance, Mohamed Hashi Elmi, has observed of aid that 'nothing is visible on the ground. It is only for generating employment for foreigners. It is mostly wasted in seminars and spent on vacations.' Somaliland's Ministry of Planning has estimated that only between 15 to 20 per cent of aid allocated actually hits the ground, the rest being consumed on overheads. Little wonder Hargeisa has forced the registration of NGOs, their number countrywide over 100.[17]

There are even more pernicious dimensions. Aid programmes are often antithetical to private sector economic development when controlled by donors who do not either understand, or like, business. Moreover, donors invariably have at least one eye fixed on a domestic agenda – for example, a powerful national lobby or electoral considerations – which further reduces the focus on the effectiveness of aid in recipient countries.

This results in good ideas becoming international NGO causes rather than business cases. The business person is seldom anywhere near this process: rather, community power brokers, local 'notables' or others with an axe to grind become professional aid recipients and dole out the resultant assistance to their supporters. In Afghanistan, professional (but fake) 'tribal elders' have specialised in gaining assistance of various kinds for villages, selling their services on a consultancy basis. The real elders remain in the background, while local business people are crowded out. As Clare Lockhart and Ashraf Ghani have shown, in Afghanistan this economic distortion effect resulted in a village-level brain drain, with local traditional civil servants and entrepreneurs flocking to become drivers, translators or fixers for the international aid community. For example, much of the focus of counter-insurgency and peace-building campaigns has dwelt on illicit activities as an impediment to good governance. Afghanistan's opium trade is a perfect example, where the incomes generated help pay insurgents and fuel corruption. Yet, the money involved pales in comparison to what can be hived off aid programmes. Afghanistan's poppy trade is worth no more than $300 million inside Afghanistan, in terms of money paid to farmers who grow the crop. By comparison, as noted in Chapter 12, the principal Host Nation Transport contract to support the International Security Assistance Force (ISAF) totalled over $2 billion in 2010.[18] Aid is part of the political economy of war.

Equally, the view elsewhere of the assets that infect and distort the political economy is also sometimes off the mark. Zimbabwe's Marange diamonds, for example, have been viewed as the most pernicious element in that country's misery, the proceeds enabling President Robert Mugabe's ZANU-PF party to circumvent the fiscus and stay in power. No doubt the gems, said to be the biggest diamond find in 100 years since South Africa's Kimberley fields, are a massive earner, likely realising over $1 billion in annual export receipts.[19] But cigarette (and to a lesser extent other forms of) smuggling are Zimbabwe's equivalent of ISAF's Afghan trucking contracts, where the money but not the international attention is.[20] South Africa's cigarette industry comprised 29 billion sticks annually in 2011, or over 11 million per day, worth an estimated R30 billion. Of this, 30 per cent is made up of illicit flows, mainly from Zimbabwe and Dubai. This costs the South African exchequer, since excise duties on cigarettes amounted to nearly R11 billion in 2011, despite the seizure of 1.2 billion sticks in 2011. But it costs good governance and democracy more, being a major source of income for ZANU-PF elites. In other words, to fully appreciate how Zimbabwe's political economy operates, an eye should be on Zimbabwe's smuggling per se, not just Marange's diamonds.

Truck on

Tensions are exacerbated where donor strategies are not harmonised but instead clash. The existence in 2010 of three distinct seed distribution programmes in Helmand and Kandahar provinces in Afghanistan, each under a different lead nation, is a case in point. This may also be one impact, paradoxically, of over-resourcing in an economy that lacks absorptive capacity, due to decades of conflict. In this environment, donors have more money to spend than there are good projects and local capacity to spend it on, leading inter alia to engagement fratricide – individuals and communities game the system, collecting donor money from multiple sources for the same projects. The dumping of cash on communities with limited absorptive capacity, and with little accountability, creates incentives for corruption and can overload fragile local systems of governance.

By 2010 the international community was spending more than $10 billion in development aid annually in Afghanistan, amounting to $333 per Afghan man, woman and child per year. In some areas, such as the restive southern provinces, the concentration was much higher.[21] Yet, given the lack of development impact – as measured by the existence of an indigenous economy outside that supported by donor money – it may have been better (and considerably more efficient) if the international community had bombed the country with bundles of money. As Angus Deaton has noted, it would take an astonishingly small sum of money – he calculates about 15 US cents a day from each adult in the rich world – to bring everyone up to at least the 'destitution line' of a dollar a day.[22] Of course, this is no solution, given that the donors want to have control over where the money is spent, and citizens in the recipient countries need government, as Deaton observes, to lead better lives. While 'taking government out of the loop might improve things in the short run', it would leave unsolved underlying problems, not least since poor countries 'cannot forever have their health services run from abroad'.

Needless to say, not every Afghan has received this allocation of aid. Much of it has gone into just a few hands. Much has been spent on consumptive rather than productive areas of investment aimed at expanding business and creating jobs. The scale of the failure and waste has been staggering, even among hardened aid types. 'Aid expenditure in Afghanistan is highly distributive,' remarked one seasoned expert in Kabul. 'There is too much money. It is so gross in its volume that the effort is mostly to disperse it rather than disperse it in a wise, sustainable way.'[23] Much of this expenditure, of course, has benefited aid middlemen (implementing partners or expatriate contractors) from the donor countries themselves. An Afghan business person from Kandahar observed, 'Afghans call international assistance "aeroplane aid" – the money flies to Afghanistan, touches down, and flies right back where it came from.'[24]

Moreover, of course, not all aid programmes are explicitly designed to help the recipient population. USAID, for example, was established 50 years ago in September 1961 as an instrument of American foreign policy. It was explicitly designed to promote what some have called 'instrumental' assistance (designed to generate favourable effects for US foreign policy), rather than 'fundamental' assistance that helps develop and modernise local economies. This does not mean that instrumental aid does not also bring fundamental benefits, as indicated by the overlap between poverty, conflict, water scarcity and geography. Still, seldom, if ever, is foreign assistance explicitly used to create economic opportunities and to improve competitiveness, the substance of economic growth and prosperity.[25] This world is not standing still either.

How the aid world is changing

The apogee of the aid world was likely reached at the Gleneagles G8 summit in July 2005. At that event agreement was reached to double aid globally to $100 billion and cancel debt for eighteen countries, plus achieve universal access to HIV drugs in Africa by 2010.

Bob Geldof was among those campaigning for the increase. He has since lauded then UK Prime Minister Tony Blair (and his chancellor Gordon Brown) for the outcome of Gleneagles for shaping 'not only our politics but that of the world' by cancelling debt and doubling aid. This act, he claims, released 'tens of millions of children into schooling, setting off an intellectual stampede in the continent with the fastest-growing middle class in the world.'[26]

'Aid', he says, 'sent money into basic health, education and agriculture, providing stability at a fundamental community level and allowing stretched societies a moment to pause ... while helping governments acquire the capacity they needed to govern.' The timing, he claims, was critical since it was exactly at this moment the Chinese became interested in Africa and a digital take-off occurred.

Geldof, like his Irish colleague Bono, is undoubtedly a humanitarian activist. He is also an egotist, a celebrity economist and quite wrong on Africa and aid.

As the lead singer of the Boomtown Rats once had a big hit with 'I Don't like Mondays', Geldof sprung to global prominence with his role in the 1984 Band Aid supergroup and its 'Do they know it's Christmas' number one song and the Live Aid concerts the following year, both to raise money for the Ethiopian famine. The former sold nearly 12 million copies; the latter raised £150 million.

For these efforts, Geldof received an honorary knighthood. He was also in the process elevated to a spokesperson for African development. Never one to mince his words – he famously used the f-word on television in exhorting people to fund his cause – in 2006 he reportedly described Russell Brand as a four-letter bit of a woman's anatomy, to which the colourful presenter responded, 'It's no wonder Bob Geldof knows so much about famine. He's been dining out on "I Don't Like Mondays" for 30 years.'[27]

The reason for the famine that catapulted him to prominence had more to do with the Ethiopian government policy to withhold food shipments to rebel areas than the weather, and to spend nearly half of its GDP on its military. Aid became a tool of the government's counter-insurgency strategy, being left to rot or distributed according to political objectives.

The same political issues shape African development choices today and these, not external activism on aid, are key to understanding the continent's future trajectory. African development solutions, like the problems themselves, are principally domestic, and also have to be founded in sustainable business logic, not political gestures or NGO activism.

Beijing's needs, not the proselytising of Bob or Blair, have transformed Africa from a problem to be solved through aid to a commercial opportunity to be entertained through investment.

It is Chinese investment and its demand for natural resources, not aid, that has been behind the 2000s' African growth surge. Nor has aid infused government capacity, allowing cellphones to revolutionise African communications and business. Indeed, the latter has occurred precisely because government is out of the way for once. It has nothing to do with the Western aid industry, as difficult as that is for them to accept.

Regardless, Geldof claims that 'I have no doubt that it is because of Gleneagles that I and colleagues were able to raise hundreds of millions of dollars to invest in Africa and create jobs'. To the contrary, it is precisely in spite of Gleneagles and its reinforcement of a helpless continent deserving charity that private investment has been raised.

What Bob does not seem to realise is that, while there is a role for humanitarian spending in difficult cases and, indeed, for development agencies as sources of loans and financing, the role for giving away money as a tool for development is at best dubious.

This is why aid agencies continually shift their methods and focus from agriculture and infrastructure to governance and back again. Such inefficiencies, along with the premium on administering aid through Byzantine bureaucracies (not for nothing has the World Bank's staffing increased from 650 people in 1960 to 10 000 today, two-thirds of whom are based in the centre of the poverty-stricken world, Washington, D.C.) help to explain why, as the economist Bill Easterly has pointed out, donor countries have absurdly argued to spend over $3 500 annually to lift the income of extremely poor people to above $365 per year.[28]

This is why remittances from Africans abroad, which do not have to go through many of these costly bureaucratic hoops and which some estimates have put as high as $60 billion annually (or double the flow of donor money), are a more efficient source of external financing than aid. This reflects the growing importance of remittances per se. Global remittance flow grew nearly 11 per cent, for example, between 2011 and 2012, to $514 billion, according to the World Bank, with now more than 215 million people, or 3 per cent of the world's population, living outside their countries of birth, many of them from fragile countries.[29] The top recipients of officially recorded remittances for 2012 were India ($70 billion), China ($66 billion), the Philippines and Mexico ($24 billion each) and Nigeria ($21 billion). Other large recipients include Egypt, Pakistan, Bangladesh, Vietnam and Lebanon.

To the contrary, however, Sir Bob has argued that 'surely now the [aid] model has been proved'. But nowhere does he mention the aspect of widening democracy, key to Africa's developmental and growth success and to improving governance. Little wonder. The record of development spending is that it can distort accountability of governments more than it improves governance, underwriting the very bad governance practices that are at the heart of underdevelopment.

Africans themselves realise this. This is one reason why the debate in and about the continent has shifted from perennial questions of what others can do for Africa, to one where Africa helps itself. Short-term Band-Aids have given way to longer-term development plans, at the heart of which are local political challenges, arguments and compromises.

This reflects changes in the importance, too, of aid overall. In 2011, for example, members of the Development Assistance Committee of the OECD[30] provided $133.5 billion of net official development assistance, representing 0.31 per cent of their combined gross national income. This was a 2.7 per cent drop in real terms compared to 2010, the year it reached its peak.[31] As a comparison, EU members pledged to reach a collective aid target of 0.56 per cent of GDP by 2010, and 0.7 per cent by 2015. Aid has also, more importantly, declined relative to global capital flows and sources of domestic financing.[32]

Two 2013 African events illustrate how much the landscape for development finance has changed – and what role the World Bank, for example, might play in the future.

In May, the Bank's president, Jim Yong Kim, pledged $1 billion to help bring peace to the Great Lakes region. Kim's pledge was made in the Democratic Republic of Congo's capital Kinshasa on a trip in the company of UN Secretary General Ban Ki-moon, which also took in neighbouring Rwanda and Uganda. Earmarked for financing health and education services, hydroelectric projects and cross-border trade, the loan is intended as an incentive for peace because of the Congo's ongoing violence, especially in its eastern reaches, and in spite of endemically poor governance – as noted, the DRC ranked behind only Somalia in *Foreign Policy's* 2013 Failed States Index.

Only a month before, in April, Rwanda had gone to the international capital market to raise $400 million in a debut bond offering. Orders reached $3.5 billion, over eight times the bond's issue. Rwanda is far from alone in finding a new source of capital. African countries were slated for offering $7 billion in fresh government debt in 2013, as more governments, including Tanzania and Kenya, strive to get access to private money. Once seen as the preserve of autocrats and corruption, today some countries in Africa are seen as the new, high-yield investment frontier.

Low returns in the developed world have led to investors aggressively searching for yield. Whereas ten-year US Treasuries offered 1.66 per cent, Rwanda promised 6.875 per cent at the time of its bond issue, though this was little more than Slovenia has had to offer or the rate at which Spain was battling to borrow.

Other factors have also been at work. Many African countries have experienced substantial growth in recent years (albeit off extremely low bases) and are becoming attractive bets (albeit still in the high-risk, high-return quadrant). Rwanda's economy, for example, has grown over 7 per cent a year over the last decade.

Thus, for the first time in many years, African countries have been able to raise capital independent of donors and their governance and political conditions. Rwanda, with half of its budget provided by donors, has been particularly vulnerable to changes in international mood. It faced a cash-flow crisis when donors switched off the taps on the grounds of Kigali's support for Congolese rebels, an issue BNP Paribas and Citigroup (who co-managed the offering) are less likely to be concerned with.

China's growing role on the continent has also provided Africans with new options. China's African investment stake is officially $15 billion, though this figure may be three times greater if money flows from tax shelters are factored in. Additionally, Beijing has promised a further $75 billion on aid and development projects in the past decade, though the amount actually delivered is, as with Western counterparts, less clear. But it is less the impact of Chinese aid than Chinese demand for African resources that has changed Africa's twenty-first-century growth trajectory for the good and helped, in the process, to quash the idea that Africa's fate is tied to Western donors – still the operating assumption of many celebrities.

The resulting decline in the World Bank's importance as a tool for development can be seen in its own figures. In 1990, at the end of the Cold War, private investment flows ($21.1 billion) were in the ballpark of World Bank grants and loans ($17.7 billion) to developing countries globally. By 2000, this had changed dramatically to nearly 8 to 1 ($144.5 billion to $18.5 billion). By 2011, foreign investment in low-income countries far outstripped World Bank spending by a factor of 19 to 1 ($612 billion versus $32 billion). In Africa, which is considered the investment laggard among developing countries and the most in need of aid, World Bank spending was just $5.6 billion in 2011 versus over $46 billion in foreign direct investment flows. This gap has increased from $2 billion in disbursements and $9 billion in investment in 2000.[33]

These changes raise a complicated question: what is the proper role of the World Bank, and the appropriate division between private finance and traditional, multilateral lending? While access to private financing should continue to improve as long as these economies grow, the current low interest rate environment that has driven investors to purchase government bonds from Rwanda and other countries will not continue indefinitely.

'Ideally, the World Bank should succeed until it is out of business. If aid is truly effective,' says Donald Kaberuka, president of the African Development Bank, 'it will progressively do itself out of a job.' Even though bureaucracies tend to find new missions, the Bank – like other development institutions – should increasingly become a lender of last resort. And it should continually be a voice for good governance, a cause that private interests will not trumpet as long as they are being paid back.

However, providing money to countries such as the DRC sends a very mixed message. Indeed, at the same moment that the Bank's new money was announced, the IMF was cutting its loan programmes to Congo due to concerns about governance. The Bank's president argues, 'There are always going to be problems and downsides with the governance of places that are fragile and conflict-affected like the DRC.' But he says, 'The point is that by investing, and by helping governments get better, over time we can both reduce the conflict and improve governance overall.'[34]

But that argument assumes that the World Bank can actually improve governance by spending more. Kinshasa has not felt compelled to improve governance because of all the other billions spent on it and it is not clear why the Bank's new effort might be different.

Five steps to more effective aid

Overall, it is important to get the basics right: to see conflict – and the process of recovery – afresh. Without this, as Collier's research reminds us, the prospect of countries sliding from post-war conditions back into conflict within a decade are around 50 per cent. The Oxford economist has also demonstrated that economic growth is the single most important factor in reducing a return to civil conflict after a war ends.[35] Getting post-conflict reconstruction right lies in creating the conditions that essentially replicate the development stories of the donors themselves – increasing the absorptive capacity of local economies, better use of capital, improving productivity of labour, a focus on infrastructure, prudential management, rule of law and transparency and accountability, along with adherence to the macroeconomic 'basics' of openness and steady liberalisation.

The second, related step is to change the geographic focus of aid and public expenditure, complementing rural development with urban and peri-urban infrastructure and small business. Although Afghanistan is a war fought primarily in rural areas, this pattern is anomalous. Since mid-2008, more than 50 per cent of humans on the planet now live in a city, and the rate of urbanisation is increasing. Africa, home to three-quarters of UN peacekeeper deployments, will be an urban continent by 2025, passing the 50 per cent urbanisation threshold, up from 40 per cent in 2010. This environment is self-reinforcing. As the March 2011 McKinsey report mapping the economic power of cities suggests, the agglomeration benefits of cities and the capacity to attract talented workers and higher investments drives higher GDP growth and, in cyclical fashion, urbanisation.[36]

Since war is fundamentally a human social and political activity, conflict occurs where people are – and the people are in cities. Just as populations are rapidly urbanising, likewise war is changing from a rural struggle involving agrarian peasant populations to a clash among urban dwellers. Baghdad, Basra, Grozny, Gaza, Beirut and Mogadishu are the future. Of course, there will be exceptions. Conflict involving refugees or displaced persons will still arise well beyond urban centres. And in an increasingly resource-constrained planet, outbreaks of violence over access to water or land are almost inevitable in some rural areas. Nevertheless, the trend towards urban conflict is clear.

Third is the need to decentralise fiscal authority. The authority of the central government needs to be balanced by the requirement to devolve budgetary responsibilities to village, district and provincial levels. Moreover, donors must be sensitive to the ways that budget support can negatively impact the rule of law, good governance and the functioning of the private sector. In the past, budget support has often served to enrich government elites and their patronage networks at the expense of national development. Again, a renewed emphasis on 'outcomes' will promote greater accountability.

Fourth is the need to get down to the granular specifics in aid projects. Electrical power can transform many aspects of social life, including health, education and security, and is one of the most important short-term factors in increasing economic capacity. At a more mundane level, the recycling of plastic bags – the national flower of governance-free zones, and plastic water bottles – the detritus of international relief and military presence – offers not only visible change and environmental improvement, but provides jobs in the process.

But even these two disparate areas – power and plastic – have proven hopelessly difficult for most aid projects to deliver, especially in conflict-affected areas.

Thus, a number of broad guidelines stand out. As already noted, spending on key infrastructure such as electrical power offers economies of scale as well as multiplier potential. Commercial sustainability of investments is essential. Commercialism not only helps to ensure a local stake in the preservation of projects, but can assuage local suspicions as to why money – and goods – are apparently 'given' away. Commercial development may, however, require catalytic investment to encourage it, in the form of upstream interventions out of sight of beneficiary populations. Such subsidies might ultimately prove cheap, compared to the cost of foreign military forces *in situ* to keep the peace. Furthermore, rather than spending on delivery of projects by foreigners, care has to be taken to incentivise local entrepreneurs to start businesses that deliver projects to acceptable standards, and for government to maintain and monitor these standards.

Finally, fifth, it is important to get the metrics right. Outcomes, rather than just inputs or outputs, must be measured. Assistance is about far more than just the volume of money dedicated and spent, even though this is usually the easiest metric. Changing the way in which donor contracts are awarded could be a key means of both demonstrating a different way of doing business, and ensuring that risk is averted as money is spent better. Some, but not all, aid agencies operate a contractual 'scorecard' for donor contracts to ensure that not only are contractors seen to be complying with governance requirements but that they are cognisant of the need to spread the wealth around. Such a scorecard can insist either that contractors require a certain number of points to be eligible or receive a discount on their tender, dependent on their score. There is a need also to move the measurement of aid beyond adherence to principles only, or through subjective criteria (including interviews with leadership and anecdotal reporting) to more objective standards, both in the pre- and post-implementation assessment phases. Thus, it may be appropriate to investigate establishing a scorecard for aid and NGO effectiveness, including quantitative (and not just *qualititative*) metrics, such as the number of jobs created (when measured against predictions at the outset of the project), increases in tax revenue and improvements in doing business or other competitiveness indicators.[37]

On aid results, there is a further temptation, which is for donors to give money to authoritarian leaders because 'they get things done' and there is a visible result. Hence, the preference they have had for Meles Zenawi's Ethiopia and Paul Kagame's Rwanda, for example, as partners. Of course, this implementation ability does not only reflect their leadership style, but an inherent social organisation among these populations. But it does run counter to professed support for democracy and such a 'Kigali consensus' is unlikely to be sustainable in economic and political terms.

Getting under the iceberg

In Rwanda, as in much of Africa, one frequently encounters foreign, usually American, philanthropists visiting and trying to 'do good'.

They hang out for few days in Kigali's luxury hotels, often paying homage at the genocide museum and taking in the obligatory visit to the Virunga gorillas, perhaps even a soirée or prayer breakfast with the president. Often affiliated to a church group, they are intent, usually, on feeling good about helping others. Much less often do they apparently go beyond platitudinous refrain and earnest looks and dip into their own pockets.

Of course, the Rwanda government has been completely wise to this. These modern-day missionaries bring little in the way of readies, and they certainly are not going to shape a regime that, under Kagame, knows exactly what it wants. That has not stopped some of them from trying very hard to impart their styles and fringe ideas, often infused with an extraordinarily patronising belief that local systems worked as badly as they did because they lacked their personal enlightenment. Like many other advisers they fail to appreciate that things do not happen for a reason. Regardless, the visitors offered a precious commodity – diplomatic protection and credibility for a regime with limited resources, under constant scrutiny and, as has recently been reminded over the Congo, with a sometimes controversial and unpopular view of how it ensures its own interests.

There is a plethora of advisers across Africa, among them traditional consultants offering advice on technical issues including security, NGO activists pressing home a particular agenda from AIDS to climate change, experts hired as part of the conditions of aid to ensure donor money is well spent and, more recently a new group, the 'celebronsultants' – celebrity former politicians, scruffy rock stars and actors rubbing shoulders with political leaders and frequently refugees, providing photo-snap evidence of their 'time in Africa'. Another is the group of usually young people taking time out to work on 'worthy' projects for little pay but with little justification – what one colleague described as 'first-year university for adults: sex, drugs, alcohol and no one to answer to'.

One benchmark to the growth of this advisory 'industry' is in their cost – in South Africa R3 billion (then $400 million) was spent on consultants in 2012,[38] many of them replicating the functions carried out, at least on paper, by civil servants. If one takes the UK percentage of aid expenditure on consultants as the norm across Africa, then $2.9 billion of the $33 billion in aid to Africa in 2011 was spent on advisers by donors alone.[39]

How useful are these actors? Are there some things they do better than others? Can the undoubted energies and the considerable wealth they expend be better harnessed by the very people they are supposedly there to help?[40]

There are many examples of the decline of Western influence in steering failures onto a better path, for example in delivering an acceptable 'free and fair' election outcome in Zimbabwe in July 2013. Despite sanctions against key individuals in Mugabe's ruling ZANU-PF party and multilateral and bilateral donor support for the good governance cause of the opposition Movement for Democratic Change, the election went wholly against the MDC. Similar questions could be asked as to whether outsiders can influence the overall philosophy of governments; whether, for example, they can be made more amenable to private sector interests and in so doing limit the role of the state.

As was highlighted in the Introduction, and has been seen throughout the case studies, policy choices are shaped by local political and other impulses, the 'stuff' below the tip of the (policy) iceberg. Foreigners can only usefully make policy suggestions that take root if local actors have the will to do so. The extent of such willingness reflects whether their domestic political instincts and fortunes align with the content of these external inputs. Shaping the stuff below the iceberg – customs, traditions, institutional culture and politics – depends thus less on the overall logic of the suggestion than the calculation made by leadership in assessing its political impact.

Presidential advisory bodies can have a role to play in establishing the 'ideological climate' or 'enabling environment'. Opportunity is greatest early on when presidential will and ownership are fresh and strong and opportunity to mobilise opposition not yet galvanised. Since institutional and policy reform takes perseverance, setting a climate of thinking is perhaps one of greatest contributions of such bodies.[41] There is also evidence of local players being energised by sharing best-practice ideas from open skies to the establishment, in the Rwandan case, of the national economic Development Board, modelled as it was on my laptop and in consultation with colleagues in Singapore, El Salvador and Costa Rica. Sharp interventions on specific policy aspects can also help to establish a hierarchy of priorities, and helps to hold both government and the advisory body accountable to an issue.

There remain, however, clear limits to the policy advisory role, including that of local business. Even though no country has prospered without being business-friendly, for ideological and historical reasons, there remains widespread animus to business and their views, exacerbated by the thin dividing line between advice and vested interest, although this tension applies to other advisers, too. Too often business bodies provide governments with an excuse that they have consulted with this sector, than actually hold the feet of government to the fire on specific issues. These tensions reflect government seeing business as a competitor for resources, especially true in weak states.

Even when one does get through the door, where there is willingness there is often a paucity of government capacity, notable again in weak states, which can lack the human and financial resources to digest advisory inputs made. Governments are simply overwhelmed on occasion by outsiders, most whom are disinterested in coordinating their own services, wanting to claim responsibility for success and a special relationship with local actors.

The vagaries and granularity of domestic institutional politics is sometimes less about national-international, insider-outsider issues than institutional issues, and is often the principal hurdle to sound advice gaining traction. This 'swarm' effect is worsened by 'everyone wanting to be a [Lionel] Messi' in government, to building and managing their own empires, with ministers and civil servants intent on protecting their vested institutional importance and personal ambitions, aside from the national interest. The decisions of presidents are often ignored against such inertia. 'Most politicians,' said one seasoned African official who has seen many advisers come and go, 'look first at their bellies, and are keener to listen to people in their own ministries than to their own leadership'. It is, in other words, difficult for politicians to take decisions that are not in their interests and are either not theirs or seen to be theirs.

Where more successful, external interventions not only complement indigenous domestic processes, but are cognisant of local capacity constraints, containing programmes to build local expertise and skills, and local political sensitivities over ownership. An example of this approach was in the role played by Dr Albert Winsemius in Singapore's development, the Dutch economist who became a trusted adviser of Lee Kuan Yew. He served for 23 years, assisting in shaping policy on key issues such as the establishment of the Economic Development Board. He visited Singapore twice a year, the island-state paying for his air ticket and hotel bills but nothing else. His usual methodology, recalled Lee, was to meet with officials, executives of multinational and Singaporean companies and trade unionists. He would then submit a report and brief the prime minister, his advice being characterised by a 'pragmatic, hands-on approach ... and a knack for getting to grips with the basic issues, ignoring the mass of details'.[42]

Embedded technical support can also help. Receptiveness to such a semi-permanent role is shaped partly by their origin, local 'outsiders' in government being preferred to foreign outsiders, even if they are funded internationally. Generally, however, embedded support is preferable to outsider pundits parachuting in sporadically. It improves the 'sense of ownership and respect among the locals', as one official has noted, 'as well as sustainability and usefulness'.

When things are really desperate there has been a role for outsiders in promoting corrective economic reforms, though this has proven a highly unpopular role, politically and ideologically contentious, and subject to reversal when the tough going gets better.

In the view of the World Bank chief economist for Africa, Shantanayan Devarajan,[43] in 2013, 'There is no question that one of the major reasons for Africa's growth over the last 10–15 years is because macroeconomic policies have improved. Average inflation is half of what it was in the 1990s. Fiscal deficits are down; current account deficits are down. The reason,' he says, 'is that African policymakers followed Structural Adjustment Programmes over the last 10–15 years. It worked, it delivered results. It delivered economic growth and poverty reduction. You can't dispute that.' He explains the criticism of structural adjustment policies as 'not that the policies were wrong' but that they were 'designed in Washington, London and Paris' rather than 'Abuja, Yaoundé and Nairobi'. Instead the Bank has picked up criticism, for example, for its structural adjustment policies, being accused of a 'major source of poverty' of encouraging a 'race to the bottom' in terms of labour prices and living standards, and of maintaining 'dependency and poverty'.[44] The plan that African leaders came up with on debt relief in many respects mirrored the much-maligned conditionalities of structural adjustment, yet they were home-grown solutions, not imposed, and thus acceptable, not least since few other policy options remained.

The greatest cost of advisory efforts is twofold: first in maintaining the illusion that the solution, like the problem, is external. And second, by a focus on reforming bits of the system, when the problem is in the nature of the overall system – the political economy. For example, Blair's African Governance Initiative (AGI), which, by 2013, was operating in seven African countries,[45] focuses on improving government communication and organisation specifically within the various presidencies. There is nothing wrong with that per se, that is if it does not prove a distraction and a diplomatic fig leaf for the need to make difficult political decisions about economic choices; simply tinkering with rather than overhauling the system of government that got them into trouble in the first instance. The problems are not technical – they are fundamentally political, requiring much more than improved flow charts and messaging from '100 brilliant people from over 15 countries and across the public, private and third sectors', according to the AGI,[46] scuttling about earnestly in the offices of African governments. Blair's term in office, after all, should have reminded of the limits of spin doctors.

Volumes of anodyne papers on security and governance, and, especially, visits by insufferable celebrities have proven of little help in shifting political debates and, especially, in fabricating solutions. Regardless, the celebrity and consultancy business is unlikely to change. Brace yourself for more visits by ageing rockers and the odd airhead actress. Their focus will, in time, shift with public attention, as leaders and causes fall out of and into favour. They largely remain a tool for domestic political leadership to prove their international credentials; occasionally useful idiots to sometimes malign political causes.

In summary, outsiders to government can make a difference if their advice aligns with wider public concerns and synchs with government interests and intent. This was the case, for example, with the 'High Road, Low Road' scenarios prepared by Anglo American in the late 1980s, which helped simultaneously to prepare the domestic mood for political change and provide pressure on Pretoria to do so.[47] The success of policy advice, however, depends more often than not on its intrinsic soundness, rather the relationships that enable access and thereby can give reason and comfort to decision-makers. In other words, the best ideas count for nought if you cannot get through the door, and even then, while you might get a hearing, the argument is less about national interests than personal political advantage, Formal structures – including business organisations and presidential advisory and policy groups – may help, but largely inasmuch as they offer access to build these often highly personalised relationships, where access and traction seems, from experience, to hinge less on institutions than reputations and personal dynamics.

The search for quiet professionals

So, how to win the peace? This chapter suggests that the current narrative on aid – that it promotes economic development and economic development promotes stability – starts from a flawed premise. Aid itself has become part of the problem because too little consideration has been given to the way it is distributed, especially in post-conflict environments.

Foreign aid and assistance can only help facilitate the conditions that permit members of the society itself to develop locally appropriate forms of responsive government and achieve reconciliation between former adversaries. There is no substitute for bottom-up buy-in in this context: outsiders can never achieve what locals themselves are not willing to follow through on.

But pure bottom-up efforts rarely work alone. External assistance could therefore be better focused on 'stability multipliers': enabling new business formation; electricity, water and roads are key; as is assistance aimed at improving the professionalism of civil government, police and the military, ensuring that they do not become predatory institutions.

Promoting the growth of local small and medium business needs a more prominent place in the planners' repertoire. Such entities can often scale up without considerable investment in time and skills. Even in immediate post-conflict environments, or in the aftermath of major natural disasters when civil society seems prostrate and incapable, it is almost always better to work through local private sector business, providing opportunities for small, self-defined and community-generated projects, than to funnel assistance solely through government structures. Paying individuals on a cash-for-work basis is vastly less beneficial than helping people set up their own local businesses, creating cross-sectional interests and making people stakeholders in stability rather than entrepreneurs in the business of rent-seeking and the manipulation of foreign assistance.

Perhaps the greatest challenge is in tackling the vested institutional and personal interests that keep the donor and NGO system as it is. A $33-plus billion annual aid tranche to Africa (almost a quarter of the overseas development assistance annual total pledged worldwide) provides at least as many opportunities for enrichment to those giving as those on the receiving end. An unfortunate element of the 'aid business' is the rush to plaster every 'good deed' with some signpost indicating the donor. While understandable, it is also part of an unsightly game that has more to do with capturing budget shares and professional rivalries among donors than making concrete impacts on the ground.

Instead of advertising what is being provided by outsiders, media communications strategy should aim to engage with the issues affecting the local population, strengthening the local governance dimension. Recognising the need to put local interests first rather than those of donors is a crucial step, as is guarding against the tautology that the aid world can become.

*

'Give a man a fish,' goes the cliché, 'and you will feed him for a day. Teach him to fish, and you will feed him for life.' In post-conflict reconstruction there is little disagreement about the need to teach people to fish. The question, however, is for how long? How many times do you have to teach before cutting people loose? To stretch the analogy further, what of the potential problems of overfishing and the tensions between fishing communities? But teaching people to fish also offers the prospect of helping them set up businesses, of selling fish and selling them fishing equipment. And so begins a reinforcing cycle of recovery and prosperity.

There is a wealth of engineering and other expertise available to work in such situations, one of the positive if unintended consequences of Iraq and Afghanistan. These are men and women in the mould of the frontier diplomat as described by Peter Hopkirk in *The Great Game*.[48] Young officers, British and Russian, risked their lives promoting imperial interests in a difficult region, a contest described on the Russian side as 'this tournament of shadows'. Disguised as holy men, horse traders, or in Captain Arthur Conolly's case a doctor, they mapped secret passes, gathered intelligence and negotiated alliances and deals with powerful khans. It was a mission fraught with danger, some never returning. Hopkirk's tale opens with the execution of Colonel Charles Stoddart and the man who coined the term 'Great Game' many years before Kipling made it famous in *Kim*, Captain Conolly, in the dusty great square behind the emir's palace in the central Asian town of Bokhara in June 1842. 'Their arms were tied tightly behind their backs, and they were in a pitiful condition. Filthy and half-starved, their bodies were covered with sores, their hair, beards and clothes alive with lice ... [They] were paying the price of engaging in a highly dangerous game ... Moments after Stoddart's beheading, Conolly was also dispatched, and today the two men's remains lie, together with the Emir's many other victims, in a grisly and long-forgotten graveyard somewhere beneath the square.' Conolly, of the 6th Bengal Native Light Cavalry, was one of the first of the British empire's 'young bloods' sent into the field to reconnoitre the 'military and political no-man's-land between the Caucasus and the Khyber'.[49]

Equally, the twenty-first-century version demanded people capable of 'making a plan', ever being resourceful, learning on the job and relying on intuition perhaps beyond all else in being tossed into difficult if not near-impossible circumstances. As Rory Stewart, who as a young man was expected to assume a position of such 'authority' as part of a team tasked with bringing stability and reconstruction to Amara in the south of Iraq in 2003, observes: 'I had acquired near-absolute authority over eight hundred and fifty thousand people. A CPA [Coalition Provisional Authority] governorate co-ordinator ranked theoretically as a one-star general.'[50]

New methods for aid delivery and new roles for donors should not be invented simply to prolong their mission, however, whatever the bureaucratic imperative or personal self-interest. Herein is a critical related lesson for fragile states in particular: it is not enough to get just the hardware (ports, roads, railways and airports) right, which donors can deliver at least in part, but also the human software systems. Both combine to shape the prospects for growth and development. 'Softer' issues relate to mindset, child nutrition and food security, skills, public administration, the utility and functioning of borders, the extent to which identity questions or policy issues shape political choices, self-respect and the ability fundamentally to develop employment opportunities beyond the state, requiring a private sector and policies and practices that encourage its growth. To conclude: the positive, long-term impact of the role of donors – their role beyond assisting with stabilisation – fundamentally depends on whether they stop funding and whether the locals take responsibility.

33

THE PRIVATE SECTOR

Melting the Iceberg and the Zen Master

*

In *Charlie Wilson's War*, Congressman Wilson, played by Tom Hanks, and CIA case officer Gust Avrakotos (Philip Seymour Hoffman) are chatting on the balcony of Wilson's Watergate condo in the afterglow of the Soviet retreat from Afghanistan in February 1989. While the party celebrates inside, Wilson says, 'Well, I told you … all we had to do [was] shoot down the helicopters.' Avrakotos cautions him with his story of the Zen master: 'There's a little boy and on his fourteenth birthday he gets a horse,' he says, 'and everybody in the village says, "How wonderful. The boy got a horse." And the Zen master says, "We'll see." Two years later, the boy falls off the horse, breaks his leg, and everyone in the village says, "How terrible." And the Zen master says, "We'll see." Then, a war breaks out and all the young men have to go off and fight except the boy can't cause his leg is all messed up, and everybody in the village says, "How wonderful."' Wilson chips in: 'Now the Zen master says, "We'll see."' Gust: 'So you get it?' Charlie: 'No. No, cause I'm stupid.' Gust: 'You're not stupid, you're just in Congress.'

The point the CIA man was making is that the really hard work is not in stopping a war or defeating an adversary, but what comes after the guns fall silent. 'Start with the roads, move on to the schools, restock the sheep herds, give 'em jobs, give 'em hope,' Gust implores. 'I'm trying,' says Wilson. 'Try harder,' tests Avrakotos. Wilson, the unlikely activist who had virtually single-handedly mobilised Congressional funding for the mujahidin, responds: 'I took you from five million [dollars in aid] to a billion. I broke this ice on this thing – I got a Democratic congress in lockstep behind a Republican president.' Gust: 'That's not good enough. Because I am about to hand you a code-word classified NIE [national intelligence estimate] right now and it's gonna tell you that the crazies have started rolling into Kandahar like it's a fuckin bathtub drain.' 'Jesus, Gust, you could depress a bride on her wedding day,' retorts Wilson.

The failure to backfill with development after the retreat of the Soviets was not lost on the larger-than-life Representative from Texas, who later attempts to explain this challenge to his Congressional colleagues: 'Half the population of that country is under the age of fourteen ... now think how fuckin dangerous that is. They are going to come home and find their families are dead, their villages have been napalmed.' In response to his colleague's interjection that 'we helped kill the guys who did it', Wilson says, 'But they don't know that, Bob, cause they don't get home delivery of the *New York Times*. And even if they did, it was covert, remember. This is what we always do. We go in with our ideals and we change the world. And then we leave. We always leave.'

Whereas Wilson had lobbied successfully to fund the mujahidin, he failed in his subsequent Congressional struggle for the US to remain engaged in Afghanistan, creating in his mind the power vacuum that allowed the rise of the Taliban, a safe haven for Al-Qaeda and the events of 9/11. As Wilson (rather than his movie version) put it, 'These things happened. They were glorious and they changed the world. And then we fucked up the end game.'

The wording might be a little different, but he is not alone in these sentiments. Testifying before the US Congress in December 2009, Robert Gates, the defence secretary under presidents George W. Bush and Barack Obama, criticised the decision to pull back support twenty years earlier, saying that the US 'abandoned that country only to see it descend into chaos and into Taliban hands'.[1] Secretary Gates said earlier that 'I feel a certain sense of personal responsibility' in testifying before the House Armed Services Committee in December 2007. 'I was deputy director of CIA and then deputy national security advisor during the period when the Soviets did withdraw from Afghanistan, and the United States essentially turned its back on Afghanistan. And five years later came the first attack on the World Trade Center. And so, you know, one of the lessons that I think we have is that if we abandon these countries, once we are in there and engaged, there is a very real possibility that we will pay a higher price in the end.'

Gates has stressed: 'We will not repeat the mistake – we must not repeat the mistake of 1989, and turn our backs on these folks. And when we've got the security situation with them under control, then the civilian and the development part must be the preponderant part of our relationship far into the future.'

This is easier said than done, however, not least since success is beyond the power alone of the US.

As was noted in the previous chapter, the economic realm is perhaps the most neglected and least understood patch of the post-conflict and recovery landscape. Yet, economic growth is critical in determining whether a country successfully emerges from failure or conflict and becomes stable and peaceful, or instead lapses back into war. In particular, the private sector in such environments is often weak or compromised, alienated from local governments and viewed with suspicion by donors, so incapable of becoming the engine of growth that it has successfully proven in other development examples.

How might this positively change, all the way from stability to development?

Stopping fighting

Political instability and especially conflict nearly always damage economic growth. The GDP of Libya, for instance, contracted by as much as 60 per cent in 2011. War also increases poverty. The World Bank notes that 'for every three years that a country is affected by major violence … poverty reduction lags behind by 2.7 percentage points'.[2] Liberia's President Ellen Johnson Sirleaf has said that 'there is no development without peace and security'.[3] This may be so, but equally there is no long-term security without development. The huge expenditure of military resources, of blood and treasure, in Iraq and Afghanistan, teaches of the limits of a security-led solution.

Certainly, there have been times that peace leads to prosperity. Think only of Japan or Germany after the Second World War. Nevertheless, in both these cases external assistance and peace built on the solid foundations of previously well-organised and managed, skilled societies. Frequently, development success after conflict is not the rule. From South Sudan to Afghanistan, Congo to Somalia, it has proven very difficult to get war-torn economies back up and running, and independent from outside aid. The period of recovery has also proven as a rule as least as long as the period of decline, and even then, it is not certain that countries will recover.

This is among the most elemental of all the lessons to emerge from international interventions of the past quarter-century of post-Cold War years, the first generation of peace-building missions and the countless workshops, studies, papers, consultancies and conferences they have in turn spawned. As has been seen in this volume, the security, or stabilisation, aspect of such missions follows a well-trodden path: a ceasefire (or military victory), a political settlement that is often the outcome of international facilitation and local negotiations, elections followed sometimes by a unity government, and the disarmament, demobilisation and reintegration of former combatants. All this does not, of course, occur in an economic vacuum. This explains why donor money is usually employed to get things up and running.

A complex mix of ingredients is therefore necessary for this process to keep moving forward, but often insufficient for success. Success with stability does not only depend on improved security, or better governance, or a responsive and responsible government, or better technical skills, or more money or efficient infrastructure: it demands all of these things, and more. It requires a strategic conceptualisation of the problem that got these countries into trouble in the first instance, which invariably goes to the nature of the political economy – where the primary intention is usually to promote narrow interests, to pamper elites, to favour the middleman over creating a middle class. This illustrates the paucity of independent sources of wealth creation and the ineffectiveness of government policy in developing the private sector.

No matter the 'formula' or recipe for external engagement, success is unlikely without addressing the deeper issues that lie behind conflict.

Cementing stability

A half-century of reform teaches that development relies on sustaining a virtuous cycle in which economic recovery and political stability are mutually reinforcing. Economic recovery has a number of political jobs to do: in the short run, it is needed to placate or neutralise political opposition (both in terms of ex-combatants and the parliamentary legislature); build support for government in both the non-urban areas and the capital (that will last beyond the first term); and to signal a return of confidence and change for the better.

To achieve this, it must, firstly, return per capita GDP to pre-conflict levels (adjusted for population growth and changed commodity prices). Secondly, it must build the revenue base of the government to levels that

602 — WHY STATES RECOVER

allow public investment and service delivery to normalise. Thirdly, it must increase labour absorption to promote political and social stability and reduce poverty. Lastly, it must build the minimum infrastructure base for a modern economy, which requires focusing on power, roads and ports.

Along with ensuring peace and security, stability can be helped and economic growth accelerated by reinstating traditional economic drivers (usually mineral and agriculture commodities) along with improving basic infrastructure and services. This can be boosted by sectoral reforms, especially freeing up those areas of infrastructure – transport and ports – that clog trade and those, such as electricity, that otherwise hinder the creation of skills and the working of industry. While a lot of effort is spent on addressing barriers to trade, the greater rewards, at least in the short term, are more likely to come from better logistics, not adjusted tariffs. This requires, first, dealing with soft infrastructure issues, notably customs, and synchronising these, later, with longer-term, 'hard' infrastructural priorities and purchases.

Immediate improvements can create both a reform 'aroma' – a sense of progress and thus domestic confidence and political support for the recovery, along with more income and jobs. That is seldom enough, however, especially where expectations are high and fuelled by global media access. It is also necessary to devise and create a new economic model, which offers the opportunity for more inclusive growth. The elite-driven, self-enrichment model, where vested interests trump national development needs, has to be broken, in part by addressing corruption and influence of such interests.

Here is a key dilemma. The very people who take over after conflict has subsided are often interested in perpetuating the same predatory system that led to collapse in the first instance, albeit with a different cast (or hierarchy) of characters. They are more focused on the transactional aspect of investment, where they can make money, rather than in the development value of the inflows. Think here the Democratic Republic of Congo, for example, where there has been little difference in this respect between the Belgians, Mobutu and the two Kabilas, father and son, Laurent-Désiré and Joseph.

Melting the iceberg

From international experience the steps to recovery are clear. Development is not a mystery, hence rapid change over decades, especially in Southeast Asia. There are many examples to follow, for big and small countries, and for those both resource rich and poor, and along the full spectrum from outright state collapse and civil war to economic reform and diversification. Those who recover quickly, whatever the nature of that recovery, 'have a good crisis', whether this be Costa Rica after its currency and debt crisis in the mid-1980s; El Salvador's 22-year civil war that left 75 000 dead and where its GDP fell 20 per cent; Singapore in 1965 with the dissolution of the Malay Federation and internal political and economic turmoil; Colombia in 2002 with the guerrillas moving to a semi-conventional phase of warfare when together they and the Escobarian drug lords had gained the upper hand over the government; or Vietnam in the mid-1980s where its command economy had seen widespread famine and ushered in the period of *doi moi* reforms, leading to 7 per cent growth for nearly three decades. From 1992, Salvador followed a path of privatisation, tax reform, dollarisation in 2001, and trade liberalisation, reducing poverty in 20 years from 60 per cent to 34 per cent. Costa Rica went quickly from producing bananas as its main export to producing, by 2010, one quarter of the world's computer chips, where exports rose 10 per cent per annum from $870 million in 1983 to over $10 billion in 2008, built on openness to trade and capital, with brains and common sense as the principal policy tools.[4]

In each of these and other cases, governments were successful at reforms when they acted fast, instituted tough reform, and did not spare their own political constituencies, notably the civil service. Insiders need to admit and identify failures, not just outsiders.

There is also a general need for proactivity, since we know that, especially in situations of extreme poverty, there may not be clear warning signs of a crisis that could cause collapse. Many governments have been surprised at the speed and suddenness of failure. During the 2000s, examples include the coup against the regime in Mali, once lauded as a model, if unlikely, African reformer; Arab states during the 'Spring' from 2010; and even, four years later, the crisis in Ukraine. Often it is too late to act when the need for change becomes clear. In all these cases, reforms were not undertaken piecemeal but as a whole batch – affecting governance, public spending and private sector growth – at once.

But more is necessary. As was argued in the Introduction, recovery of states is akin to an iceberg. The stuff that can be seen, the tip, is the terrain on which outsiders attempt to work with insiders in changing for the better, by shaping policy through a 'formula' of technical and advisory assistance, and better and smarter aid targeting. Yet, recovery demands far more than just better policy, as important as that is. State recovery is a systemic problem, a problem with a political economy, one solved not just by removing a few personalities and tinkering with governance niceties. There are several other dimensions to this aspect of change, which involve both policy matters and the things, too, under the iceberg – culture, tradition and, especially, politics. The system that gives rise to conflict and failure centres usually around elite enrichment, ethno-political agendas and exclusion, an inability to grasp the centrality of international economic competiveness, burgeoning population growth and related urbanisation, and widening inequality.

This is the model where the aforementioned middleman rules, the trader, the licensing or customs official, the handler of agricultural goods between the seller and purchaser, the politician who relies on access and preferences to safeguard business interests, or the monopoly passing on costs to the consumer, the transport companies acting as fronts for politicians and officials. Fundamentally, this necessitates acting against corruption, and putting the civil service in its place. In other words, there can be no sacred cows for reform to deliver.

Part of this 'cultural' shift includes overcoming any aversion to the private sector, which is likely to determine the impact of reforms and the speed of recovery. As we have seen, failure stems in part from when the government – or at least the political hierarchy – is in many circumstances unwilling to lessen their grip on the levers of control, power, patronage and wealth. Take Egypt as an example. As noted, at the turn of the century, the public sector comprised more than half of all investments. While by 2014, this had turned around to where private investors supplied two-thirds, the sectors of energy, health care and transport were relatively devoid of private involvement, and remain poor performers. On average, globally half of health expenses are met 'out of pocket', that is, by the patient. The average of such personal 'out of pocket' expenditure in high-income countries is just 13 per cent, the bulk being met by health insurance. But the figure in Egypt is 98 per cent. In other words, the majority of Egyptians are dependent on exceptionally poor public (rather than private) health care, a burden on the state that could be offset by allowing the private sector in.[5]

Private sector recovery requires, as is argued above, getting corrupt government out of the way, and this includes efforts by donor governments to prevent predatory extraction by local governments, as well as efforts to reduce direct government involvement in business activity. Good governance is absolutely essential. But what governments must do is regulate and support, not expropriate and extract. The private sector should be regulated in a way that *minimises* risk to investors, citizens and governments alike and *maximises* opportunity for local entrepreneurs, and lowers the cost of the formalisation of businesses. By helping to turn informal businesses into formal ones, the state can increase its tax revenues while entrepreneurs will have greater access to finance and security. Crucially, however, the state must ensure that tax regimes are kept as straightforward as possible and rates high enough to build necessary state capacity, but reciprocated by affordable service delivery to especially the poor and vulnerable, institutional systems and ethics, ensuring transparency and accountability as a quid pro quo to revenue collection.

The preference for state control is usually not only because other options do not exist. Frequently, it can be because it is instinctively what countries want to provide to their citizens, both out of responsibility as well as out of the desire for 'cradle to grave' control. It can take a variety of forms, not least in heavy government borrowing (for example, as in Zambia or Malawi) to pay recurrent expenditures, such as civil service salaries, rather than to make investments in health, education and other long-term public goods. This has the impact of driving up interest rates, compounding the challenges facing private entrepreneurs in borrowing money for their businesses.[6] Thus, the term 'crowding out' refers both to government spending that uses up resources that would otherwise be used by the private sector, or to a situation where government attempts to deliver a service or good that could be provided by private enterprise.

As has been observed in the variety of case studies, this 'crowding out' feature cuts across more extreme and pernicious forms of state involvement, such as that in illicit activities.

Undoing illicit networks

A key part of stabilisation is in undoing the influence of those who profit from instability – Afghanistan's power brokers, Congolese warlords, and Colombian or Burmese drug smugglers. There is a wealth of material available as to how criminal networks have penetrated weak states to their advantage, building up and employing international networks.[7]

West Africa is one instance, where the global cocaine trade (peaking at 47 tonnes in 2007, and worth several billion dollars) and methamphetamine production along with regional weapons flows and migrant smuggling into Europe are core areas of transnational criminal activity.[8] In East Africa, to take another example, according to a 2013 United Nations Office on Drugs and Crime (UNODC) report, more than 100 000 people were smuggled out of that region in 2012, generating an estimated $15 million for organised criminal networks employing the maritime crossing from the Horn of Africa. Ivory poaching, amounting to around 150 tonnes annually, created an additional $30 million in illicit revenue from Asian markets alone, with up to 15 000 elephants poached in the eastern African region annually. Up to 22 tonnes of heroin is, according to the UNODC, trafficked to and through the region every year. Piracy out of bases in the north of Somalia was assessed by the UNODC to be worth an estimated $150 million in 2011, equivalent to almost 15 per cent of that country's GDP, though this had come down given changes both in Somalia and on the high seas with a comprehensive international naval response.

Such activities can directly challenge state authority. As noted in the case of Mali, both criminal and political groups have taken advantage and profited from the weakness of the central government in Bamako, leading to the overthrow of the democratic state. This was in part a consequence, as has been seen, of Muammar Gaddafi's violent departure from power in Libya in 2011, as the Tripoli regime was a key source of income for Mali and a brake on insurgent movements. Colombia offers another example, but one where the state has successfully fought back in breaking the link between an insurgency and narco-trafficking.

These illustrations are not unique as explanations of the relationship between state fragility and illicit criminal networks, even though they are among the more obvious portrayals. In other instances, the state is the deliberate target for sophisticated capture rather than avoidance or for deliberate attack.

Overall, three overlapping types of state interaction with criminal elements can be identified in this regard – in so-called 'liberation states', where there are ongoing insurgencies, and in fragile states.

In states where liberation movements have taken over (including Angola, Mozambique, Zimbabwe and South Africa) and remain in power, old networks and attitudes combined with fresh post-liberation access to state contracts produce one category of criminal (or at least quasi-criminal) activity. During the 1980s, for example, elements of the South African liberation movements were (allegedly) engaged in extensive smuggling activities centring around vehicles out of South Africa and drugs, among other goods. Crime syndicates and liberation structures thus worked hand-in-hand, enabling the liberation movement to in- and ex-filtrate armed cadres, as well as getting weapons past border patrols. Ironically, the South African (apartheid) state itself, was at the same time, creating unusual business bedfellows of political foes in order to obtain weapons and oil for a country confronted by international sanctions. It should be noted that international sanctions, irrespective of how well intended, often has had this as a consequence, namely that domestic crime syndicates and international organised crime groups gained a foothold that would later prove to be difficult to undo: for crime and country it seems.

Today, informed by an entitlement culture, and infused by access to government contracting and a disregard for state authority, this activity continues in different ways: at the more benign end of the scale in the form of 'tenderpreneuring' (contracts for pals), at the more extreme, the links between the state and organised crime networks.[9] What may be defined by some as organised crime, for others is simply justifiable reward in this situation, reflecting also neo-patrimonial, redistributive state tendencies in the use of its revenue base and institutional legitimacy as a means for patronage and clientelism.

The peculiar nature of the Angolan, Zimbabwean and Mozambican political economy each produces specifics in this regard, but the overall ethos is the same: the state is at the centre of these relationships and the aim is its maintenance, contractual health and revenue base. A strong and independent private sector is a potential threat, given its challenge as a competitor to these relationships, hence at an extreme the deliberate and insidious 'crowding out' of its activities and use of ideological pretexts (notions of the development state, for example) in limiting its latitude for operating.

There is a difference in tone between the first generation of liberation movements (in southern Africa in the main) and the second elsewhere in sub-Saharan Africa, such as Ethiopia, Rwanda and Uganda, where insurgent leaders who fought against their own (rather than colonial) governments have taken over. But the same control features pervade, along with access to and the distribution of preferential contracts.

This first category, where the state is strong and a key distributive node, is different, however, from a second type: that of the insurgent state. In this regard, there is a need to distinguish between nationalistic movements (those fighting for capture of the state only, such as the Revolutionary Armed Forces of Colombia or FARC) and those with a wider transnational agenda (for example, Islamic movements in the Sahel such as Al-Qaeda in the Islamic Maghreb) or elements of both (such as Nigeria's Boko Haram or Al-Shabab in Somalia/Kenya/Uganda). In both, however, the methods and the aims (to gain control of the state or states) are similar. Advantage is taken of ungoverned spaces and porous borders. The range of activities and income includes piracy to drug and cigarette smuggling to skimming remittance flows.

The third instance is that of the failing or failed state. Here there are limited opportunities for state contracting. The aim, unlike in the case of the insurgent state, is not to overthrow the state per se, but rather to use both its weakness and legitimacy and protection it affords to engage in transnational criminal activities, including drugs (Guinea-Bissau is an example), charcoal (Al-Shabab in Somalia, in areas that it has physically controlled) or minerals (Congo). International connectivity, state atrophy and the penetration and control of its institutions are key attributes to the criminal, not least since key changes in the African state came at the same time as shifts in both the global licit and illicit economy, whether this be the growing cocaine market in Europe or the growth in the Asian middle class, and the subsequent demand for rhino horn, ivory and wood, that have transformed criminal flows in Africa and corrupted institutions. Criminality does not then demand fragility. But fragility can be exacerbated by state weakness in a number of respects: by funding rebel or criminal groups, challenging state authority, providing incentives both for policy-makers to focus away 'from law enforcement to appropriation' and for others to engage in violence, and by instigating conflict between competing groups.[10]

In this third category of state, war economies morph into criminal economies. Illicit networks used to supply armed groups, such as those in the Congo, have transitioned into those for criminal gain. Security institutions stand at the centre of this network and in essence become criminal enterprises in their own right, leading not only to inefficiency but to internal conflict, creating an ability to exist outside of the fiscus, and promoting alignment with corrupt political actors.[11]

In all three categories, the political economy can be described as closed (keep the private sector out) if paradoxically open to illicit forms of trading activity and dominated by the informal sector and a 'rentier' state.[12] In all three of these types, it is unclear where the state ends and crime begins, and whether a strong state (with greater efficiencies) will produce more crime or less, given that the revenue and contractual opportunity advantages this offers have to be balanced against the impact of more effective institutions. But in all three, it demands electorates managing the financial urges of elites.

Private sector donor alignment

Getting the politics right is thus crucial, not only in terms of a peace settlement, but also the economics. Outsiders seeking to influence these countries in a positive direction have to show that democracy, the rule of law and liberal economics makes sense, not crony capitalism and authoritarianism or radicalism.

In broken societies, where local resources are often minimal and, like confidence, public and private investment low, there is a need to attract foreign inflows. This requires understanding what attracts and deters investment. The work by Ricardo Hausmann, Dani Rodrik and Andrés Velasco[13] identifies three sources of such constraints: the cost and/or scarcity of capital (which link to poor integration with global markets, poor financial intermediation or low domestic saving), low productivity (relating to human capital, infrastructure or geography), or poor institutions (including high tax rates, corruption and macro risks). Such an analysis is important as is an understanding of where the highest returns exist for post-conflict environments in terms of growth and jobs. Here, construction lends itself to high returns while, at the same time, not only visibly offering a perspective of change but in so doing removing longer-term infrastructure constraints. This is not to suggest, however, that post-conflict recovery and prosperity is dependent on the sort of innovation required by developed economies; on the contrary, success will largely be measured in terms of reinstating the traditional drivers of growth and improving quantities (rather than qualities) of production of existing goods.

As noted in the previous chapter, donors can improve their role to benefit failed states. As time progresses, and as a fragile state turns its attention from reinstating the drivers of growth and setting the stage for private sector investment, the role for donors inevitably turns to infrastructure financing and policy advice.

For example, Collier, again, has detailed a number of ways in which donors can help fragile states through 'pioneer investments'. Assisting with the establishment of competent and transparent local bureaucratic capability is one aspect, with the aim to reduce corruption and rent-seeking while developing key areas of capacity, including in tax collection. Another is to subsidise key areas of infrastructure, such as electricity provision. He has recommended the evolution of development agency private finance arms (such as the International Finance Corporation, the Dutch Entrepreneurial Development Bank and the Commonwealth Development Corporation) so that they are capable of integrating commercial and economic criteria into their investment decisions. In terms of reducing the political risk barriers to investment, current providers such as the US government's Overseas Private Investment Corporation and the World Bank's Multilateral Investment Guarantee Agency, could be better integrated into the work of their associated development agencies, enabling development finance to be used to subsidise the provision of political risk to private investors.[14]

There is also a need to craft regional solutions. For example, border flows of people, weapons, diamonds and other goods, and issues have defined the Mano River Union encompassing Côte d'Ivoire, Liberia, Guinea and Sierra Leone. As the deputy commander of the UN mission in Côte d'Ivoire has noted, 'Just as the problems lie regionally, so do the solutions.' This is not only in terms of the flow of weapons and cross-border problems, but practicality in terms of, he says, 'the ease of raising money as an integrated group rather than as individual states'.[15]

Fixing such economies is thus very difficult. Not only, as with Zimbabwe, does it demand straightening out the macroeconomic issues, an often delicate task given the vested political and commercial interests in keeping things in these places as unstable as they mostly are. It additionally requires giving the locals a stake in change, even though they might not have the capacity to carry out this change themselves. And it means fixing these economies within the very state structures that gave rise to these crises in the first instance.

Moving along the recovery spectrum

What should follow once the fighting has stopped and stability is in place? How could economies easiest move from donor life support to prosperity and self-sufficiency?

A high-growth development 'story' for fragile states involves addressing both comparative and competitive advantages, of (usually) digging things out the ground on the one hand, and making them on the other. The former especially demands regulatory clarity and predictability, the avoidance of over-bureaucratisation, lower infrastructure costs and reducing policy uncertainty (that is, if you threaten to nationalise, forget it).

The latter, which centres on improving competitiveness, requires all of these things and more. At the outset, at its foundation, skills are essential. Getting educational establishments to provide this is, at least in fragile states, often a difficult, expensive and tedious task. They seem to give very little bang for considerable buck. But educational establishments are not the only way to create these. People learning in jobs is one other way.

Singapore's transformation, like the other sustained high-growth Asian and Latin American as well as some east European experiences, emphasises key policy and societal aspects in progressing from stabilisation to development. Naturally, every situation has its nuances and variances, and it is important not to attempt to apply these, exactly templatically again, from one case to another, as Harvard's Matt Andrews has reminded.[16] Regardless, there are certain reform commonalities, without which development, as measured in the growth of sustainable jobs and not only GDP, is difficult to envision, including:

Jobs, incentives and wealth creation: Jobs are created, at least over the long term, by countries attracting those businesses that can go anywhere with their investment. This is done through a combination of sound and predictable policy, including the tax rates, a labour regime that equates skills with costs via productivity on a global basis, a political regime that minimises days lost to strikes and seeks to give ongoing leadership and comfort to investors, and the provision of cheap and reliable hard and soft infrastructure. All this requires not only a competitive policy but political regime, with all the necessary checks and balances that go with it.

This policy approach is sometimes disparaged as a race to the bottom in terms of labour rates; but this argument conveniently (since this is usually politically or ideologically driven) overlooks that the rise 'upwards' is fundamentally dependent on skills – or perhaps this argument is used to let governments and their people off this hook of responsibility? Governments should also avoid picking winners in creating state industries or in backing private industry with incentives, since the market does this better than any other mechanism. Indeed, the provision of incentives without the emphasis on the other aspects above can only ultimately be a race to the bottom, as countries outbid each other in desperate attempt to buy jobs. This sort of state behaviour can also incentivise the wrong sort of corrupt, rent-seeking elite practices. Incentives – and their corollary, disincentives – have to be carefully thought through in other dimensions. Aid can also distort accountability, drive government energy in a direction that has limited rewards compared to private capital, and be unsustainable without subsidies. And what incentive is there to be attractive to all capital when there are other, perhaps less politically palatable, alternatives out there?

Competitiveness, benchmarking and innovation: In addition to the factors highlighted above, there is a continuous need for reinvention and keeping ahead of country competitors with regard to productivity. Competitiveness is, after all, a marathon with no finishing line. Benchmarking is needed on key indicators – the time taken (rather than the number of steps) for clearances at border posts and ports is one that explains a plethora of efficiencies. But there should not be too many of these, since the greater the number, the greater the governmental wiggle room and the skewing of measurements. 'We are the best at giving credit' is not the same as 'we are the fastest at customs clearance' or 'most reliable, widespread or cheapest electricity provider'. And in this there is a requirement for human efficiency. As Lee Kuan Yew has noted, the 'single decisive factor' in Singapore's success has been the 'ability of its ministers and high quality of civil servants who supported them'.[17]

Openness and capital: Despite the lukewarm attitudes in some capitals towards the benefits of globalisation, successful rapid-development countries adopted an attitude of openness to trade and capital, with brains and common sense as the principal policy tools. For example, until India dropped its xenophobia towards free enterprise, free markets and foreign trade and investments, it was doomed to experience a 'Hindu rate of low growth'. As the (Indian) co-founder of the IT giant Infosys, Nandan Nilekani, has noted, 'Openness [is] ... a no-brainer, especially considering that a still-developing economy needs multipliers like trade to give our entrepreneurs the markets they need to expand and our price-sensitive consumers the widest possible choice of goods.'[18] Dropping chauvinism abroad requires doing so also at home: success demands ensuring equal access for women since no country can develop when it hinders, or even disqualifies, half its population from full participation.

Natural resource management: Often, as was seen in the first section of this book on state pathologies, these endowments are prevalent among fragile states. They can provide a catalyst for development, a boost to exports and government revenue. To do so, such resources and their proceeds have to be carefully managed to provide the sustained basis for development everywhere, that is, jobs and private wealth creation. And this is especially so in an increasingly capital-intensive mining environment, where direct mining jobs are going to become more scarce, especially where business prefers their mechanical reliability over union volatility. It is also crucial not to confuse elite wealth accumulation with broad-based empowerment, a burring usually preferred by those preaching resource nationalism.

Get the philosophical basics right: All of the above stresses getting the basics right. If countries get rich by making things that others want to buy and selling them, there is a need to be better organised, more efficient and more competitive than others. This requires recognition that growth has to be driven by entrepreneurs, not the state, and yet that development depends on working together, and on a united and determined leadership. There is a need for 'coalitions of growth', having champions of reform, in and out of government. Failure is guaranteed where there are oligarchic, out of touch elites lording it in conditions of extreme inequality, where states live constantly beyond their means (such as Argentina) and with no responsibility, or where the country goes for glamour projects (such as airlines over agriculture, foreign travel over infrastructure, or politically expedient, if expensive, technological solutions without addressing the human interface). This can only serve to divert scarce talent and scant resources. Social cohesion – *inclusiveness* – is important, as is ending conflict, given that it stunts potential and drains resources.

In all of the above, the establishment of macroeconomic fundamentals is taken for granted, including: balanced budgets, low inflation, stable monetary regime and policy predictability. Fiscal prudence and discipline begins at home, at the top with leadership setting the best example, and in government. The overall mantra has to be to make the country an easier place to do business, with stability in policy regimes and easy access. This has to be motivated by a positive narrative of national-driven governance and development, with a vision that citizens can identify with and relate to, and a sense of leadership and energy in that direction.

From emergency to transformation – managing elites

Luisa Dias Diogo has enjoyed an extraordinary political career in Mozambique. The country's first female prime minister (2004–10), she served previously as minister of planning and finance.[19] She joined government in the Finance Ministry in 1980, which she left on her appointment as deputy finance minister in 1994. At the time of the end of the civil war in 1992, which had raged since 1977, she was the budget director in the Treasury.

'The civil war cost the country,' says the former prime minister, 'one million dead along with six million displaced people and 1.5 million refugees, all this from a population of some twelve million. It was a disaster for Mozambique. Some 70 per cent of the health network was destroyed, 60 per cent of the country's educational facilities, and there was no movement between the north and south.' In places, she says, 'the roads had become jungles, and only 35 per cent of the territory was reachable.

'When President [Joaquim] Chissano became president in 1986 I was the deputy director of the budget in the Finance Ministry. We started to plan for financing the new army, which would come out of the peace process that started in the late 1980s. Of course,' she smiles, 'military commanders always like to give you three figures when they talk about their strength: the salaries they pay, the mouths they have to feed and the actual number of combatants. The last number is always 10 per cent of the first one.'

A peace agreement followed in October 1992, negotiated by the Community of Sant'Egidio with the support of the UN. 'We discovered that there were between 80 000 to 90 000 soldiers, which we needed to demobilise. While we provided a demobilisation "kit" for farming, there was also a need to give them money to give them a cushion for two-and-a-half years while they changed their mindset back to being civilians once more.'

Annual per capita GDP had halved to under $140 by the war's end, but bounced back quickly. 'I went to Washington in 1993 and said to the IMF that we would have 19 per cent growth. They thought I was exaggerating to get more money. Actually they found out it was 22 per cent. This was because people started to travel and trade again.'

Thus, the next stage involved infrastructure reforms and 'integrating the 400 NGOs in the country with more than 4 800 projects, into the government programme. Then we moved through elections [27–28 October 1994] before establishing essential priorities with the donors in Paris. Here we disagreed with the NGOs who said that macroeconomic stability and low inflation – our inflation was running at 76 per cent at the end of 1994 – was not essential. I said that the lives of people were aggravated by such high inflation, and we set our priorities accordingly, along with a focus of spending on infrastructure, human resources, education and health.

'But we also had to reduce expenditure in non-essential areas, where we were wasting money, to be able to control inflation, such as in giving subsidies to things that could be done by the private sector.' Hence, the country adopted an aggressive privatisation programme of 4 000 state-owned enterprises and liberalised prices, 'which was resisted by the hardliners'.

Diogo identifies three phases to recovery. The first is moving from emergency to reconstruction. The second focuses on the 'in-depth reforms, such as privatisation'. And the final stage is that of 'transformation'. The missing link to Mozambique's recovery is in this third phase, she believes. 'For example if you don't improve agriculture, where 80 per cent of the population works, you will not improve the lives of the majority of Mozambicans. There is in this a need,' she emphasises, 'to manage the sectors better, which create jobs. Is it,' she asks, 'better to put up a hotel with state financing, which costs, with "commissions", $250 million, or to spend that money on agriculture? The reason why we spend it on hotels is that the elites benefit. They are more interested in making money than creating jobs.'

Rent-seeking has increasingly defined Mozambique's politics. This explains why the country has enjoyed high growth, yet over half the population remains locked in poverty.

The need to ensure the political economy makes choices to the benefit of the many and not just the few is heightened by the growth in population numbers (Mozambique's population doubled between 1985 and 2013) produced in part by peace. The economic growth versus poverty disjuncture is worsened, too, by the failure of big projects (such as in Mozambique's Mozal aluminium smelter in Maputo, the Moatize coal projects in the central Tete province or the northern Rovuma offshore gas fields) to produce direct jobs. Even if these mega-projects have benefited government tax revenues, employing this usefully and widely requires a combination, at least, of good planning, bureaucratic efficiencies and sound ethics.

Transformation, to use Diogo's terminology, requires a leadership committed to a 'national project', to popular welfare, and intent on putting the country and not their personal interests first.

*

Mohammed, an ebullient Afghan trader and marketing expert guiding me around the Kabul juicing plant, put the country's problems succinctly and inadvertently. 'In the United States,' he said, 'you make $100 and keep $20 for yourself. In Afghanistan, you make $100 but keep $90 for yourself. This is the better place to do business.'[20]

Yes, Mohammed, but the problem is that the $100 in Afghanistan comes from the tax paid by the American. It is hardly sustainable.

Here is the key problem with Afghanistan's economic development. Most Afghans are locked into the politics of survival, a feudal-style system where security depends not on independence but patronage and servitude. This is compounded where the space for entrepreneurs is so limited and money-making opportunities are given over, in the main, to political operators.

But what might Afghanistan make and sell that will create additional jobs and ensure a greater stake in stability by Afghans, blunting the insurgency and recruits to that cause?

The international community is very poor at delivering development, especially in post-conflict countries. This should not be surprising since the donors themselves developed through internal rather than external actions. All development, to paraphrase the cliché on politics, is local.

Where jobs are created by donors, this is usually in services, most notably construction. But sustainability is problematic, especially when the gush of donor funding is inevitably cut.

Combined with a pathological tendency to examine rather than 'to do', attempts to create jobs in Afghanistan (as elsewhere) follow a pattern: an idea followed by a scoping study, usually backed up by a consultative process, an evaluation process producing a commission to conduct fieldwork to deliver a detailed report, 'workshopped' along the way by various representative constituents and appraised by peer reviewers in 'deep-dive longitudinal' processes. And the product has to be matched by a business plan, which, usually after a period involving at least one turnover of donor staff, is condemned to a dusty plight on a shelf, forgotten when the idea is revived later and the process started over again. The traditional route of an entrepreneur with a good idea borrowing money and starting a business is lost in the focus on easy money, where talents are diverted to tapping soft donor sources. Finally, as Mohammed's insight into the donor world has hinted, there is a deeper and more intractable generational issue that has been exacerbated by conflict and aid regimes. It lies in changing attitudes and ingraining a culture of personal responsibility; that is the biggest challenge to be gripped if Afghans, Liberians, Somalis and Sierra Leoneans, among others, are to ascend the recovery ladder from peace-building to prosperity.

CONCLUSION

*

BUY, HOLD, FIX

I skate to where the puck is going to be, not where it has been.

— Wayne Gretzky

You must always think three moves ahead, what happens not now, but ten years from now.

— Lee Kuan Yew

Myanmar is a revelation among fragile states. Finding small-scale industry adding value to basic agricultural products in the most rural of settings tells a story about a country lifting itself out of poverty after years of isolation and statism. There were no NGOs helping the bandage and rubber manufacturers, or consultants writing studies or business plans, and nor did the locals demand aid expenditure on new roads or, in the case of the rubber plantation, even electricity since it relied on man-cranked machinery. They were not waiting for someone to help; they were helping themselves.

The case studies suggest that a key aspect to fixing failure is the need for action by locals to address the causes. In some cases, this means finding the means to end conflict, in others the imposition of better policies, enabling producers to earn more by working harder.

But it also demands a comprehensive approach since in many cases the problem is the nature of the system, a political economy based on primitive rent-seeking, where far from holding their leaders accountable, citizens seek primarily to engage in the trade of favours and contracts for support. Establishing a virtuous cycle of state recovery requires not only higher levels of efficiency in government, imposition of the rule of law, the safeguarding of land rights, the ending of monopolies and the (de)regulation of labour and credit markets, but the establishment of an environment that spurs an innovative and transformational culture. There is no point, after all, in recovering to the same place where precipitous decline began. Instilling these tenets necessitates institutions capable of restraining political excesses, and making investment in people through education and in hard, physical infrastructure. It requires incentives for people to save, invest and innovate.

This is easier said than done; it is easier to describe the problem and the condition than provide a route map out of it. Getting from one stage requires an elite having little to gain from their own continued dominance of politics or the economy, or little to fear from pluralism and democracy, and much to fear from their electorate. Always outsiders should be wary of setting a raft of operating guidelines and conditions, but instead focus on a few clear 'red lines' over which local partners should not transgress, giving them the space necessary to pursue recovery. Rather than focusing on perfecting their tactical responses, outsiders should be much less linear and far more strategic in building the alliances between states, and relationships with personalities and citizens necessary. Such a human component is often lost in the contemporary lexicon about 'stabilisation', 'comprehensive approaches', 'peace-building', 'recovery' and 'development', and arguments about the definition of state 'failure', 'fragility', 'weakness' or 'vulnerability'.

Overall, there is a need for outsiders and insiders alike to keep the spotlight on domestic actions if they are serious about fixing such situations. This is difficult when there is an 'industry' specifically to give out assistance and there are high stakes in ensuring short-term stability through a flood of aid, heightened by threats of terrorism or, less dramatically, a flood of refugees. Outsiders letting go of the urge to help and insiders similarly relaxing the levers of state control, allowing the economy to grow and people to prosper, are perhaps not only the hardest but also the best things to do.

This highlights the most important aspect of all. Local leadership has to realise that the extractive rent-seeking model of government that lies behind most instances of failure is unsustainable. Corruption is destructive, unproductive and ultimately self-defeating, whether this be on Wall Street, in corporate boardrooms in Europe or in Africa's presidential palaces. Changing this system and culture demands leadership, in business as in government, taking a longer-term 'buy, hold, fix' rather than 'buy, sell' care-less view.

Doing so also requires a long-term principled commitment and stance overcoming any desire to gain short-term domestic political dividends; a clarity and constancy of purpose, not an urge by politicians especially to be loved. As Bernard Ingham wrote in this regard of Margaret Thatcher, 'She was a politician with the courage to follow her instincts. And she never ceased to find a way forward to a better world, not by smarm or flattery but by a fierce determination.' And as her former press secretary said of the 'Iron

Lady' on her death on 8 April 2013, 'This week has shown how she came to be respected, not least paradoxically by those celebrating her death. If she had not counted for something, they would not have bothered.'[1] Thatcher's contribution to politics in Britain was significant in part because she was the daughter of a shopkeeper, and injected issue over class, substance over identity in the nation's politics. She was seen as divisive precisely because she could not be pigeonholed and because she sought people to make choices, not simply to seek lame consensus. As she put it in 1969, 'it is wrong to talk of "taking the big issues out of politics"'.[2] Or as another tough woman in politics, South Africa's veteran parliamentarian Helen Suzman, put it: 'Like everyone else, I long to be loved. But I am not prepared to make any concessions whatsoever.'[3]

Such iron will and firm leadership is increasingly an anathema in a consensus-driven, media-ridden, carefully choreographed world, yet all the more notable when it occurs. What is surprising is how little people do to make a lasting mark on the wellness of all – a community, a country, a world – in their short earthly sojourns, even though they may receive so much more than they risk in return. What holds them back? Why so self-defensive and lacking in imagination? Why so few Trumans, willing to take the tough stand, Thatchers, willing to break the class and glass ceilings, Martin Luther Kings, ready to walk in the valley and suffer, or Gandhis, trodding barefoot to dine one night with Muslim, the next with Hindu? These are paths available to many; why, in a time of peril and possibility, do so few leaders walk them?

*

The presence and even the extent of challenges should not preordain countries to a particular future. They can, as Singapore, Colombia, Kosovo, Sierra Leone and Vietnam among others have shown, change for the better despite a disastrous inheritance, internal division, volatile politics, difficult geography and no apparent advantages. This is especially the case for those states at the bottom, many of whom are described in this book, not least because expectations like per capita income are so low. Things can change quickly and with far-reaching consequences. Higher rates of economic growth and greater prosperity can significantly reduce population growth rates over a generation when it goes hand in hand with women gaining authority over their own lives.

Thus, what might internal and external actors do better, singly and in partnership, to create a positive, virtuous cycle in setting the conditions for ending state fragility and ensuring conditions of stability and prosperity?

Here it is useful to return to the typologies of failure outlined at the start of this volume: outright collapse; where there is no state; and where there is democratic failure.

State failure

State-building is nearly always a messy business. As Jim Bailey, philanthropist, one-time proprietor of *Drum* magazine and decorated Second World War pilot reminds, 'War and peace are not separate existences. Wars are made in peace-time and peace shaped and justified out of the harvesting of war. The carnage of one is more spectacular than the other but in the poorer countries there is not much to choose.'[4] Indeed, such messiness was true for Europe, as late as the Balkan wars of the 1990s.

In this process, security, as has been seen from various case studies presented here, is a first order priority, and one where outsiders can in the right circumstances play a useful role. Without stability, other components of success including better governance and economic growth are insufficient components by themselves. But the security aspect cannot succeed alone. Iraq and Afghanistan illustrate that there is no such thing as a 'security solution' to a country's problems. A political and economic solution is required for even medium-term stability.

This demands understanding the motives behind conflict, from those fought over national interests, grievances or even over resources and greed. There are also wars where violence has its own tautology: conflicts that never end, otherwise termed the 'forever wars'.[5] For example, while the number of conflicts in Africa declined appreciably in the 2000s, there are a number of wars that have a seemingly endless logic to them – the Lord's Resistance Army in Uganda, various struggles in the Congo, the armed groups in the Niger Delta and the rebels running across borders in the Sahel. At one time, most of Africa's armed struggles had a cause: fighting colonialism, apartheid, a lack of democracy, ethnic exclusion and other forms of injustice. Some of these elements still persist, but some warring groups fight as a way of life, exactly because there is no state. This reminds that countries, not armies, win wars and end conflict, the point that Senator John McCain has made about the American experience in Vietnam: while the US never lost a battle against North Vietnam, it ultimately lost the war.[6] Americans tired of the dying and the killing before the Vietnamese did. Political support is vital to military success, domestically and internationally.

Just as the reasons for conflict and failure are rooted in regional issues cutting across borders, whether this be 'AfPak' – Pakistan-Afghanistan – in South Asia, across Central America in the 1980s, or today in the Mano River Union in West Africa, the solution has to be regionally focused and driven. This is not just for reasons of managing people flows, ensuring regional transport integration and cleaning up illicit trade, but also given that regional projects involving more than one country are often not only more cost-effective but easier to source funds for.

Whatever the short-term role for outsiders, state recovery hinges on stopping doing things for the locals. This is counter-intuitive in a number of ways. To remind, as Paul Collier has pointed out, such states are not usually characterised by governments that are 'reasonably representative' of the interests of their citizens, and 'reasonably competent' in managing public spending. If they were, they would probably not be fragile.[7] Philosophically this contradicts a statist instinct of recovery led by governments and multilateral agencies, which centres on infusing institutions and capacity paradoxically not present in fragile situations.

This realisation is also counter-intuitive to most energetic, motivated, dynamic officers, especially those in the military, who often finds themselves in these situations and who are programmed to take initiative and to resolve problems, 'sorting things out', 'getting things moving and done', kicking up dust, creaking state machinery into life. Paradoxically, the success of such external missions, from Afghanistan to Africa and in Haiti and elsewhere, depends not on largely subjective external judgements about security or development, but to stress the point, on whether the locals can sort things out themselves or not. Whatever the route, absent such caution and changing the incentives for violent conflict, external interveners – from those giving aid to those going in hard – can only risk becoming 'prisoners of their conquest'.[8]

Many military contingents also wrongly assume these missions will be easy. On the contrary – these are usually wars. Moreover, to be successful, interventions require domestic and international legitimacy. With the intervener, moral authority, which comes with legitimacy, is often more important than military might.

The arrival of a 'swarm'[9] of external actors, advisers and donors can also easily overwhelm the limited capacity of the governments and people they are trying to help. Care has to be taken among the donors to not establish 'armies of expats' on fat, tax-free salaries brought in to a theatre, who, rather than 'achieving and leaving', orient their advice towards preserving their own jobs or securing follow-up consultancies. Instead, transferring ownership of imported ideas to local politicians is necessary for good ideas to take root. This requires building capacity among technocrats and politicians. And the swarm, at a minimum, has to ensure that they do no harm.

Additionally, donors have to guard, too, against the metrics being pinned, not at GDP growth or remedying the failure that underlies the conflict, but money expended. In this there is a need to separate out 'bounce-back' growth – where stability and aid can provide a sudden economic growth surge once the fighting stops, such as the 30 per cent Afghan growth in 2003 – from the needs for reforms geared to improving local efficiencies and productive investment. Holding court, being busy with meetings and driving big cars is equally a sign of the miscarriage of the development mission, and the failure of donor agencies to appreciate that sustainable salvation is not going to happen as a result of welfare from foreign taxpayers, but when locals themselves take on this responsibility.

No state at home

What to do in the circumstances where there is insufficient state capacity, where it has been hollowed out or never existed to begin with? These are the countries of sullen, inefficient, unhelpful and corrupt border guards, police, military and other government officials, the ones who greet you aggressively on arrival, as if you are taking something away from their country by spending money in it, or policemen who stop you for 'some tea' in Kenya, 'help' in South Africa, 'air time' in Zimbabwe, or *gaseosa* (soda) in Angola.

These are the countries where a lack of funds or capacity apparently exists to carry out basic tasks, yet they its leadership never lacks the capacity to grasp opportunities for self-enrichment, or to expedite their own travel by first class or charter aircraft. They may be loser states for the majority of their citizens, but far from it for the elites. Rent-seeking defines their political economy; mediocrity not meritocracy their politics and administration.

Such a cycle of despair and state failure can be envisaged also at the level of the individual. People can be locked into a cycle of poverty – where unemployed or uneducated people produce offspring to whom they can devote little in the way of resources or time. Without an extraordinary event or specially gifted individuals, this routinely means reinforcing patterns of delinquency and poverty. The invisible hand of social culture plays a part in shaping peoples' fortunes, at least as much as state institutions. This is an environment of urban slums, chronic inequality in access to opportunity, collapsing infrastructure, weak government, poor governance, little infrastructure, limited human and institutional capacity, and much, often daily, violence.

This is the environment where key groups benefit from chaos, where puzzlement over a lack of progress can often be explained by the logic of elite interests. This is the environment where, like Kenya, you can have a fantastic private sector but a terrible state, where the former prospers largely in spite of the rent-seeking and corruption of the latter. That does not mean that they do not cooperate, and sometime with cost to the overall economy. The political connections of road hauliers, for example, explain why railways do not work properly. The same rationale explains, perversely, why goods move so slowly through ports, a case of, to paraphrase Winston Churchill, so much cost for so many for the benefit of so few.

These can be countries where there is little or no violence, but years of low economic growth, where the state employs the numbers but has none of the capacity for efficiency and dynamic reform. Think Malawi, the archetypal walking society.

So where to start?

Donors should, in this regard, not expect others to develop differently. This especially applies to donors who somehow believe that the target states can develop through aid, though they themselves developed through private sector action and growth. Why should they? While some countries have stabilised with external assistance (think the Marshall Plan, but which worked on the solid foundations of existing local expertise), no country has developed through aid. Building a state depends on the presence of market fundamentals, from assistance for revenue collection to private sector growth, whether this is in London or Lusaka.

Here the creation of the mutually beneficial relationship in a short time between China and Africa shows, among other things, that Western donor-driven growth is not the only route to development, or indeed, necessarily a useful route at all. Rather, it is necessary for domestic governments to create certainty beyond their tenure for investors through the rule of law and

626 — WHY STATES RECOVER

to develop a vision – a story – of growth and development for locals and internationals to follow. And there is a need to reduce the mistrust often felt between governments and the private sector. Weak states need to develop, in sum, a vision of what private sector companies will be able to do in and for their societies, and sell that vision to investors, local and foreign.

It is abundantly clear to policy-makers what is required in technocratic terms to inspire growth. As the African Development Bank's president, Donald Kaberuka, has explained, 'We know the policies that lead to growth; and we know the policies that kill you.'[10] It is clear, too, that the gaps between vision (of which there is much about), planning (less, but still plentiful) and execution capacity and ability (in short supply) has to be narrowed. Why then are these solutions not implemented? It is partly because politicians lack the will to do so, or because it is not in their short-term political or personal financial self-interest. Political economy is, after all, about making choices. Local voters have the main role to play in keeping politicians honest in this regard; and politicians should themselves focus on building constituencies for growth to enable the space and support for difficult choices to be made.

Also, domestic actors must guard against adopting a zero-sum outlook to reforms and to the world outside, since things do not work like this. Viewing it as such not only focuses on the wrong problem, but misses the best opportunity for recovery through enhanced trade, investment flows and (some) aid. Rather than a focus on competitiveness and global engagement as a means of upliftment, weak states are often concerned predominantly with using perceptions of social and global exclusion to justify its rule and populism. This is used as a counter to a failure to improve legitimacy through economic growth, as has been the case in East Asia, for example. Such mercantilism is very Malthusian in believing that there are insufficient resources for all, that productivity increases can never match expectations or even demand, where wealth relies on taking resources from someone else. It is a pre-Industrial Revolution view of the world, and it is one aligned with a failure to diversify economies, create jobs and, indeed, to state failure itself.

Equally, there is a need to avoid Manichean debates between the state as the solution and market fundamentalism, if you will, between the Berlin Wall and Lehman Brothers, between left- or right-wing maximalist or minimalist versions of government. Of course, functioning states (and governments) need effective states, since many fragile states already exist in a weak-state, low-tax, low-capacity environment, and this condition is not very appealing. But equally they do not need the Soviet Union or a European welfare variant, choking individual entrepreneurship. For those countries striving to recover, there is thus no luxury in labelling choices as 'left wing' or 'neoliberal' or 'conservative'. The basics, as Elton Mangoma, once the economic planning minister in the unity government in Zimbabwe, says, 'defy such terms. The basics are all about macroeconomic stability.'[11]

Overwhelmingly, there is a need to focus on the conditions that encourage private sector growth, employment creation and individual prosperity. Of course there are crooked people who take advantage of the freedoms inherent in free market capitalism. However difficult this may be for its ideological rivals to swallow, there is no other economic system that has created comparable wealth over generations by permitting people the space to use their talents. Other recipes, the record equally shows, have proven disastrous. As noted, the necessary conditions include macroeconomic fundamentals (low inflation, fiscal rectitude, stable monetary regime) along with conducive labour relations, suitable infrastructure and bureaucratic efficiency and congeniality. It also means championing business. A focus on jobs – and housing – offers a stake in stability; security begets economic growth and vice versa. This aspect of personal security is crucial to economic growth as countries stabilise, reform and recover, and can create its own economic dividend in so doing.

To enable this, there is a need, as was outlined in the previous chapter, to get the basics right. People have the same universal aspirations everywhere: security and prosperity. External engagement has to set these priorities accordingly. For example, modern sewerage and plumbing or electrification would do more than seminars on human rights or treatises on gender empowerment, especially in the overcrowded, underinvested urban environments in which most fragile populations find themselves. Success requires not only having the right resources, or of doing the right thing, but of doing the right things with the right resources.

People work better and more productively when they are incentivised to do so. At the most basic level this involves ownership and the retention of profits. For this to work at its foundation requires getting the market to set prices. In the run up to Malawi's 2014 election, one of the opposition leaders, Reverend Dr Lazarus Chakerwa, was quoted as saying at a political rally in Malingunde on the outskirts of Lilongwe City: '*Ukakhala ndi nkhukunsudikira ogula adzakuuze mtengo ayi, umanena ndiwe* (You don't wait for a buyer to tell you the price of a chicken you are selling). Why should we wait for external forces to determine our tobacco prices?' He added: 'This is why we are saying that we will not bow down to external forces to determine the prices of our agricultural products, especially tobacco. A buyer cannot decide the price of tobacco but the seller, in this case the farmers.'[12]

No matter how politically tempting and convenient, this is just rubbish and reckless.

Just as it is important to build champions of domestic reform, there is also an imperative to avoid a constituency of losers. It is important not to perpetuate a situation where you continuously have one group or another, defined often by race, religion, ethnicity or even gender, left out from the benefits of participation. This encourages low and poor involvement in institutions, sets a low threshold for violence, and can ensure that societies remain highly unequal and fragmented politically.

Democratic failure

This book has consistently illustrated how weak and failed states are characterised by a highly extractive, rent-seeking elite, weak domestic governance institutions, high levels of corruption, and family- or tribe-based organisation of the political economy.[13] Yet countries do not have to be trapped by their pasts. Transitions from failure to success require leadership willing to take a long view, and local citizens willing to be more active and to pressure them to do so.

Again, the reason for failure, as with success, is inherently political. This requires crafting political solutions, not just attempting a military or economic one. From South Asia to South Africa, this volume shows that, in terms of the mechanics of making peace, there is a need for method, subtlety, finesse, brinkmanship and a sense of timing since, after all, these negotiations are between enemies not friends. Success demands more than just a ticket-punching exercise; to reiterate what Tony Blair has remarked of Mandela, 'It was not just what he did, but the way he did it.'

In this, however, to reiterate: recovery is an iceberg. Policy matters can be imagined as the tip, what we can see and attempt to mould, shape and change. Still, other equally important issues below the surface need to be addressed, including culture, mindset, customs, tradition and, of course, politics, the reasons that give rise to such policy choices in the first instance. And while the focus is unsurprisingly on the national and even the community levels for the solutions, Guinea reminds that the trouble can begin at the smaller, family nuclear unit. Recovery has at times to include the installation of traditional values.

From Venezuela to Zimbabwe, the adaptability of elites should not be underestimated, which includes their using democratic transitions and frustrations over inequality to their advantage. They usually have interests in strengthening, not diluting, their power, and the proper functioning (rather than the simple facade) of democratic institutions usually runs counter to patronage and other preferred mechanisms for doing so. Democracy, like free markets, is not self-regulating. It requires hard work by civil society and parliamentary opposition to keep it alive and valuable. But the rewards are clear: authoritarian capitalist success is the exception and not the rule.

Given the primacy of politics, there is a need to find the means to support agents of domestic change. The Arab Spring and its aftermath illustrate that pushing all aid towards development, humanitarian causes and civil society must be challenged. This has become a never-ending treadmill, an industry for civil society that can alleviate the worst problems but never resolve the undergirding issues. It does not make sense to spend billions of dollars on patching up the socio-economic environment or humanitarian situation while tossing only a few crumbs the way of politics. Those seeking to influence these countries in a positive direction have to show that democracy, the rule of law and liberal economics makes sense, not crony-capitalism and authoritarianism or radicalism. Given the role of social media in these political events in the first instance, those seeking to ensure positive change should disseminate ideas through both the mass media and social platforms, and should be aggressively engaged in supporting change agents.

Building a local civil society is thus a critical aspect, and not simply acting as an expeditor of development spending in the absence of a capable or corrupt government. The nurturing and support of voices outside of government is an important check and balance on executive power.

Countries are not poor, Francis Fukuyama reminds, because they lack resources, but because they lack effective (and accountable) political institutions.[14] To move from failure to function, countries require a combination of effective states, the rule of law and accountable government. The development of such government institutions parallels the change from tribal, race or religious identity to issue-based politics and merit-based governance. The aim is not to get political institutions out of the way since that is what has happened in many of our weak states already to their cost, but rather to institutionalise the necessary foundations of a modern society and economy:

a free press, rule of law, property rights and active civil society, to complement but not to replace an efficient and effective government.[15] Thus, the antidote for identity politics – an extractive rather than inclusive economic environment – fundamentally revolves around improving the level of political rights.[16]

Buy, hold, fix

The challenges facing fragile states are very specific, reflecting their circumstances and shaping the expectations as to the likely trajectory. With some countries, the focus is simply on maintaining a degree of political stability and preventing widespread radicalism. Conversely, it is less the rebuilding of the state than its capture that is the aim of radical groups, for example, in Egypt, Pakistan, Libya and Afghanistan. In other cases, the focus is on ending widespread conflict through external assistance, as in the Congo or Somalia, or extending government territorial control through domestic-led action as with Colombia. In these cases the military leads in the search for a solution. Congo, Somalia and Sierra Leone have faced the challenge of building the state, at least in parts, from scratch. Others will, to escape fragility, have to create a different sort of state, less elitist and rentier, and more inclusive along the Asia model. This group includes South Africa, Kenya and, indeed, much of Africa. For some there is a related need to change the development 'story', in placing the country on a higher growth path, without which the state will be ultimately, if not already, overcome in the mismatch between the population's expectations and the government's ability to supply and deliver.

In all the cases of weakness and failure there are, however, common themes. Little progress can be made without security, although security by itself is not enough to ensure recovery, and it has to be integrated closely with civilian action around the economy and governance, and be part of a wider political framework. The crisis that leads to failure usually offers an opportunity to change things in a positive way, but this moment has to be seized. Singapore had a very good crisis. So did Vietnam in the 1980s, which started its *doi moi* (renovation) process, and Costa Rica around the same time.

Since the period of recovery from failure has proven historically at least as long as the period of decline, reformist speed is of the essence. Of course, there is a need to guard against the temptation of short-term expediency – where donors and domestic politicians overlook the need for governance in the interests of stability, or to genuflect to redistribution over policies favouring growth, even though welfare through redistribution, where possible, can be a buffer against extreme poverty and political instability.

There are deeper issues that need to be addressed beyond only tinkering with policy, as noted above, encompassing politics, tradition and mindset. Identity politics have, as a rule, been a sure determinant of weakness and failure. To take another example, recovery requires avoiding being pigeonholed by outsiders as a 'failure'. In Haiti, as has been seen, race has conditioned the way the rest of the world relates to the island and its citizens to the world, in that they expect the world to come to their assistance, and the world expects and wants to do so. While initially politically attractive, and potentially lucrative in terms of immediate aid appeals, this avenue can narrow the options for dealing with crises and consistently limits the constituencies reformers can appeal to.

Finally, whatever the position of states on the 'spectrum' of failure, successful recovery demands political leadership interpreting the reasons for failure as primarily internal, not external, and thus requiring far-reaching, sometimes painful domestic changes. It is precisely the sort of 'Buy, Hold, Fix' leadership, one – to use John Lewis Gaddis's phraseology[17] – that has a 'destination' of a different state in mind that is necessary to solve problems and ensure state recovery.

NOTES

✳

INTRODUCTION

1 Estimate of the OECD, http://www.oecd.org/dac/
incaf/factsheet%202013%20resource%20flows%20
final.pdf.

2 See http://edition.cnn.com/2014/04/02/world/
europe/italy-migrants-rescue/index.html?utm_
source=feedburner&utm_medium=feed&utm_
campaign=Feed%3A+rss%2Fcnn_world+%28RSS%3
A+World%29.

3 The Human Development Index's bottom twenty
(in 2013) are, worst to better, Niger, DRC,
Mozambique, Chad, Burkina Faso, Mali, Eritrea,
Central African Republic, Guinea, Burundi, Sierra
Leone, Guinea-Bisssau, Afghanistan, Liberia,
Ethiopia, Zimbabwe, Sudan, Malawi, Comoros
and Côte d'Ivoire. Rwanda is in 21st place. See
'Migrants from Niger Found Dead in Sahara', *New
York Times*, 1 November 2013.

4 The fraction of the world's population in extreme
poverty fell from 84 to 24 per cent between
1820 and 1992. See Francois Bourguignon
and Christian Morrisson, 'Inequality Among
World Citizens: 1820–1922', *American Economic
Review* 92(4), 2002, pp.727–44, cited in Angus
Deaton, *The Great Escape*. Princeton and Oxford:
Princeton University Press, 2013, p.167.

5 According to *The Economist*, 'Poverty rates started
to collapse towards the end of the 20th century
largely because developing-country growth
accelerated, from an average annual rate of 4.3
per cent in 1960–2000 to 6 per cent in 2000–10.
Around two-thirds of poverty reduction within
a country comes from growth. Greater equality
also helps, contributing the other third.' See
'Towards the End of Poverty', *The Economist*,
1 June 2013, http://www.economist.com/news/
leaders/21578665-nearly-1-billion-people-have-
been-taken-out-extreme-poverty-20-years-world-

should-aim. China pulled 680 million people
out of misery in 1981–2010, and reduced its
extreme-poverty rate from 84 per cent in 1980
to 10 per cent by 2013.

6 Deaton, *The Great Escape*, p.219.

7 See the OECD definition at http://www.oecd.org/
dac/incaf/FragileStates2013.pdf.

8 Reported at http://www.defenceweb.co.za/index.
php?option=com_content&view=article&id=
34253:armed-violence-costs-africa-18-billion-
a-year-oxfam&catid=56:Diplomacy%20&%20
Peace&Itemid=111 on 3 April 2014.

9 See http://www.nytimes.com/
interactive/2011/09/08/us/sept-11-reckoning/
cost-graphic.html?_r=0. This is made up of
$55 billion in physical damage; $123 billion in
economic impact; homeland security, $589 billion;
$1 649 billion in war and related costs; and $867
billion in future war and veteran costs.

10 These comparisons were relayed by Moises Naim
in his talk to HSBC, New York, 7 November
2013. See also his book, *The End of Power: From
Boardrooms to Battlefields and Churches to States,
Why Being In Charge Isn't What It Used to Be*. New
York: Basic Books, 2013.

11 Cited in Thomas Ricks, *The Generals: American
Military Command from World War II to Today*.
New York: Penguin, 2013, pp.47–48.

12 Agreed through the G7+ group of nineteen fragile
and conflict-affected countries at the fourth global
high-level forum on aid effectiveness held in
South Korea in November 2011.

13 William Easterly, 'Stop Sending Aid to Dictators',
Time, 24 March 2014.

14 This figure was provided in circular
correspondence by the Integrated Regional
Information Networks (IRIN) of the UN Office
for the Coordination of Humanitarian Affairs,

3 April 2014.

15 By the admission of the World Bank, aid to fragile states has often propped up corruption, rather than weakened it. See http://www.irinnews.org/report/94502/aid-policy-spotlight-on-new-deal-for-fragile-states.

16 The New Deal is, for example, built around three pillars: five peace-building and state-building goals; inclusive and country-led transitions out of fragility; and relationship-building with donor partners. The five goals are: inclusive and legitimate politics, security, justice, economic foundations, revenues and services.

17 Howard French, 'The Not-So-Great Professor: Jeffrey Sachs' Incredible Failure to Eradicate Poverty in Africa', Pacific Standard, 13 September 2013, http://www.psmag.com/culture/smart-guy-jeffrey-sachs-nina-munk-idealist-poverty-failure-africa-65348/.

18 Discussion, Mepal, 10 January 2014.

19 Cited in Thomas Ricks, The Generals, p.23.

20 See, for example, the 2013 OECD report on 'Fragile States and Resource Flows' and the Overseas Development Institute's 'Development, Security and Transitions in Fragile States: A Meeting Series Report' of March 2010, http://www.odi.org.uk/publications/4772-development-security-transitions-fragile-states-meeting-series-report.

21 See http://siteresources.worldbank.org/INTWDRS/Resources/WDR2011_Overview.pdf.

22 See http://databank.worldbank.org/data/download/GNIPC.pdf.

23 The bottom ten countries listed were Congo, Burundi, Malawi, Niger, Liberia, Ethiopia, Madagascar, Uganda, Eritrea and Guinea.

24 Where the term Congo is used, this refers to the Democratic Republic of Congo (DRC), known as Zaire under Mobutu Sese Seko from October 1971 until his overthrow in May 1997. The Republic of Congo (otherwise known as Congo-Brazzaville) is denoted differently throughout.

25 See the World Bank country databank, http://data.worldbank.org/country. Unless otherwise cited, this is the source of World Bank statistics.

26 See 'Water Shortages in Malawi', IRIN, 12 December 2013.

27 See http://www.un.org/africarenewal/magazine/october-2008/harvest-hope-african-farmers.

28 See http://www.theguardian.com/world/2013/apr/11/malawi-madonna.

29 For a discussion of these factors, see Francis Fukuyama, The Origins of Political Order. New York: Farrar, Straus and Giroux, 2011.

30 Mancur Olson, Power and Prosperity: Outgrowing Communist and Capitalist Dictatorships. New York: Basic Books, 2000.

31 Rising from the Ashes is the title of the documentary film describing the remarkable role of the Team Rwanda cycling initiative.

32 I am grateful to Terry McNamee for this metaphor.

33 Samuel P. Huntington, Keynote Address at Colorado College's 125th Anniversary Symposium, 'Cultures in the 21st Century: Conflicts and Convergences', 1999, cited in Bo Malmberg, 'Demography and the Development Potential of Sub-Saharan Africa', http://www.diva-portal.org/smash/get/diva2:241196/FULLTEXT01.pdf.

34 See http://www.nytimes.com/1993/08/10/opinion/yes-there-is-a-reason-to-be-in-somalia.html?scp=2&sq=%22failed+state%22&st=nyt.

35 See http://www.theguardian.com/global-development/poverty-matters/2013/sep/23/development-jargon-decoded-fragile-failed-states.

36 See http://www.theguardian.com/global-development/poverty-matters/2012/jul/02/failed-states-index-policy-dustbin.

37 See, for example, Clare Leigh, 'Telling Countries They're the Worst in the World Doesn't Really Help Them', The Guardian Poverty Matters Blog, http://www.theguardian.com/global-development/poverty-matters/2013/jul/15/fragile-states-south-sudan.

38 Interview, Monrovia, September 2013.

39 The OECD's 47 fragile states are Afghanistan, Cameroon, Angola, Bangladesh, Republic of Congo, Bosnia and Herzegovina, Burundi, Côte d'Ivoire, Iran, Central African Republic, Georgia, Chad, Iraq, Comoros, Kiribati, Democratic Republic of Congo, Kosovo, Eritrea, Marshall Islands, Ethiopia, Micronesia, Guinea, Nigeria, Guinea-Bissau, Pakistan, Haiti, Solomon Islands, Kenya, South Sudan, Democratic Republic of Korea, Sri Lanka, Kyrgyzstan, Sudan, Liberia, Timor-Leste, Malawi, West Bank and Gaza, Myanmar, Yemen, Nepal, Niger, Rwanda, Sierra Leone, Somalia, Togo, Uganda and Zimbabwe.

40 See http://www.oecd.org/dac/incaf/factsheet%202013%20resource%20flows%20final.pdf.

41 For a critique of this, see http://www.globaldashboard.org/2013/02/03/what-the-oecd-does-not-understand-about-fragile-states/.

42 The reliability of African data, among other fragile states, is frequently suspect both in terms of its consistency between countries and over time, can have ancient base foundations on which they are calculated and sometimes can be subject to guesstimates. For example, Morten Jervon has calculated that in more than half of sub-Saharan countries the base formulations are over a decade old, while there is also a paucity in collection of data, especially given the informal nature of much of African economies (and thus a failure to collect relevant revenue, investment and profit figures, which leads to unreliable GDP growth calculations). See Morten Jervon, Poor Numbers: How We Are Misled by African Development Statistics and What to Do about It. Cornell: Cornell University Press, 2013. However, for a reliable analytical view of Africa, see Africa in Fact: The Journal of Good Governance Africa at www.gga.org.

43 See Danny Dorling's *Population 10 Billion: The Coming Demographic Crisis and How to Survive It.* London: Constable, 2013, esp. pp.104–51.

44 See http://www.valuewalk.com/2012/01/africa-to-have-worlds-largest-population-in-2040/; and http://corporate.exxonmobil.com/en/energy/energy-outlook/global-fundamentals/population-and-progress. According to the latter report by Exxon-Mobil, from 2010–40, the world's population is projected to rise from seven billion to nearly nine billion, and the global economy to more than double. Over that same period, global energy demand is likely to rise by about 35 per cent.

45 For an explanation of the drivers of this new world and likely outcomes, see David Kilcullen, *Out of the Mountains: The Coming Age of the Urban Guerrilla.* New York: Oxford University Press, 2013, esp. pp.184–87.

46 See Moises Naim, *The End of Power.*

47 See 'Principles for Good International Engagement in Fragile States', http://www.oecd.org/document/46/0,3343, en_2649_33693550_35233262_1_1_1_1,00.html.

48 With thanks to Dave Kilcullen for this point.

49 Paul Collier, *The Bottom Billion: Why the Poorest Countries are Failing and What Can Be Done About It.* Oxford: Oxford University Press, 2007.

50 Collier's Bottom Billion include Afghanistan, Angola, Azerbaijan, Benin, Bhutan, Bolivia, Burkina Faso, Burundi, Cambodia, Cameroon, Central African Republic, Chad, Comoros, the Democratic Republic of Congo, Republic of the Congo, Ivory Coast, Djibouti, Equatorial Guinea, Eritrea, Ethiopia, the Gambia, Ghana, Guinea, Guinea-Bissau, Guyana, Haiti, Kazakhstan, Kenya, Kyrgyzstan, Laos, Lesotho, Liberia, Madagascar, Malawi, Mali, Mauritania, Moldova, Mongolia, Mozambique, Myanmar, Nepal, Niger, Nigeria, North Korea, Rwanda, Senegal, Sierra Leone, Somalia, Sudan, Tajikistan, Tanzania, Togo, Turkmenistan, Uganda, Uzbekistan, Yemen, Zambia and Zimbabwe.

51 See http://www.foreignpolicy.com/failed_states_index_2012_interactive.

52 The countries with 'high-alert' status in the 2013 edition of the Failed States Index are: Somalia, Democratic Republic of Congo, Sudan, South Sudan, Chad, Yemen, Afghanistan, Haiti, Central African Republic, Zimbabwe, Iraq, Ivory Coast, Pakistan, Guinea, Guinea-Bissau, Nigeria, Kenya, Niger, Ethiopia, Burundi, Syria, Uganda, North Korea, Liberia, Eritrea, Myanmar, Cameroon, Sri Lanka, Bangladesh, Nepal, Mauritania, East Timor, Sierra Leone, Egypt and Burkina Faso.

53 See, for example, http://abcnews.go.com/Politics/libya-military-intervention-costs-us-taxpayers-millions-dollars/story?id=13193525.

54 See http://www.aafjournal.co.za/news/au-wants-more-troops-somalia-un-needs-more-everywhere.

55 Fukuyama, *The Origins of Political Order*, p.15.

56 See Paul Theroux, *The Last Train to Zona Verde: Overland from Cape Town to Angola.* Johannesburg: Penguin, 2013, pp.8 and 13.

57 See 'Preventing Conflict in the Next Century' in D. Fisburn (ed.), *The World In 2000.* London: Economist Publications, 1999, p.91.

58 See Joseph Siegle, Michael Weinstein and Morton Halperin, 'Why Democracies Excel', *Foreign Affairs* 83(5), 2005, pp.57–71. See also Morton Halperin, Joseph Siegle and Michael Weinstein, *The Democracy Advantage: How Democracies Promote Prosperity and Peace.* London: Routledge, 2010.

59 Takaaki Masaki and Nicolas van de Walle, 'The impact of democracy on economic growth in sub-Saharan Africa, 1982–2012', WIDER Working Paper 2014/057, March 2014.

60 See 'Ten Things You Should Know About Fragile States', http://www.afdb.org/fileadmin/uploads/afdb/Documents/Generic-Documents/Ten%20Things%20You%20Should%20Know%20About%20Fragile%20States.pdf. This figure varies. The G7 denotes eighteen states as fragile. Others have the figure at 28, of which 23 are in Africa. See Joseph Siegle, 'Stabilizing Fragile States', *Global Dialogue* 13(1), Winter/Spring, 2011, cited at the 2013 Lake Tana Security Forum.

61 According to Freedom House, the number of electoral democracies worldwide stood at 118 in 2012, an increase of one compared to 2011. Three countries, Bhutan, Georgia and Libya, achieved electoral democracy status, while two were dropped from the category, Mali and the Maldives. Four countries moved from Partly Free to Free: Lesotho, Senegal, Sierra Leone and Tonga. Three countries rose from Not Free to Partly Free: Côte d'Ivoire, Egypt and Libya. Mali fell two tiers, from Free to Not Free, and Guinea-Bissau dropped from Partly Free to Not Free. Of the 47 countries designated as Not Free, nine have been given the survey's lowest possible rating of 7 for both political rights and civil liberties: Eritrea, Equatorial Guinea, North Korea, Saudi Arabia, Somalia, Sudan, Syria, Turkmenistan and Uzbekistan. Two territories, Tibet and Western Sahara, were also ranked among the worst of the worst. See http://www.freedomhouse.org/report/freedom-world/freedom-world-2013.

62 Remarks made at the Third Tana Forum, Bahir Dar, Ethiopia, 26 April 2014.

63 See William J. Dobson, *The Dictator's Learning Curve: Tyranny and Democracy in the Modern World.* London: Vintage, 2013.

64 Cited in Dobson, *The Dictator's Learning Curve.*

65 Larry Devlin, *Chief of Station, Congo: Fighting the Cold War in a Hot Zone.* New York: Public Affairs, 2007.

66 Alex Boraine, *What's Gone Wrong? On the Brink of a Failed State.* Johannesburg: Jonathan Ball, 2014, p.142.

67 See http://www.ted.com. With thanks to Eddie and Gary Keizan for highlighting Sinek's argument.

68 As cited in the film, *Jobs.*

PART 1:
PATHOLOGIES AND THREADS
OF FAILURE

1 For a background on Sudan's wars, see Douglas Johnson, *The Root Causes of Sudan's Civil Wars: Peace or Truce*. London: James Currey, 2011.
2 South Sudan was visited in November 2010 and again, in the company of Tim Carson and Patrick Mazimhaka, in April 2013. The quotations are derived from meetings during these visits.
3 For a detailed summary of the challenges of statehood for South Sudan, see Matthew Arnold and Matthew LeRiche, *South Sudan: From Revolution to Independence*. London: Hurst, 2012.
4 With thanks to Jeffrey Herbst for this axiom.
5 See http://www.bbc.co.uk/news/world-africa-25427965.
6 See https://www.cia.gov/library/publications/the-world-factbook/rankorder/2002rank.html?countryname=South Sudan&countrycode=od&regionCode=afr&rank=3#od.
7 See https://www.cia.gov/library/publications/the-world-factbook/geos/od.html.
8 See http://www.bbc.co.uk/news/world-africa-25454168.
9 Cited by Shaukat Abdulrazak of Kenya's National Commission for Science, Technology and Innovation at the Kenyan Institute for Management conference on 'Governance, Leadership and Management', Diani Beach, Kenya, 5 September 2013.
10 See http://www.bbc.co.uk/news/world-africa-24433996.
11 World Bank. 'Africa Overview', Washington, D.C., http://www.worldbank.org/en/region/afr/overview.
12 Robert Rotberg, 'Failed and Weak States Defined', *Africa and Asia: The Key Issues*, 11 February 2013, http://robertrotberg.wordpress.com/2013/02/11/failed-and-weak-states-defined/. Rotberg has helpfully defined these categories as strong, weak, failed and collapsed states. Strong states (numbering around 60 to 70), include the Finlands, New Zealands and Singapores of the world, plus the US, bits of Asia and Latin America, and most of Europe, where there is respect for democracy, institutions and the individual. 'Weak' states (some 80 to 90 or more) are those that supply less-than-adequate political and socio-economic goods to their populations. This includes a wide spectrum of countries, which may be further divided into a sub-type of those that tend towards 'failing'. It includes those that may appear strong but 'mask their weaknesses through systematic repression and therefore display a fake strength'. Such states include North Korea, Turkmenistan, Syria, Equatorial Guinea, Uzbekistan, Belarus, Saddam Hussein's Iraq, and, before 2011, Egypt, Burma, Libya, Syria and Tunisia. Next are 'failed' states, which 'lack security, are unsafe, honour rules of law in the breach, are robustly corrupt, deny participation or voice most of the time to most of their people, discriminate within their countries against classes and kinds of citizens, offer sustainable economic opportunity only to ruling elites and other cronies, and provide human development (educational and health services) sparingly or not at all'. The final category is that of 'collapsed' states, including Somalia, Liberia under Charles Taylor, and Sierra Leone during its civil war, where there are defined (if not always guarded or recognised) borders but no government and governance.

1 ARGENTINA

1 See http://www.bbc.co.uk/news/world-latin-america-22044970. Most of the material here was gathered during a research visit to Argentina from 6–13 July 2011. Thanks are especially due to Tony Leon and Lyal White for assistance in this regard. Unless otherwise indicated, the interviews quoted here were conducted during this visit.
2 See http://web.worldbank.org/WBSITE/EXTERNAL/TOPICS/EXTPOVERTY/EXTPA/0,,contentMDK:20206704~menuPK:435735~pagePK:148956~piPK:216618~theSitePK:430367~isCURL:Y~isCURL:Y,00.html.
3 See http://en.mercopress.com/2013/04/25/official-poverty-in-argentina-2.5-million-people-private-estimate-11-million.
4 The tequila effect was the term given to the impact of the 1994 Mexican economic crisis caused by a sudden devaluation of the peso on other South American countries, which caused their own currencies to decline. The peso was propped up by a $50-billion US loan.
5 Discussion, Buenos Aires, June 2011.
6 This amount comprised, in 2001, 53 million tonnes in soya, 22 million tonnes in maize, 10.6 million tonnes in wheat, 3.62 million tonnes in sunflower, 3.61 million tonnes in citrus, 3 million tonnes in sorghum and 0.57 million tonnes in peanuts.
7 'Which Emerging Economies are at Greatest Risk of Overheating?', *The Economist*, 2 July 2011.
8 See 'Don't Lie to Me Argentina', http://www.economist.com/node/21548242.
9 See http://www.reuters.com/article/2012/04/18/us-spain-argentina-ypf-eu-idUSBRE83G0QU20120418.
10 See http://www.bbc.co.uk/news/business-26349207.
11 See http://www.bbc.co.uk/news/business-17732910.
12 See http://www.euractiv.com/energy/repsol-expropriation-eating-arge-analysis-519304.
13 The interviews with Cavallo, De La Rúa, Menem and Prat-Guy were conducted in Buenos Aires in July 2011.

2 GUINEA

1 This chapter is based on a research trip undertaken to Guinea in April 2013 with Daniel Pinhassi. The interviews cited here were conducted during this time in Conakry.

2 With thanks to Dr Peter Pham for his input into the history of politics under Sékou Touré.

3 Stephen Ellis, email correspondence, 6 April 2014.

4 The others being Burundi, Liberia, Guinea-Bissau, Central African Republic and Liberia. See http://www.un.org/en/peacebuilding/.

5 See Patrick Radden Keefe, 'Buried Secrets', New Yorker, 8 July 2013, http://www.newyorker.com/reporting/2013/07/08/130708fa_fact_keefe?printable=true&currentPage=all#ixzz2fiX7hKqN.

6 Radden Keefe, 'Buried Secrets'.

7 See http://www.bbc.co.uk/news/world-africa-24590091.

3 HAITI

1 See http://jphro.org/. This chapter is based on a research trip to Haiti and the Dominican Republic in January 2013. Where not referenced, interviews were conducted during this visit, the same approach taken with other chapters.

2 See http://www.time.com/time/world/article/0,8599,1953959,00.html.

3 This is based partly on a trip to Aruba in November 2013, and a meeting with the prime minister of Aruba in Haiti in January 2013.

4 See.http://svs.gsfc.nasa.gov/vis/a000000/a002600/a002640/haiti_still_web.jpg.

5 See http://www.undp.org/content/undp/en/home/presscenter/articles/2012/05/21/undp-helps-haiti-and-dominican-republic-reforest-shared-border.html.

6 See http://www.un.org/en/peacekeeping/missions/minustah/.

7 See http://www.foreign.senate.gov/imo/media/doc/Simon-Barjon%20testimony.pdf.

8 See http://reliefweb.int/sites/reliefweb.int/files/resources/has_aid_changed_en.pdf.

9 'Haiti Earthquake Recovery: Where Did All The Money Go?', Huffington Post, 11 January 2012, http://www.huffingtonpost.com/2012/01/11/haiti-earthquake-recovery_n_1197730.html.

10 See http://www.brown.edu/Facilities/John_Carter_Brown_Library/remember_haiti/race_moreau-de-saint-mery.php.

11 François 'Papa Doc' Duvalier ruled from 1957 until his death in 1971, and Jean-Claude 'Baby Doc' from his father's death until his overthrow in 1986.

12 See Ian Thomson, Bonjour Blanc: A Journey Through Haiti. New York: Vintage, 2004.

13 See Michel Laguerre, Voodoo and Politics. New York: St Martin's Press, 1989. Tonton Macoute was created in 1959 by François 'Papa Doc' Duvalier. The force was so named after the Haitian Creole mythological Tonton Macoute ('Uncle Gunnysack') bogeyman, who kidnaps and punishes unruly children by putting them in a gunnysack (macoute) and abducting them off to be consumed at breakfast.

14 Email exchange, January 2013.

15 Jonathan Katz, The Big Truck that Went By: How the World Came to Save Haiti and Left Behind a Disaster. New York: Random House, 2013, p.2.

16 See http://www2.webster.edu/~corbetre/haiti/misctopic/leftover/headstate.htm.

17 Interview, Port-au-Prince, 23 January 2013.

18 This section is based on a visit to Dominican Republic in January 2013.

19 Laura Jaramillo and Cemile Sancak, 'Growth in the Dominican Republic and Haiti: Why has the Grass Been Greener on One Side of Hispaniola?' IMF Working Paper 07/63, http://www.imf.org/external/pubs/ft/wp/2007/wp0763.pdf.

20 See http://www.doingbusiness.org/rankings.

21 See http://www.transparency.org/cpi2013/results.

22 Interview, La Romana, January 2013.

23 See http://www.dallasnews.com/entertainment/books/20130104-review-two-insightful-looks-at-haitis-eternal-troubles.ece.

24 See Kathy Klarreich and Linda Polman, 'The NGO Republic of Haiti', http://www.thenation.com/article/170929/ngo-republic-haiti.

25 See http://www.economist.com/node/21532299.

26 See http://www.economist.com/node/21532299.

27 Email correspondence, 23 January 2013.

28 This agreement provides fuel at preferential financing rates to seventeen Caribbean countries, including Haiti. Under these terms, Haiti can import 14 000 barrels of oil a day and has three months to pay for 60 per cent of each oil shipment, and 25 years to pay the balance at just one interest point.

4 KENYA

1 The visit to Kibera occurred in March 2014 in the company of Lyal White.

2 See https://www.cia.gov/library/publications/the-world-factbook/geos/ke.html. This chapter is, in part, based on two trips to Kenya in February 2013, working with Prime Minister Raila Odinga's office on a post-election development approach, and again when the train diagnostic was undertaken in August–September 2013.

3 See http://www.africaresearchinstitute.org/publications/policy-voices/urban-planning-in-kenya/.

4 Unless otherwise cited, quotes are taken from these various first-hand trips.

5 With thanks to Edward Clay for this point.

6 See, for example, http://www.globalpost.com/dispatches/globalpost-blogs/groundtruth/state-of-the-union-income-inequality-kenya-kansas-obama.

7 See, for example, http://www.un.org/africarenewal/magazine/april-2008/east-africa-feels-blows-kenyan-crisis.

8 According to research by the Kenyan Institute for

Public Policy Analysis and Research, as reported in *The East African*, 15–21 March 2014.

9 See http://www.farwell-consultants.com/ commentaries/arresting-income-inequality-in-kenya-and-perspectives-for-the-wider-east-africa.

10 See, for example, http://geography.about.com/od/economic-geography/a/Rostow-S-Stages-Of-Growth-Development-Model.htm.

11 With thanks to Professor Hiroyuki Hino for pointing out the census data. See also in this regard http://www.esk.co.ke/resources/72-analysis-of-the-2009-kenyan-population-census-report.html.

12 Jeremy Paxman, *Empire*. London: Penguin, 2012, p.150.

13 Paxman, *Empire*, p.151.

14 See http://www.millspublishing.com/books.aspx?book=3.

15 Discussion, Diani, 6 September 2013.

16 'RVR at a Crossroads as East Africa goes for Standard Gauge to Fix Infrastructure Mess', *The East African*, 31 August – 6 September 2013.

17 See http://www.monitor.co.ug/Business/Technology/RVR+completes+73km+Mombasa++ +Nairobi+stretch+/-/688612/1895802/-/u3xsdy/-/index.html.

18 'RVR at a Crossroads'.

19 See Michela Wrong, *It's Our Turn to Eat*. London: Fourth Estate, 2010.

20 See https://www.cia.gov/library/publications/the-world-factbook/geos/ke.html.

21 See http://www.cipe.org/blog/2009/01/21/democracy-is-more-than-elections/.

22 See http://www.statehousekenya.go.ke/speeches/kibaki/2002301201.htm.

23 Discussion at his home, Nairobi, February 2013.

24 'Nairobi Pays Price as EA Peers do Better Job on Payroll Costs', *The East African*, 15–21 March 2014.

25 See http://www.theeastafrican.co.ke/magazine/-/434746/486376/-/view/printVersion/-/14skfudz/-/index.html.

26 See http://en.wikipedia.org/wiki/Paul_von_Lettow-Vorbeck.

27 With thanks to Dave Kilcullen for this statistic.

28 See http://www.ideels.uni-bremen.de/nairobi.html.

29 Email correspondence, 27 September 2013.

30 See http://www.theguardian.com/commentisfree/2013/sep/23/kenya-behind-terror-rampant-corruption/print.

31 Part of Kenya's Vision 2030, LAPSSET includes the following infrastructural components: a port at Manda Bay, Lamu; standard gauge railway lines to Juba and Addis Ababa and parallel road network; oil pipelines to Southern Sudan and Ethiopia; an oil refinery at Bargoni; three airports; and three resort cities at Lamu, Isiolo and on the shores of Lake Turkana.

32 See '"Little Something" Takes Big Toll on Kenya's People', http://articles.latimes.com/2002/feb/07/news/mn-26745.

33 Where the Kenyan government subsidised exports of gold 35 per cent over their foreign currency earnings, estimated to cost Kenya the equivalent of more than 10 per cent of the country's annual GDP.

34 The supply of a new passport printing system was awarded to a UK-based firm with links to the Moi regime, the Anglo Leasing and Finance Company Limited, who allegedly subcontracted a French firm to do the work for around half the tendered amount.

35 See http://www.transparency.org/cpi2013/results.

36 See http://www.transparency.org/cpi2010/results.

37 Discussion, Nairobi, March 2014.

38 The cost of the line for the first 485-kilometre phase from Mombasa to Nairobi reportedly rose by Sh107 billion (approximately $1.2 billion at the prevailing exchange rate) between July 2012 and November 2013 when the first track was laid, to Sh327 billion. This compares unfavourably, too, with the construction on the new railway in Ethiopia. For Kenya, rolling stock that includes 56 diesel locomotives, 1 620 freight waggons, 40 passenger coaches and one simulator are to cost Sh101 billion. Ethiopia's 35 electric engines, six diesel shunting locomotives, 1 100 freight waggons, 30 passenger coaches and one simulator are estimated to cost Sh20.24 billion. Ethiopia's budget to build 756 kilometres from Addis Ababa to Djibouti port on the Red Sea coast is Sh323 billion. See http://www.kenyaengineer.co.ke/index.php/n-e/ln/1730-price-controversy-haunts-standard-gauge-railway-project.

39 'Nairobi Pays Price as EA Peers do Better Job'.

40 For the impact of technology on birth rates, see http://www.geocurrents.info/population-geography/indias-plummeting-birthrate-a-television-induced-transformation.

41 Discussion, 20 March 2014.

5 NIGERIA

1 The term 'Cauldron of Superlatives' is taken from Richard Dowden's excellent *Africa: Altered States, Ordinary Miracles*. London: Portobello, 2009. This section is based partly on a research trip to Lagos and the Niger Delta in the company of Anthony Arnott, Dianna Games and Leila Jack during April 2013. Grateful appreciation is also expressed to Afeikhena Jerome and Michael Faborode for their insights.

2 See http://blogs.cfr.org/campbell/2013/10/09/is-the-military-winning-against-boko-haram/#cid=soc-facebook-at-blogs-is_the_nigerian_military_winni-100913.

3 With thanks to Anton Roux for this factoid.

4 See http://web.amnesty.org/library/index/ENGAFR440172006?open&of=ENG-NGA.

5 Cited in *The Economist*, 27 April – 3 May 2013, p.49.

6 See http://www.informationng.com/2013/04/president-jonathan-endorses-trust-fund-for-niger-delta.html.

7 See http://premiumtimesng.com/opinion/128652-
amnesty-for-boko-haram-dancing-with-ghosts-
ignoring-the-dead-by-okey-ndibe.html.

8 Peter Lewis, 'Nigeria: Assessing Risks to
Stability', Centre for Strategic and International
Studies, June 2011, http://csis.org/files/
publication/110623_Lewis_Nigeria_Web.pdf.

9 For details on the background to the conflict,
see Frederick Forsyth, *The Making of an African
Legend: The Biafra Story*. London: Penguin, 1978.
For the view from the frontlines of the federal
side, see Olusegun Obasanjo, *My Command:
An Account of the Nigerian Civil War, 1967–70*.
Ibadan: Heinemann, 1980.

10 Peter Lewis, 'The Dysfunctional State of Nigeria'
in Nancy Birdsall, Milan Vaishnav and Robert L.
Ayers (eds), *Short of the Goal: US Policy and Poorly
Performing States*. Washington, D.C.: Center for
Global Development, 2006.

11 Lee Kuan Yew, *From Third World to First:
The Singapore Story: 1965–2000*. New York:
HarperCollins, 2008, p.395.

12 Dowden, *Africa*, p.463.

13 Lewis, 'The Dysfunctional State of Nigeria'.

14 See Nicholas Shaxson, *Poisoned Wells: The Dirty
Politics of African Oil*. London: Palgrave, 2008, p.4.

15 See Morten Jervon, 'What Does Nigeria's GDP
Number Actually Mean?', *African Arguments*,
8 April 2014.

16 See http://www.washingtonpost.com/blogs/
worldviews/wp/2013/07/16/the-amazing-
surprising-africa-driven-demographic-future-of-
the-earth-in-9-charts.

17 Discussion, Port Harcourt, April 2013.

18 See, for example, African Institute for Applied
Economics, 'Nigeria: Macroeconomic
Assessment and Agenda for Reforms', http://
www.usaid.gov/ng/downloads/reforms/
macroeconomicassessment.pdf.

19 Dowden, *Africa*, p.459.

20 Dowden, *Africa*, p.465–66.

21 See http://www.thenigerianvoice.com/
nvnews/49811/1/nigeria-records-biggest-gap-
between-electricity-su.html.

22 See http://www.ft.com/cms/s/0/61fb070e-bf90-
11e1-a476-00144feabdco.html.

23 See http://www.bdlive.co.za/africa/africannews/
2013/05/02/solving-nigerias-power-woes-may-
take-decades.

24 Research consultants Frost and Sullivan cited in
African Business, April 2013, p.34.

25 See http://www.indexmundi.com/g/g.
aspx?c=ni&v=66.

26 See http://www.bbc.com/news/world-
africa-26873233; http://www.budde.com.au/
Research/Nigeria-Mobile-Market-Overview-
Statistics-and-Forecasts.html.

27 These recollections and views were gathered in a
meeting with President Obasanjo, 3 July 2013.

28 Lewis, 'The Dysfunctional State of Nigeria'.

29 See, for example, Olu Ajakaiye and Afeikhena
Jerome, 'The Role of Institutions in the
Transformation of the Nigerian Economy'.
Unpublished paper, 2013.

6 TUNISIA

1 Self-immolation is not a new form of protest
to Tunisia. After two brutal wars with rival
Rome, the second of which famously featured
Hannibal's march over the Alps with his elephants,
600 years of Carthaginian rule were ended in the
third Punic war around 149 BC. Some 50 000
citizens of Carthage were taken prisoner, their
buildings levelled and lands sown symbolically
with salt. While he sensibly surrendered, the wife
and children of their commander, Hasdrubal,
committed suicide by self-immolation. Another
300 years lapsed before Carthage rose again to
become the third-largest imperial city behind
Rome and Alexandria. Sidi Bouzid is the site of
a battle between US forces and German Panzer
divisions in February 1943, the start of what
became known as the Battle of the Kasserine Pass.

2 This section is based on research trips to Tunisia
in March and September 2013, and March 2014,
and to Mali in May 2011 and February 2013. The
discussion with Ayed was conducted at the Villa
Didon in Carthage in March 2014.

3 See https://www1.oecd.org/mena/49036903.pdf.

4 Discussion, African Development Bank,
Tunis, March 2013.

5 See http://www.bbc.com/news/
business-26336738.

6 This figure on GDP loss was provided by
Liz Martins at the HSBC Emerging Markets
conference, New York, 7 November 2013. It is
based on Central Bank and HSBC data.

7 Andrew Lebovich, 'Mali's Bad Trip', *ForeignPolicy.
com*, 15 March 2013, http://www.foreignpolicy.
com/articles/2013/03/15/mali_s_bad_trip?wp_
login_redirect=0.

8 Interview, Conakry, Guinea, April 2013.

9 See Lebovich, 'Mali's Bad Trip'.

10 See, for example, 'The Political Economy of
Conflicts in Northern Mali', ISS ECOWAS
Reports, April 2013, http://www.issafrica.org/
uploads/ECOWAS_Report_2_-_ENG.pdf.

11 Discussion, Tana Forum, 26 April 2014.

12 I am grateful to Mark Shaw for this point. For
a further explanation of this argument, see
the Global Initiative's paper on Mali at www.
globalinitiative.net.

13 With thanks to Stuart Doran for his insights here.

14 See http://www.worldbank.org/en/news/press-
release/2014/02/28/world-bank-group-support-
tunisia-2014.

15 See Asher Susser, 'Tradition and Modernity
in the Arab Spring', *INSS Strategic Assessment*
15(1), April 2012.

7 UGANDA

1 This section is in part based on a research trip to

Kampala, Entebbe and Gulu in May 2012 in the company of Dr Jeffrey Herbst, Sharon Polansky and Janet Wilson. The visit was kindly organised through the good offices of Svend K. Jensen of the ABI Trust. For details on the politics of Uganda, see Adam Seftel (comp.), *Uganda: The Bloodstained Pearl of Africa and its Struggle for Peace*. Kampala: Fountain Publishers, 1994. I am grateful to Adrian Kitombo for his inputs into this section.

2 For further reading, see Heike Behrend, *Alice Lakwena & the Holy Spirits: War In Northern Uganda 1986–97*. Athens, OH: Ohio University Press, 2000; Tim Allen and Koen Vlassenroot, *The Lord's Resistance Army: Myth and Reality*. London: Zed Books, 2010; Peter Eichstaedtm, *First Kill Your Family: Child Soldiers of Uganda and the Lord's Resistance Army*. Chicago: Chicago Review Press, 2009; Sverker Finnstrom, *Living with Bad Surroundings: War, History, and Everyday Moments in Northern Uganda: The Cultures and Practice of Violence*. Durham: Duke University Press, 2008.

8 VENEZUELA

1 This chapter is partly based on interviews conducted in Venezuela in November 2013 in the company of Ambassador (retired) Malcolm Ferguson. Thanks are expressed particularly to Ambassador Thaningi Shope-Linney and Schoeman du Plessis of the South African Embassy in Caracas for their professional assistance in this regard. Unless otherwise indicated, the interviews cited here were conducted during this trip.

2 Comisión de Administración de Divisas (CADIVI or the Commission for the Administration of Currency Exchange) is the government body administering currency exchange in Venezuela.

3 See http://www.bbc.co.uk/news/world-latin-america-24185342.

4 See http://www.bbc.co.uk/news/world-latin-america-22526622.

5 See Steve Hanke's analysis, http://www.cato.org/blog/venezuelas-house-cards.

6 See http://www.bbc.co.uk/news/world-latin-america-24897407.

7 *El Universal*, 14 November 2013.

8 See http://www.bbc.com/news/world-latin-america-26985114.

9 For an excellent summary of the Chávez phenomenon, see Rory Carroll, *Comandante: Hugo Chávez's Venezuela*. London: Penguin, 2013.

10 See the BBC Radio Documentary on the toilet paper crisis, September 2013, http://downloads.bbc.co.uk/podcasts/worldservice/docarchive/docarchive_20130926-0100a.mp3.

11 Bart Jones, *Hugo! The Hugo Chávez Story from Mud Hut to Perpetual Revolution*. Hanover, New Hampshire: Steerforth Press, 2007, cited at http://en.wikipedia.org/wiki/Hugo_Ch%C3%A1vez#Jon07.

12 Carroll, *Comandante*.

13 Made with Felipe Acosta Carles, Jesús Urdaneta and Raul Isaias Baduel, based on the oath made by Simón Bolivar in Monte Sacro.

14 For the historical details, including the controversy around registration and the voting and tabulation process, see http://en.wikipedia.org/wiki/Venezuelan_recall_referendum,_2004.

15 For a discussion on these developments, see http://www.newyorker.com/online/blogs/newsdesk/2013/11/chavezs-successor-sees-a-trilogy-of-evil.html.

16 See http://en.rsf.org/venezuela-rctvi-yields-in-order-to-resume-23-02-2010,36202.

17 This is the May 2013 figure. See http://www.eluniversal.com/economia/130612/venezuelan-oil-output-slides-246-in-may.

18 With thanks to Alberto Trejos for these figures. Statistics are notoriously unreliable and politicised in Venezuela and a source of much dispute.

19 With thanks also to Professor Trejos for this point.

20 By 2012 the US was importing 40 per cent of Venezuela's oil production, some 760 000 barrels per day, with China estimated at 500 000 barrels per day. See http://www.nasdaq.com/article/venezuela-awash-in-oil-but-riddled-with-corruption-inefficiency-cm122707.

21 See http://www.nytimes.com/2013/03/09/world/americas/venezuelas-role-as-oil-power-diminished.html?_r=0.

22 See http://www.bbc.co.uk/news/business-19813533.

23 See http://www.bbc.co.uk/news/business-19813533.

24 See http://www.reuters.com/article/2013/05/14/us-venezuela-crime-idUSBRE94D01120130514.

25 See http://www.transparency.org/cpi2013/results.

26 See http://www.doingbusiness.org/rankings.

9 ZIMBABWE

1 This chapter is based, in part, on a research trip to Zimbabwe in August–September 2012. Unless otherwise indicated, the information and interviews presented here were gathered at that time.

2 Remittances into Zimbabwe were, by 2013, estimated to flow at anywhere from $1 million per day to three times this amount, given the difference between formal and informal channels. For a diary of events detailing the disintegration of the Zimbabwe economy, see Andrew Meldrum, *Where We Have Hope*. London: John Murray, 2004.

3 Discussion, January 2014.

4 See 'A New Rand?' in Thomas Pakenham, *The Scramble for Africa*. Johannesburg: Jonathan Ball, 1991, p.372.

5 Cited in *The Times*, 11 January 2014.

6 With thanks to Stuart Doran for this insight.

7 With thanks to John Robertson for this point.

8 Discussion, Tswalu Kalahari Reserve, November 2013.

9 For an overview of the reasons behind Zimbabwe's decline, see Terrence Kairiza, 'Unbundling Zimbabwe's Journey to Hyperinflation and Official Dollarization', GRIPS Discussion Paper 9/12, http://www3.grips.ac.jp/~pinc/data/09-12.pdf.

10 As cited in William Dobson, The Dictators, London: Vintage, 2013, p.127.

11 Dobson, The Dictators, p.9.

12 James A. Robinson and Daron Acemoğlu, Why Nations Fail: The Origins of Power, Prosperity and Poverty. London: Profile, 2013.

13 The words of a senior manufacturing sector executive in Harare, August 2012.

14 Dobson, The Dictators, p.9.

15 Dobson, The Dictators, p.11. It should not be forgotten that until 2011, the Middle East was the only region that lacked a single democracy save Israel, where the average leader ruled for not less than sixteen years. And the democratic wave started in the most unlikely of places, Tunisia, considered to be one of the 'sturdiest' autocracies in the region.

16 See, for example, 'How ZANU-PF Stays in Power', http://africanarguments.org/2013/05/09/how-zanu-pf-stays-in-power-%E2%80%93-by-simukai-tinhu/. See also http://www.news24.com/Africa/Zimbabwe/Zanu-PFs-Chinamasa-just-making-noise-20121017.

17 See, for example, http://mg.co.za/article/2014-01-14-un-cuts-food-aid-for-one-million-zimbabweans.

18 See http://mg.co.za/article/2014-01-14-un-cuts-food-aid-for-one-million-zimbabweans.

19 A further indication of the extent of corruption can be gauged from the reputed cost of a minibus passenger from Harare-Johannesburg at R1 500 (£120 at the time in September 2012) sans travel papers, and just R400 return.

20 As a guide, at the start of October 2013, the ZAR exchange rate was R10 to the US dollar, R16 to the UK pound and R13.5 to the euro.

PART 2:
INSTANCES OF INTERVENTION

1 Cited in Joshua Levine, Forgotten Voices of the Somme. London: Ebury, 2008, p.143.

2 See John Lewis-Stempel, Six Weeks: The Short and Gallant Life of the British Officer in the First World War. London: Orion, 2011.

3 Patrick Bishop, Bomber Boys. London: HarperCollins, 2008, p.xxxviii. Estimates of the deaths caused on the ground in Germany and elsewhere in occupied Europe range from 300 000–600 000.

4 See, for example, Antony Beevor, Berlin: The Downfall 1945. London: Penguin, esp. p.424.

5 See Duff Hart-Davis, The War That Never Was. London: Century, 2011.

6 John Simpson, BBC TV, 1 March 2014.

7 See http://www.un.org/en/peacekeeping/resources/statistics/factsheet.shtml.

8 These missions include: United Nations Mission for the Referendum in Western Sahara (MINURSO) since April 1991, with a strength of 485, and budget (07/2012–06/2013) of $61 299 800; United Nations Stabilization Mission in Haiti (MINUSTAH) since June 2004, strength 11 324, budget (07/2012–06/2013) $648 394 000; United Nations Organization Stabilization Mission in the Democratic Republic of the Congo (MONUSCO) since July 2010, strength 23 638, budget (07/2012–06/2013) $1 347 538 800; African Union-United Nations Hybrid Operation in Darfur (UNAMID), since July 2007, strength 24 505, budget (07/2012–06/2013) $1 448 574 000; United Nations Disengagement Observer Force (UNDOF) in Syria since June 1974, strength 1 055, budget (07/2012–06/2013) $45 992 000; United Nations Peacekeeping Force in Cyprus (UNFICYP) since March 1964, strength 1 088, budget (07/2012–06/2013) $56 106 200; United Nations Interim Force in Lebanon (UNIFIL) since March 1978, strength 11 802, budget (07/2012–06/2013) $524 010, 000; United Nations Interim Security Force for Abyei (UNISFA) since June 2011, strength 4 123, budget (07/2012–06/2013) $257 932 000; United Nations Mission in the Republic of South Sudan (UNMISS) since July 2011, strength 9 857, budget (07/2012–06/2013) $839 490 000; United Nations Operation in Côte d'Ivoire (UNOCI), since April 2004, strength 12 414, budget (07/2012–06/2013) $575,017,000; United Nations Interim Administration Mission in Kosovo (UNMIK) since June 1999, strength 382, budget (07/2012–06/2013) $46 963 000; United Nations Mission in Liberia (UNMIL) since September 2003, strength 9 944, budget (07/2012 – 06/2013) $496 457 800; United Nations Military Observer Group in India and Pakistan (UNMOGIP) since January 1949, strength 110, appropriation (biennium 2012–13) $21 084 400; United Nations Truce Supervision Organization (UNTSO) in Middle East since May 1948, strength 386, appropriation (biennium 2012–13) $70 280 900.

9 See http://www.telegraph.co.uk/news/worldnews/northamerica/usa/9961877/Cost-to-US-of-Iraq-and-Afghan-wars-could-hit-6-trillion.html.

10 United Nations Department of Public Information, 30 November 2007, http://www.un.org/Depts/dpko/dpko/bnote.htm.

11 The UK bill alone is estimated at over $300 million. See http://www.huffingtonpost.co.uk/2011/12/08/libya-operations-cost-treasury-212m_n_1135952.html.

12 See 'The Report of the Panel on UN Operations', Brahimi Report, 2003, http://www.un.org/peace/reports/peace_operations/.

13 At the 2005 World Summit, UN member-states included R2P in the Outcome Document agreeing

to Paragraphs 138 and 139. These paragraphs state: '(138). Each individual State has the responsibility to protect its populations from genocide, war crimes, ethnic cleansing and crimes against humanity. This responsibility entails the prevention of such crimes, including their incitement, through appropriate and necessary means. We accept that responsibility and will act in accordance with it. The international community should, as appropriate, encourage and help States to exercise this responsibility and support the UN in establishing an early warning capability. (139). The international community, through the UN, also has the responsibility to use appropriate diplomatic, humanitarian and other peaceful means, in accordance with Chapters VI and VIII of the Charter, to help protect populations from genocide, war crimes, ethnic cleansing and crimes against humanity. In this context, we are prepared to take collective action, in a timely and decisive manner, through the Security Council, in accordance with the Charter, including Chapter VII, on a case-by-case basis and in cooperation with relevant regional organizations as appropriate, should peaceful means be inadequate and national authorities manifestly fail to protect their populations from genocide, war crimes, ethnic cleansing and crimes against humanity. We stress the need for the General Assembly to continue consideration of the responsibility to protect populations from genocide, war crimes, ethnic cleansing and crimes against humanity and its implications, bearing in mind the principles of the Charter and international law. We also intend to commit ourselves, as necessary and appropriate, to helping States build capacity to protect their populations from genocide, war crimes, ethnic cleansing and crimes against humanity and to assisting those which are under stress before crises and conflicts break out.' In contemplating the threshold for military action, consideration should be given, it is argued (for example, by the non-binding International Commission for Intervention and State Sovereignty Report of 2001), to various criteria, including just cause, final resort, the key intention to prevent civilian deaths, proportional means and the reasonable prospect of success. See http://en.wikipedia.org/wiki/Responsibility_to_ protect.

14 See, for example, http://abcnews.go.com/Politics/ libya-military-intervention-costs-us-taxpayers-millions-dollars/story?id=13193525.

15 See, for example, http://www.rand.org/ publications/randreview/issues/ summer2003/ nation3.html.

16 See Jeremy Greenstock, http://www. middleeastmonitor.com/resources/ interviews/7277-jeremy-greenstock-on-syria-qiraq-wmd-was-a-big-turn-off-of-peoples-trust-in-government-assertion-and-that-cant-be-put-back-in-the-boxq.

17 See http://www.iol.co.za/news/politics/ letter-sparks-diplomatic-damage-control-1.59038?ot=inmsa.ArticlePrintPageLayout.ot. See also http://www.telegraph.co.uk/news/worldnews/ africaandindianocean/southafrica/1319582/ Mbeki-pledge-to-support-Zimbabwe.html.

10 AFGHANISTAN

1 This chapter is based partly on research conducted while on secondment to ISAF in Kandahar in April–May and September–October 2010 and to Kabul in October–November 2012. Thanks are expressed to Anthony Arnott, Major General Dickie Davis and Brigadier General Ewen McLay, in particular, for their support during these assignments, and to Lieutenant General Nick Carter, in 2010 commanding the division in the south of Afghanistan and in 2012 DCOM ISAF, for his invitation and hospitality in this regard.

2 The Dasht-e – otherwise known as Dashti Margo, Dasht-e Mārgow, Dasht-e Margoh or 'Desert of Death' – is the desert region in the southern provinces of Helmand and Nimruz in Afghanistan.

3 The number of ISAF troops peaked at 145 000 in 2011, and was down to 87 207 from 49 contributing nations by 1 August 2013, the US providing some 60 000 and the United Kingdom 7 700 of this total. At the same time, Afghan National Army and Afghan National Police numbers increased from 100 000 and 93 000 respectively in 2009 to 152 000 and 118 000 two years later, and totalled 350 000 by the start of 2013.

4 Stefanie Nijssen, 'The Afghan Economy: A Brief History', October 2010, http:// www.cimicweb. org. See also Mark N. Katz, 'Lessons of the Soviet Withdrawal from Afghanistan', Middle East Policy Council Commentary, 2012, http://www.mepc. org/articles-commentary/commentary/lessons-soviet-withdrawal-afghanistan?print, and Open Source Works, 'Afghanistan: Lessons of the Soviet War', 27 March 2009, http://info.publicintelligence. net/CIAafghanlessons.pdf.

5 See, for example, Walter Cronkite's 'Vietnam War', CBS News, 2003.

6 This is based on detainee transcripts studied in Helmand, November 2013.

7 For an excellent historical narrative, see Bijan Omrani and Matthew Leeming, Afghanistan: A Companion and Guide. New York: Odyssey, 2005.

8 Barnett R. Rubin, 'Lineages of the State in Afghanistan', Asian Survey 28(11), November 1988.

9 Karzai was selected to serve a six-month term as chairman of an interim administration during the December 2001 International Conference on Afghanistan held in Berlin. During the 2002 Loya Jirga held in Kabul he was chosen as interim president for a two-year term. He was declared the winner of the 2004 presidential election and again

in 2009, serving two terms as president of the Islamic Republic of Afghanistan.

10 Afghanistan places 175th and last on Transparency International's 2013 Corruption Perception Index, tying with North Korea and Somalia. It ranks 164/189 on the World Bank's 2014 Ease of Doing Business Indicators.

11 See http://www.nytimes.com/2012/07/21/opinion/afghanistans-economic-challenges.html.

12 Barnett Rubin, 'The Political Economy of War and Peace in Afghanistan', http://elmu.umm.ac.id/file.php/1/jurnal/UVW/World%20Development/Vol28.Issue10.Oct2000/1060.pdf.

13 Discussions, Kabul, 31 October and 1 November 2012 respectively.

14 See Barnett Rubin, Afghanistan in the Post-Cold War Era. New York: Oxford University Press, 2013, p.68.

15 Telephonic discussion, 7 May 2013.

16 International Development Committee, 'Sixth Report Afghanistan: Development Progress and Prospects after 2014', http://www.publications.parliament.uk/pa/cm201213/cmselect/cmintdev/403/40305.htm.

17 Daron Acemoğlu and James Robinson, Why Nations Fail: The Origins of Power, Prosperity and Poverty. London: Profile, 2012. See also the review by Paul Collier, The Guardian, 11 March 2012.

18 See http://www.bbc.co.uk/news/world-asia-china-20233101.

19 Cited in Edward Luce, In Spite of the Gods. London: Abacus, 2011, p.64.

20 See http://www.telegraph.co.uk/news/worldnews/asia/afghanistan/8559898/Afghanistan-troop-withdrawal-Robert-Gates-warns-against-short-term-thinking.html.

21 See http://www.ft.com/intl/cms/s/0/9c525462-4cad-11e1-8b08-00144feabdco.html#axzz2BlDOkkR3.

22 Interview, New Delhi, October 2012.

23 See http://www.cfr.org/pakistan/us-pakistan-military-cooperation/p16644.

24 Though this was put on hold in 2014. See http://www.scmp.com/news/world/article/1453375/chinas-mcc-turns-back-us3b-mes-aynak-afghanistan-mine-deal.

25 Anatol Lieven, Pakistan: A Hard Country. London: Penguin, 2012.

26 Cited in Lieven, Pakistan.

27 See http://www.economist.com/news/asia/21565246-country-faces-three-momentous-transitions-how-it-handles-them-will-determine-its-future-all.

28 Not his real name.

29 See http://cso.gov.af/Content/files/External%20Trade(1).pdf.

30 Sir Rodric Braithwaite, Afghantsy: The Russians in Afghanistan, 1979–89. London: Profile, 2011, p.8.

31 Braithwaite, Afghantsy, p.12.

32 This section relies on David Fivecoat's excellent analysis on the Soviet withdrawal. David G. Fivecoat, 'Leaving the Graveyard: The

Soviet Union's Withdrawal from Afghanistan', Parameters, Summer 2012, http://www.carlisle.army.mil/USAWC/parameters/Articles/2012summer/Fivecoat.pdf.

33 Cited in Fivecoat, 'Leaving the Graveyard'.

34 Braithwaite, Afghantsy, pp.223–24.

35 By October 2012, the Afghan army was said to be fighting in nine-tenths of all operations and leading nearly half of them, taking four or five times the casualties of ISAF. See http://www.economist.com/news/asia/21565246-country-faces-three-momentous-transitions-how-it-handles-them-will-determine-its-future-all.

36 Christian F. Ostermann (ed.), 'Notes from Politburo Meeting, 21–22 January 1987', The Cold War International History Project (CWIHP) Bulletin 14/15 (2003–2004), p.146, cited in Fivecoat, 'Leaving the Graveyard'.

37 The AfPak Hands programme was created by the US Department of Defence in September 2009 to develop a cadre of military and senior civilian experts specialising in the complexities of Afghanistan and Pakistan – the language, culture, processes and challenges. By 2012, they had embedded themselves across a number of key Afghan ministries with the aim of playing a facilitating role between ISAF and the Government of the Islamic Republic of Afghanistan.

38 Braithwaite, Afghantsy, p.152.

39 The Afghan Air Force circa 2012 comprised 4 956 personnel flying 33 Mi-17 and nine Mi-35 attack helicopters, with a planned expansion to 8 000 personnel and 145 aircraft, including additional attack helicopters and twenty A-29 Super Tucano fixed-wing attack aircraft.

40 Artemy M. Kalinovsky, A Long Goodbye: The Soviet Withdrawal from Afghanistan. Cambridge, MA: Harvard University Press, 2011, p. 107, cited in Fivecoat, 'Leaving the Graveyard'.

41 See http://cso.gov.af/Content/files/External%20Trade(1).pdf.

42 Open Source Works, 'Afghanistan: Lessons of the Soviet War', 27 March 2009, http://info.publicintelligence.net/CIAafghanlessons.pdf.

43 Mark N. Katz, 'Lessons of the Soviet Withdrawal from Afghanistan', Middle East Policy Council Commentary, 2012, http://www.mepc.org/articles-commentary/commentary/lessons-soviet-withdrawal-afghanistan?print.

44 Fivecoat, 'Leaving the Graveyard'.

45 See, for example, my article 'Talk to the Taliban', New York Times, 18 September 2006.

46 See Jon Boone and Declan Walsh, 'US Scrambles to Restore Afghan Relations after WikiLeaks Revelations', The Guardian, 3 December 2010, cited in Fivecoat, 'Leaving the Graveyard'.

47 Open Source Works, 'Afghanistan'.

48 Clare Lockhart, 'Struggling for Government Leadership: The Relationship between Afghan and International Actors in Post-2001 Afghanistan' in James Mayall and Ricardo Soares de Oliveira

(eds), *The New Protectorates: International Tutelage and the Making of Liberal States*. London: Hurst, 2012, p.261.

49 See http://www.nytimes.com/2012/07/21/opinion/afghanistans-economic-challenges.html?_r=0.

50 See 'Afghans say US Team Found Huge Potential Mineral Wealth', http://www.bbc.co.uk/news/10311752. This is reportedly made up of iron, $421 billion; copper, $274 billion; niobium, $81 billion; cobalt, $51 billion; and gold, $25 billion. Other sources put reserves as high as $3 trillion. See http://www.guardian.co.uk/global-development/poverty-matters/2011/oct/12/afghanistan-transparency-vast-mineral-deposits.

51 Acemoğlu and Robinson, *Why Nations Fail*.

52 The tax base has increased from 3 per cent to 11 per cent over the course of the international intervention to total £1.65 billion in 2010–11, up 26 per cent, for example, from the previous year. See House of Commons International Development Committee, 'Afghanistan: Development Progress and Prospects after 2014', Sixth Report of Session 2012–13, 12 September 2012.

53 David Fowkes, 'Review of Why Nations Fail', *Focus* 66, October 2012, http://www.hsf.org.za/resource-centre/focus/issues-61-70/Focus66web.pdf/view.

54 With thanks to Anthony Arnott for his input into this section.

55 For an excellent overview of this aspect focusing on one project, see Samia Waheed Altaf, *So Much Aid, So Little Development*. Baltimore: Johns Hopkins University Press, 2011.

56 Discussion, Kabul, October 2010.

57 Discussion, Turquoise Mountain Foundation, Kabul, 1 May 2010.

58 See Report of the Majority Staff, Committee on Oversight and Governmental Reform, 'Warlords Inc.: Extortion and Corruption Along the US Supply Chain in Afghanistan', US House of Representatives, June 2010.

59 Discussion, Kabul, 2 May 2010.

60 Survey conducted in Kandahar City, 2 May 2010.

61 'Let There Be Lights: Kandahar Residents Want Power Instead of Cdn Polio Shots', 25 April 2010, http://news.aol.ca/article/let-there-be-lights-kandahar-residents-want-power-instead-of-cdn-polio-shots/796221/.

62 Each MW/h (using Sri Lanka as regional benchmark) can add up to $1 740 to the economy. Thus one MW could, using this benchmark, add $15 million to the economy over the course of a single year.

63 Conducted on 3 May 2010.

64 Discussion, Gandamack Lodge, Kabul, 2 May 2010.

65 Weish, 16 April 2010.

66 Speech at UN, 2 October 2008.

67 For example, a police chief's post is rumoured to 'cost' $50 000, this money being collected in turn through informal 'taxation'.

68 Her story achieved literary fame in *The Sewing*

Circles of Herat: My Afghan Years. New York, Flamingo, 2003.

69 The Iranian rial fell 40 per cent in September 2012, while Tehran altered its subsidy policy from goods to individuals, favouring nationals over foreign workers in the process.

70 Email correspondence, David Kilcullen, 15 November 2012.

71 Nick Dowling, *Small Wars Journal*, 6 May 2009, http://smallwarsjournal.com/blog/travels-with-nick-3.

72 Telephonic discussion, 7 May 2013.

73 As cited in Henry Kamm, 'Kabul Army Looks Strong, Russian Says', *New York Times*, 30 November 1988. I am grateful to Dominic Medley for pointing this out.

74 *The Wall Street Journal*, 19 September 2013.

75 'Dateline Saigon', Walter Cronkite's CBS series on the Vietnam War.

76 See Thomas E. Ricks, *The Generals: American Military Command from World War II to Today*. New York: Penguin, 2013, p.293.

77 Cited in Ricks, *The Generals*, p.322.

11 THE DEMOCRATIC REPUBLIC OF CONGO

1 The visit to meet Nkunda took place in 2008.

2 See Jeffrey Gettleman's article by the same title in *Foreign Policy*, February 2010, http://www.foreignpolicy.com/articles/2010/02/22/africas_forever_wars.

3 See http://www.economist.com/blogs/dailychart/2010/12/urbanisation_africa.

4 See http://www.un.org/en/peacekeeping/missions/monusco/facts.shtml.

5 Correspondence, December 2012.

6 For an early evaluation of the performance of the UN intervention brigade and the implications, see http://www.voanews.com/content/united-nations-intervention-brigade-drc-conflict/1788997.html.

7 Discussion, regional security adviser, 5 April 2014.

8 This example is drawn from 'Analysis: Where is the State in North Kivu?', *IRIN Reports*, 9 August 2013. See also http://www.opendemocracy.net/opensecurity/karen-b%C3%BCscher-koen-vlassenroot/humanitarian-industry-and-urban-change-in-goma, a March 2013 paper by the Conflict Research Group on the role of aid organisations.

9 See http://www.voanews.com/content/congo-president-rejects-british-mp-accusations-of-mining-fraud-135509493/149482.html.

10 See http://hdr.undp.org/en/media/HDR2013_EN_Statistics.pdf.

11 Email and telephonic communication with the Union for Democracy and Social Progress, December 2011.

12 See http://www.france24.com/en/20120224-democratic-republic-congo-election-legislative-kabila-carter-center.

13 See http://www.google.com/hostednews/afp/
article/ALeqM5jlkk3cyN2vLEDkZp1-H5sTJU5x
pw?docId=CNG.104a1c9e9c71e179b33042a465
c95d6c.711.
14 See http://www.congoplanet.com/news/1926/dr-
congo-presidential-election-results-not-truthful-
cardinal-monsengwo.jsp.
15 This section is based in part on the series of
three articles on the Congo with Jeffrey Herbst in
Foreign Policy, March 2009, August 2009 and June
2013.
16 See http://www.economist.com/node/18617876.
17 BBC Radio Four, 10 January 2014.
18 See https://www.cia.gov.
19 See http://www.transparency.org/country#COD.
20 See http://www.heritage.org/index/ranking.
21 Email correspondence, May 2013.
22 See http://www.state.gov/documents/
organization/160453.pdf.
23 Discussion, 3 July 2013.
24 See Jeremy Paxman, Empire. London: Penguin,
2012, p.23. Slavery practised by local elites
was abolished in Sierra Leone only in 1928, a
place established for freed slaves, though one
study has found practices of domestic slavery
still widespread in rural areas in the 1970s.
See Paul Richards, Memoranda submitted on
'British Peacemaking Policy in West Africa' to
the House of Commons Select Committee on
International Development, January 2006, http://
www.publications.parliament.uk/pa/cm200506/
cmselect/cmintdev/923/923m21.htm.

12 IRAQ TO SYRIA

1 Private email correspondence, 2 December 2013.
2 See http://edition.cnn.com/2013/12/26/politics/
us-iraq-missiles/.
3 This chapter is based partly on interviews with
serving and retired coalition military officers,
during, between and after three visits to that
country: the first as a 'unilateral' journalist
in March 2003; and two fieldwork trips courtesy of
the UK Ministry of Defence in January–February
and September–October 2004.
4 See http://www.theguardian.com/politics/2003/
mar/18/foreignpolicy.iraq1.
5 See http://www.publications.parliament.
uk/pa/cm201314/cmhansrd/cm130829/
debtext/130829-0001.htm.
6 Paul Wolfowitz, 'Iraq: It's Too Soon to Tell', Asharq
Al-Awsat, 9 April 2013.
7 See Steve Hull, 'Remembering the Invasion
of Iraq: "A Colossal Strategic Error"', National
Security Forum Occasional Commentary, http://
nationalsecurityforum.org. For an excellent
insight into the challenges of fighting a counter-
insurgency war in the midst of wider, national
challenges, see David Kilcullen, The Accidental
Guerrilla. New York: Oxford University Press, 2011.
8 See, in this regard, Emma Sky, 'Iraq War: Six
Lessons We Still Need to Learn', http://www.

guardian.co.uk/commentisfree/2013/mar/11/iraq-
war-lessons-intervention.
9 See George W. Bush, Decision Points. New York:
Crown, 2010, pp.223–24.
10 Bush, Decision Points, p.229.
11 See Dick Cheney, In My Time: A Personal and
Political Memoir. New York: Threshold, 2011,
p.368–69.
12 Interviewed at http://downloads.bbc.
co.uk/podcasts/worldservice/docarchive/
docarchive_20130917-0905a.mp3.
13 See http://wais.stanford.edu/Iraq/iraq_
deathsundersaddamhussein42503.html.
14 See http://www.nytimes.com/2003/01/26/
weekinreview/the-world-how-many-people-has-
hussein-killed.html?pagewanted=all&src=pm.
15 Interviewed at http://downloads.bbc.
co.uk/podcasts/worldservice/docarchive/
docarchive_20130917-0905a.mp3.
16 See http://edition.cnn.com/ALLPOLITICS/
stories/1998/12/16/transcripts/clinton.html.
17 UNMOVIC (United Nations Monitoring and
Verification Commission) Report, 27 January
2003, http://www.iraqwatch.org/un/unmovic/
unmovic-blix-012703.htm.
18 Bush, Decision Points, p.247.
19 Bush, Decision Points, p.242.
20 Bush, Decision Points, p.262.
21 Donald Rumsfeld, Known and Unknown. New
York: Sentinel, 2011, p.449.
22 The Iraq Survey Group was a multinational
1,400-strong team set up and sent into Iraq after
the 2003 invasion to find WMD and supporting
research programmes and infrastructure to
develop such weapons. Its final report is known
as the Duelfer Report.
23 Cited in Karen de Jong, Soldier: The Life of Colin
Powell. New York: Alfred Knopf, 2006, p.508.
24 There is contentious evidence that both the head
of Iraqi intelligence at the time, Tahir Habbush
Al Tikriti, and the Iraqi foreign minister, Naji
Sabri, were on the CIA's payroll. The wearing of
a handmade CIA-supplied suit by the foreign
minister at his September 2002 UN General
Assembly address was designed to show to the
US administration that he was a reliable source
concerning his information about the presence
of WPD. The CIA case officer, Bill Murray,
responsible for Sabri, claimed that the report
had been doctored to show that Sabri said there
were WMD, when he had said that there were
in fact no WMD. The former foreign minister,
once a professor of English literature, is today
teaching journalism in Qatar; Habbush is living
in Jordan, having reputedly received a $5-million
CIA resettlement package. Discussion with Ron
Suskind, Bellagio, May 2013. See also http://www.
telegraph.co.uk/news/worldnews/middleeast/
iraq/9937516/Iraq-war-the-greatest-intelligence-
failure-in-living-memory.html.
25 The Iraq War: After the Fall, BBC Series, Part
One, http://downloads.bbc.co.uk/podcasts/

worldservice/docarchive/docarchive_20130917-0905a.mp3.

26 Correspondence, 4 October 2013.

27 Part One of the 2013 BBC series.

28 Discussion, Bellagio, Italy, 3 May 2013. See also Ronald Suskind, *The One Percent Doctrine: Deep Inside America's Pursuit of Its Enemies since 9/11*. New York: Simon & Schuster, 2006, esp. pp.163–91.

29 Bush, *Decision Points*, p.253.

30 See http://downloads.bbc.co.uk/podcasts/worldservice/docarchive/docarchive_20130917-0905a.mp3.

31 See http://downloads.bbc.co.uk/podcasts/worldservice/docarchive/docarchive_20130917-0905a.mp3.

32 See http://downloads.bbc.co.uk/podcasts/worldservice/docarchive/docarchive_20130917-0905a.mp3.

33 Cited in http://downloads.bbc.co.uk/podcasts/worldservice/docarchive/docarchive_20130917-0905a.mp3.

34 See http://downloads.bbc.co.uk/podcasts/worldservice/docarchive/docarchive_20130917-0905a.mp3.

35 Cited in http://downloads.bbc.co.uk/podcasts/worldservice/docarchive/docarchive_20130917-0905a.mp3.

36 See http://en.wikipedia.org/wiki/Iraq_War.

37 Including future health care benefits for civilians.

38 Bush, *Decision Points*, pp.248–49.

39 Bush, *Decision Points*, p.250.

40 Bush, *Decision Points*, p.268.

41 Cross and Garner's comments are taken from *The Iraq War: After the Fall*, BBC Series, Part Two, http://downloads.bbc.co.uk/podcasts/worldservice/docarchive/docarchive_20130917-0905a.mp3.

42 Cited in *The Independent*, 4 January 2010.

43 Cross and Garner, *The Iraq War*.

44 Interviewed in Cross and Garner, *The Iraq War*.

45 Rumsfeld, *Known and Unknown*, p.513.

46 Rumsfeld, *Known and Unknown*, p.508.

47 De Jong, *Soldier*, p.462.

48 De Jong, *Soldier*, p.520.

49 As put by Walter Slocombe of the CPA, reported in the BBC podcast, http://downloads.bbc.co.uk/podcasts/worldservice/docarchive/docarchive_20130917-0905a.mp3.

50 Discussion, Ambassador Malcolm Ferguson, Chief Director: Middle East, South African Department of Foreign Affairs, October 2013.

51 Cited in De Jong, *Soldier*, p.460.

52 Cited in De Jong, *Soldier* p.461.

53 This is derived from a series of interviews in Iraq during 2003 and 2004, and subsequent email correspondence with, inter alia, Generals Bill Rollo and Andrew Stewart, both of whom headed the British-led operation in Basra in 2003–05. See also Jack Fairweather, *A War of Choice: The British in Iraq, 2003–09*. London: Jonathan Cape, 2011.

54 See Office of the Special Inspector General for Iraq Reconstruction, *Hard Lessons: The Iraq Reconstruction Experience*. Washington, D.C.: US Government Printing Office, 2009.

55 Cited in Thomas E. Ricks, *The Gamble: General Petraeus and the Untold Story of the American Surge in Iraq, 2006–2008*. New York: Allen Lane, 2009, p.22.

56 Telephonic discussion, 7 May 2013.

57 See Ricks, *The Gamble*, pp.437–38.

58 See http://www.doingbusiness.org/rankings.

59 See his testimony to the 2009 British Iraqi inquiry, http://www.telegraph.co.uk/news/worldnews/middleeast/iraq/6669634/Iraq-inquiry-war-not-legitimate-Sir-Jeremy-Greenstock-tells-inquiry.html.

60 Email correspondence, Major General (retired) Andrew Stewart, 8 May 2013.

61 On Fareed Zakaria's *GPS*, 17 March 2013.

62 Wolfowitz, 'Iraq'.

63 *Fox News*, 28 April 2013.

64 *WMAL*, 14 June 2012.

65 *Fox News*, 28 April 2013.

66 See http://www.nytimes.com/2013/09/19/world/middleeast/gates-and-panetta-critical-of-obama-on-syria.html?_r=0.

67 See http://edition.cnn.com/2013/09/10/politics/obama-syria/index.html.

68 With thanks to David Richards for this observation.

69 See http://www.economist.com/blogs/economist-explains/2013/06/economist-explains-12.

70 See http://www.nytimes.com/2013/06/15/us/politics/pressure-led-to-obamas-decision-on-syrian-arms.html?pagewanted=all.

71 The Gulf of Tonkin incident is the name given to two separate incidents involving then North Vietnam and the US in the waters of the Gulf of Tonkin. On 2 August 1964, the destroyer USS *Maddox* engaged three North Vietnamese navy torpedo boats in international waters (according to the US) or territorial waters (according to the North Vietnamese). A second similar incident was claimed by the US government to have occurred two days later. The outcome of these incidents was the passage by Congress of the Gulf of Tonkin Resolution, granting President Lyndon B. Johnson the authority to assist any Southeast Asian country whose government was considered to be jeopardised by 'communist aggression'. This became the legal justification for deploying US conventional forces against North Vietnam. Later investigations found that while the *Maddox* had engaged the North Vietnamese navy on 2 August, there were no North Vietnamese vessels present during the second incident.

72 As per the calculation in *The Fog of War: Eleven Lessons from the Life of Robert S. McNamara*. Sony Pictures, 2003.

13 KOSOVO

1 See, for example, http://www.academia.
edu/1461300/The_Legendary_Commander_the_
construction_of_an_Albanian_master-narrative_
in_post-war_Kosovo_2006_.
2 See http://www.un.org/peace/kosovo/pages/
kosovo12.htm.
3 See http://www.europeanforum.net/country/
kosovo.
4 This chapter is based on two trips to Kosovo and
Macedonia in December 2009 and May 2013.
5 A recommendation for admission from the
Security Council requires affirmative votes from
at least nine of the council's fifteen members,
with none of the five permanent members voting
against. The Security Council's recommendation
must then be subsequently approved in the
General Assembly by a two-thirds majority vote of
its 193 (May 2013) members.
6 See http://www.globalpost.com/dispatch/news/
regions/europe/130219/kosovo-independence-
anniversary#1.
7 See http://www.bbc.co.uk/news/world-
europe-20138687.
8 Serbian enclaves, with their own currency (dinars,
not euros) and cellphone network, are still dotted
throughout the country, most notably in the
northern part of Mitrovica.
9 See Bedri Durmishaj, Sylejman Hyseni and Ferat
Shala, Trepca Minerals Atlas. Prishtina: University
of Kosovo, 2011.
10 The figure is 17 per cent. See http://www.
worldbank.org/en/country/kosovo.
11 See http://www.theodora.com/wfbcurrent/
kosovo/kosovo_economy.html.
12 Nicholas Schmidle, 'Bring up the Bodies',
6 May 2013, http://www.newyorker.com/
reporting/2013/05/06/130506fa_fact_
schmidle?currentPage=all.
13 See http://www.nytimes.com/2011/10/07/world/
europe/death-of-war-crimes-witness-casts-cloud-
on-kosovo.html?_r=0.
14 See http://www.bbc.co.uk/news/world-
europe-20418824. See also http://assembly.
coe.int/CommitteeDocs/2010/20100622_
ProtectionWitnesses_E.pdf.
15 See http://www.balkaninsight.com/en/article/
fatmir-limaj-indicted-for-corruption.
16 Schmidle, 'Bring up the Bodies'.
17 See http://www.bbc.co.uk/news/world-
europe-20536318. See also Schmidle, 'Bring up
the Bodies'.
18 Cited in Schmidle, 'Bring up the Bodies'.
19 See, for example, Matt McAllester, 'Kosovo's
Mafia: How the US and Allies Ignore Allegations
of Organized Crime at the Highest Levels of a
New Democracy', Globalpost, 27 March 2011,
http://www.globalpost.com/dispatch/news/
regions/europe/110321/kosovo-hashim-thaci-
organized-crime?page=full.
20 Schmidle, 'Bring up the Bodies'.
21 Schmidle, 'Bring up the Bodies'.
22 See http://www.newyorker.com/
reporting/2013/05/06/130506fa_fact_schmidle.

14 LIBERIA

1 This chapter is based on several visits to Liberia
from 2006 to 2013, including more recently
in September 2013. Grateful thanks are expressed
to Anthony Arnott for his research assistance
in this regard, and to the former UN Special
Representative of the Secretary General Alan
Doss and Deputy Special Representative of the
Secretary General Jordan Ryan for their help in
this regard. Where not specifically cited, quotes
are taken from interviews conducted in September
2013.
2 See http://www.un.org/en/peacekeeping/missions/
unmil/facts.shtml.
3 Interview, UNMIL HQ, 3 September 2013.
4 For details of this history and the failed Libyan
effort to revive the hotel, see http://blogs.aljazeera.
com/blog/africa/liberia-libya-war-peace-and-
hospitality.
5 Discussion, 27 August 2013.
6 With thanks to Stephen Ellis for this insight.
7 With thanks to Stuart Doran for this insight.
8 See Helene Cooper, The House at Sugar Beach:
In Search of a Lost African Childhood. New
York: Simon & Schuster, 2009.
9 See, for example, 'An Evaluation of the National
Democratic Institute (NDI) Legislative
Strengthening Program in Liberia', USAID Report,
Washington, D.C., March 2013.
10 Discussion, Royal Hotel, Monrovia, 2 September
2013.
11 Interview, Ministry of Foreign Affairs, Monrovia,
3 September 2013.
12 See https://www.princeton.edu/
successfulsocieties/content/data/policy_note/
PN_id203/Policy_Note_ID203.pdf.
13 See http://www.imf.org/external/pubs/ft/survey/
so/2010/car062910a.htm.
14 Correspondence with Steve Radelet, 3 September
2013.
15 The Kimberley Process grew out of discussions
in May 2000 in Kimberley, South Africa, among
interested governments, the international
diamond industry and civil society, as a unique
initiative to combat 'conflict diamonds' – rough
diamonds used to finance conflicts in the 1990s
in some of Africa's diamond-producing countries.
The Kimberley Process is backed by the UN.
In December 2000, the UN General Assembly
adopted a resolution supporting the creation of
an international certification scheme for rough
diamonds. In November 2002, an agreement was
reached on the Kimberley Process Certification
Scheme. This system imposes extensive
requirements on all participants to control all
imports and exports of rough diamonds and to
put in place internal controls over production
and trade to ensure that conflict diamonds could

not enter the legal trade. In its first four years, the Kimberley Process helped to reduce the amount of conflict diamonds to a fraction of just 1 per cent of world trade. At the time of Liberia's accession, the Kimberley Process Certification Scheme had 46 participants (with the European Community counting as a single participant), totalling 72 countries, including all major diamond-producing, trading and polishing centres, and counts on the active participation of civil society and industry groups. See http://www.eu-un. europa.eu/articles/en/article_7000_en.htm and www.kimberleyprocess.com.

16 By September 2013, the international training component included 40 US officers and one UK colonel.

17 'An Evaluation of the National Democratic Institute'.

18 Discussion, Stephen Ellis, 3 April 2014. Ellis is the author, inter alia, of *The Mask of Anarchy: The Destruction of Liberia and the Religious Dimension of an African Civil War*. New York: New York University Press, 2001.

19 After fleeing the country after the 1980 Doe coup (she had served as a minister of finance from 1979 in the Tolbert government), Johnson Sirleaf worked for the World Bank in Washington. In 1981 she moved to Nairobi as vice president of the African Regional Office of Citibank, moving to Equator Bank four years later. In 1992 she was appointed as the director of the United Nations Development Programme's Regional Bureau for Africa, from which she resigned in 1997 to run for president in Liberia, which she lost to Charles Taylor. During her time at the UN she was chairperson of the Open Society Initiative for West Africa and a visiting professor of Governance at the Ghana Institute of Management and Public Administration.

20 I am grateful to Stephen Ellis for these insights.

21 See http://www.huffingtonpost.com/2013/08/27/students-fail-university-liberia-exam_n_3823895.html.

22 See http://africajournalismtheworld.com/2013/08/10/liberian-corruption-saga-take-new-twist-over-defence-minister-tapes/.

23 Discussion, foreign diplomat, Monrovia, 4 September 2013.

24 Discussion, Monrovia, 4 September 2013.

15 LIBYA

1 Interview, 30 May 2013.

2 BBC News, 31 May 2013.

3 For a background to these events, see Frederic Wehrey, 'Libya's Revolution at Two Years: Perils and Achievements', *Mediterranean Politics*, 11 February 2013, http://carnegieendowment.org/2013/02/11/libya-s-revolution-at-two-years-perils-and-achievements/ff7s.

4 See http://en.wikipedia.org/wiki/History_of_Libya_as_Italian_colony.

5 Gaddafi reportedly spent nine months in 1966 on an English-language course in Buckinghamshire, a signal instructors' course at Bovington Camp in Dorset and an infantry signal instructors' course at Hythe in Kent. See http://en.wikipedia.org/wiki/Muammar_Gaddafi.

6 For an excellent summary of the history of Libya, see the *Lonely Planet* guide to the country.

7 Discussion, Tunis, March 2014.

8 See http://www.dailymail.co.uk/news/article-1367764/David-Cameron-tells-Gaddafi-time-UK-jets-prepare-lead-UN-force.html#ixzz2UyrUQEvO.

9 See, for example, Claudia Gazzini, 'Trial by Error: Justice in Post-Qadhafi Libya', *Middle East/North African Report* 140, 17 April 2013, http://www.crisisgroup.org/en/publication-type/media-releases/2013/mena/trial-by-error-justice-in-post-qadhafi-libya.aspx.

10 See, for example, http://www.libyaherald.com/2012/12/17/ld-500-million-project-being-prepared-by-warriors-affairs-commission-to-get-revolutionaries-ready-for-business/.

11 See http://www.foxnews.com/politics/2011/10/14/terrorists-seeking-missing-libyan-missiles-us-official-says/.

12 Global Resources News, see also graph on p.289.

13 Heritage Foundation, '2012 Index of Economic Freedom', http://www.heritage.org/index/.

14 See http://epp.eurostat.ec.europa.eu/cache/ITY_PUBLIC/2-29042013-CP/EN/2-29042013-CP-EN.PDF.

15 Interview, 31 May 2013.

16 See http://www.libyaherald.com/2013/05/30/cabinet-meeting-forms-committee-on-subsidies-zeidan/.

17 Interview, 31 May 2013.

18 See http://www.presstv.ir/detail/2013/05/28/305865/nato-to-give-technical-support-to-libya/.

19 See http://www.islamtimes.org/vdcgz79x7ak93w4.5jra.html.

20 See http://unsmil.unmissions.org/Default.aspx?tabid=3545&language=en-US.

21 'Humanitarian Aid in Libya: How Much Has Each Country Donated?', *The Guardian*, 22 August 2011.

22 See http://news.xinhuanet.com/english2010/world/2011-07/23/c_131003411.htm.

23 See http://www.huffingtonpost.com/2011/07/03/libya-rebels-turkey-aid_n_889580.html.

24 See http://nbcpolitics.nbcnews.com/_news/2012/09/14/13866898-how-much-are-taxpayers-spending-on-egypt-and-libya?lite.

25 Interview, Palm City, Tripoli, 31 May 2013.

26 Interview, Tripoli, 2 June 2013.

27 See http://www.guardian.co.uk/politics/wintour-and-watt/2011/oct/02/libya-muammar-gaddafi.

28 Wehrey, 'Libya's Revolution at Two Years'.

29 With thanks to Thomas Will for this point.

30 With thanks to Peter Pham for this point.

31 Interview, Tripoli, 31 May 2013.

32 Fareed Zakaria, 'How the Lessons of Iraq Paid Off in Libya', *Time*, 5 September 2011.

16 MALAWI

1 See http://www.huffingtonpost.com/2012/04/06/bingu-wa-mutharika-hospital_n_1407857.html.

2 Paul Theroux, *The Last Train to Zona Verde: Overland from Cape Town to Angola.* Johannesburg: Penguin, 2013, p.62.

3 For example, see http://news.bbc.co.uk/2/hi/africa/139596.stm.

4 Discussion, December 2013.

5 See Alec Russell, *Big Man, Little People.* London: Pan Books, 2000. Kamuzu Banda died on 25 November 1997, aged 99, although there is some confusion over his exact age. This section is based on several research trips to Malawi, including an interview with President Joyce Banda on 13 December 2013.

6 See 'Malawi Tries Ex-Dictator in Murder', *Los Angeles Times*, 21 May 1995, http://en.wikipedia.org/wiki/Hastings_Banda#cite_note-LATimes-3.

7 I am grateful to (Lord) John Roper for this quote.

17 SIERRA LEONE

1 This chapter is based on several research visits to Sierra Leone, most notably in August–September 2008 and August–September 2013. See also David Richards, 'Sierra Leone: Pregnant with Lessons' in David Richards and Greg Mills (eds), *Victory Among People: Lessons from Countering Insurgency and Stabilising Fragile States.* London: RUSI, 2011. With thanks also to Anthony Arnott for his research assistance, and Palo Contech, Yero Baldeh and Hugh Blackman for their help in setting up meetings in Freetown.

2 See http://www.hrw.org/reports/1999/sierra/SIERLE99-04.htm.

3 Eeben Barlow, *Executive Outcomes: Against All Odds.* Johannesburg: Galago, 2008, p.319.

4 Barlow, *Executive Outcomes*, p.363.

5 *The Economist*, 13 May 2000.

6 See Paul Richards, 'British Peacemaking Policy in West Africa', Memoranda submitted to the House of Commons Select Committee on International Development, January 2006, http://www.publications.parliament.uk/pa/cm200506/cmselect/cmintdev/923/923m21.htm.

7 The country produced more than 400 000 carats of diamonds in 2010, making it the world's tenth-largest producer and accounting for nearly half of the nation's total exports. See, for example, http://www.revenuewatch.org/countries/africa/sierra-leone/overview.

8 See, for example, http://en.wikipedia.org/wiki/Economy_of_Sierra_Leone.

9 Daron Acemoğlu and James Robinson, *Why Nations Fail: The Origins of Power, Prosperity and Poverty.* London: Profile, 2013, p.338.

10 See Simon Akam, 'The Vagabond King', *New Statesman*, 2 February 2012.

11 See http://www.africa-confidential.com/special-report/id/4/Chronology_of_Sierra_Leone.

12 Akam, 'The Vagabond King'.

13 Telephonic discussion, 22 September 2013.

14 Discussion, Pretoria, 27 September 2013. Executive Outcomes was unusual among private security companies in that it was deployed as a fighting force rather than to, as is more common, provide convoy or point protection. Whatever the regulatory environment, it is unlikely that its type will, however, be seen again – not least given the ageing of the generation of southern African military skills from which it was drawn, who are willing to accept risk and hardship virtually unheard of in the contemporary private security business.

15 Executive Outcomes' air support in Sierra Leone comprised its own Mi-8 'Hip' and Mi-17 helicopters along with HS 748 transport and a Cessna 337 spotter aircraft. Russian pilots were flying the Mi-24 'Hind' gunship, 'which we were supposed to fly', recalls Janeke, 'but after their one pilot shot himself in it on the hard stand, we were not allowed anywhere near it'. Executive Outcomes pilots were eventually allowed to fly the Mi-24, becoming at that time the first non-Soviet pilots to operate it in combat conditions.

16 Chapter VI of the UN Charter deals with peaceful settlement of disputes. This Chapter authorises the Security Council to issue recommendations, but does not allow it to make binding resolutions. Chapter VII of the Charter allows the Council to 'determine the existence of any threat to the peace, breach of the peace, or act of aggression' and to take military and non-military action to 'restore international peace and security'.

17 See Tony Blair, *A Journey.* London: Random House, 2010, pp.247–48.

18 By chance Bernard Miyet, the head of the UN's Department of Peacekeeping Operations, was in Freetown when the British arrived. There is no doubt that his presence and pragmatism eased the way for what potentially could have been a very difficult relationship between the UN and UK forces.

19 HMS *Illustrious* arrived off Freetown on 11 May and the HMS *Ocean* group on 14 May 2000.

20 This was the direction to the force commanders, and specifically those officers with responsibility for the campaign's information operation, Freetown, 10 October 2000.

21 With thanks to Defence Minister Palo Conteh for providing these figures. See also, for example, https://www.google.co.uk/#fp=493odabd5e0ocfce&q=sierra+leone+GDP+per+capita&stick=H4sIAAAAAAAAAGOovnz8BQMDoz0HjxKHfq6-gVlxvJGWY3aylX5OfnJiSWZ-nn5xCZAuLslMTsyJLopNBwpZpacUxOfl52bmAYUKUovikxMLMksS48vzi3JS4pMS87K7GH254OYJUdE8k4yqLGqaZ1aSXk4F82bd-7n9gqDDDDvbNa2uNw8MnSnwu-woAqn-Y5VwBAAA.

22 This figure is supplied by the African Development Bank; government puts it twice as high.

23 Taken from a document supplied by Defence Minsiter Palo Conteh.
24 See http://www.doingbusiness.org/rankings.
25 Again the government figure is higher, at $4.6 billion.
26 Information supplied by the African Development Bank, 20 September 2013.
27 Discussion, Country Lodge Hotel, Freetown, 31 August 2013.
28 *East African*, 15–21 March 2014.
29 See http://www.imdb.com/title/tto116695/quotes.
30 See http://www.moibrahimfoundation.org/ibrahim-prize/.

18 SOMALIA

1 Conrad Norton and Uys Krige, *Vanguard of Victory: A Short Review of South African Victories in East Africa – 1940–1941*. Pretoria: Government Printer, 1941, p.35. An earlier, longer version of this chapter appeared in *Somalia: Fixing the World's Most Failed State*. Cape Town: Tafelberg, 2013, authored with J. Peter Pham and David Kilcullen.
2 This chapter is based on three research trips each to Somalia (December 2011, June–July 2012 and September 2012) and Somaliland (June 2010, May 2011 and September 2012). Where not specifically footnoted, the quotes are taken directly from meetings during these visits.
3 For a most readable literary summary involving descriptions of modern Somalia and the harrowing life this produces, see Nuriddin Farah, *Crossbones*. Johannesburg: Penguin, 2012. See also Peter D. Little, *Somalia: Economy without State*. Bloomington, IN: Indiana University Press, 2003.
4 See, for example, http://www.foreignpolicy.com/failedstates2012.
5 Political scientist Robert Rotberg even invented a special category of 'failed state' to describe Somalia: the 'collapsed state', which he defined as a 'rare and extreme version of the failed state' that is 'a mere geographical expression, a black hole into which a failed polity has fallen', where 'there is dark energy, but the forces of entropy have overwhelmed the radiance that hitherto provided some semblance of order and other vital political goods to the inhabitants (no longer the citizens) embraced by language or ethnic affinities or borders'. Robert I. Rotberg, 'The Failure and Collapse of Nation-States: Breakdown, Prevention, and Repair' in Robert I. Rotberg (ed.), *When States Fail: Causes and Consequences*. Princeton: Princeton University Press, 2004, pp.9–10.
6 See http://www.unhcr.org/pages/49e483ad6.html.
7 See http://www.bbc.co.uk/news/world-africa-24783828.
8 Somalia's total aid flow was $497 million in 2010, of which $239 million was in humanitarian assistance. See http://www.globalhumanitarianassistance.org/countryprofile/somalia. By 2012, this had increased substantially.

Turkey, for example, is supplying $300 million in direct aid (projects conducted by Turks), including refugee camps, roads, hospitals and schools. The UN requested $1.5 billion in 2012, partly to prevent a return to famine. For example, the World Food Programme was, by 2012, bringing in 5 000 tonnes of food aid into Mogadishu alone each month. See http://www.cbsnews.com/8301-202_162-20092927.html. This fed around 420 000 people on a continuous basis. See http://article.wn.com/view/2012/08/18/Somalia_food_support_for_420,000_people_in_Mogadishu/. The benefits of such aid are, however, held to be dubious. See 'Help Somalia's President: Cut Off Aid', http://www.bloomberg.com/news/2012-09-11/help-somalia-s-new-president-cut-off-aid.html.
9 The army seized power on 21 October 1969 (the day after the funeral of President Abdirashid Ali Shermarke who had been shot dead by one of his own bodyguards), headed by Major General Siad Barre, the army commander.
10 Interview, Tswalu Kalahari Reserve, South Africa, August 2006.
11 See http://www.bbc.co.uk/news/world-africa-14094503.
12 See http://www.globalhumanitarianassistance.org/countryprofile/somalia.
13 Correspondence, UN official, 9 April 2014.
14 For details on humanitarian funding, see http://fts.unocha.org/pageloader.aspx?page=Pooled-SummaryPoolFunds.
15 Discussion, Mogadishu, September 2012.
16 UNSCR 2124 wording on SNA support is: 'Takes note of the Secretary-General's recommendation of the need to provide targeted support to front line units of the Somali National Army (SNA), requests UNSOA to support the SNA through the provision of food and water, fuel, transport, tents and in theatre medical evacuation, decides that this exceptional support shall be provided only for joint SNA operations with AMISOM and which are part of AMISOM's overall Strategic Concept, further decides that funding for this support will be provided from an appropriate United Nations trust fund, and encourages Member States to make uncaveated contributions to the trust fund.'
17 See http://www.economist.com/node/21560905.
18 See, for example, Ken Menkhaus, 'The Somali Spring', *Foreign Policy*, September 2012, http://www.foreignpolicy.com/articles/2012/09/24/the_somali_spring?page=0,1. See also J. Peter Pham, 'State Collapse, Insurgency, and Famine in the Horn of Africa: Legitimacy and the Ongoing Somali Crisis', *Journal of the Middle East and Africa* 2(2), 2011, pp.153–87.
19 See http://www.aljazeera.com/programmes/insidestory/2012/07/201272081233390153.html. The UN report found inter alia that of every $10 received by Somalia's transitional government between 2009 and 2010, $7 are unaccounted for. In May 2012, the World Bank reported that

$131 million in government revenues were unaccounted for from that same period. The UN report notes almost a quarter of government spending in 2011 – over $12 million – was 'absorbed' by the office of the president, prime minister and the parliamentary speaker, noting that a further $40 million in government revenues in 2011 could be missing.

20 Discussion, Turkish ambassador, Mogadishu, 27 September 2012.

21 Cited in the (Kenyan) *Daily Nation*, 24 September 2012.

22 Menkhaus, 'The Somali Spring'.

23 See David Lamb, *The Africans: Encounters from the Sudan to the Cape*. London: Methuen, 1983, p.197.

24 Henry Kissinger, *Does America Need a Foreign Policy? Toward a Diplomacy for the 21st Century*. New York: Simon & Schuster, 2002, p.265. With thanks to Jeff Sims for pointing this out.

25 With grateful acknowledgement to Christopher Clapham for his input into this section.

26 Originally described thus to Burton by a visiting Ugandan. See Richard Dowden's 'Don't Force Statehood on Somalia', http://africanarguments. org/2011/10/20/don%E2%80%99t-force-statehood-on-somalia-by-richard-dowden/.

27 Though there are two major sub-clans to consider in this regard, the Majeeteen (based around Puntland) and the Marehan (Siad Barre's clan).

28 Discussion, Villa Somalia, Mogadishu, 26 September 2012.

29 I.M. Lewis, 'Visible and Invisible Difference: The Somali Paradox', *Africa* 74(4), November 2004, p.492.

30 Little, *Somalia*, p.1.

31 See Little, *Somalia*, p.2. For a most readable summary involving descriptions of modern Somalia and the harrowing life this produces, see Farah, *Crossbones*.

32 This information was sourced during a visit to the airport on 27 September 2012, and discussions with Ska Air personnel. The *qat* trade that morning was flown by two De Havilland Dash 8 aircraft registered to Bluebird Aviation, based in Kenya and currently operating a fleet of fifteen aircraft. See http://www.planespotters.net/ Production_List/De-Havilland-Canada/DHC-8_Dash-8/4024,5Y-VVZ-Blue-Bird-Aviation.php.

33 See http://www.telegraph.co.uk/news/worldnews/ africaandindianocean/somalia/9563506/Somalias-Islamist-war-chest-being-boosted-by-UN-funds. html.

34 See http://www.thenational.ae/news/uae-news/ charcoal-exports-from-somalia-banned.

35 Little, *Somalia*.

36 Taken from Green's 'Laissez Faire in Africa', an unpublished paper dated 1998, cited in Little, *Somalia*, p.124.

37 Little, *Somalia*, p.124.

38 These figures are from 2009, and were supplied by the Somali Chamber of Commerce and Industry.

39 See http://www.doingbusiness.org/rankings and http://www.transparency.org/cpi2013/results.

40 With thanks to Dave Kilcullen for this insight.

41 See Adrian Leftwich, *States of Development: On the Primacy of Politics in Development*. London: Polity, 2000.

42 See Jonathan Katzenellenbogen's review of Leftwich's works, http://www.politicsweb.co.za/ politicsweb/view/politicsweb/en/page72308?oid= 376417&sn=Marketingweb+detail&pid=90389.

43 Discussion held at the Tana Forum, 26 April 2014. For background on the Puntland president, see http://www.bbc.com/news/world-africa-14114749.

44 See J. Peter Pham, 'Let's Give Somalia's Government the Non-Recognition It Deserves,' http://www.atlanticcouncil.org/blogs/new-atlanticist/let-s-give-somalia-s-government-the-non-recognition-it-deserves.

45 Discussion, Hargeisa, September 2012.

PART 3

ILLUSTRATIONS OF RECOVERY

1 See 'Zambia might be best avoided', *Business Day*, 12 December 2013.

2 This section is based on several research trips to Zambia in 2012 and 2013.

3 The Brenthurst Foundation was established by the Oppenheimer family in 2005 to help strengthen African economic performance fundamentally through better policy.

4 From Zambia's own 2012 budget figures, First Quantum's Kansanshi mine contributed three-quarters of the total tax paid by all corporations in Zambia and 16 per cent of all the tax collected. The effective tax rate on the mines was already about 65 per cent, being made up of the overall rate of 30 per cent plus the 12 per cent variable profits tax, the 20 per cent 'free carry' of Zambian Consolidated Copper Mines, and a royalty of 6 per cent. This information was gathered in discussions with mining, retail and tourism executives in Zambia during March 2013.

5 See http://www.lusakatimes.com/2012/09/13/ zambia-raised-750-million-debut-10year-eurobond/.

6 I am grateful to Mark Pearson for these insights. See also http://www.bloomberg.com/news/2013-10-29/zambia-considering-1-billion-eurobond-after-rating-cut.html; and http://www.bdlive. co.za/africa/africanbusiness/2014/03/14/zambias-eurobond-costs-rise-on-soaring-deficit.

7 As of 2014, there are 1 850 MW available from 1 988 MW installed capacity in Zambia. Supply has to be tightly balanced, with a national demand of some 1 750 MW. New supply, including Kariba Extension, is expected to add 660 MW by the end of 2015, and perhaps another 160 MW by the end of 2016. The Kafue Gorge Lower scheme will, it is planned, kick in around 2020 with a further

750 MW. At independence in October 1964, Zambia produced just shy of 500 MW, the joint (with then Rhodesia) Kariba (South) Dam scheme providing 333 MW. Today Kariba North Bank provides 720 MW, of a countrywide estimated total hydro capacity of 6 000 MW.

8 See http://www.doingbusiness.org/rankings.
9 Discussion, Nevers Mumba, leader of the Movement for Multiparty Democracy, 9 December 2013.
10 See http://www.lusakatimes.com/2012/12/26/nevers-mumba-arrested-issuing-alarming-statement-breach-peace/.
11 See http://www.lusakatimes.com/2012/08/13/upnd-leader-hakainde-hichilema-arrested/; and http://zambiareports.com/2013/02/26/hichilema-arrested-in-livingstone/.
12 Discussion, Lusaka, August 2012.
13 See http://www.bbc.co.uk/news/health-15433140.

19 ANGOLA

1 This chapter is in part based on three trips to Angola in 2003, 2011 and 2013 when a number of interviews were conducted. Unless otherwise indicated, these are the sources of the direct quotes and information.
2 See, for example, 'Global Humanitarian Emergencies 1996', http://reliefweb.int/report/world/global-humanitarian-emergencies-1996.
3 See http://www.guardian.co.uk/world/1999/aug/14/unitednations.
4 Simon Jenkins, SAIIA Annual British Council Lecture, Jan Smuts House, Johannesburg, 21 February 2000.
5 Edward Luttwak, 'Give War a Chance', Foreign Affairs, July/August 1999, http://www.foreignaffairs.com/articles/55210/edward-n-luttwak/give-war-a-chance.
6 See Douglas Hurd, The Search for Peace: A Century of Peace Diplomacy. London: Warner, p.42 and p.200.
7 Andrew Williams, Failed Imagination? New World Orders of the Twentieth Century. Manchester: Manchester University Press, 1998.
8 Cited in Andreas Osiander, The States System of Europe, 1640–1990: Peacemaking and the Conditions of International Stability. Oxford: Clarendon Press, 1994, p.254, see also pp.7–8.
9 Discussion, 28 June 2013.
10 See http://www.rnw.nl/africa/bulletin/angolas-savimbi-still-haunts-10-years.
11 See http://data.worldbank.org/indicator/SI.POV.GINI/.
12 The remainder being won by the Social Renewal Party, which scooped three seats, and the FNLA, which won two.
13 'Deception in High Places: The Corrupt Angola-Russia Debt Deal', http://www.cw-uk.org/wp-content/uploads/2013/04/The-Corrupt-Russian-Angolan-Debt-Deal-Executive-Summary.pdf. For comment on this, see, for example, http://

www.dailymaverick.co.za/article/2013-04-17-angola-russia-corruption-and-a-world-in-crisis/.
14 Discussion, Mozambique, 24 January 2014.
15 Speech to the Atlantic Basin Initiative, Luanda, 23 June 2013.

20 BURKINA FASO

1 This chapter is based on a research trip to Burkina Faso in April 2013 in the company of Daniel Pinhassi and Anthony Arnott.
2 Per International Water Management Institute, of 235 800 hectares of irrigable lane, 32 per cent is exploited, which works out to 14 per cent of all land.
3 See http://www.doingbusiness.org/rankings.
4 See http://www.transparency.org/cpi2013/results.
5 With thanks to Anthony Arnott for his observations in this section.

21 BURUNDI AND RWANDA

1 See https://www.cia.gov/library/publications/the-world-factbook/geos/rw.html; and https://www.cia.gov/library/publications/the-world-factbook/geos/by.html.
2 See http://www.doingbusiness.org/data/exploreeconomies/rwanda/.
3 See http://www.transparency.org/cpi2013/results.
4 See http://en.wikipedia.org/wiki/Burundian_Genocide.
5 In Burundi, members of the royal family were not technically classified as Tutsi, but as Ganwa, a class apart and above. Similarly, the military rulers – Micombero, Bagaza and Buyoya – were all from a sub-caste in Burundi known as Hima. So unlike in Rwanda, the spectrum of Tutsi in Burundi is usually broken down into these three sub-classes: Ganwa, Tutsi and Hima.
6 Reported at http://www.executedtoday.com/2009/06/30/1962-georges-kageorgis-assassin/.
7 Interviewed at the Hôtel Club du Lac Tanganyika, Bujumbura, October 2011.
8 See http://www.un.org/en/peacekeeping/missions/past/onub/.
9 The Marshall Plan amounted to $15 billion over four years from 1947. See http://en.wikipedia.org/wiki/Marshall_Plan.
10 See Carol Lancaster, 'Africa in World Affairs' in John W. Harbeson and Donald Rothchild (eds), Africa in World Politics: The African State System in Flux. Colorado: Westview, 2000, p.212; and Nicolas van der Walle, 'Africa and the World Economy: Continued Marginalisation or Re-engagement?' in Harbeson and Rothchild, p.271.
11 See http://bnub.unmissions.org/Default.aspx?tabid=2961&ctl=Details&mid=5312&ItemID=389154&language=en-US.
12 This chapter is based on a stint living and working in Rwanda in 2007/08, along with several subsequent research trips, the most recent

being in October 2013; and four research trips to Burundi, including most recently in 2011 and 2013. Where not directly cited, the quotes are taken from these meetings. With thanks also to Mauro de Lorenzo for his detailed review of this chapter.

13 As in Bernard Fall's classic, *Hell in a Very Small Place: The Siege of Dien Bien Phu*. New York: De Capo Press, 2002.

14 Pasteur Bizimungu, a Hutu who had been a civil servant under the government of Habyarimana before fleeing to join the RPF, was appointed president. Kagame remained commander-in-chief of the army and de facto ruler of Rwanda. After Kagame accused Bizimungu of corruption and poor management, the president resigned in March 2000. A number of Hutu politicians, including Prime Minister Pierre-Célestin Rwigema, left the government at around the same time as Bizimungu. The latter started his own party following his resignation, but this was quickly banned for 'destabilising the country'. He was subsequently arrested, convicted of corruption and inciting ethnic violence, and imprisoned until 2007, when he was pardoned by Kagame.

15 Neither the letter nor spirit of the law in Rwanda bans discussion of ethnic categories, nor attempts to erase these identities from people's memory. What is outlawed is the politicisation of the categories or acts of incitement around them.

16 See http://en.wikipedia.org/wiki/Paul_Kagame.

17 Paul Kagame, 'Rwanda and the New Lions of Africa', *The Wall Street Journal*, 19 May 2013, http://online.wsj.com/news/articles/SB10001424127887324767004578485234078541160.

18 Stephen Kinzer, *A Thousand Hills: Rwanda's Rebirth and the Man Who Dreamed it*. Hoboken, NJ: John Wiley & Sons, 2008.

19 See, for example, William Blum, *America's Deadliest Export: Democracy – The Truth About US Foreign Policy and Everything Else*. London: Zed Books, 2013.

20 *New Times*, 24 March 2011, http://www.responsibilitytoprotect.org/index.php/crises/190-crisis-in-libya/3337-paul-kagame-allafricacom-rwandans-know-why-gaddafi-must-be-stopped-.

21 See http://www.bbc.co.uk/news/world-africa-24228425; and see his speech to the 2013 Tana Forum, http://www.newsofrwanda.com/featured1/18198/kagame-lectures-west-on-democracy-and-governance/.

22 Kinzer, *A Thousand Hills*.

23 Kinzer cites the case of four former Kagame allies – former chief of staff and ambassador to Washington, Théogène Rudasingwa, Gerald Gahima, Rwanda's former prosecutor general and vice president of the supreme court, Colonel Patrick Karegeya, former director of Rwanda's external security services, and Genenal Kayumba Nyamwasa, a former army chief of staff – who were found guilty *in abstentia* in January 2011

of forming a terrorist group, threatening state security, undermining public order, promoting ethnic divisions and insulting the president. They received symbolic sentences between 20 and 24 years. Evidence was taken in part from a 'Rwanda Briefing' issued by the four just as President Kagame began his second term. In this they asserted there is 'more to Rwanda and Paul Kagame than new buildings, clean streets, and efficient government ... Rwanda is essentially a hardline, one-party, secretive police state with a façade of democracy.' To move from 'the brink of an abyss' the four urged a 'genuine, inclusive, unconditional and comprehensive national dialogue' to create a new 'national partnership government'. Kinzer suggested that Kagame who 'trusted them once ... should heed their warning and seek their counsel'. Karegeya was found dead, apparently murdered, in a hotel room at the start of 2014 in Johannesburg, where he had lived in exile for six years. See http://www.theguardian.com/commentisfree/cifamerica/2011/jan/27/rwanda-freedom-of-speech.

24 With thanks to Paul Collier for this point.

25 Famously described in Roméo Dallaire's *Shake Hands with the Devil*. London: Arrow, 2005.

26 See http://news.bbc.co.uk/2/hi/africa/3573229.stm.

27 As per the detailed notes of that meeting taken by Lieutenant General Chris Brown, dated 23 July 2007.

28 Cited in Patricia Crisafulli and Andrea Redmond, *Rwanda Inc.: How a Devastated Nation became an Economic Model for the Developing World*. New York: Palgrave Macmillan, 2012.

29 Cited in Crisafulli and Redmond, *Rwanda Inc.*, p.207.

30 See, for example, the article by Jeffrey Gettleman, 'The Global Elite's Favorite Strongman', *New Yorker*, 4 September 2013, http://nyti.ms/19fPVCr.

31 Cited in Crisafulli and Redmond, *Rwanda Inc.*, p.i.

32 As per RwandAir's publicity video, viewed 25 October 2013.

33 Cited at http://www.theguardian.com/world/2010/dec/31/tony-blair-rwanda-paul-kagame.

34 See Magnus Taylor, http://africanarguments.org/2013/10/08/debating-rwanda-under-the-rpf-gap-between-believers-and-unbelievers-remains-wide-by-magnus-taylor/.

35 See http://www.doingbusiness.org/data/exploreeconomies/rwanda/.

36 Crisafulli and Redmond, *Rwanda Inc.*

37 The discussion with the permanent secretary took place in Kigali on 25 October 2013. The tightening aid world helps to explain Kigali's launch of a $400-million government bond in April 2013.

38 See http://www.economist.com/news/leaders/21587787-too-many-dinosaurs.

39 Reportedly 2 000 Uganda People's Defence Force troops were killed in the 1999 clash. See http://www.ugandacorrespondent.com/articles/2010/09/revealed-2000-updf-troops-died-in-kisangani/.

654 — 22 CHILE TO ZAMBIA

40 See http://www.theguardian.com/world/2012/oct/17/rwanda-minister-leader-congo-rebels-kabarebe.

41 See http://www.bbc.co.uk/news/world-africa-24424868.

42 Cited in Fareed Zakaria, 'A Conversation with Lee Kuan Yew', *Foreign Affairs*, March/April 1994, http://www.foreignaffairs.com/articles/49691/fareed-zakaria/a-conversation-with-lee-kuan-yew#.

43 Lee Kuan Yew, *From Third World to First: The Singapore Story: 1965–2000*. New York: HarperCollins, 2008, p.342.

44 Lee, *From Third World to First*, pp.22–23.

45 See http://www.cbc.ca/news/canada/toronto/toronto-visit-by-rwanda-s-paul-kagame-divides-expats-1.1871512.

46 With thanks to Stuart Doran for this insight.

47 With thanks to Colgate University's Susan Thomson for this point.

48 Lee, *From Third World to First*, p.763.

49 British defence spending in Singapore accounted for, by Lee's figures, in 1968 some 20 per cent of GDP, and gave employment directly to 30 000 workers and indirectly to 10 000 more. See Lee, *From Third World to First*, p.23.

50 See http://www.gov.rw/The-19th-Commemoration-of-the-1994-Genocide-against-Tutsi-will-be-marked-in-each-Umudugudu-village-under-the-theme-Let-us-commemorate-the-Tutsi-Genocide-as-we-strive-for-self-reliance.

51 See http://www.newsofrwanda.com/featured1/18198/kagame-lectures-west-on-democracy-and-governance/.

52 Discussion, Bujumbura, 23 October 2013.

53 See J.P. Landman, *The Long View: Getting Beyond the Drama of South Africa's Headlines*. Johannesburg: Jacana, 2013, p.93.

22 CHILE TO ZAMBIA

1 For an excellent summary of the historical relationship between state-building and the mining sector, see Martin Meredith, *Diamonds, Gold and War: The Making of South Africa*. London: Pocket Books, 2007.

2 Jeremy Paxman, *Empire*. London: Penguin, 2012, p.158.

3 Brian Roberts, *Kimberley*. Cape Town: David Philip, 1976.

4 SA History Online, http://www.sahistory.org.za/'The%20rock%20on%20which%20the%20future%20will%20be%20built'.

5 The English novelist Anthony Trollope's impressions from a visit in 1877, as cited in Meredith, *Diamonds, Gold and War*, pp.54–55.

6 Cited in Meredith, *Diamonds, Gold and War*, p.158.

7 See http://www.sahistory.org.za/'The%20rock%20on%20which%20the%20future%20will%20be%20built'.

8 Meredith, *Diamonds, Gold and War*, p.35.

9 Meredith, *Diamonds, Gold and War*, p.155.

10 See http://www.sahistory.org.za/'The%20rock%20on%20which%20the%20future%20will%20be%20built'.

11 Sol Plaatje, *Native Life in South Africa, Before and Since the European War and the Boer Rebellion*, 1916, http://hsf.org.za/resource-centre/focus/focus-70-on-focus/focus-70-oct-politicsweb.pdf/download.

12 Cited in Meredith, *Diamonds, Gold and War*, p.523.

13 See http://hsf.org.za/resource-centre/focus/focus-70-on-focus/focus-70-oct-politicsweb.pdf/download.

14 *Hansard*, 15 May 1913, http://hsf.org.za/resource-centre/focus/focus-70-on-focus/focus-70-oct-politicsweb.pdf/download.

15 Cited in Meredith, *Diamonds, Gold and War*, p.161.

16 Cited in Meredith, *Diamonds, Gold and War*, p.264.

17 Cited in Meredith, *Diamonds, Gold and War*, p.474.

18 See http://www.health-e.org.za/2000/03/27/violence-and-alcohol-tear-northern-cape-apart/.

19 See http://www.info.gov.za/speech/DynamicAction?pageid=461&sid=34665&tid=100302.

20 See http://www.bdlive.co.za/national/politics/2013/06/05/superficial-shake-up-mires-northern-cape-in-ineptness-says-da.

21 This section is based on a trip to Windhoek in October 2013 in the company of Thomas Vester and Robert Lloyd George. For details on the diamond production and history, see http://www.worlddiamondcouncil.org/download/resources/documents/Fact%20Sheet%20(Diamond%20Mining%20in%20Africa).pdf.

22 See http://www.namdeb.com/about_namdeb_history.php.

23 With thanks to Robert Lloyd George, grandson of the former British prime minister, for relating this anecdote.

24 See http://www.worlddiamondcouncil.org/download/resources/documents/Fact%20Sheet%20(Diamond%20Mining%20in%20Africa).pdf.

25 See http://www.tradingeconomics.com/namibia/rural-population-wb-data.html.

26 These and other quotes were taken from discussions in Windhoek on 3–4 October 2013.

27 See http://www.doingbusiness.org/data/exploreeconomies/namibia/.

28 See http://www.confidente.com.na/2013/03/28/namibias-economic-competitiveness-drops-on-wef-report/.

29 SWAPO has been the governing party in Namibia since independence in 1990. For example, it won 75.25 per cent of the popular vote and 54 out of 72 seats in the parliamentary election held in November 2009.

30 With thanks to Alberto Trejos for this insight.

31 See http://atlasnetwork.org/blog/2010/08/transforming-the-americas-the-chilean-experience/.

32 Ricardo Ffrench-Davis, *Reforming the Reforms in Latin America*. London: Macmillan, 2000.
33 Including Hernan Buchi (see http://www.hacer. org/chile/?page_id=15), José (Pepe) Pinera, regarded as the architect of the pension reform and brother of Sebastian Pinera, the president from 2010, Carlos Cáceres Contreras, Cristián Larroulet, Hernán Felipe Errázuriz and Miguel Kast.
34 See Ricardo Ffrench-Davis, *Economic Reforms in Chile: From Dictatorship to Democracy*. New York: Palgrave Macmillan, 2010. See also his blog, http://triplecrisis.com/the-chilean-model/.
35 Mantos Blancos accounted in 1990 for about 70 000 tonnes, Disputada 100 000, which together with various other small private sector mines, made up 250 000. CODELCO's production was made up of Chuquicamata (500 000 tonnes), El Teniente (150 000 tonnes), Salvador (50 000 tonnes) and Andina (approximately 70 000 tonnes).
36 With thanks to Patrick Esnouf for these figures. See also http://minerals.usgs.gov/minerals/pubs/country/2010/myb3-2010-ci.pdf.
37 Eduardo Frei Montalva served as the 28th president of Chile from 1964 to 1970. His eldest son, Eduardo Frei Ruiz-Tagle, was elected president of Chile in 1994 and served until 2000.
38 For details, see http://www.hacienda.gov.cl/english/investor-relations-office/incentives-for-foreign-investment/legal-framework.html.
39 See http://www.foreigninvestment.cl/index.php?option=com_content&view=article&id=123.
40 For an assessment of these reforms, see http://www.oecd-ilibrary.org/social-issues-migration-health/pension-reform-in-chile-revisited_224473276417.
41 For the Corruption Perception Index results, see http://www.transparency.org/research/cpi/cpi_2001.
42 For details of this transaction and the subsequent dispute between Anglo and CODELCO, see http://www.theglobeandmail.com/globe-investor/anglo-american-codelco-settle-copper-row/article4495320/.
43 The biggest private sector mines in Chile circa 2010 being Escondida at 1.4 million tonnes, and Disputada, Collahuasi and Pelambres, each at 400 000 tonnes.
44 See http://www.miningweekly.com/article/mine-nationalisation-lost-zambia-45bn-eunomix-study-finds-2013-03-22.
45 With thanks (again) to Patrick Esnouf for this point and for his overall help and input into the section on Chile.
46 With thanks to Stuart Doran for this point.
47 Conversation, Bellagio, 30 April 2013.
48 See http://www.ft.com/intl/cms/s/0/62be6d98-05df-11e3-ad01-00144feab7de.html#axzz2gwfmyj6n.
49 Cited in Meredith, *Diamonds, Gold and War*, p.163.
50 See Robert Rotberg, 'Worst Crisis You've Never Heard of: CAR Non-State about to Explode', 4 October 2013, http://robertrotberg.wordpress.com/2013/10/04/worst-crisis-youve-never-heard-of-car-non-state-about-to-explode/.
51 See http://eiti.org/extractive-industries-transparency-initiative-0.

23 COLOMBIA

1 This chapter is based on research conducted in Colombia in December 2006, March 2009, December 2010 and November 2013, including in Bogotá, Medellin and rural Antioquia, Cartagena, Norte de Santander and Cali. Grateful thanks are expressed to Juan Carlos Pinzón, Juan Carlos Echeverry, Lyal White and others who assisted with these trips. The interviews with the former president, Uribe, were conducted in the Dominican Republic in January 2013, and in Pereira in Colombia in November 2013. Unless otherwise referenced, the quotations are from discussions and interviews during the above research-gathering trips.
2 See Steven Dudley, *Walking Ghosts: Murder and Guerrilla Politics in Colombia*. New York: Routledge, 2006, p.2.
3 Information supplied by the Police Intelligence Division, Bogotá, 10 December 2010.
4 Discussion, Bogotá, 9 December 2010.
5 Reported at http://edition.cnn.com/2014/04/10/world/un-world-murder-rates/.
6 The source for these figures is the Ministerio de Defensa Nacional de Colombia.
7 See http://www.globalsecurity.org/military/world/war/colombia.htm.
8 See https://www.cia.gov/library/publications/the-world-factbook/fields/2212.html.
9 See http://www.abcolombia.org.uk/mainpage.asp?mainid=76.
10 Police Intelligence, Bogotá, 10 December 2010.
11 Policy for the Consolidation of National Security, 2007, Ministry of National Defence, Republic of Colombia.
12 See http://www.reuters.com/article/latestCrisis/idUSN06348039.
13 In the 1960s the FARC had a term for their strategy: *la combinación de todas la formas de lucha* (the combination of all forms of the struggle). While they would have left-wing politicians, unionists, students and others representing their interests in formal chambers, the guerrillas would take the fight to the government in the mountains and hills.
14 Dudley, *Walking Ghosts*, p.8.
15 See http://www.bbc.co.uk/news/world-latin-america-24920394.
16 Speech to the group of African officials organised by the Brenthurst Foundation, Bogotá, March 2009.

24 MYANMAR

1 Although the name change from Burma to Myanmar in 1989 is still not recognised by groups inside and outside the country, this remains the official name.

2 As a comparison with global figures, according to the UN, the global balance tilted from rural to urban areas in 2007. At the turn of the nineteenth to twentieth century, just two of every ten people lived in an urban area. By 1990, less than 40 per cent of the global population lived in a city. By 2030, six out of every ten people worldwide will live in urban areas. In China, as a comparative figure, this share is anticipated to be 70 per cent.

3 For two outstanding guides to historical and contemporary developments in Mynamar, see Thant Mynit-U, *The River of Lost Footsteps: A Personal History of Burma*. New York: Farrar, Straus and Giroux, 2008; and Benedict Rogers, *Burma: A Nation at the Crossroads*. Sydney: Random House, 2012.

4 See the Asian Development Bank report, 'Mynamar in Transition: Opportunities and Challenges', August 2012, http://blogs.wsj.com/searealtime/2012/08/20/myanmars-growing-but-has-a-long-way-to-go/.

5 This section is based, in part, on a visit to Myanmar in November–December 2013. With thanks to Al Leithead, Robert Lloyd George, Anthony Bergin, High Commissioners Graeme Wilson and Matthew Neuhaus, and to Ambassador Myint Naung and Hlaing Phone Myint at the Myanmar Embassy in South Africa for their help in organising meetings and providing other information.

6 McKinsey Global Institute, 'Myanmar's Moment: Unique Opportunities, Major Challenges', June 2013, http://www.telenor.com/wp-content/uploads/2013/08/MGI_Myanmar_Full_report_June2013.pdf.

7 Thant Myint-U, *The River of Lost Footsteps*, p.220.

8 See Charles McMoran Wilson, *Churchill: Taken from the Diaries of Lord Moran*. Boston: Houghton Mifflin, 1966, http://en.wikipedia.org/wiki/Orde_Wingate#cite_note-61.

9 Frank McLynn, *The Burma Campaign: Disaster into Triumph*. Vintage: London, 2010.

10 Cited in the excellent *Myanmar: The Insight Guide*. Apa Publications, 2013, p.37.

11 McLynn, *The Burma Campaign*, p.6.

12 U Thant, who took over the UN's top position on Dag Hammerskjöld's death in the Ndola plane crash in September 1961, served as U Nu's private secretary from 1951 to 1957.

13 George Orwell, *Burmese Days*. London: Penguin, 1986.

14 See the introduction by Emma Larkin to Orwell, *Burmese Days*, p.vii.

15 Larkin in Orwell, *Burmese Days*, pp.viii–ix.

16 Larkin in Orwell, *Burmese Days*, p.vi.

17 See Association of Myanmar Architects, *30 Heritage Buildings of Yangon: Inside the City that Captured Time*. Chicago: Serindia, 2013; and Jacques Maudy and Jimi Casaccia, *Yangon: A City to Rescue*. Self-published, 2013.

18 Discussion, Yangon, 29 November 2013.

19 The Pyidaungsu Hluttaw (Assembly of the Union) is the bicameral legislature of Myanmar, made up of two houses, the Amyotha Hluttaw (House of Nationalities), a 224-seat upper house, as well as the Pyithu Hluttaw, a 440-seat lower house (House of Representatives).

20 See http://www.lowyinterpreter.org/post/2013/10/30/Aung-San-Suu-Kyis-risky-strategy.aspx.

21 Discussion, Institute of Southeast Asian Studies, Singapore, 5 December 2013.

22 With thanks to Al Leithead, former BBC correspondent to the region, for these insights.

23 Email correspondence with Andrew Selth, 28 November 2013.

24 See http://www.dvb.no/analysis/suu-kyi-is-fighting-but-how-long-for/14223.

25 Email correspondence, 2 January 2013.

26 See http://www2.irrawaddy.org/article.php?art_id=2768.

27 Thant Myint-U, *The River of Lost Footsteps*, p.245.

28 See http://blogs.wsj.com/searealtime/2012/08/20/myanmars-growing-but-has-a-long-way-to-go/.

29 *Myanmar Times*, 25 November – 1 December 2013, p.23.

30 Discussion, Yangon, 29 November 2013.

31 Thant Myint-U, *The River of Lost Footsteps*, p.340.

32 Discussion, Thant Myint-U, Yangon, 29 November 2013.

25 SINGAPORE

1 As of December 2013, Temasek owns 54 per cent of Singapore Airlines, and 100 per cent of the Singapore Port Authority. This section is based on several trips to Singapore, most recently during November–December 2013 as a Distinguished Visitor of the Ministry of Foreign Affairs.

2 Discussion, Jaloul Ayed, Tunis, 26 March 2014.

3 Presentation, Urban Renewal Authority, Singapore, 3 December 2013.

4 See http://news.asiaone.com/News/AsiaOne+News/Singapore/Story/A1Story20110117-258649.html.

5 See http://wp.sg/2013/02/a-dynamic-population-for-a-sustainable-singapore-reclaiming-back-singapore-mp-sylvia-lim/.

6 Meeting, Singapore, May 2008.

7 Discussion, HDB, Singapore, 5 December 2013.

8 See http://www.juronggrc.sg/goh_Keng_swee.

9 Matt Andrews,*The Limits of Institutional Reform in Development*. Cambridge: Cambridge University Press, 2012.

10 For details on his life story, see S.R. Nathan, *An Unexpected Journey: Path to the Presidency*. Singapore: Editios Didier Millet, 2011. The direct quotes are taken from a personal interview

undertaken in Singapore, 2 December 2013.
11 See Barry Desker and Chong Guan Kwa, *Goh Keng Swee: A Public Career Remembered.* Singapore: RSIS and World Scientific Publishing, 2012.
12 See Lee Kuan Yew, *From Third World to First: The Singapore Story: 1965–2000.* New York: HarperCollins, 2008.
13 Private correspondence, 15 September 2013.
14 Taken from a video presentation, National Museum of Singapore, 7 December 2013.
15 His answer to my question at the S. Rajaratnam Lecture, Raffles City Convention Centre, 2 December 2013.

26 SOMALILAND

1 This chapter is based on visits to Somaliland in September 2003, June 2011, September 2012 and, again, April 2014. Unless otherwise indicated, the interviews were conducted during these visits. For a background to Somaliland, see Ioan Lewis, *Understanding Somalia and Somaliland: Culture, History, Society.* London: Hurst, 2011.
2 See Mark Bradbury's excellent *Becoming Somaliland.* London: Progressio, 2008, p.3.
3 Bradbury, *Becoming Somaliland.*
4 With thanks to Dr John Mackinlay for this allegory of a 'swarm' of foreign actors.
5 The full list of UN organisations present in Somaliland in 2011 was: UNDP, DSS, FAO, UN-HABITAT, ICAO, IOM, OCHA, UNESCO, UNFPA, UNHCR, UNICEF, UNOPS, UNPOS, WFP, WHO, UNCDF, UNMAS and UNIDO, plus the World Bank, which is a member of the UN Country Team. The non-resident agencies were UNODC, ILO, UNAIDS and UNWOMEN.
6 After Abdirahman Ahmed Ali Tuur (28 May 1991 until 16 May 1993), Muhammad Haji Ibrahim Egal (16 May 1993 to 3 May 2002) and Dahir Riyale Kahin (3 May 2002 to 27 July 2010).
7 Somaliland's problem is that, unlike the split up of Czechoslovakia or secession of Eritrea, its original marriage partner, Somalia, does not agree to a divorce, even though it does not function to all intents and purposes as a proper state. Moreover, this ignores the political and legal arguments. South Africa's then department of foreign affairs concluded in 2003 that '[i]t is undeniable that Somaliland does indeed qualify for statehood, and it is incumbent on the international community to recognise it'. The African Union, which has sent two missions to Somaliland in 2005 and 2008, has said Somaliland fulfils many of the aspects of state recognition. 'Objectively viewed,' the 2005 report states, 'the case should not be linked to the notion of "opening a Pandora's box"' – the source of African misgivings about the recognition of new states in the continent. See, for example, the African Union reports of 2005 and 2008: 'Resumé: AU Fact-Finding Mission to Somaliland', 30 April – 4 May 2005; and Nicolas Bwakira, 'Visit of the

African Union Special Representative for Somalia', Hargeisa, 12–14 September 2008.

27 SOUTH AFRICA

1 With thanks to Sir Edward Clay.
2 Statement made outside Downing Street as reported on BBC TV, 5 December 2013. See also http://www.bbc.co.uk/news/world-africa-25250082.
3 *Radio Today* podcast, accessed 7 December 2013, http://downloads.bbc.co.uk/podcasts/radio4/today/today_20131206-1020a.mp3.
4 See http://www.bbc.co.uk/news/world-africa-20734941.
5 BBC TV, 6 December 2013.
6 See http://mg.co.za/article/2013-12-06-00-tutu-we-thank-god-for-madiba.
7 Cited in Hugh Macmillan, *The Lusaka Years: The ANC in Exile in Zambia.* Johannesburg: Jacana, 2013, p.12.
8 See Rian Malan's perceptive 'Nelson Mandela: He was Never Simply the Benign Old Man', *Daily Telegraph*, 6 December 2013, http://www.telegraph.co.uk/news/worldnews/nelson-mandela/10502173/Nelson-Mandela-he-was-never-simply-the-benign-old-man.html?fb.
9 As he put it on BBC TV on the occasion of Mandela's death, 6 December 2013.
10 Cited in Allister Sparks, *Tomorrow is Another Country: The Inside Story of South Africa's Negotiated Revolution.* Johannesburg: Struik, 1994, p.95.
11 Discussion, Johannesburg, 18 January.
12 *Leadership*, March 1989.
13 See http://www.weeping.info/Weeping-lyrics.html.
14 For an excellent summary of these negotiations, see Sparks, *Tomorrow is Another Country*, esp. pp.68–90 and pp.109–19. The following section is based partly on a personal discussion and email exchange with F.W. de Klerk during 18–20 December 2013.
15 Sparks,*Tomorrow is Another Country*, p.98.
16 Sparks, *Tomorrow is Another Country*, p.108.
17 Discussion, Tana Forum, 26 April 2014.
18 Discussion with Olusegun Obasanjo, Sao Paolo, June 2012.
19 SAPA, 9 December 2013. With thanks to Ray Hartley for this source.
20 As cited in *The Wall Street Journal*, 5 December 2013.
21 SAPA, 9 December 2013.
22 In the words of Thabo Mbeki's published eulogy on Mandela's death: 'Nelson Mandela engaged in struggle both as a frontline combatant and a senior member of the general staff during the defining period in our history from the accession of the National Party to power in 1948, to its defeat in 1994.' See http://www.iol.co.za/news/south-africa/farewell-madiba-1.1617819.
23 See http://en.wikipedia.org/wiki/

South_African_apartheid_referendum,_1992.

24 Email correspondence, 7 January 2014.

25 See https://s3.amazonaws.com/vookflow-sf-prd/
Nelson_Mandela_-_Making_Peace.pdf.

26 Discussion at his offices, Tyger Valley, Cape Town,
18 December 2013.

27 Malan, 'Nelson Mandela'.

28 See http://www.npr.org/templates/story/story.
php?storyId=249454377.

29 See http://www.nybooks.com/articles/
archives/2013/jun/06/mandela-communism-
exchange/?pagination=false.

30 See Daniel Silke, 'How Mandela's Passing Changes
SA Politics', http://www.politicsweb.co.za/
politicsweb/view/politicsweb/en/page72308?oid=
483584&sn=Marketingweb+detail&pid=90389.

31 For details, see *Two Decades of Freedom: A 20-Year
Review of South Africa*. Johannesburg: Goldman
Sachs, 2013.

32 *Two Decades of Freedom*.

33 For example, see Alex Boraine, *What's
Gone Wrong? On the Brink of a Failed State*.
Johannesburg: Jonathan Ball, 2014.

34 Mike Cohen, 'Manuel Pledges Loyalty to ANC
as he Quits South African Politics', *Bloomberg*,
11 March 2014.

35 See 'The Contradictions of Mandela', *New York
Times*, 5 December 2013, http://www.nytimes.
com/2013/12/06/opinion/the-contradictions-of-
mandela.html?smid=tw-nytimes&_r=1&.

36 Discussion, 16 April 2014.

28 VIETNAM

1 This chapter is based on several trips to Vietnam,
in 1994, 2004, 2005, 2007, 2010 and 2011. I
am grateful for the input of Do Duc Dinh to
this chapter, and to his collegial support and
companionship during these trips.

2 See http://www.state.gov/r/pa/ei/bgn/4130.htm.

3 See http://moeaitc.tier.org.tw/idic/mgz_topic.nsf/
0/54f372825f4887ac4825676a002abac9.

4 See http://www.davifo.dk/userfiles/file/pdf/
International%20NGOs%20in%20Vietnam8.pdf.

5 David Lamb, *Vietnam, Now: A Reporter Returns*.
New York: Public Affairs, 2003, p.55.

6 See http://www.pep-net.org/fileadmin/medias/
pdf/files_events/ngoc.pdf.

7 Human Rights Watch Asia Director Phil
Robertson cited at http://www.bbc.com/news/
world-asia-27019624.

1 For a sympathetic account of the origins of the
Brotherhood, see John Calvert, *Sayyid Qutb
and the Origins of Radical Islamism*. New York:
Columbia University Press, 2010.

2 See Phebe Marr (ed.), *Egypt at the Crossroads:
Domestic Stability and Regional Role*. London:
Create Space, 2012, pp.39–40.

3 Interview, Cairo, 28 March 2014.

4 Discussion, Cairo, 28 March 2014.

5 Mary Anne Weaver, *A Portrait of Egypt: A Journey
Through the World of Militant Islam*. New York:
Farrar, Straus and Giroux, 2000.

6 See http://www.theguardian.com/media/
pda/2011/may/18/google-wael-ghonim-mubarak.
See also http://www.vocativ.com/world/egypt/
where-in-the-world-is-wael-ghonim/.

7 See Wael Ghonim, *Revolution 2.0: The Power of
the People is Greater than the People in Power*. New
York: Houghton Mifflin Harcourt, 2012.

8 Discussions, February 2011.

9 Tarek Osman, *Egypt on the Brink: From the Rise
of Nasser to the Fall of Mubarak*. New Haven: Yale
University Press, 2011, pp.242–43.

10 Omar Ashour, 'Egypt: Return to a Generals'
Republic?', http://www.bbc.com/news/world-
middle-east-23780839.

11 Discussion, Tivoli Food Court, Cairo, 26 March 2014.

12 For details on the impact of the fuel subsidy – and
shortages – see Max Reibman, 'Fueling Egypt's
Economy', *Sada Journal*, 27 March 2014, http://
carnegieendowment.org/sada/2014/03/27/fueling-
egypt-s-economy/h5yp.

13 The official figure for Egypt was 5 854 million
in 2010, of which one-third were in the
capital. See http://english.ahram.org.eg/
NewsContent/3/12/18085/Business/Economy/
Egypt-vehicles-up-per-cent-in-,-new-figures-
show.aspx.

14 These figures were provided by the Ministry of
Finance, 27 March 2014. See also 'Arab Spring
Break', http://www.economist.com/news/
business/21577089-turmoil-has-scared-all-
rugged-and-russians-arab-spring-break.

15 Discussion, Dcode, Cairo, 31 March 2014.

16 The government has relied on petroleum and
stimulus packages from Saudi Arabia, the United
Arab Emirates and Kuwait to reduce the deficit
and pay bills to foreign and domestic creditors.
See Ann Lesch, 'Egypt: Resurgence of the Security
State', FPRI E-note, 28 March 2014. This was also
discussed with the Ministry of Finance, Cairo,
27 March 2014.

17 Information supplied in correspondence with
Dcode, 4 April 2014.

18 Cited in Ann Lesch, 'Playing with Fire: The
Showdown in Egypt between the General and
the Islamist President', FPRI E-note, March 2014,
http://www.fpri.org/articles/2014/03/playing-fire-
showdown-egypt-between-general-and-islamist-
president.

19 See 'Demoralized Cairo Slum Longs for Army Chief as President', http://www.reuters.com/ article/2014/01/12/us-egypt-referendum-imbaba-idUSBREA0B07F20140112.
20 Interview with journalists, Cairo, 28 March 2014.
21 See Mostafa Hashem, 'The Dangers of Alienating Egypt's Youth', http://carnegieendowment.org/ sada/2014/03/06/dangers-of-alienating-egypt-s-youth/h2l2.
22 Discussion, Cairo, 28 March 2014.
23 Information supplied by Dcode, Cairo, 31 March 2014.
24 Discussion, Mohammed Omran, Executive Chairman, Egyptian Exchange, 31 March 2014.
25 For a comprehensive statistical background on Egypt, see African Development Bank, *Egypt Economic Quarterly Review* 5, 2014.
26 Discussion, Cairo, 28 March 2014.
27 See, for example, http://www.egyptindependent. com/news/air-pollution-indoors-and-outdoors-high-threaten-health-and-environment.
28 See http://www.aljazeera.com/news/ middleeast/2014/03/sisi-resignation-speech-full-201432620163812390 5.html.
29 Ashour, 'Egypt'.
30 Steve A. Cook, 'Echoes of Nasser', *Foreign Policy*, 16 July 2013, http://www.foreignpolicy.com/ articles/2013/07/16/echoes_of_nasser_egypt_ muslim_brotherhood_history.
31 See Calvert, *Sayyid Qutb*.
32 See http://www.youtube.com/ watch?v=TX4RK8bj2W0.
33 Osman, *Egypt on the Brink*, pp.54–56.
34 Osman, *Egypt on the Brink*, p.76.

29 THE PRIOR QUESTION

1 See, for example, Angus Deaton, *The Great Escape*. Princeton and Oxford: Princeton University Press, 2013, p.219.
2 For data on global poverty comparisons, see Martin Ravallion, 'A Comparative Perspective on Poverty Reduction in Brazil, China and India', World Bank Development Research Group, October 2009, http://elibrary.worldbank. org/doi/pdf/10.1596/1813-9450-5080.
3 Deaton, *The Great Escape*, p.234.
4 Milton Osborne, *Southeast Asia: An Introductory History*. Sydney: Allen & Unwin, 2013, p.45. To an extent with the exception of Vietnam, where there was always much greater state control from the centre.
5 Osborne, *Southeast Asia*, p.43.
6 Osborne, *Southeast Asia*, p.111.
7 Osborne, *Southeast Asia*, p.107.
8 Tana Forum, 26 April 2014.
9 This debate is advanced in Greg Mills, *Why Africa is Poor: And What Africans Can Do About It*. Johannesburg: Penguin, 2010.
10 See 'Towards the End of Poverty', *The Economist*, 1 June 2013, http://www.economist.com/news/ leaders/21578665-nearly-1-billion-people-have-

been-taken-out-extreme-poverty-20-years-world-should-aim.
11 Ha-Joon Chang, 'Economic History of the Developed World: Lessons for Africa', address given to the African Development Bank, 26 February 2009.
12 International Trade Statistics, http://www. intracen.org/exporters/statistics-export-country-product/.
13 Cited in Devesh Kapur, John Prior Lewis and Richard Charles Webb, *The World Bank: History*, Washington, D.C.: Brookings, 2008, p.145.
14 With thanks to Barry Desker for this observation. See also William Easterly, 'Explaining Miracles: Growth Regressions Meet the Gang of Four', Policy Research Working Paper 1250, World Bank, February 1994, http://williameasterly. files.wordpress.com/2010/08/7_easterly_ explainingmiracles_bc.pdf. See also World Bank, *The East Asian Miracle*. New York: Oxford University Press, 1993; World Bank, *Sustaining Rapid Development in East Asia and the Pacific*. Washington, D.C.: Office of the Vice President, East Asia and Pacific Region, 1993.
15 Jared Diamond, *Collapse: How Societies Choose to Fail or Survive*. New York: Penguin, 2011.
16 David Lamb, *The Africans*. New York: Random House, 1987, p.17.
17 See http://www.mbendi.com/land/p0007.htm.
18 With thanks to Christopher Clapham for this point.
19 With thanks to Johnny Clegg for highlighting this. See also http://www.nomadsed.de/fileadmin/ user_upload/redakteure/Dateien_Publikationen/ Mitteilungen_des_SFB/owh6sigrist.pdf.
20 Jeffrey Herbst, *States and Power in Africa*. Princeton: Princeton University Press, 2001.
21 See his 1999 paper, 'The Political Economy of State Failure', http://www.iig.ox.ac.uk/output/ articles/OxREP/iiG-OxREP-Collier.pdf.
22 See Dambisa Moyo, *Dead Aid: Why Aid is Not Working and How There is a Better Way for Africa*. New York: Farrar, Straus and Giroux, 2009.
23 Ines Ferreira and Marta Simoes, 'Aid and Growth: A Comparative Study between Sub-Saharan Africa and Asia', *Applied Econometrics and International Development* 13(1), 2013. This is the source, too, of the aid per capita table as representing World Bank World Development Indicator data for 2012.
24 See, for example, R. Ram, 'Recipient Country's "Policies" and the Effect of Foreign Aid on Economic Growth in Developing Countries: Additional Evidence', *Journal of International Development* 16, 2004, pp.201–11; S. Robinson and F. Tarp, 'Foreign Aid and Development: Summary and Synthesis' in Finn Tarp and Peter Hjertholm (eds), *Foreign Aid and Development: Lessons Learnt and Directions for the Future*. London: Routledge, 2000; Paul Collier and David Dollar, 'Aid Allocation and Poverty Reduction', *European Economic Review* 26, 2002, pp.1475– 1500; Paul Collier and Anke Hoeffler, 'Aid,

Policy, and Growth in Post-Conflict Societies',
Policy Research Working Paper No. 2902, World
Bank, 2002; Mark McGillivray, 'Is Aid Effective?',
WIDER, Helsinki, 2004, http://www.oecd.org/
dev/34353462.pdf.

25 Herbst, States and Power in Africa, p.15.

26 As in the Bedouin saying: 'Me and my brothers
against my cousins, me and my cousins against
the world.'

27 See http://www.oecd.org/dac/incaf/
FragileStates2013.pdf.

28 See Seth Kaplan's critique, http://www.
fragilestates.org/2013/01/29/what-the-oecd-does-
not-understand-about-fragile-states/.

29 See http://www.guardian.co.uk/books/2011/
may/20/francis-fukuyama-origins-political-order-
review. For example, recent research suggests that
religious composition is important. The armed
conflict trend for Muslim-majority countries
(about one-half the population of non-Muslim/
non-Western countries) was at about one-half
the magnitude for the non-Muslim countries
until the late 1970s. Thereafter, violence trends
in Muslim-majority countries increases very
sharply in the late 1970s and early 1980s and
very quickly surpasses the level for non-Muslim
countries (making the Muslim countries about
twice as likely as non-Muslim countries to
experience armed conflict until about 2001 when
this likelihood doubles once again to about four
times as likely). See http://www.systemicpeace.
org/conflict.htm.

30 See Robert Rotberg, 'Failed and Weak States
Defined', Africa and Asia: The Key Issues,
11 February 2013, http://robertrotberg.wordpress.
com/2013/02/11/failed-and-weak-states-defined/.

31 Associated Press, 12 July 2009.

32 Osborne, Southeast Asia, p.158.

33 Paul Collier, 'The Political Economy of State
Failure', 1999, http://www.iig.ox.ac.uk/output/
articles/OxREP/iiG-OxREP-Collier.pdf.

34 Tsvangirai's remarks were made at the launch of
Africa's Third Liberation, Johannesburg, August
2012.

35 These perspectives were gathered in the course of
several trips to Ethiopia, most recently in April
2014. See http://www.bloomberg.com/news/2013-
02-18/ethiopian-military-run-corporation-seeks-
more-foreign-partners.html.

36 Discussion, Addis Ababa, 19 March 2014.

37 Befekadu Wolde Gabriel, 'EPRDF, Developmental
State, and Rent Seeking', http://www.aigaforum.
com/articles/EPRDF-DS-RS.pdf.

38 Meles Zenawi, 'Africa's Development: Dead Ends
and New Beginnings', http://cgt.columbia.edu/
files/conferences/Zenawi Dead_Ends_and_New_
Beginnings, 2006, as cited by Wolde Gariel.

39 See 'Ethiopia: Rent Seeking Discourse Seeks
Achievable Targets', 28 April 2013, http://allafrica.
com/stories/201304300518.html.

40 For example, 'Eyes on Ethiopia: Kenyan Investors
want Addis to Ease Market Restrictions', East

African, 22–28 March 2014.

41 See 'Ethiopia is Open for Investment but not
Everyone is Welcome', East African, 22–28 March
2014.

42 William Easterly, 'Stop Sending Aid to Dictators',
Time, 24 March 2014.

43 Remarks delivered to the Tana Forum, 26 April
2014.

44 These arguments are more fully explored in
Jeffrey Herbst and Greg Mills, Africa's Third
Liberation: The New Search for Jobs and Prosperity.
Johannesburg: Penguin, 2012.

45 Nandan Nilekani, Imagining India: Ideas for the
New Century. New Delhi: Penguin, 2007, p.18.

46 See, for example, Meredith Woo-Cumings,
The Developmental State. Ithaca, NY: Cornell
University Press, 1999; and Stephen Haggard,
Pathways from the Periphery: The Politics of
Growth in the Newly Industriailizing Countries.
Ithaca, NY: Cornell University Press, 1990.

47 Jagdish Bhagwati, The Economics of
Underdeveloped Countries. New York: McGraw-
Hill, 1966.

48 For an excellent overview of these arguments
on which this sections draws, see Takaaki
Masaki and Nicolas van de Walle, 'The Impact of
Democracy on Economic Growth in Sub-Saharan
Africa, 1982–2012', WIDER Working Paper
2014/057, March 2014.

49 Chalmers Johnson, MITI and the Japanese
Miracle. California: Stanford University Press,
1982. See also http://www.e-ir.info/2008/06/15/
the-developmental-state-and-economic-
development/ for a summary of these arguments.

50 See http://www.forbes.com/sites/
kenrapoza/2012/10/03/is-russia-ready-for-life-
after-oil/.

51 See http://www.indexmundi.com/venezuela/
economy_profile.html.

52 Deemed as part of China for this purpose.

53 See, for example, Douglass North, Institutions,
Institutional Change and Economic Performance.
Cambridge: Cambridge University Press, 1990;
Adam Przeworski, Democracy and Development:
Political Institutions and Well-Being in the World.
Cambridge: Cambridge University Press, 2000;
Adam Przeworski and Fernando Limongi,
'Political Regimes and Economic Growth', Journal
of Economic Perspectives 7(3), 1993, pp.51–69;
and Nic van de Walle, 'Economic Reform in a
Democratizing Africa', Comparative Politics 32(1),
1999, pp.21–41.

54 See Benno Ndulu and Stephen O'Connell,
'Governance and Growth in Sub-Saharan Africa',
Journal of Economic Perspectives, 13(3), 1999,
pp.41–66.

55 Jon S.T. Quah, Curbing Corruption in Asian
Countries: An Impossible Dream? Singapore:
Institute for Southeast Asian Studies, 2013.

56 Of the 175 countries polled in the 2013 Index,
Cambodia was at 160th position, Myanmar 157,
Laos 140, observer states East Timor 119 and

Papua New Guinea 144, Indonesia 114, Thailand 102 and the Philippines 94. Singapore was at fifth position, Brunei 38 and Malaysia 53.

57 See http://cpi.transparency.org/cpi2013/results/.

58 Interview, Institute for Southeast Asian Studies, Singapore, 5 December 2013.

59 See Kerry A. Dolan and Rafael Marques de Morais, 'Daddy's Girl: How an African "Princess" Banked $3 Billion in a Country Living on $2 a Day', Forbes, 2 September 2013.

60 Collier, 'The Political Economy of State Failure'.

61 With thanks to Jeffrey Herbst on this point.

62 See http://www.washingtonpost.com/blogs/worldviews/wp/2013/07/16/the-amazing-surprising-africa-driven-demographic-future-of-the-earth-in-9-charts/.

63 See http://www.economist.com/blogs/dailychart/2010/12/urbanisation_africa.

64 See http://www.africaresearchinstitute.org/publications/policy-voices/urban-planning-in-kenya/.

65 This section is based on research in Mozambique from 2005 to 2014, including most recently in January 2014. For a thorough historical overview of the country, see Malyn Newitt, A History of Mozambique. London: Hurst, 2009, especially pp.517–77.

66 See World Bank database, http://data.worldbank.org/country/mozambique.

67 See http://www.gfmag.com/gdp-data-country-reports/215-mozambique-gdp-country-report.html#axzz2r7h9go4j.

68 See James Zahn, 'Making Foreign Investment Work: Lessons from Mozambique', The Guardian, 30 July 2013, http://www.theguardian.com/global-development-professionals-network/2013/jul/30/mozambique-foreign-direct-investment-unctad; see also 'Mozambique: Growth has not Led to Economic Transformation', http://allafrica.com/stories/201401250143.html?page=2.

69 See also Pedro Martins, 'Growth, Employment and Poverty in Africa: Tales of Lions and Cheetahs', Overseas Development Institute Background Paper for the World Development Report, February 2013, http://www.odi.org.uk/publications/7294-growth-employment-poverty-africa-tales-lions-cheetahs.

70 See http://allafrica.com/stories/201310031211.html.

30 THE FRAGILITY 'INDUSTRY'

1 This chapter draws on the excellent essays by Rory Stewart and Gerald Knaus in Can Intervention Work? New York: W.W. Norton, 2011; See also http://www.da.mod.uk/recommended-reading/warfare/readingitem.2013-03-08.3547506354#_ednref20.

2 Stewart and Knaus, Can Intervention Work?

3 Bush cited in Michael Mazarr, 'The Rise and Fall of the Failed-State Paradigm: Requiem for a Decade of Distraction', Foreign Affairs, January/February 2014, http://www.foreignaffairs.com/articles/140347/michael-j-mazarr/the-rise-and-fall-of-the-failed-state-paradigm.

4 See http://georgewbush-whitehouse.archives.gov/nsc/nss/2002/.

5 Francis Fukuyama, State-Building: Governance and World Order in the 21st Century. Cornell: Cornell University Press, 2004, cited in Mazarr, 'The Rise and Fall of the Failed-State Paradigm'.

6 From July 1983 an insurgency was waged against the Sri Lanka government by the Liberation Tigers of Tamil Eelam (also known as the Tamil Tigers), which fought to create an independent ethnic Tamil state in the north and east of the island, reflecting a history of ethnic discrimination and exclusion of the minority (8.5 per cent) Tamils by the majority (74 per cent) Sinhalese. With allegations of atrocities and human rights violations on both sides, as many as 100 000 people were killed as a consequence, with several times this number displaced. The Tigers came to be listed as a terrorist organisation by more than 30 countries worldwide, suicide bombings their military trademark. Despite several ceasefires and attempts at an internationally facilitated political settlement (led notably by the Norwegian government), after a 26-year war, the Sri Lankan military defeated the Tigers in May 2009, bringing the civil war to an end.

7 See Conor Cruise O'Brien, 'Bosnia: Hands Off', The Atlantic, November 1992, http://www.theatlantic.com/magazine/archive/1992/11/bosniahands-off/5341/, cited in Stewart and Knaus, Can Intervention Work?

8 See, for example, Sean Rayment, 'General Sir David Richards: "We Can't Afford to Lose the War in Afghanistan"', Telegraph, 4 October 2009. http://www.telegraph.co.uk/news/worldnews/asia/afghanistan/625, cited in Stewart and Knaus, Can Intervention Work?

9 Mazarr, 'The Rise and Fall of the Failed-State Paradigm'.

10 See Rory Stewart: "The Secret of Modern Britain is There is No Power Anywhere', The Guardian, 3 January 2014, http://www.theguardian.com/politics/2014/jan/03/rory-stewart-interview.

11 See, for example, http://www.brookings.edu/research/papers/2011/11/fragile-states-chandy; http://www.weforum.org/content/global-agenda-council-fragile-states-and-conflict-prevention-2012-2014; http://www.lse.ac.uk/internationalDevelopment/research/crisisStates/download/publicity/CitiesBrochure.pdf; http://economics.ouls.ox.ac.uk/13009/1/workingpaper51.pdf; http://wws.princeton.edu/centers_programs/states/; http://www.ifad.org/english/fragilestates/; http://www.odi.org.uk/sites/odi.org.uk/files/odi-assets/publications-opinion-files/1955.pdf; and http://www.u4.no/themes/fragile-states/; http://www4.carleton.ca/cifp/ffs.htm.

12 See, for example, Seth Kaplan, Fixing Fragile

States: A New Paradigm for Development.
Westport, CT: ABC-CLIO, 2008; Charles T. Call
and Vanessa Wyeth (eds), *Building States to Build
Peace.* Boulder: Lynne Rienner, 2008; Robert
I. Rotberg (ed.), *When States Fail: Causes and
Consequences.* Princeton: Princeton University
Press, 2004; Ashraf Ghani and Clare Lockhart,
*Fixing Failed States: A Framework for Rebuilding a
Fractured World.* Oxford: Oxford University Press,
2008; and James Mayall and Richard Soares de
Oliveira (eds), *The New Protectorates: International
Tutelage and the Making of Liberal States.* London:
Hurst, 2011.

13 Robert Dallek, *Nixon and Kissinger: Partners in
Power.* New York: HarperCollins, 2007, p.106.

14 With thanks to John Mackinlay for this analogy.

15 This can happen sometimes in unintended
and hard-to-discern ways. For example, in
Afghanistan, ISAF's arrival had the effect, inter
alia, of hollowing out the rural, village-level
intelligentsia, where an estimated 150 000 people
traipsed to Kabul and other centres for better-
paying, internationally supported jobs. In 2010,
donor salaries were, as a guide, twice as high
as those in the business community, let alone
government. With thanks to David Kilcullen for
pointing this out.

16 See http://www.middleeastmonitor.com/
resources/interviews/7277-jeremy-greenstock-on-
syria-qiraq-wmd-was-a-big-turn-off-of-peoples-
trust-in-government-assertion-and-that-cant-be-
put-back-in-the-boxq.

17 Stewart and Knaus, *Can Intervention Work?*

18 'How to Stop Fighting, Sometimes', *The Economist*,
9 November 2013.

19 Cited in Karen de Jong, *Soldier: The Life of Colin
Powell.* New York: Alfred Knopf, 2006, p.469.

20 The Iraq surge refers to the increase of 28 000
US troops starting in early 2007, initially
concentrated in Baghdad and Anbar province in
Iraq, to assist Iraqi army units 'clear and secure
neighbourhoods, to help them protect the local
population, and to help ensure that the Iraqi
forces left behind are capable of providing the
security'. The surge was decided by President
George W. Bush in response to the deteriorating
security situation, followed from the December
2006 report of the bipartisan Iraq Study Group
(co-chaired by his father's secretary of state,
James Baker), and was influenced, too, by the US
experience in Vietnam of the disjuncture between
military actions and the lack of support in
Congress and among the American public.

21 Interview, ISAF HQ, Kabul, October 2010.

22 Cited in George Packer, 'The Last Mission', *The
New Yorker*, 28 September 2009, cited in Stewart
and Knaus, *Can Intervention Work?*

23 John Lewis Gaddis, *The Cold War.* New York:
Penguin, 2005.

24 Tony Leon, http://www.politicsweb.co.za/
politicsweb/view/politicsweb/en/page72308?oid=
397097&sn=Marketingweb+detail&pid=90389.

25 Richard Stengel, 'Mandela's Way: Lessons on Life',
http://www.leadershiponline.co.za, as cited in the
Leon speech above.

26 Jerome Booth, BBC Radio Four, 11 January 2014.

27 Stewart and Knaus, *Can Intervention Work?*

28 Afghanistan, Burundi, Central African Republic,
Chad, Comoros, Democratic Republic of Congo,
Guinea, Guinea-Bissau, Haiti, Côte d'Ivoire,
Liberia, Papua New Guinea, Sierra Leone,
Solomon Islands, Somalia, South Sudan, Timor-
Leste and Togo.

29 The eight Millennium Development Goals –
which range from halving extreme poverty rates
to halting the spread of HIV/AIDS, improving
maternal health, and providing universal primary
education, all by the target date of 2015 – formed
a blueprint agreed to by all the world's (then 189)
countries and leading development institutions at
the UN summit held in September 2000. The eight
goals have 21 targets.

30 See http://www.pbsbdialogue.org/
documentupload/49151944.pdf.

31 See http://web.worldbank.org/WBSITE/
EXTERNAL/EXTDEC/EXTRESEARCH/EXTWD
RS/0,,contentMDK:23252415~pagePK:478093~pi
PK:477627~theSitePK:477624,00.html.

31 CONFRONTING AUTHORITARIAN DEMOCRACY

1 See http://www.enca.com/africa/mugabe-if-you-
lose-you-must-surrender.

2 See http://www.crisisgroup.org/en/publication-
type/media-releases/2013/africa/zimbabwes-
elections-mugabes-last-stand.aspx.

3 See http://www.bbc.co.uk/news/world-
africa-23550191.

4 See, for example, http://www.csmonitor.
com/World/Africa/2013/0806/
Africans-now-say-Mugabe-election-in-
Zimbabwe-free-but-not-fair-video?utm_
source=feedburner&utm_medium=feed&utm_ca
mpaign=Feed%3A+feeds%2Fcsm+(Christian+Sci
ence+Monitor+%7C+All+Stories).

5 See http://www.politicsweb.co.za/politicsweb/
view/politicsweb/en/page72308?oid=476581&sn=
Marketingweb+detail&pid=90389.

6 See Peter Fabricius, 'In the Beginning, there was
Mugabe, always Mugabe', *The Star*, 6 August 2013.

7 See https://www.mmegi.bw/index.
php?sid=10&aid=1488&dir=2013/July/Tuesday23.

8 See John Lewis Gaddis, *The Cold War.* New York:
Penguin, 2005, p.2.

9 See Steven Budlender and Nic Ferreira, 'The
DA's Case Against the SABC', *Politicsweb*,
12 April 2014, http://www.politicsweb.co.za/
politicsweb/view/politicsweb/en/page72308?
oid=589036&sn=Marketingweb+detail&pid
=90389&utm_source=Politicsweb+Daily+He
adlines&utm_campaign=c1ee44e256-DHN_
April_14_2014&utm_medium=email&utm_

term=0_a86f25db99-c1ee44e256-130059649.
10 Alex Boraine, *What's Gone Wrong? On the Brink of a Failed State.* Johannesburg: Jonathan Ball, p.58.
11 See Vince Musewe, 'Liberation Politics will Never Deliver', http://www.politicsweb.co.za/politicsweb/view/politicsweb/en/page72308?oid=406613&sn=Marketingweb+detail&pid=90389.
12 David Lamb, *The Africans.* New York: Random House, 1987.
13 Peter Carrington, *Reflect on Things Past.* London: Collins, 1988, p.294.
14 Government employment increased in South Africa by 44 000 in the first quarter of 2013 to 3 072 000 employees or 22.6 per cent of total employed persons, replacing the trade sector (which contracted by 66 000 over the same period), as the single biggest employer. See http://www.becker-posner-blog.com/2011/09/too-many-government-workersposner.html. This section also draws on William Dobson, *The Dictators.* London: Vintage, 2013.
15 According to the SA Chamber of Commerce and Industry, http://www.politicsweb.co.za/politicsweb/view/politicsweb/en/page72308?oid=374732&sn=Marketingweb+detail&pid=90389.
16 The names of millions of pro-opposition supporters who signed the 'recall petitions' (seeking to remove Chávez from office) during 2002–03, and the names of pro-government supporters who signed counter-petitions, were made public in 2004 in the Maisanta list, so-named after Pedro Pérez Delgado, known as Maisanta, a Venezuelan activist and great-grandfather of Chávez. For details see Chang-Tai Hsieh, Edward Miguel, Daniel Ortega and Francisco Rodriguez, 'The Price of Political Opposition: Evidence from Venezuela's Maisanta', National Bureau for Economic Research Working Paper No. 14923, April 2009, http://www.nber.org/papers/w14923. Voters who were identified as Chávez opponents experienced a 5 per cent drop in earnings and a 1.5 percentage point drop in employment rates after the voter list was released. GDP shrank as a result by an estimated 3 per cent of GDP. As Chávez put it in a nationally televised address on 17 October 2003, 'Whoever signs against Chávez … their name will be there, registered for history, because they'll have to put down their first name, their last name, their signature, their identity card number, and their fingerprint.'
17 Dobson, *The Dictators*, p.92.
18 See Eddie Cross, 'The Failure of Zimbabwe's Civil Society Institutions', 7 April 2014, http://www.politicsweb.co.za/politicsweb/view/politicsweb/en/page72308?oid=587029&sn=Marketingweb+detail&pid=90389&utm_source=Politicsweb+Daily+Headlines&utm_campaign=89e4b956bf-DHN_April_8_2014&utm_medium=email&utm_term=0_a86f25db99-89e4b956bf-130059649.
19 See 'Iran's Rouhani: High Hopes, Narrow Remit', IISS Strategic Comment, 19 November 2013.
20 Margaret Thatcher, *Daily Telegraph*, 17 March 1969.
21 Discussion, Bellagio, 7 May 2013.
22 See Michela Wrong, 'Election Aid Fiasco', *The Spectator*, 20 April 2013, http://www.spectator.co.uk/features/8890471/the-technological-fix/.
23 With thanks to Wilmot James for this point.
24 See http://www.iol.co.za/news/politics/fransman-ethnic-division-a-reality-in-cape-1.1590115.
25 See http://mg.co.za/article/2013-10-16-white-jewish-land-ownership-comments-cant-be-verified.
26 Statement issued by the Department of Sport and Recreation, South Africa, 4 April 2014, http://www.politicsweb.co.za.
27 See the transcript of his interview, as president, on eTV, 24 April 2001, http://www.thepresidency.gov.za/pebble.asp?relid=1944.
28 Remarks made at the Tana Forum on Security in Africa, 21 April 2013.
29 With appreciation to Jeremy Paxman, *Empire.* London: Penguin, 2012, pp.3–4.
30 See 'Generation Jobless', *The Economist*, 27 April 2013, p.59.
31 See 'The Middle of the Pyramid: The Dynamics of the Middle Class in Africa', 20 April 2011, http://www.afdb.org/fileadmin/uploads/afdb/Documents/Publications/The%20Middle%20of%20the%20Pyramid_The%20Middle%20of%20the%20Pyramid.pdf. Africa is not alone: Venezuela's rich and middle class make up just 3 and 18 per cent respectively of the population, and the poor and extremely poor number a total of 79 per cent. See Dobson, *The Dictators*, p.88.
32 With thanks to Thomas Claiborne for this point.
33 Lee Kuan Yew, *From Third World to First: The Singapore Story: 1965–2000.* New York: HarperCollins, 2008, p.409.
34 See his Desmond Tutu International Peace lecture at the University of the Western Cape, October 2013, http://www.ghanaweb.com/GhanaHomePage/NewsArchive/artikel.php?ID=288182.
35 Lee, *From Third World to First.*
36 With thanks to Rick Menell for this anecdote.
37 See http://archive.kremlin.ru/eng/speeches/2008/11/05/2144_type70029type82917type127286_208836.shtml.

32 THE QUIET PROFESSIONALS

1 This chapter is based in part on the article of the same title by David Kilcullen, Greg Mills and Jonathan Oppenheimer, which appeared in the *RUSI Journal* 156(4), August 2011.
2 The US government spends more than $58 billion a year in foreign assistance through more than twenty agencies. Aid managed by the State Department and USAID amounted to $37 billion in the 2012 fiscal year. Peace and security received the greatest contribution, nearly $11 billion, with health ($9.4 billion) and economic development

($4.7 billion) next up, followed by humanitarian assistance ($4 billion) and democracy promotion ($3.3 billion). See the USAID 'Dashboard', http://www.foreignassistance.gov/.

3 See his paper on 'The Role of Donors in Fragile African States', African Development Bank High-Level Panel on Fragile States, Monrovia, 2 September 2013.

4 Colin Gray, *Defining and Achieving Decisive Victory*. Carlisle, PA.: US Army War College, Strategic Studies Institute, 2002.

5 William C. Martel, *Victory in War: Foundations of Modern Military Policy*. New York: Cambridge University Press, 2007.

6 US Agency for International Development, 2010, 'Theories of Change and Indicator Development in Conflict Management and Mitigation', http://pdf.usaid.gov/pdf_docs/PNADS460.pdf.

7 Carol Hirschon Weiss, 'Nothing as Practical as Good Theory: Exploring Theory-based Evaluation for Comprehensive Community Initiatives for Children and Families' in James Connell et al. (eds), *New Approaches to Evaluating Community Initiatives: Concepts, Methods, and Contexts*. Washington, D.C.: Aspen Institute, 1995.

8 See Dambisa Moyo, *How the West was Lost: Fifty Years of Economic Folly – And the Stark Choices that Lie Ahead*. New York: Farrar, Straus and Giroux, 2001; and *Dead Aid: Why Aid is Not Working and How There is Another Way for Africa*. New York: Farrar, Straus and Giroux, 2001.

9 See William Easterly, *The White Man's Burden: Why the West's Efforts to Aid the Rest Have Done So Much Ill and So Little Good*. New York: Penguin Press, 2006.

10 Paul Collier, *The Bottom Billion: Why the Poorest Countries are Failing and What Can Be Done About It*. Oxford: Oxford University Press, 2007.

11 Eli Berman, Joseph Felter and Joseph Shapiro, 'Can Hearts and Minds be Bought? The Economics of Counterinsurgency in Iraq', *Journal of Political Economy*, April 2011.

12 Andrew Wilder and Stuart Gordon, 'Money Can't Buy America Love', *Foreign Policy*, 1 December 2009.

13 Charles Wolf, *Insurgency and Counterinsurgency: New Myths and Old Realities*, Santa Monica, CA: RAND Corporation, July 1965.

14 As put in his CBS *The Vietnam War* television series released in DVD format, 2008.

15 Christopher Hitchens, 'From Abbottabad to Worse', *Vanity Fair*, June 2011.

16 See Hilton Root, *Alliance Curse: How America Lost the Third World*. New York: Brookings Institution Press, 2008.

17 Interviews, Hargeisa, 15 and 16 June 2011.

18 See 'Warlords Inc.': Extortion and Corruption Along the US Supply Chain in Afghanistan', Report of the Majority Staff, Committee on Oversight and Governmental Reform, US House of Representatives, June 2010.

19 See, for example, 'Zimbabwe: Diamond Revenue – Zimbabwe Misses IMF Target', 8 September 2013, http://allafrica.com/stories/201309080243.html.

20 See, for example, http://mg.co.za/article/2012-05-18-the-tobacco-industry-by-the-numbers.

21 See also Greg Mills and David Richards, 'The Binds That Tie Us: Overcoming the Obstacles to Peace in Afghanistan', *Foreign Affairs*, 24 November 2010.

22 'Weak States, Poor Countries', 24 September 2013, http://www.project-syndicate.org/commentary/economic-development-requires-effective-governments-by-angus-deaton.

23 Interview, USAID: ISAF HQ, Kabul, September 2010.

24 Interview, Kabul, 7 December 2009.

25 This point is made by Dr Reuben Brigety. His Center for American Progress drafted a National Strategy for Global Development outlining multiple definitions for global assistance: fundamental assistance (to improve the lives of civilians); instrumental assistance (to improve the lives of civilians to achieve another strategic or tactical end); and diplomatic assistance (assistance primarily to governments for a US national diplomatic objective, which may not improve the lives of civilians). See http://www.usaid.gov/km/seminars/2009/admin_forum_civ_mil_seminar09.html.

26 See his article in *The Observer*, 2 March 2013.

27 See http://www.mirror.co.uk/3am/celebrity-news/russell-brands-top-10-most-352295.

28 William Easterly, 'The Cartel of Good Intentions', http://koreamosaic.net/elp/extras/seniors/aideasterly.pdf.

29 See, for example, http://gulfnews.com/business/economy/global-remittance-flow-grows-10-77-to-514-billion-in-2012-world-bank-1.1172693.

30 The OECD was formed in 1960, when eighteen European countries plus the US and Canada created an organisation dedicated to global development. As of September 2013 membership comprised 34 countries: Australia, Austria, Belgium, Canada, Chile, Czech Republic, Denmark, Estonia, Finland, France, Germany, Greece, Hungary, Iceland, Ireland, Israel, Italy, Japan, Korea, Luxembourg, Mexico, the Netherlands, New Zealand, Norway, Poland, Portugal, Slovak Republic, Slovenia, Spain, Sweden, Switzerland, Turkey, the UK and the US.

31 See http://www.oecd.org/newsroom/developingcountriesfallsbecauseofglobalrecession.htm.

32 See http://dgff.unctad.org/chapter1/1.2.html.

33 These figures are calculated from the World Bank website. I am grateful to Anthony Arnott for his assistance in this regard. This section is also based, in part, on Jeffrey Herbst and Greg Mills, 'The World Bank's Diminishing Role in Africa', *International Herald Tribune*, 11 July 2013.

34 See http://www.bloomberg.com/news/2013-05-23/congo-rwanda-must-commit-to-peace-for-

world-bank-s-1-billion.html.
35 Collier, *The Bottom Billion*.
36 See http://www.mckinsey.com/mgi/publications/
urban_world/pdfs/MGI_urban_world_exec_
summary.pdf.
37 See also Mills and Richards, 'The Binds That Tie
Us'.
38 With thanks to Tim Harris MP, South Africa's
shadow minister of trade and industry, for this
figure.
39 See http://www.bbc.co.uk/news/uk-
politics-20265583.
40 These views are based on the findings of a
meeting of African private sector government
interlocutors, hosted by the Brenthurst
Foundation and held at Laro in Kenya
in December 2012.
41 With thanks to Mike Spicer for this point.
42 Lee Kuan Yew, *From Third World to First:
The Singapore Story: 1965–2000*. New York:
HarperCollins, 2008, p.79.
43 See *Think Africa Press*, 7 May 2013, http://
thinkafricapress.com/development/world-bank-
devarajan.
44 See, for example, http://www.globalissues.org/
article/3/structural-adjustment-a-major-cause-
of-poverty.
45 South Sudan, Liberia, Rwanda, Malawi, Sierra
Leone, Guinea and Nigeria.
46 See http://www.africagovernance.org/africa/news-
entry/AGIs-CEO-reflects-on-5-years-supporting-
effective-governance/.
47 With thanks to Eddie Keizan for this point.
48 Peter Hopkirk, *The Great Game: The Struggle for
Empire in Central Asia*. New York: Kodansha,
1994.
49 Hopkirk, *The Great Game*, p.123.
50 Rory Stewart, *Occupational Hazards*. London:
Picador, 2006, pp.30–31.

33 THE PRIVATE SECTOR

1 See http://abcnews.go.com/blogs/
politics/2009/12/secretary-gates-and-the-zen-
master/.
2 World Development Report 2011, http://
wdronline.worldbank.org/worldbank/a/c.html/
world_development_report_2011/overview.
3 African Development Bank, High Level Panel
on Fragile States Meeting, Monrovia, September
2013.
4 With thanks to Luis Membreno and Alberto
Trejos for this information.
5 These figures were supplied by Dcode, Cairo,
31 March 2014.
6 Or, in the case of South Africa, to take another
example, a very high percentage of expenditure
goes on social welfare payments – R410 billion
over three years in a R1-trillion annual budget
(compared in 2014/15 to R15.2 billion on
the economic competitiveness and support
package, R22.9 billion to upgrade commuter rail

services and R143.8 billion to support municipal
infrastructure) – as a means both of alleviating
conditions for the poorest citizens and delivering
on the government's political promises. Of course,
there is another way to achieve the latter: to
deregulate the economy, including salaries, but
that is politically difficult.
7 See the wealth of UNODC reports, for
example, http://www.unodc.org/toc/en/reports/
TOCTAWestAfrica.html and http://www.un.org/
apps/news/story.asp/www.unaids.org/en/html/
story.asp?NewsID=45775&Cr=trafficking&Cr1#.
U0RVN38aySM.
8 See, for example, Laura Ralston, 'Guns, Drugs
and Development', http://blogs.worldbank.org/
futuredevelopment/guns-drugs-and-development.
9 As in the relationship between Glen Agliotti
and South African police commissioner Jackie
Selebi. See Peter Piegl and Sean Newman, *Glen
Agliotti: A Biography*. Johannesburg: Penguin,
2013. See also Adriaan Basson, *Finish & Klaar:
Selebi's Fall from Interpol to the Underworld*. Cape
Town: Tafelberg, 2010; and Mandy Wiener, *Killing
Kebble: An Underworld Exposed*. Johannesburg:
Pan Macmillan, 2011.
10 Ralston, 'Guns, Drugs and Development'.
11 With thanks to Mark Shaw for this point.
12 A 'rentier' state is a term coined by Hossein
Mahdavy in describing economic development
in Iran, today used to depict those states that
derive all or a substantial portion of their revenue
from the rent of indigenous resources to external
clients.
13 Ricardo Hausmann, Dani Rodrik and Andrés
Velasco, 'Growth Diagnostics', Harvard University,
2004.
14 Paper prepared for the African Development Bank
High-Level Panel on Fragile States, Monrovia,
2 September 2013.
15 Discussion, Monrovia, 4 September 2013.
16 Matt Andrews, *The Limits of Institutional
Reform in Development*. Cambridge: Cambridge
University Press, 2012.
17 Lee Kuan Yew, *From Third World to First:
The Singapore Story: 1965–2000*. New York:
HarperCollins, 2008, p.737.
18 Nandan Nilekani, *Imagining India: Ideas for the
New Century*. New Delhi: Penguin, 2007.
19 For details on her career, see Luisa Dias Diogo,
*Soup Before Sunrise: From the Reforms to Economic
and Social Transformation in Mozambique,
1994–1999*. Maputo: DANIDA/SDC, 2013.
20 The visit to the Kabul juice factory was
undertaken in September 2010.

CONCLUSION: BUY, HOLD, FIX

1 See http://www.thesun.co.uk/sol/homepage/
news/politics/4886003/Sir-Bernard-Ingham-
remembers-Mrs-Thatcher.html. See also Charles
Moore, *Margaret Thatcher: The Authorized
Biography*. London: Penguin, 2013.

2 See http://www.margaretthatcher.org/ document/101650. See also Moore, *Margaret Thatcher*.

3 Cited in Robin Renwick, *Helen Suzman: Bright Star in a Dark Chamber*. Johannesburg: Jonathan Ball, 2014.

4 Jim Bailey, *The Sky Suspended*. London: Bloomsbury, 1990, p.183.

5 See Jeffrey Gettleman's article by the same title in *Foreign Policy*, February 2010, http://www. foreignpolicy.com/articles/2010/02/22/africas_ forever_wars.

6 He made this point on the death of the Vietnamese general and strategist Vo Nguyen Giap in October 2013. See http://www.huffingtonpost. com/2013/10/08/john-mccain-op-ed_n_4063699. html.

7 Paul Collier, 'The Role of Donors in Fragile African States'. Paper prepared for the African Development Bank High-Level Panel on Fragile States, Monrovia, 2 September 2013.

8 This phrase is taken from James Ambrose Brown's *War of a Hundred Days: Springboks in Somalia* to describe the plight of the Italian conquerors of Abyssinia.

9 With thanks (again) to John Mackinlay for this allegory.

10 Discussion, Tswalu Kalahari Reserve, November 2013.

11 Discussion, Johannesburg, 21 January 2014.

12 *Nyasa Times*, 13 March 2014.

13 Daron Acemoğlu and James Robinson, *Why Nations Fail: The Origins of Power, Prosperity and Poverty*. London: Profile, 2013, p.345.

14 Francis Fukuyama, *The Origins of Political Order*. New York: Farrar, Straus and Giroux, 2011, p.14.

15 Fukuyama, *The Origins of Political Order*, p.13.

16 See J.P. Landman, *The Long View: Getting Beyond the Drama of South Africa's Headlines*. Johannesburg: Jacana, 2013, p.93.

17 John Lewis Gaddis, *The Cold War*. New York: Penguin, 2005.

INDEX

＊